PENGUIN CLASSICS

BLACK PANTHER

A regular contributor to Marvel's letter columns as a teen, DON MCGREGOR broke into comics writing short stories for Warren's Publishing black-and-white magazines *Creepy*, *Eerie*, and *Vampirella*. Making the jump to Marvel Comics as a writer-editor in the mid-1970s, he combined a penchant for densely descriptive prose captions and character-driven narrative with the excitement of super hero drama on the first solo series devoted to the adventures of the Black Panther. His groundbreaking run brought a new social relevance to the series, and McGregor's vision of T'Challa, his people, and the nation of Wakanda remains influential to this day. Concurrent with his work on the Panther, McGregor collaborated with artist P. Craig Russell on Killraven in *Amazing Adventures*: a science-fiction romance about an earthbound hero's struggles against Martian invaders. In this series, too, McGregor pushed back against the presumptions of racism: Killraven featured mainstream comics' first interracial kiss.

His later works include the graphic novel and subsequent series *Sabre* (with artist Paul Gulacy) and *Detectives Inc.* (with Marshall Rogers and Gene Colan), both published by Eclipse, and a pair of well-received noir detective miniseries, *Nathaniel Dusk* (also illustrated by Colan) for DC comics. The 1980s would also see McGregor return to Killraven and Black Panther; the former in a lushly illustrated graphic novel with P. Craig Russell, the latter following up storylines from *Jungle Action* in the *Marvel Comics Presents* anthology and a four-issue miniseries, *Black Panther: Panther's Prey.*

McGregor has also written the syndicated *Zorro* newspaper strip, and published the prose fictions *Dragonflame & Other Bedtime Nightmares* and *The Variable Syndrome*, among other works.

RICH BUCKLER (1949–2017) was a versatile artist who drew hundreds of pages for Marvel, DC, Archie, Warren, and others, during his long career. Among his most notable work for Marvel: In the 1970s he helped introduce Deathlok in the pages of *Astonishing Tales*; penciled several storylines in *Peter Parker, the Spectacular Spider-Man*; and enjoyed runs on *Fantastic Four*, *Thor*, and other monthly titles, including the first solo series featuring the Black Panther. Buckler's DC work includes *Lois Lane*, *The Secret Society of Super-Villains*, and *World's Finest*, as well as the groundbreaking *Superman vs. Shazam*. Buckler was also editor of the short-lived Solson Publications and wrote two books on comic book art.

BILLY GRAHAM (or the "Irreverent Billy Graham," as he was known around the Marvel Bullpen, a play on the name of the popular evangelist) was one of the industry's brightest young talents in the 1970s. He honed a style born out of his love of fantasy stylists such as Frank Frazetta and Al Williamson and his adoration of comic art legend Jack Kirby. Like many young artists from the 1970s, Billy got his start on Warren's line of black-and-white horror mags *Creepy*, *Eerie*, and *Vampirella*. Impressed by Graham's all-around talent as an artist and storyteller, publisher James Warren made Graham art director for the Warren line, a position he held until he jumped over to Marvel Comics. The first book handed to him was *Hero for Hire*; he penciled, co-plotted, and/or inked the first sixteen issues of Luke Cage's title, Marvel's first ongoing series following the solo adventures of a Black character. Joining Don McGregor on the Black Panther in *Jungle Action* for his next assignment, Graham—the first Black creator to work on the character—would help to define the Wakandan warrior king for a generation of readers.

Graham later reunited with McGregor for the writer's Eclipse series, *Sabre*, in the mid-1980s. His final comics work appeared in 1985's *Power Man and Iron Fist* #114. Graham was also a playwright, theatrical set designer, stage and film actor, and commercial artist. He passed away in 1997 at the age of sixty-one.

Writer-editor STAN LEE (1922–2018) and artist Jack Kirby made comic book history in 1961 with *The Fantastic Four* #1. The success of its new style inspired Lee and his many collaborators to develop a number of super heroes, including, with Jack Kirby, the Incredible Hulk and the X-Men; with Steve Ditko, the Amazing Spider-Man and Doctor Strange; and with Bill Everett, Daredevil. Lee oversaw the adventures of these creations for more than a decade before handing over the editorial reins at Marvel to others and focusing on developing Marvel's properties in other media. For the remainder of his long life, he continued to serve as a creative figurehead at Marvel and as an ambassador for the comics medium as a whole. In his final years, Lee's signature cameo appearances in Marvel's films established him as one of the world's most famous faces.

Born Jacob Kurtzberg in 1917 to Jewish-Austrian parents on New York's Lower East Side, JACK KIRBY came of age at the birth of the American comic book industry. Horrified by the rise of Nazism, Kirby co-created the patriotic hero Captain America with Joe Simon in 1940. Cap's exploits on the comic book page entertained millions of American readers at home and inspired US troops fighting the enemy abroad. Kirby's partnership with Simon continued throughout the 1940s and early '50s; together, they produced comics in every popular genre, from Western to romance. In 1958, Kirby began his equally fruitful collaboration with writer-editor Stan Lee, and in 1961 the two men co-created the foundational text of the modern Marvel Universe: *The Fantastic Four.* Over the next decade, Kirby and Lee would introduce a mind-boggling array of new characters—including the Avengers, the Hulk, Thor, Iron Man, the Silver Surfer, and the X-Men. Kirby's groundbreaking work with Lee formed the foundation of the Marvel Universe. In the early 1970s, Kirby moved to DC Comics, where he created his interconnected Fourth World series, as well as freestanding titles such as *The Demon.* He returned to Marvel in 1975, writing and illustrating The Black Panther and Captain America and introducing series such as Devil Dinosaur and the Eternals. Kirby died in 1994. Today, he is generally regarded as one of the most important and influential creators in the history of American comics. His work has inspired multiple generations of writers, artists, designers, and filmmakers, who continue to explore his vast universe of concepts and characters. He was an inaugural inductee into the Eisner Hall of Fame in 1987.

NNEDI OKORAFOR is a Nigerian American author of African-based science fiction, fantasy, and magical realism for children and adults. Her works include *Who Fears Death* (currently in development at HBO into a TV series), the Binti novella trilogy, *The Book of Phoenix*, the Akata books, and *Lagoon.* She is the winner of Hugo, Nebula, World Fantasy, Locus, and Lodestar Awards, an Eisner Award nominee, and her debut novel *Zahrah the Windseeker* won the prestigious Wole Soyinka Prize for Literature. Nnedi has also written comics for Marvel, including *Black Panther: Long Live the King* and *Wakanda Forever* (featuring the Dora Milaje) and the Shuri series. Her science fiction comic series *LaGuardia* (from Dark Horse) is an Eisner and Hugo Award winner, and her memoir, *Broken Places & Outer Spaces*, is a Locus Award nominee. Nnedi holds two MAs (literature and journalism) and a PhD (literature).

QIANA J. WHITTED is a professor of English and African American Studies at the University of South Carolina. She is the author of the Eisner Award–winning book *EC Comics: Race, Shock, and Social Protest* and co-editor of the collection *Comics and the U.S. South.* She is also the editor of *Inks: The Journal of the Comics Studies Society* and chair of the International Comic Arts Forum.

BEN SAUNDERS is a professor of English at the University of Oregon. He is the author of *Desiring Donne: Poetry, Sexuality, Interpretation* and *Do the Gods Wear Capes?: Spirituality, Fantasy, and Superheroes*, as well as numerous critical essays on subjects ranging from the writings of Shakespeare to the recordings of Little Richard. He has also curated several museum exhibitions of comics art, including the record-breaking multimedia touring show *Marvel: Universe of Super Heroes*—a retrospective exploring the artistic and cultural impact of Marvel Comics from 1939 to the present.

## BLACK PANTHER

As Black Panther and the leader of the hidden African nation of Wakanda, King T'Challa combines the legendary stealth of his namesake with the strength and intelligence to overcome his adversaries while earning the trust of his people. This anthology includes the Panther's 1966 origin story by Stan Lee and Jack Kirby, and the critically acclaimed "Panther's Rage" from the character's 1970s solo series, by Don McGregor, Rich Buckler, and Billy Graham; both series were produced during a turbulent moment in America's struggle for civil rights, and they reflect that struggle in different ways.

The Penguin Classics Marvel Collection presents these influential comics in a scholarly context for the first time. The detailed introduction offers insight into the thematic development of the Black Panther, along with the social and cultural influences that shape the world he inhabits. This volume features a new foreword by Nnedi Okorafor.

## PENGUIN CLASSICS MARVEL COLLECTION

It is impossible to imagine American popular culture without Marvel Comics. For decades, Marvel has published groundbreaking visual narratives that sustain attention on multiple levels: as explorations of the relationship between power and responsibility; as metaphors for the experience of difference and otherness; as meditations on the pain of adolescence and the fluid nature of identity; as examinations of the meaning, and limits, of patriotism; as ironic juxtapositions of the cosmic and the quotidian; as resources for the understanding of political and social history; and as high-water marks in the artistic tradition of American cartooning.

These carefully curated collections present the foundational tales and characters of the Marvel Universe as Penguin Classics. Scholarly introductions and supplemental materials provide essential context for the modern reader, while forewords by contemporary authors speak to the enduring significance of Spider-Man, the Fantastic Four, the X-Men, and many other iconic creations. The Penguin Classics Marvel Collection serves as a testament to Marvel's transformative and timeless influence on an entire genre of fantasy.

DON McGREGOR,
RICH BUCKLER, BILLY GRAHAM,
STAN LEE, AND JACK KIRBY

# Black Panther

*Foreword by*
NNEDI OKORAFOR

*Introduction by*
QIANA J. WHITTED

*Series Editor*
BEN SAUNDERS

PENGUIN BOOKS

PENGUIN BOOKS
An imprint of Penguin Random House LLC
penguinrandomhouse.com

ISBN 9780143135807 (hardcover)
ISBN 9780143135814 (paperback)

Printed in China
1 3 5 7 9 10 8 6 4 2

Set in Sabon LT Pro

# Contents

# Series Introduction

If you were suddenly gifted with powers that set you apart from ordinary humanity, what would you do?

For the first generation of comic book super heroes, launched in the late 1930s, the answer was obvious: You used your special abilities for the benefit of others. You became a "champion for the helpless and oppressed" and waged an "unceasing battle against evil and injustice."[1]

It was a fantasy predicated on the effortless fusion of moral certainty with aggressive action, the national appetite for which only increased after America's entry into the Second World War in 1941. More than seven hundred super-powered do-gooders debuted in the boom years of 1938–1945.[2] Collectively, they helped to transform the comic book business from a vestigial limb of print culture into a muscular arm of the modern entertainment industry.[3] With the social tensions and abiding inequalities of US culture temporarily obscured by the Nazi threat, super heroes even came to emblematize the (sometimes contradictory) principles of individualism, democracy, and consumerism: the American way.[4]

After the war, comics remained big business—the genres of romance, Western, crime, horror, and humor all thrived—but audiences turned decisively away from super heroes.[5] Indeed, by the summer of 1953, the costumed crime-fighter appeared on the verge of extinction. Of the hundreds of characters that had once crowded the newsstands, only five still had their own titles: Quality Comics' Plastic Man and DC Comics' Superman, Superboy, Batman, and Wonder Woman.[6] Old-fashioned products of a simpler time, they were ripe targets for satire.[7] There were sporadic attempts to revive the craze, of course—most notably in 1954, when a wave of national hysteria over the putatively negative effects of crime and horror comics on younger readers led several publishers to seek more parent-friendly alternatives. The companies of Ajax, Atlas, Charlton, Harvey, Magazine Enterprises, Prize, and Sterling all tried out a few super hero books in an effort to recapture a small portion of the market that they once had dominated. Significantly, all failed.[8]

No single factor can definitively explain this shift in popular taste, but clearly times had changed. Against the background of the wasteful and inconclusive war in Korea, the vicious theater of McCarthyism, and the ugly response to the first stirrings of the civil rights movement in Montgomery, Alabama, the moral simplicity of the super hero fantasy looked naïve at best and reactionary at worst. Clearly, if super heroes were going to be revived successfully, they would have to be reinvented.

The process began at DC Comics, the only American comic book publisher to have a real stake in the genre at the time, with the return of the Flash in mid-1956.[9] Writer Bob Kanigher revised the concept (which dated back to 1940), adding a self-reflexive element; his hero, Barry Allen, had a nostalgic fondness for old Flash comics. Kanigher thereby acknowledged and incorporated DC's earlier Flash stories while simultaneously placing them at an ironic distance—making his own tale seem more authentic and contemporary. The summer of 1959 saw a similar modernization of the Green Lantern. The origin story of the first Lantern, from almost twenty years prior, had been a messy Orientalist hodgepodge; the new version drew on science fiction tropes more suited to the age of the space race. In late 1959, these revitalized heroes joined forces with Superman, Batman, and Wonder Woman to form a team: the Justice League of America.

The strong sales of the JLA made other publishers sit up and take notice. Among them was Martin Goodman, the owner of the company not yet known as Marvel.[10] Goodman had enjoyed plenty of success with super hero comics in the 1940s and owned the rights to such former hits as Captain America, the Human Torch—somewhat misnamed, as he was actually a flame-powered android—and Namor the Sub-Mariner. (A true original, the Sub-Mariner was perhaps the only super-powered character of the first generation to regard ordinary humanity with open hostility.) But Goodman had canceled all his super hero books in 1949 to pursue more popular trends.[11] Now, at the dawn of the '60s, half the titles in his comics division were romances or "teen humor" titles, while the other half was divided among war, Western, and "monster" books—anthologies that served up a different B-movie-style menace month after month—without a single super hero in the bunch.

Goodman decided that he needed a super team of his own on the shelves, fast, and assigned the job to a writer-editor named Stanley Lieber, better known today as Stan Lee. A cousin of Goodman's wife, Lee had joined the company in 1939 at the age of seventeen, rising to oversee Goodman's entire line. He'd grown up in the comic book industry, knew all its formulas and limitations, and longed to transcend them—but by his own account, he was starting to wonder if he ever would. When Goodman told him to create a copycat Justice League, Lee turned for help to Jack Kirby, a veteran artist who had co-created Captain America (among many other super heroes) with Joe Simon back in the 1940s. The result of their collaboration would be far more than a knockoff of the latest trend, however. Drawing inspiration from multiple sources, the two men managed to blend a whole new pop-cultural cocktail: a transformative take on the super hero. The comic was called The Fantastic Four, and in its pages, Lee and Kirby would also map out the basic contours of the Marvel Universe.

The Fantastic Four focused on a super team that was also a family. This simple choice immediately brought a new level of emotional dynamism to the super hero genre. The members of the Four loved one another fiercely, but like all families (and unlike the super friends of the JLA), they also bickered and fought. They were distinct individuals, with their own virtues and, more important, their own flaws. Lee and Kirby also added a previously unexplored dimension of tragedy to the generic mix with the character of the Thing—who was crippled with self-loathing after his transformation into a hideous behemoth. At the same time, Lee and Kirby took the potential for self-reflexivity that Kanigher had glimpsed in his revival of the Flash to even greater heights: playing with conventions, occasionally breaking the fourth with a protective layer of irony. The result was surprisingly tonally complex—a self-conscious mixture of comedy and drama for which there really was no precedent in super hero comics.[12]

The Fantastic Four was the first bona fide hit that Goodman's company had enjoyed in a while. Galvanized by success, Lee and Kirby co-created several more of their new breed of super heroes between late 1961 and late 1963—introducing the characters of Ant-Man, the Incredible Hulk, the Mighty Thor, Iron Man, Sergeant Nick Fury, and the X-Men in that short span. (It should be noted that Lee's brother, Larry Lieber, wrote the first scripts for Ant-Man, Thor, and Iron Man after receiving short synopses from Lee. Similarly, artist Don Heck drew the first Iron Man story after receiving a character design from Kirby.) Lee and Kirby also somehow found time to unite several of these new characters in a title called The Avengers (launched in July 1963 on the same day as the X-Men), and to bring back a war-traumatized version of Captain America in the fourth issue. All the while, they continued to create new stories and characters every month in the pages of the Fantastic Four. As if that were not enough, working in collaboration with artist Steve Ditko, Lee co-created and launched Spider-Man and Doctor Strange during the same period.[13]

It was an astounding burst of creativity over the course of which Goodman's company forged a new brand identity: Marvel Comics. Developing and extending the formula of the Fantastic Four, Marvel's new characters were "Super Heroes with Super Problems."[14] At times they struggled to do the right thing—and frequently they did not seem to know whether to regard their powers as a blessing or as a curse. Nor were they necessarily regarded with respect and admiration in their communities, but were just as likely to be regarded as criminals or monsters. Suddenly, it was no longer quite so obvious how you were supposed to respond if you were granted powers beyond those of ordinary humanity—or how ordinary humanity would respond to you.

Marvel's reinvention of the super hero comic book did not end with these changes, however. As the overseer of all of Marvel's titles, Lee also decided to locate the new characters in the same story-world. Events in one comic could thus be referenced in another, and characters could cross over from title to title—giving the impression that every comic in the line was part of one huge story. This development of what we might call "lateral continuity" across different titles was matched with more extended forms of linear continuity within the individual series. The dominant mode of comic book narrative at the time, even in the most enduring franchise, was that of the self-contained episode—so that it hardly mattered in what order one read, say, the Batman comics published in any given year. Now Lee, Kirby, and Ditko began to experiment with long-running subplots, such as the arc of Reed and Sue's romance in the Fantastic Four, or the mystery of the Green Goblin's identity in the Amazing Spider-Man—storylines that were developed over months and even years, in the manner of a soap opera.

These ever more elaborate forms of continuity rewarded the most-devoted readers—something that Lee was quick to recognize and embrace as one of several tools he would employ to feed the flames of Marvel fandom. Indeed, Lee's skillful fostering of fan culture was every bit as important to the success of the company as was his work as a writer. He began to address the growing readership in a distinctive editorial voice, combining the hyperbole of a carnival barker with the hipster flippancy of a rock and roll DJ, and cultivating a (largely fictitious) image of a carefree office space—the "Marvel Bullpen"—in which "Jolly" Jack Kirby and "Sturdy" Steve Ditko and the rest of the gang assembled the machinery of the "Marvel Revolution." (In fact, Ditko had his own office space, while Kirby generally worked at home.)

As the public face of Marvel, Lee was brilliant: compellingly persuasive with regard not only to his faith in Marvel's products but also to the potential of comics as an aesthetic form. Long after he had ceased to create comics, he remained a great ambassador for Marvel and for the medium as a whole. But among the many hundreds of journalists with whom Lee spoke over the years, few actually understood the process whereby Marvel Comics were produced. Frequently, he was treated as the sole author of the franchise, rather than a key member of a creative organization. These misunderstandings would later become a source of bitterness between Lee and several of his closest artistic partners—particularly Jack Kirby and Steve Ditko, who continued to labor in relative obscurity throughout the 1970s and '80s, while Lee became that most unlikely of things: a comic book celebrity.

But the true origins of Marvel Comics were fundamentally collaborative, as Lee himself acknowledged to an audience of fans at the San Diego Comic-Con in 1975:

> The way we worked, for those of you who don't know, is not the way they work at other companies, where the writer writes the script, and it's given to an artist, and the artist draws it, and that's the end of it. With us, it's a marriage of talents. The artist and writer will discuss the plots together, then the artist goes off to his little nook where he works, and he—without benefit of script—only with this vague, ridiculous plot that he's discussed—goes and draws the whole story all by himself. . . . Then, when the writer has to put in the copy, just imagine how much easier it is to look at a drawing and suit the dialogue perfectly to the expression of the character's face—to what the drawing represents—than to try and write perfect dialogue when you're looking at a blank sheet of paper, trying to imagine what the drawing will be like. . . .
>
> The artists are great storytellers themselves. They know which sequence to enlarge upon, which to cut short. . . . They'd put in characters I knew nothing about. . . . The competition still hasn't learned [that] this technique gives our stories a certain freshness, a spirit, that I think is Marvel.[15]

This way of working eventually became known as the "Marvel Method," and as these comments make clear, Lee liked it precisely because it gave artists such as Kirby and Ditko more control than the traditional "full script" method, where the details of page breakdowns and dialogue were decided by the writer beforehand. As Lee also acknowledges here, he was happy to place a very significant amount of storytelling responsibility in the artists' hands—to the point that they would add numerous elements that he had not anticipated and "knew nothing about." In addition, Lee felt that this profoundly collaborative creative process was essential to the "spirit" of Marvel and helped to set the company apart from the competition.

But understanding the Marvel Method is only the first step in appreciating the extent to which artistic labor was broadly distributed at Marvel in the 1960s. There was certainly room for key creators such as Lee, Kirby, and Ditko to place their distinctive, individual stamp upon the work, but they made their comics within a factory system where many vital tasks were dispersed across multiple hands. Their astonishing rate of productivity would not otherwise have been possible. Besides Lee's regular reliance on his brother, Larry, for scripting assistance, for example, we have to consider the fact that Kirby almost never inked his own work; his penciled pages were "embellished" (as the process was sometimes called) by numerous different artists, including Dick Ayers, Vince Colletta, Paul Reinmann, George Roussos, Joe Sinnott, and Chic Stone. Consequently, when we look at a page by Kirby, it is actually almost never by him alone. (This does not diminish Kirby's status as one of the most significant comic book creators of the past century, but it does make the task of thinking critically about his achievement that much more complex.) Lettering and coloring were also separate but highly skilled jobs—the former task generally handled at Marvel in the early days by Artie Simek or Sam Rosen, while Stan Goldberg and Marie Severin were responsible for the latter. Marvel's cultural ascendance over the course of the '60s was then further abetted by a number of talented creators who continued to develop the properties that Lee, Lieber, Kirby, Ditko, and Heck had launched—John Buscema, Gene Colan, John Romita Sr., Jim Steranko, Herb Trimpe, and Roy Thomas chief among them.[16]

To summarize their collective achievements in a single sentence:

together, these creators expanded the emotional and aesthetic horizons of an entire genre of fantasy in ways that continue to reverberate across the popular culture of the twenty-first century. The works that they produced were long ago accorded "classic" status by comic book fans and industry professionals alike—and as the primary source material for the Marvel Cinematic Universe, their influence has only grown, registering now on a global scale. And moreover—as teachers and scholars in numerous disciplines are now beginning to realize—these classic super hero stories can sustain intellectual scrutiny on multiple levels: as explorations of the relationship between power and responsibility; as intriguing metaphors for the experience of racial difference; as meditations on the pain of adolescence; as examinations of the meaning, and limits, of patriotism; as reflections on the joys and challenges of family life; as experiments in the juxtaposition of the cosmic and the quotidian; as the artistic working through of a variety of forms of trauma; as unexpected resources for the understanding of our political and social history; as revealing representations of our shifting attitudes toward various categories of identity; and as high aesthetic watermarks in the semiotically rich tradition of American cartooning. As such, these comics not only continue to give pleasure to readers everywhere but also merit our deepest critical engagement—something that this Penguin Classics Marvel Collection is designed to foster.

BEN SAUNDERS

# Foreword

My path to writing the big black cat started with a fat orange cat.

I've always been attracted to comics. Even before the word, it was the black line that drew me (pun intended). It began when I was about seven years old in the early '80s with . . . *Garfield*. My father was an avid *Chicago Sun-Times* newspaper reader, and every day he would sit at the dinner table and read it. It was while hanging around him that I noticed that there was a comics page every day. *The Family Circus*, *Hi and Lois*, *Bloomsbury*, *Calvin and Hobbes*, *Momma*, *Ziggy*—there were so many I enjoyed. And, oh man, on Sunday, there were pages of comics, and they were in *color*! I loved these little stories told in pictures. But I became most obsessed with *Garfield*.

It was more than the hijinks and jokes. There was something about those dark lines, how they looped and swirled to create images and how those images melded with the "drawings" of letters that were words, communicating thoughts and ideas with the pictures. Even before I was writing stories using prose I was marveling at the dance of symbolic representations of sound and images.

Nevertheless, I didn't arrive at comic books until much later in life. When I was a kid, I'd see the local comic book shops. I was interested and so, yes, I'd walk in there. I had seen boys at school with comic books and their colorful covers with titles in electrical-looking fonts. The excitement of those boys and their flimsy books intrigued me. And since I was very little, I'd always had dreams of flying. Heroes in capes with super powers were definitely in my realm of wonder.

However, when I'd push that comic book shop door open, the bell on the top of the door would ring and then something problematic would happen. I'd like to compare it to that moment when Luke and Obi-Wan walk into the bar or that record-scratch moment in Westerns when the stranger walks into the saloon. The comic book shop was always full of white boys; the person behind the counter was always a white guy. None of this bothered me; I'd grown up in a white neighborhood. What bothered me was their reaction to me. The staring, and *staring*.

I'd slowly walk in, trying not to make eye contact with anyone. However, the silent scrutiny and feeling that I had invaded a place where I wasn't welcome would be so strong that I'd leave soon after. On top of this, I was unfamiliar with comic books, how they were shelved, so I didn't even know what I was seeking. Let alone the fact that when I glanced at all the covers, I didn't see anyone black or female or outside a male gaze.

It was the late '80s. I was between eight and twelve years old in those years, the child of Nigerian immigrants, an athlete playing and grandly excelling in the sport of tennis. I was navigating through a lot of blatant racism, prejudice, and xenophobia. I knew when to avoid a space, even if I didn't fully understand the depth of it. Comic book shops remained an unwelcoming place on several levels for many years. I can't state it enough: to be white and male was such a privilege if you loved or wanted to love comic books.

My discovery of super heroes didn't happen until I was nineteen years old and paralyzed from spinal surgery complications when doctors tried to straighten out my acute scoliosis. That's a lot crammed in one sentence, I know. I wrote a whole book about it called *Broken Places & Outer Spaces*. I was a semipro tennis player and a track star with severe scoliosis that was increasing in severity every year. I was eventually told that I could either have the spinal surgery to straighten it out or become crippled by twenty-five and have a much shorter life due to compressed organs. When I had the surgery, I was in the anomalous 1 percent of patients who mysteriously respond to the surgery with paralysis. So I went from super athlete to paralyzed from the waist down in a matter of nine hours. I'd lost my super powers.

It took me months to regain sensation in my legs (and the doctors didn't know whether I would until it gradually happened). After a month in the hospital, and then another several weeks of rigorous physical therapy, I got out of that wheelchair and began using a walker. Eventually I graduated to a half walker, then cane, then finally using only my own two legs. But that summer, while I was still using the walker, I spent a lot of time in front of the TV. And that's when I discovered the X-Men. I especially loved Storm, who could fly. But the one who intrigued me most was Wolverine because he was so angry and he had a skeleton that was unbreakable. As a twenty-year-old who'd just lost her super powers and was now trying to figure out who the heck she was, this discovery gave me strength. It was the first time I understood why so many loved super heroes. The first super hero comic I read was *Wolverine*.

I went on to consume comics through graphic novels, including *Persepolis*, *A Contract with God*, *Bone*, and two more iconic cat narratives in *The Rabbi's Cat* and *We3*. I read these while I earned my second MA and then PhD. I came to more super heroes through Grant Morrison's *Animal Man* and *Vixen* and Alan Moore's *Watchmen*. And then, years later, while I was a professor at the University at Buffalo, I learned about a country in Marvel's Africa called Wakanda and I said, "Hmmm, interesting." I thank Ta-Nehisi Coates for introducing me to King T'Challa. Yes, yes, I was late, but we can't always be on time.

Writing *Black Panther: Long Live the King* (2017–2018) was a marvelous experience. Initially, I came to it looking at King T'Challa and the country of Wakanda out of the side of my eye. I'm Igbo (a Nigerian ethnic group), and among the Igbo there's a common saying, "*Igbo enwe eze*," which means, "The Igbo have no king." Being a series of democratic societies consisting of small independent communities, historically, Igbos didn't have a centralized government or royalty.

I grew up hearing this phrase, and between this and also being an American, any type of monarchy gets my side-eye of disapproval . . . even a mythical one. Then I realized, in writing *Black Panther*, I could affect him and his country. I could enter into direct conversation and be heard. It was like visiting a country for the first time, and not as a tourist, but as a diplomat. I couldn't be passive during my visit, and that made my visit even more interesting. I got to listen to, know, and speak to T'Challa and the people and land of Wakanda.

*Black Panther* and Wakanda hold a powerful place in the Marvel Universe. I've always viewed Wakanda as a proper return of African Americans (the direct descendants of enslaved Africans during the Transatlantic Slave Trade) to the continent of Africa. Because one can never go back in the past, the gaze is into the future, and that was where the reconciliation was made . . . at least the beginning of one. There's a sense of homecoming and belonging in *Black Panther* that is celebratory. One gets to claim Wakanda as a space and make an African connection.

One of the reasons I agreed to write T'Challa, Shuri, the Dora Milaje, and Wakanda was because I wanted to further develop that bridge. I focused on bringing T'Challa closer to the common people of Wakanda and later, when I wrote Shuri as the Black Panther, bringing her to the rest of Africa. Comics are powerful indeed. King T'Challa, the mantle of Black Panther, and the country of Wakanda have all evolved *so much* over the decades. I look forward to what comes next.

Nigerian writer Ben Okri once wrote in his book *Birds of Heaven*, "The happiness of Africa is in its nostalgia for the future, and its dreams of a golden age." I think this is true both on the continent and in the Black Diaspora beyond. Wakanda Forever.

NNEDI OKORAFOR

# Volume Introduction

Long after night has fallen, the lone figure of the Black Panther staggers into the fog of a Georgia swamp and over gnarled tree roots before collapsing in the marsh. The smoldering cinder of a broken cross is strapped to his back, and his skin blisters beneath a midnight blue costume that he drags through the muck and slime. In this harrowing scene from the 1976 issue of *Jungle Action* featuring the Black Panther, King T'Challa has ventured far from his beloved home in the fictional African country of Wakanda. He can barely move or speak after having depleted his tremendous strength in single-handedly fighting back the hooded white supremacists who tried to burn him alive. The mental and physical devastation is so great that a flare of uncertainty breaches his thoughts: "Why survive? Why not succumb to the language of the pain?" Still he rises from the swamp, and what pushes his body forward is a deeper, more restorative jolt of defiance: "Come on, he speaks angrily, chiding himself . . . you have travelled this *identity labyrinth* before. Is it a *journey* you must return to endlessly . . . seeking resolutions to problems your past convinced you were resolved?" (JA 21.7).

T'Challa is a king, a warrior, a scientific genius, and under the mantle of Black Panther, he is the divinely sanctioned leader of an unconquered African people. Yet his continual return to the labyrinth of identity speaks to the fundamental predicament that has accompanied his character across the pages of Marvel Comics since 1966. No matter the threat to his sovereignty, no matter the villains to be overcome, doubt is the adversary that never tires; the inner journey of discovery will always demand the mighty hunter's utmost attention. To know one's self and remain steadfast in the face of ignorance and resentment. To find an unconditional place of belonging and extend its welcome to others. To wield immense power with skill, conviction, and reverence. These are the death-defying feats that make the Black Panther not just a reigning monarch but a super hero.

The Black Panther, created by Stan Lee and Jack Kirby, is widely heralded as the first high-profile Black super hero in mainstream American comic books. The decades prior to his thrilling appearance in the two *Fantastic Four* issues that open this collection saw a number of notable precursors, including Prince Lothar from the *Mandrake the Magician* newspaper comic strip in the 1930s, Lion Man from *All-Negro Comics* #1 in 1947, and Waku, Prince of the Bantu in *Jungle Tales* from Marvel's predecessor, Atlas Comics. Lee and Kirby would also include African American soldier Gabe Jones as a series regular in *Sgt. Fury and His Howling Commandos* starting in 1963. Yet the Black Panther's status as a super hero distinguished his recurring character, along with his prominence as one of the Earth's Mightiest Heroes in Marvel's team, the Avengers, and his appearance in a successful solo series starting in the 1970s.

T'Challa joined the Marvel Comics Universe as the ruler of a hidden African kingdom where tribal traditions merge seamlessly with scientific and technological advancements. The character was developed as part of a larger effort to connect with Black readers and bring more diversity to Marvel's stories. His earliest images were based on Kirby's concept sketches of a Black hero that he and Lee called the Coal Tiger. Staring confidently with a smile, the Coal Tiger had the imposing physique of a boxing champ in a black-and-yellow-striped costume and red cape. By the time the character appeared on newsstands, he was clad in the all-black attire and enigmatic stealth of a panther.

Born and raised in Wakanda and educated abroad with a PhD in physics, T'Challa leads the inhabitants of his country in protecting the rare and powerful sound-absorbing metallic ore called Vibranium. The material is mined from the region's sacred mound, created by a meteor that fell to Earth thousands of years ago. Holding everything together is the mythical Panther God and the sacred powers of the heart-shaped herb that heightens the senses and reflexes and endows the body with exceptional strength, stamina, speed, and healing abilities. The Black Panther is a powerful combination of an ancestral bloodline and a spiritual bounty, a super hero with a title that is marked by constant tests and trials of leadership, duty, and community obligation.

The origins of the Black Panther are also rooted in the social and political transformations that occurred in the United States and around the world in the mid-1960s. While the nonviolent protest campaigns of the civil rights movement resulted in meaningful legislative changes, including the landmark Civil Rights Act of 1964, the struggle for African Americans to freely exercise their rights as citizens remained urgent and necessary. A rising generation of activists were increasingly dissatisfied with the movement's methods given the persistence of racial terrorism, voter intimidation, and entrenched economic barriers, along with the prolonged impact of the Vietnam War. "Black Power" became a rallying cry that leaders such as Stokely Carmichael of the Student Nonviolent Coordinating Committee (SNCC) used to galvanize a new sense of racial pride and self-reliance within Black communities. Even embracing the term *Black* (rather than *Negro* or *Colored*) signaled a more radical identity for the 1960s activists who consigned assimilationist aims to the past and linked people of African descent in America with the revolutionaries who had rejected colonial rule in Ghana, Kenya, the Democratic Republic of Congo, and other countries across the African continent.

Months prior to the Black Panther's first comic book appearance in July 1966, SNCC organizers worked with local Black residents in Lowndes County, Alabama, to form a political party called the Lowndes County Freedom Organization (LCFO). In defiance of the white rooster that the state's Democratic Party adopted as a badge of white supremacy, the LCFO used the black panther to identify their organization on the ballot. Although Lee and Kirby have stated that the political symbol was not the basis for their character, scholars Adilifu

Nama, Crystal Am Nelson, and Charles W. Henebry note that Marvel's creative team was undoubtedly aware of the conversations surrounding the social and political upheavals in the South, whether or not they had direct knowledge of the Lowndes County group or the Clark College mascot on which the LCFO panther emblem was based.[1] Other sources such as Dennis Culver point to earlier inspirations, including Harry Wills, the World Colored Heavyweight Championship boxer who was called the Black Panther during the 1910s and 1920s. A few decades later, the US Army's 761st Tank Battalion, the first predominately African American armored unit to engage in combat during World War II, would be dubbed the Black Panthers, too.[2]

Clearly, then, many people regarded the dark-colored large feline from Africa, Asia, and the Americas to be an inspiring and provocative symbol: from the armed forces to the world of politics and sport. What matters most is the cultural climate in which these ideas about racial justice and equality circulated, ultimately generating an affirming visual rhetoric of Black courage and self-determination that coalesce in the panther. The summer debut of Marvel's super hero is bookended between these earlier iterations and the founding of the Black Panther Party for Self Defense by Huey P. Newton and Bobby Seale in Oakland, California, in October 1966. While the organization's paramilitary style and views on armed self-defense often dominated media coverage, their extensive platform advocated for economic, social, and political power within Black communities; spoke out against police brutality; and instituted social programs for job training, medical access, and food assistance. In his speech at a conference called "Black Power and Its Challenges," Carmichael explained: "We chose for the emblem a black panther, a beautiful black animal which symbolizes the strength and dignity of Black people, an animal that never strikes back until he's back so far into the wall, he's got nothing to do but spring out. Yeah. And when he springs he does not stop."[3]

Such sentiments were echoed in the uprisings in Watts, New York, Chicago, and Cleveland, but also through unprecedented Black civic engagement and in artistic movements that eschewed white Western ways of thinking to embrace aesthetic traditions grounded in the African diaspora. Several scholars see Lee and Kirby's decision to locate T'Challa's home across the Atlantic Ocean as an effort to distance the character from the more immediate tumult taking place in the United States.[4] Others such as Nama regard the Black Panther's African identity as central to his embrace among readers as a progressive symbol and "a triumphant vision of Afrofuturist blackness."[5] The fact remains that Marvel's Black Panther emerged at a pivotal moment during the 1960s, when America was confronting the deep historical consequences of race and racism in a well-trodden identity labyrinth of its own.

In turn, T'Challa's earliest appearances seem marked by a pronounced ambivalence: Is the Black Panther friend or foe? Just as *Fantastic Four* #52 was being stocked on newsstands, marketing teasers hinted at the debut of this "mystery villain," while the published cover heightens the suspense by depicting the Black Panther masked and menacing in mid-leap, grasping for Reed Richards (aka Mr. Fantastic) and his companions. His dark body looms larger on the opening page beneath a foreboding promise that the Fantastic Four will be "trapped" in his realm. Initially the unsuspecting team is awestruck by T'Challa's gift of an ultramodern jet and an invitation to travel to Africa. But instead of the safari vacation that the heroes expected, the Fantastic Four become unwitting prey in the "man-made jungle" of Wakanda, where the dense tropical vegetation shimmers and hums with dials, wires, and computer technology. As Ben Saunders notes, *Fantastic Four* served "as Kirby and Lee's primary laboratory, a space for fearless experimentation and invention."[6] Mysterious interactions with unknown people and species were a key part of the team's explorations, from the Mole Man and the shape-shifting Skrulls to Namor the Sub-Mariner from Atlantis. Readers eventually learn that the Fantastic Four were brought to Africa as part of an elaborate training exercise to test the Wakandan warrior's skill as he prepares to take revenge on the merciless villain named Klaw, the Master of Sound, who murdered T'Challa's father, King T'Chaka.

Questions about the Black Panther's allegiances would continue to surface, notably after he is offered a place among the Avengers. T'Challa is forced to use his stealth to sneak into their locked New York mansion in *Avengers* #52, only to be arrested after discovering the dead bodies of Hawkeye, Goliath, and the Wasp inside. The triple murder would turn out to be a hoax orchestrated by another villain known as the Grim Reaper. In every instance, the Black Panther proves himself to be honorable and trustworthy. T'Challa's debut even concludes with the king expressing a willingness to set aside the mantle of Black Panther and renounce his throne in order to pledge "my *fortune*, my *powers*—my very *life*—to the service of all mankind!" (FF 53.20). The shift from the so-called provincial interests of Wakanda to a global crusade affirmed that the Black Panther's commitments would ultimately align with the broader vision of Marvel's more established heroes. And given the fears of the Cold War era and incidents such as the Congo Crisis, scholar Martin Lund argues further that T'Challa's vows in these early appearances helped to tamp down Western anxieties over whether an independent African nation would resist communism and use its valuable resources to uphold democratic ideals. "Black Panther is an engineer-genius," notes Lund, "who represents Africa's potential postcolonial self-renewal."[7] To realize this potential, the comics often suggested that the implied threat of the "mighty, masked jungle mystery man" (FF 52.20) could be neutralized by enlisting his talents in a worldwide struggle against evil.

To fully appreciate the shape and substance of the world that Marvel imagined for the Black Panther also requires some understanding of how comic book genres were evolving in the period during the 1960s and 1970s known as the industry's Silver Age. Black Panther's creative team ironically reworked earlier tropes and character types from well-known "jungle" comics. Edgar Rice Burroughs's Tarzan adventures were among the most popular of this genre, and adaptations of the stories ran as a newspaper comic strip and various comic book serials for several decades starting in 1929. Historians Mike Benton and Bradford Wright note that this success prompted publishers such as Fiction House, Inc. and Fox Feature Syndicate to produce their own titles that dramatized the exploits of white adventurers in remote lands facing off against angry natives, ferocious animals, and greedy hunters. As Wright explains, "Paternalistic, imperialistic, and racist, the jungle comics showed the reductionist comic book style at its ugliest."[8] The indigenous Black and brown people who populated these comics as secondary characters often remained fixed within the bounds of stoicism and savagery.

While many of these series were canceled by the mid-1960s, the familiar settings and caricatures of jungle comics would continue to shape readers' expectations for the Fantastic Four's mysterious trip to Africa. Lee and Kirby strategically use Ben Grimm (aka the Thing) to give voice to these assumptions through his surly misconceptions about the Black Panther and his home. Once Ben learns that the sleek new aircraft that Mr. Fantastic is piloting is from an African chieftain, his perplexed reply is revealing: "But how does some refugee from a *Tarzan* movie lay his hands on *this* kinda gizmo?" (FF 52.2). He goes on to boast of having seen "a million *jungle movies*" and claims to have little interest in hearing T'Challa's story, since after all, he can recite "half'a the *Bomba, the Jungle Boy* books by *heart*!" (FF 53.5–6). To reach Ben, and comic book readers like him, the story lingers on the astonishing convergences of the Black Panther's kingdom, reworking the cliché of the noble savage into "the collision of ancient civilizations and futuristic technologies" that would generate a more dynamic story-world.[9]

Indeed, what moves the Thing from skepticism to grudging respect is not only T'Challa's sense of honor but also the ingenuity of Wakandan engineering and science. Ramzi Fawaz makes the case that the plot is punctuated by ironic "moment[s] of misrecognition" and "visual reversals"[10] to prove that the people of Wakanda are "*not* the ordinary native tribe they *seem* to be!" (FF 53.1). For instance, Fawaz notes that during the hero's ceremony, Lee and Kirby disrupt the white colonizing gaze by positioning the Fantastic Four and their Native American friend, Wyatt Wingfoot, at the foot of T'Challa's throne as they marvel at a "socially and economically independent Africa." Likewise, the unmistakable evidence of Wakanda's technological innovation and the Black Panther's exceptional abilities makes the "cross-cultural encounter" between him and the Fantastic Four mutually beneficial.[11]

Several years later, after traveling the globe alongside Captain America and the Avengers, the Black Panther returns to an icy welcome in Wakanda. First he defeats M'Baku, the Man-Ape in *Avengers* #62, only to face a daunting new rival. Erik Killmonger attempts to seize T'Challa's title and end his life with an ensemble of ruthless challengers who make the king a stranger in his own home. The story, called "Panther's Rage," extended for thirteen issues, from September 1973 to November 1975, in *Jungle Action*, resulting in one of the earliest examples of a self-contained narrative arc in mainstream American super hero comic books. Writer Don McGregor collaborated with a team of artists, including Rich Buckler, Billy Graham, and Gil Kane, on the critically acclaimed story, all of which is included in this collection.

As with the Black Panther's *Fantastic Four* appearance, Marvel's editors chose to build the foundation of the super hero's first solo adventures out of the remnants of an outdated genre. When *Jungle Action* was relaunched in 1972, it contained reprints of 1950s stories featuring white adventurers such as Lorna the Jungle Queen and Jann of the Jungle. Cheap to produce, the series was merely intended "to capture shelf space from the growing competition in the comics market."[12] By then other Black characters were making their way through the door that T'Challa had opened years earlier, including Captain America's companion the Falcon (1969), DC's John Stewart as Green Lantern (1971), and Luke Cage in his own series in 1972. Historian David Taft Terry notes that Marvel even began to incorporate Black supporting characters into their comics, including Dr. Bill Foster (later known as Black Goliath) and *Daily Bugle* city editor Joseph "Robbie" Robertson.[13] McGregor, a copy editor and staff writer at Marvel, was disturbed to see the stories in *Jungle Action* still in circulation. "I wasn't particularly thinking about the Black Panther," he admits. "I hadn't given it any thought more than that I hated them reprinting a lot of those terribly insulting, often racist stories."[14] When McGregor was assigned to write Black Panther stories for the title instead, he saw an opportunity to build a richer, more complex narrative, one that explored King T'Challa's life and struggle from the inside out.

Revamping a minor title that generated little profit may not have seemed like a particularly controversial venture in 1973. Yet McGregor took creative risks that would build on the foundation that Lee and Kirby established in order to chart a new direction for Marvel's African Avenger, prompting scholar Rebecca Wanzo to cite "Panther's Rage" as "the major first step in decolonizing the character."[15] The story takes place entirely in Wakanda, starting with the sixth issue of *Jungle Action* featuring the Black Panther. And with no cameo appearances from the rest of the Avengers and only a single white supporting character, the series featured a virtually all-Black cast for its two-year run. In making this decision, McGregor offered sound logic ("This is a hidden, technologically advanced African nation. Where are the white people supposed to come from?!") while also insisting on the integrity and agency of the story's protagonist. As he writes in the essay that appears in this volume: "I did not want the black hero to have to rely on white heroes to save the day for him."[16]

Instead readers see T'Challa benefiting from his relationships with his trusted advisors W'Kabi, Taku, and Zatama. By his side is Monica Lynne, the soul songstress and social worker from America, who became his first romantic interest. Also appended to each installment were detailed maps, concept sketches, story recaps, and other back matter that were solicited to ensure that there would be no more room for 1950s jungle reprints. Taken together, as media studies scholar Todd Steven Burroughs notes, "McGregor expanded T'Challa's fictional universe greatly, giving Wakanda a distinct look and culture, a geography, religious rituals, tribal rivalries, and, perhaps most importantly, a royal court for King T'Challa. With McGregor's Panther, you could read a comic about a universe that, up until 1973, was unthought of: one starring an African king in an African land, separate from the Avengers."[17]

Artists Rich Buckler and Billy Graham joined McGregor in redefining the hero's presence on the page. In the second skin of his costume, the Black Panther moves with the long agile strides and graceful leaps of a gymnast. The narrative drawings depict his stamina and stealth against a teeming landscape that includes humid jungle forests and swamps, deep caverns and snow-topped mountain ranges, modest villages and the opulent rooms of the royal palace. Graham, who would pencil most of the issues, was the first African American artist to work on a Black Panther title. He became a part of the creative team after spending the previous year on *Luke Cage, Hero for Hire* and prior to that working as art director at Warren Publishing, where he and McGregor first became friends. On "Panther's Rage," Graham became well-known for the comic's striking title pages and action sequences. Writer James Heath Lantz notes that "McGregor's storytelling style seemed to be in sync with Graham's larger-than-life images."[18] While the Vibranium-enriched technologies and scientific advancements of earlier Black Panther stories are less apparent in *Jungle Action*, the creators—including colorist Glynis Oliver—worked together to relay what McGregor has called the "distinct, magical reality" of Wakanda.[19]

This visual aesthetic further distinguished Black Panther from other 1970s Black comic book heroes, who tended to operate in urban spaces where reality was defined by the economic blight and racial disparities of the American ghetto. Luke Cage's series is often singled out for approximating the speech, fashion, and social awareness of popular Blaxploitation cinema in films such as *Shaft* (1971), *Blacula* (1972), and *Cleopatra Jones* (1973). Yet David Taft Terry points out that Marvel relied on "black militant" stock characters to integrate numerous titles, adapting the hypermasculine attitudes and oversimplified renderings of Black Power ideology that independent filmmakers helped to make so notorious during the early 1970s.[20] Buckler and Graham also found ways to incorporate aspects of modern African American popular culture into their renderings of the Panther. In his throne room, for example, King T'Challa is draped in a modified version of the gold-chain outfit worn by singer Isaac Hayes for the Watts, Los Angeles, community benefit concert that was released as the 1973 documentary film *Wattstax*. Such visual allusions allowed "Panther's

Rage" to indirectly reference the soundtrack of Black unity created by the Stax Records concert that, according to the promotional poster, drew "100,000 brothers and sisters turning on to being black . . . telling it like it is!"

This time, however, the Black Panther's loyalty is called into question by a fellow Wakandan. Killmonger was born N'Jadaka in a village near the mountains on the country's western border. Orphaned in his early years and enslaved by Klaw in the Vibranium mines, he was kidnapped and transported to the United States against his will. When Killmonger returns to Africa, he is determined to take control of the country's people and resources for vengeful ends. Readers see evidence of Killmonger's power in the fierce symmetry that finds the two opponents clashing high atop Warrior Falls both at the start and the finish of the story's main twelve chapters. Joining him in the battle to dethrone T'Challa in the intervening issues are American snake charmer Venomm and Wakandans Malice and Lord Karnaj. The henchmen duo Kazibe and Tayete provide a measure of comic relief through their run-ins with the "Panther Devil," while a supernatural world comes to life in Baron Macabre, Sombre, and King Cadaver. Just as striking are the beasts of nature that challenge the Black Panther: rhinos, alligators, gorillas, and even prehistoric dinosaurs.

While the Black Panther emerges victorious from each battle, the toll that these altercations take on his mind and body is a recurring theme throughout "Panther's Rage." McGregor, Buckler, and Graham extend the meticulous world-building of Wakanda to the architecture of T'Challa's interior life, and as a result, the impact of every accusation, every betrayal and disappointment, lands on his shoulders like a body blow. As the king's country splinters, his own advisory council begins to openly wonder about his allegiances, too. Compounding their suspicions about his time away in foreign lands is his devotion to Monica, an "out-worlder" who is unfamiliar with Wakandan traditions and rituals. Killmonger exploits these vulnerabilities in his quest for dominance, forcing T'Challa to defend his crown on multiple fronts and leading scholars like Julian C. Chambliss to conclude that "in McGregor's tale T'Challa is a king first and a hero second."[21] Just as the heart-shaped herb that bestows the sacred Panther powers must be replenished, so T'Challa's lineage only enables access to the throne; the kingdom's trust must be earned by its leader, again and again.

Critics often comment on McGregor's generous use of the omniscient narrative voice to relay the Black Panther's thoughts and emotions during the *Jungle Action* run. His narration amplifies Buckler and Graham's dynamic page layouts with a contemplative writing style that can transform any encounter into a multivolume treatise on the responsibilities of power and the human costs of war. Ultimately McGregor's approach reveals what lies beneath the principled composure that is Black Panther's signature character trait. Readers are offered a glimpse of the hero's tactical deliberations as well as his rare moments of apprehension and righteous anger. The setting further reflects T'Challa's inner turmoil, and as scholar José Alaniz suggests, "During his grueling journey back to civilization, its changing landscapes mirror the protagonist's growing desperation and will to triumph. To a degree not seen before in superhero comics, the natural setting entails the character."[22]

One example comes at the start of issue #10, when a stretch of quiet finds the king on the banks of a Wakandan river. Even as the hostile world edges closer (in this case, the twenty-foot-long crocodile behind him), we are invited to observe T'Challa "staring into the waters at *his* reflection [. . .] as if he has forgotten who he once *was* or who he now *is*!" (JA 10.1). Soon the crocodile strikes and the panels on the next three pages depict the gaping jaws ripping through his flesh in a series of doubled images that show man and animal twisting in and out of the churning lake. The "fragmented vision" of the water becomes a revelation, one that we are told generates "a *stabbing clarity* the mirror-perfect figure *lacked*!" (JA 10.3). Is it only in the midst of such desperate fights for survival that the Black Panther can remember who he is?

The unrelenting physical trials that T'Challa faces are a crucial part of his story. In Graham's illustrations, the Black Panther can scarcely make it through a single issue without his costume being torn to shreds by everything from wolves to cactus thorns to the armies of the undead. Scholars such as Rob Lendrum and Anna Peppard make the case that while most comic book super heroes draw meaning from the body in crisis, the Black Panther's race and gender invest the graphic depictions of his suffering with added significance. When he strikes back, as a Black male hero with animalistic panther-like qualities, he runs the risk of being narrowly defined as a "super-savage."[23] Readers must decide if spectacles like the crocodile attack double down on the stereotypes of hypermasculine Blackness or draw our attention instead to the humanity beneath the tattered remains of his clothing. The Wakandan king's own willfulness must also be taken into account, since as Peppard points out, "Black Panther is very rarely passive in his suffering; in the vast majority of his spectacles of bondage, the narration and the ways in which Graham's often intricate linework dramatically contorts, stretches, and enlarges the Panther's muscles emphasize[s] his active resistance."[24]

This kind of active resistance would carry over into McGregor and Graham's second *Jungle Action* arc, "The Panther vs. the Klan." (Three issues of the story are included here.) In the comic, T'Challa travels with Monica to Georgia to help investigate the murder of her sister. While this is not the Black Panther's first time in the United States or his first encounter with white supremacist violence, the story is a fascinating thought experiment that considers how a Black super hero with a royal African lineage might change the calculus of racial terrorism in the South. Would he be able to find the answers that have eluded Monica's family and white allies like *Georgia Sun* reporter Kevin Trueblood? Could he deliver justice against the bigots who treated Black American southerners as second-class citizens?

The Black Panther's intervention achieves unprecedented results, although the series was canceled mid-story with *Jungle Action* #24.[25] King T'Challa hurls the bodies of Ku Klux Klansmen through windows, uses their own weapons against them, and sends them retreating on their horses and motorcycles. At one point, Monica's mother tells the story of a cousin who was murdered after the Civil War by a group of former Confederate death riders. McGregor and Graham stage a flashback that contrasts Mrs. Lynne's memory of her cousin Caleb, proud but defenseless, with a new ending that Monica supplies as she listens. In her vision, the Black Panther and Caleb take a stand together, defending his family from humiliation and fighting back bullets and the lynch rope. Monica's Reconstruction-era fantasy turns into a self-reflexive exercise that uses the super hero narrative to envision freedom for Black bodies and imaginations.

Significantly, "The Panther vs. the Klan" also makes a point to show how Monica and T'Challa's affection for each other grows. She acquires a richer personality and a more complex past as he learns about her family. While Monica was often treated as a liability in Wakanda, in Georgia she becomes his guide and cultural translator. It is the Black Panther who is the fish out of water, pushing a grocery cart down aisle three of a local supermarket (in full costume) or watching the Wakandan Sonar Glider land next to the Lynne family's front porch after dinner.

Still, some obstacles prove to be more difficult for T'Challa to overcome. In his attempt to protect Monica from an attack, local deputies assume the Black Panther is a criminal and join an angry mob in beating him until the sheriff intervenes. The police brutality that the Black Panther endures is an important indictment of the American justice system (and brings to mind his wrongful arrest at the Avengers mansion years before). This and other critical issues are invoked throughout the series with references to the writings of James Baldwin and Eldridge Cleaver. At the same time, the social realities of the comic are offset by the introduction of arcane occult figures. In addition to the KKK, T'Challa and the Lynne family are harassed by another "clan," a multiracial group of hooded vigilantes called the Dragon's Circle. The sometimes-confusing presence of both groups and the erratic pacing of the murder plot blemishes an unfinished story that is otherwise compellingly rendered.

One of the most remarkable scenes portrays the Black Panther interrupting a late-night Klan rally in the middle of the Devouring Swamp. A stunning full-page sequence shows his lithe dark blue form leaping among the tree branches high above, only to pause and spring out fighting through the torches below. As the hooded figures swarm around him with shotguns and ropes, the comic makes clear that this is a battle that our hero could actually lose. He is strapped to a cross, and later, when his body is set ablaze, his inner voice resurfaces. Finding the courage to fight and to live in this moment means acknowledging that his flesh is not Christ-like nor invulnerable to hurt: "Don't you understand, a man can only take so much!" (JA 21.4). T'Challa allows himself to feel the grief, the tears, and the anger without succumbing to the "language of pain." His mind keeps fighting and his legs keep moving, swinging high enough to crack in half the wood that binds him.

Subsequent writers and artists in the decades to come would take the Black Panther through different variations of this identity labyrinth. Kirby returned to write and illustrate a solo *Black Panther* title during the late 1970s that revived the more science-fictional elements of the super hero in a cosmic, time-traveling adventure. A limited series during the 1980s by Peter B. Gillis and Denys Cowan forced T'Challa to fend for himself after being abandoned by the Panther Spirit. McGregor resumed the writing duties on *Marvel Comics Presents* and sent the Black Panther to confront apartheid in South Africa and reunite with his stepmother, Ramonda. In the character's longest run, from 1988 to 2003, writer Christopher Priest and artists such as Mark Texeira, Sal Velluto, and Bob Almond sharpened T'Challa's commanding presence as a monarch and wealthy philanthropist visiting New York City. This acclaimed series also introduces U.S. State Department staffer Everett K. Ross and the corps of Wakandan women selected from the country's eighteen tribes to protect the king, called the Dora Milaje. Starting in 2005, Reginald Hudlin and a host of artists including John Romita Jr., Scot Eaton, and Francis Portela expanded our understanding of Wakanda with a deeper accounting of the spiritual practices and political traditions that shape the country. In the process, Hudlin's run introduced T'Challa's younger sister, Shuri (who would take on the mantle of Black Panther at one point), and featured his brief marriage to Storm of the X-Men. King T'Challa would continue to face his nemeses Klaw and Killmonger during these years, while the long-simmering tensions with the Avengers, and particularly King Namor of Atlantis, would erupt in various crossover events such as *Avengers vs. X-Men* in 2012.

When *Black Panther* relaunched in 2016 with writer Ta-Nehisi Coates and artist Brian Stelfreeze, T'Challa faces a civil war within Wakanda, one that forces him to reevaluate the monarchy in favor of a more democratic system. The series would be joined by a host of spin-offs such as *World of Wakanda*, *Black Panther & the Crew*, *Rise of the Black Panther*, and *Black Panther: Long Live the King*. And for the first time in the character's history, these titles featured an unprecedented number of Black women creators, including Roxane Gay, Yona Harvey, Nnedi Okorafor, Alitha Martinez, and Afua Richardson.

Each artist, writer, and editor, starting in 1966 with Lee and Kirby, has been instrumental in creating the Black Panther that we know today. Their contributions would come together in the award-winning 2018 motion picture, *Black Panther*, directed by Ryan Coogler and starring Chadwick Boseman in the title role. It would swiftly join the ranks of the top-grossing movies of all time, making more than $1.3 billion worldwide and becoming the first Marvel Comics Universe film to earn an Academy Award. The live-action production breathes new life and a rich cultural vitality into the Wakandan landscape that was unveiled so many years ago in the *Fantastic Four*, while the contours of T'Challa's personality and his righteous struggle in the face of Killmonger's resolve are indebted to the narrative constructed by McGregor, Buckler, and Graham. The film flawlessly dramatizes the enduring elements of the Black Panther's story that make this collection of comic books a Marvel classic. Across shifting political grounds and thorny paths of duty and conscience, T'Challa's journey bears witness to the capacity of established super heroes to develop both the vast and intricate dimensions of character over time. On these pages, the journey of the Black Panther begins.

QIANA J. WHITTED

# Black Panther

# *FANTASTIC FOUR* #52,

# JULY 1966

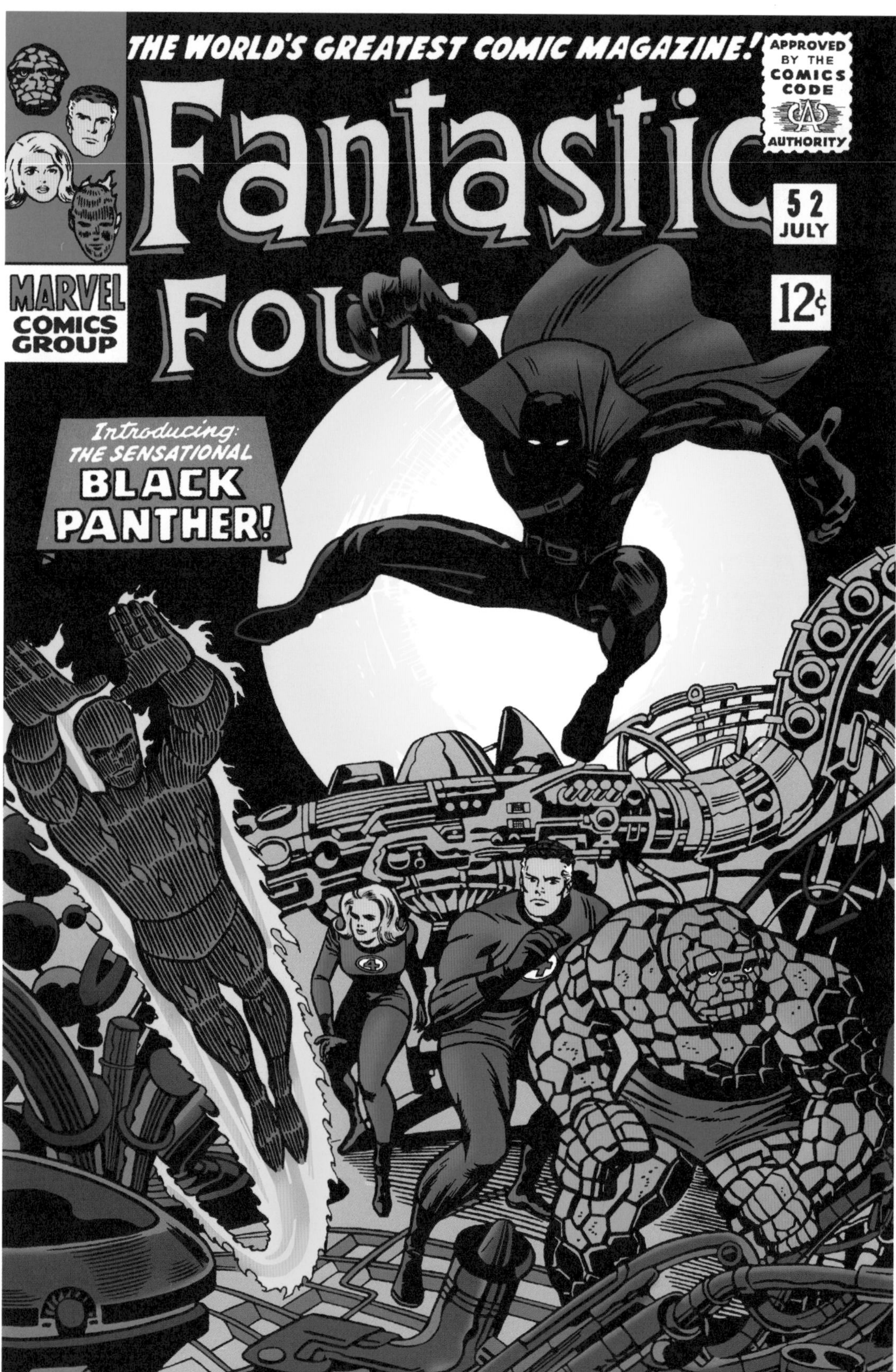
THE WORLD'S GREATEST COMIC MAGAZINE!
APPROVED BY THE COMICS CODE AUTHORITY
Fantastic Four
52 JULY
MARVEL COMICS GROUP
12¢
Introducing: THE SENSATIONAL
BLACK PANTHER!

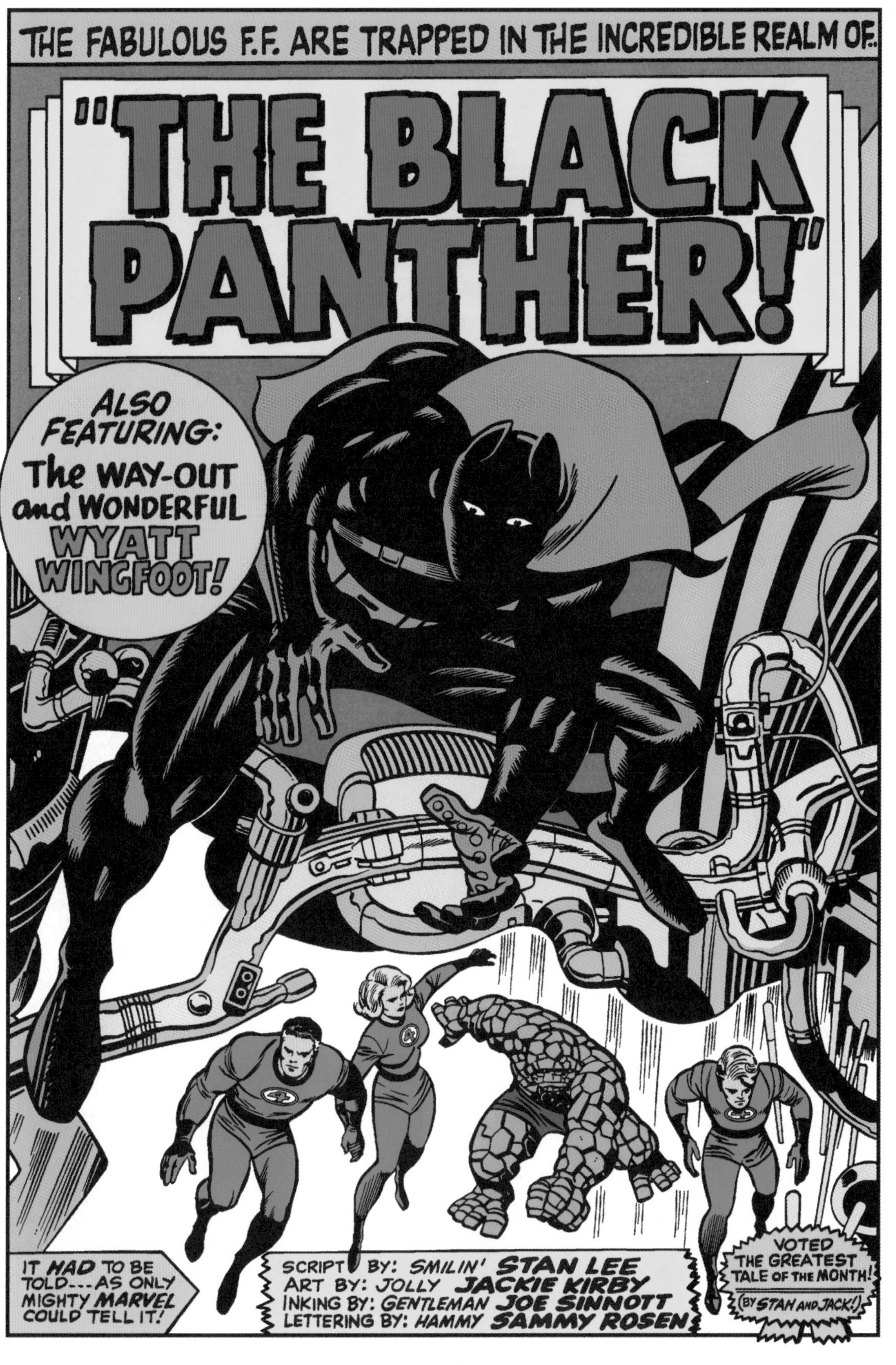
THE FABULOUS F.F. ARE TRAPPED IN THE INCREDIBLE REALM OF..
"THE BLACK PANTHER!"
ALSO FEATURING: The WAY-OUT and WONDERFUL WYATT WINGFOOT!
IT HAD TO BE TOLD---AS ONLY MIGHTY MARVEL COULD TELL IT!
SCRIPT BY: SMILIN' STAN LEE
ART BY: JOLLY JACKIE KIRBY
INKING BY: GENTLEMAN JOE SINNOTT
LETTERING BY: HAMMY SAMMY ROSEN
VOTED THE GREATEST TALE OF THE MONTH! (BY STAN AND JACK!)

WHEN YOU OR I GO FOR A SPIN, PUSSYCAT, WE HOP INTO THE OL' HOT ROD AND TAKE OFF! BUT, YOU WOULDN'T EXPECT THE F.F. TO BE AS CONVENTIONAL AS THAT, NOW, WOULD YOU?
HEY, STRETCH... WHEN DID YOU HAVE TIME TO DREAM UP A JAZZY FLYIN' FASTBACK LIKE THIS BABY?
I DIDN'T, BEN!
IT WAS AN UNEXPECTED GIFT... SENT TO ME BY AN AFRICAN CHIEFTAIN, CALLED... THE BLACK PANTHER!
IF ONLY JOHNNY WERE HOME FROM COLLEGE! HE'D BE IN SEVENTH HEAVEN BY NOW!
NEVER HEARD OF 'IM! BUT HOW DOES SOME REFUGEE FROM A TARZAN MOVIE LAY HIS HANDS ON THIS KINDA GIZMO?
'N WHY WOULD HE GIVE IT TO YOU?

HEY, EGGHEAD... WHAT HAPPENED? DIDJA LOSE CONTROL?
NO, BEN! RELAX... I JUST WANT TO SEE WHAT THIS SHIP WILL DO! ITS MANEUVER-ABILITY IS AMAZING!

IT SEEMS TO BE POWERED BY SOME SORT OF MAGNETIC WAVES...
AND, THESE PUSH-BUTTON CONTROLS MAKE HANDLING IT AS EASY AS DIALING A PHONE!
I WONDER HOW THE BLACK PANTHER... WHOEVER HE IS... GOT POSSESSION OF SUCH A SHIP?

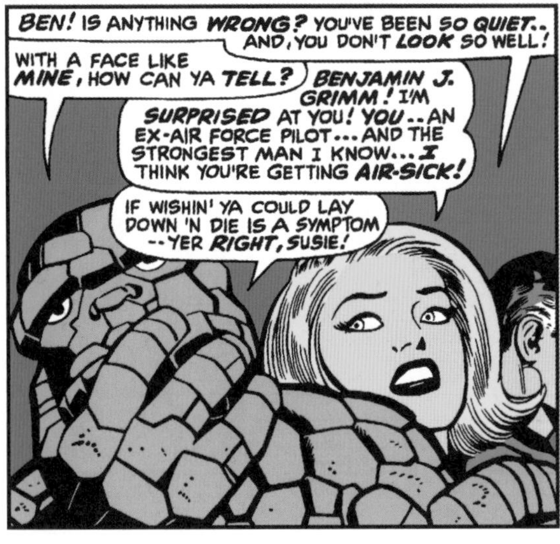
BEN! IS ANYTHING WRONG? YOU'VE BEEN SO QUIET.. AND, YOU DON'T LOOK SO WELL!
WITH A FACE LIKE MINE, HOW CAN YA TELL?
BENJAMIN J. GRIMM! I'M SURPRISED AT YOU! YOU.. AN EX-AIR FORCE PILOT... AND THE STRONGEST MAN I KNOW... I THINK YOU'RE GETTING AIR-SICK!
IF WISHIN' YA COULD LAY DOWN 'N DIE IS A SYMPTOM --YER RIGHT, SUSIE!

I THINK BEN'S PUTTING YOU ON, HONEY!
BUT, I'LL HEAD FOR THE BAXTER BUILDING NOW, ANYWAY! THE BLACK PANTHER'S EMISSARY IS WAITING FOR US ON THE LANDING-ROOF..!
I'M ANXIOUS TO HAVE HIM TELL ME MORE ABOUT OUR MYSTERIOUS BENEFACTOR!
2.

THUS, A FEW SECONDS LATER...
THE SKY-CRAFT IS YOURS TO KEEP, MR. RICHARDS, IF YOU ACCEPT MY CHIEFTAIN'S INVITATION!
HE WISHES THE FAMOUS FANTASTIC FOUR TO BE HIS GUESTS IN THE KINGDOM OF WAKANDA!
THERE, HE SHALL ARRANGE THE GREATEST HUNT OF ALL TIME...IN HONOR OF YOUR VISIT!
WELL, WE COULD USE A VACATION!
BEN! DID YOU HEAR THAT? WE'RE GOING TO... OH, DEAR! YOU WEREN'T FOOLING!
YOU REALLY WERE AIR-SICK!
YOU'RE TELLIN' ME!

VERY WELL! AS SOON AS MY WIFE GIVES THE THING SOME DRAMAMINE FOR HIS AIR-SICKNESS, WE'LL BE DELIGHTED TO ACCEPT YOUR OFFER!
EXCELLENT, SIR!

I SHALL COMMUNICATE THESE GLAD TIDINGS TO THE BLACK PANTHER AT ONCE!
HE TOOK A METAL DEVICE FROM INSIDE HIS TOGA! BUT, IT'S SO SMALL..!
CAN HE ACTUALLY TRANSMIT A MESSAGE HALF-WAY 'ROUND THE GLOBE... WITH THAT?

YOU SEEM SURPRISED, SIR! ACTUALLY, THIS APPARATUS OPERATES BY C.C.W. ...COSMIC CHANNEL WAVES WHICH CAN BLANKET ALL OF EARTH!
AND NOW, BY YOUR LEAVE... AT THE MERE PRESS OF A BUTTON...
...I SHALL CONTACT MY CHIEFTAIN... IN WAKANDA!

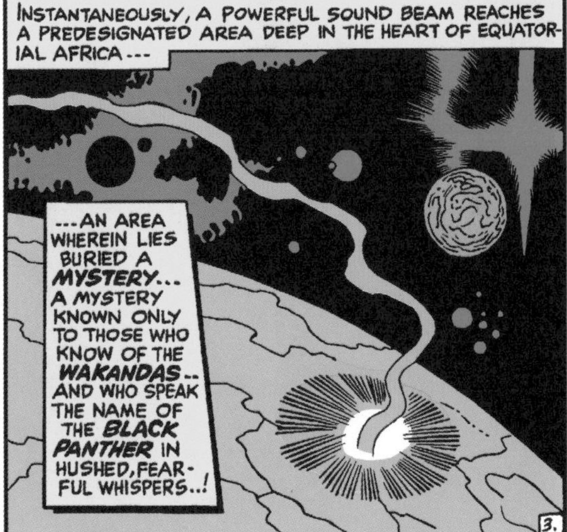
INSTANTANEOUSLY, A POWERFUL SOUND BEAM REACHES A PREDESIGNATED AREA DEEP IN THE HEART OF EQUATORIAL AFRICA---
...AN AREA WHEREIN LIES BURIED A MYSTERY... A MYSTERY KNOWN ONLY TO THOSE WHO KNOW OF THE WAKANDAS.. AND WHO SPEAK THE NAME OF THE BLACK PANTHER IN HUSHED, FEARFUL WHISPERS..!
3.

BUT NOW, AS THE *FANTASTIC FOUR* PREPARE FOR THEIR MOMENTOUS JOURNEY, LET US DO WHAT FEW WESTERN MEN HAVE EVER DONE... LET US GAZE UPON THE ENTHRONED FIGURE OF HIM WHO RULES THE WAKANDAS...

MIGHTY CHIEFTAIN! THE SIGNAL HAS BEEN RECEIVED! YOUR OFFER IS ACCEPTED! THE *FANTASTIC FOUR* WILL COME TO WAKANDA!

AS I *KNEW* THEY WOULD! IT IS *GOOD*!

NOW, LET THE *PREPARATIONS* BEGIN! THIS SHALL BE THE *GREATEST HUNT* OF ALL!

RAISE THE TOTEM! LET THE RITUAL BEGIN!
THE TIME HAS COME FOR THE BLACK PANTHER TO STALK ONCE MORE!

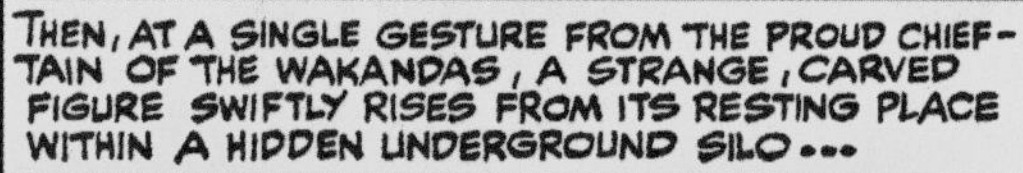

THEN, AT A SINGLE GESTURE FROM THE PROUD CHIEFTAIN OF THE WAKANDAS, A STRANGE, CARVED FIGURE SWIFTLY RISES FROM ITS RESTING PLACE WITHIN A HIDDEN UNDERGROUND SILO...

HO! YOUR BROTHER GREETS YOU THIS DAY! THE HUNT IS ABOUT TO BEGIN!
4.

DEFTLY PUSHING A SERIES OF DELICATE CONTROL BUTTONS AT THE BASE OF THE GIGANTIC, FELINE FIGURE, THE POWERFULLY-BUILT MONARCH EXPOSES A BANK OF ELECTRONIC COMPUTERS, WITH WHICH HE CONTROLS THE MYRIAD WONDERS OF HIS MYSTERIOUS JUNGLE EMPIRE--!
ALL DEVICES ARE FULLY OPERATIONAL!
AND SO I REMOVE MY STALKING COSTUME FROM ITS CAREFULLY CONCEALED COMPARTMENT!

NOW, LET THE FANTASTIC FOUR COME!
THE BLACK PANTHER SHALL GREET THEM--- AS THEY HAVE NEVER BEEN GREETED BEFORE!

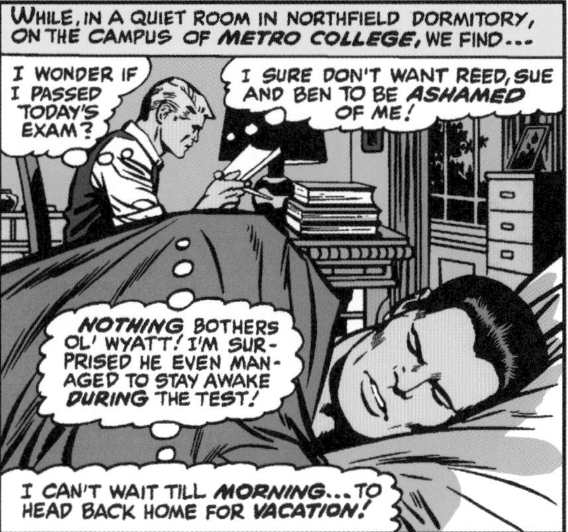
WHILE, IN A QUIET ROOM IN NORTHFIELD DORMITORY, ON THE CAMPUS OF METRO COLLEGE, WE FIND---
I WONDER IF I PASSED TODAY'S EXAM?
I SURE DON'T WANT REED, SUE AND BEN TO BE ASHAMED OF ME!
NOTHING BOTHERS OL' WYATT! I'M SURPRISED HE EVEN MANAGED TO STAY AWAKE DURING THE TEST!
I CAN'T WAIT TILL MORNING... TO HEAD BACK HOME FOR VACATION!

IT'S HARD---HARDER THAN I THOUGHT IT WOULD BE--- TO CONCENTRATE ON MY COURSES... WHEN I CAN'T GET CRYSTAL OUT OF MY MIND!
BUT, I'VE GOT TO KEEP TRYING! UNTIL REED CAN FIND SOME WAY TO BREAK THE BARRIER THAT HOLDS HER PRISONER,* THERE'S NOTHING I CAN DO!
NOTHING BUT HOPE---AND DREAM--- AND PRAY!
I'VE GOT TO SNAP OUT OF IT... AND I WILL! IF ONLY THE EVENINGS WEREN'T SO LONG..!
* IF YOU MISSED F.F. #48, DON'T TELL US! YOU KNOW HOW UPSET WE GET! --- SHAKY STAN.

HEY!! HOLY HANNAH!! WHAT THE...?!!
SURPRISE!

HIYA, JOE COLLEGE! WHAT'S THE GOOD WORD, LITTLE ITTY BITTY BUDDY?
I'LL ITTY BITTY BUDDY YOU, YOU BLUE-EYED BIRDBRAIN!!
I KNOWED YA'D BE AS GOOD-NATURED AS EVER, JUNIOR!
LEGGO, BEFORE I GIVE YOU A HOT-FOOT BETWEEN WHERE YOUR EARS OUGHTTA BE!
5.

WHAT KINDA CRUMMY COLLEGE *IS* THIS? YA DON'T LOOK ANY MORE EJJICATED TO *ME!*
OH, JOHNNY-- JOHNNY! IT'S SO *GOOD* TO SEE MY LITTLE KID BROTHER AGAIN!
SAME HERE, SIS! BUT YOU DON'T HAVETA BREAK MY RIBS TO *PROVE* IT!
GIMME *FIVE*, NEW BROTHER-IN-LAW! BUT TELL ME--- HOW'D YOU ALL *GET* HERE SO FAST?
IT WAS A *BREEZE*, JOHNNY! WE FLEW IN BY LIGHTNING-FAST *MAGNETIC WAVES!*
GOSH, REED--- YOU'VE TURNED INTO A GREAT *KIDDER* WHILE I WAS GONE, HUH?
I'M NOT KIDDING, LAD!

IT'S A NEW SHIP--- OPERATES ON A BRAND NEW PRINCIPLE! IT WAS THE GIFT OF AN AFRICAN CHIEFTAIN!
NOW I *KNOW* YOU'RE CONNIN' ME! HOW DOES AN AFRICAN CHIEFTAIN LATCH ONTO A PLANE THAT FLIES BY MAGNETIC WAVES?
*THAT*, LITTLE PARTNER, IS JUST WHAT WE'RE GOING TO *FIND OUT!*
WE'RE LEAVING FOR *WAKANDA*.. RIGHT AWAY! AND *YOU'RE* GOING WITH US!

LIKE *WOW*, BROTHER-IN-LAW! THAT'S THE *GEAREST!*
BUT LOOK--- CAN I BRING MY BUDDY, *WYATT WINGFOOT?* HE'LL *FLIP!*
SURE, JOHNNY!

ANY BUDDY OF *YOURS* IS A BUDDY OF *OURS*, JOHNNY BOY!
*ONE* THING GOOD ABOUT 'IM--- ANY GUY WHO CAN SLEEP LIKE *THAT* AIN'T GONNA BE KEEPIN' US AWAKE BY *JAWIN'* ALL NIGHT!
HEY, KID--- HE'S *ALIVE*, AIN'T HE?
IT'S HARD TO TELL, BEN! WYATT DOESN'T *MOVE* VERY FAST... UNLESS HE *WANTS* TO! BUT WHEN HE *DOES*--- *WATCH OUT!*

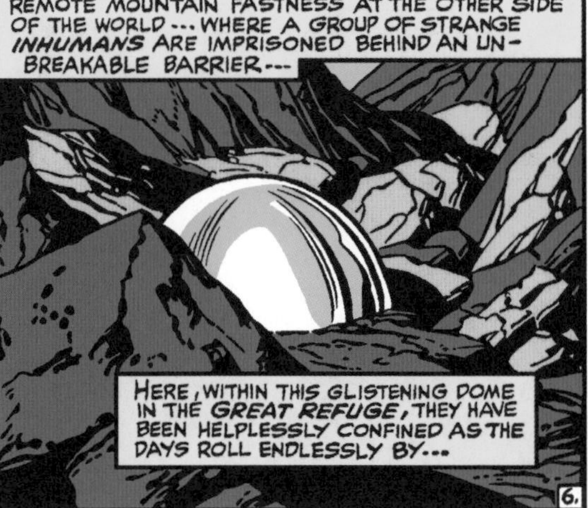
AND NOW, LEST YOU THINK WE'VE FORGOTTEN ABOUT THEM, LET US BRIEFLY TURN OUR ATTENTION TO A REMOTE MOUNTAIN FASTNESS AT THE OTHER SIDE OF THE WORLD--- WHERE A GROUP OF STRANGE *INHUMANS* ARE IMPRISONED BEHIND AN UN-BREAKABLE BARRIER---
HERE, WITHIN THIS GLISTENING DOME IN THE *GREAT REFUGE*, THEY HAVE BEEN HELPLESSLY CONFINED AS THE DAYS ROLL ENDLESSLY BY--
6.

BUT, THOUGH THEIR PLIGHT SEEMS TRULY HOPELESS, THEY REFUSE TO DESPAIR...
YOU WASTE YOUR TIME, KARNAK! EVEN YOUR POWER CANNOT SHATTER A NEGATIVE ZONE!
IT COULD, GORGON..IF I COULD FIND THE ONE WEAK SPOT! PERHAPS I NEED MORE PRACTICE!
BUT YOU'VE BEEN SHATTERING THOSE DIAMOND BLOCKS FOR MONTHS!
I MUST KEEP MY HAND IN! WE MUST NEVER STOP TRYING!

EVERYTHING HAS ONE WEAK SPOT!! EVERYTHING!! EVEN THIS SEEMINGLY INDESTRUCTIBLE DIAMOND BLOCK!
BUT, A NEGATIVE ZONE IS DIFFERENT! IT CAN REPEL ANY POSITIVE MATTER!
NO! I'LL FIND A WAY! NOTHING CAN RESIST THE POWER OF KARNAK!

NOTHING!!
CLAKK!

IF I CAN SHATTER THE HARDEST SUBSTANCE KNOWN ON EARTH... WHY CAN'T I FREE US FROM THE PRISON OF THIS ACCURSED NEGATIVE ZONE??! WHY? WHY? WHY?
OH, KARNAK...IF ONLY YOU COULD! IF ONLY WE COULD ONE DAY REJOIN THE HUMAN RACE..!
STAND BACK! I'LL TRY AGAIN..!
IF I COULD SEE JOHNNY STORM ONCE MORE... FEEL HIS ARMS AROUND ME AGAIN...JUST ONCE MORE...
I'VE TOLD YOU, CRYSTAL.. YOU MUST FORGET HIM! YOU MUSTN'T TORTURE YOURSELF SO!

ARRRHHHH!
NO MORE, KARNAK... NO MORE! YOU'LL BREAK YOUR HAND! THERE MUST BE ANOTHER WAY!!

THEN, FROM A SECURELY-LOCKED CELL, HIGH ABOVE, THE MAD, CACKLING LAUGHTER OF MAXIMUS... THE POWER-CRAZED BROTHER OF BLACK BOLT.. TAUNTS THE DESPERATE LITTLE BAND WHOM WE KNOW AS... THE INHUMANS!
YOU'LL NEVER BE FREE! NEVER! NEVER! NEVER!
I AM THE RIGHTFUL KING... NOT BLACK BOLT!!
AND MY SUBJECTS MUST REMAIN WITH ME... FOREVER!!
7.

WHAT MONUMENTAL IRONY! ONLY MAXIMUS KNOWS THE SECRET OF ESCAPING FROM THE NEGATIVE ZONE!! THUS, THE KEY WILL BE ETERNALLY LOCKED IN A MADMAN'S BRAIN!
AHH, BLACK BOLT.. IT IS YOU WHO ARE THE MIGHTIEST AMONG US... AND EVEN YOU STAND HELPLESS!
'TIS ALMOST GOOD THAT YOU HAVE LOST THE POWER OF SPEECH... FOR, OF WHAT USE ARE WORDS TO US..NOW?
WE MUST NEVER ABANDON HOPE! I KNOW THE MAN I LOVE WILL NOT FAIL US! SOME DAY... SOMEHOW..BLACK BOLT WILL FIND THE WAY TO FREE US ALL!
BUT, FOR ME, IT MAY BE... TOO LATE! WHAT IF JOHNNY STORM HAS FOUND ANOTHER?
I'LL NEVER STOP TRYING! NEVER! NEVER..!

AND THAT, FRANTIC ONE, IS ALL WE'LL SEE OF THE INHUMANS THIS ISH! WE JUST WANTED TO WHET YOUR APPETITE A BIT! BESIDES, IT'S TIME TO VISIT WAKANDA... SO C'MON..THE SAFARI'S JUST LEAVING...
SHIP APPROACHES! ALL GOES AS PLANNED!
AS THE CHIEFTAIN HAS PROMISED... THIS WILL BE HIS GREATEST HUNT!

THE JUNGLE LOOKS SO PRIMITIVE... SO UNDEVELOPED! ARE YOU SURE WE HAVE REACHED WAKANDA TERRITORY?
WE ARE VIRTUALLY AT OUR DESTINATION, MR. RICHARDS!
AND YOU WOULD DO WELL TO REMEMBER... IN THIS LAND, THINGS ARE NOT ALWAYS... AS THEY SEEM!

IT'S SO HARD TO BELIEVE THAT A SHIP SUCH AS THIS ONE COULD HAVE COME FROM A LAND WITH NO SIGN OF TECHNOLOGY ...OF INDUSTRIAL DEVELOPMENT..!
BEFORE YOUR VISIT IS ENDED, MRS. RICHARDS, YOU WILL FIND MANY MORE SURPRISING FACETS OF OUR LITTLE KINGDOM!
I DON'T LIKE IT! THERE'S SOMETHING OMINOUS IN THE AIR... AND YET, I DON'T WANT TO ALARM SUE!
IT'S TOO LATE TO TURN BACK NOW! I'LL JUST HAVE TO REMAIN ON GUARD!

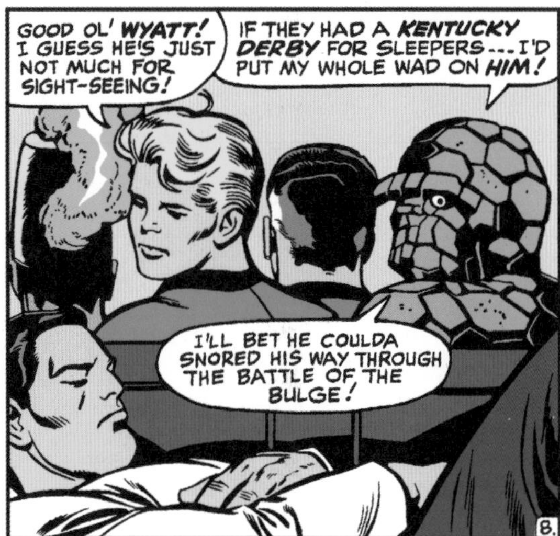
GOOD OL' WYATT! I GUESS HE'S JUST NOT MUCH FOR SIGHT-SEEING!
IF THEY HAD A KENTUCKY DERBY FOR SLEEPERS... I'D PUT MY WHOLE WAD ON HIM!
I'LL BET HE COULDA SNORED HIS WAY THROUGH THE BATTLE OF THE BULGE!
8.

SUDDENLY... THERE IS A BREAK IN THE DENSE FOLIAGE BELOW---AND WITH UNERRING PRECISION, THE GRIM-LIPPED NATIVE PILOT GUIDES HIS SILENT SHIP INTO... A WORLD OF SHEER WONDERMENT..!
IT'S A STRANGE NEW LAND... HIDDEN FROM ABOVE BY A CONCEALING COVER OF GIANT TREES.
IT'S TRULY A JUNGLE...BUT LIKE NOTHING EVER SPAWNED BY NATURE! IT'S A MAN-MADE JUNGLE!
INDEED, YOU ARE CORRECT! THE ENTIRE TOPOGRAPHY AND FLORA ARE ELECTRONICALLY-CONTROLLED MECHANICAL APPARATUS! THE VERY BRANCHES ABOUT US ARE COMPOSED OF DELICATELY-CONSTRUCTED WIRES..
WHILE THE FLOWERS WHICH ABOUND HERE ARE HIGHLY COMPLEX BUTTONS AND DIALS! EVEN THE BOULDERS CAN BE HEARD TO HUM WITH THE STEADY PULSE OF COMPUTER DYNAMOS!
THEN, NO SOONER DOES THE AMAZING SHIP COME TO A VIBRATIONLESS HALT, THAN...
OUR GUIDE!! HE'S GONE! HE VANISHED BEHIND A NETWORK OF TUBES AND COILS!
STAY TOGETHER... ALL OF YOU! WHOEVER CREATED THIS ELECTRONIC NIGHTMARE HAS KEPT IT A SECRET FOR SOME DEADLY REASON!
PHOOEY! IT'LL TAKE MORE'N A MESS'A CHROME-PLATED NUTS 'N BOLTS TO SCARE ME!
9.

HEY, LOOK! IT'S LAUGHIN' BOY! THAT'S WHERE HE DISAPPEARED TO! HE'S MAKIN' A GETAWAY DOWN THAT BLAMED ELEVATOR!
LUMBERING FOOL! YOU'LL NEVER REACH ME IN TIME!

I WON'T, HUH?
OKAY, SO YA MANAGED TO GIT DOWN TO YER RAT HOLE! I'LL RIP THE BLAMED PLATFORM RIGHT OUTTA THE GROUND, 'N THEN ---
AGGHHH-HHHH!
BEN!

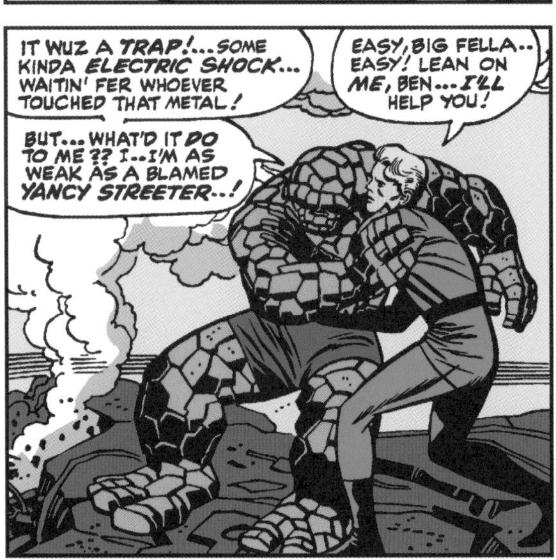
IT WUZ A TRAP!...SOME KINDA ELECTRIC SHOCK... WAITIN' FER WHOEVER TOUCHED THAT METAL!
EASY, BIG FELLA.. EASY! LEAN ON ME, BEN...I'LL HELP YOU!
BUT...WHAT'D IT DO TO ME?? I..I'M AS WEAK AS A BLAMED YANCY STREETER..!

YOU WASTE YOUR TIME, JOHNNY STORM! NOTHING CAN HELP ANY OF YOU NOW!
THOSE ELECTRIC VOLTS HAVE CAUSED A CHAIN REACTION IN HIS BLOOD CELLS WHICH WILL WEAKEN HIM FOR FIVE MINUTES!
AND THAT IS ALL THE TIME THE BLACK PANTHER SHALL NEED!

'TWAS I WHO INVITED YOU FOR THE HUNT!
BUT, I NEGLECTED TO TELL YOU ONE THING ---
IT IS YOU WHO SHALL BE HUNTED!
10.

MISTER, IF THIS IS YOUR IDEA OF A JOKE, YOU MAY HAVE NOTICED... WE'RE NOT LAUGHING!
HE DUCKED UNDER MY BLOW WITH THE EASE OF THE BEAST FOR WHICH HE'S NAMED!
WINGFOOT! STAY BACK! THIS ISN'T YOUR FIGHT!
I WOULDN'T BET ON THAT, MR. RICHARDS!

HOLD IT, WYATT! WHEN MR. FANTASTIC BARKS AN ORDER... THAT'S IT, PAL!
ANYWAY, THIS KINDA THING IS MORE IN THE LINE OF THE HUMAN TORCH!
FLAME ON!

YOUR FIERY ATTACK DOES NOT IMPRESS THE BLACK PANTHER! LET US SEE WHETHER YOUR BLAZING POWER CAN MATCH MY FELINE AGILITY!
WOW! HE'S NOT KIDDIN'! HE'S AS NIMBLE AS A TWO-LEGGED CAT!

HA! YOU REACTED JUST AS I KNEW YOU WOULD... PLUNGING HEADLONG INTO THE FIREPROOF TRAP I'VE SO CARE-FULLY PREPARED!
UH OH! JOHNNY BOY... WHAT HAVE YOU BLUNDERED INTO THIS TIME?

AN ASBESTOS DOOR--- AUTO-MATICALLY LOCKED BEHIND ME...CAN'T GET OUT!
VACUUM BLASTS! PUTTING OUT MY FLAME ... WEAKENING ME!! NO DEFENSE AGAINST THEM...! UHHHHH!

TWO MIGHTY MEMBERS OF THE FAMED FANTASTIC FOUR DEFEATED IN AS MANY MINUTES BY THE BLACK PANTHER!
NOW TO LOWER YOUR TRAP INTO THE GROUND... WHILE I COMPLETE MY NEWEST AND GREATEST HUNT!
11.

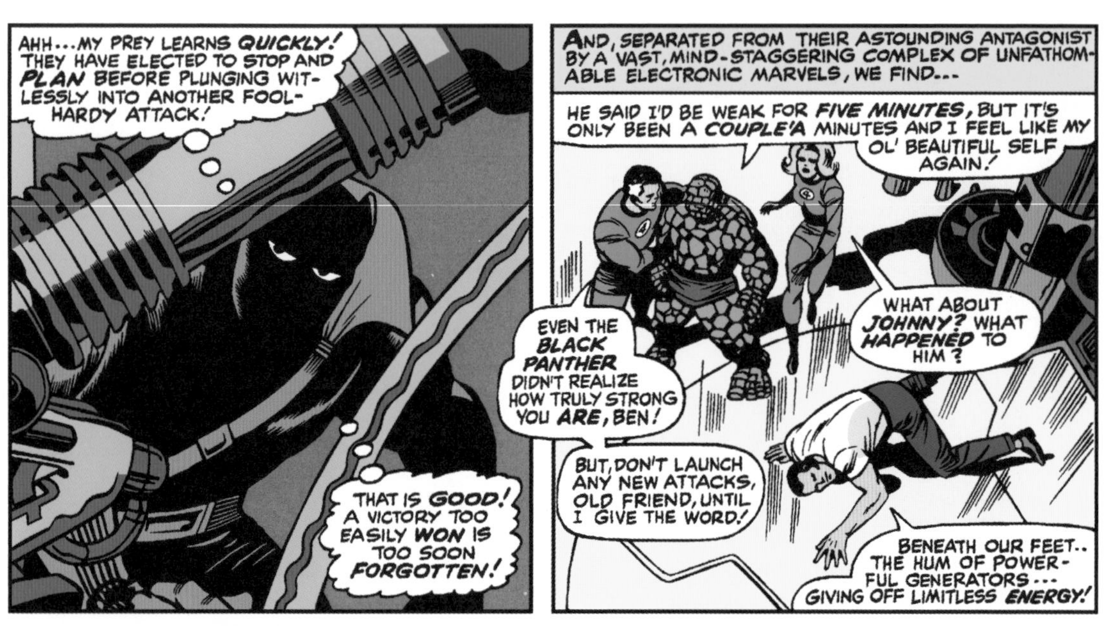
AHH...MY PREY LEARNS QUICKLY! THEY HAVE ELECTED TO STOP AND PLAN BEFORE PLUNGING WIT-LESSLY INTO ANOTHER FOOL-HARDY ATTACK!
THAT IS GOOD! A VICTORY TOO EASILY WON IS TOO SOON FORGOTTEN!
AND, SEPARATED FROM THEIR ASTOUNDING ANTAGONIST BY A VAST, MIND-STAGGERING COMPLEX OF UNFATHOM-ABLE ELECTRONIC MARVELS, WE FIND...
HE SAID I'D BE WEAK FOR FIVE MINUTES, BUT IT'S ONLY BEEN A COUPLE'A MINUTES AND I FEEL LIKE MY OL' BEAUTIFUL SELF AGAIN!
EVEN THE BLACK PANTHER DIDN'T REALIZE HOW TRULY STRONG YOU ARE, BEN!
BUT, DON'T LAUNCH ANY NEW ATTACKS, OLD FRIEND, UNTIL I GIVE THE WORD!
WHAT ABOUT JOHNNY? WHAT HAPPENED TO HIM?
BENEATH OUR FEET.. THE HUM OF POWER-FUL GENERATORS... GIVING OFF LIMITLESS ENERGY!

BEN--WAIT! WHAT ARE YOU DOING?!!
DON'T DO IT, MR. GRIMM! PUT THAT IRON DEVICE DOWN! PUT IT DOWN!
RELAX, STRETCHO! I'M JUST TESTIN' MY EVER-LOVIN' STRENGTH!

YOU GOTTA BE KIDDIN'!
THE ONLY GUY-WHO GIVES ME ORDERS IS A GUY WHO CAN LICK ME!
AND THERE AIN'T NO SUCH ANIMAL!

LOOK, SIR... I'M NOT PRESUMING TO GIVE ORDERS TO ANYONE!
BUT, IT'S PATENTLY OBVIOUS THAT A SUPERIOR INTELLECT BUILT THIS ELECTRONIC JUNGLE... AND EVERY-THING YOU TOUCH MIGHT BE A FATAL BOOBY TRAP!
USE YOUR HEAD, BEN! WINGFOOT IS DEAD RIGHT!
OUR FIRST JOB IS TO LEARN MORE ABOUT WHAT WE'RE UP AGAINST!
AND I'M THE ONE TO DO THAT FOR YOU, SIR!
THE BLOOD OF MY ANCESTORS-- THE GREATEST SCOUTS OF ALL TIME... FLOWS STRONG IN MY VEINS!
NO WONDER JOHNNY TOOK A SHINE TO THAT JOE! THE KID'S GOT WHAT IT TAKES!
WE'LL STAY TO-GETHER HERE TILL YOU RE-TURN, SON!
12

SUE, DARLING ... DON'T WORRY ABOUT JOHNNY.. YET! THE PANTHER IS JUST TOYING WITH US NOW ... TAUNTING US!
IF ONLY WE COULD LEARN HIS MOTIVE!
THE ODDS SEEM SO HOPELESS! WE'RE ON HIS HOME GROUND.. IN A FIGHT WHERE HE MAKES THE RULES ... WHERE HE HAS PLANNED EVERYTHING BEFOREHAND!
SHEESH! YA WANNA BORROW MY CRYIN' TOWEL ?!!
HEY.. LISTEN! WHAT'SAT?

DRUMS!! LOUD 'N CLEAR! IT MUST BE MOOD MUSIC TO BE CLOBBERED BY!
LOOK SHARP!! IT'S AN ATTACK SIGNAL OF SOME SORT!
THANKS FER TELLIN' US! WE MIGHTA THOUGHT IT WAS LAWRENCE WELK!

TAKE YOUR POSITIONS!! READY YOUR POLARITY GUNS! RELEASE SAFETY! AIM!
CLICK!
CLICK!
CLICK!

FIRE!
WHAT'SIS ... A GAG? DO THEY EXPECT TO POLISH US OFF BY SHOOTIN' FLASHLIGHT BEAMS AT US?
THEY'RE NOT LIGHT BEAMS, BEN! FEEL THAT VIBRATION? WE'VE BEEN HIT BY MAGNETIC ANTI-POLARITY BEAMS!
WHAT DOES IT MEAN? WHAT ARE THEY..?

THEY MAKE OBJECTS REPEL EACH OTHER! WE CAN'T STAY TO-GETHER ... TILL THEY WEAR OFF!
THE PANTHER WANTS TO SEPARATE US ... TO ATTACK US INDIVIDUALLY! TURN INVISIBLE WHEN YOU LAND, SUE!
IT'S GETTIN' SO THAT YA CAN'T POKE YER SNOOT OUTTA THE HOUSE WITHOUT RUNNIN' INTA SOME NEW REJECT FROM MAD SCIENTISTS, INCORPORATED!
THWUP!
13.

I'M SLOWING DOWN! THE POLARITY GETS WEAKER ...THE FURTHER I GO FROM THE OTHERS!
AS SOON AS I TOUCH THE GROUND, I'LL TURN INVISIBLE AS REED SAID!

A LAUDABLE EFFORT, MRS. RICHARDS... BUT YOU CANNOT HOPE TO EVADE THE BLACK PANTHER SO EASILY!
IT'S HIM! HE KNOWS I'M HERE!
I MUST BE PREPARED FOR ANY-THING!

IT IS NOT FOR NOTHING I AM CALLED THE BLACK PANTHER!
FOR, MY SENSES ARE SHARP AS A JUNGLE CAT'S!
I CAN'T TRUST INVISIBILITY ALONE!..MUST RUN!

THOUGH A PANTHER MIGHT NOT SEE YOU, DO YOU THINK HE'D FAIL TO HEAR YOUR SOFT FOOT-FALLS?
HE'S RIGHT! MY ONLY CHANCE IS TO STAND STOCK STILL!

I OUTSMARTED HIM! BY STANDING NEAR THIS PULSATING GENERATOR, THE SOUND OF MY OWN FRANTIC BREATHING IS DROWNED OUT!
BUT... WHY IS HE STOPPING?

I APPLAUD YOUR CLEVERNESS, MRS. RICHARDS! BUT, YOU OVER-LOOKED ONE THING! EVEN WHEN A PANTHER CANNOT HEAR HIS VICTIM---HE CAN ALWAYS DETECT THE SCENT!
HE'S STARTING TO TURN! HE'S FOUND ME!

AH! YOU HAVE OBLIGINGLY TURNED VISIBLE! THAT MEANS YOU ARE ABOUT TO RESORT TO YOUR DEFENSIVE FORCE FIELD, WHICH CAN ONLY BE EMPLOYED WHEN YOU LOSE YOUR INVISIBILITY!
YOU SEE, I HAVE MADE AN EXHAUSTIVE STUDY OF THE STRANGE POWERS OF YOUR FAMOUS TEAM!
HE WAS TOO FAST! HE LEAPED INSIDE MY FORCE FIELD BEFORE I COULD SEAL IT!
A STUDY WHICH HAS SERVED ME IN GOOD STEAD!
14.

YOU ARE FORTUNATE IN ONE RESPECT, YOUNG LADY! UNLIKE THE CLAWS OF MY NAMESAKE, MINE HAVE THE POWER TO EMIT A HARMLESS SLEEP GAS.!
OHHHH...!

BY THE TIME YOU AWAKEN, THE HUNT WILL BE OVER AND THE BLACK PANTHER SHALL HAVE WON HIS GREATEST VICTORY!
BY NOW, THE BLUNDERING THING SHOULD HAVE STUMBLED INTO THE SECOND TRAP I'VE PREPARED FOR HIM!

THE TIMING IS PERFECT!
THERE HE IS... REFRESHING HIMSELF BY WASHING HIS FACE AT WHAT SEEMS TO BE A FOUNTAIN OF CRYSTAL-CLEAR WATER--!
I TRUST YOU'VE ENJOYED SPLASHING A DANGEROUS AMOUNT OF DEVITALIZING FLUID UPON YOURSELF!
GLURRGLE! ...HUH..??

THAT LIQUID IS BUT ONE OF MANY TRAPS I'VE PREPARED TO SAP YOUR STRENGTH..!
...SAP IT JUST ENOUGH SO THAT WE TWO CAN BATTLE, HAND-TO-HAND!
FOR, IN ANY EQUAL MATCH, THE BLACK PANTHER IS CERTAIN TO WIN!

SAY, YOU 'N RICHARDS DIDN'T GO TO THE SAME PREP SCHOOL OR SOMETHIN', DIDJA?
IT'S MOST UNLIKELY! ---WHY?
YA BOTH GOT THE SAME CORN-BALL HABIT...

...YA CAN TALK A GUY TO DEATH WHILE YER FIGHTIN' 'IM!
PERHAPS, BUT I CAN DO FAR MORE THAN TALK..
..AS YOU SHALL SEE..!

AMONG OTHER THINGS, I HAVE LONG BEEN THE BOXING CHAMPION OF THIS ENTIRE CONTINENT!
WOK!
WELL GOODY FER YOU!..URPPP!
15.

JUST STAY THERE, WISE GUY... TILL I GIT TO MY FEET! THAT'S ALL I ASK!
I SHALL BE HAPPY TO OBLIGE YOU!

FOR, AFTER ALL... UNTIL YOU STAND, I'LL BE DENIED THE EXQUISITE PLEASURE OF FLOORING YOU AGAIN!
GOTTA STEADY MY-SELF! CAN'T FALL APART JUST 'CAUSE HE WEAKENED ME WITH THAT PHONY WATER!

THEN SUDDENLY... WITH FEROCIOUS SPEED TOTALLY BELYING HIS MAMMOTH BULK, THE THING STRIKES BACK..!
POW
MEBBE THIS'LL SHUT YER YAP FER A WHILE!

NUTS! IF NOT FER DRINKIN' THAT BLASTED WATER, I'DA DEMOLISHED 'IM WITH THAT WHAP! BUT, I'LL BEAT 'IM ANYHOW!
YOUR COURAGE IS TRULY A MATCH FOR YOUR FAME!
BUT YOUR SKILL, ALAS, CANNOT NEARLY COMPARE WITH MINE!
YEAH? WE'LL SEE ABOUT THAT!

HE'S CHARGING INTO ME LIKE A MADDENED RHINO! I'VE GOT TO SIDESTEP, AND THEN...
LOOK OUT!! IF YOU UPSET THAT HIGH-VOLTAGE REFRIGERATION UNIT, IT'LL FREEZE YOU ALIVE WITHIN SECONDS!
BAM!
UNHHH! NOW YA TELL ME!!
TOO LATE!!

YOU ARE INDEED FORTUNATE, THING!
YOUR OWN MASSIVE STRENGTH WAS BEGINNING TO RETURN AGAIN AT THE EXACT MOMENT OF IMPACT!
THUS, YOU WILL SURVIVE THE DEEP FREEZE... THOUGH IT WILL TAKE YOU A WHILE TO THAW OUT!

AND NOW FOR YOUR LEADER... THE ONE WHOM I CONSIDER THE MOST DANGEROUS FOE OF ALL!
BUT, EVEN THE FABULOUS MR. FANTASTIC WILL BE NO MATCH FOR ME!
16

MEANWHILE, WHAT OF WYATT WINGFOOT? (...WE THOUGHT YOU'D NEVER ASK!)
SO! THE EDGE OF THE REAL JUNGLE, AT LAST! BUT, WHAT'S THIS?
A HIDDEN OBSERVATION POST... THE WAKANDAS HAVE BEEN SECRETLY MONITORING THE F.F.!
OUR CHIEFTAIN MUST DEFEAT ONLY ONE MORE TO ACHIEVE HIS GOAL OF TOTAL VICTORY!
THE BLACK PANTHER SHALL NOT FAIL!

BUT THEN, WITH THE STEALTHY SILENCE OF HIS PROUD, RED-SKINNED FOREBEARS, THE INDIAN YOUTH STRIKES!
IF I CAN CRIPPLE THE BLACK PANTHER'S COMMUNICATIONS, IT MAY HELP THE F.F.!
BAM!

LUCKY FOR ME THEY WEREN'T EXPECTING AN ATTACK! NOW IF THEY'LL JUST STAY OUT LONG ENOUGH..!
THERE! THEY WON'T BE ABLE TO SPY ON ANYONE ELSE WITH THESE ELECTRONIC SCANNERS!
AND NOW, I'D BETTER GET BACK TO THE OTHERS... WHILE I STILL CAN!
KRAK!

I'VE GOT TO FIND THEM AGAIN, AND LEAD THEM OUT OF THIS ARTIFICIAL JUNGLE INTO THE REAL ONE!
SO LONG AS THEY'RE SURROUNDED BY ALL OF THE BLACK PANTHER'S ELABORATE TRAPS, THE ODDS MUST BE AGAINST THEM!

BUT, MINUTES LATER, AS THE COURAGEOUS YOUTH REACHES HIS DESTINATION...
I'M TOO LATE!! THEY'RE GONE!
WAIT...WHAT'S THIS? THE GROUND...IT FEELS WARM!
IS THERE SOME SORT OF DYNAMO BENEATH ME, OR..CAN IT BE..?!!

THE INTENSITY OF THE HEAT KEEPS VARYING! THERE CAN BE ONLY ONE EXPLANATION...
IT'S THE TORCH! HE'S TRAPPED BENEATH ME... AND HE'S TRYING TO SIGNAL..TO CATCH MY ATTENTION!
NO MATTER WHAT..I MUSTN'T FAIL HIM!
17.

IF YOU CAN KEEP TRACK OF WHERE WE LEAVE EVERYONE DURING THESE STACCATO SCENE CHANGES, YOU'RE BETTER THAN WE ARE, FRANTIC ONE! —ANYWAY...
ONCE I HAVE BESTED YOU, RICHARDS, THE HUNT WILL BE ENDED!
MY WIFE!! WHERE IS SHE? IF YOU'VE HARMED HER..?
SHE IS SAFE ENOUGH... FOR NOW! I DO NOT CONSIDER FEMALES TO BE FAIR GAME!

HE'S POISED TO LEAP! IF I CAN LASSO HIM FIRST--!
I CAN DIVINE YOUR PURPOSE.. BUT YOU WILL FIND THAT I AM NOT SO EASILY OUT-MANEUVERED!
KLIK!

HE PLUNGED THE AREA INTO TOTAL DARKNESS! I CAN'T SEE!
REMEMBER... THE PANTHER IS ONE OF THE MOST DEADLY OF CATS!

AND, UNLIKE A MERE HUMAN, THE CAT IS NEVER SIGHTLESS IN THE DARK!
UHHHH..!

MR. FANTASTIC... LEADER OF THE FANTASTIC FOUR... HELPLESS BEFORE THE POWER OF THE BLACK PANTHER! MY HOUR OF TRIUMPH AT LAST!

BUT, ALTHOUGH UNABLE TO SEE HIS TAUNTING FOE... THE VALIANT REED RICHARDS CONTINUES TO STRUGGLE ...TO FIGHT BACK...TO LASH OUT IN A DESPERATE, RAGING FURY...
YOU HAVEN'T WON YET, PANTHER! NOT WHILE I HAVE ONE BREATH OF LIFE LEFT..!
I HAVE TO DODGE HIS ARMS..FOR ANOTHER FEW SECONDS..!
18.

HERE I AM, RICHARDS! HERE I AM! IF YOU WANT ME, JUST REACH OUT--I'M WAITING FOR YOU!
HE'S DELIBERATELY GOADING ME--TRYING TO TRICK ME IN SOME WAY! BUT I MUST KEEP GROPING FOR HIM---I MUST GET HIM---SOMEHOW--!
I DON'T KNOW YOUR MOTIVE FOR ANY OF THIS---BUT YOU'LL LEARN--AS SO MANY HAVE LEARNED BEFORE YOU---THAT NOBODY ATTACKS THE FANTASTIC FOUR--
---NOT WITHOUT PAYING FOR THAT PRIVILEGE.. AND PAYING IN FULL!
CLICK!
HE SWITCHED THE LIGHTS BACK ON! I CAN SEE AGAIN!

I KNEW YOUR GROPING HANDS WOULD EVENTUALLY FIND THEIR WAY INTO MY SPECIALLY-PREPARED TITANIUM CUFFS!
TLAK!
TLAK!
AND SO, THE TABLEAU ENDS! THE HUNT IS OVER!

THE BLACK PANTHER HAS WON!
NOT YET YOU HAVEN'T, MASKED MAN!
WHO SAID THAT?!!

WHY NOT JUST TAKE A WILD GUESS?!!
THE HUMAN TORCH! YOU'RE FREE AGAIN! BUT---HOW--??
YOU MEAN THERE'S SOMETHING YOU DON'T KNOW?!

LEMME BURN THOSE NUTTY CUFFS OFF YOU, BROTHER-IN-LAW!
NOW THAT MY SWINGIN' STRENGTH'S BACK, I JUST WANT ONE GOOD POKE AT 'IM!
I'LL KEEP HIM BUSY WITH A BOBBING FORCE FIELD, DARLING!
YOU'VE ALL BEEN LIBERATED FROM MY TRAPS! IT-IT CANNOT BE---!
WE SHOULD HAVE WARNED YOU, PANTHER ---THE F.F. DOESN'T MAKE A HABIT OF LOSING!
19.

YOU CAN RELEASE YOUR FORCE FIELD NOW, SUE! HE'S LOST THE ELEMENT OF SURPRISE... AND, WITHOUT THAT, HE'S NO MATCH FOR US!
C'MON... TAKE A SWING AT ME! YA WANT ME TO GIT FRUSTRATED?!!
SURRENDER, PANTHER! IT'S THE ONLY CHOICE LEFT TO YOU!
HOW? HOW DID YOU DO IT? I MUST KNOW!

IT WAS OL' WYATT! HE FREED ME, AND I FREED THE OTHERS!
YOU TOOK EVERY PRECAUTION AGAINST THE GREATEST SUPER-POWERED TEAM IN THE WORLD...
...BUT, YOU OVER-LOOKED ONE FACTOR! SOMETIMES A MAN WITH NO SUPER POWERS CAN TIP THE SCALES FOR, OR AGAINST YOU!
ORDER YOUR MEN BACK, PANTHER! I DON'T WANT TO HURT ANY OF THEM..!

THEN, MINUTES LATER, AFTER THE MIGHTY, MASKED JUNGLE MYSTERY MAN HAS ACCEPTED THE STARTLING TURN OF FATE..!
WHAT HAPPENS TO HIM NOW?
HE PROMISED NOT TO LAUNCH ANY NEW ATTACK AGAINST US!
WE CAN ALL STAND BACK NOW...
A MAN SUCH AS THE BLACK PANTHER DOES NOT GIVE HIS WORD LIGHTLY ---NOR DOES HE DISHONOR IT, ONCE GIVEN!

BUT, I THINK YOU MIGHT REMOVE YOUR MASK NOW...AND TELL US WHAT THIS IS ALL ABOUT!
I SHALL DO AS YOU SAY..!
MY MASK IS NOT FOR CONCEAL-MENT.. BUT RATHER A SYMBOL OF MY PANTHER POWER!

NOW THAT THE HUNT IS OVER..THE GAME IS ENDED...I SHALL OFFER YOU THE EXPLANATION...FOR YOU HAVE EARNED IT INDEED!

I AM, AS YOU SEE ME...HEREDITARY CHIEFTAIN OF THE WAKANDAS... AND PERHAPS THE RICHEST MAN IN ALL THE WORLD!
BUT, IT WAS NOT ALWAYS SO! MY TALE IS ONE OF TRAGEDY... AND DEADLY REVENGE..!
NEXT ISSUE: "THE REASON WHY!"
20.

# *FANTASTIC FOUR* #53,
# AUGUST 1966

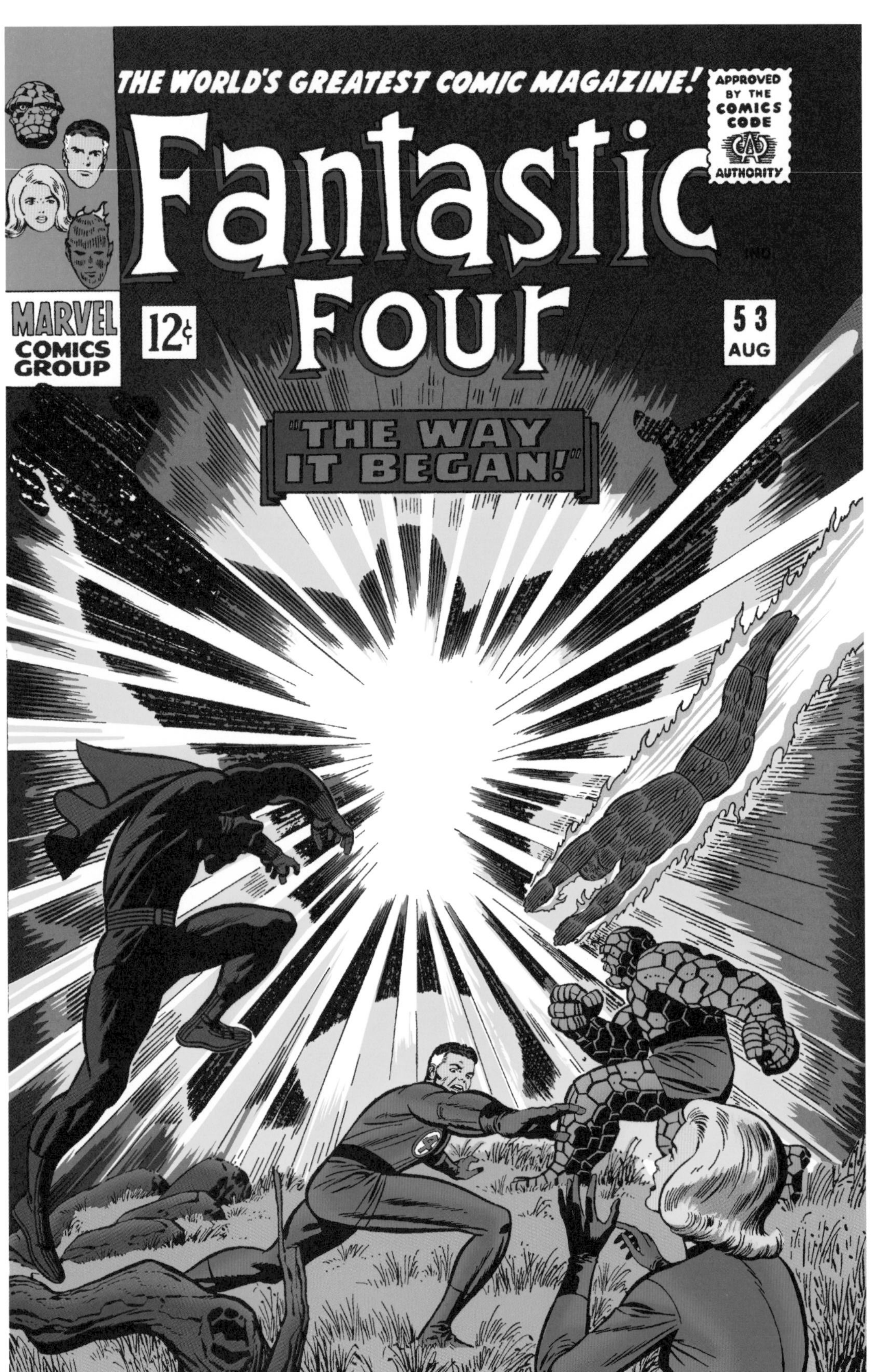
THE WORLD'S GREATEST COMIC MAGAZINE!
APPROVED BY THE COMICS CODE AUTHORITY
Fantastic Four
MARVEL COMICS GROUP
12¢
53 AUG
"THE WAY IT BEGAN!"

THE FABULOUS F.F. LEARN THE SECRET OF THE BLACK PANTHER
"THE WAY IT BEGAN!"...
HAVING SUCCESSFULLY EVADED ALL THE UNCANNY TRAPS OF THE BLACK PANTHER, THE TRIUMPHANT FANTASTIC FOUR, ACCOMPANIED BY WYATT WINGFOOT, ARE AWARDED A HEROES' CEREMONY---
LET THE DANCE OF FRIEND-SHIP BEGIN!
THOUGH THE WAKANDA TRIBE LIVES IN THE TRADITION OF THEIR FOREFATHERS, THEY POSSESS MODERN, SUPER-SCIENTIFIC WONDERS WE CAN ONLY MARVEL AT! THERE'S AN INCREDIBLE MYSTERY HERE--AND ONLY THE BLACK PANTHER HIM-SELF KNOWS ALL THE ANSWERS!
THEY ARE NOT THE ORDINARY NATIVE TRIBE THEY SEEM TO BE!
SHEESH! A BUNCH'A FRED ASTAIRES THEY AIN'T!
RELAX, BEN! IT'S BETTER'N BEING SHOT AT BY THEM!
SCRIPT: STAN LEE
ART: JACK KIRBY
INKS: JOE SINNOTT
LETTERING: ARTIE SIMEK
NATIVE DANCES: THE BALLET FORBUSH TERPSICHOREAN TROUPE
1

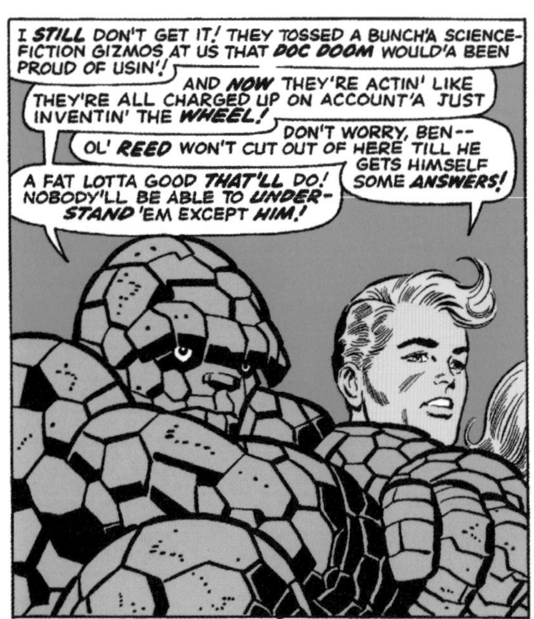
I STILL DON'T GET IT! THEY TOSSED A BUNCH'A SCIENCE-FICTION GIZMOS AT US THAT DOC DOOM WOULD'A BEEN PROUD OF USIN'!
AND NOW THEY'RE ACTIN' LIKE THEY'RE ALL CHARGED UP ON ACCOUNT'A JUST INVENTIN' THE WHEEL!
DON'T WORRY, BEN-- OL' REED WON'T CUT OUT OF HERE TILL HE GETS HIMSELF SOME ANSWERS!
A FAT LOTTA GOOD THAT'LL DO! NOBODY'LL BE ABLE TO UNDER-STAND 'EM EXCEPT HIM!

AWRIGHT, BREAK IT UP--BREAK IT UP! WHAT'RE YA ALL GAPIN' AT, ANYWAY?
AINTCHA NEVER SEEN A BASHFUL, BLUE-EYED THING BEFORE?!!
LET'S GO, BEN! THE BLACK PANTHER IS INVITING US TO HIS PRIVATE QUARTERS!

WOW! WOTTA PAD! I'LL BET EVEN HUGH HEFNER COULDN'T IMPROVE ON THIS LAYOUT!
MAN! IF YA GOTTA LIVE IN THE JUNGLE, THIS SURE IS THE WAY TA DO IT! THERE MUST BE A LOTTA DOUGH IN BLACK PANTHERIN'!
STILL ANOTHER EXAMPLE OF THE OLD AND THE NEW, DARLING! LOOK AT THAT ELABORATE STEREO MUSIC SYSTEM--COMPLETE WITH TAPE RECORDER!
I JUST CAN'T BELIEVE WE'RE IN THE HEART OF THE JUNGLE!
MY GUESTS AND I DO NOT WISH TO BE DISTURBED!

YOU SEEM PUZZLED BY WHAT YOU HAVE SEEN! YOU SHOULDN'T BE!
AFTER ALL, I CAN AFFORD TO PAMPER MYSELF--TO INDULGE MY EVERY WHIM--ENJOY EVERY LUXURY! I'M ONE OF THE RICHEST MEN IN THE WORLD!
REMEMBER, I'VE SEEN, I BELIEVE YOU! BUT, THERE'S MORE TO YOUR STORY THAN MERE WEALTH--
YOU ARE PERCEPTIVE INDEED, RICHARDS!

ACTUALLY, THE BLACK PANTHER LIVES UNDER A TRAGIC CURSE!
BUT, MY TALE REALLY BEGINS WITH THE SPEAR AND SHIELD OF MY FATHER--T'CHAKA, THE WARRIOR KING!
2

BUT, EVEN AS THE DRAMATIC BLACK PANTHER BEGINS HIS REVELATION, TWO MEMBERS OF THE TERRITORIAL PATROL COME UPON A STAGGERING DISCOVERY--
THE ENTIRE AREA SEEMS TO HAVE BEEN RIPPED UP--AS THOUGH BY GIANT HANDS! THERE ARE NO ANIMALS--NO BIRDS!! EVERY FORM OF LIFE HAS BEEN FRIGHTENED AWAY!
AND THESE HOLES IN THE GROUND--IMPOSSIBLE THOUGH IT SEEMS, THEY CAN ONLY BE TRACKS--THE FOOTPRINTS OF SOME GARGANTUAN CREATURE!
CAN IT BE THAT THE RUMORS OF MONSTROUS BEASTS ROAMING THE JUNGLE ARE TRUE?!!

AT FIRST, I THOUGHT THEY WERE JUST SUPERSTITION--OLD WIVES' TALES TO FRIGHTEN LITTLE CHILDREN! BUT NOW--I CAN ALMOST SENSE THE DANGER UPON US!
HOLD IT! DID YOU JUST FEEL THE GROUND TREMBLE--AS THOUGH BENEATH THE PRESSURE OF SOME TITANTIC WEIGHT?!!
THERE! I FELT IT AGAIN!! THERE'S NO DOUBT ABOUT IT--SOMETHING IS BEHIND US!

SWIFTLY TURNING, THE TWO MEN RECOIL IN MUTE SHOCK AT THE AWESOME SIGHT THAT GREETS THEIR EYES--AS THEY FIRE WILDLY--DESPERATELY, AT THAT WHICH CONFRONTS THEM--!
IT'S LIKE A GIGANTIC GORILLA--AN UNBELIEVABLE CRIMSON ANTHROPOID!!
CRAK!
CRAK
KEEP FIRING! OUR ONLY CHANCE IS TO FRIGHTEN HIM AWAY WITH OUR GUNSHOTS!! IT'S TOO LATE TO RUN!

HOWEVER, THE GUNFIRE OF THE TWO COURAGEOUS PATROLMEN CAUSES A PHENOMENON FAR DIFFERENT THAN EITHER OF THEM EXPECTS--!
IT-IT SEEMED TO EXPLODE--RIGHT BEFORE OUR EYES!!
IT'S IMPOSSIBLE! IT CAN'T BE--!
AND YET--I SAW IT, TOO!
3

THIS IS FAR STRANGER THAN ANYTHING WE EXPECTED!! MUCH BIGGER THAN THE TWO OF US CAN HANDLE!
YOU'RE RIGHT! WE'VE GOT TO GET BACK TO THE OUTPOST--REPORT IT TO HEADQUARTERS!
BOK!

RRR!
LISTEN! BEHIND US--THAT NOISE--FAR LOUDER THAN BEFORE!!
PERHAPS THE RED GORILLA HAS RETURN---! NO! LOOK!
IT'S EVEN BIGGER THAN THE GORILLA--MORE POWERFUL--MORE DANGEROUS!!

RRRRR RRRRRR

IT CANNOT BE!! THERE ARE NO SUCH BEASTS!! IT IS NOT POSSIBLE! WE MUST BE GOING MAD!

I ALMOST WISH THAT WERE THE ANSWER--BUT WE BOTH KNOW WE SEE IT!

THERE IS MUCH MADNESS HERE--BUT, IT DOES NOT LIE WITH US!

4

THE GIANT ELEPHANT HURLS TREES ABOUT AS THOUGH THEY ARE MERE TWIGS! BUT, HE DOES NOT PURSUE US! WE ARE VIRTUALLY BENEATH THE NOTICE OF A CREATURE SO HUGE!
BUT WHERE DID IT COME FROM--AND WHAT IS IT?? WE'VE GOT TO FIND OUT!! WE'VE GOT TO LEARN WHAT'S HAPPENING IN THERE--LEARN HOW MANY MORE OF THOSE CRIMSON MONSTERS THERE ARE!
THIS IS THE EDGE OF WAKANDA COUNTRY! PERHAPS THE ANSWER LIES THERE--!

AND, SPEAKING OF THE WAKANDAS, IT'S TIME ONCE AGAIN TO REJOIN THE BLACK PANTHER AS HE CONTINUES HIS NARRATIVE--
MY FATHER WAS THE GREATEST, WISEST CHIEFTAIN IN ALL OF AFRICA!
AND, HIS SKILL AS A HUNTER WAS SECOND TO NONE!

YAWWWWW!
BEN! CUT THAT OUT!
AWW, I CAN'T HELP IT! I SAW THIS IN A MILLION JUNGLE MOVIES!
SO! I'M BORING YOU, AM I?
SUPPOSE I TELL YOU YOU'RE SITTING ON TWENTY MILLION DOLLARS!

DO YOU MEAN THIS MARBLE BENCH BENEATH US?
I DIDN'T EVEN PAY ANY ATTENTION TO IT! BUT, MARBLE ISN'T WORTH THAT MUCH MONEY!
LOOK CLOSELY, JOHNNY! THAT ISN'T MARBLE--!
YOU'RE RIGHT, SUE! IT'S SOME SORT OF GLISTENING METALLIC ORE!
SAY IT IN ENGLISH--JUST FER ONCE!
THE NAME OF THAT METAL IS VIBRANIUM!

EVEN I KNOW THAT COMES FROM THE WORD VIBRATE! WHAT'S IT DO--SHIVER UP A STORM IF YA TOUCH IT?
EXACTLY THE OPPOSITE, IRASCIBLE ONE! IT ABSORBS VIBRATIONS--YOU MIGHT EVEN SAY IT SWALLOWS THEM!
BUT, WHAT MAKES IT SO VALUABLE?
DON'T YOU SEE, DEAR--?
IT CAN BE WORTH A FORTUNE TO OUR MISSILE PROGRAM ALONE! ROCKETS MADE OF VIBRANIUM WOULD NEVER GO OFF COURSE DUE TO VIBRATIONS!
THAT IS CORRECT, RICHARDS!
5

OUR VIRTUALLY INEXHAUSTIBLE SUPPLY OF VIBRANIUM COMES FROM THAT SACRED MOUND WHICH HAS BORDERED THE LAND OF THE WAKANDAS SINCE THE DAWN OF TIME!

EVERY WAKANDA CHIEFTAIN IS PLEDGED TO PROTECT THE SACRED VIBRANIUM WITH HIS LIFE--JUST AS MY FATHER WAS SO PLEDGED!
ALL HAIL T'CHAKA--GUARDIAN OF THE ETERNAL PEAK!

"MY FATHER WAS THE GREATEST CHIEFTAIN OF ALL! WISE IN COUNCIL--JUST IN JUDGEMENT--AND BRAVE IN BATTLE!"
"WHEREVER THERE WAS DANGER, THERE TOO WAS T'CHAKA--ALWAYS IN THE FOREFRONT--!"

"TO ME, HE WAS MORE THAN FATHER--MORE THAN WARRIOR--TO ME, HE WAS LIKE A GOD!"
ONE DAY I TOO SHALL BE CHIEFTAIN, FATHER!
AND I SHALL BE WORTHY OF ALL YOU HAVE TAUGHT ME!
BUT NOW, IT IS BEDTIME FOR THE LITTLEST CHIEFTAIN OF ALL!

LOOK, KIDDO--WHY DON'TCHA SAVE YER-SELF THE TROUBLE? I KNOW THE REST BY HEART! EVERY-THING WUZ HUNKY DORY UNTIL THE GREEDY IVORY HUNTERS MADE THE SCENE!
BEN! FOR THE LAST TIME, WILL YOU REMEMBER THAT WE'RE HIS GUESTS?!
DO NOT BE CON-CONCERNED, REED RICHARDS! I REALIZE MY TALE MAY SOUND CONTRIVED TO YOU!
YOU AINT JUST WHISTLIN' WATUSI, PAL!

YER TALKIN' TO A GUY WHO SEEN EVERY TARZAN MOVIE AT LEAST A DOZEN TIMES! AND I CAN RECITE YA HALF'A THE BOMBA, THE JUNGLE BOY BOOKS BY HEART!
SO YER LITTLE BEDTIME STORY AINT IMPRESSIN' ME! LET'S GIT TO THE PUNCHLINE, HUH?
THAT'S ENOUGH, BEN!
6

I DO NOT MIND THE **THING'S** INTERRUPTIONS!

PERHAPS MY TALE **DOES** FOLLOW THE USUAL PATTERN, EXCEPT FOR ONE THING! IT WAS NOT A GREEDY **IVORY HUNTER** WHO CAME TO OUR LAND! NO, IT WAS ONE FAR MORE **DANGEROUS**--FAR MORE **EVIL**--!

HE CALLED HIMSELF **KLAW**, THE **MASTER OF SOUND!**--AND HE POSSESSED A WEAPON THE LIKE OF WHICH NO MAN HAD EVER SEEN BEFORE--A WEAPON WHICH COULD CONVERT **SOUND** INTO MASS!

THE **FOOLS!** THEY **MOCKED** ME WHEN I SAID THAT **VIBRANIUM** EXISTED! BUT NOW I HAVE **FOUND** IT, HERE IN THIS JUNGLE--AND, IT MUST BE **MINE!**

**VIBRANIUM!!** THE ONE ELEMENT I NEED--THE ONE ELEMENT WHICH WILL POWER MY **SOUND TRANSFORMER**--SO THAT I MAY CHANGE THE BASIC ENERGY OF **SOUND** INTO ANY LIVING **FORM** I DESIRE!

"I STILL REMEMBER THE SIGHT OF KLAW, THE UNSMILING--KLAW, THE MERCILESS--ORDERING MY FATHER TO GIVE UP OUR SACRED MOUND--OUR PRECIOUS ETERNAL ROCK--!"
YOU HAVE NO CHOICE! ONCE I GAIN POSSESSION OF THE WORLD'S ONLY SUPPLY OF VIBRANIUM, ALL THE RICHES OF EARTH SHALL BE MINE!
BEGONE! THIS LAND IS OURS! SO SPEAKS T'CHAKA, THE CHIEFTAIN!
THEN T'CHAKA SHALL SPEAK NO MORE!
GUN HIM DOWN--NOW!

"IT WAS THE FIRST TIME I HEARD THE SOUND OF GUNFIRE--A SOUND I WAS TO REMEMBER ALL THE DAYS OF MY LIFE--!"
CRACK! CRACK!
FATHER!! FATHER!
THEY HAVE SLAIN T'CHAKA!
BUT, HIS DEATH SHALL BE AVENGED!
7

"I, WHO HAD LIVED IN THE JUNGLE SINCE BIRTH, HAD NEVER SEEN SUCH VIOLENCE AS I BEHELD THAT MOMENT--WHILE THE MACHINE-GUN FIRE OF KLAW FELL UPON OUR WARRIORS WITHOUT MERCY--!"
WE ARE HELPLESS BEFORE THE WITHERING FIRE OF THE INVADERS!!
FLEE, MY BRAVE ONES--FLEE! WE MUST LIVE TO FIGHT ANOTHER DAY!

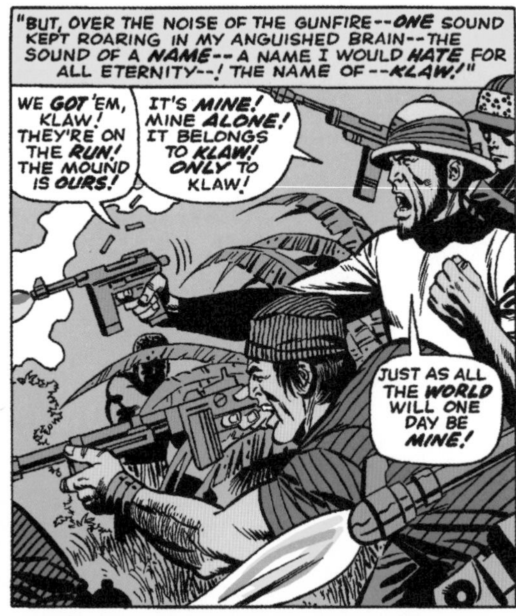
"BUT, OVER THE NOISE OF THE GUNFIRE--ONE SOUND KEPT ROARING IN MY ANGUISHED BRAIN--THE SOUND OF A NAME--A NAME I WOULD HATE FOR ALL ETERNITY--! THE NAME OF --KLAW!"
WE GOT 'EM, KLAW! THEY'RE ON THE RUN! THE MOUND IS OURS!
IT'S MINE! MINE ALONE! IT BELONGS TO KLAW! ONLY TO KLAW!
JUST AS ALL THE WORLD WILL ONE DAY BE MINE!

"SECONDS LATER, THE FIRING HAD CEASED--BUT, THE DEADLY SILENCE WHICH FOLLOWED WAS MORE DEAFENING--MORE FRAUGHT WITH DREAD--THAN ALL THE THUNDER THAT HAD GONE BEFORE!"
FATHER!
MY FATHER--!

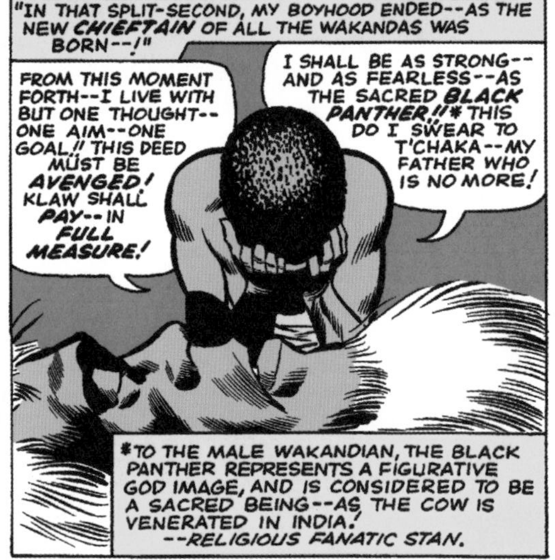
"IN THAT SPLIT-SECOND, MY BOYHOOD ENDED--AS THE NEW CHIEFTAIN OF ALL THE WAKANDAS WAS BORN--!"
FROM THIS MOMENT FORTH--I LIVE WITH BUT ONE THOUGHT--ONE AIM--ONE GOAL!! THIS DEED MUST BE AVENGED! KLAW SHALL PAY--IN FULL MEASURE!
I SHALL BE AS STRONG--AND AS FEARLESS--AS THE SACRED BLACK PANTHER!! * THIS DO I SWEAR TO T'CHAKA--MY FATHER WHO IS NO MORE!
* TO THE MALE WAKANDIAN, THE BLACK PANTHER REPRESENTS A FIGURATIVE GOD IMAGE, AND IS CONSIDERED TO BE A SACRED BEING--AS THE COW IS VENERATED IN INDIA! --RELIGIOUS FANATIC STAN.

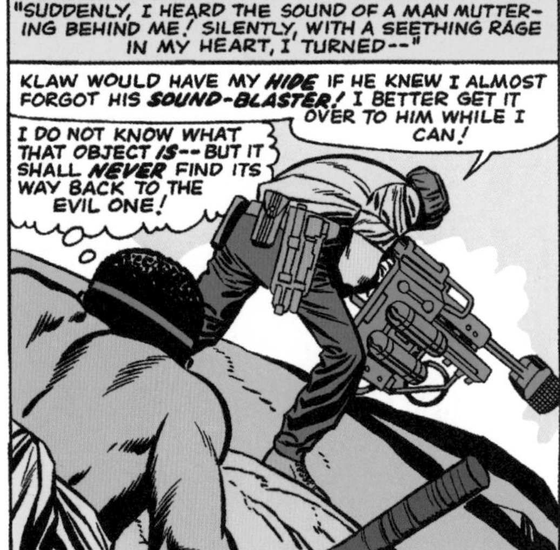
"SUDDENLY, I HEARD THE SOUND OF A MAN MUTTERING BEHIND ME! SILENTLY, WITH A SEETHING RAGE IN MY HEART, I TURNED--"
KLAW WOULD HAVE MY HIDE IF HE KNEW I ALMOST FORGOT HIS SOUND-BLASTER! I BETTER GET IT OVER TO HIM WHILE I CAN!
I DO NOT KNOW WHAT THAT OBJECT IS--BUT IT SHALL NEVER FIND ITS WAY BACK TO THE EVIL ONE!

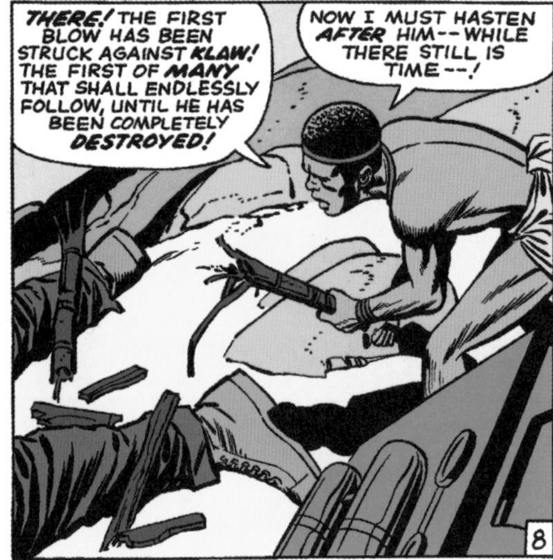
THERE! THE FIRST BLOW HAS BEEN STRUCK AGAINST KLAW! THE FIRST OF MANY THAT SHALL ENDLESSLY FOLLOW, UNTIL HE HAS BEEN COMPLETELY DESTROYED!
NOW I MUST HASTEN AFTER HIM--WHILE THERE STILL IS TIME--!
8

"FINDING THE STRANGE WEAPON SURPRISINGLY LIGHT IN WEIGHT, I LIFTED IT, CARRYING IT WITH ME, UNTIL I REACHED THE GATES OF OUR VILLAGE, WHERE MY EYES BEHELD KLAW'S FINAL ACT OF VILLAINY--!"
MY PEOPLE-- FLEEING FOR THEIR LIVES!! OUR VILLAGE IN FLAMES!!
THIS IS NO MAN I SEEK TO BATTLE!! TRULY, HE IS EVIL INCARNATE!! HIS VERY PRESENCE BEFOULS THE EARTH UPON WHICH HE STANDS!
OUT! DRIVE THEM OUT! THE MOUND OF VIBRANIUM MUST BELONG TO KLAW! ONLY I AM DESTINED TO BE SUPREME! ONLY I AM MASTER OF SOUND!

"WITHOUT CONSCIOUS THOUGHT, I AIMED THE FEARSOME OBJECT IN MY ARMS DIRECTLY AHEAD OF ME --WHILE MY FINGER BEGAN TO TIGHTEN ON THE TRIGGER, AS I CRIED--"
YOU HAVE SLAIN MY FATHER! YOU HAVE PUT THE TORCH TO OUR VILLAGE! AND NOW YOU MUST PAY--!
THE SOUND BLASTER!! HE'S ABOUT TO FIRE IT!
STOP HIM! HE DOESN'T KNOW WHAT HE'S DOING--!!

TOO LATE! HE DETONATED IT!
IT WAS AN ACCIDENT! HE DOESN'T EVEN KNOW HOW TO AIM IT! THE SHOT FELL SHORT!
I'LL MAKE SURE HE GETS NO SECOND CHANCE!
VAK

YOU LITTLE FOOL! YOU CANNOT REALIZE THE FORCES YOU ARE TAMPERING WITH! THE DEVICE YOU HOLD CONVERTS SOUND INTO PURE ENERGY! IN THE WRONG HANDS, IT CAN WREAK UNMENTIONABLE HAVOC!!
YOURS ARE THE HANDS THAT ARE WRONG, EVIL ONE--NOT MINE!
LOOK OUT! HE'S GONNA FIRE AGAIN!
THE LITTLE SAVAGE WOULDN'T DARE!
I SEE YOU STARTING TO SQUEEZE YOUR TRIGGER! BUT, YOU ARE TOO LATE--!

THIS IS FOR T'CHAKA-- THE WARRIOR KING!
MY HAND!
VAK
9

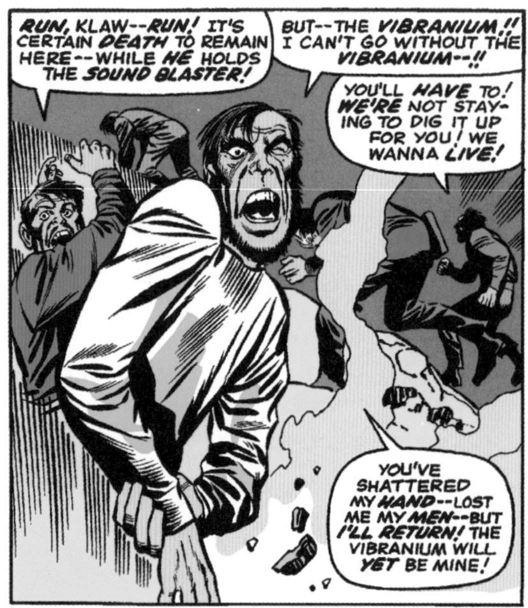
RUN, KLAW--RUN! IT'S CERTAIN DEATH TO REMAIN HERE--WHILE HE HOLDS THE SOUND BLASTER!
BUT--THE VIBRANIUM!! I CAN'T GO WITHOUT THE VIBRANIUM--!!
YOU'LL HAVE TO! WE'RE NOT STAYING TO DIG IT UP FOR YOU! WE WANNA LIVE!
YOU'VE SHATTERED MY HAND--LOST ME MY MEN--BUT I'LL RETURN! THE VIBRANIUM WILL YET BE MINE!

THAT WAS TEN YEARS AGO--TO THE DAY!
I COULD NOT THEN PURSUE HIM, FOR THE SHOCK OF FIRING THOSE TWO MIGHTY BURSTS HAD DRAINED MY YOUTHFUL STRENGTH!
BUT, I KNOW HE WILL RETURN--I CAN SENSE THAT THE TIME HAS COME!
AND THIS TIME--I SHALL BE READY!
Y'KNOW--THAT STORY'S JUST PLAIN NUTTY ENUFF TO BE TRUE!

IT IS TRUE! I SOLD SMALL PORTIONS OF VIBRANIUM TO VARIOUS SCIENTIFIC FOUNDATIONS, ENABLING ME TO AMASS A FORTUNE--THE EQUAL OF ANY ON EARTH!
SO THAT'S HOW YA COULD AFFORD THAT FAR-OUT MECHANIZED JUNGLE OF YOURS!
THAT? I JUST DID IT FOR A LARK!

IT WAS A SIMPLE EXERCISE, TO TEST MY SKILL--FOR I HAD ATTENDED THE FINE UNIVERSITIES OF BOTH HEMISPHERES!
HOW ABOUT YER PANTHER POWER--THE WAY YA SEE IN THE DARK, 'N STUFF--!
A SECRET--HANDED DOWN FROM CHIEFTAIN TO CHIEFTAIN!

WE EAT CERTAIN HERBS--AND UNDERGO RIGOROUS RITUALS--OF WHICH I AM FORBIDDEN TO SPEAK!
BUT, WHY THE HECK DIDJA TRY TO TRAP US?!!
I HAD TO! YOU FOUR WERE THE SUPREME TEST!
IF I COULD FIGHT YOU TO A STANDSTILL, THEN I AM READY FOR--KLAW!

ALTHOUGH HE HAS KEPT HIDDEN FROM ME ALL THESE YEARS, I KNOW HE IS PLANNING TO--
WAIT!!
IT HAS COME! THE LONG AWAITED, CRITICAL DANGER SIGNAL!!
WHEEE
WHEEEEE
WHEEEEE
WHEEEEE
CLICK
NOW WHAT?

WOTTA DEAL! YA MOVE ONE OF THEM CRAZY PANTHER STATUES, AND THE WHOLE BLASTED WALL SLIDES BACK!
QUIET! THIS SENSA-SCOPE IS RECORDING THE APPROACH OF A NAMELESS MENACE --FROM THE DIRECTION OF OUR SACRED MOUND!
KLAW HAS RETURNED!
10

AND, JUST A SHORT DISTANCE AWAY, LUMBERING AWESOMELY INTO WAKANDA TERRITORY, WE SEE--
A GIGANTIC CRIMSON GORILLA! THE FORCE CANNON-- FIRE IT! FIRE!!
WHOOM!
IT IS PREDICTED THAT KLAW, THE SOUND MASTER, WILL RETURN THIS DAY! BUT SUCH A SIGHT AS THIS--NONE COULD HAVE EXPECTED!
WE MUST STAND FAST WHILE WE MAY!
THE BLACK PANTHER WILL BE HERE WITHIN MINUTES!
WHAT IS AMISS? WHY DOES THE FORCE GUN NOT STOP HIM--??

EVEN AS THE FORCE BOLT STRIKES HIM, HE SEEMS TO BE GATHERING ITS ENERGY WITHIN HIS BODY--AND NOW-- IT-IT IS NOT POSSIBLE--!

--HE TOOK THE FULL IMPACT OF THE BLOW-- AND HURLS IT BACK AT US!
HE HAS DEMOLISHED OUR ADVANCE OUTPOST--WITH OUR OWN WEAPON!

WE DON'T KNOW WHAT'S UP, PANTHER--BUT IT'LL BE MORE FUN FIGHTING WITH YOU THAN AGAINST YOU!
FLAME ON!
THERE IS NO NEED FOR YOU TO SHARE THE DANGER! THIS IS A BATTLE FOR THE SON OF T'CHAKA!
HENCE, I SHALL DON MY RITUALISTIC GARB, AS THE BLACK PANTHER STALKS AGAIN!
IF EVERYONE ELSE CAN BE A CORNBALL, SO CAN I!
IT'S CLOBBERIN' TIME!
A LITTLE ACTION WILL BE GOOD FOR JOHNNY-- TO STOP HIM FROM BROODING OVER CRYSTAL!
WAIT FOR ME, REED! WHATEVER IS OUT THERE-- WE'LL FACE IT TOGETHER!
I'VE COME THIS FAR WITH THE F.F.--I MIGHT AS WELL GO ALL THE WAY!
11

SECONDS LATER, AS THE TORCH IS FIRST TO REACH THE GIGANTIC CRIMSON MONSTER--
WHAT CAN IT BE? IT'S SHAPED LIKE A GORILLA--BUT IT'S HAIRLESS--AND COLORED RED--AND LOOK AT THE SIZE OF IT--!

BUT THEN, SUDDENLY, THE FIERY YOUTH COMES TO A STARTLING REALIZATION--
HE SEEMS ALIVE--BUT HE ISN'T! HE CAN'T BE!
EVERY BEAST THAT LIVES FEARS MY FLAME--BUT HE DOESN'T!

AT THAT MOMENT...
LOOKA THAT, STRETCH! THEY MUST BE FILMIN' A NEW KING KONG!
BUT WHO EVER HEARD OF A RED, HAIRLESS GORILLA?
IT'S NOT A GORILLA, BEN! IT'S SOMETHING FAR MORE DANGEROUS!
WHAT DARLING? WHAT IS IT??

WHAT'SA DIFFERENCE? I'M GOIN' AFTER 'IM!
ANYTHING'S BETTER'N STAYIN' THERE 'N LISTENIN' TO ANOTHER ONE OF BIG DOME'S EXPLANATIONS!

BEN--STAY BACK! YOU CAN'T HURT HIM! LOOK HOW HE IGNORES MY FLAME!
FLAME, SHMAME! NOW WE'LL SEE IF HE CAN IGNORE A FISTFUL O' KNUCKLES!
NOBODY'S MAKIN' AN ACCORDION OUTTA MY LITTLE BUDDY!
I GOTTA MOVE FAST! NO TELLIN' WHAT HE MIGHT DO TO THE KID!
12

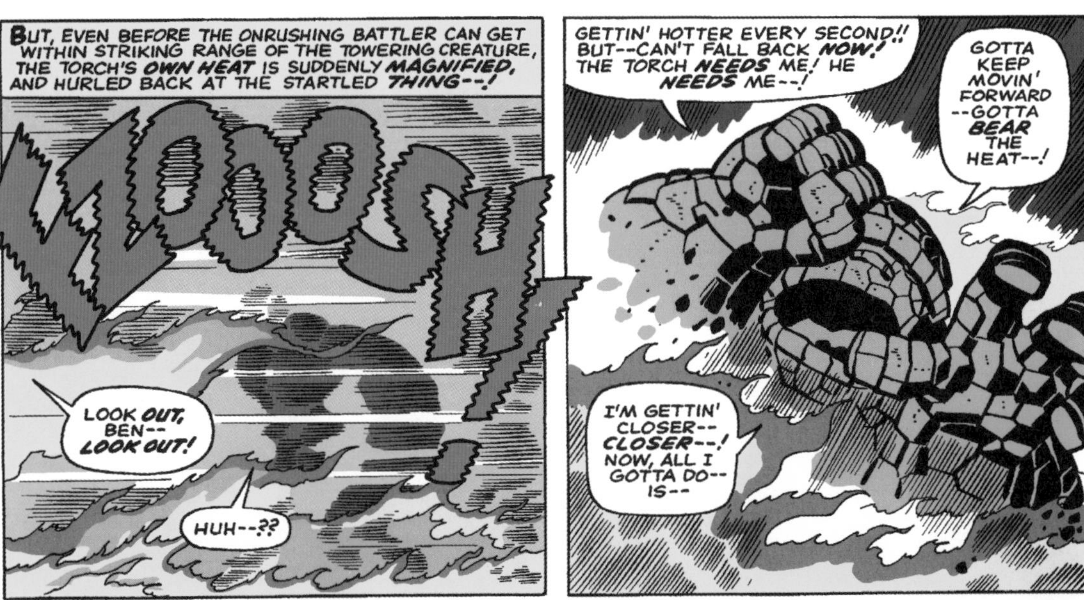
BUT, EVEN BEFORE THE ONRUSHING BATTLER CAN GET WITHIN STRIKING RANGE OF THE TOWERING CREATURE, THE TORCH'S OWN HEAT IS SUDDENLY MAGNIFIED, AND HURLED BACK AT THE STARTLED THING--!
ZOOOSH!
LOOK OUT, BEN-- LOOK OUT!
HUH--??
GETTIN' HOTTER EVERY SECOND!! BUT--CAN'T FALL BACK NOW! THE TORCH NEEDS ME! HE NEEDS ME--!
GOTTA KEEP MOVIN' FORWARD --GOTTA BEAR THE HEAT--!
I'M GETTIN' CLOSER-- CLOSER--! NOW, ALL I GOTTA DO-- IS--

--LAND ONE SOLID SOCK-- THAT'S ALL I-- HEY! I DID IT!
JUST IN TIME, BENJY! YOUR PUNCH MADE HIM LET ME GO!
BTOOOM!
BUT, BEFORE THE ORANGE-SKINNED CLOBBERER CAN ENJOY HIS VICTORY-- LOOK WHAT HAPPENS--

THAT NOISE!! IT ALMOST DEAFENED ME! WHA-WHAT WAS IT?
DON'TCHA KNOW A SONIC BOOM WHEN YA HEAR ONE, JUNIOR! BUT, I DON'T GET IT-- IT CAME FROM THAT OVER-SIZE APE--!
HOW IN THUNDERATION DID HE BREAK THE SOUND BARRIER!??

I'LL ANSWER YOU LATER, BIG BUDDY! RIGHT NOW, I WANNA ENJOY SINKING INTO SUSIE'S FRIENDLY LITTLE FORCE FIELD!
DIDJA EVER HAVE A FEELIN' YA GOT STUCK IN THE WRONG NIGHTMARE?
I GOT THEM, REED! JUST IN TIME!
13

GET THEM DOWN QUICKLY, SUE! THEY DON'T KNOW WHAT THEY'RE FIGHTING!
WHAT IS IT, DARLING? SOME SORT OF A GIANT ROBOT?
NO! IT'S MORE UNCANNY THAN THAT! IT'S SOMETHING THAT CANNOT EXIST!
RUMBLINGS! IN THE DISTANCE! COMING CLOSER--!

JOHNNY'S LAPSED INTO UNCONSCIOUSNESS! BUT HE'LL BE ALL RIGHT! IT'S JUST THE SHOCK OF HIS FLAME BEING SNUFFED OUT SO SUDDENLY!
THANK HEAVENS THAT'S ALL IT IS! BUT, WHAT DO WE DO NEXT?
ME, I FEEL LIKE FINDIN' OUT ONCE 'N FER ALL IF BUFFERIN WORKS FASTER THAN ASPIRIN!

QUICK--TAKE COVER! SOMETHING IS COMING! JUDGING BY ALL THE SIGNS, IT'S SOMETHING ENORMOUS!
THERE'S NO PLACE WE CAN RUN TO! WE'LL JUST HAVE TO STAND FAST AND FIGHT IT!
BUT, REED-- WHAT IS IT? WHAT WAS THAT HORRIBLE RED CREATURE?
YOU SOUNDED BEFORE AS IF YOU KNEW!
I DO KNOW!--THOUGH I ALMOST WISH I DIDN'T!

WHATEVER'S HEADING THIS WAY, NOTHIN'S SO BIG THAT I CAN'T STOP 'IM WITH A ROCK IN THE HEAD!
YOU'RE WASTING YOUR TIME, BEN!
DON'T YOU REALIZE --IT MAGNIFIES WHATEVER STRIKES IT--AND FEEDS THAT SAME FORCE BACK--MORE DEADLY THAN EVER --TO ITS OWN ATTACKER!

BUT, WHY DON'T NOTHIN' HURT IT??
THINK, BEN!! HOW CAN YOU HURT-- A SOUND?
A SOUND?!!
EXACTLY! DON'T YOU REMEMBER THE BLACK PANTHER TELLING US THAT KLAW CALLED HIMSELF THE MASTER OF SOUND!
DIDN'T HE HAVE A METHOD OF CONVERTING SOUND INTO LIVING MATTER??

BUT, EVEN AS REED RICHARDS BEGINS HIS ASTOUNDING EXPLANATION, THE BLACK PANTHER, EMULATING HIS NAMESAKE, TAKES TO THE TREES IN SEARCH OF HIS PREY--
KLAW COULD NEVER CREATE HIS DEMONIACAL SOUND MONSTERS WITHOUT THE AID OF MANY COMPLEX SCIENTIFIC MACHINES!
AND, IN ALL OF WAKANDA TERRITORY, THERE IS BUT ONE PLACE WHERE SUCH EQUIPMENT COULD BE HIDDEN--!
IT IS THERE, I KNOW, THAT I SHALL FIND THE ONE I MUST DESTROY!
14

SOFTLY, SILENTLY, THE BLACK PANTHER DROPS TO THE GROUND, A FEW MINUTES LATER--LANDING WITH THE GRACE AND EASE OF A TRUE FELINE--!
THIS PORTION OF MY BELOVED JUNGLE--LAID WASTE BY THE POWER OF KLAW, AND HIS DEADLY CREATIONS!
BUT, FROM THIS MOMENT ON --HE WILL DESTROY NO MORE!

THIS HIDDEN CAVE-- THE LARGEST IN WAKANDA--HE COULD SAFELY CONCEAL ANYTHING WITHIN ITS DEPTHS!
EVEN IN THE SHADOWS-- EVEN IN THE GLOOM--HE IS UNMISTAKABLE! I HAVE FOUND MY QUARRY!

FIRST, I'LL DISPOSE OF THESE TWO UNSUSPECTING GUARDS!
AND THEN, THE REAL CHALLENGE WILL COME--WHEN I'M FACE-TO-FACE WITH KLAW, AT LONG LAST!

I WAS RIGHT! IT IS HIM!
AND THAT MUST BE HIS MASTER CONVERSION SYSTEM FOR CHANGING BASIC SOUND INTO LIVING MATTER!
AT LAST I'M READY TO LAUNCH MY MAIN ATTACK!

FOR YOU, KLAW, THERE SHALL BE NO MORE ATTACKS! FOR YOU--THERE IS ONLY RETRIBUTION!
THAT VOICE!! I LAST HEARD ONE LIKE IT TEN YEARS AGO-- BUT I CAN NEVER FORGET IT!

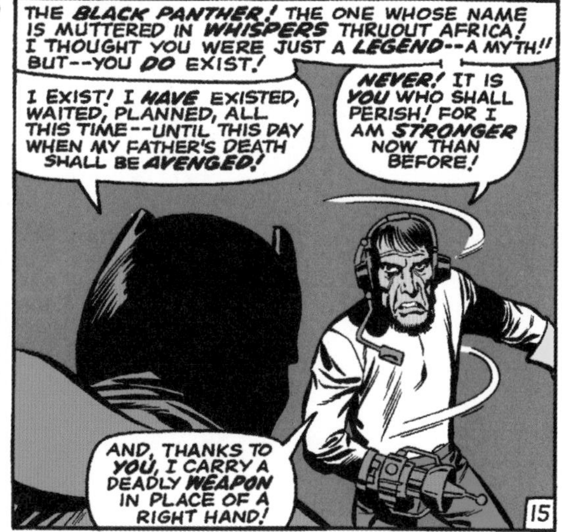
THE BLACK PANTHER! THE ONE WHOSE NAME IS MUTTERED IN WHISPERS THRUOUT AFRICA! I THOUGHT YOU WERE JUST A LEGEND--A MYTH!! BUT--YOU DO EXIST!
I EXIST! I HAVE EXISTED, WAITED, PLANNED, ALL THIS TIME--UNTIL THIS DAY WHEN MY FATHER'S DEATH SHALL BE AVENGED!
NEVER! IT IS YOU WHO SHALL PERISH! FOR I AM STRONGER NOW THAN BEFORE!
AND, THANKS TO YOU, I CARRY A DEADLY WEAPON IN PLACE OF A RIGHT HAND!
15

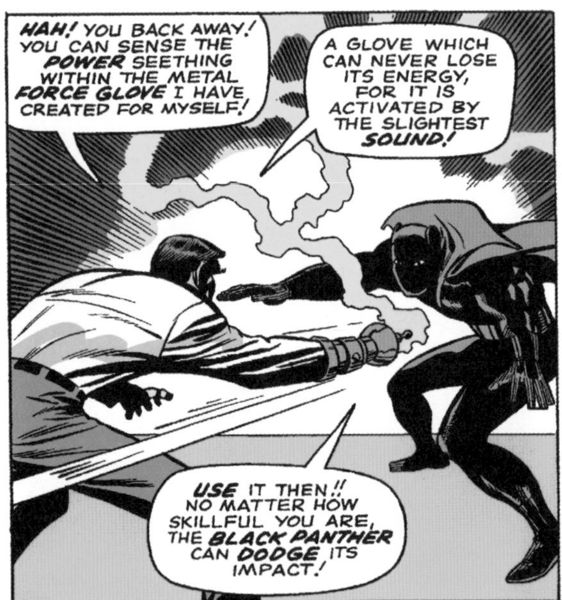
HAH! YOU BACK AWAY! YOU CAN SENSE THE POWER SEETHING WITHIN THE METAL FORCE GLOVE I HAVE CREATED FOR MYSELF!
A GLOVE WHICH CAN NEVER LOSE ITS ENERGY, FOR IT IS ACTIVATED BY THE SLIGHTEST SOUND!
USE IT THEN!! NO MATTER HOW SKILLFUL YOU ARE, THE BLACK PANTHER CAN DODGE ITS IMPACT!

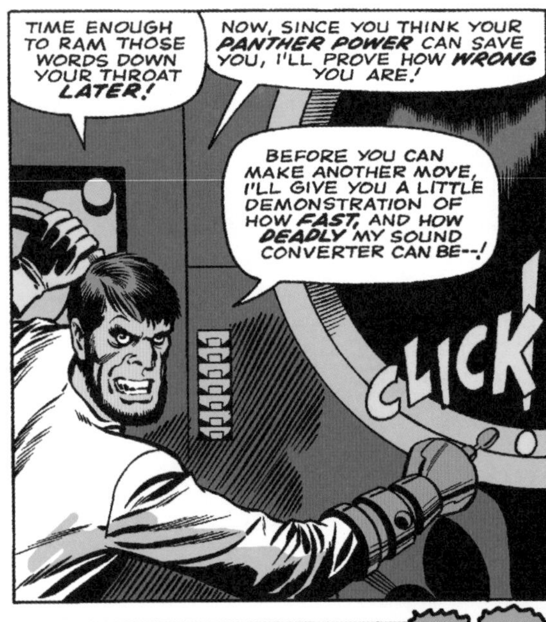
TIME ENOUGH TO RAM THOSE WORDS DOWN YOUR THROAT LATER!
NOW, SINCE YOU THINK YOUR PANTHER POWER CAN SAVE YOU, I'LL PROVE HOW WRONG YOU ARE!
BEFORE YOU CAN MAKE ANOTHER MOVE, I'LL GIVE YOU A LITTLE DEMONSTRATION OF HOW FAST, AND HOW DEADLY MY SOUND CONVERTER CAN BE--!
CLICK!

ONLY KLAW CAN INSTANTANEOUSLY CHANGE THE BASIC ENERGY OF SOUND--AND TRANSFORM IT INTO A SIMULATION OF ANY LIVING CREATURE--

AND, WHAT CAN BE MORE IRONIC-- MORE JUST--THAN HAVING YOU MEET YOUR FATE BENEATH THE TALONS OF ANOTHER BLACK PANTHER--A FAR SUPERIOR ONE!
THUS, DOES THE MASTER OF SOUND EXACT HIS FINAL REVENGE!

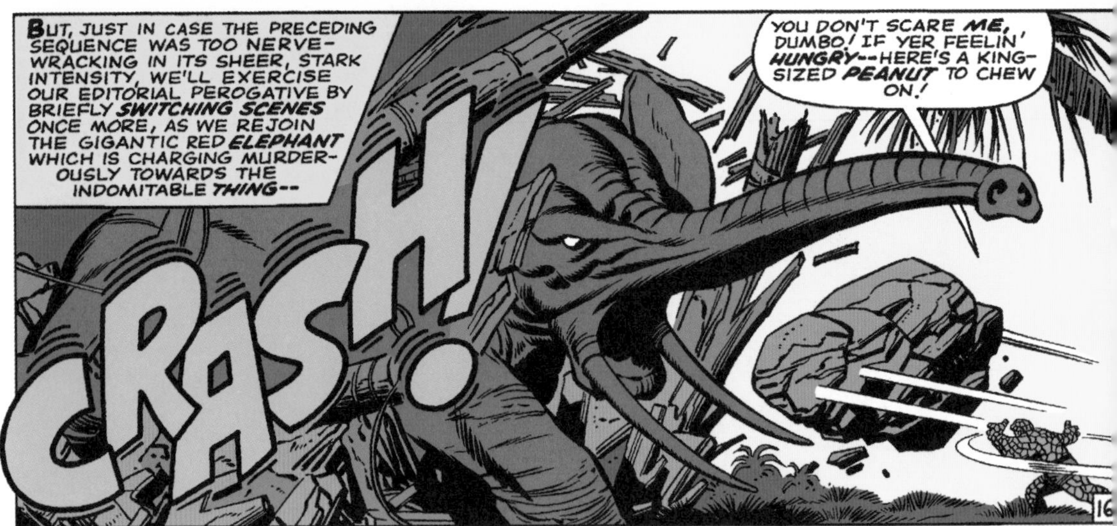
BUT, JUST IN CASE THE PRECEDING SEQUENCE WAS TOO NERVE-WRACKING IN ITS SHEER, STARK INTENSITY, WE'LL EXERCISE OUR EDITORIAL PEROGATIVE BY BRIEFLY SWITCHING SCENES ONCE MORE, AS WE REJOIN THE GIGANTIC RED ELEPHANT WHICH IS CHARGING MURDEROUSLY TOWARDS THE INDOMITABLE THING--
YOU DON'T SCARE ME, DUMBO! IF YER FEELIN' HUNGRY--HERE'S A KING-SIZED PEANUT TO CHEW ON!
CRASH!
16

BUT, NO SOONER DOES THE MOUNTAINOUS BOULDER STRIKE THE CHARGING BEAST, THAN IT CRUMBLES INTO A THOUSAND SMALLER FRAGMENTS, RICOCHETTING BACK AT THE DUMBFOUNDED HUMAN POWERHOUSE--!
WHOOM!

IF THERE'S ONE THING THAT REALLY BUGS ME, IT'S A WISE-GUY ELEPHANT!
IT'S THE ONES LIKE YOU THAT MAKE A JOKE OUTTA "BE KIND TO DUMB ANIMALS WEEK"!

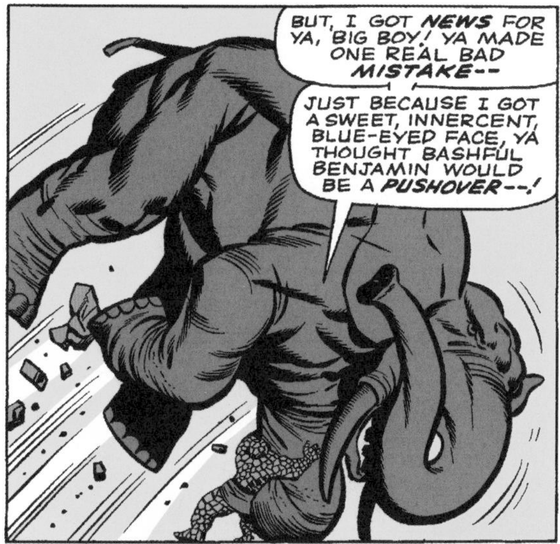
BUT, I GOT NEWS FOR YA, BIG BOY! YA MADE ONE REAL BAD MISTAKE--
JUST BECAUSE I GOT A SWEET, INNERCENT, BLUE-EYED FACE, YA THOUGHT BASHFUL BENJAMIN WOULD BE A PUSHOVER--!

BUT, NOW I'M GONNA--
HEY! WHAT'S GOIN' ON?? THIS IS CRAZY!! IT-IT DON'T MAKE SENSE--!
THE MORE PRESSURE I PUT ON 'IM, THE MORE IT HURTS ME--JUST LIKE HE'S REFLECTIN' IT ALL BACK-- LIKE A MIRROR!

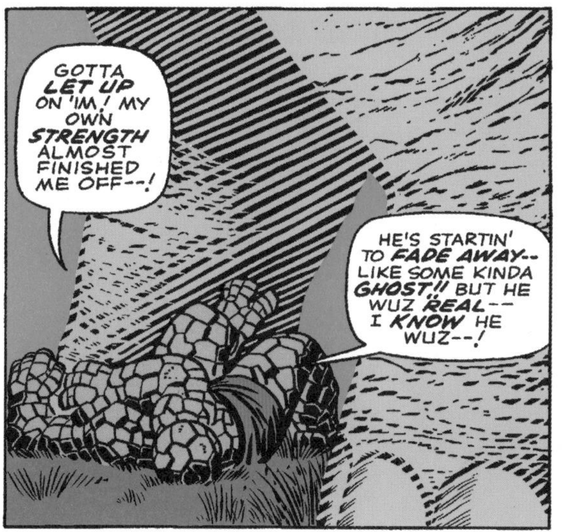
GOTTA LET UP ON 'IM! MY OWN STRENGTH ALMOST FINISHED ME OFF--!
HE'S STARTIN' TO FADE AWAY-- LIKE SOME KINDA GHOST!! BUT HE WUZ REAL-- I KNOW HE WUZ--!

WYATT! THE ELEPHANT'S GONE! SEE IF BEN NEEDS ANY HELP--WHILE I LOWER SUE AND JOHNNY TO THE GROUND!
HE SEEMS ALL RIGHT, MR. RICHARDS! HE'S STARTING TO GET UP!
'COURSE I'M AWRIGHT! I WUZ JUST TRYIN' TO FIND ME A FOUR-LEAF CLOVER!
17

LEGGO MY PAW, KID! I CAN GIT UP BY MY LONE-SOME!
I WOULDN'T HAVE BELIEVED ANYBODY COULD BATTLE A GIANT ELEPHANT TO A STANDSTILL!
THEY CAN'T! BUT I AINT ANYBODY!
I MUST'A BEEN UNCONSCIOUS! WHAT HAPPENED TO BIG BEN?
HE'S ALL RIGHT, JOHNNY! HE TRIED TO TACKLE THAT CRIMSON ELEPHANT SINGLE-HANDED, EVEN THOUGH I WARNED HIM IT WAS HOPELESS!

YOU SEE, BEN--THERE ARE SOME PROBLEMS THAT RAW STRENGTH ALONE JUST WON'T SOLVE!
WELL, IF YA EXPECT TO GIT RID'A THEM LIVIN' ANIMAL CRACKERS BY RECITIN' POETRY AT 'EM, COUNT ME OUT!
REED, DARLING-- WHAT CAN WE DO? IT ALL SEEMS SO HOPELESS!
THE BLACK PANTHER! HE'S THE ONE WHO HOLDS THE KEY TO ALL THIS! BUT--WHERE IS HE? WHAT HAPPENED TO HIM?

REED RICHARDS MAY NOT KNOW WHAT HAPPENED TO THE MYSTERIOUS WAKANDA CHIEFTAIN, BUT WE DO--DON'T WE--?
IT ISN'T POSSIBLE! HE'S OUT-FIGHTING MY OWN GIANT PANTHER!
HIS SPEED--HIS STRENGTH--HE'S LIKE A HUMAN PANTHER HIMSELF!

ENOUGH! I SEE NOW THAT I MAY TOY WITH YOU NO LONGER! IT IS TIME FOR MY SUPREME WEAPON TO BE BROUGHT INTO PLAY!
HE MERELY PUSHED A LEVER-- AND THE BEAST IS VANISHING-- AS THOUGH HE HAS NEVER EXISTED!
IT WAS NO ILLUSION, SON OF T'CHAKA! I HAVE MERELY RECONVERTED HIM --BACK TO BASIC SOUND!

AND NOW, USING MY SOUND-POWERED FORCE GLOVE, I'LL CHANGE THE BASIC STRUCTURE OF YOUR BODY!
THEN, WITH THE BLACK PANTHER GONE, I'LL SEIZE THE TREASURE OF THE WAKANDAS! THE SACRED MOUND OF VIBRANIUM WILL BE MINE--AT LAST!
NEVER--WHILE A TRIBESMAN LIVES!
THEN THEY MUST DIE--STARTING WITH YOU--!
18

BUT, BEFORE THE MAD MASTER OF SOUND CAN ACTIVATE HIS STRANGE WEAPON, THE BLACK PANTHER, MOVING AS SWIFTLY AS HIS NAMESAKE, HURLS THE FATAL POWER SWITCH WHICH HIS NIMBLE FINGERS HAD BEEN SILENTLY GROPING FOR--!
MY CONVERTER! IT-IT'S BEING BLOWN APART!!
IT HAS TO END THIS WAY-- IN THE NAME OF JUSTICE!
YOU DID NOT REALIZE-- I AM A SCIENTIST, TOO--!

THUS, I COULD TELL WHICH LEVER TO THROW IN ORDER TO OVERLOAD YOUR DELICATE ELECTRONIC CIRCUITS!
AND NOW, ONLY MY PANTHER SPEED CAN SAVE ME FROM THE HOLOCAUST WHICH IS ABOUT TO BEFALL--!

IT'S OVER! THE CAVE IS DESTROYED! NEVERMORE SHALL THE MASTER OF SOUND'S UNCANNY MONSTERS THREATEN MY LAND!
MAY YOUR ETERNAL SLEEP BE A PEACEFUL ONE, T'CHAKA MY FATHER!! THIS DAY YOU HAVE BEEN AVENGED!

AT THAT MOMENT, THOUSANDS OF YARDS AWAY, FIVE PAIR OF STARTLED EYES SEE THE ELECTRIFYING UPHEAVAL--
THAT ENTIRE HILL-- IT'S BEEN SHATTERED INTO NOTHING-NESS!
WHAT IS IT, REED? WHAT DOES IT MEAN?
I'M NOT SURE, JOHNNY--BUT I HAVE A FEELING THAT THE BLACK PANTHER IS SOMEHOW RESPONSIBLE!
THE SOUND IS DEAFENING!! IT'S LIKE THE END OF THE WORLD! HOLD ME, MY DARLING--!
HEY! LOOK--OVER THERE! A COUPLE MORE OF THEM REFUGEES FROM GOD-ZILLA!

BUT--THEY'RE FADING AWAY!! THEY MUST SOMEHOW BE LINKED TO THE EXPLOSION!
WHATEVER IT WAS THAT HAS BEEN DESTROYED, MUST HAVE BEEN THE THING THAT CREATED THEM!
19

IT WAS KLAW WHO CREATED THEM--KLAW, WHO, IN HIS MADNESS, LEARNED THE INCREDIBLE SECRET OF TRANSFORMING SOUND INTO MASS!
BUT, I DESTROYED HIS ELECTRONIC EQUIPMENT! IT WOULD TAKE HIM A LIFETIME TO REPLACE IT--IF HE SURVIVED!
SO THAT'S WHY THEM NUTTY ANIMALS FADED AWAY!
THEN YOUR MISSION IS ENDED!

YES--THE MASTER OF SOUND HAS BEEN DEFEATED!
BUT, SOMEHOW, I CANNOT BELIEVE IT IS OVER! I CANNOT BELIEVE THAT THE BLACK PANTHER WILL STALK NO MORE!
DON'T GIT ALL SHOOK UP, PAL! MEBBE THE YANCY STREET GANG CAN USE YA!
BENJAMIN J. GRIMM! THAT WASN'T FUNNY!
WELL, YA CAN'T WIN EM ALL!

THERE'S NO REASON FOR THE BLACK PANTHER'S CAREER TO COME TO AN END! THE WORLD WILL ALWAYS HAVE NEED OF A DEDICATED, POWERFUL FIGHTER AGAINST INJUSTICE!
REED'S RIGHT, FELLA! THE WAY THINGS ARE GOING TODAY, YOU NEVER HEAR OF A SUPER-HERO BEING OUT OF WORK!
I SHALL DO IT! I PLEDGE MY FORTUNE, MY POWERS--MY VERY LIFE--TO THE SERVICE OF ALL MANKIND!
ANYWAY, WITH A COSTUME LIKE THAT, YA CAN ALWAYS BECOME A RASSLER, OR A NEW KINDA FOLK SINGER!

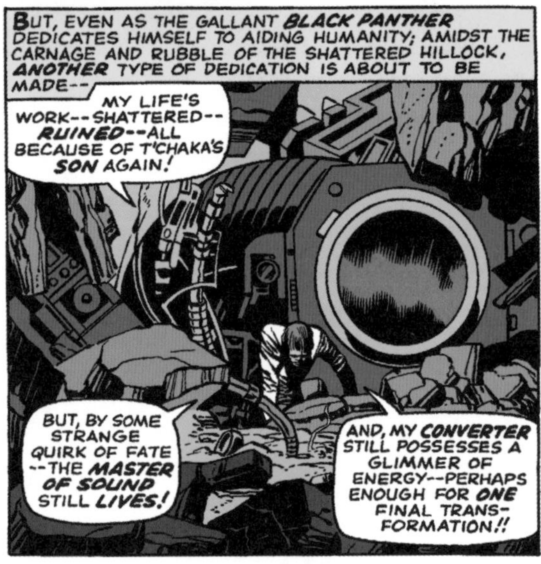
BUT, EVEN AS THE GALLANT BLACK PANTHER DEDICATES HIMSELF TO AIDING HUMANITY; AMIDST THE CARNAGE AND RUBBLE OF THE SHATTERED HILLOCK, ANOTHER TYPE OF DEDICATION IS ABOUT TO BE MADE--
MY LIFE'S WORK--SHATTERED--RUINED--ALL BECAUSE OF T'CHAKA'S SON AGAIN!
BUT, BY SOME STRANGE QUIRK OF FATE--THE MASTER OF SOUND STILL LIVES!
AND, MY CONVERTER STILL POSSESSES A GLIMMER OF ENERGY--PERHAPS ENOUGH FOR ONE FINAL TRANS-FORMATION!!

THERE IS ONE EXPERIMENT I NEVER DARED TO MAKE--ONE CHALLENGE I NEVER DARED ACCEPT!
I NEVER LEARNED WHAT WOULD HAPPEN IF--A HUMAN ALTERED HIS OWN BASIC STRUCTURE VIA MY SOUND TRANSFORMER!!
20

IF I SURVIVE, I'LL EMERGE WITH POWERS FAR DIFFERENT THAN THOSE EVER POSSESSED BY MORTAL MAN--!

POWERS ENOUGH TO ENABLE ME TO DESTROY THE ACCURSED BLACK PANTHER--
--AND, AFTER HIM--ANY-ONE ELSE I SO CHOOSE!
IT IS NOT UNLIKELY THAT WE SHALL MEET THE BLACK PANTHER AND HIS ARCH-FOE, KLAW, ONCE AGAIN--BUT, TILL WE DO, DON'T MISS THE START OF A BRAND-NEW STORY LINE NEXT ISH! YOU KNOW HOW IT UPSETS US WHEN YOU'RE NOT IN AT THE BEGINNING!

# *JUNGLE ACTION* #6,
# SEPTEMBER 1973

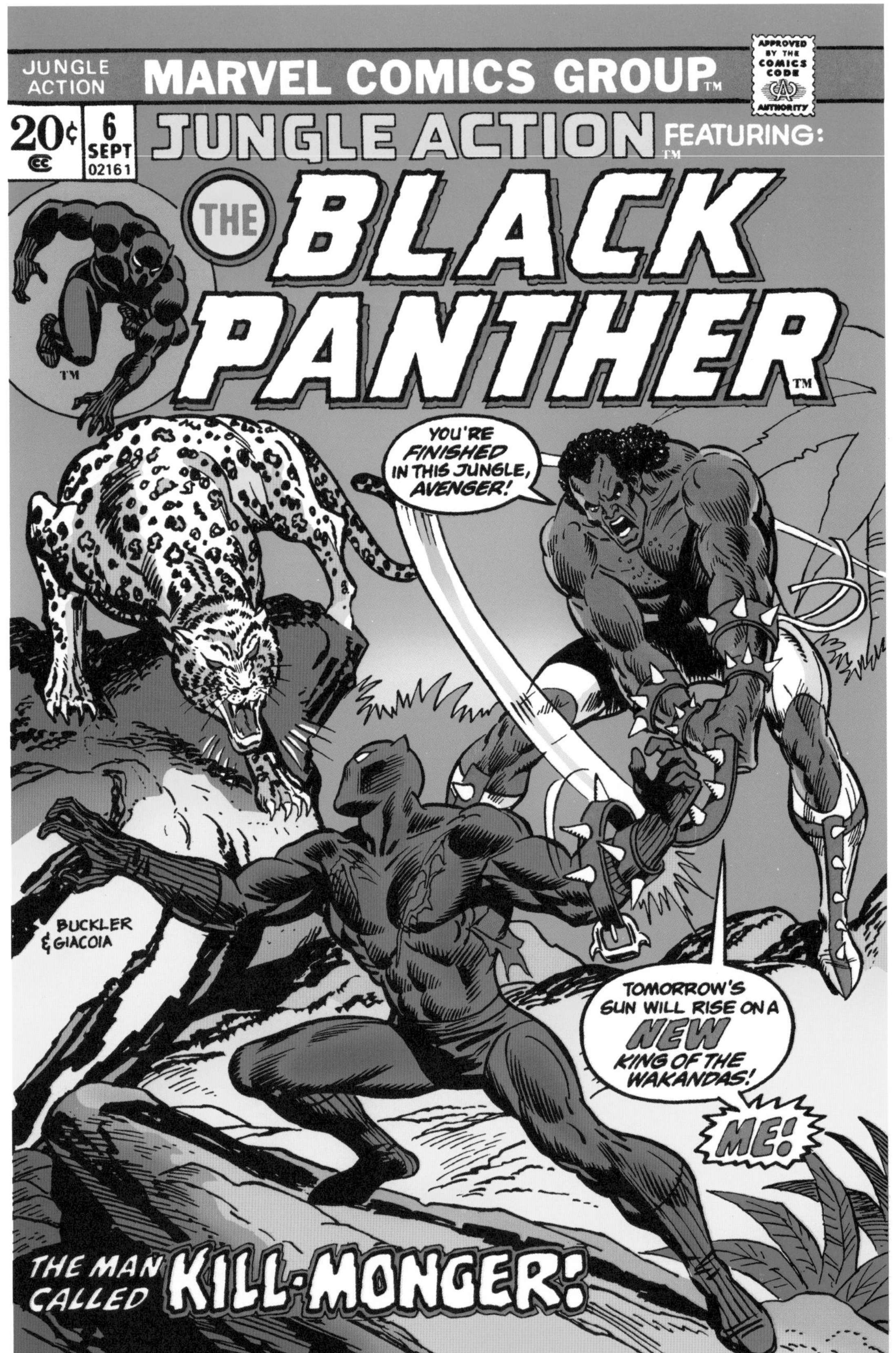
JUNGLE ACTION
MARVEL COMICS GROUP
APPROVED BY THE COMICS CODE AUTHORITY
20¢
6 SEPT 02161
JUNGLE ACTION FEATURING:
THE BLACK PANTHER
YOU'RE FINISHED IN THIS JUNGLE, AVENGER!
BUCKLER & GIACOIA
TOMORROW'S SUN WILL RISE ON A NEW KING OF THE WAKANDAS!
ME!
THE MAN CALLED KILL-MONGER!

Stan Lee PRESENTS: THE BLACK PANTHER!™

DON McGREGOR WRITER / RICH BUCKLER ARTIST / KLAUS JANSON INKER / TOM ORZECHOWSKI, LETTERER GLYNIS WEIN, COLORIST / ROY THOMAS EDITOR

PANTHER'S RAGE
THIS LITHE, OMINOUSLY GARBED FIGURE THAT PASSES AMONG THE HIGH BRANCHES IS NOT ONE OFTEN SUBJECT TO UNREASONING, TOTAL RAGE...
...FOR THIS IS THE BLACK PANTHER, KNOWN IN THIS FERTILE, RESPLENDENT JUNGLE GLADE OF THE WAKANDIAN NATION, AS T'CHALLA...
COME, WIZEND ONE, SPARE YOURSELF PAIN!
YOU'LL ANSWER KILLMONGER'S QUESTIONS!
TAYETE! ABOVE US!
THERE'S NOTHING BUT BIRDS...
TAYETE... THIS IS NO BIRD.
...AND HE HAS ALSO BEEN KNOWN AS A MAN OF COMPASSION... BUT NOW, HE IS FILLED WITH A SEETHING RAGE, EVOKED BY THE CASUAL CRUELTY THAT HIS GLARING, MENACING EYES WITNESS!
A MOMENT BEFORE, HE WAS RE-COMMUNICATING WITH THIS LAND THAT IS MORE THAN HIS IN NAME, RE-ESTABLISHING THE LINK THAT HAS WEAKENED SINCE HIS ABSENCE FROM HIS KINGDOM!
NOW THAT SENSE OF SERENITY IS SWEPT ASIDE... AND THIS REASONABLE MAN, THIS NOBLE MAN... CONSIDERS TERRIBLE RETRIBUTION!

KCHUNK!
STAY YOUR HANDS, SCAVENGERS!
YOU'VE ENJOYED YOUR CRUEL GAMES, BUT YOU'LL TASTE THE POISON OF CRUELTY...
...AND YOU'LL TASTE IT...NOW!

AND YOU...
...YOU LOOK LOST WITHOUT YOUR "SECURITY BLANKET!"
ME?

SO I'LL JUST GIVE IT BACK!
KA-CHOK

A SLIGHT, DEADLY MECHANICAL CLICK BEHIND HIM ALERTS THE PANTHER TO A NEW DANGER--
--AND HE MOVES FLUIDLY, DIVING UNDER THOSE THUNDERING, LETHAL GUN BLASTS--
BRRRAT!
--SOUNDS AS ALIEN TO THIS SUN-SCORCHED GLADE--

--AS ARE THE TORTURED GASPS OF THE MAN BOUND INSIDE THE BAMBOO CAGE--

--AND BOTH SOUNDS FEED THE PANTHER'S RAGE!
YOU'LL NEED BETTER COMMAND OF YOUR CIVILIZED WEAPON IF YOU HOPE TO FELL THE KING OF WAKANDA.
I CAN BREAK YOU AS EASILY AS THIS GUN!
WAIT, PANTHER DEVIL--
IT'S BEEN LONG SINCE YOU BREATHED WAKANDIAN AIR--
--BUT YOU'LL NOT BREATHE ANY AIR MUCH LONGER!
PLEAS FOR MERCY AND ACTS OF TREACHERY--
--HOW OFTEN THE TWO BECOME UNWILLING COMPANIONS!
FLEE WHILE YOU HAVE THE CHANCE! THIS SCORE IS NOT YET SETTLED!
THE NOISE OF BATTLE FADES, REPLACED BY A KEENING WAIL THAT HAS BEEN EVER-PRESENT BUT OVERSHADOWED BY THE HARSH CONFLICT.
BUT THAT CAN WAIT TILL AFTER I'VE USED ONE OF THEIR HIDEOUS TOOLS FOR LESS DESTRUCTIVE PURPOSES.

T'CHALLA--
THERE ARE FEW CAGES ON WAKANDAN SOIL, LOYAL FRIEND -- FOR THEY CAGE THE SPIRIT AS WELL AS THE BODY--
--AND I SHALL FREE BOTH FOR YOU!
PERHAPS THE BODY, YES...
-- MY CHIEFTAIN!
... BUT THE SPIRIT... SEEKS ITS OWN FLIGHT.

THE PANTHER KNEELS BEFORE A SIGHT THAT BURNS HIS VISION...
WHY DID THEY DO THIS TO YOU?
BECAUSE OF THE TERRIBLE TROUBLE THAT THREATENS WAKANDA! THEY SOUGHT TO LEARN WHAT ROYAL ORDERS WERE GIVEN FROM YOUR THRONE WHILE YOU WERE IN ABSENCE!
THEY DID NOT KNOW IT WAS YOUR EXPECTED COMING THAT STIRRED CENTRAL WAKANDA SO.

MANY OF THE PEOPLE SAID YOU'D NEVER COME BACK...

...THAT THE WAKANDAS HAD LOST THEIR KING! ...THAT YOU WOULD DESERT US!
BUT I KNEW THEY WERE WRONG.

YOU MUST BELIEVE... I NEVER LOST FAITH IN YOU, T'CHALLA!
I ALWAYS... BELIEVED.

IT IS A LONG TREK BACK INTO THE CENTER OF THE WAKANDA VILLAGE...
...AND AS THE PANTHER STEPS OUT OF THE LUSH FOLIAGE INTO THE SUN-BURNT DUST SURROUNDING THE WOOD AND STRAW HUTS, ANOTHER DISTURBING THOUGHT CLAIMS HIM:
HE HAS BEEN AWAY TOO LONG.

ONCE, HE WAS ACUTELY ATTUNED TO THIS LAND... ...ONCE, HE WAS PART OF IT AND IT WAS A PART OF HIM...
...BUT NOW HE IS AWARE THAT THERE HAS BEEN A SUBTLE, UNDEFINABLE CHANGE...
...AND HE IS NO LONGER AN INTEGRAL PART OF HIS HERITAGE!

THE KNOWLEDGE OF THIS AND OF THE DESTROYED HUMANITY HE HOLDS IN HIS ARMS IS REFLECTED IN HIS WALK.
A SOMBER WAKE FORMS THIS SILENT PROCESSION, ALL MUTE WITH ONE EMOTION:
MOURNING!

T'CHALLA--
WE'VE BEEN LOOKING ALL OVER FOR YOU.
WHAT HAS HAPPENED, MY CHIEFTAIN?
I'M NOT SURE, W'KABI. I HAD HOPED YOU WOULD KNOW MUCH OF WHAT TEARS WAKANDA APART.
WHAT TEARS AT US IS A WHISPERED THREAT-- THAT LEAVES TERROR IN HIS WAKE! ERIK KILLMONGER!
YOUR WORDS ARE HARSH, W'KABI.
PERHAPS IF YOU'D SPENT MORE TIME HERE, YOU WOULD NOT HAVE HAD TO ASK!
WE SHALL TALK ON THIS AND MORE AFTER YOU SEND SOME WARRIORS INTO THE NORTHERN HILLS.

THEY WILL FIND A GLADE THERE-- AND A MECHANICAL WEAPON.
I WANT TO KNOW WHERE THE MOUNTAIN DWELLERS GOT SUCH A DEADLY DEVICE.
YOUR 'GUEST' FROM THE FAR-AWAY SHORES APPROACHES. IT MIGHT BE BEST SHE DID NOT HEAR SUCH TRIBAL CONCERNS!
YOU DONE PLAYING YOUR JUNGLE LORD ACT, TA-CHARLIE.
WOULD YOU LIKE ME TO PLAY JANE-MONICA?
MY CHIEFTAIN, YOU CANNOT ALLOW THIS OUTSIDER TO DISRUPT THE DIGNITY OF THIS COURT.
DIG HIGH AND MIGHTY, HERE. FROM FIRST TAKE HE'S BEEN GIVING ME DAGGER EYES AND...
OOOHH!
HER NAME IS MONICA LYNNE... AND ONCE SHE WAS A SONGSTRESS, A MINOR-GRADE ARETHA FRANKLIN...

T'CHALLA, I... I'M SORRY!
...AND MORE RECENTLY SHE SPENT HER DAYS AS A SOCIAL WORKER...
...UNTIL THE WORDS OF THIS QUIET, ELOQUENT MAN CONVINCED HER SHE MIGHT LEARN MORE ABOUT DIFFERENT LIFE-STYLES AND HERSELF HERE IN THIS JUNGLE PARADISE.
MONICA, HE TRUSTED ME...
... AND I DIDN'T EVEN KNOW HIS NAME.
SHHH... DON'T TALK.
JUST TRY TO ACCEPT IT...
...JUST FOR NOW!

BUT THE TIME FOR ACCEPTANCE IS SHORT, AND THE NEXT DAY DAWNS CRIMSON OVER RIVERS TAINTED THEIR OWN VERSION OF RED...
IT IS THE SCENE OF A MASSACRE, THE SLAUGHTER OF A GENTLE PEOPLE WHO LIVED OFF THE TEPID WATERS...
...AND WHO HAVE NOW DIED THERE!
THE PAIN AND HURT AND LOSS ARE A SHATTERING REALITY--
--THE DESTRUCTION OF A LEADER'S DREAM.
HOW HAVE SUCH ATROCITIES BEEN ALLOWED TO HAPPEN, W'KABI?
YOU ALLOWED IT TO HAPPEN!
HAVE A CARE, W'KABI. THIS IS NOT A TIME FOR DISPUTE!
YOU HAVE ALWAYS BEEN TOO LENIENT, TAKU!
THESE SUBJECTS ARE NOT THE CONCERN OF A MERE COMMUNICATIONS ADVISOR!
PERHAPS YOU CAN ANSWER MY QUESTION, TAKU-- AND ALSO EXPLAIN W'KABI'S HOSTILITY!
WAKANDA EXPANDS, T'CHALLA!
THERE ARE MANY SMALL VILLAGES AS THIS ONE.
CONSIDER... WHEN WAS THE LAST TIME YOU VISITED ANY OF THE ISOLATED MOUNTAIN SETTLEMENTS?
THEY REMAIN SECLUDED, GOVERNED MOSTLY BY THEIR OWN LEADERS--
--AND ONE HAS ARISEN FROM THAT VASTNESS-- ONE FIERCER THAN ALL OTHERS.
YOU WERE A WISE AND JUST LEADER IN YOUR EARLY DAYS-- WHEN FIRST WE DECIDED HOW TO USE OUR NATURAL RESOURCES OF VIBRANIUM.
BUT NOW WAKANDA SEPARATES-- AND ONE WONDERS--ARE YOU STRONG ENOUGH TO PULL IT BACK TOGETHER!
YOU NEARLY OVERSTEP YOUR POSITION, W'KABI!
BEWARE-- THESE ARE NOT MOMENTS TO PUSH ME!

TAKU, USE THE REMOTE AND CONTACT THE HOSPITAL--
--TELL THEM TO SEND MORE MEDICAL TEAMS HERE, IMMEDIATELY. THE GRIM RUMORS ARE, UNFORTUNATELY, TRUE!
THIS MUST BE MORE OF KILLMONGER'S WORK!


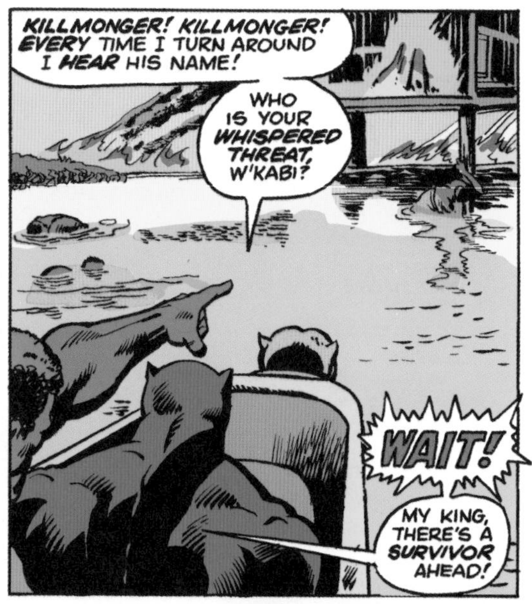

KILLMONGER! KILLMONGER! EVERY TIME I TURN AROUND I HEAR HIS NAME!
WHO IS YOUR WHISPERED THREAT, W'KABI?
WAIT!
MY KING, THERE'S A SURVIVOR AHEAD!

THERE, W'KABI, IS THAT NOT THE ACTIONS OF THE KING YOU ONCE RESPECTED BACK WHEN YOU WERE BUT A PALACE GUARD?

WHO HAS DONE THIS TERRIBLE BARBARISM?
THERE WERE MANY OF THEM-- AND THEY SPOKE VERY LITTLE-- BUT THEIR LEADER WAS A VENGEFUL GIANT--
I HEARD HIS NAME ABOVE THE SCREAMS-- ERIK... ERIK KILLMONGER!
SO YOU WERE RIGHT, W'KABI!
YOUR THREAT HAS SPILLED THE BLOOD OF MY PEOPLE...
...AND I CAN TRY TO DO NO LESS TO HIM!

A PITY IT HAS TAKEN SUCH DRASTIC EVENTS TO STILL YOUR OBSESSION WITH THOSE FOREIGN SHORES...
BUT IF YOU DO GO FOR KILLMONGER, MY CHIEF-TAIN, BE CAREFUL--
--FOR HE'LL CUT YOU INTO STRIPS OF BACON AND LEAVE YOU TO FRY IN THE AFRICAN SUN!
HE'LL BREAK EVERY BONE IN YOUR BODY JUST TO ENJOY HEARING THEM SNAP...
...AND HE WON'T EVEN FEEL ANY REMORSE!
THAT'S KILLMONGER, T'CHALLA--

YOU SOUND LIKE HIS PUBLICITY AGENT, W'KABI.
MY CHIEFTAIN, A CALL COMES FROM WARRIOR FALLS-- A GROUP OF MEN HAVE BEEN SPOTTED-- LED BY A GIANT MAN WITH-- A WHITE LEOPARD!
AS A CHILD, WARRIOR FALLS WAS A WORK OF WONDER TO T'CHALLA'S YOUNG EYES-- AND NOW, THOUGH HE HAS SEEN MANY WONDERS SINCE, THE CASCADING FALLS STILL INSPIRE AWE; THEIR ROAR IS LIKE THE RAGE THAT CONSUMES HIM!
TAYETE--
IF WE RUN INTO THAT PANTHER DEVIL AGAIN, I'M GOING TO RIP HIM LIMB FROM LIMB!
--NOT AGAIN.
HE'D RATHER LICK TONGUES WITH A COBRA THAN TANGLE WITH ME!
KAZIBE, WHAT ARE YOU MUM-BLING ABOU...!
I WILL ASK BUT ONCE: WHERE IS YOUR LEADER?
JUNGLE BRED INSTINCTS, NURTURED AND AIDED BY HERBAL MEDICINES AND RIGOROUS, OFT-REPEATED RELIGIOUS CEREMO-NIES, CUT THROUGH THE PANTHER'S RAGE--
--AND ALERT HIM TO A SHIFTING OF SHADOWS-- A SLIGHT RUSTLE OF EXOTIC FERNS--AND THE INSTINCTIVE KNOWLEDGE THAT DEATH IS ABOUT TO STRIKE!

THE PANTHER HAD ONLY HALF BELIEVED W'KABI'S DIRE PREMONITIONS, FOR WHISPERED THREATS HINT OF MELODRAMA...
... BUT HE DOES NOT DOUBT THOSE WORDS ANY LONGER!
PTNCHH
MY DIVERSION DID NOT KEEP YOU OCCUPIED AS I'D HOPED!
BUT, IF YOU DESIRE MY PRESENCE, THEN LOOK WELL-- FOR IT'LL BE YOUR LAST KINGLY ACT!
KILLMONGER IS--HERE!!

YOU ATTACKED THAT VILLAGE... EXACTED THAT CARNAGE... JUST TO DIVERT US?
YOU SOUND OUT-RAGED, T'CHALLA!
IT'S ALMOST AS IF YOU'VE FORGOTTEN THAT WE'VE MET BEFORE--!
IT HAS BEEN A LONG TIME SINCE I'VE HEARD YOUR MORAL INDIGNATION, GRANTED...
...BUT WHAT ARE YOU LOOKING FOR? A METHOD OF ESCAPE? THERE...
... ISN'T...
... ANY!
THAT'S ONLY PARTIAL REPAYMENT. PERHAPS JUST ONE OF US WALKS FROM HERE TODAY!
WHAT'S THIS?
YOU'RE STILL STANDING!
IS THAT THE BEST YOU CAN DO, T'CHALLA?
IF SO, I'M DISAP-POINTED.
MY CAT, PREYY...
...MAKES SHORT WORK OF MY DISAPPOINTMENTS!
THE LEOPARD HURTLES INTO THE PANTHER--A SNARL FOLLOWING ITS LUNGE...
...AND THE COPPER-WARM AIR FLASHES BEFORE HIS EYES AS HE BUCKLES UNDER THE ON-SLAUGHT!

THIS IS THE HOUR OF YOUR DEFEAT, T'CHALLA--
--I'D NOT EXPECTED IT TO HAPPEN THIS QUICKLY!
THE PANTHER BARELY HEARS KILLMONGER'S WORDS, FOR THE RUSHING WATER SPILLS THUNDEROUSLY OVER THE PRECIPICE--
--ECLIPSING EVEN THE INSISTENT GROWLS OF THE BEAST WHOSE FANGS SEEK TO RIP INTO HIS JUGULAR VEIN!
FOR ONE MOMENT THE PANTHER KNOWS FEAR-- THEN CONQUERS IT--HIS FINGERS QUESTING THROUGH FUR FOR A VULNERABLE OPENING.
YOU COULD NOT HAVE HOPED TO WIN!
WAKANDA BECAME A TOY TO YOU-- A BRIGHT SHINING GEM--
--AND ON THE DAY THAT HAPPENED YOU LOST YOUR KINGDOM!
THE PANTHER IGNORES THE ACCUSATIONS, FINGERS PROBING, PRYING APART THE ANIMAL'S SLAVERING JAWS.
COME, PREYY! FINISH THIS FARCE QUICKLY!
FOR A MOMENT, BOTH OPPONENTS HOLD THEIR OWN-- AN INCREDIBLE CONTEST OF STRENGTH--
SNAPPP!
-- UNTIL SLOWLY, SURELY, HIS GLOVED FINGERS, SLICKENED BY HIS OWN BLOOD AND THE CREATURE'S SALIVA, THE PANTHER FORCES THE GAPING MOUTH TO ITS LIMIT, NEARLY BREAKING ITS NECK!

NO!!
AWAY, PREYY!
I'LL NOT ALLOW PREYY TO DIE AT YOUR HANDS, T'CHALLA!
YOU AND YOUR FATHER'S REIGN HAVE TAKEN TOO MUCH FROM ME ALREADY!
YOUR LINE OF DESCENT ENDS WITH YOU, AND YOU'LL TAKE NOTHING FROM ME EVER AGAIN!
GOOD BYE, GREAT AND MIGHTY KING!
YOU'VE RETURNED TO THE LAND OF YOUR BIRTH--
--ONLY TO DIE HERE!
NEXT:
DEATH REGIMENTS BENEATH WAKANDA
AND VENOMM

# MAP OF THE LAND OF THE WAKANDA

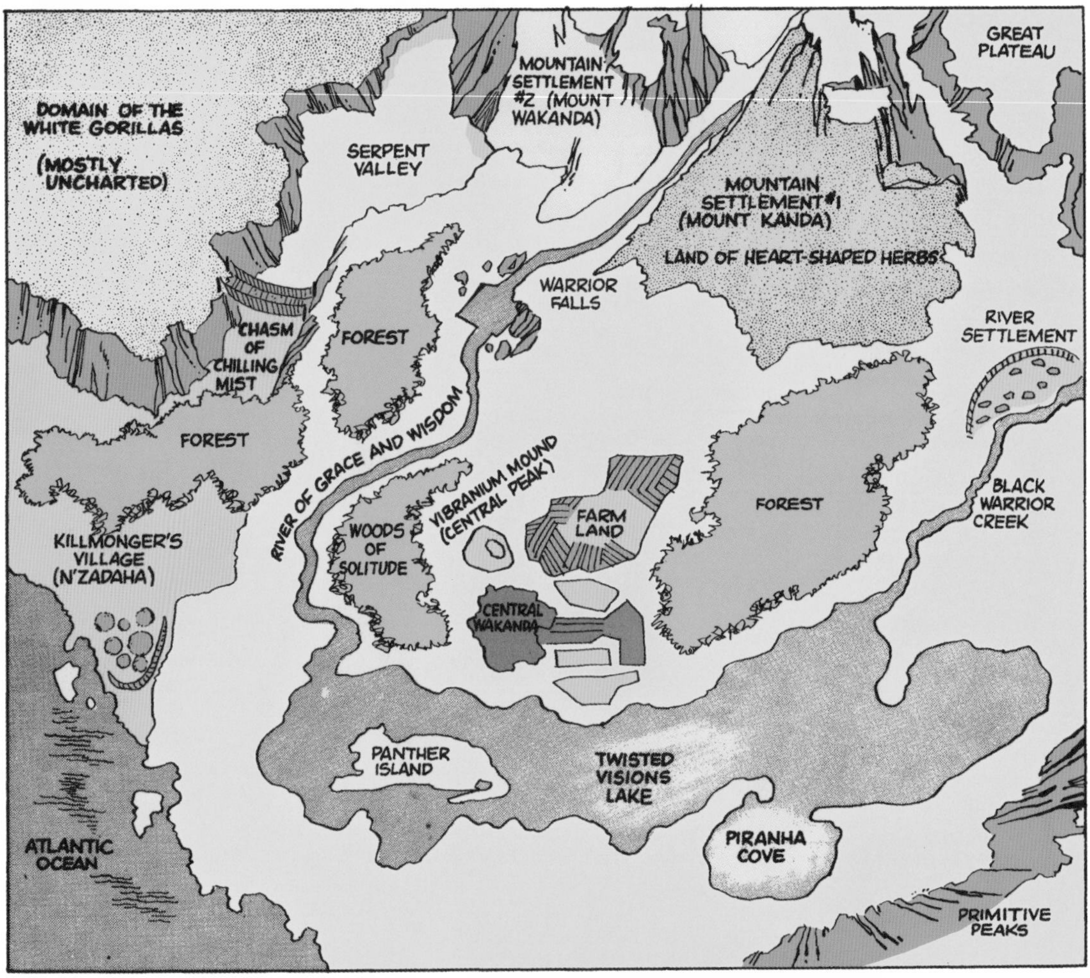

DOMAIN OF THE WHITE GORILLAS
(MOSTLY UNCHARTED)
SERPENT VALLEY
MOUNTAIN SETTLEMENT #2 (MOUNT WAKANDA)
GREAT PLATEAU
MOUNTAIN SETTLEMENT #1 (MOUNT KANDA)
LAND OF HEART-SHAPED HERBS
WARRIOR FALLS
CHASM OF CHILLING MIST
FOREST
RIVER SETTLEMENT
FOREST
RIVER OF GRACE AND WISDOM
VIBRANIUM MOUND (CENTRAL PEAK)
BLACK WARRIOR CREEK
FARM LAND
FOREST
WOODS OF SOLITUDE
KILLMONGER'S VILLAGE (N'ZADAHA)
CENTRAL WAKANDA
PANTHER ISLAND
TWISTED VISIONS LAKE
PIRANHA COVE
ATLANTIC OCEAN
PRIMITIVE PEAKS

# CENTRAL WAKANDA

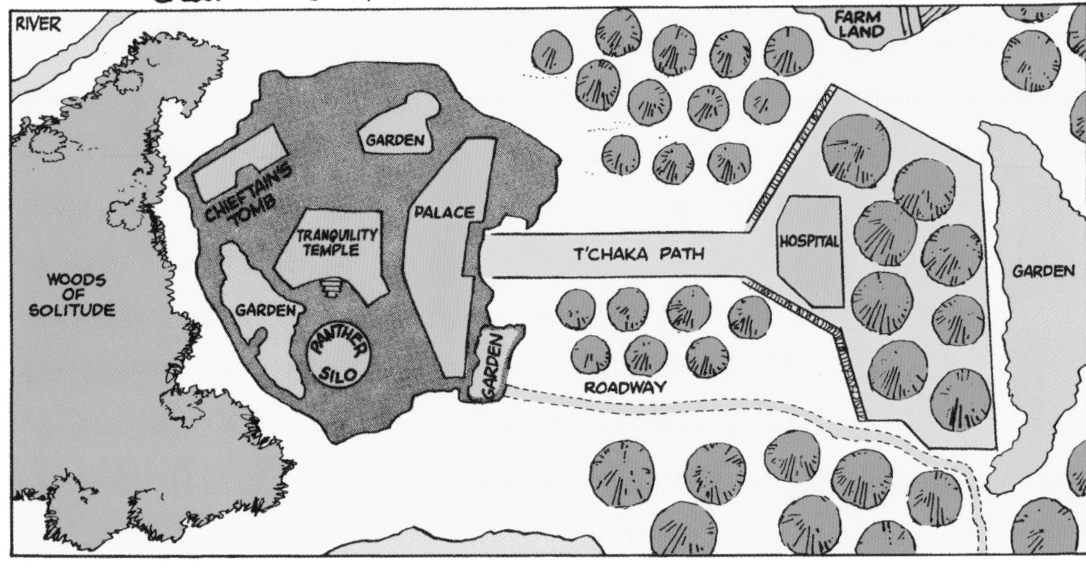

# *JUNGLE ACTION* #7,
NOVEMBER 1973

JUNGLE ACTION
MARVEL COMICS GROUP
APPROVED BY THE COMICS CODE AUTHORITY
20¢
7 NOV
02161
JUNGLE ACTION FEATURING:
THE BLACK PANTHER
STRIKE, MY PETS! STRIKE-- AND SLAY!
THE BLACK PANTHER MUST DIE!
AND--IF I DON'T MOVE EVEN FASTER THAN THOSE VIPERS--
--THAT'S JUST WHAT'LL HAPPEN!
BUCKLER & JANSON
VENOMM IS HIS NAME-- AND MURDER IS HIS GAME!

Stan Lee PRESENTS: THE BLACK PANTHER!
PANTHER'S RAGE CONTINUES...
THE BLACK PANTHER IS BACK-- BACK IN WAKANDA-- BUT IT IS NOT A JOYOUS RETURN--
--FOR THIS HIDDEN JUNGLE PARADISE WHERE HE IS KNOWN AS T'CHALLA, KING OF THE WAKANDAS, IS NOT THE LAND HE LEFT!
THE PANTHER'S RULE IS THREATENED BY ERIK KILLMONGER!
KILLMONGER-- A VIOLENT LEADER WHO HAS ARISEN FROM ONE OF THE NUMEROUS MOUNTAIN SETTLEMENTS SURROUNDING CENTRAL WAKANDA!
A TOP WARRIOR FALLS, THE PANTHER AND KILLMONGER CLASH FOR THE FIRST TIME-- A CONFLICT THAT ENDS ABRUPTLY--
--AND IS PERHAPS, THE LAST SUCH CONFLICT THE PANTHER WILL EVER HAVE!
GOOD BYE, GREAT AND MIGHTY KING!
YOU'VE RETURNED TO THE LAND OF YOUR BIRTH--
--ONLY TO DIE HERE!
DON McGREGOR WRITER
RICH BUCKLER ARTIST
KLAUS JANSON INKER
T. ORZECHOWSKI, LETTERER
GLYNIS WEIN COLORIST
ROY THOMAS EDITOR

THE PANTHER HAS ALWAYS RESPECTED THE MAJESTIC POWER OF WARRIOR FALLS.
HE HAS EARLY MEMORIES OF THIS CRUELLY BEAUTIFUL DOWNWARD PLUNGE OF WATER!
THE THUNDERING SWEEP OF WATER BATTERS THE PANTHER WITH INSENSATE FURY-- AS IF A LIVING ENTITY RUN AMOK!
AN IMAGE FLASHES THROUGH THE SWIRL OF WATER, AND IT IS THAT OF HIS FATHER, T'CHAKA, HOLDING HIM WHEN HE WAS BUT FOUR YEARS OLD--
DEATH REGIMENTS
--AND HIS FATHER'S WORDS COME TO HIM THROUGH THE DEAFENING ROAR OF THE CATARACT--
--THAT HE SHOULD NOT FEAR THIS RAGING SPECTACLE--
--BUT THAT HE MUST NEVER UNDERESTIMATE

BENEATH
SACRED WAKANDAN CEREMONIES TO BECOME THAT WHICH HE IS-- THE BLACK PANTHER, KING OF THE WAKANDAS--
--AND NOW, THOUGH THE BRUTAL CURRENT FLOODS HIS LUNGS WITH SUFFOCATING FORCE--
--HE DOES WHAT LITTLE HE CAN TO SAVE HIMSELF!
HE KICKS OFF THE JAGGED, MOSS COVERED ROCKS THAT LIE UNDER THE CHURNING, FOAMING SURFACE--STRATEGICALLY CONTROLLING HIS PANIC AND NEED FOR AIR!
THE SAVAGE DESCENT CONTINUES--
--UNTIL HE GLIMPSES THE FINAL UPTHRUST ROCKS BELOW, POINTING UP LIKE ETERNAL GRANITE SPIKES THAT HAVE WAITED PATIENTLY--
--TO PIERCE HIS FLESH... AND END HIS LIFE!
WAKANDA
COME, KAZIBE AND TAYETE!
WE MUST TAKE ADVANTAGE OF THE CONFUSION THAT WILL ARISE OVER THEIR CHIEFTAIN'S DEATH!
LONG BEFORE THEY ARE AWARE OF IT--
--WE SHALL HIT THEM WITH THE MOST SHOCKING EVENT OF ALL!

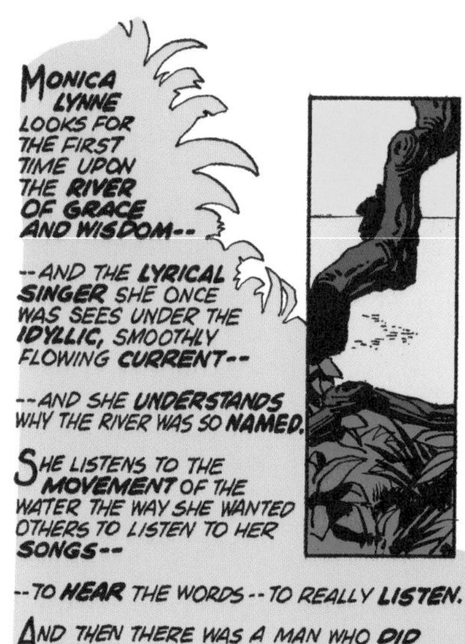
MONICA LYNNE LOOKS FOR THE FIRST TIME UPON THE RIVER OF GRACE AND WISDOM--
--AND THE LYRICAL SINGER SHE ONCE WAS SEES UNDER THE IDYLLIC, SMOOTHLY FLOWING CURRENT--
--AND SHE UNDERSTANDS WHY THE RIVER WAS SO NAMED.
SHE LISTENS TO THE MOVEMENT OF THE WATER THE WAY SHE WANTED OTHERS TO LISTEN TO HER SONGS--
--TO HEAR THE WORDS--TO REALLY LISTEN.
AND THEN THERE WAS A MAN WHO DID LISTEN... AND THAT IS WHY SHE IS HERE!

YOU WILL FIND THE WATER MOST WARM AND PLEASING AT THIS SPOT, MISS LYNNE.
IT'S A BEAUTIFUL PLACE. I THANK YOU FOR BRINGING ME HERE.
BUT, TANZIKA, WHY IS IT I GET SO MANY BAD VIBES FROM YOU?
YOU TALK MOST STRANGELY... MISS LYNNE!

CALL ME MONICA.
I'LL BE AWAITING YOU UP IN THE AMBER PAGODA.
IF YOU SHOULD NEED ANYTHING, JUST CALL...
...MISS LYNNE.

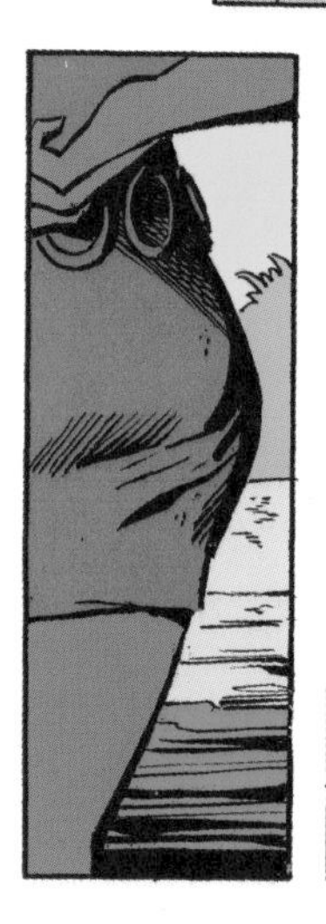

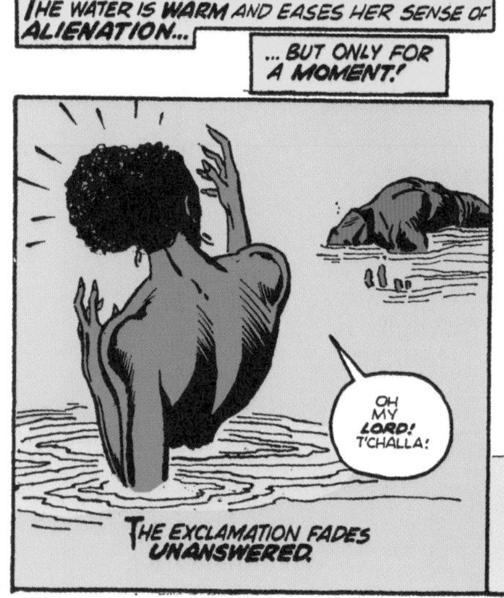
THE WATER IS WARM AND EASES HER SENSE OF ALIENATION...
...BUT ONLY FOR A MOMENT!
OH MY LORD! T'CHALLA!
THE EXCLAMATION FADES UNANSWERED.

TEARS FILL MONICA'S EYES--
--AND SHE FEARS THAT THE MAN WHO HAD LISTENED--WILL NEVER HEAR ANYTHING... AGAIN!

DUSK FALLS OVER THE ISOLATED VILLAGE OF N'JADAKA, AND A SIBILANT, MUSICAL SOUND WAVERS IN THE HUMID AIR--

--REACHING INTO THE SHELTERED HUTS WHERE THE SETTLEMENT'S INHABITANTS REACT SUSPICIOUSLY.

SOME GLANCE FEARFULLY TOWARD THE COLORLESS MAN WITH THE HIDEOUS FACE--

--AND SHUDDER!

BUT THE MAN WHO INTONES THAT WHISPERING CARESS MOVES SLOWLY AND HYPNOTICALLY, A HALF-ENTRANCED MYSTIC--

--WHO PLAYS TO HIS AUDIENCE!

HE KNOWS THESE REPTILES WELL--

--AND HE KNOWS THE VIPERS CANNOT HEAR ANY SOUND AT ALL!

IT IS ONLY CHEMICAL POTIONS, HYPNOTIC ABILITY, AND DEDICATED EXPERIMENTATION THAT MAKES THEM DOCILE AND MANAGEABLE--

--A POISON-FANGED ARSENAL, TRIGGERED AND AWAITING THE SILENT COMMAND OF HIS HANDS!

IT WAS A LONG--BUT TRIUMPHANT TREK FROM WARRIOR FALLS, WAS IT NOT, TAYETE?

COME!
REST FOR A MOMENT.
YOU ARE WATCHING A MASTER AT WORK. IT'S SELDOM A SIGHT ONE GETS TO SEE HERE IN N'JADAKA.
I... I DON'T KNOW WHAT YOU SEE IN A GUY THAT WRAPS THEM THINGS ABOUT HIM FOR RELAXATION!

WHY, SNAKES DON'T BOTHER YOU... DO THEY, TAYETE?
OF... OF COURSE NOT.
SO I THOUGHT.
COME, VENOMM! YOUR ACT BECOMES MORE FLAMBOYANT EACH PERFORMANCE!
AND HE'LL FRIGHTEN THE CHILDREN... RIGHT, TAYETE?

N'JADAKA--
I DISCARDED THAT NAME--IT'S NOW KILLMONGER. YOU SHOULD RECALL THAT, HORATIO!
YOU'RE RIGHT! BECAUSE I CHOSE THIS NAME--
--VENOMM!
IT'S A BITTER TASTE--
--AN' IT KEEPS LINGERIN' IN MY MIND.
I PROMISED YOU, FRIEND, A PLACE WHERE YOU COULD CARRY ON YOUR REPTILIAN PRACTICES--
--BUT ALSO A PLACE WHERE YOU WOULD BE ACCEPTED.
THAT PLACE IS HERE! THE TIME IS NOW!
I'VE HEARD THE MELODY BEFORE--
--NEVER CARED FOR THE REFRAIN!
THOSE AREN'T IMPASSIONED PROMISES FOR THE FOLLOWERS!
THE ATTACK UPON THE RIVER SITE AT BLACK WARRIOR CREEK DID NOT DIVERT OUR MAJOR OBSTACLE, THE PANTHER--
--AND AS A RESULT THE WAKANDAN'S DARLING IDOL IS NO LONGER ANY OBSTACLE AT ALL!
BUT, ENOUGH ARROGANCE. YOU SHOULD BE ON YOUR WAY TO THE MINES, VENOMM!
WE ARE ABOUT TO HIT THE WAKANDANS RIGHT WHERE THEY LIVE!
WHAT I DON'T UNDER-STAND--
--IS WHY YOU PUT THAT ANEMIC FREAK IN CHARGE OF THE DEATH REGIMENTS INSTEAD OF..
KA-POW!
YOU, TAYETE?
THAT'S NOT A QUESTION THAT NEEDS ANSWERING.
AND YOU SHOULD BEWARE, TAYETE, LEST VENOMM EVER OVERHEAR YOUR SENTIMENTS.
HE DOES NOT WEAR THOSE SERPENTS AS DECORATIONS!

IT IS A LONG, HOT WEEK IN CENTRAL WAKANDA--AND THERE IS A TENSE EXPECTANCY ABOUT THE CEREMONIAL CHAMBERS.
TORCHES FLARE NIGHTLY FROM THE ORNATELY CARVED TRANQUILITY TEMPLE... FLICKERING FLAMES THAT PAY TRIBUTE TO THE SLAIN WAKANDANS FROM BLACK WARRIOR CREEK!
AND THE PANTHER MENDS REMARKABLY FAST DURING THOSE DAYS.
AT WEEK'S END, HUGE TORTOISE SHELLS ARE SCRAPED CLEAN AND FILLED WITH EXOTIC WAKANDAN DELICACIES, SMOKED OVER RITUALISTIC FIRES OF LAMENT!
T'CHALLA LOOKS AT THE COURT ASSEMBLAGE:
TANZIKA, NOTING HER COOL INDIFFERENCE TOWARD...
...MONICA, WHO SEEMS AWARE THAT THE TRIBUNAL PRESENCE REGARDS HER AS AN INFERIOR OUTWORLDER.
TAKU, REMAINING STOIC AND NEUTRAL--
--BUT W'KABI, HIS SECOND IN COMMAND, WAITS IMPATIENTLY--
--AND ZATAMA'S EYES SEETHE WITH RIGHTEOUS REBELLION.
THEY ARE ALL WAITING FOR HIM TO SPEAK--AS IF THEY THINK HE HAS ALL THE ANSWERS
I HAD HOPED THAT THE FIRST FEASTS UPON MY RETURN WOULD BE ONES OF GAIETY--
--BUT GAIETY HAS BECOME SOMETHING LOST TO OUR SHORES.
IF ONE MAN CAN STEAL SUCH AS THAT...
... THAT MAN IS... ERIK KILLMONGER!
"THOUGH, WHEN WE FIRST MET, I KNEW HIM AS N'JADAKA--NOT KILLMONGER. HE APPROACHED ME, W'KABI, WHILE I WAS IN MONICA'S HOMELAND--BUT HIS ORIGINS ARE WAKANDAN! HE TOLD ME THAT DURING KLAW'S INITIAL ATTACK UPON OUR SOIL* THAT HE WAS BADLY BEATEN!
"DURING THE RAID THAT KILLED MY FATHER, KLAW'S MEN SAVAGELY DECIMATED THE SMALLER VILLAGE SITES, FORCING THE YOUNG MEN AWAY IN CHAINS, TO BE USED AS SLAVES IN MINING OUR VALUABLE VIBRANIUM ORE!
*SHOWN IN FANTASTIC FOUR #53.--ROY.
"N'JADAKA WAS AMONG THOSE CAPTURED!

"AS FOR MYSELF, I CAN RECALL LITTLE MORE THAN MY FATHER LYING AT MY FEET-- HIS WARMTH FADING BENEATH MY HANDS.

"I HAD NEVER REALLY TOLD HIM I'D LOVED HIM-- I GUESS BECAUSE LOVE IS AN EMOTION WE ARE EMBARRASSED TO ADMIT. IT MAKES US VULNERABLE!

"AND NOW THEY WERE WORDS HE WOULD NEVER HEAR!

"AS MY FATHER'S BLOOD DRIED UPON MY HANDS, I DESTROYED KLAW'S EFFORTS TO STEAL OUR PRECIOUS VIBRANIUM METAL WHICH ABSORBS ALL ENERGY--

"--BUT THE MERCENARY PAWNS KLAW HAD USED FLED, TURNING THOSE CAPTIVES INTO THEIR PAWNS!

"N'JADAKA ESCAPED THEIR CLUTCHES AFTER REACHING AMERICAN SHORES--

"--AND WAS UNDERSTANDABLY EMBITTERED AND DISPLACED-- WITHOUT ANY IDEA HOW TO GET BACK TO THE HIDDEN LANDS OF WAKANDA.

WHEN I FOUGHT ALONGSIDE THE AVENGERS, IN AMERICA, HE RECOGNIZED MY WAKANDAN COSTUME AND CONTACTED ME!

"I BROUGHT HIM BACK WITH ME DURING THAT TIME WE HAD THE TROUBLE ON PANTHER ISLAND -- AND HE VANISHED INTO THE WILDERNESS!"

NOW HE REAPPEARS WITH THE NAME ERIK KILLMONGER.
I CANNOT GUESS HOW HE HAS BECOME SO POWERFUL IN SO FEW YEARS--
--BUT HE WILL PAY FOR THE SUFFERING HE HAS CAUSED!
VIOLENCE!! THAT'S ALWAYS YOUR ONLY ANSWER, T'CHALLA!

MY CHIEFTAIN, WHY DO YOU ALLOW ZATAMA'S DISRESPECT?
CALM YOURSELF, W'KABI!
ZATAMA'S RADICAL DISPLAY IS OFT A HEALTHIER SIGN--
--THAN APATHY! FOR APATHY IS A SUBTLE KILLER!

THAT'S NO ANSWER, T'CHALLA!
PERHAPS, ZATAMA, YOU DON'T UNDERSTAND THE QUESTION.
WHAT'S WRONG, TAKU?
THE REMOTE COMMUNICATIONS UNIT SIGHTS MORE ACTIVITY AT WARRIOR FALLS-- PANICKY VOICES CLAIM THEY'VE SEEN--
--A DEATHLY LEGION!

THEY ARE LED BY AN APPARITION -- A DEATH FIGURE WITH FLESH OF A CORPSE -- AND SERPENTS SPIRALLED ABOUT HIS BODY!
AS QUICKLY AS THEY APPEARED, THEY WERE GONE -- WITHOUT A TRACE!
T'CHALLA -- YOUR ISSAC HAYES "GET-UP" DON'T MAKE YOU JOHN SHAFT!
YOUR WOUNDS--
-- ARE FAR DEEPER THAN PHYSICAL SCARS, MONICA.
W'KABI, DOUBLE THE GUARDS ABOUT THE ETERNAL PEAK--
KILLMONGER MUST NEVER EXTINGUISH THE FLAMES OF THAT SACRED MOUND!

I'LL TELL YOU ONE THING, KAZIBE--
TAYETE, DON'T YOU THINK WE SHOULD MOVE WITH STEALTH?
WHAT FOR? REMEMBER? THERE'S NO MORE... PANTHER DEVIL!

HE OUGHT TO THANK HIS GODS THAT KILLMONGER FINISHED HIM OFF!
SURE, TAYETE.
I'D'VE MANGLED HIM!

I WOULDN'T HAVE BEEN SO...

...MERCIFUL!
GGHHAAARRKK

PERHAPS, THEN, I'LL NOT BE MERCIFUL EITHER.
KAZIBE... TELL ME IT ISN'T TRUE!

THE DEATH REGI-MENTS ARE RIGHT BEHIND US!
YOU'D BEST LET US GO!
SINCE YOU DEMAND IT!
DEATH REGIMENTS?
THEY'LL CERTAINLY BE OF MORE USE THAN EITHER OF YOU!

A PRETERNATURAL HUSH DESCENDS OVER THE UNTAMED HIGHLAND--

--AS IF THE MYRIAD JUNGLE LIFE SENSES WITH ANTENNAE, SCENT, AND HIDDEN EYES... THE ESSENCE OF DEATH PASSING BY--

--TERRIFYING SPECTERS THAT TREAD MALEVOLENTLY INTO A SIDE INLET CAUSED BY BLACK WARRIOR FALLS--

--BECOMING INCREASINGLY SPECTRAL AS THE MIST SWALLOWS AND DISTORTS THEIR OMINOUS FORMS!

THEY HAVE BEEN CALLED DEATH REGIMENTS--

--AND THEIR NAME FITS THEM WELL.

AND THIS IS AN ACT THEY HAVE DONE MANY TIMES--

--EXCEPT THIS TIME--
--THEY ARE NOT ALONE!

DESPITE THE FACT THAT TORN LIGAMENTS AND BRUISED MUSCLES SIGNAL THEIR ACHE--
--THE PANTHER FOLLOWS!
HIS CAT-LIKE EYES REGISTER THE ROCK HEWN WALLS--
--AND A STARTLING PREMONITION TELLS HIM WHERE THIS SHADOW-FRAUGHT PASSAGE LEADS!
THE PANTHER MOVES OUT, MUCH LIKE HIS NAMESAKE--
--AND THOUGH THESE CAVERN WALLS WOULD NORMALLY MAGNIFY ALL SOUND--
--HIS PURSUIT IS ABSOLUTELY SILENT!
BUT AT THE TRAIL'S END, THE SIGHT THAT SEARS HIS EYES--
--IS EVEN MORE STAGGERING THAN HIS EARLIER FEAR!
IT IS AN IMMENSE MINING OPERATION--
--BATHED IN EERIE ILLUMINOSITY, THE VALUABLE ORE STREAKING THROUGH THE STONE WALLS RADIATING A BLUISH OVERCAST!
THE PANTHER KNOWS HE IS DIRECTLY UNDER THE SACRED MOUND OF VIBRANIUM--
--AND THAT ALL THE GUARDS THAT STAND VIGILANCE OVER THIS SUBSTANCE WHICH ABSORBS ALL VIBRATIONS--
--WILL NEVER REALIZE THAT THE VERY MOUND UPON WHICH THEY STAND--
--IS BEING HOLLOWED OUT BENEATH THEIR FEET!
WHIIIIRRRRRRRRRRRR
CRACK!
AND THEN THERE IS A SINISTER SOUND--JUST BEFORE A DOUBLE-PRONGED BULLWHIP RIPS ABOUT HIS THROAT AND CHEST!

THE PANTHER HAS ONE BLURRED IMAGE OF THE MAN BEHIND HIM, AND KNOWS THIS IS THE CORPSE WHO LEADS THE DEATH REGIMENTS!
ELONGATED, SCALY SERPENTS WRITHE ABOUT HIS BODY; RETRACTILE, FORKED TONGUES DARTING BETWEEN POISONOUS, RECURVED TEETH!
BUT IT IS THE NEARLY PALPABLE HATRED THE PANTHER SENSES MOST--
--HATRED THAT EXPRESSES ITSELF ON A FACE SCARRED SINCE INFANCY!
STATE-SIDE, HE HAD BEEN KNOWN AS HORATIO WALTERS, AND WHEN HE WAS YOUNG, HE THOUGHT THE NAME QUITE POETIC-- UNTIL SCORN AND DERISION KILLED THE POETRY IN HIM!
DURING CHILDHOOD, REJECTION WAS NOT SOMETHING HE COULD UNDERSTAND... AND AS AN ADULT IT BECAME A FORCE HE COULD NOT FACE.
HE SPENT THOSE REMAINING YEARS BUILDING AN IMMUNITY TO THE TOXIC EFFECT OF THESE REPTILES THAT HAVE BECOME AS A SECOND SKIN TO HIM--
--A SECOND, DEADLY SKIN WAITING TO STRIKE!

WELL, LOOK WHAT I CAUGHT ME HERE!
KILLMONGER SAID WE WOULDN'T HAVE TO WORRY 'BOUT YOU LURKIN' AROUND ANY MORE--
--AND HE MIGHTA BEEN WRONG ON THAT ACCOUNT--
--BUT HE WON'T BE WRONG MUCH LONGER!
GUESS AGAIN, FRIEND!
PEOPLE BEEN CALLIN' ME A SIDESHOW FREAK SINCE I CAN REMEMBER--
'CEPT NOW, I CAN STRIKE BACK!
THE NAME'S VENOMM, PANTHER--
--AND AS MY "PET'S" FANGS STRIKE--
--REMEMBER THAT NAME-- REMEMBER IT AS YOU SLOWLY DIE!
TWISTING AGILELY TO AVOID THE DEADLY LUNGE--
--THE PANTHER FEELS THE LEDGE CRUMBLE BENEATH HIS FEET!
THAT'S NOT POSSIBLE.
WHAT YOU DID JUST ISN'T POSSIBLE!
JUST AS YOU AREN'T A WALKING CORPSE AS MY LOOK-OUTS REPORTED-- THOUGH I CAN WELL UNDERSTAND HOW THEY MIGHT THINK SUCH!
NO AMOUNT OF ACROBATICS WILL HELP SURVIVE THIS FALL!

YOU JUST KEEP ON SURPRIZIN' ME!
KILLMONGER DIDN'T EXAGGERATE A BIT ABOUT YOU!
BUT THERE'S NOTHIN' LEFT TO GRAB ONTO AFTER THIS EDGE--!

YOU CAN TWIST YOURSELF INTO A PRETZEL--
BUT IT WON'T DO YOU A BIT 'A GOOD!

YOU'RE A REAL DEAD MAN THIS TIME, PANTHER!

VENOMM'S WORDS RICOCHET HAUNTINGLY OFF THE CAVERN WALLS--

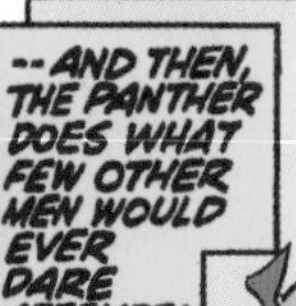
--AND THEN, THE PANTHER DOES WHAT FEW OTHER MEN WOULD EVER DARE ATTEMPT!

HE LETS HIS FREE HAND SWING AWAY FROM HIS LIFE-HOLD--

--AND FOR AN IMMENSE THREE SECONDS IS HELD FROM DEATH BY THE BOOT OF THE MAN THAT INTENDS TO KILL HIM!
AND BEFORE VENOMM CAN LIFT THAT FOOT, AND LET THE ENEMY SPLATTER UPON THE STALAGMITES BELOW--

--THE PANTHER HAS REVERSED POSITIONS!
DON'T BE AFRAID OF DYING JUST YET, VENOMM--
--THOUGH YOU MIGHT WELL WISH YOU HAD BY THE TIME I'M FINISHED WITH YOU!

I WON'T LET YOU STEAL KILLMONGER'S PROMISE!
I WON'T LET YOU STEAL MY CHANCE FOR RESPECT!

RESPECT!
SPEAK NOT TO ME OF RESPECT!

YOU'VE MADE A MOCKERY OF THAT WORD--
--AND TO ATTAIN RESPECT YOU MUST FIRST ACQUIRE SUCH ABILITY FOR OTHERS!

AND YES, VENOMM, IT'S TRUE WHAT THEY SAY--
PWOOWWWWWFFF!

--THE PANTHER IS BACK!

AND I PROMISE YOU THIS, VENOMM--

-- I SHALL NOT REST 'TILL I'VE ENDED THE TERROR KILLMONGER HAS BEGUN!

YOU HAVE LEFT A WAKE OF DESTRUCTION... AND I SHALL FOLLOW THAT BLOODY TRAIL!

I SHALL CLASH NOT ONLY WITH YOUR DEATH REGIMENTS BUT WITH ANY OTHER HELLISH THREATS KILLMONGER HAS!

THERE IS NOTHING KILLMONGER CAN DO TO KEEP ME FROM HIM!

I PROMISE YOU THAT.

NEXT: MALICE BY CRIMSON MOONLIGHT!

# *JUNGLE ACTION* #8,
# JANUARY 1974

JUNGLE ACTION
MARVEL COMICS GROUP
APPROVED BY THE COMICS CODE AUTHORITY
20¢
8 JAN
02161
JUNGLE ACTION FEATURING:
THE BLACK PANTHER
THE MOST AMAZING, MOST OFFBEAT SUPERHERO OF ALL!
BUCKLER & GIACOIA
NEVER-BEFORE-REVEALED SECRETS!
THE ALL-NEW, ALL-GREAT
ORIGIN
OF THE
BLACK PANTHER!

Stan Lee PRESENTS: THE BLACK PANTHER! TM
PANTHER'S RAGE CONTINUES
THE BLACK PANTHER STANDS IN THE CRIMSON WAKANDAN DUSK... WAITING!
HIS SENSES ARE ALERT, PROBING INTO THE SHADOWS. HE HAS KNOWN THIS EBONY MURAL OF TENSION...
... MANY TIMES SINCE HIS FATHER DIED!
THE SHADOWS TAKE DISTORTED SHAPES.
OMINOUS ARMS REACH FROM DECEPTIVE UNDER-BRUSH.
THE BLEEDING MOONLIGHT REFLECTS OFF AN UPTHRUST BLADE!
IF YOU'RE GOING TO ATTACK--
--DO IT NOW!
AND AS HIS CHALLENGE IS ACCEPTED, HE HAS ONE BRIEF AWARENESS THAT ANOTHER FIGURE PROWLS THE JUNGLE THICKET THIS BLOOD-STAINED TWILIGHT-- BUT THE NEXT MOMENT THAT AWARENESS IS LOST AS HE FIGHTS... FOR HIS LIFE!

MAL
BY
CRI
MOON
DON McGREGOR/WRITER
RICH BUCKLER AND KLAUS JANSON/ARTISTS

ICE
MSON
LIGHT
OM ORZECHOWSKI/LETTERING GLYNIS WEIN/COLORIST ROY THOMAS/EDITOR

THE AIR IS HUMID IN WAKANDA, WILTING THE MULTI-COLORED LEAFAGE--
--AND THE CRIMSON MOONLIGHT SEEMS TO HOLD ON TO THE SMOTHERING HEAT OF DAY--GLARING DOWN ON THE VIOLENCE THAT ERUPTS TWO-SCALE WITHIN THE PALACE ROYAL WALLS AND AT CENTRAL WAKANDA'S OUTER LIMITS, TORMENT FOREST!
THE PANTHER'S EYES BLAZE CAT-LIKE... HIS EARS CATCH EACH SLITHERING SOUND--
--AND HE STRIKES, PERFECTLY BALANCED, THOUGH HE HAS BARELY RECOVERED FROM WOUNDS SUSTAINED BUT TWO WEEKS EARLIER!
KRADADA, YOU'RE THE ONE THAT GOT ME INTO THIS MESS!
REMIND ME OF THAT IF WE GET OUT OF HERE IN ONE PIECE--
--OR ANY OTHER WAY!
ZATAMA HAS NEVER KNOWN ANY DANGER WITHIN THE COURTLY WALLS OF THE PALACE...
...BUT HE LOOKS UP INTO ONYX-BLACK EYES AND WOULD HAVE KNOWN DANGER WAS THERE EVEN IF THE TRIDENT-TIPPED SPEAR DID NOT PUNCTURE THE SOFT TISSUE OF HIS THROAT!
YOU'D LIKE TO GO ON BREATHING?
RIGHT?
Y--YES.
THAT'S WHAT I THOUGHT.
YOU GIVE ME ONE WRONG ANSWER... ONLY ONE... AND IT'S THE LAST ANSWER YOU'LL GIVE ANYONE.
YOU UNDERSTAND?
I... I UNDERSTAND. WH... WHO ARE YOU?

AS THE FIGURE OF KRADADA HURTLES OVER HIS SHOULDERS, THE PANTHER REMEMBERS N'BAZA... REMEMBERS THE DISTRUST HE ONCE FELT FOR THAT MAN UNTIL THE RITUALS WERE EXPLAINED TO HIM--
--AND HE ALSO REMEMBERS THAT N'BAZA IS DEAD, REMEMBERS THAT HIS FATHER IS DEAD...
...AND DEATH RUSHES IN UPON HIM, A WRAITH-LIKE REALITY HE CANNOT CONQUER.
I'M NOT GETTING MIXED UP IN THIS!
BUT YOU ALREADY ARE, MY FRIEND!
YOU ALREADY ARE!
HIS WORDS ARE HARSH WITH EMOTION... VISIONS OF A SLAUGHTERED FISHING COLONY MINGLE WITH THAT OF ONE LONE NAMELESS OLD MAN DYING IN HIS ARMS...
...AND HE KICKS OUT NOT AT THE FIGURE BEFORE HIM... BUT AT KILLMONGER... KILLMONGER, WHO HAS CAUSED ALL THIS WANTON DEATH!
THE NAME'S MALICE!
YOU UNDERSTAND WHAT THAT NAME MEANS?
YE... YES.
YOU'VE GOT ALL THE RIGHT ANSWERS SO FAR. KEEP IT UP AND YOU MIGHT EVEN SEE MORNING'S LIGHT.
KILLMONGER SENT ME HERE.
--BUT YOU PROBABLY GUESSED--
WHAT KILLMONGER DOESN'T LIKE IS THAT T'CHALLA GOT LUCKY AND CAPTURED ONE OF HIS LIEUTENANTS-- VENOMM!
I WANT TO KNOW WHERE HE IS-- AND I WANT TO KNOW NOW!

MENDINAO HAS BEEN A HERBALIST MOST OF HIS LIFE--

HE HAS WATCHED THE KING OF THE WAKANDAS GO THROUGH THESE RITES BEFORE--

--WHILE THE FORBIDDEN, HEART-SHAPED HERBS SIMMER INTO A SYRUPY PULP.

--LEARNING THE COMPLEX ART ACQUIRED BY EARLIER GENERATIONS OF HIS FAMILY.

HE FARES MUCH BETTER THAN I'D THOUGHT HE WOULD, MENDINAO.

THEN YOUR EYES SEE NOT WELL AT ALL, W'KABI.

MENDINAO'S EYES SEE WHAT'S HAPPENING.

HE FIGHTS WITH AN INNER RAGE THAT MAKES HIM SEE GHOSTS. HE USES THE TESTS TO RELEASE ALL THE TENSION IN HIM.

THERE WAS A DAY WHEN HE WOULD HAVE KEPT EVERYTHING IN CONTROL.
EVEN ANGER WOULD STAY WHERE HE COULD USE IT TO HIS ADVANTAGE!
PERHAPS THAT'S BECAUSE HE HAS SPENT SO MUCH TIME OF LATE WITH OUT-WORLDERS.

W'KABI, FOR THE HEAD OF COURT SECURITY, YOUR MOUTH HAS A TONGUE WITH KNOTS TIED IN IT.
STAY YOUR HAND, T'CHALLA, MY CHIEFTAIN...
...THE PHYSICAL TESTS ARE AT AN END!
THE BOILING JUICE EXTRACTS FROM THE HEART-SHAPED HERB ARE READY...

MENDINAO, TRUSTED FRIEND... THERE HAS NEVER BEEN A MOMENT WHEN I NEEDED THE SACRED PANTHER POWERS MORE!

I AM READY.

MALICE LISTENS TO ZATAMA'S DIRECTIONS AND HER EYES NEVER BETRAY HER THOUGHTS--
--NOT EVEN WHEN SHE USES THE STAFF END OF THE WICKED SPEAR AS A CLUB!

PURPOSEFULLY, SHE RACES PAST THE OPULENT FURNISHINGS OF THE COURT ROYALE--
--INTO THE LABYRINTH OF CORRIDORS IN THE PALACE INTERIOR.

AND HER EYES REMAIN OPAQUE EVEN AS SHE PASSES WALLS THAT FLUCTUATE FROM DELICATELY WROUGHT, HAND-PAINTED MURALS OF WAKANDAN HISTORY--
--TO FANTASY-LIKE COMPUTER BANKS... AND THEN BACK AGAIN!

A GENTLE VOICE DRIFTS UP THE CORRIDOR AND SHE STALKS ITS SOURCE--

--AND SEES TAKU. KILLMONGER HAD TOLD ALL HIS LIEUTENANTS OF T'CHALLA'S KEY PERSONNEL INSIDE THE PALACE DOMAIN--

YOU AIN'T MUCH LIKE OTHER PEOPLE, YOU KNOW THAT, TAKU?

YOU DON'T LOOK AT MY FACE THE WAY MOST OF 'EM DO. I CAN'T NEVER FORGET THE WAY THEY LOOK AT ME!

I'M GLAD WE'VE GOTTEN ON A FIRST NAME BASIS, HORATIO. AND I CAN IMAGINE THE ANGUISH YOU'VE FELT.

BUT YOU PROBABLY DON'T WANT TO TALK ABOUT IT. I DON'T BLAME YOU.

VENOMM CONSIDERS TAKU'S WORDS.

SUSPICION FLARES MOMENTARILY IN HIS EYES.

BUT THERE IS NOTHING ON TAKU'S BENIGN FACE TO FEED THAT SUSPICION...

...NEITHER PITY NOR SCORN MARK THOSE FEATURES.

THE PAST FLOODS BEFORE HIS EYES, AND HE IS VAGUELY AWARE THAT HE GIVES VOICE TO HIS PRIVATE HELL.
ONCE, I HAD A NORMAL FACE. BUT EVEN THEN I WAS SORTA WHAT YOU'D CALL A LONER.
AN' THAT DIDN'T SET SO WELL WITH SOMMA THOSE OTHER KIDS WHEN I GOT INTO JUNIOR HIGH. I DIDN'T BELONG!
IT ALL CAME TO A HEAD ONE DAY IN MY CHEM II LAB!

"BRUCE MORGAN... HE WAS THE ONE THREW THE ACID... SAID HE DIDN'T KNOW WHAT WAS IN THE BOTTLE.
"BUT HE KNEW, YOU HEAR ME, TAKU? HE KNEW!!
"ANYHOW... I BECAME A... WADDA-YACALLIT?... A RECLUSE... THAT MEANS LIKE YOU GO LIVE INSIDE YOURSELF.
"GUESS THAT'S WHY I TURNED TO SNAKES... THEY WERE SHUNNED... JUST LIKE ME.

"I WASN'T A LONER 'CAUSE I WANTED TO BE ONE ANY MORE. WOULDN'T ANYONE COME NEAR ME.
"I SCARED MYSELF WHEN I FIRST LOOKED IN THE MIRROR.
"BUT THE EXPERIMENTS WITH THE REPTILES TOOK UP ALL MY TIME. I STUDIED EVERYTHING 'BOUT ALL KINDSA CRAWLING THINGS."
"AND I BUILT UP AN IMMUNITY TO ALL BUT THE MOST FATALLY POISONOUS SERPENTS."

OUTSIDE THE PALACE, MONICA LYNNE STROLLS THE HILLS, STARING AT THE BLOOD-RED SKY--
--WONDERING IF, STATE-SIDE, A SIMILAR DUSK WOULD COLOR THE SKY-SCRAPERS OF NEW YORK.
LONELINESS ENGULFS HER AND SHE HUGS IT TO HER AS SAD SONGS FILL HER MIND.

SHE RECALLS ROBERTA FLACK'S HAUNTINGLY CLEAR VOICE SINGING "TRYING TIMES"...
...AND WISHES SHE HADN'T COMPLETELY GIVEN UP BEING A PROFESSIONAL SINGER.

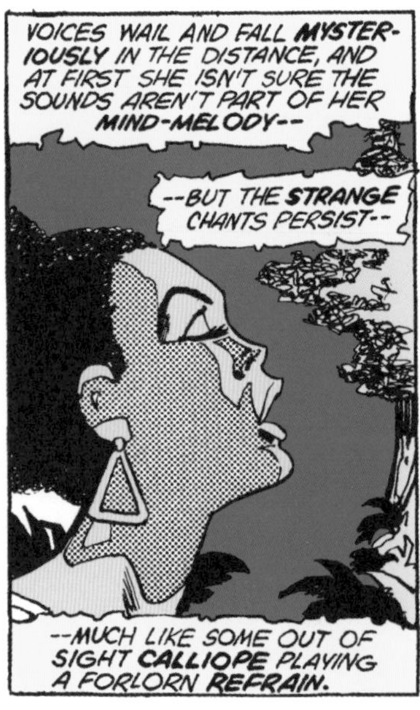
VOICES WAIL AND FALL MYSTER-IOUSLY IN THE DISTANCE, AND AT FIRST SHE ISN'T SURE THE SOUNDS AREN'T PART OF HER MIND-MELODY--
--BUT THE STRANGE CHANTS PERSIST--
--MUCH LIKE SOME OUT OF SIGHT CALLIOPE PLAYING A FORLORN REFRAIN.

MALICE'S HAND TIGHTENS ONTO HER WEAPON AS TAKU PATIENTLY URGES VENOMM TO CONTINUE.
SHE OUGHT TO KILL THE LOQUACIOUS, CORPSE-FLESHED FIGURE INSTEAD OF FREEING HIM!
YOU ATTENDED A UNIVERSITY?

"NAH! TOOK SOME NIGHT COURSES IN BIOLOGY. BOUT THE ONLY THING I WAS GOOD AT.
"THAT'S WHERE I MET KILLMONGER... ONE NIGHT WHEN THIS RADICAL GROUP DECIDED TO TEACH "THE FREAK" A LESSON--

"KILLMONGER... HE CALLED HIMSELF N'JADAKA, BACK THEN... COME FROM NOWHERE!
"YOU NEVER SEEN ANYTHING LIKE IT, TAKU.
"YOU SHOULDA SEEN 'IM TAKE THEM GUYS ON! HE WASTED 'EM WITHOUT WORKIN' UP A SWEAT.

"KILLMONGER WAS AN OUTCAST, TOO... AND BITTER LIKE AN ALMOND.
"HE SAID HE COULD USE ME, SOME DAY... AND I'LL NEVER FORGET THE OTHER WORDS HE SAID THAT NIGHT.
ONE DAY, HORATIO, I WILL TAKE YOU TO A PLACE BEYOND YOUR IMAGINATION--
--AND WE WILL TAKE THAT PLACE BY FORCE--
--AND MAKE IT OURS!

MONICA COMES UPON THE CLEARING. THE CHANTS HAVE TAKEN ON A STRANGE INTENSITY SHE CANNOT UNDERSTAND--

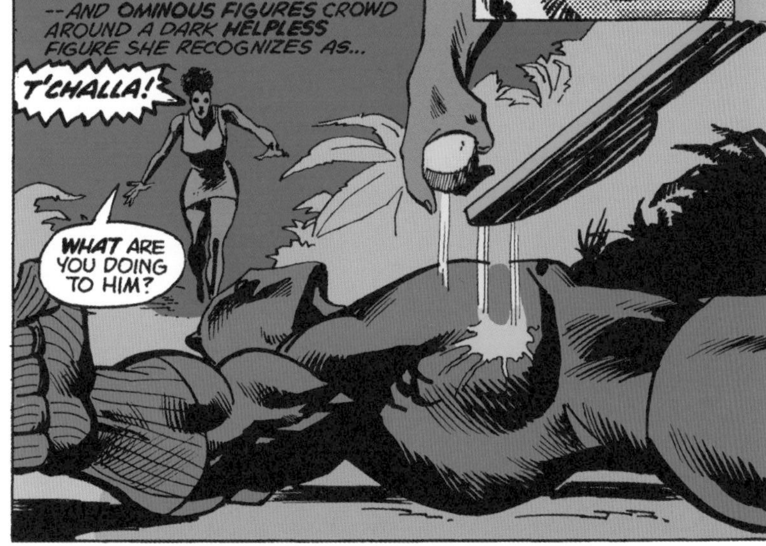
--AND OMINOUS FIGURES CROWD AROUND A DARK HELPLESS FIGURE SHE RECOGNIZES AS...
T'CHALLA!
WHAT ARE YOU DOING TO HIM?

W'KABI!!
I KNEW YOUR SOUL WAS BITTER... BUT I DIDN'T THINK YOU'D TAKE PART IN ANYTHING LIKE THIS!
KEEP BACK!
YOU MUST NOT ENTER THE SACROSANCT CIRCLE--
--NOT NOW AT THE RITUAL'S MOST IMPORTANT MOMENT!

FORGET IT, WITCH-DOCTOR!
WHAT'S THE MATTER, W'KABI? HASN'T T'CHALLA BLED ENOUGH FOR YOU SINCE HE'S COME BACK?
ARE YOU RUNNING WITH KILLMONGER'S PACK NOW?

THAT'S THE FINAL INDIGNITY, OUT-WORLDER!
YOUR VERY PRESENCE PROFANES THIS CEREMONY!
W'KABI-- I'LL TELL YOU BUT ONCE--
--TAKE YOUR HANDS OFF MISS LYNNE!
T'CHALLA! YOU... YOU'RE ABLE TO MOVE!

MY CHIEFTAIN, CERTAINLY YOU ARE NOT GOING TO DEFEND THESE ACTIONS.
YOU SAW WHAT SHE DID TO MENDINAO--AND YET YOU THREATEN ME!
MENDINAO... MY FRIEND... I HOPE YOU CAN UNDERSTAND WHAT I MUST DO NEXT...
... AND THAT MY DECISION WAS NOT AN EASY ONE. WE MUST DISCONTINUE THE RITUALS.
COME, MONICA.
I DON'T UNDERSTAND THIS...
...ANY OF IT!

A DAY OF RECKONING IS COMING RAPIDLY, MY CHIEFTAIN--
--ONE YOU'LL NOT BE ABLE TO TURN AWAY FROM!
T'CHALLA, YOU MUST COME BACK.
THE ACTIVE PRINCIPLES AND NUTRIENTS OF THE HEART-SHAPED HERB ARE AT ITS PEAK OF POTENCY.
YOU MUST NOT FORGET YOUR RESPONSI-BILITIES!
NOT EVEN MY SLEEP ALLOWS ME THE COMFORT, MENDINAO--
--BUT THIS WOMAN HAS FACED GREAT HOSTILITY, SINCE SHE'S BEEN MY GUEST--
-- AND THAT ALSO IS MY RESPONSI-BILITY!

I'LL TAKE YOU BACK TO THE PALACE, MONICA.
I GUESS I BLEW IT AGAIN, HUH?
I JUST LOST EVERYTHING WHEN I SAW YOU LYING OUT THERE.
THAT'S THE SECOND TIME I THOUGHT YOUR VOICE HAD BEEN... SILENCED.
WHY DOES W'KABI HATE ME SO?

TOO MANY PEOPLE WARP THE WORD HERITAGE, MONICA...
... THEY USE IT TO MEAN SUPERIORITY--
--WHEN IT IS ONLY MEANT TO GIVE ONE...
...IDENTITY!

WAIT!
SOME-THING'S HAP-PENED TO ZATAMA!

T'CHALLA!
WATCH OUT!!

HIS PANTHER POWERS ARE SEVERELY WEAKENED. HIS CAT-LIKE INSTINCT AND MOVEMENT MANAGE TO SAVE HIS LIFE--
--THOUGH THE TRIPLE-EDGED BLADE RIPS A GASH THROUGH HIS COSTUME AND FLESH!
I'M MALICE, PANTHER!
DON'T BOTHER TO INTRODUCE YOURSELF. I KNOW WHO YOU ARE!
AND THIS IS JUST A LITTLE TOUCH OF... MALICE!
AS THE BLOOD SPILLS FROM HIS WOUND AND THE FIRST STAB OF PAIN CUTS THROUGH HIM--
--THE PANTHER REGISTERS THE MULTI-FACETS OF THE SITUATION--
--INCLUDING THE FACT THAT HIS FOE HAS JUST SHATTERED A SOLID MARBLE COLUMN WITH HER WEAPON!
AN ABSURD THOUGHT PASSES THROUGH HIS CALCULATIONS: AREN'T THERE EVER ANY QUIET NIGHTS IN WAKANDA ANYMORE?

THE PANTHER HITS THE GROUND, SPINNING AROUND--
--ONLY TO TURN INTO A JARRING KICK THAT SNAPS HIS MOUTH CLOSED, GOUGING HIS TEETH INTO HIS TONGUE.

THE FIRST TASTE OF BLOOD IS ON HIS LIPS AS MALICE REACHES THE WALL!
I'M NOT ANYTHING LIKE VENOMM, PANTHER!

AND I'M NOT SOME PALACE HANDMAIDEN MADE SOFT BY PALACE INTRIGUES!
SHE HANDLES THE SHAFT LIKE AN EXPERT IN THE MARTIAL ARTS OF JOJITSU--

--AND THE SLIM WOODEN ROD BECOMES A LETHAL WEAPON!
THE DEADLY SHAFT SLICES THE AIR, WHISTLING DEATH--
--BUT THE PANTHER RECOVERS AMAZING-LY FAST, LEAPING OUT OF THE PATH OF THE SWING--

--UNTIL MALICE WHIPS THE SHAFT INTO THE BACK SWING--
--JABBING THE BLUNT END SAVAGELY INTO HIS RIB-CAGE!

MY MOTHER THOUGHT YOU WERE THE GREAT WIZARD KING WHO BROUGHT MAGIC TO OUR LAND!
SHE REMAINED AN IGNORANT HILL WOMAN--

-- BUT KILLMONGER HAS GIVEN ME THESE POWERS AND THE CHANCE FOR SOMETHING MORE IN MY LIFE!
AND YOUR DEATH WILL ASSURE THAT CHANCE!
NO! STOP!

MONICA'S PROTEST SEEMS TO GALVANIZE ALL THE FIGURES INTO ACTION--
--AND THE PANTHER IS THE QUICKEST TO MOVE!

YOU'D CALL MASS SLAUGHTER THE PATH TO INTELLECT, MALICE--
--THEN YOU'D BEST BEWARE, FOR IT'S A PATH LINED WITH THORNS AND LEAVES YOU, PERHAPS, MORE IGNORANT THAN YOUR PARENT EVER WAS!

MALICE! WE'VE GOT US SOME TROUBLE, BABY!
STAY HERE, MENDINAO!

THE REST OF THE TRIBUNAL WILL SPREAD OUT UNTIL MORE OF THIS ATTACK IS KNOWN!
YOUR SOFT SPOKEN WORDS WON'T GET YOU OUT OF A SITUATION LIKE THIS, TAKU!

BUT YOUR "FRIEND" WITH THE FLESH OF A CORPSE WOULD KNOW MORE OF THOSE KIND OF TACTICS THAN YOU!
MY LIMBS HAVE ACHED FOR A FOE TO BATTLE--
-- BUT YOUR KIND WOULD RATHER KILL UNSUSPECTING INNOCENTS!

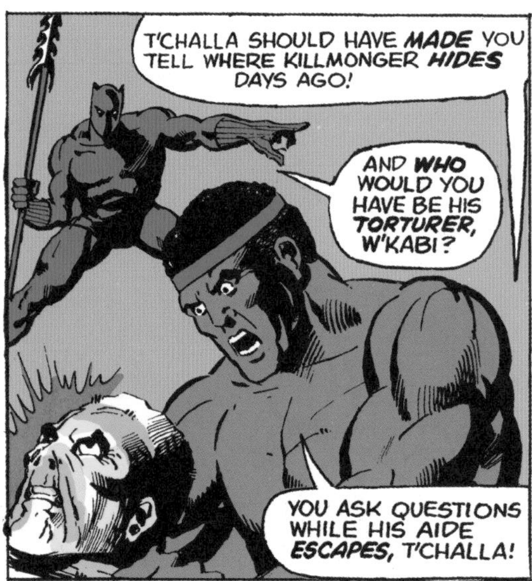
T'CHALLA SHOULD HAVE MADE YOU TELL WHERE KILLMONGER HIDES DAYS AGO!
AND WHO WOULD YOU HAVE BE HIS TORTURER, W'KABI?
YOU ASK QUESTIONS WHILE HIS AIDE ESCAPES, T'CHALLA!

YOU'VE AVOIDED THE QUESTION THIS TIME.
BUT THERE ARE QUESTIONS I WOULD ALSO LIKE TO ASK OF THIS MALICE!

AND ONE OF THEM WOULD BE TO ASK HOW KILLMONGER GAVE HER THE INCREDIBLE STRENGTH AND POWERS--
--TO HEFT AND HURL SUCH A WEAPON AS THIS THROUGH MARBLE COLUMNS!
BUT MALICE IS NOT THE ONLY ONE CAPABLE OF SUCH A STARTLING PERFORMANCE!

AS SHE DIVES GRACEFULLY OUT INTO THE CRIMSON SHADOWS, THE PANTHER UNLEASHES THAT SKULL-NOTCHED WEAPON--
-- AND WEAKENED THOUGH HIS POWERS MAY BE... IT IS AN EXHIBITION OF SHEER PERFECTION--
--PENETRATING RIGHT THROUGH SOLID STONE IN A SHATTERING DISPLAY OF SHRAPNEL!

YOU... YOU'RE GONNA KILL ME, AREN'T YA?
I REMEMBER WIDOWS WEEPING... I REMEMBER THE CRIES OF A VILLAGE SLAIN BY YOUR LEADER...
I WILL KILL YOU FOR THOSE MEMORIES!

I KNOW YOUR RAGE, W'KABI... YOU WOULD NOT BELIEVE HOW SIMILAR TO MY OWN YOURS IS.
BUT THIS DEATH WILL LEAVE YOU WITH A MEMORY AS DAMNING AS THE ONES YOU MENTION.

THIS IS NOT THE WAY. NOT THIS NIGHT...
... NOT ANY NIGHT...
... CRIMSON ...OR OTHERWISE.
NEXT
BARON MACABRÉ

# MAP OF THE LAND OF THE WAKANDA

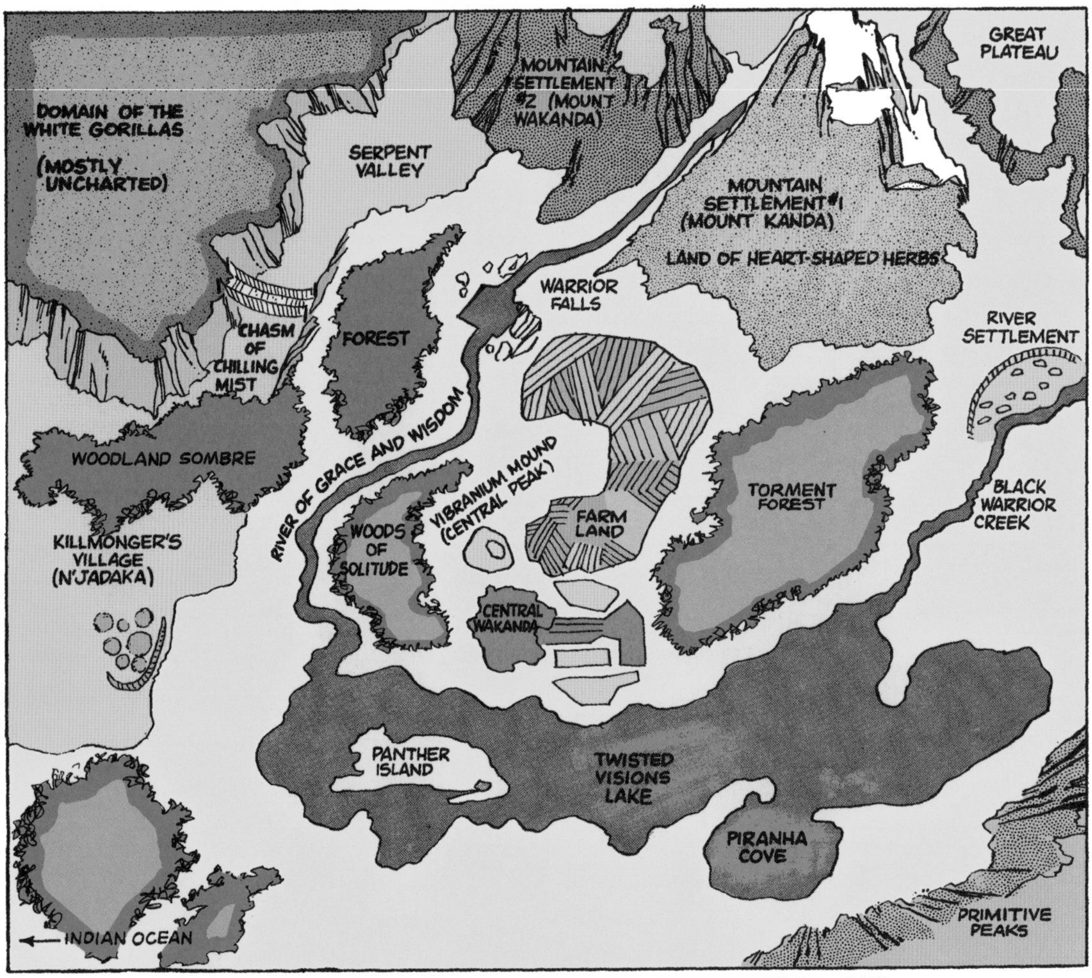

DOMAIN OF THE WHITE GORILLAS

(MOSTLY UNCHARTED)

SERPENT VALLEY

MOUNTAIN SETTLEMENT #2 (MOUNT WAKANDA)

GREAT PLATEAU

MOUNTAIN SETTLEMENT #1 (MOUNT KANDA)

LAND OF HEART-SHAPED HERBS

WARRIOR FALLS

FOREST

CHASM OF CHILLING MIST

RIVER SETTLEMENT

WOODLAND SOMBRE

RIVER OF GRACE AND WISDOM

VIBRANIUM MOUND (CENTRAL PEAK)

FARM LAND

TORMENT FOREST

BLACK WARRIOR CREEK

KILLMONGER'S VILLAGE (N'JADAKA)

WOODS OF SOLITUDE

CENTRAL WAKANDA

PANTHER ISLAND

TWISTED VISIONS LAKE

PIRANHA COVE

PRIMITIVE PEAKS

← INDIAN OCEAN

# CENTRAL WAKANDA

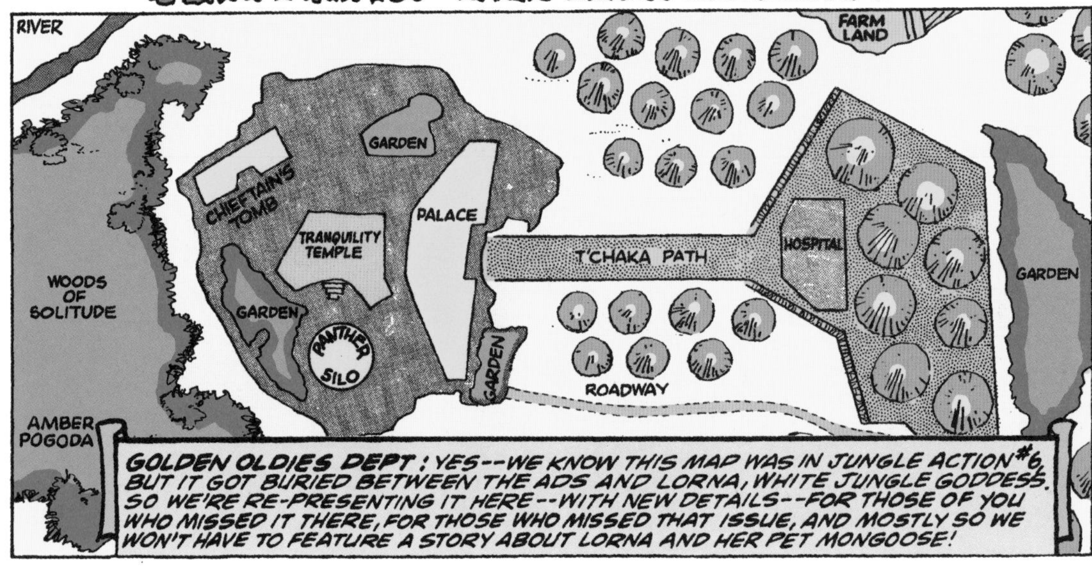
RIVER
FARM LAND
GARDEN
CHIEFTAIN'S TOMB
TRANQUILITY TEMPLE
PALACE
T'CHAKA PATH
HOSPITAL
WOODS OF SOLITUDE
GARDEN
PANTHER SILO
GARDEN
ROADWAY
GARDEN
AMBER POGODA
GOLDEN OLDIES DEPT: YES--WE KNOW THIS MAP WAS IN JUNGLE ACTION #6, BUT IT GOT BURIED BETWEEN THE ADS AND LORNA, WHITE JUNGLE GODDESS. SO WE'RE RE-PRESENTING IT HERE--WITH NEW DETAILS--FOR THOSE OF YOU WHO MISSED IT THERE, FOR THOSE WHO MISSED THAT ISSUE, AND MOSTLY SO WE WON'T HAVE TO FEATURE A STORY ABOUT LORNA AND HER PET MONGOOSE!

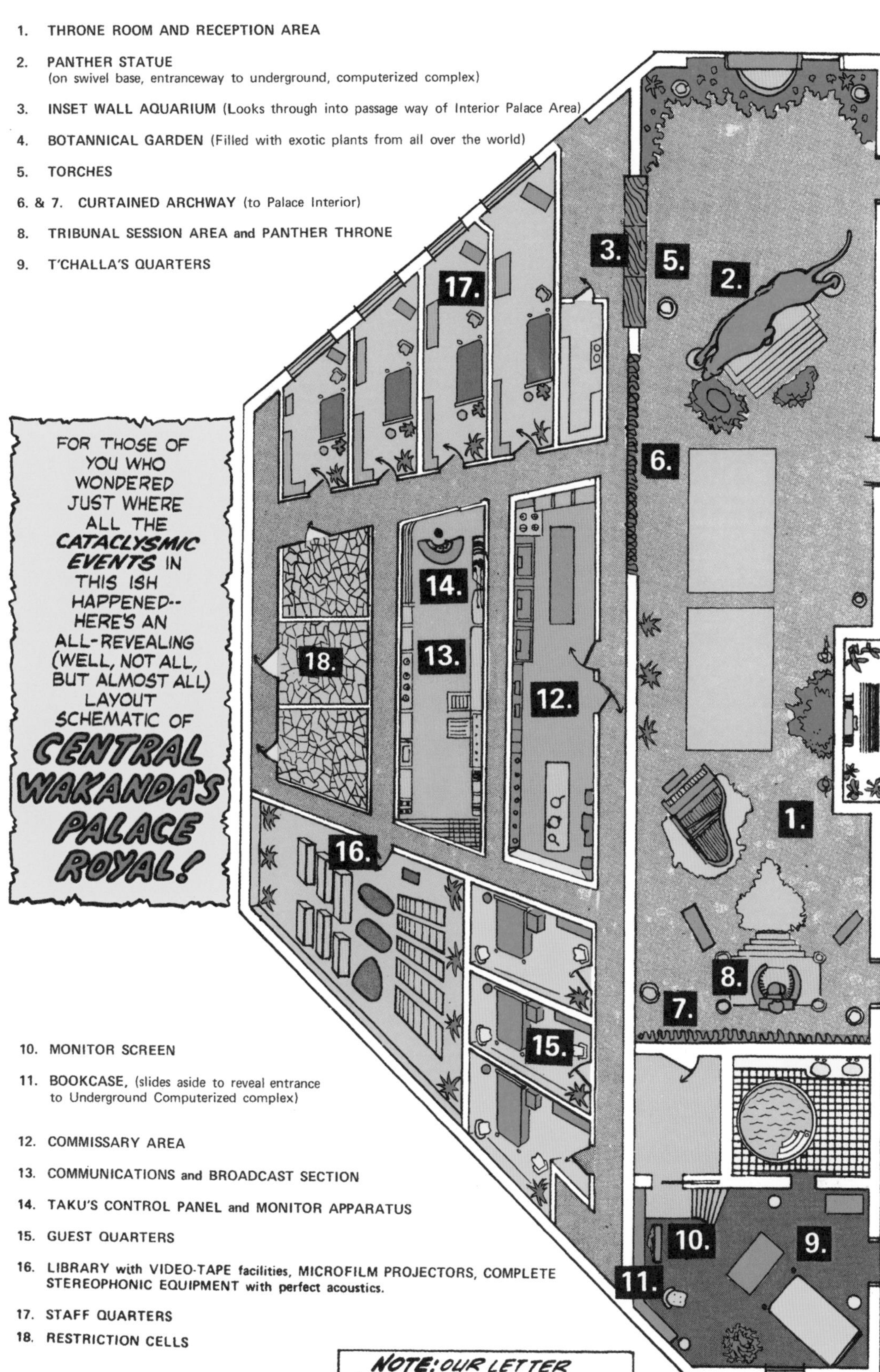

1. THRONE ROOM AND RECEPTION AREA
2. PANTHER STATUE (on swivel base, entranceway to underground, computerized complex)
3. INSET WALL AQUARIUM (Looks through into passage way of Interior Palace Area)
4. BOTANNICAL GARDEN (Filled with exotic plants from all over the world)
5. TORCHES
6. & 7. CURTAINED ARCHWAY (to Palace Interior)
8. TRIBUNAL SESSION AREA and PANTHER THRONE
9. T'CHALLA'S QUARTERS
FOR THOSE OF YOU WHO WONDERED JUST WHERE ALL THE CATACLYSMIC EVENTS IN THIS ISH HAPPENED-- HERE'S AN ALL-REVEALING (WELL, NOT ALL, BUT ALMOST ALL) LAYOUT SCHEMATIC OF
CENTRAL WAKANDA'S PALACE ROYAL!
3.
5.
2.
17.
6.
14.
13.
18.
12.
1.
16.
8.
7.
15.
10.
9.
11.
10. MONITOR SCREEN
11. BOOKCASE, (slides aside to reveal entrance to Underground Computerized complex)
12. COMMISSARY AREA
13. COMMUNICATIONS and BROADCAST SECTION
14. TAKU'S CONTROL PANEL and MONITOR APPARATUS
15. GUEST QUARTERS
16. LIBRARY with VIDEO-TAPE facilities, MICROFILM PROJECTORS, COMPLETE STEREOPHONIC EQUIPMENT with perfect acoustics.
17. STAFF QUARTERS
18. RESTRICTION CELLS
NOTE: OUR LETTER COLUMN, JUNGLE REACTION, FOLLOWS ON THE NEXT PAGE!

# *JUNGLE ACTION* #9,

# MAY 1974

JUNGLE ACTION

MARVEL COMICS GROUP™

APPROVED BY THE COMICS CODE AUTHORITY

25¢ 9 MAY 02161

JUNGLE ACTION™ FEATURING:

THE BLACK PANTHER™

NO MATTER HOW MANY I STRIKE DOWN-- THEY KEEP COMING--

THEY STALK BY NIGHT!

BARON MACABRE AND HIS DENIZENS OF DEATH!

--RISING FROM OUT OF THEIR GRAVES!

Stan Lee PRESENTS: THE BLACK PANTHER!
WAKANDA! IT IS A NATION OF PARADOXES. TECHNOLOGY COEXISTING WITH PRIMITIVE TRADITION... AND NOT ALWAYS COEXISTING PEACEFULLY. WAKANDA! ON THE OUTER PERIMETER OF ITS FARMLAND THERE IS STILL A TIME FOR SUNLIT EXPLORATIONS... A TIME BEFORE A YOUTH MUST DECIDE WHETHER TO FOLLOW THE TRADITION OF HIS ELDERS OR TO ENTER A COMPLEX WORLD OF COMPUTERIZED DYNAMICS.
KANTU MOVES WITH EXAGGERATED STEALTH...
...INTENT ON BRINGING HIS IMAGINARY PREY TO BAY. HIS INTENSE FANTASY IS SHATTERED--
--BY THE ENRAGED CHARGE OF A 3000-POUND BLACK RHINOCEROUS-- AND A DEATH-DEFYING DESCENT BY... THE BLACK PANTHER!
MOVE, SON! GET OUT OF THE WAY!
PANTHER'S RAGE CONTINUES
BUT NOW THE SPEARS ARE BROKEN
WRITER: DON McGREGOR
ARTISTS: G. KANE & K. JANSON
LETTERS: ORZ
COLORS: G. WEIN
EDITOR: ROY THOMAS

THE CREATURE WHIPS ABOUT IN SAVAGE FRENZY, INCENSED AT THIS NEW INVADER--
--AND THE PANTHER LOSES HIS GRIP UPON THE DANGEROUSLY SPIKED TUSK.
I SAID MOVE, SON! MOVE!
IN CIVILIZED MARKETS, THIS TUSK MEANS WEALTH AND ORNAMENTS. HERE, IT IS A WEAPON, A RENDING, GOUGING ARMAMENT.
HE SCRAPES OVER THE ROUGH, HAIRY HIDE, HURTLING OUTWARD, A PROJECTILE IN UNCONTROLLABLE TRAJECTORY!

THE GROUND IS SOFT, TREACHEROUS SYRUP, BUT HE HITS IT WITH HIS SHOULDER--
--USING THE MOMENTUM OF HIS FLIGHT TO PROPEL HIM UPWARD, TWISTING IN MID-FLIGHT!

THE RHINO IS THERE BEFORE HIM, UNACCOUNTABLY INFURIATED.
THERE IS NO CONSCIOUS THOUGHT PROCESS HERE, ONLY BLIND, UNREASONING FURY!

THE PANTHER DOES NOT UTTER ANY SAVAGE OATHS.

HE KNOWS THIS IS A MOMENT OF DEATH CHARGING TOWARD HIM... FOR HIS FLESH AND BONE WILL BURST AND BREAK BEFORE THIS ONSLAUGHT!

THE SWAMP AIR IS A PALPABLE, PUNGENT SMELL OF MOLD AND DECAY--

--EACH TWISTING VINE IS A REALITY ETCHED UNDER HIS SWEEPING VISION--

--EACH THUNDEROUS HOOF SHAKING THE MUCK IN ITS WAKE IS A SIGNAL--

--AND HE REPLIES TO ALL THOSE SENSES INSTANTANEOUSLY!

HE LEAPS--
--EACH SENSORY IMPRESSION AT ITS PEAK-- GLOVED HANDS GRASPING A MOSS-COVERED TREE LIMB--

--TENSED MUSCLES SOMER-SAULTING HIM THROUGH AIR AS IF GRAVITY IS NOT A LAW THAT APPLIES TO HIM!
THIS IS ANOTHER CRITICAL MOMENT, HE KNOWS. HOW OFTEN THEY OCCUR OF LATE!

FINGERS TAUT, HE TAKES **HOLD**. THIS GRIP MUST NOT WEAKEN ELSE HE WILL FALL **BENEATH** THESE POUNDING HOOVES--

--LEFT **MAIMED** AND **BLOODY** UNDER THEIR TREAD. AND HOW, HE WONDERS, WOULD THAT AFFECT HIS **KINGDOM**, HELD IN TURMOIL AS IT IS BY THE CHAOS OF KILLMONGER'S **BRUTAL INSURRECTION.**

**ERIK KILLMONGER.** MUSTN'T FORGET THE ERIK!

YET, KILLMONGER DOES FADE FROM MIND, REPLACED BY THE TASK AT HAND... AN **INSANE** TASK--

--INSPIRED BY **AMERICAN** "B" WESTERN **MYTHOS** OF HOPALONG CASSIDY VINTAGE AND OTHERS, SEEN ON IDLE SATURDAY AFTERNOONS AT **AVENGERS' MANSION.**

**THE PANTHER** BULLDOGS THIS 1½-TON MONSTROSITY--

--CARVING IT INTO THE MIRE... AND **SNAPPING** ITS VERTEBRAE!

AT LEAST THIS **ONCE**--

--IF **ONLY** THIS ONCE--

--**DEATH** HAS NOT BEEN A **VICTOR**, PROUD OR OTHERWISE--

--AND HE **COLLAPSES** WITH THE EFFORT.

NO **LOSS** THIS TIME, MONICA.

THIS TIME I WON.

KANTU SHUDDERS, HIS FEAR QUIVERING UNDER MONICA LYNNE'S TENDER HANDS--
--AND THOUGH SHE KNOWS MANY WORDS ON SUCH SUBJECTS AS FEAR AND HURT, SHE REMAINS QUIET, HOLDING HIM CLOSE--
--LETTING HER WARMTH EASE THE DREAD FROM HIM.
KANTU! KANTU, MY SON!
HE'S ALL RIGHT, KAROTA. I CAN SEE HE'S ALL RIGHT.
BEFORE THE COUPLE REACH THEM, MONICA SENSES KAROTA'S DISTRUST. IT EMANATES FROM THE WOMAN, A MATERNAL PROTECTIVENESS SOURED!

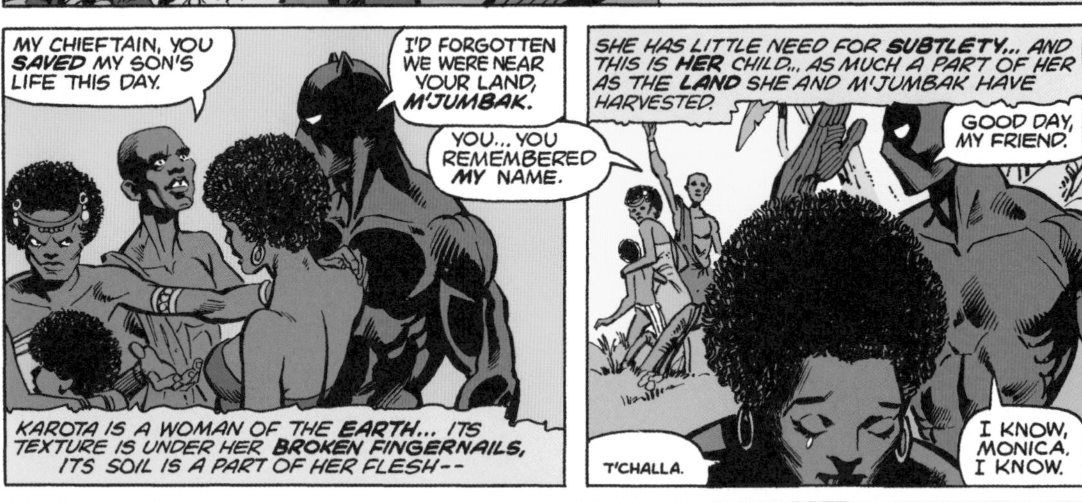
MY CHIEFTAIN, YOU SAVED MY SON'S LIFE THIS DAY.
I'D FORGOTTEN WE WERE NEAR YOUR LAND, M'JUMBAK.
YOU... YOU REMEMBERED MY NAME.
KAROTA IS A WOMAN OF THE EARTH... ITS TEXTURE IS UNDER HER BROKEN FINGERNAILS, ITS SOIL IS A PART OF HER FLESH--
SHE HAS LITTLE NEED FOR SUBTLETY... AND THIS IS HER CHILD... AS MUCH A PART OF HER AS THE LAND SHE AND M'JUMBAK HAVE HARVESTED.
GOOD DAY, MY FRIEND.
T'CHALLA.
I KNOW, MONICA. I KNOW.

DID YOU SEE THAT, M'JUMBAK? YOU KNOW WHO THAT WOMAN IS, DON'T YOU?
IT'S THAT OUT-WORLDER. THAT MOAN-A-CA!
BUT, KAROTA. HE REMEMBERED MY NAME.
LOOK AT THEM! SHAMELESS, THAT'S WHAT IT IS, M'JUMBAK.
DIDN'T YOU HEAR?
I HEARD. AND I SAW, M'JUMBAK. AND I'M ASHAMED FOR HIM.

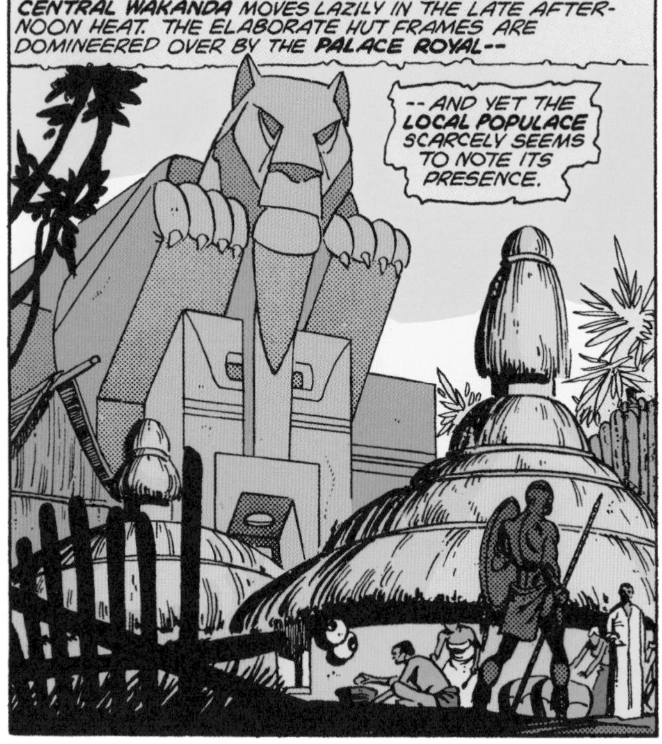
CENTRAL WAKANDA MOVES LAZILY IN THE LATE AFTER-NOON HEAT. THE ELABORATE HUT FRAMES ARE DOMINEERED OVER BY THE PALACE ROYAL--
--AND YET THE LOCAL POPULACE SCARCELY SEEMS TO NOTE ITS PRESENCE.

WITHIN THE PALACE WALLS, MONICA AND T'CHALLA SCARCELY SEEM TO NOTE THE ACTIVITY ABOUT THEM. ZATAMA PACES NEARBY, AS IF INSULTED BY THE GRANDEUR OF THEIR SURROUNDINGS--
--AND TANZIKA ENTERS THE DINING CHAMBER, STIFFLY SERVILE AS BEFITTING A COURT HANDMAIDEN, LOCKING HER HUMANITY BEHIND DARKLY LIQUID EYES.
DOES IT BOTHER YOU THAT I'M CONSIDERED A COMMONER?
I'M AFRAID THE TERM 'REGALITY' HAS ITS OWN HIDDEN TRAPS, MONICA. DELUSION IS ONE OF THEM.

HERE'S YOUR ROAST KRAAL VENISON, MY CHIEFTAIN--
--AND MISS LYNNE.

TANZIKA HAS A GREAT WAY WITH PAUSES, DOESN'T SHE--
--MONICA?

YOU ALWAYS LOOK SO ANGRY, ZATAMA.
I CAN'T BLAME YOU THOUGH. LOOK AT THE WAY T'CHALLA TOUCHES THAT OUTWORLDER'S HAIR.
THAT SEEMS TO BE WHAT EVERYONE IS CONCERNED WITH HERE. PETTY TRIVIALITIES!

THE TRIBUNAL PRESENCE KNOWS I OPPOSE T'CHALLA'S INNER COUNCIL, AND THEY ALL HATE ME FOR IT.
ESPECIALLY W'KABI. I DON'T KNOW HOW ANYBODY CAN CALL HIM HEAD OF COURT SECURITY. HE'S AS VIOLENT AS T'CHALLA.
WE'VE GOT RULERS WHO'VE ACQUIRED A TASTE FOR BLOOD.

TANZIKA DOESN'T LIKE ME. IT'S NOTHING SHE EVER COMES OUT AND SAYS IN WORDS. IT'S IN HER EYES... IN HER FACE.
I FEEL LESS LIKE A PERSON EVERY DAY I'M HERE. I'M MORE LIKE A SYMBOL TO YOUR PEOPLE... A SYMBOL OF EVERYTHING THEY'VE COME TO HATE OVER THE YEARS.
T'CHALLA--
--I DON'T WANT TO DESTROY YOU!

THERE ARE MANY KINDS OF DESTRUCTION. M'JUMBAK KNOWS LITTLE ABOUT THE KIND OF DESTRUCTION MONICA FEARS--
--BUT AS HE STROLLS REFLECTIVELY PAST A SMALL WAKANDAN BURIAL SITE, HE, TOO, THINKS OF DESTRUCTION--
--ALTHOUGH IT IS ANOTHER TYPE, ONE HE IS FAMILIAR WITH: THAT OF THE LAND DRYING UP, BECOMING A SERE PLAIN--
--AND REMEMBERS A YEAR WHEN T'CHALLA WAS BUT TEN, AS SUBJECTS AND LEADERS ALIKE SWEATED INTO THE LAND AS THEY TILLED THE VOLCANIC SOIL.

BUT DESTRUCTION, AS MENTIONED ABOVE, COMES IN MANY FORMS.
THIS ONE BEGINS WITH A SOUND--

--THE SOUND OF EARTH HIDEOUSLY SCRAPING BEFORE SOMETHING THAT CLAWS AT IT--
--RICH LOAM OF THE TYPE THAT SO FASCINATED HEMINGWAY PARTING TO REVEAL TALONED, BONY FINGERS!

AND M'JUMBAK RECOILS!
HE IS NOT A SUPERSTITIOUS MAN, BUT HE HAS HEARD THE WHISPERED TERRORS OF LATE.

HE HAS HEARD OF SUCH THINGS AS DEATH REGIMENTS... AND, OF A NAME--
BARON MACABRE! A NAME SPOKEN SURELY IN JEST. BUT JUST NOW, M'JUMBAK IS NOT SO SURE!

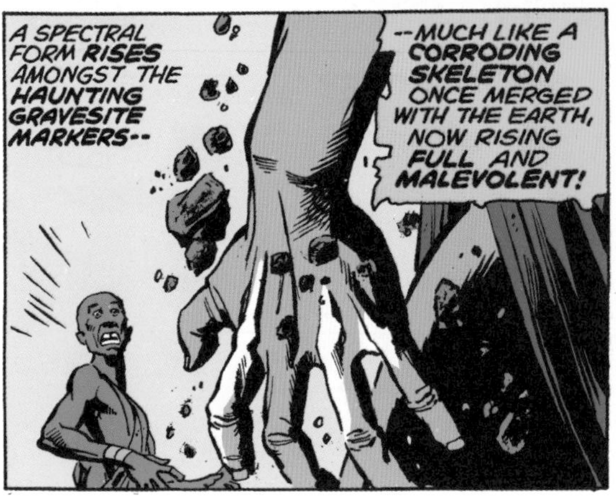
A SPECTRAL FORM RISES AMONGST THE HAUNTING GRAVESITE MARKERS--
--MUCH LIKE A CORRODING SKELETON ONCE MERGED WITH THE EARTH, NOW RISING FULL AND MALEVOLENT!

AND WHILE THE PALACE ROYAL DINES--
--M'JUMBAK FALLS VICTIM TO ANOTHER KIND OF DESTRUCTION!

YOU TALK OF DESTRUCTION, MONICA. BUT THAT IS A DECISION ALL LOVERS MUST MAKE--
--WHETHER THEIR RELATIONSHIP WILL DESTROY... OR AID AND HEAL THE OTHER.

IT'S OFTEN THE MOST DIFFICULT DECISION THEY'LL HAVE TO MAKE--
--AND, AS LOVE IS NOT A CONSTANTLY STABLE FACTOR, IT'S ONE THEY'LL HAVE TO MAKE AGAIN AND AGAIN.

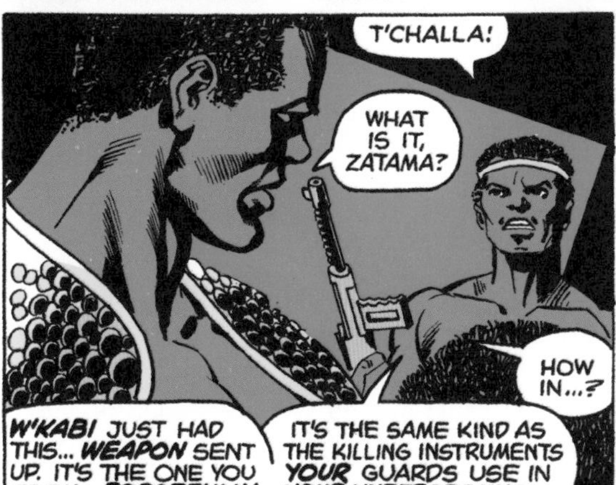
T'CHALLA!
WHAT IS IT, ZATAMA?
HOW IN...?
W'KABI JUST HAD THIS... WEAPON SENT UP. IT'S THE ONE YOU TOOK... FORCEFULLY FROM KILLMONGER'S AIDES.
IT'S THE SAME KIND AS THE KILLING INSTRUMENTS YOUR GUARDS USE IN YOUR UNDERGROUND, COMPUTERIZED JUNGLE.

W'KABI'S FOAMING AT THE MOUTH AGAIN. WANTS TO TAKE YOUR PRISONER VENOMM APART... AND THREATENED ME IN THE BARGAIN.
THE SPEARS ARE BREAKING APART ABOUT YOU, AREN'T THEY, T'CHALLA?
RIGHT NOW ONE OF YOUR SUBJECTS IS CRYING SHE MUST SEE YOU. SAYS HER NAME'S KAROTA.

MY CHIEFTAIN, M'JUMBAK... HE IS MISSING! HE WENT FOR A WALK IN THE NIGHT AIR AS HE DOES EVERY NIGHT.
HE ALWAYS RETURNS BE-FORE KANTU GOES TO SLEEP. EXCEPT TONIGHT.
I FOLLOWED HIS TRACKS AWAYS. THEY LED TOWARD THE BURIAL SITE! AND HE KNOWS IT'S HAUNTED!
HAUNTED? BY WHAT... OR WHO?

BY THE BARON, OF COURSE.
BARON MACABRE!
THE NAME SENDS THE PANTHER INTO THE COOL NIGHT--

--AND HE FINDS M'JUMBAK--
--AND SADLY RECALLS THE WARMTH OF THE FARMER'S HANDSHAKE ONLY HOURS EARLIER.

AND THAT IS THE LAST SANE THOUGHT THE PANTHER HAS TIME FOR.
MIDNIGHT SHADOWS TAKE OBSCENE FORM. HE REELS BACKWARD, CAT-LIKE EYES STUNNED, WATCHING THE EARTH GOUGE OPEN AS TWISTED LIMBS REACH FOR THE NIGHT SKY!
ONE FIGURE STANDS TALLER THAN THE REST, TOWERING SEVEN FEET INTO THE SKY, REACHING A WITHERED YET POWERFUL ARM IN THE PANTHER'S DIRECTION... WARPED FINGERS CURLING TOWARD HIM--
BURIED TOMBS YIELD SKELETAL FIGURES, WHITE BONE AND BROWN FLESH GLEAMING IN THE BLEAK MOONLIGHT!
IT IS A NIGHTMARE TAKING ROOT IN THE SOIL OF THIS CEMETERY, A CORRUPT BUDDING OF DECAY AND MOLD THAT FILLS THE DARK!

--AND A VOICE COMES FROM THE LIPLESS MOUTH, A VOICE MOCKING WITH THE CHILL OF DEATH!
AHHH... MY DEAR PANTHER... WE'VE EXPECTED YOU WOULD SHOW HERE SOONER OR LATER.
MYSELF AND THE OTHERS HAVE BEEN WAITING--
--QUITE IMPATIENTLY!
INSTINCTIVELY, THE PANTHER KNOWS: THIS IS THE VOICE OF
BARON MACABRE!

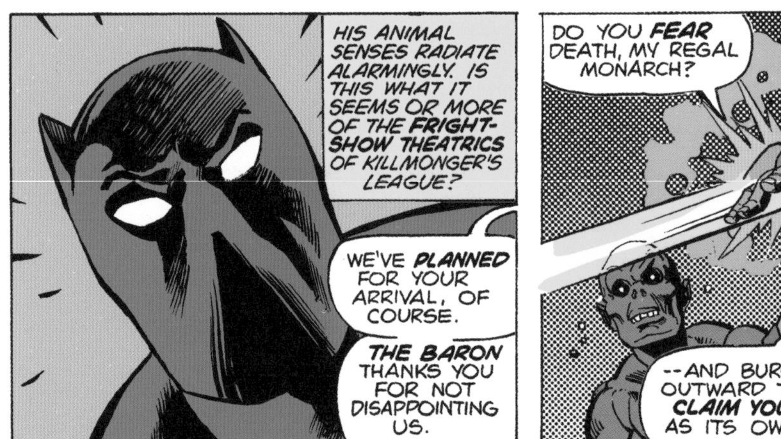
HIS ANIMAL SENSES RADIATE ALARMINGLY. IS THIS WHAT IT SEEMS OR MORE OF THE FRIGHT-SHOW THEATRICS OF KILLMONGER'S LEAGUE?
WE'VE PLANNED FOR YOUR ARRIVAL, OF COURSE.
THE BARON THANKS YOU FOR NOT DISAPPOINTING US.

DO YOU FEAR DEATH, MY REGAL MONARCH?
THE BARON DOES NOT FEAR DEATH... FOR DEATH EXISTS IN MY LIMBS--
--AND BURSTS OUTWARD TO CLAIM YOU AS ITS OWN!

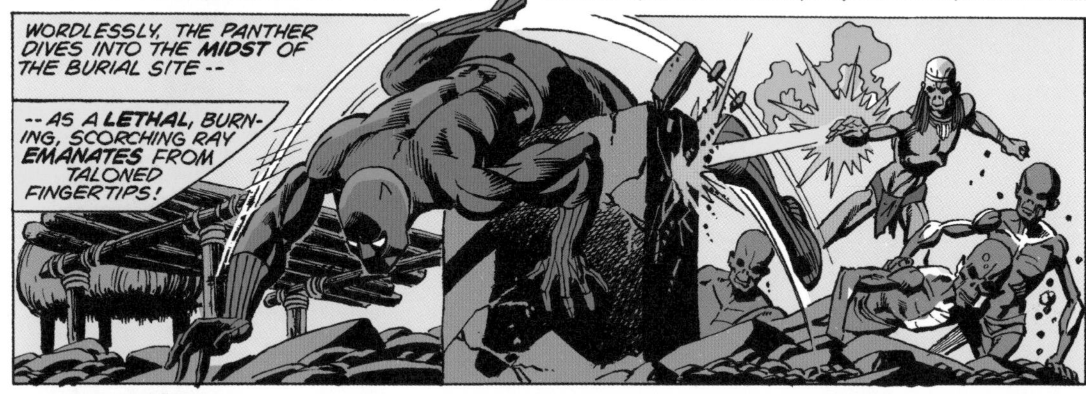
WORDLESSLY, THE PANTHER DIVES INTO THE MIDST OF THE BURIAL SITE --
-- AS A LETHAL, BURNING, SCORCHING RAY EMANATES FROM TALONED FINGERTIPS!

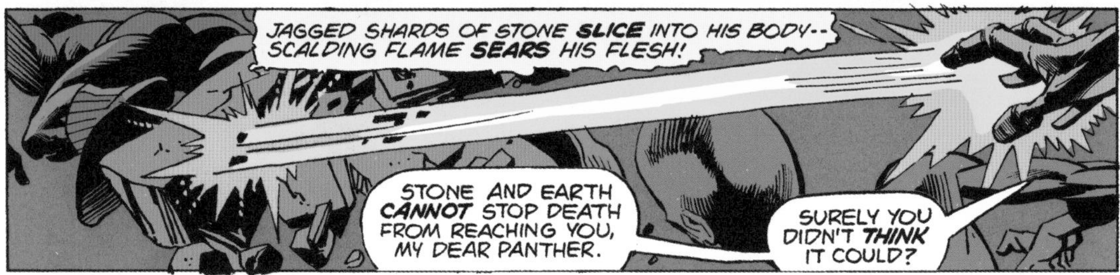
JAGGED SHARDS OF STONE SLICE INTO HIS BODY-- SCALDING FLAME SEARS HIS FLESH!
STONE AND EARTH CANNOT STOP DEATH FROM REACHING YOU, MY DEAR PANTHER.
SURELY YOU DIDN'T THINK IT COULD?

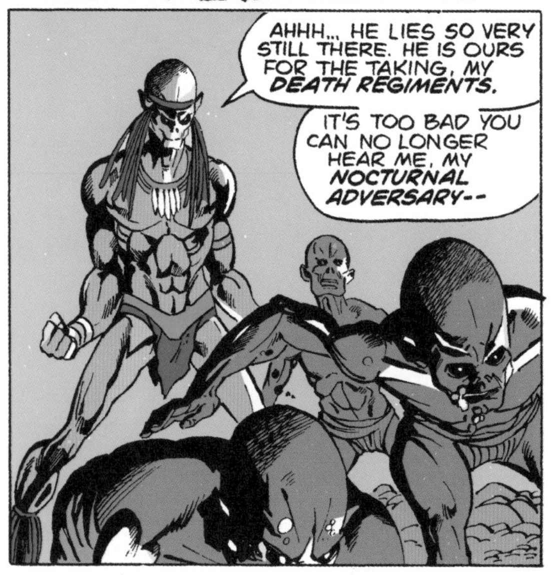
AHHH... HE LIES SO VERY STILL THERE. HE IS OURS FOR THE TAKING, MY DEATH REGIMENTS.
IT'S TOO BAD YOU CAN NO LONGER HEAR ME, MY NOCTURNAL ADVERSARY--

-- FOR THERE ARE OTHER REASONS THE BARON DOES NOT FEAR DEATH!
FOR THE BARON IS EMISSARY OF DEATH INCARNATE--
--KING CADAVER!!
AND LIMBS, REEKING OF DAMP EARTH, CARRY THE PANTHER FORWARD-- AND THE BLOOD FROM HIS WOUNDS SPILLS ONTO THEIR HANDS!

CONVERGING EVENTS. SO MANY OF THEM TAKING A VIOLENT TWIST IN WAKANDA THESE PAST FEW MONTHS--
--A SIMULTANEOUS DEATH MOSAIC THAT NOW INCLUDES ZATAMA.
ZATAMA, WHO WAS BORN NEAR THESE PALACE WALLS... THOUGH AT HIS BIRTH THERE WEREN'T ANY IMPOSING WALLS HERE, BUT ONLY THE FOLIAGE RISING IN SPLENDID COLOR ABOUT STRAW AND WOOD AND MUD-BAKED HUTS.

ZATAMA, WHOSE YOUNG EYES WATCHED THOSE STONE COLUMNS TAKE SHAPE... WHOSE PLAYGROUND THUNDERED WITH MECHANIZED HORRORS THAT WOKE HIM SCREAMING IN THE NIGHT.
TONIGHT, HE WILL DIE HERE.

HE SITS REFLECTIVELY. MIND IMAGES FLASH MENTAL RECORDINGS.
W'KABI, NEAR READY TO KILL VENOMM WHEN KILLMONGER SENT ONE OF HIS SUPERB SQUADRON, MALICE, TO FREE THE PANTHER'S PRISONER.
A SOFT, BUT INSISTENT, KNOCK AT HIS DOOR, INTERRUPTS HIS REVERIE.

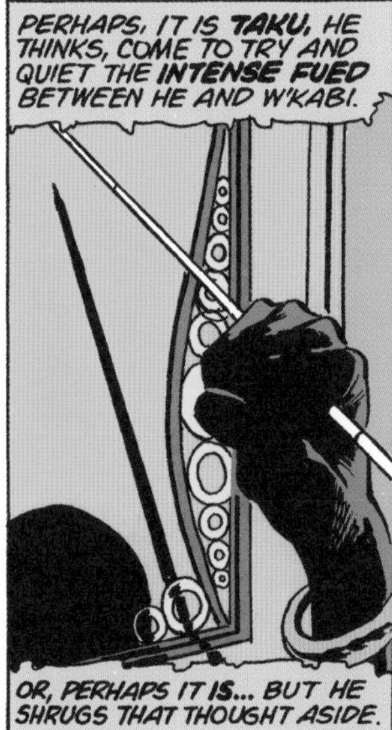
PERHAPS, IT IS TAKU, HE THINKS, COME TO TRY AND QUIET THE INTENSE FUED BETWEEN HE AND W'KABI.
OR, PERHAPS IT IS... BUT HE SHRUGS THAT THOUGHT ASIDE.

TAKU, IS THAT YOU?
LOOK, I ALREADY KNOW THE...
WAIT...! PLEASE, WAIT! DON'T DO THIS!
PLEASE, DON'T DO THIS!

HE SCREAMS THE WORD PLEASE ONCE MORE, AN INSTINCTIVE WORD THAT HAS LITTLE OTHER MEANING.

ZATAMA WAS BORN NEAR THESE PALACE WALLS.
TONIGHT, HE HAS DIED HERE.

LIKE PIECES OF AN ERRATIC PUZZLE REFUSING TO LINK INTO ONE PICTURE, THE DEATH-MOSAIC SPREADS OUTWARD.
A SEGMENT OF THE MOSAIC RECALLS ZATAMA SPEAKING SARDONICALLY, "THE SPEARS ARE BREAKING APART ABOUT YOU, AREN'T THEY, T'CHALLA?"
IT WOULD CERTAINLY APPEAR THEY HAVE!
YOU NEVER HAD A CHANCE, MY POOR KINGLY WRETCH.

YOU DON'T SAY?
OH... YOU DO SAY?
NOW THAT IS TRULY AN AMAZING STUNT, HURTING AS YOU MUST BE!

WELL SOMEHOW, BARON, I HARDLY THINK THAT'LL BOTHER YOU MUCH LONGER.
AHHH... I THOUGHT YOUR DEMISE A BIT TOO EASY.
THAT WAS, INDEED, A CLEVER RUSE!

I REALLY ENJOYED IT, MY DEAR PANTHER!

I REALLY DID!
BUT THE TIME FOR HUMOR IS PAST--
--AND ONE DOES NOT TOUCH DEATH--
DEATH TOUCHES OTHERS!
BONE SEEMS TO GLINT BENEATH MACABRE'S PARCHMENT-DRIED FLESH, BUT THE ARM IS LIKE COILED WIRE, SWEEPING OUT, TEARING THE PANTHER'S GRIP FROM THE MOLD-SLICK, GAUNT FORM!

HIS BACK IS SLICK WITH THE BLOOD THAT THROBS FROM THE WOUND CARVED INTO HIS FLESH BY MACABRE'S DEATH-BLAZE... AND HE CANNOT PRY THOSE DECAYING FINGERS FROM HIS THROAT.
FEEL THE TOUCH OF DEATH NOW-- FOR THE POWER OF BARON MACABRE IS DEATH ITSELF--
--AND THE BARON IS THE INSTRUMENT OF DEATH TO ANY WHO WOULD ENTER THE KING'S DOMAIN!

YELLOWED TEETH FILL THE PANTHER'S BLURRING VISION.
DARKENED, SUNKEN EYE-SOCKETS KINDLE A MAD BLAZE DEEP IN THEIR INTERIOR.

THERE IS A FEELING OF MORTALITY WHEN ONE ENTERS A NORMAL PLACE SET ASIDE FOR THE DEAD. THIS PLACE RADIATES SOMETHING FAR LESS SUBTLE.
THE TWO FIGURES THAT MOVE ALONG THE OUTER RIM OF THIS TRY MOVING WITH FURTIVE STEALTH. AND THEY ARE FAILING...
...MISERABLY.
I HEARD SOMETHING, TAYETE. DON'T YOU HEAR WHAT I HEAR?
HEAR WHAT? I DON'T HEAR ANYTHING, KAZIBE.

IT... IT'S COMING FROM OVER THERE.
THAT'S YOUR PROBLEM, KAZIBE. YOU AREN'T EVER GOING TO GET ANYWHERE WITH KILLMONGER 'CAUSE YOU'RE AFRAID OF EVERYTHING.
AREN'T YOU AFRAID OF THIS BARON MACABRE?

I'M NOT AFRAID OF HIM. I'M NOT AFRAID OF THAT PANTHER DEVIL. THING IS, KAZIBE, THEY BETTER FEAR ME.
EVERY TIME YOU SAY THINGS LIKE THAT, TAYETE... WE END UP GETTING STOMPED ON, AND I...
...I... I...

TAYETE, TELL ME YOU DON'T SEE WHAT I SEE.
IN FACT, TELL ME I DON'T SEE WHAT I SEE.
KAZIBE?
I'M SEEING IT, AREN'T I?

THE PANTHER HAS **NOT** BEEN ABLE TO **BREATHE** FOR **OVER FIVE MINUTES**, BUT HE RIDES THE CREST OF FEAR--
--AND DOES **NOT** TRY TO PRY THOSE INHUMAN HANDS APART, **INSTEAD** HE GRASPS THOSE **MURDEROUS** WRISTS TIGHTER.

IT IS A MOVEMENT FEW MEN WOULD **CONSIDER** ATTEMPTING.
THE PANTHER DOES **MORE** THAN CONSIDER IT. HE DRAWS MACABRE TO HIM, FEET KICKING INTO THE HOLLOW BELLY, AND DRIVING HIS FOE **OVER** HIS HEAD.

INCINERATE HIM!
BURN HIS FLESH TO THE **MARROW!**
THAT **WON'T** STOP ME, BARON!
I'LL BE **BACK.** YOU CAN **COUNT** ON THAT!
EMBER-HUED RAYS **FOLLOW** THE PANTHER'S MOVE-MENTS--

--MOVEMENTS SO **ACUTELY TIMED** THAT EVEN AN ACCIDENTAL ARRIVAL SEEMS PART OF A **COMPLETELY CHOREOGRAPHED VIOLENT BALLET!**
HEY, YOU CAN'T...
UHHH... TAYETE?
ARE YOU STILL **HERE,** TAYETE?

MOMENTUM AND **EXTREME GRACE** MAKE THE FANTASTIC ACTS SEEM ALMOST **NATURAL**--
--AT **ONE** WITH THE FLOURISH OF VINE AND TREE LIMB, FERN AND PETAL LEAF.

HE DOES NOT HAVE TO TALK ABOUT BEING ONE WITH NATURE.
A HALF HOUR PASSES, AND HE IS A HUMAN IN FLIGHT--
--WHO DROPS SWIFTLY WHEN HE REACHES THE OUTER PARAPETS OF THE PALACE ROYAL.

HE HAS BARELY ENTERED THE WINDOW WHEN W'KABI'S HARSH VOICE FILLS THE CHAMBER INTERIOR.

W'KABI! TAKU!
WHAT'S GOING ON HERE? WHERE ARE YOU TAKING MONICA... AND WHY?
I'VE WARNED YOU BEFORE, W'KABI. I WON'T HAVE MY GUESTS MISTREATED.
YOU'D BEST HAVE A GOOD REASON FOR YOUR ACTIONS.

IS THIS REASON GOOD ENOUGH, MY CHIEFTAIN? SHE MURDERED ZATAMA!
YOU HAVE ALLOWED THIS OUTWORLDER TO DESECRATE SACRED RITES... IT IS ONLY LAST NIGHT YOU FINISHED THE SACROSANCT PANTHER CEREMONY!
YOU HAVE ALLOWED HER PRESENCE IN TRIBUNAL MATTERS. YET TIME AND AGAIN YOU DEFEND HER.
BUT NO LONGER, MY CHIEFTAIN.

TONIGHT, SHE MURDERED ZATAMA--
--AND HER FINGERPRINTS ARE ALL OVER THE SPEAR THAT STOLE ZATAMA'S LIFE!

NEXT
KING CADAVER IS DEAD
...AND LIVING IN WAKANDA!
KING CADAVER: HE'LL STEAL YOUR MIND! HE'LL STEAL YOUR SOUL! AND THEN, IF YOU'RE LUCKY, HE'LL STEAL YOUR LIFE!
NEXT

# *JUNGLE ACTION* #10,
# JULY 1974

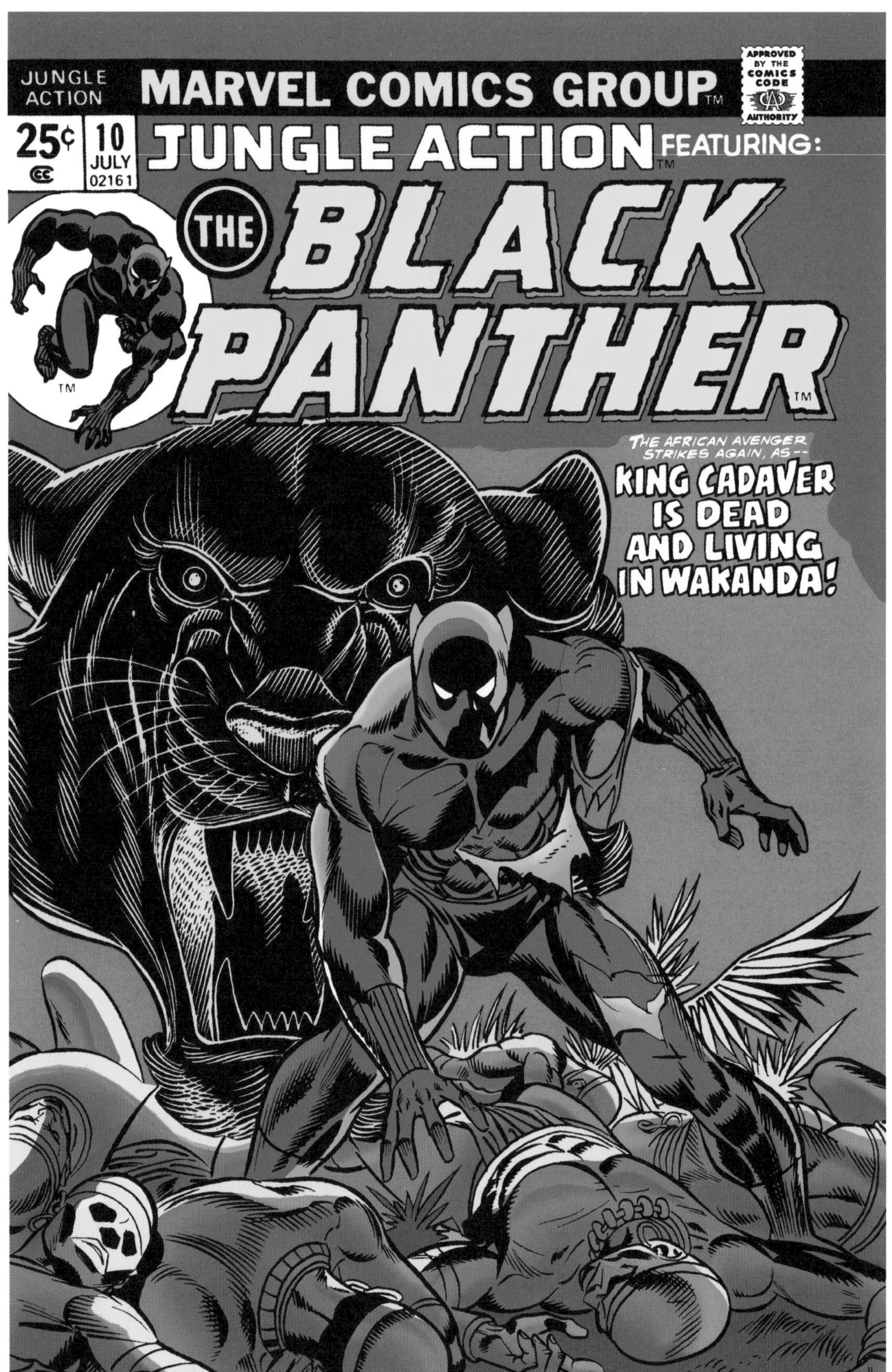
JUNGLE ACTION
MARVEL COMICS GROUP
APPROVED BY THE COMICS CODE AUTHORITY
25¢
10
JULY
02161
JUNGLE ACTION FEATURING:
THE BLACK PANTHER
THE AFRICAN AVENGER STRIKES AGAIN, AS--
KING CADAVER IS DEAD AND LIVING IN WAKANDA!

Stan Lee PRESENTS: **THE BLACK PANTHER!** TM

DON McGREGOR / WRITER | BILLY GRAHAM and KLAUS JANSON / ARTISTS | DAVE HUNT, LETTERER / GLYNIS WEIN, COLORIST | ROY THOMAS / EDITOR

THE SETTING SUN DRIPS BLOOD ONTO THE RIVER OF GRACE AND WISDOM, EACH DROP SPLATTERING IN BRILLIANT REFLECTION FROM THE MIRROR SURFACE OF THE WATER, ESCORTING NIGHT-TIDE OVER THE JUNGLE GROWTH THAT FLOURISHES ABOUT THE RIVER'S BANKS.
THE BLACK PANTHER SITS ALONE IN THE GATHERING TWILIGHT, STARING INTO THE WATER AT HIS REFLECTION... AND HARDLY RECOGNIZES HIMSELF--AS IF HE HAS FORGOTTEN WHO HE ONCE WAS OR WHO HE NOW IS!
HE IS NOT AWARE OF THE 20 FOOT LONG CROCODILE UNTIL IT IS UPON HIM... AND THEN IT IS TOO LATE TO DO ANYTHING BUT BATTLE FOR--
SURVIVAL!!
PANTHER'S RAGE CONTINUES:
KING CADAVER IS DEAD AND LIVING IN WAKANDA!

THE CROCODILE'S TEETH ARE THICK WITH **SLIME**, AND THE PANTHER'S GLOVED FINGERS SEEK **DEFENSE** WITHIN THE FETID **MUSH INTERIOR** OF ITS MOUTH!

HE CAN FEEL **DEAD LEECHES**, DRIED TO DEHYDRATED SHELLS, BENEATH HIS FINGERS--

--LEECHES THAT HAVE **INFESTED** THE BEHEMOTH'S MOUTH, WHICH IS PROBABLY WHY IT WAS **LANDWARD** TO BEGIN WITH, SPENDING THE AFTERNOON HOURS WITH ITS JAWS AGAPE, THE **AFRICAN SUN** SUCKING THE JUICES FROM THE **PARASITES** THAT INFECT ITS GUMS!

A SOUND RISES ABOVE HIS **HARSH BREATHING**, ONE HE CAN'T QUITE IDENTIFY, BUT **HUMAN** IN ORIGIN--

--AND JUST BEFORE HE **PLUNGES** UNDER THE WATER, CLINGING ALGAE COVERING HIM IN A **MURKY GELATIN**--

--HE KNOWS IT IS **TAKU**, HIS **COMMUNICATIONS COMMANDER**.

TAKU, WHO IS USUALLY **QUIET** AND OBSERVING--

TAKU, WHO **LISTENS** INSTEAD OF INFLICTING HIS PERSONALITY UPON **OTHERS**.

**T'CHALLA!**

TAKU, SOUNDING **UNLIKE** HE HAS EVER HEARD THE MAN SPEAK!

MY CHIEFTAIN!

TAKU'S EXCLAMATIONS **FADE**, AND ONLY THE SAVAGE, GUTTURAL SOUNDS OF THE BRUTAL ORDEAL **REMAIN**--

--THE PANTHER'S ARM **LOCKING** ABOUT THE LOWER MOUTH, THE LEFT ARM STIFFENED INTO **STEEL**, ALTHOUGH THE CREATURE'S TEETH RIP THE **FLESH** INTO RIVULETS OF **BLOOD**!

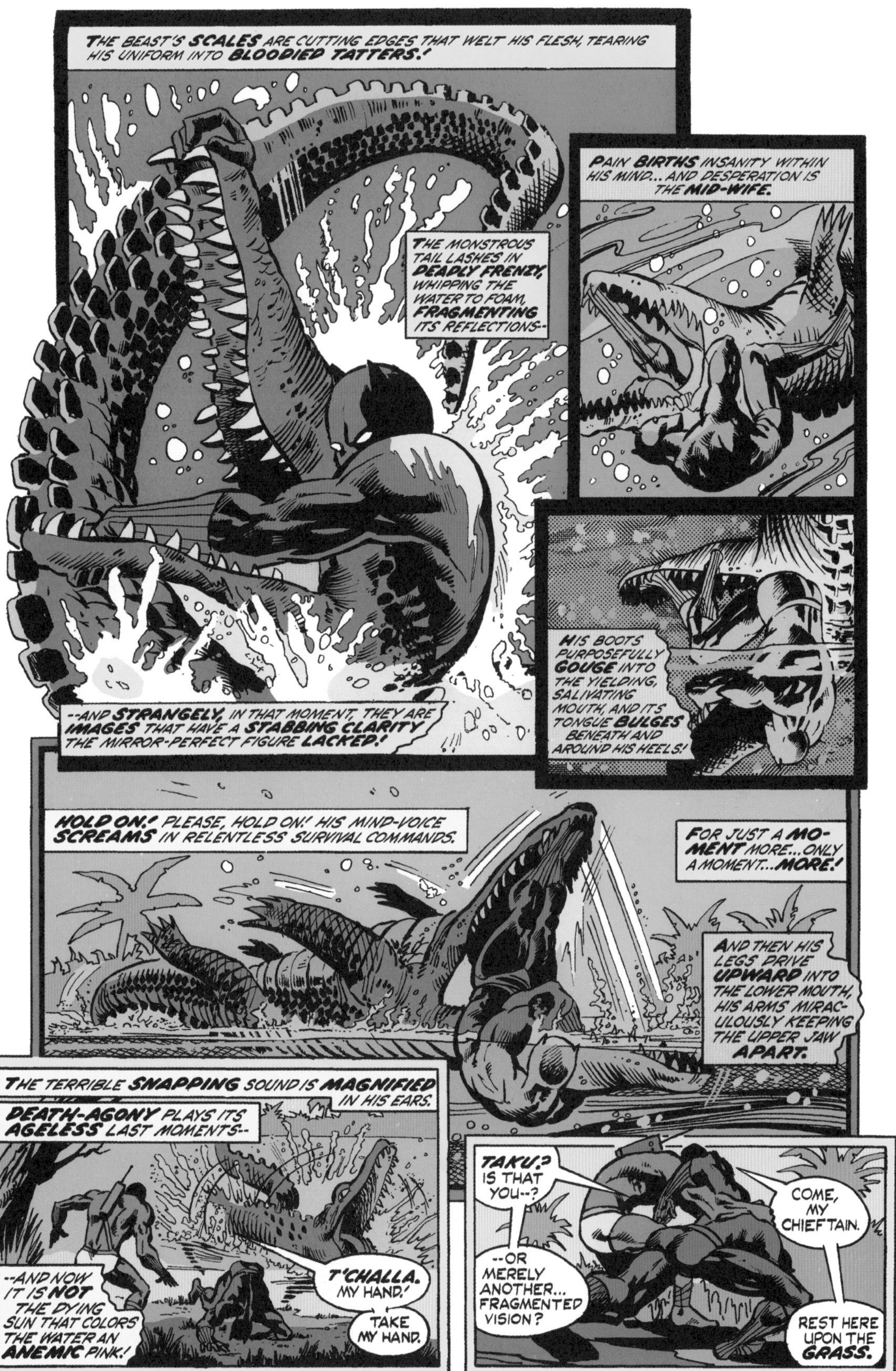
THE BEAST'S SCALES ARE CUTTING EDGES THAT WELT HIS FLESH, TEARING HIS UNIFORM INTO BLOODIED TATTERS!
THE MONSTROUS TAIL LASHES IN DEADLY FRENZY, WHIPPING THE WATER TO FOAM, FRAGMENTING ITS REFLECTIONS--
--AND STRANGELY, IN THAT MOMENT, THEY ARE IMAGES THAT HAVE A STABBING CLARITY THE MIRROR-PERFECT FIGURE LACKED!
PAIN BIRTHS INSANITY WITHIN HIS MIND... AND DESPERATION IS THE MID-WIFE.
HIS BOOTS PURPOSEFULLY GOUGE INTO THE YIELDING, SALIVATING MOUTH, AND ITS TONGUE BULGES BENEATH AND AROUND HIS HEELS!
HOLD ON! PLEASE, HOLD ON! HIS MIND-VOICE SCREAMS IN RELENTLESS SURVIVAL COMMANDS.
FOR JUST A MOMENT MORE... ONLY A MOMENT... MORE!
AND THEN HIS LEGS DRIVE UPWARD INTO THE LOWER MOUTH, HIS ARMS MIRACULOUSLY KEEPING THE UPPER JAW APART.
THE TERRIBLE SNAPPING SOUND IS MAGNIFIED IN HIS EARS.
DEATH-AGONY PLAYS ITS AGELESS LAST MOMENTS--
--AND NOW IT IS NOT THE DYING SUN THAT COLORS THE WATER AN ANEMIC PINK!
T'CHALLA. MY HAND!
TAKE MY HAND.
TAKU? IS THAT YOU--?
--OR MERELY ANOTHER... FRAGMENTED VISION?
COME, MY CHIEFTAIN.
REST HERE UPON THE GRASS.

I SAW YOU LEAVE THE PALACE EARLIER. YOU WERE FARTHER DOWN-STREAM THAN I THOUGHT YOU'D BE.
I SUPPOSE W'KABI WOULD TELL YOU THAT YOU SHOULD HAVE STAYED UP-RIVER. THE CROCODILES ARE SELDOM SIGHTED NEAR THE AMBER PAGODA.
A MAN GOES TO BROOD WHERE IT'S MOST ISOLATED, TAKU. UNLESS HE HAS SOMEONE TO LISTEN TO HIS SILENCES.
THAT'S WHY I CAME LOOKING FOR YOU, T'CHALLA. IT'S ABOUT MISS LYNNE... YOUR GUEST...
I STOPPED BY THE CELL THE INNER COUNCIL HAS LOCKED HER IN SINCE--
--THEY ACCUSED HER OF MURDERING ZATAMA. SHE ASKED TO SEE YOU.

I COULDN'T RELEASE HER.
NO, YOU'RE RIGHT. W'KABI WOULD THINK I SIDED WITH THE "OUT-WORLDER" ONCE AGAIN.
HOW DID I LOSE HIM, TAKU?

HE WAS ONCE MY RIGHT HAND. HEAD OF COURT SECURITY. WAS IT ONLY MY ABSENCE FROM OUR LAND THAT SEPARATED US, TAKU?
PERHAPS YOU LEFT HIM STANDING ON THE SHORELINE, MY CHIEFTAIN.
THE CURRENT CONTINUES TO TRAVEL. IT IS DIFFICULT TO RETURN TO THE SHORE-LINE IT HAS PASSED.
IT ANGERS HIM THAT I'VE BROUGHT MONICA TO OUR HIDDEN LAND, BUT GUESTS WERE NEVER UNWELCOME BEFORE.

PART OF IT IS KILLMONGER. SURELY YOU KNOW THAT?
KILLMONGER. THE MAGNIFICENT REBEL ... BUT HE HAS NO CONCERN FOR THE FRAILTY OF THE VICTIMS HE MAIMS!

HE WOULD GOVERN THIS LAND, IF THAT'S WHAT YOU'D CALL IT... BUT HE WOULD ONLY BE CONCERNED WITH HIS OWN DESIGNS.
THE QUESTION YOU MUST ASK YOURSELF, MY CHIEFTAIN, IS IF YOU--
--HAVE BEEN ANY DIFFERENT.

IT IS AN OPULENT CAGE, BUT STILL A CAGE, THINKS T'CHALLA. THE COLUMNS AND INLAID TILES, THE TAPESTRIES AND BOTANICAL GARDENS ARE ALL DIMINISHED BY THE BARRED WINDOWS AND DOORS.
I JUST KEEP LOOKING AT THIS WEAPON THAT HAS YOUR PRINTS ON IT, MONICA. THEY ARE YOUR PRINTS AND THIS IS THE SPEAR THEY FOUND IN ZATAMA'S BODY.
I KEEP LOOKING AT IT TRYING TO FIGURE OUT HOW THE REAL MURDERER MANAGED THAT LITTLE TRICK.
THERE'S SOME-THING FAMILIAR AND NAGGING ABOUT THIS SPEAR BUT I CAN'T PLACE WHAT.
CAN'T PLACE THIS GREASY SUBSTANCE SMEARED ON IT, EITHER.
T'CHALLA... I'VE SEEN A DOZEN FLICKS WHERE THE LOCAL YOKELS GO OUT FOR THE BLOOD OF THE STRANGE DUDE IN TOWN... NEVER THOUGHT I'D BE PLAYING THAT ROLE.
I'M FRIGHTENED.
ONCE WAKANDA DID NOT MIMIC LIFE, ONCE THEY LIVED IT.
IN THAT TIME, I DO NOT THINK THIS WOULD HAVE HAPPENED.
I KNOW THIS LAND IS IN YOUR BLOOD, T'CHALLA.
BLOOD VESSELS ARE LIKE A RIVER, MONICA. BOTH KEEP ALIVE THAT THROUGH WHICH THEY FLOW.
OH, HEY, THAT'S HIP, T'CHALLA. YOU AN' THAT KUNG FU GUY OUGHTTA GET TOGETHER AND EXCHANGE PROVERBS!
I'M SORRY, MONICA.
I KNOW YOUR FEAR.
I'M SORRY TOO. I REALLY WANTED TO SAY...
I NEED YOU.

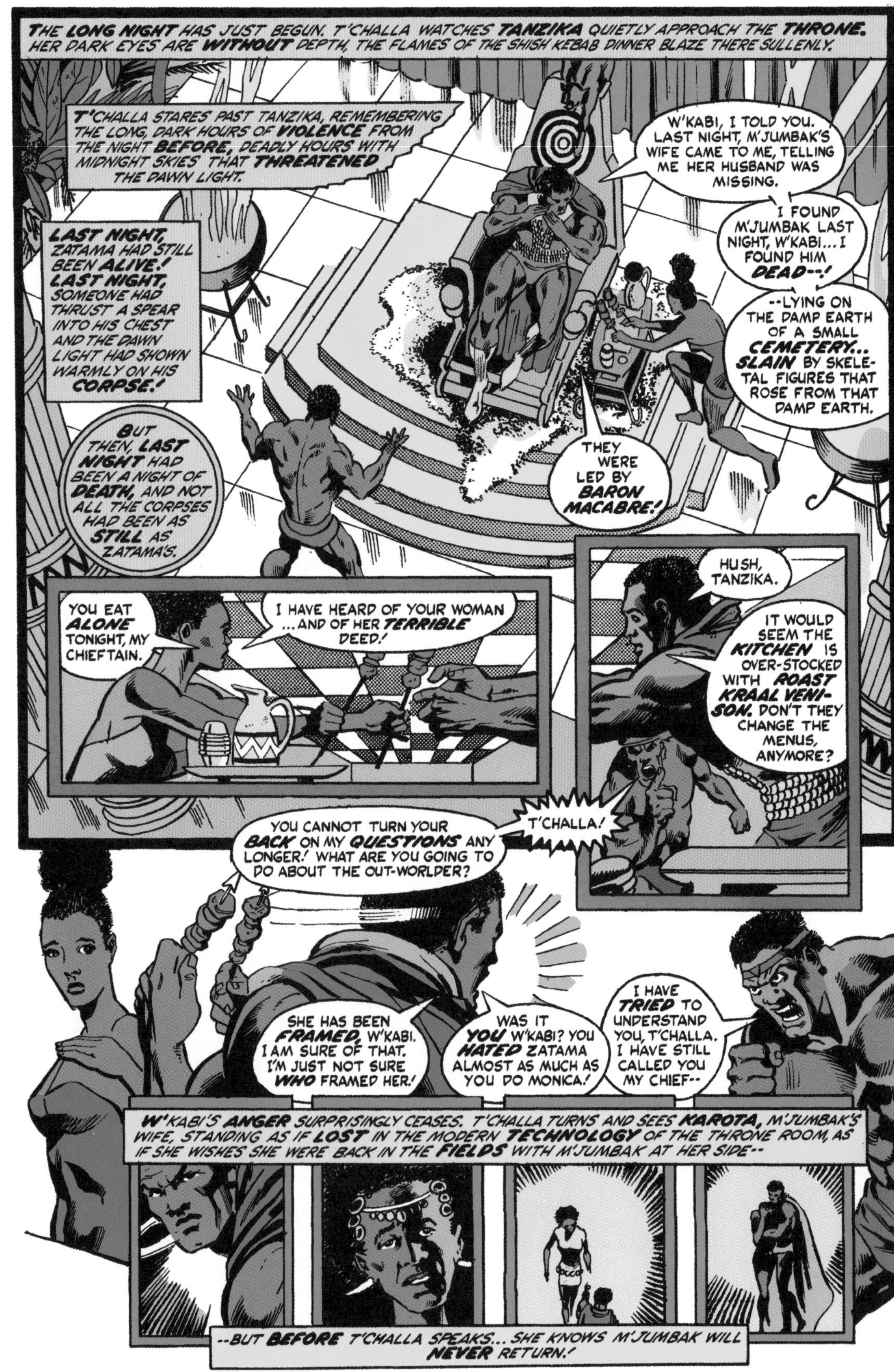

THE LONG NIGHT HAS JUST BEGUN. T'CHALLA WATCHES TANZIKA QUIETLY APPROACH THE THRONE. HER DARK EYES ARE WITHOUT DEPTH, THE FLAMES OF THE SHISH KEBAB DINNER BLAZE THERE SULLENLY.
T'CHALLA STARES PAST TANZIKA, REMEMBERING THE LONG, DARK HOURS OF VIOLENCE FROM THE NIGHT BEFORE, DEADLY HOURS WITH MIDNIGHT SKIES THAT THREATENED THE DAWN LIGHT.
W'KABI, I TOLD YOU. LAST NIGHT, M'JUMBAK'S WIFE CAME TO ME, TELLING ME HER HUSBAND WAS MISSING.
I FOUND M'JUMBAK LAST NIGHT, W'KABI... I FOUND HIM DEAD--!
--LYING ON THE DAMP EARTH OF A SMALL CEMETERY... SLAIN BY SKELETAL FIGURES THAT ROSE FROM THAT DAMP EARTH.
LAST NIGHT, ZATAMA HAD STILL BEEN ALIVE! LAST NIGHT, SOMEONE HAD THRUST A SPEAR INTO HIS CHEST AND THE DAWN LIGHT HAD SHOWN WARMLY ON HIS CORPSE!
BUT THEN, LAST NIGHT HAD BEEN A NIGHT OF DEATH, AND NOT ALL THE CORPSES HAD BEEN AS STILL AS ZATAMA'S.
THEY WERE LED BY BARON MACABRE!
YOU EAT ALONE TONIGHT, MY CHIEFTAIN.
I HAVE HEARD OF YOUR WOMAN ...AND OF HER TERRIBLE DEED!
HUSH, TANZIKA.
IT WOULD SEEM THE KITCHEN IS OVER-STOCKED WITH ROAST KRAAL VENISON. DON'T THEY CHANGE THE MENUS, ANYMORE?
T'CHALLA!
YOU CANNOT TURN YOUR BACK ON MY QUESTIONS ANY LONGER! WHAT ARE YOU GOING TO DO ABOUT THE OUT-WORLDER?
SHE HAS BEEN FRAMED, W'KABI. I AM SURE OF THAT. I'M JUST NOT SURE WHO FRAMED HER!
WAS IT YOU W'KABI? YOU HATED ZATAMA ALMOST AS MUCH AS YOU DO MONICA!
I HAVE TRIED TO UNDERSTAND YOU, T'CHALLA. I HAVE STILL CALLED YOU MY CHIEF--
W'KABI'S ANGER SURPRISINGLY CEASES. T'CHALLA TURNS AND SEES KAROTA, M'JUMBAK'S WIFE, STANDING AS IF LOST IN THE MODERN TECHNOLOGY OF THE THRONE ROOM, AS IF SHE WISHES SHE WERE BACK IN THE FIELDS WITH M'JUMBAK AT HER SIDE--
--BUT BEFORE T'CHALLA SPEAKS... SHE KNOWS M'JUMBAK WILL NEVER RETURN!

T'CHALLA HOLDS KAROTA FOR A LONG MOMENT, MURMURING VEHEMENTLY, "I WILL AVENGE M'JUMBAK'S DEATH!" BUT THEY ARE WORDS THAT MEAN NOTHING TO HER.
AND THEN HE KNOWS HE CAN AVOID THE TASK NO LONGER! HE RETURNS TO THE SMALL CEMETERY BORDERING M'JUMBAK'S FARMLAND... AND DROPS INTO THE MIDDLE OF THE DEATH SITE.

M'JUMBAK'S BODY IS BRITTLE, CURIOUSLY REMINDING HIM OF THE LEECHES INSIDE THE CROCODILE'S MOUTH, THEIR JUICES SUCKED DRY INTO HOLLOW SHELLS.
I AM SORRY I COULD NOT RETURN FOR YOU SOONER, M'JUMBAK.
TONIGHT ...TONIGHT, I WILL TAKE YOU BACK HOME... AND AWAY FROM THIS HELLISH PLACE!
HE HEARS THE FIRST FAINT CLAWINGS THEN--

--AND TURNS, SEEKING THEIR SOURCE, PREPARING HIMSELF FOR THE GRUESOME SPECTACLE!
HE IS IN THE MIDST OF THE NIGHTMARE ONCE MORE! AS THEY DID THE NIGHT BEFORE, CORPSE-LIKE LIMBS THRUST FROM THE FRESHLY FILLED GRAVES--
--TALONED FINGERS STREAKED WITH BLOOD THAT MARK THEIR EFFORTS TO FREE THEMSELVES FROM THEIR TOMBS!
IT BEGINS ANEW, M'JUMBAK--!

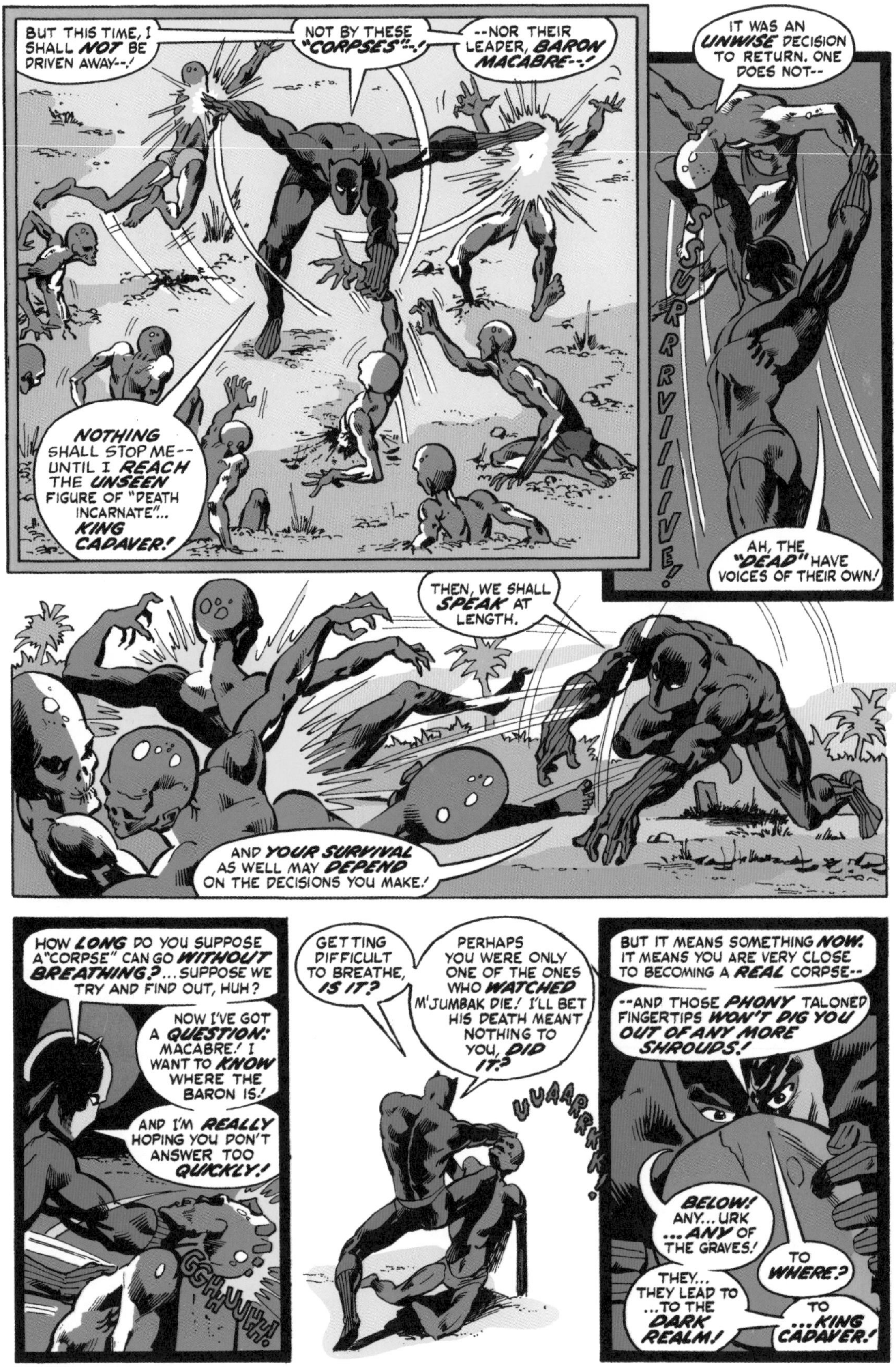

BUT THIS TIME, I SHALL *NOT* BE DRIVEN AWAY--!
NOT BY THESE *"CORPSES"*--!
--NOR THEIR LEADER, *BARON MACABRE*--!
*NOTHING* SHALL STOP ME-- UNTIL I *REACH* THE *UNSEEN* FIGURE OF "DEATH INCARNATE"... *KING CADAVER!*

IT WAS AN *UNWISE* DECISION TO RETURN. ONE DOES NOT--
SSURRRRVIIIIIVE!
AH, THE *"DEAD"* HAVE VOICES OF THEIR OWN!

THEN, WE SHALL *SPEAK* AT LENGTH.
AND *YOUR SURVIVAL* AS WELL MAY *DEPEND* ON THE DECISIONS YOU MAKE!

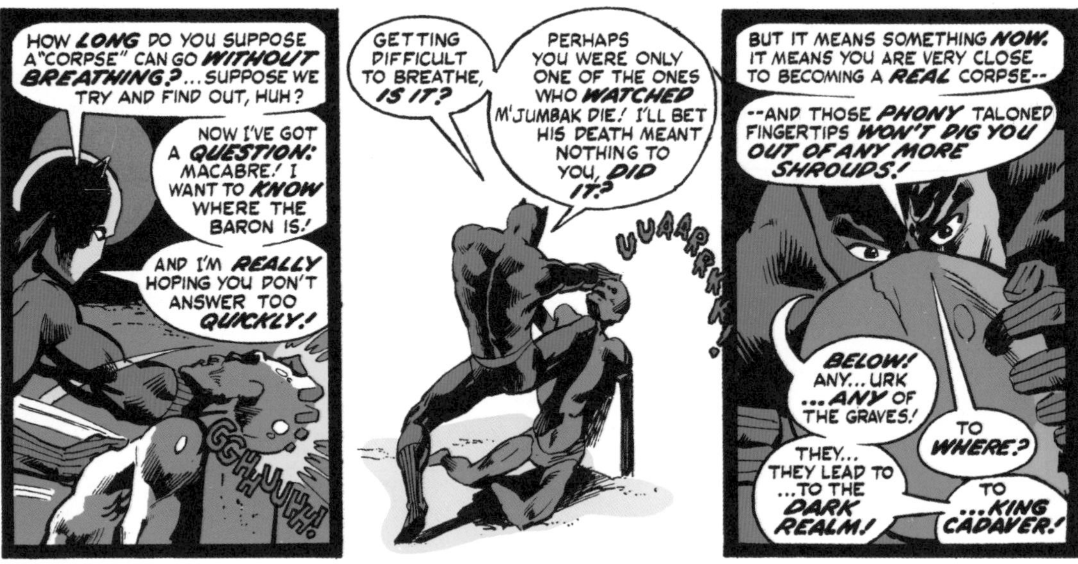

HOW *LONG* DO YOU SUPPOSE A "CORPSE" CAN GO *WITHOUT BREATHING?*... SUPPOSE WE TRY AND FIND OUT, HUH?
NOW I'VE GOT A *QUESTION:* MACABRE! I WANT TO *KNOW* WHERE THE BARON IS!
AND I'M *REALLY* HOPING YOU DON'T ANSWER TOO *QUICKLY!*
GGHHUUHH!
GETTING DIFFICULT TO BREATHE, *IS IT?*
PERHAPS YOU WERE ONLY ONE OF THE ONES WHO *WATCHED* M'JUMBAK DIE! I'LL BET HIS DEATH MEANT NOTHING TO YOU, *DID IT?*
UUAARRKK!
BUT IT MEANS SOMETHING *NOW.* IT MEANS YOU ARE VERY CLOSE TO BECOMING A *REAL* CORPSE--
--AND THOSE *PHONY* TALONED FINGERTIPS *WON'T DIG YOU OUT OF ANY MORE SHROUDS!*
*BELOW!* ANY... URK ...*ANY* OF THE GRAVES!
TO *WHERE?*
THEY... THEY LEAD TO ...TO THE *DARK REALM!*
TO ...*KING CADAVER!*

HIS VICTIM'S EYES **GLAZE** BENEATH THE **SKULL-MASQUE**, AND THE PANTHER HAS TROUBLE REMINDING HIMSELF THAT THIS IS ONLY A GUISE OF **MAKE-SHIFT DETERIORATION**--

--THAT THE FLESH GLEAMING WITH **VOLCANIC EARTH**, THAT THE TALONED FINGERS **DRIPPING SCARLET** GORE AND MOIST DIRT TO FORM A **COAGULATING VENEER OF BLOOD** ARE ONLY **FURTHER** EXAMPLES OF KILLMONGER'S SENSE OF **DRAMATICS!**

**ANGRILY,** IMAGINING THE CALLOUSNESS THEY MUST HAVE DISPLAYED AT M'JUMBAK'S **FINAL MOMENTS,** THE PANTHER FLINGS THE UNDERLING ASIDE... AND **HARDLY NOTICES** THE OTHERS THAT **TRY** TO STOP HIM AS HE APPROACHES THE NEAREST GRAVE.

I WILL BE BACK, M'JUMBAK--

--ONLY MY OWN DEATH WILL PREVENT THAT!

HE DROPS DOWN A GOOD THIRTY FEET, LANDING QUIETLY UPON A PASSAGE-WAY HEWN FROM THE VOLCANIC EARTH--
--AND THE TEMPERATURE DROPS, A COLD, NEAR UNEARTHLY CHILL THAT PENETRATES FLESH.
HE STANDS STILL FOR A MOMENT, NEAR INVISIBLE, BLENDING WITH THE SHADOWS. HIS EYES ARE DRAWN FIRST TO THE BECKONING LIGHT WAY IN THE DISTANCE, LIGHT THAT HINTS AT REVELATIONS!

SLOWLY, MOVING AS HIS NAMESAKE DOES IN THE EARLY MORN HOURS OF STALKING, THE PANTHER WARILY HEADS TOWARD THE TANTALIZING LIGHT.

THE TUNNEL SHIFTS AND ALTERS, A MAZE TURNING BACK IN UPON ITSELF... BUT ALWAYS THE LIGHT IS THERE... AND EACH STEP CLOSER INCREASES HIS CAUTION!
HE HAS VAGUE PREMONITIONS OF SUPRA-NORMAL FIGURES WAITING WITHIN THE LIGHT, WEAVING KILLMONGER'S ENEMY TACTICS!
BUT, BEFORE THOSE SENSES ARE HALF-FORMED, THE LIGHT ABRUPTLY EXPANDS ...EXPLODING BLINDINGLY!

THE PANTHER CROUCHES AS THE LIGHT LANCES THROUGH HIS EYES INTO HIS BRAIN!
HE HEARS THE VOICES FIRST, VOICES THAT HAVE NO APPARENT POINT OF ORIGIN.
HIS VISION ADAPTS TO THE INTENSE, NEON-BRIGHT GLARE... AND HE TURNS, A SNARL TWISTING HIS LIPS, TURNING INTO HIS OWN IMAGE.
SUPERIMPOSED OVER HIS COWLED FACE IS ANOTHER FIGURE AND FACE, A PRESENCE THAT DWARFS HIS OWN. IT IS A TERRIFYING SIGHT, FLESH MALIGNANTLY SWOLLEN, AN OBSCENE FACE, BLOATED WITH SAC-LIKE GLANDS!
KING CADAVER!!
THE KING'S EYES ARE EVERYWHERE! THE PANTHER SEES THEM A HUNDRED TIMES IN REFLECTIONS OF REFLECTIONS! AND THEY ARE BULGING, MESMERIZING, LINED WITH VEINS THAT PULSE WITH CONCENTRATION!
MACABRE! I KNEW YOU'D BE HERE--
--BUT THIS...!

AS HIS VOICE FADES, TWO OTHERS FILL THE CHAMBER. ONE, THE PANTHER RECOGNIZES AS BELONGING TO THE GAUNT, SKELETAL FIGURE IN THE MIRRORS: THE BARON!
AH, MY DEAR PANTHER, I TOLD THE KING WE COULD EXPECT YOU TONIGHT.
BUT IT IS KING CADAVER'S VOICE THAT SHOCKS HIM. FOR IT IS A VOICE THAT BELIES HIS GROTESQUE ABNORMALITY.
FROM LIPS WET WITH SALIVA AND TORN RAW IN THE BLISTERED FACE COMES THE VOICE OF AN ORATOR--
--SOFT AND PLEASANT--
--WITH A POLITICIAN'S ELOCUTION--
--A GENTLY PERSUASIVE TONE THAT PROBES, INSISTENTLY PROBING FOR THE PANTHER'S IDENTITY--
--RIPPING INTO HIS PSYCHE, THREATENING TO TEAR THAT VERY IDENTITY FROM HIM--
--EYES AND MOUTH WORKING TOWARD ONE PURPOSE, THE EYES STEALING ACROSS EGO-VALLEYS, ID CENTERS, AND SUPER-EGO RESERVOIRS!
--WHILE THE VOICE CALMS AND COAXES, CORROSIVELY EATING AWAY AT THE PANTHER'S RESISTANCE.
TURN, PANTHER. TURN WHICHEVER WAY YOU CHOOSE!
IT DOES NOT MATTER WHICH WAY YOU TURN. KING CADAVER'S EYES WILL SEEK YOU OUT.
YOU CANNOT HIDE FROM THEM!
YOU KNOW YOU CANNOT HIDE FROM THEM!

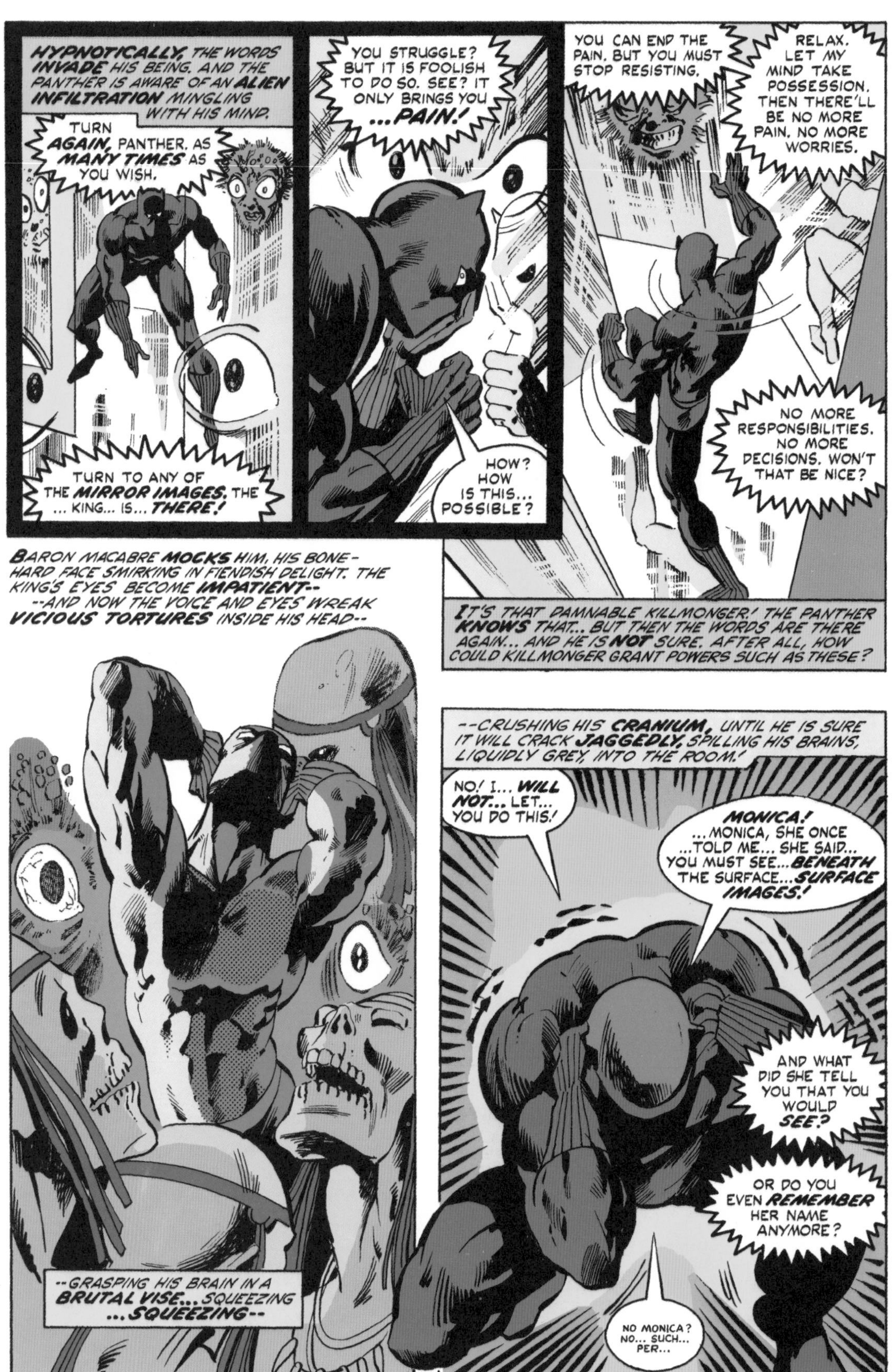
HYPNOTICALLY, THE WORDS INVADE HIS BEING, AND THE PANTHER IS AWARE OF AN ALIEN INFILTRATION MINGLING WITH HIS MIND.
TURN AGAIN, PANTHER, AS MANY TIMES AS YOU WISH.
TURN TO ANY OF THE MIRROR IMAGES, THE ... KING... IS... THERE!
YOU STRUGGLE? BUT IT IS FOOLISH TO DO SO. SEE? IT ONLY BRINGS YOU ...PAIN!
HOW? HOW IS THIS... POSSIBLE?
YOU CAN END THE PAIN. BUT YOU MUST STOP RESISTING.
RELAX. LET MY MIND TAKE POSSESSION. THEN THERE'LL BE NO MORE PAIN, NO MORE WORRIES.
NO MORE RESPONSIBILITIES. NO MORE DECISIONS. WON'T THAT BE NICE?
BARON MACABRE MOCKS HIM, HIS BONE-HARD FACE SMIRKING IN FIENDISH DELIGHT. THE KING'S EYES BECOME IMPATIENT-- --AND NOW THE VOICE AND EYES WREAK VICIOUS TORTURES INSIDE HIS HEAD--
IT'S THAT DAMNABLE KILLMONGER! THE PANTHER KNOWS THAT... BUT THEN THE WORDS ARE THERE AGAIN... AND HE IS NOT SURE. AFTER ALL, HOW COULD KILLMONGER GRANT POWERS SUCH AS THESE?
--GRASPING HIS BRAIN IN A BRUTAL VISE... SQUEEZING ...SQUEEZING--
--CRUSHING HIS CRANIUM, UNTIL HE IS SURE IT WILL CRACK JAGGEDLY, SPILLING HIS BRAINS, LIQUIDLY GREY, INTO THE ROOM!
NO! I... WILL NOT... LET... YOU DO THIS!
MONICA! ...MONICA, SHE ONCE ...TOLD ME... SHE SAID... YOU MUST SEE... BENEATH THE SURFACE... SURFACE IMAGES!
AND WHAT DID SHE TELL YOU THAT YOU WOULD SEE?
OR DO YOU EVEN REMEMBER HER NAME ANYMORE?
NO MONICA? NO... SUCH... PER...

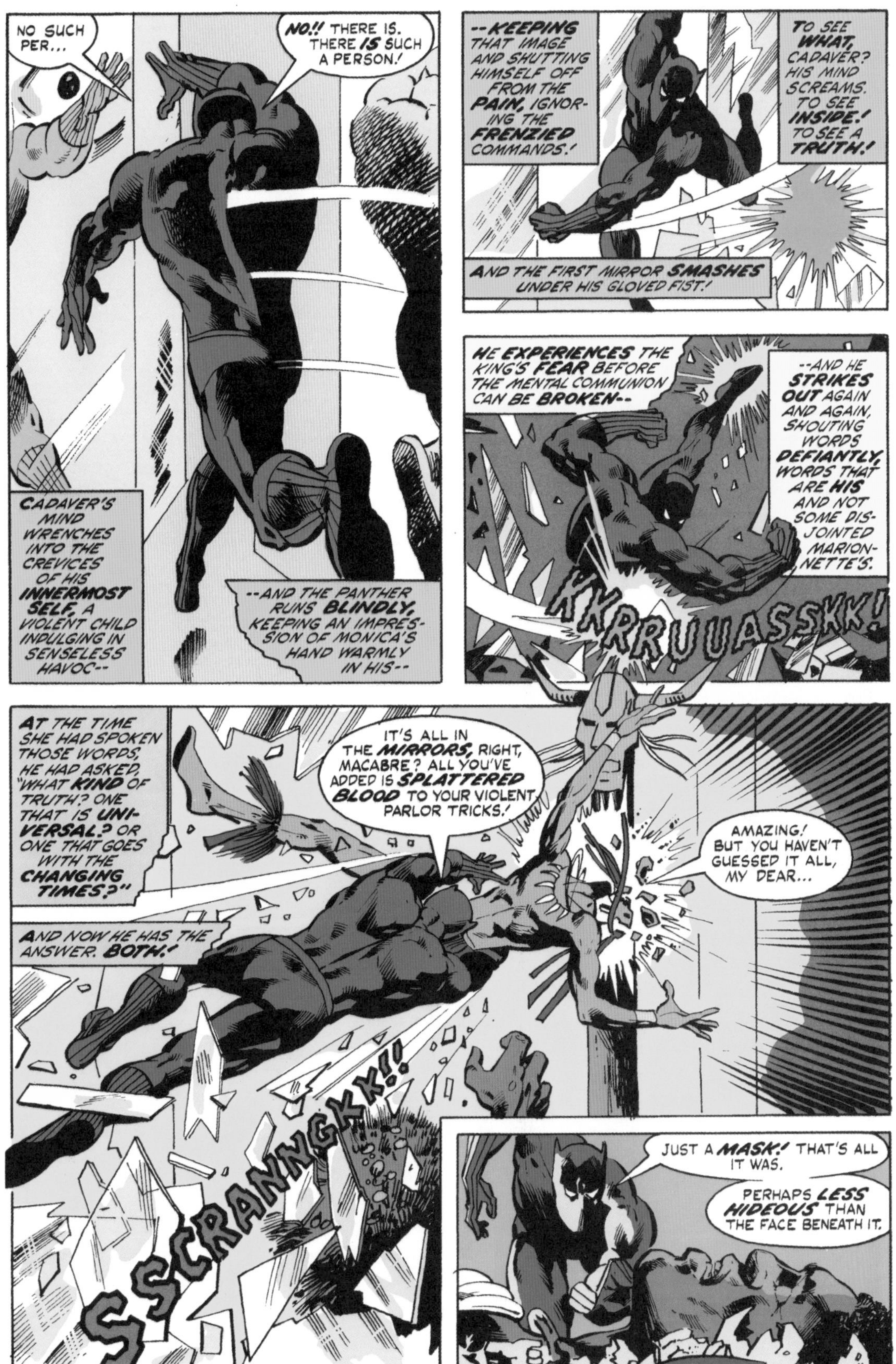
NO SUCH PER...
NO!! THERE IS. THERE IS SUCH A PERSON!
CADAVER'S MIND WRENCHES INTO THE CREVICES OF HIS INNERMOST SELF, A VIOLENT CHILD INDULGING IN SENSELESS HAVOC--
--AND THE PANTHER RUNS BLINDLY, KEEPING AN IMPRESSION OF MONICA'S HAND WARMLY IN HIS--
--KEEPING THAT IMAGE AND SHUTTING HIMSELF OFF FROM THE PAIN, IGNORING THE FRENZIED COMMANDS!
TO SEE WHAT, CADAVER? HIS MIND SCREAMS. TO SEE INSIDE! TO SEE A TRUTH!
AND THE FIRST MIRROR SMASHES UNDER HIS GLOVED FIST!
HE EXPERIENCES THE KING'S FEAR BEFORE THE MENTAL COMMUNION CAN BE BROKEN--
--AND HE STRIKES OUT AGAIN AND AGAIN, SHOUTING WORDS DEFIANTLY, WORDS THAT ARE HIS AND NOT SOME DISJOINTED MARIONNETTE'S.
KKRRUUASSKK!
AT THE TIME SHE HAD SPOKEN THOSE WORDS, HE HAD ASKED, "WHAT KIND OF TRUTH? ONE THAT IS UNIVERSAL? OR ONE THAT GOES WITH THE CHANGING TIMES?"
IT'S ALL IN THE MIRRORS, RIGHT, MACABRE? ALL YOU'VE ADDED IS SPLATTERED BLOOD TO YOUR VIOLENT PARLOR TRICKS!
AMAZING! BUT YOU HAVEN'T GUESSED IT ALL, MY DEAR...
AND NOW HE HAS THE ANSWER. BOTH!
SSCRANNGKK!!
JUST A MASK! THAT'S ALL IT WAS.
PERHAPS LESS HIDEOUS THAN THE FACE BENEATH IT.

IT IS NOT ALL OVER. AND THE BARON IS CORRECT. YOU HAVE NOT GUESSED ALL OF IT.
I DON'T KNOW WHY KILLMONGER HAD YOU AND MACABRE AND THOSE DEATH REGIMENTS GUARDING THIS PLACE...
THEN YOU'D BETTER MAKE IT FAST, CADAVER! BECAUSE I'M COMING FOR YOU... NOW!!
I DO NOT NEED THE MIRRORS TO TAKE YOUR WILL FROM YOU. THEY MERELY MAGNIFY MY EMANATIONS.
THIS TIME I SHALL ENTER YOUR MIND-- AND I SHALL BATTER IT UNTIL YOU CANNOT CONTROL ANY OF YOUR LIMBS...UNTIL YOUR MOUTH CAN SPEAK ONLY MY WORDS!
...BUT I'M GOING TO FIND OUT AS SOON AS I RIP THIS MASK OFF YOUR...
FACE.
THE SWOLLEN INHUMAN FACE SQUIRMS BENEATH HIS CLUTCHING HANDS--
--AND HIS VOICE IS LOST! CADAVER'S FACE IS NOT A MASK!
A DEFORMED HAND WITH FLESH THAT HAS THE TEXTURE OF MOLD FORMING ON A CULTURE DISH HOLDS HIM STILL--
--AND THE VOICE AND EYES BEGIN THEIR ASSAULT!
YOUR ASTONISHMENT WILL MAKE THIS ALL THE EASIER!
I MAY LET YOU DIE THIS NIGHT, PANTHER... BUT IT WON'T BE AN EASY DEATH!

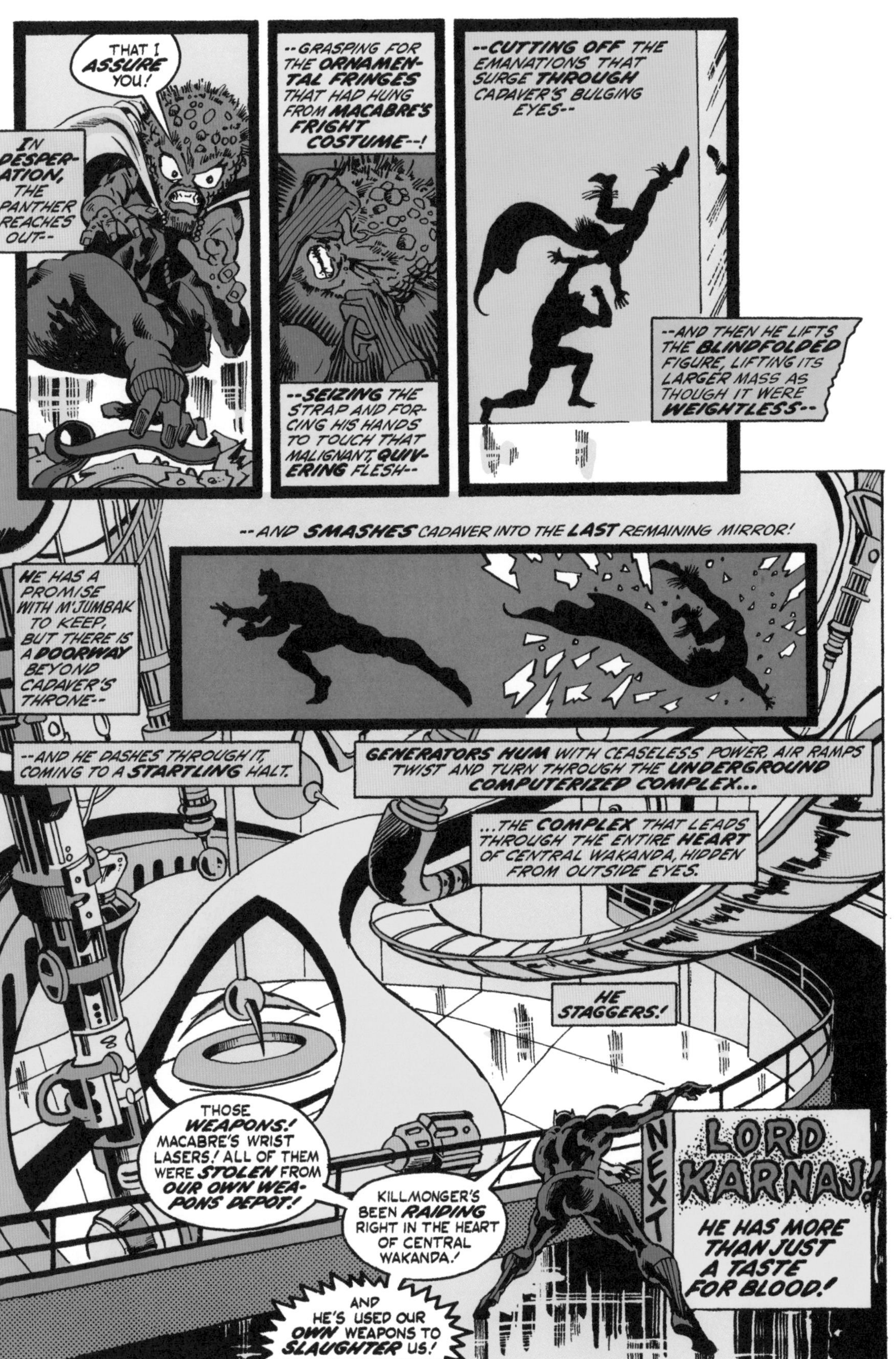
THAT I ASSURE YOU!
IN DESPERATION, THE PANTHER REACHES OUT--
--GRASPING FOR THE ORNAMENTAL FRINGES THAT HAD HUNG FROM MACABRE'S FRIGHT COSTUME--!
--SEIZING THE STRAP AND FORCING HIS HANDS TO TOUCH THAT MALIGNANT, QUIVERING FLESH--
--CUTTING OFF THE EMANATIONS THAT SURGE THROUGH CADAVER'S BULGING EYES--
--AND THEN HE LIFTS THE BLINDFOLDED FIGURE, LIFTING ITS LARGER MASS AS THOUGH IT WERE WEIGHTLESS--
--AND SMASHES CADAVER INTO THE LAST REMAINING MIRROR!
HE HAS A PROMISE WITH M'JUMBAK TO KEEP, BUT THERE IS A DOORWAY BEYOND CADAVER'S THRONE--
--AND HE DASHES THROUGH IT, COMING TO A STARTLING HALT.
GENERATORS HUM WITH CEASELESS POWER, AIR RAMPS TWIST AND TURN THROUGH THE UNDERGROUND COMPUTERIZED COMPLEX...
...THE COMPLEX THAT LEADS THROUGH THE ENTIRE HEART OF CENTRAL WAKANDA, HIDDEN FROM OUTSIDE EYES.
HE STAGGERS!
THOSE WEAPONS! MACABRE'S WRIST LASERS! ALL OF THEM WERE STOLEN FROM OUR OWN WEAPONS DEPOT!
KILLMONGER'S BEEN RAIDING RIGHT IN THE HEART OF CENTRAL WAKANDA!
AND HE'S USED OUR OWN WEAPONS TO SLAUGHTER US!
NEXT
LORD KARNAJ!
HE HAS MORE THAN JUST A TASTE FOR BLOOD!

HERE IT IS, PEOPLE! JACK KIRBY'S ORIGINAL COSTUME FOR THE BLACK PANTHER! ONLY WOULDJA BELIEVE THAT BACK IN THOSE HALCYON DAYS STAN AND JACK WERE CALLING HIM THE COAL TIGER!
BLACK PANTHER Artistry
YOU'VE NO DOUBT NOTICED A FEW SLIGHT CHANGES IN T'CHALLA'S ATTIRE AND NAME WHICH GIVES YOU JUST A VAGUE IDEA WHAT KIND OF VISUAL PREPARATIONS AND CHARACTER ATTITUDES ARE CONSIDERED BEFORE ONE OF OUR SCINTILLATING HEROES BURST FULL BLOWN INTO COMIC BOOK REALITY.
SO HERE IT IS, MARVEL-ITES! FEAST YOUR EYES ON THIS RARE COLLECTOR'S ITEM PRESENTED FOR THE FIRST TIME EVER!
KINDA GETS TO YOU, DOESN'T IT?

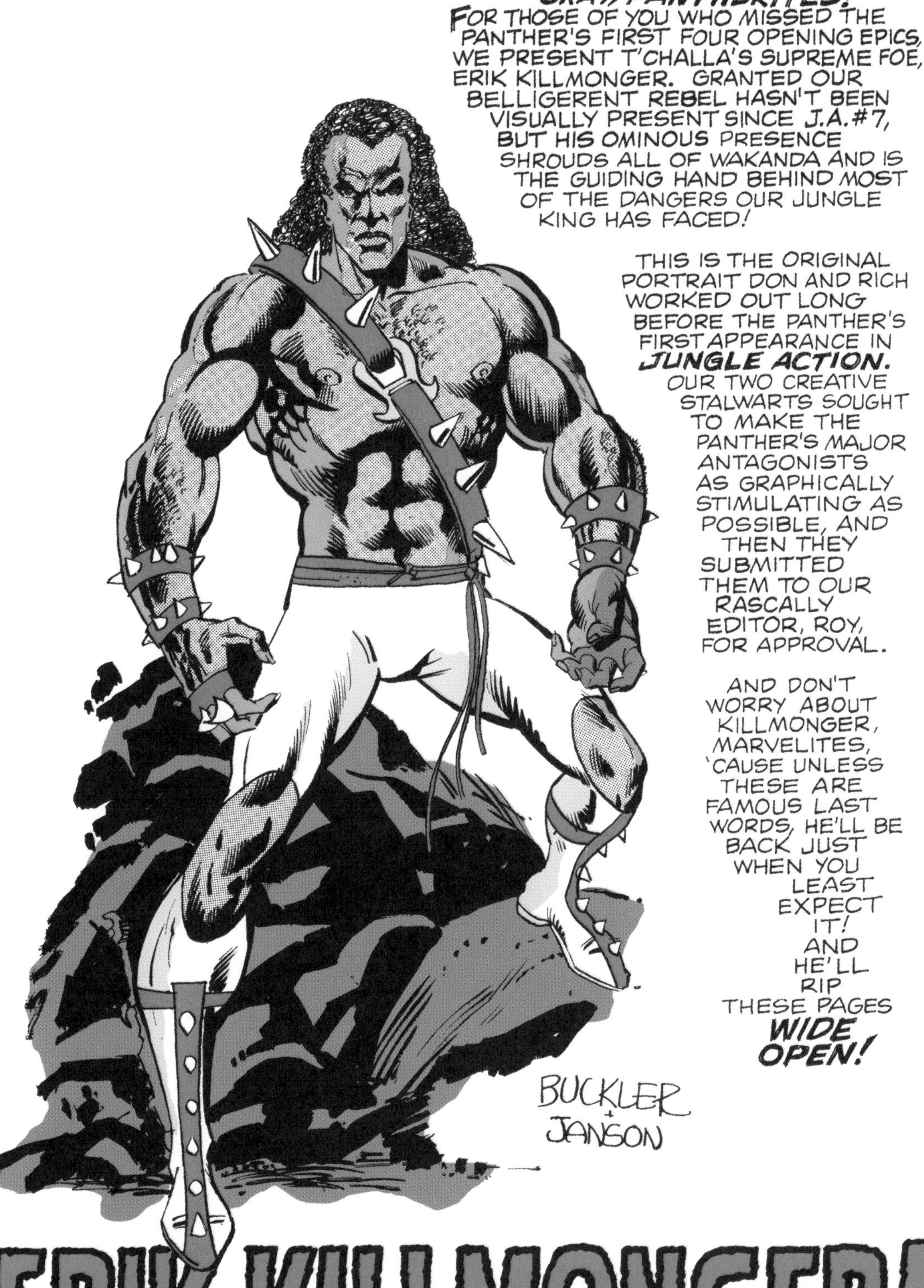

OKAY, PANTHERITES!
FOR THOSE OF YOU WHO MISSED THE PANTHER'S FIRST FOUR OPENING EPICS, WE PRESENT T'CHALLA'S SUPREME FOE, ERIK KILLMONGER. GRANTED OUR BELLIGERENT REBEL HASN'T BEEN VISUALLY PRESENT SINCE J.A. #7, BUT HIS OMINOUS PRESENCE SHROUDS ALL OF WAKANDA AND IS THE GUIDING HAND BEHIND MOST OF THE DANGERS OUR JUNGLE KING HAS FACED!
THIS IS THE ORIGINAL PORTRAIT DON AND RICH WORKED OUT LONG BEFORE THE PANTHER'S FIRST APPEARANCE IN JUNGLE ACTION. OUR TWO CREATIVE STALWARTS SOUGHT TO MAKE THE PANTHER'S MAJOR ANTAGONISTS AS GRAPHICALLY STIMULATING AS POSSIBLE, AND THEN THEY SUBMITTED THEM TO OUR RASCALLY EDITOR, ROY, FOR APPROVAL.
AND DON'T WORRY ABOUT KILLMONGER, MARVELITES, 'CAUSE UNLESS THESE ARE FAMOUS LAST WORDS, HE'LL BE BACK JUST WHEN YOU LEAST EXPECT IT! AND HE'LL RIP THESE PAGES WIDE OPEN!
BUCKLER + JANSON

# ERIK KILLMONGER!

## VERY FEW PEOPLE CALL HIM ERIK!

# *JUNGLE ACTION* #11, SEPTEMBER 1974

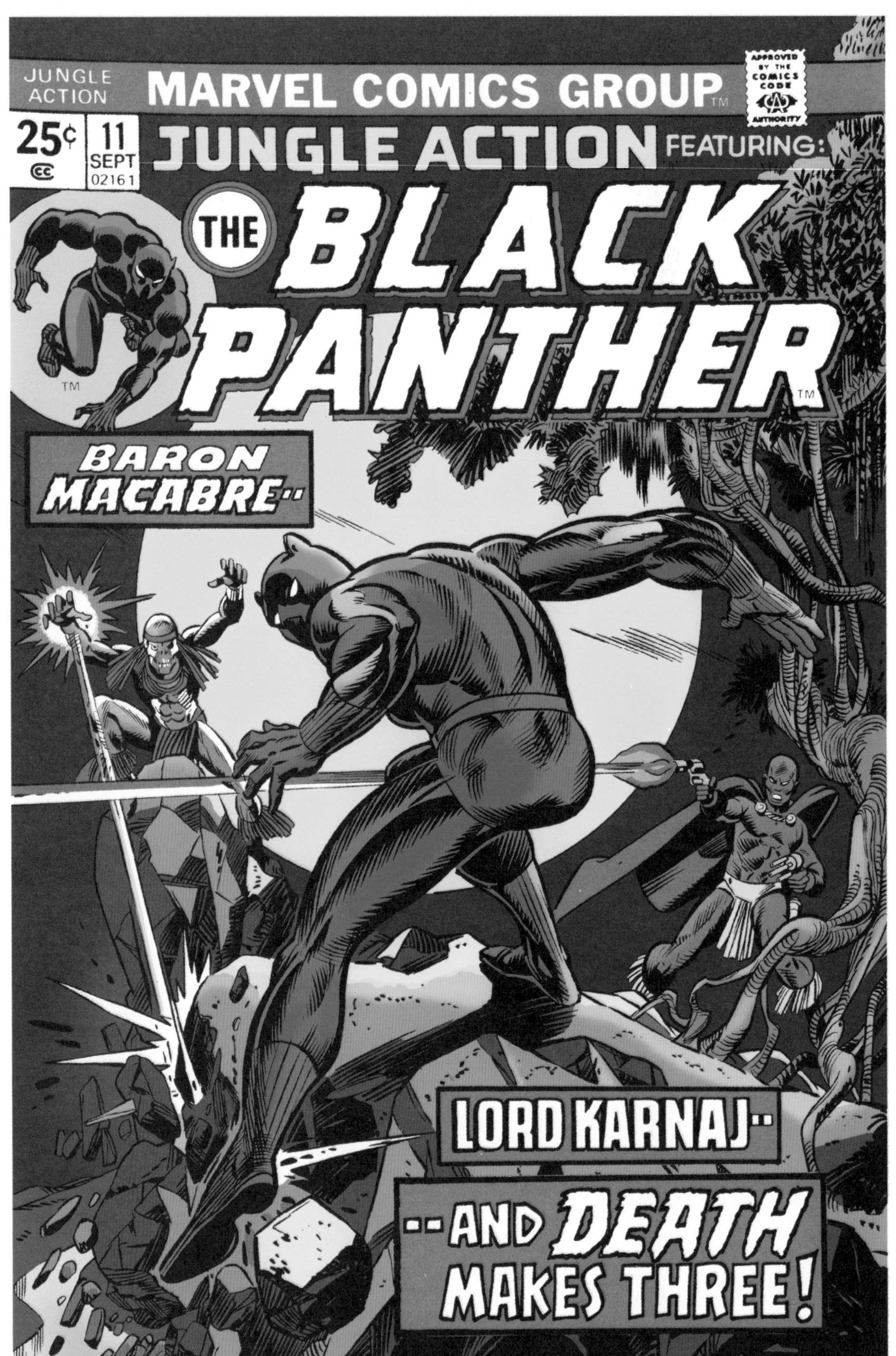
JUNGLE ACTION
MARVEL COMICS GROUP
APPROVED BY THE COMICS CODE AUTHORITY
25¢
11 SEPT
02161
JUNGLE ACTION FEATURING:
THE BLACK PANTHER
BARON MACABRE--
LORD KARNAJ--
--AND DEATH MAKES THREE!

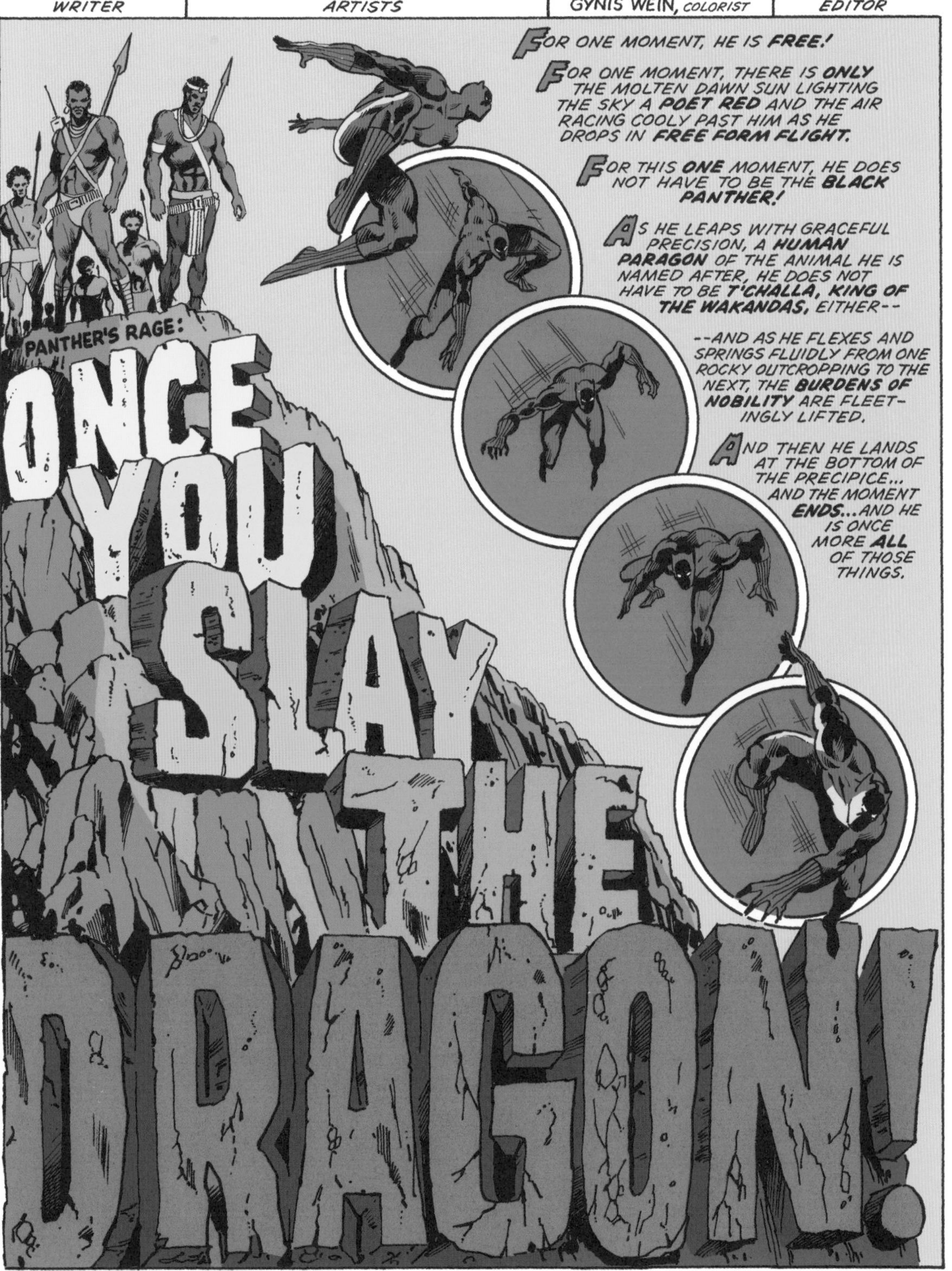
Stan Lee PRESENTS: THE BLACK PANTHER! TM
DON McGREGOR WRITER
BILLY GRAHAM & KLAUS JANSON ARTISTS
ARTIE SIMEK, LETTERER
GYNIS WEIN, COLORIST
ROY THOMAS EDITOR
FOR ONE MOMENT, HE IS FREE!
FOR ONE MOMENT, THERE IS ONLY THE MOLTEN DAWN SUN LIGHTING THE SKY A POET RED AND THE AIR RACING COOLY PAST HIM AS HE DROPS IN FREE FORM FLIGHT.
FOR THIS ONE MOMENT, HE DOES NOT HAVE TO BE THE BLACK PANTHER!
AS HE LEAPS WITH GRACEFUL PRECISION, A HUMAN PARAGON OF THE ANIMAL HE IS NAMED AFTER, HE DOES NOT HAVE TO BE T'CHALLA, KING OF THE WAKANDAS, EITHER--
--AND AS HE FLEXES AND SPRINGS FLUIDLY FROM ONE ROCKY OUTCROPPING TO THE NEXT, THE BURDENS OF NOBILITY ARE FLEETINGLY LIFTED.
AND THEN HE LANDS AT THE BOTTOM OF THE PRECIPICE... AND THE MOMENT ENDS...AND HE IS ONCE MORE ALL OF THOSE THINGS.
PANTHER'S RAGE:
ONCE YOU SLAY THE DRAGON!

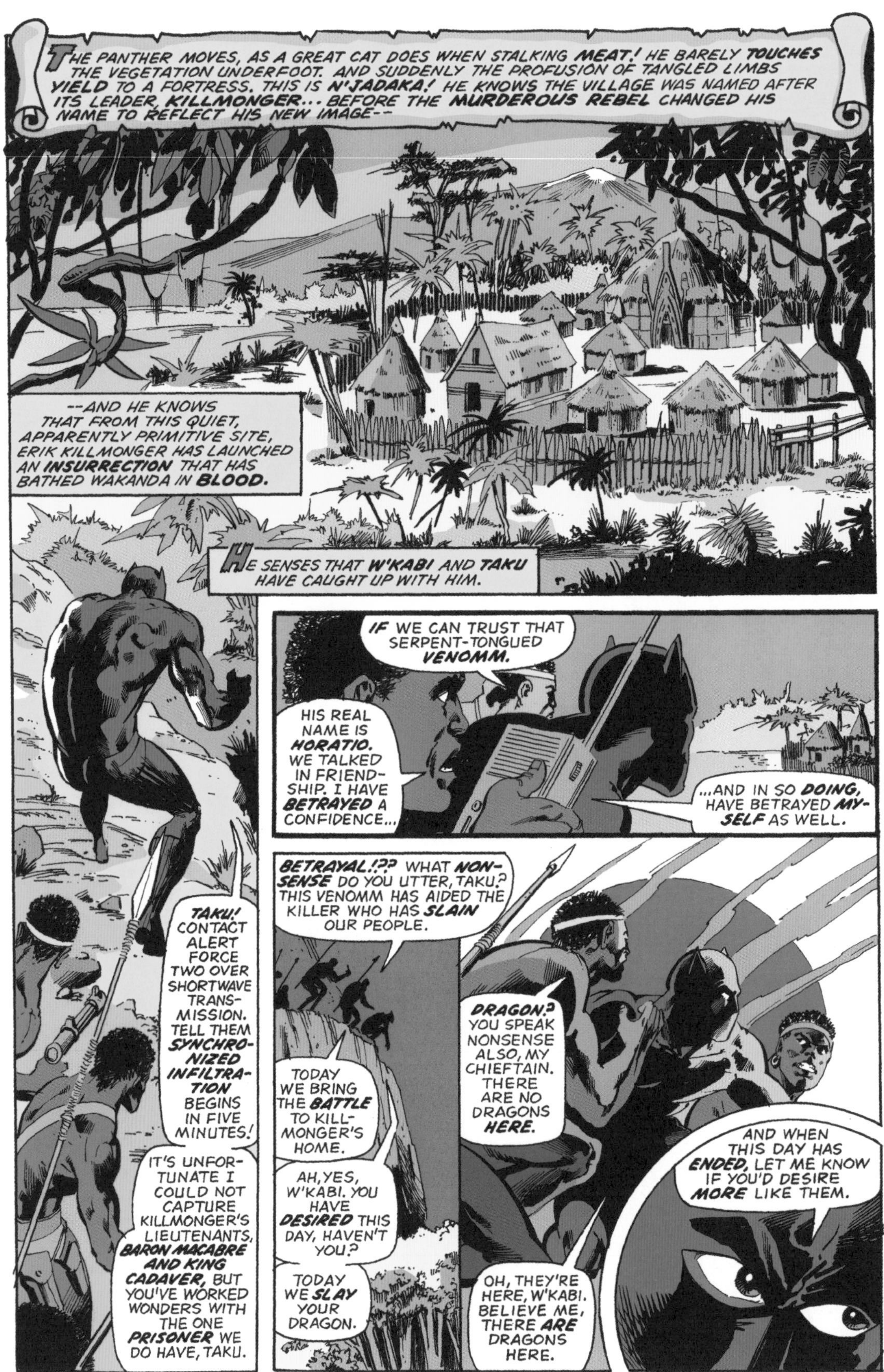
THE PANTHER MOVES, AS A GREAT CAT DOES WHEN STALKING MEAT! HE BARELY TOUCHES THE VEGETATION UNDERFOOT. AND SUDDENLY THE PROFUSION OF TANGLED LIMBS YIELD TO A FORTRESS. THIS IS N'JADAKA! HE KNOWS THE VILLAGE WAS NAMED AFTER ITS LEADER, KILLMONGER... BEFORE THE MURDEROUS REBEL CHANGED HIS NAME TO REFLECT HIS NEW IMAGE--
--AND HE KNOWS THAT FROM THIS QUIET, APPARENTLY PRIMITIVE SITE, ERIK KILLMONGER HAS LAUNCHED AN INSURRECTION THAT HAS BATHED WAKANDA IN BLOOD.
HE SENSES THAT W'KABI AND TAKU HAVE CAUGHT UP WITH HIM.
TAKU! CONTACT ALERT FORCE TWO OVER SHORTWAVE TRANSMISSION. TELL THEM SYNCHRONIZED INFILTRATION BEGINS IN FIVE MINUTES!
IT'S UNFORTUNATE I COULD NOT CAPTURE KILLMONGER'S LIEUTENANTS, BARON MACABRE AND KING CADAVER, BUT YOU'VE WORKED WONDERS WITH THE ONE PRISONER WE DO HAVE, TAKU.
IF WE CAN TRUST THAT SERPENT-TONGUED VENOMM.
HIS REAL NAME IS HORATIO. WE TALKED IN FRIENDSHIP. I HAVE BETRAYED A CONFIDENCE...
...AND IN SO DOING, HAVE BETRAYED MYSELF AS WELL.
BETRAYAL!?? WHAT NONSENSE DO YOU UTTER, TAKU? THIS VENOMM HAS AIDED THE KILLER WHO HAS SLAIN OUR PEOPLE.
TODAY WE BRING THE BATTLE TO KILLMONGER'S HOME.
AH, YES, W'KABI. YOU HAVE DESIRED THIS DAY, HAVEN'T YOU?
TODAY WE SLAY YOUR DRAGON.
DRAGON? YOU SPEAK NONSENSE ALSO, MY CHIEFTAIN. THERE ARE NO DRAGONS HERE.
OH, THEY'RE HERE, W'KABI. BELIEVE ME, THERE ARE DRAGONS HERE.
AND WHEN THIS DAY HAS ENDED, LET ME KNOW IF YOU'D DESIRE MORE LIKE THEM.

TAYETE HAS FLINCHED ONLY ONCE DURING THE NIGHT... WHICH ISN'T A BAD RECORD. HE HAS NOT ONCE ADMITTED TO HIS COMPANION, KAZIBE, THAT PANTHERISH EYES HAVE HAUNTED THE MAZES OF HIS DREAMS, AND HE FEELS EXTREMELY SECURE NOW AS THE VILLAGE AWAKENS.
THE PUNGENT AROMA OF MATOKE, MASHED AND STEAMED BANANAS, FILL THE COMPOUND.
YES, IF THERE IS ANY PLACE THAT IS SAFE FROM THAT PANTHER DEVIL... THIS IS THE PLACE!
TAYETE! LOOK QUICK!!
LOOK AT WHAT?
DIDN'T YOU SEE THEM?
SEE WHAT?
THOSE FIGURES RIGHT...
THERE?
I'VE NO TIME FOR YOUR CHILDISH GAMES, KAZIBE. LORD KARNAJ WILL SUMMON US SOON, AND I INTEND FOR MY BELLY TO BE FULL WITH MATOKE BEFORE HE CALLS.
TAYETE, WHERE'D THAT SHADOW COME FROM?
YOU MUST BE SEEING THINGS. YOU'VE BEEN HAVING NIGHTMARES SINCE THAT NIGHT IN THE CEMETERY.
I SAW HOW THAT PANTHER DEVIL AND EVEN OUR OWN MAN, BARON MACABRE, FRIGHTENED YOU.
COURSE, THEY DIDN'T BOTHER ME AT ALL.
TAYETE! ON THE ROOF!!
AND WHAT ARE YOU SEEING THERE? MORE SHADOWS?
NO, TAYETE. IT'S JUST THAT PANTHER DEVIL YOU'RE NOT AFRAID OF.
AND I THOUGHT YOU WERE GOING TO PUT THAT MATOKE IN YOUR BELLY... NOT ALL OVER YOUR FACE.

"NOT HERE," WHIMPERS TAYETE, A WHIMPER HE WILL NOT RECALL IN FUTURE TELLINGS OF THIS MOMENT. "HE CAN'T BE HERE!" BENEATH THE MASK, THE PANTHER ALMOST SMILES.
THE SMILE NEVER APPEARS. FROM THE CENTRAL EDIFICE, WARRIORS APPEAR, AND THE GAY DISPLAY OF PLUMAGE AND WOOD BURNISHED SHIELDS BELIES THE PURPOSE OF THEIR DRESS.
THE FAINT TRACE OF HUMOR LEAVES HIS EYES. THROUGH THE MASK SLITS, THE PUPILS OF HIS EYES SEEM TO BURN IN AMBER AGONY. THIS IS NOT A DAY FOR HAPPY MEMORIES!
KEEP YOUR WEAPONS STILL, WARRIORS, AND LISTEN TO MY WORDS--
--OR ELSE THIS PLACE WILL BECOME A BATTLEGROUND BATHED IN BLOOD!
THIS IS A DAY OF DEATH!
W'KABI, HAVE YOUR FORCE KEEP THEIR AUTO-MATIC DEVASTATIONERS AT THE READY!
YOU MAY THINK THESE STRANGE WEAPONS ARE LESS DEADLY THAN YOUR SPEARS. THEY AREN'T!
AND THEY'VE YET TO BUILD A WEAPON THAT WILL NOT KILL!
YOU'D DO WELL TO REMEMBER THAT YOURSELF, T'CHALLA.
AND REALLY... DID YOU ACTUALLY HOPE TO TAKE US UNPREPARED?
ALLOW ME TO INTRO-DUCE MYSELF--
--AFTER THE HYDRAULIC SYSTEMS STRIP AWAY THE FACADE OF PRIMITIVISM YOU SO OBVIOUSLY FELL FOR.
ERIK... THAT'S KILLMONGER, T'CHALLA... ERIK CALLS ME LORD KARNAJ. AND IF IT PLEASES HIM, SO BE IT.
JUST NOW, HE'S NOT HERE, BUT I'LL EXTEND THE COURTESY I'M SURE HE'D WISH FOR YOU!
KARNAJ THRUSTS ASIDE THE ROBES, AND WEAPONS UNLIKE ANY THE PANTHER HAS SEEN BEFORE COME UNSHEATHED IN A BLUR OF DESTRUCTION.

IN EVERY WAR, THERE MUST BE A FIRST VICTIM.
THE FIRST SCREAM OF DEATH LIFTS INTO THE MORN AIR; THE FIRST SPLASH OF BLOOD IS UNEXPECTED, AS IF THEY THOUGHT VIOLENT DEATH RESIDED IN SOME ANTISEPTIC FANTASY LAND!
KRADADA! THEY'VE KILLED KRADADA!
THESE ARE SONIC DISRUPTORS, IF YOU'RE WONDERING. AND THEY ARE AS SUPERIOR TO YOUR AUTOMATIC DEVESTATIONERS AS THEY ARE TO THE SPEARS.
THE NAME IS LORD KARNAJ, T'CHALLA. AND IF ERIK CALLS ME THAT, THERE'S NO REASON WHY YOU CAN'T... WHILE YOU'RE STILL ABLE TO SPEAK!
BY THE VERY NATURE OF YOUR NAME, THERE SEEMS LITTLE CHANCE YOU'D LISTEN TO REASON.
WELL, LOOK, KARNAJ. WE WEREN'T TAKEN UNAWARE EITHER.
THAT'S A SECOND TASK FORCE, HITTING YOUR VILLAGE FROM THE OPPOSITE SIDE!
COME, COME, T'CHALLA, YOU SHOULDN'T PRIDE YOURSELF FOR SO SIMPLE A MANEUVER!
KRADADA'S DEATH WILL NOT GO UNAVENGED!
PERHAPS YOU'D CARE TO JOIN HIM IN HELL!
BUT JUDGING FROM YOUR HASTY MOVEMENT, I'D SAY NOT.
WITHOUT A DOUBT, YOU MUST BE W'KABI... T'CHALLA'S HEAD OF COURT SECURITY.
OH, DON'T LOOK SURPRISED, ERIK HAS MADE QUITE SURE ALL HIS LIEUTENANTS KNOW T'CHALLA'S KEY PERSONNEL BY SIGHT.
LASERS! THEY ARE USED IN MICRO-SURGERY, THEY ARE USED TO PIERCE DIAMONDS! AND THEY ARE ALSO USED AS ARMAMENT! THE DEADLY LASERS ON BARON MACABRE'S WRIST CAN BURN A THREE INCH HOLE THROUGH A HUMAN BODY WITHOUT EVEN AN INCREASE IN INTENSITY.
AND HE AIMS THOSE LASERS AT W'KABI'S VULNERABLE FLESH!

WAR DISORIENTS A MAN.
WHEN THE ACTUAL COMBAT FINALLY BEGINS THERE ARE SO MANY MINOR CONFLICTS WITHIN THE WHOLE THAT HE CANNOT KEEP TRACK OF THEM ALL.

SCATTERED VIOLENT INTERPLAYS RESOLVE THEMSELVES WHILE HE CONFRONTS HIS OWN CONFLICT. MOST OF THE INTERPLAYS ARE RESOLVED BY DEATH OR MAIMING.
THE HEAT FROM THE LASERS SCORCHES W'KABI'S FLESH, AND THE ONLY THING HE IS SURE OF IS THAT THE BLAST DID NOT COME FROM LORD KARNAJ.
SO YOU DON'T BELIEVE IN BARON MACABRE, HUH, W'KABI?

W'KABI TURNS TO SEE A HURTLING FIGURE OF PANTHERISH GRACE--

--TO WATCH AN ELBOW SNAP BACK AS IF A CONTINUATION OF THE FIRST SWING--

--TO SEE MACABRE'S SKULL-MASQUE BATTERED THRICE IN THE AMOUNT OF TIME IT WOULD HAVE TAKEN HIM TO THROW ONE PUNCH.

THE FIRST TIME HE HAD SEEN T'CHALLA IN THE SACROSANCT RELIGIOUS GARB OF THE PANTHER, IT HAD TAKEN HIS BREATH AWAY.
THE SAME REACTION HAPPENS NOW.
THERE WASN'T A CHANCE TO INTRODUCE YOU FORMALLY, W'KABI. BUT THAT WAS BARON MACABRE.
HE AND KING CADAVER WERE THE ONES WHO HELPED KILLMONGER RAID OUR HIDDEN UNDERGROUND MAN-MADE JUNGLE. UNFORTUNATELY, THEY FLED WHILE I WAS MAKING THAT DISCOVERY.

YOU'VE SURPRISED ME NO END SINCE YOU GAINED THAT SECRET. YOU ACT LIKE THE PANTHER I REMEMBER OF OLD, MY CHIEFTAIN.

IT'S BEEN A LONG TIME SINCE YOU'VE SAID THAT TITLE BY ANYTHING MORE THAN ROTE, W'KABI.

W'KABI'S HANDSHAKE IS FIRM; AND IN THE CLASPING OF HANDS SEVERED CAMARADERIE IS FORGED ANEW.

THE PRESENT BLURS, FADING TO ANOTHER TOUCH, OTHER EYES ASKING SOMETHING OF HIM.

PAST BECOMES REAL AS PRESENT--

--AND MIND-IMAGES, INCREDIBLY VIVID, REPLAY THEMSELVES. EACH NUANCE OF MONICA LYNNE'S VOICE COMES CLEARLY WITH THE MEMORY, DROWNING OUT THE DEATH-HYMN OF BATTLE.
THESE DAYS THE MADNESS OF THE OUTSIDE WORLD AFFECTS WAKANDA, MONICA.
THEY SEEM TO FEAR ANY BELIEFS DIFFERENT THAN THEIR OWN--AS IF THE VERY EXISTENCE OF A BELIEF CONTRARY TO THEIRS WOULD NEGATE OR THREATEN THEIR WAY OF LIFE.
NO, T'CHALLA, IT'S MORE THAN A CONFLICT OF IDEOLOGIES, NOW. I'VE SEEN SUSPICIONS AND BIGOTRY ERUPT INTO RIPPED FLESH AND DEAD BODIES...AND FOR LESS REASON THAN YOUR PEOPLE THINK THEY HAVE!
THEY BELIEVE SOME HEATHEN FOREIGNER KILLED ONE OF THEIR PEOPLE. MY FINGERPRINTS ON THAT WEAPON PUT ME RIGHT UP THE PROVERBIAL CREEK!
MAYBE A HUNDRED YEARS FROM TODAY, THEY'LL CHASTISE THEMSELVES FOR THEIR ACTIONS AND HAVE TALK SHOW DEBATES ABOUT THEIR ANCESTORS' BARBARISM.

BUT FOR TODAY, THEY NEED A VICTIM. AND I'M IT!!
THAT'S QUITE A SCRIPT AND ROLE YOU'VE GIVEN YOURSELF. BUT IT'S NOT GOING TO TURN OUT THAT WAY.
BECAUSE I KNOW HOW YOU WERE FRAMED FOR ZATAMA'S MURDER, MONICA! AND SOON...I'LL HAVE EVIDENCE THAT WILL PROVE IT!

LIKE THE SHUTTER-EFFECT ON A SLIDE PROJECTOR CLICKING FROM ONE PAST IMAGE TO THE NEXT, EACH SCENE COMPLETE UNTO ITSELF IN ONE SEARING FLASH, THE PANTHER RECALLS THE LONELY NIGHT HOURS AFTERWARD.

HE CROUCHES. PATIENTLY.
AT FIRST, THE PASSING SHADOWY WILD-LIFE GIVES HIM WIDE BERTH--
--BUT AS THE HOURS STRETCH TO MIDNIGHT AND BEYOND, HE BECOMES A PART OF THE JUNGLE LAND-SCAPE.
UNTIL THE ROUTINE IS BROKEN...BY THE APPROACH OF A LESS CAUTIOUS HUMAN.

HE IS AS A BROTHER TO THE NIGHT.
WITHOUT PANIC, WITHOUT HASTE, HE USES THE BRANCH AS A SPRINGBOARD TO LAUNCH HIM-SELF, A NOCTURNAL MISSILE THAT HITS ITS TARGET WITH STUNNING IMPACT!

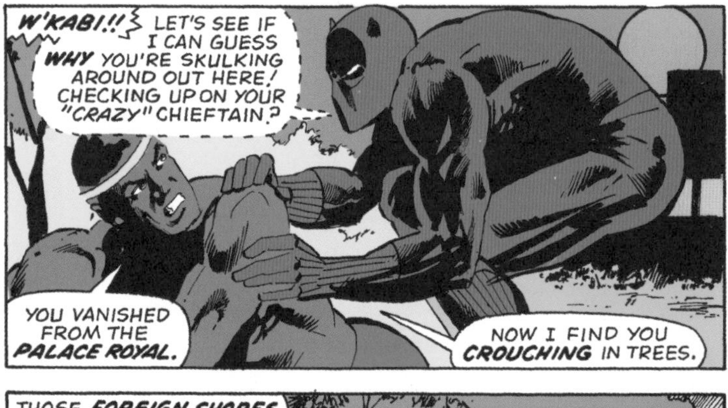
W'KABI!!
LET'S SEE IF I CAN GUESS WHY YOU'RE SKULKING AROUND OUT HERE! CHECKING UP ON YOUR "CRAZY" CHIEFTAIN?
YOU VANISHED FROM THE PALACE ROYAL.
NOW I FIND YOU CROUCHING IN TREES.

THOSE FOREIGN SHORES HAVE CHANGED YOU.
YOU ARE NOT THE SAME MAN WHO TOOK OVER AS THIS COUNTRY'S LEADER WHEN HIS FATHER WAS MURDERED BY OUTWORLDERS!

YOU'RE RIGHT, W'KABI.
I AM FAR WISER THESE DAYS. ONLY MY WISDOM COMES TOO SLOWLY--
--AND PERHAPS TOO LATE!

BE STILL, W'KABI!
I HAVE BEEN WAITING FOR ZATAMA'S MURDERER--
--AND TO USE ONE OF THOSE OUTWORLDER'S PHRASES, I THINK THE "GAME'S AFOOT!"

WITH TWO QUICK STEPS, HE SPRINGS, RISING AN INCREDIBLE 10 FEET INTO THE AIR AMONG THE SPIDERY NETWORK OF TREE LIMBS!

HE HEARS THE FAINT TREAD OF FURTIVE MOVEMENT--

--A BUSH CARELESSLY BRUSHED AGAINST--
--A THORN SCRAPING FLESH!
THE PANTHER WAITS. HE IS THE CAT ONCE MORE.

HE LANDS SILENTLY, READY TO POUNCE UPON HIS PREY. THE FIGURE MOVES, UNAWARE THAT IT IS BEING STALKED--
--MOVES OUT ONTO THE SOFT SAND THAT LIES PAST THE AMBER PAGODA. BEYOND, THE RIVER OF GRACE AND WISDOM'S SERENE CURRENT CARRIES ITS TITLE DOWNSTREAM.

HIS SHADOW REACHES FORWARD AS HE CLOSES IN.
THE PANTHER SUPPOSES HE SHOULD LAUGH IN THE OBSCENE MANNER OF AN AMERICAN PULP HERO--
--AND HE FROWNS, REALIZING THERE IS SOME TRUTH IN W'KABI'S RANTINGS.

THE CRIMSON MOONLIGHT SPILLS THE PANTHER'S SHADOW FURTHER--
--TOUCHING NEAR THE HOLE IN THE EARTH THAT HAS BECOME THE "MAGUFFIN" OF THE ACT, AS HITCHCOCK WOULD PUT IT!
DAMN! HE THINKS. MUST ALL OF HIS REFERENCE POINTS BE SO FOREIGN TO HIS NATIVE LAND?

ENOUGH TIME SPENT ON SELF-RECRIMINATION!
RECOGNIZE THIS, TANZIKA?
T'CHALLA!
I ASKED FOR AN ANSWER, TANZIKA. I KNOW WHO I AM. AND I ALSO KNOW THIS IS THE WEAPON YOU USED TO KILL ZATAMA!
W'KABI THOUGHT THIS WAS A SPEAR. BUT HE WAS WRONG! IT'S A SIMPLE TWO-SECTION SHISH KEBAB STICK THAT MONICA USED WHEN YOU SERVED DINNER...OR AT LEAST IT WAS--

--UNTIL YOU UNSCREWED THE TWO SECTIONS AND ADDED A THIRD SECTION TO THE MIDDLE--
--LEAVING MONICA'S PRINTS ALL OVER THE HANDLE OF YOUR MURDER WEAPON!
YOU CAN'T PROVE ANY OF THAT!
NOT FAST ENOUGH, TANZIKA!
I BAITED YOU EARLIER TONIGHT WITH THOSE LINES ABOUT EVIDENCE...HOPING THERE WAS SOME AND THAT YOU'D PANIC.
IT WAS THE MOTIVE I NEEDED. AND HERE IT IS!

PICTURES TAKEN AT A ROMANTIC TRYST? KEEPING MEMENTOES OF YOUR DAYS WITH ZATAMA, WERE YOU, TANZIKA?
KNOWING ZATAMA, HE'D WANT A THING LIKE THIS KEPT QUIET. ROMANTIC INTERLUDES WITH THE PALACE ROYAL'S LADIES MIGHT HAVE DILUTED HIS GOAL AS A SELF-MADE REVOLUTIONARY.
SPOILS THE IMAGE. RIGHT?

HE CALLED ME A CHILD.
HE CALLED ME PETTY AND IGNORANT! ME?!!
I TOLD HIM HE COULDN'T JUST USE ME AND THROW ME AWAY.
AND I'LL BE DOING WAKANDA A FAVOR PUTTING YOU OUT OF YOUR MISERY!
CLOSE SHOT! BUT CLOSE ISN'T GOOD ENOUGH, TANZIKA.
AND THOUGH I CAN SENSE YOUR PAIN, I CANNOT EXCUSE HOW YOU USED MONICA'S VULNERABILITY..
--AND IT DISTURBS ME THAT YOU WILL NEVER REALIZE HOW YOU CALLOUSLY USED HER IN MUCH THE MANNER YOU FEEL ZATAMA USED YOU!

TRANSITIONS. PAST TO PRESENT.
HATRED EXPRESSING ITSELF IN DARK EYES IS REPLACED BY A REAFFIRMATION OF TRUST.
AND A SELF-INDULGENT FEROCITY FEEDING GLUTTONOUSLY UPON ITS OWN SPITE FADES--
--FADES BACK INTO MEMORY...
...THAT RANDOM COLLECTION OF PERSONAL DATA THAT SHAPES AND MOLDS FUTURE DECISIONS.
THAT MOMENT OF OBLIVION HAS A QUIET INTENSITY FOR BOTH MEN THAT IS FAR LONGER THAN THE TOTAL OF ITS SECONDS.
THE WAR HAS CLAIMED THEM AGAIN, SWEPT THEM UP INTO ITS MIDST.
MALICE!!
KEEP CLEAR OF THAT TRIDENT, MY CHIEFTAIN!
IT'S BEEN SOME TIME SINCE OUR LAST MEETING, PANTHER. I SEE YOU'VE BEEN KEEPING YOURSELF FIT!
IF I HADN'T, I WOULDN'T BE AROUND TO HEAR YOUR WARNING, W'KABI!
THERE'S AN ABSURD REALITY ABOUT WAR.
YOU PREPARE FOR IT IN THE LONG WAITING HOURS BEFORE IT ACTUALLY BEGINS ONLY TO LEARN IT IS AN EXPERIENCE THAT CANNOT BE PREPARED FOR.
UNLIKE W'KABI, TAKU HAS NOT LOOKED FORWARD TO THIS DAY. HE HAS KNOWN IT MUST COME, AND HE HAS INTELLECTUALLY STEELED HIMSELF FOR THE ATROCITIES HE KNOWS MUST OCCUR.
EXCEPT THERE IS A BIG DIFFERENCE BETWEEN KNOWING SOMETHING INTELLECTUALLY AND HAVING TO EXPERIENCE THE BRUTALITY FIRST HAND.

WAR CANNOT BE CONTAINED WITHIN BOUNDARIES. NOR CAN IT BE EASILY DIRECTE
YOU'VE TURNED YOUR BACK ON ME, T'CHALLA. YOU MUST ADMIT, THAT'S VERY CARELESS OF YOU.
OR PERHAPS I HAVEN'T WON YOUR RESPECT YET. ERIK HAS SAID YOU ARE QUITE POMPOUS, AND ALSO A PRETENTIOUS QUOTER OF NONSENSICAL RHETORIC.
WHATEVER THE CASE MAY BE, I THINK ONCE YOUR FLESH TASTES THE BITE OF MY SONIC DISRUPTORS, I'LL EARN YOUR RESPECT.
ALAS, YOU'LL PROBABLY BE IN YOUR DEATH THROES BY THEN.
NOT QUITE, KARNAJ.
BUT YOU'VE MADE YOUR POINT. DON'T FEEL LEFT OUT. I'M DEALING WITH YOU NEXT!
YOU OUGHT TO W
THERE ISN'T ANYO
WHO HAS MALIC
UNDER CONTROL.
REMEMBER THA
IN WAR, THERE IS NO USE CRYING, "I WANT NOTHING TO DO WITH YOUR FEUD. I DO NOT WA
TO DIE!" WORDS, UNFORTUNATELY, CAN NOT SAVE YOU IN THE MIDST OF COMBAT; AND COMB
ALSO UNFORTUNATELY, HAS LITTLE RESPECT FOR AGE OR RACE OR SEX OR SHOE SIZE.

WAR NOT ONLY AFFECTS ITS PERPETRATORS AND ITS PARTICIPANTS. IT RAVAGES ALL IT TOUCHES, AND SCARS MUCH PAST THAT.
INNOCENTS DIE ALONGSIDE WARRIORS, AND SOME WARRIORS ARE AS INNOCENT AS THE CIVILIANS WHOSE FATES AWAIT THE OUTCOME OF THE CONFLICT.
I'VE GOT MALICE UNDER CONTROL, MY CHIEFTAIN!
WAR, AT TIMES, IS VERY COSMOPOLITAN!

THIS IS TAKU...
WHACK!
HE WAS A GENTLE, SENSITIVE MAN.

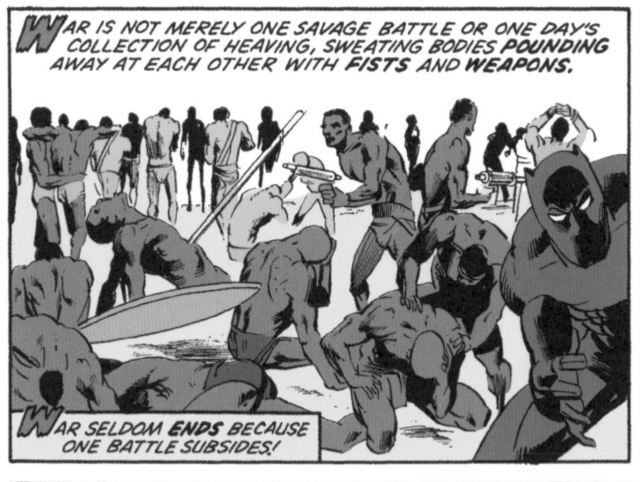
WAR IS NOT MERELY ONE SAVAGE BATTLE OR ONE DAY'S COLLECTION OF HEAVING, SWEATING BODIES POUNDING AWAY AT EACH OTHER WITH FISTS AND WEAPONS.
WAR SELDOM ENDS BECAUSE ONE BATTLE SUBSIDES!

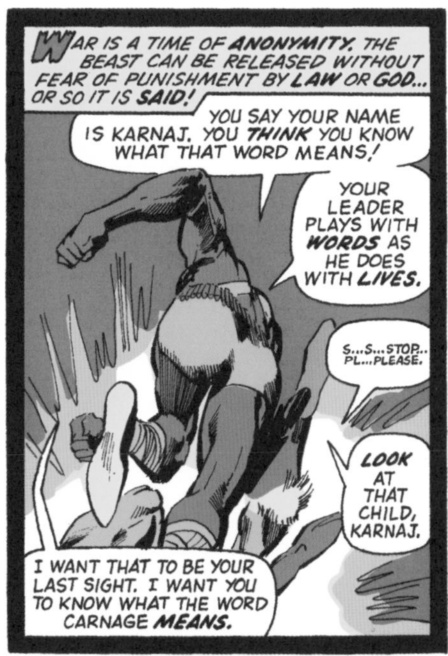
WAR IS A TIME OF ANONYMITY. THE BEAST CAN BE RELEASED WITHOUT FEAR OF PUNISHMENT BY LAW OR GOD... OR SO IT IS SAID!
YOU SAY YOUR NAME IS KARNAJ. YOU THINK YOU KNOW WHAT THAT WORD MEANS!
YOUR LEADER PLAYS WITH WORDS AS HE DOES WITH LIVES.
S...S...STOP... PL...PLEASE.
LOOK AT THAT CHILD, KARNAJ.
I WANT THAT TO BE YOUR LAST SIGHT. I WANT YOU TO KNOW WHAT THE WORD CARNAGE MEANS.

TAKU, OLD FRIEND.
LET ME GO, MY CHIEFTAIN. I'M GOING TO KILL HIM.
WOULD THAT MEAN YOU ARE NO LONGER THE OBSERVER?
THE CHILD...

YOU'VE SEEN MEN GROW LOST IN THE JOURNEY TO VENGEANCE.
W'KABI'S DRAGON. REMEMBER?

I STILL DO NOT UNDERSTAND YOUR MEANING, MY CHIEFTAIN.
BUT I HAVE SEEN A SIDE OF TAKU TODAY THAT I THOUGHT HE LACKED--
--A SIDE I NOW WISH HE DID NOT HAVE.
THIS IS THE DAY YOU DESIRED, W'KABI. WAS IT ANYTHING LIKE YOU EXPECTED?
THEY WERE EVIL! WE COULD NOT LET THIS CONTINUE.
YOUR POINT IS WELL TAKEN, W'KABI--
--BUT OFT-TIMES, ONCE YOU SLAY THE DRAGON--
ITS BLOOD STAINS MORE THAN YOUR HANDS!
NEXT LAND OF THE CHILLING MISTS

# *JUNGLE ACTION* #12,
NOVEMBER 1974

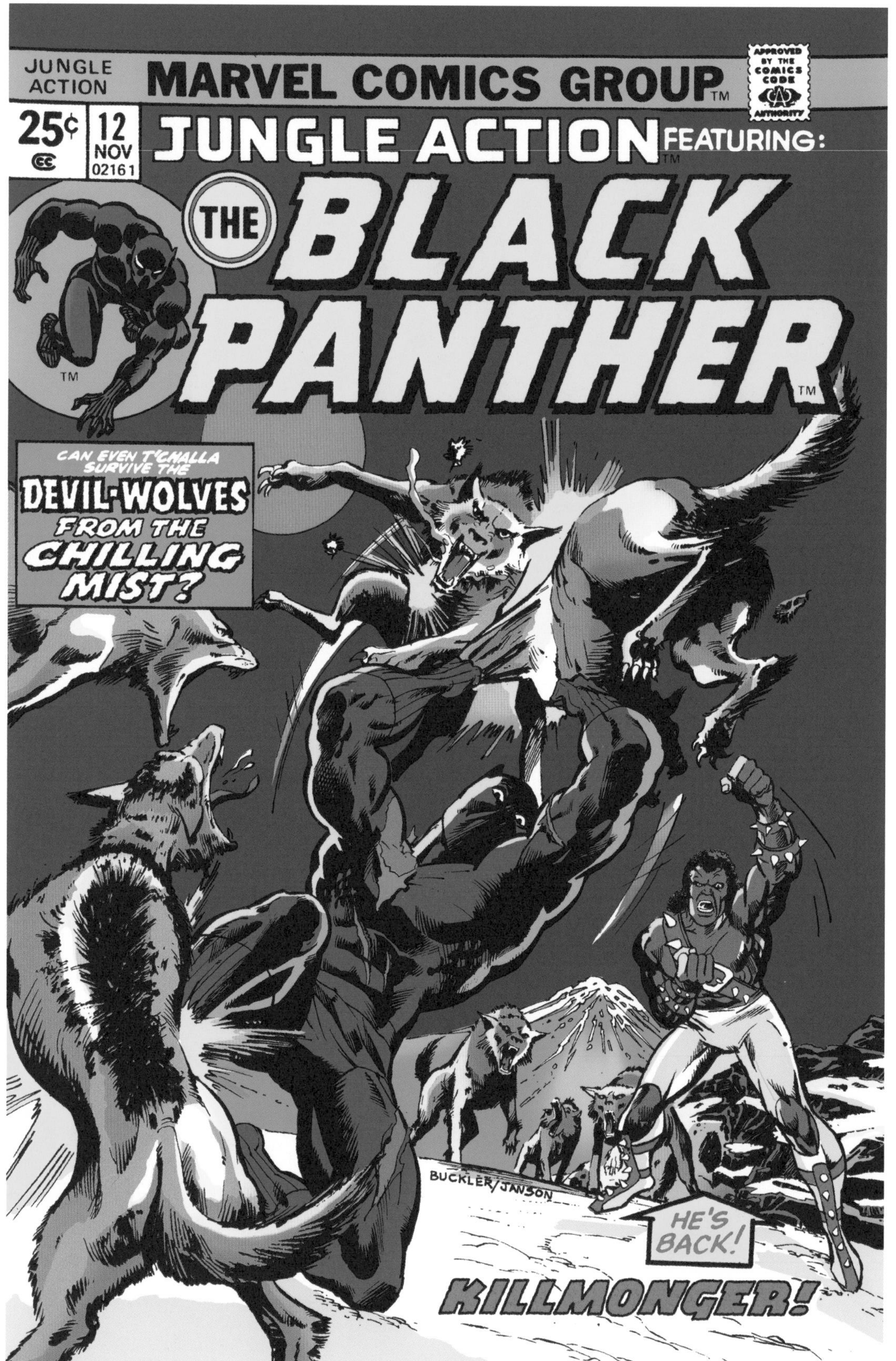
JUNGLE ACTION
MARVEL COMICS GROUP
APPROVED BY THE COMICS CODE AUTHORITY
25¢
12 NOV
02161
JUNGLE ACTION FEATURING:
THE BLACK PANTHER
CAN EVEN T'CHALLA SURVIVE THE
DEVIL-WOLVES
FROM THE
CHILLING
MIST?
BUCKLER/JANSON
HE'S BACK!
KILLMONGER!

Stan Lee PRESENTS: THE BLACK PANTHER! TM
THE MIST IS CARNIVORE PINK... A LIVING, WRITHING ENTITY THAT DEVOURS THE SWAYING BRIDGE AT ITS MIDSECTION. ITS DESTINATION IS OBLITERATED!
THE MIST THREATENS TO DEVOUR THE TWO TINY CRAFTS WHICH PENETRATE ITS OMINOUS VEIL... A PROTECTIVE, VINDICTIVE MOTHER PROTECTING ITS BROOD.
THE BLACK PANTHER STANDS POISED ON THE SONAR-SKIMMER... AND TO THE TWO UNWILLING PASSENGERS INSIDE THE CRAFT, HE IS NOT HUMAN... HE IS MORE LIKE THE GREAT BLACK CAT, PROWLING IN THE NIGHT SHADOWS, AMBER EYES TAKING IN EVERYTHING... WITHOUT ONCE EVER MOVING!
PANTHER'S RAGE:
BLOOD STAINS ON VIRGIN SNOW!
DON McGREGOR, WRITER
BILLY GRAHAM & KLAUS JANSON, ARTISTS
GLYNIS WEIN, COLORIST
DAVE HUNT, LETTERER
ROY THOMAS, EDITOR
WHAT'S HE DOING NOW, TAYETE?
DON'T LOOK, KAZIBE! YOU DON'T WANT TO SEE!!
I'M NOT WEAK LIKE YOU, KAZIBE, BUT EVEN I HAVE TROUBLE BEARING UP UNDER THIS STRAIN. WE'RE GOING TO CRASH! I KNOW IT!
I KNOW IT!

THE MID-MORNING AFRICAN HEAT COOLS, LIKE WARMTH FADING FROM THE FLESH OF A CORPSE. AFRICA IS A LAND OF EXTREME ATMOSPHERIC CONTRASTS, AND THE HIDDEN NATION OF WAKANDA IS SUBJECT TO THAT CLIMATE DICTATE.
BUT THERE IS SOMETHING MORE THAN NATURE THAT CAUSES THE CHILL RISING FROM THE FATHOMLESS DEPTHS. THE FOG-SHROUDED MOUNTAINTOPS GLISTEN TIMELESS HOARFROST.
BEYOND, AT THE OTHER EDGE OF INFINITY, LIES THE LAND OF THE CHILLING MIST!
ALL RIGHT, TAYETE. WE'RE HERE! NOW WE'LL LEARN IF YOU YOU HAVE SPOKEN THE TRUTH.
WH...WHAT DO YOU MEAN, PANTHER-DEVIL?
I MEAN THAT YOU'RE GOING INTO THE LAND OF THE CHILLING MIST WITH ME.
BUT I'M SURE THAT DOESN'T FRIGHTEN YOU, DOES IT, TAYETE?

IT'S NOT FRIGHT THAT CAUSES ME TO SPEAK, PANTHER-DEVIL, BUT THERE ARE OTHER THINGS YOU MUST... UHM...
...CONSIDER?
I'VE CONSIDERED ALL THAT YOU'VE TOLD ME IN THE PAST WEEK, TAYETE, REMEMBER THAT!!
PERHAPS IT WAS DREAMS OF POWER THAT RULED YOUR THOUGHTS, TAYETE AND KAZIBE, WHEN YOU DECIDED TO FOLLOW ERIK KILLMONGER IN HIS REVOLUTION.

I'D LIKE TO BELIEVE YOU DID NOT KNOW KILLMONGER WOULD BE SO RUTHLESS IN HIS STRATEGEMS...
...TO OVERTHROW MY REIGN OF WAKANDA. HE WOULD NOT DEBATE. HE WOULD SLAUGHTER!
AND NOW YOU TELL ME HE HAS GONE INTO THESE MYTHICAL MISTS... WITH KING CADAVER.
YOU'D BETTER BE AFRAID. IF YOU'VE LIED TO ME, I'LL UNLEASH MY RAGE FOR KILLMONGER UPON YOU!

MONICA LYNNE WATCHES HIM APPROACH. EBON ANGER DARKENS HIS AMBER EYES.
YOU DON'T HAVE ANY IDEA WHAT COULD GO DOWN OUT THERE, DO YOU, T'CHALLA?
NO, MONICA. BUT I MUST MAKE THIS TREK.
BUT WHY ALONE? AT LEAST TAKE W'KABI WITH YOU.
W'KABI IS CHIEF OF COURT SECURITY. AND WITH ALL OUR PRISONERS AT THE PALACE THERE IS MUCH FOR HIM TO MAKE SECURE.
BESIDES, ULTIMATELY, THIS BATTLE IS BETWEEN KILLMONGER AND I, AND IF HE HAS GONE INTO THIS FORBIDDEN LAND ...THERE IS A REASON FOR IT. KILLMONGER DOES NOTHING THAT DOES NOT HAVE A PURPOSE!

TAYETE, WHY IS HE TAKING OFF OUR CHAINS?
OBVIOUSLY, KAZIBE, IT'S BECAUSE... WHY ARE YOU FREEING US?
THE WORLD CHANGES IN AWESOME UPHEAVALS, AS IF TO REFLECT MY STATE OF MIND.
HOW DOES A LEADER TEACH HIS PEOPLE SUCH A THING AS A RESPECT FOR LIFE?

...AND HOW DOES HE KEEP THAT PRINCIPLE FIRM UNTO HIMSELF WHEN CALLOUS ATROCITIES TRANSPIRE AROUND HIM.
MANY OF YOUR PEOPLE HAVE THAT RESPECT. BUT THERE ARE NO SIMPLE ANSWERS.
T'CHALLA SAYS TO GIVE YOU THIS SPEAR. I DON'T AGREE WITH OUR CHIEFTAIN...
...BUT THEN I'VE BEEN WRONG ABOUT HIM BEFORE.
COMPASSION ISN'T ALWAYS AN INSTINCTIVE TRAIT IN THE HUMAN ANIMAL.
ME?
YOU.
YOU'RE RIGHT, AS USUAL. I HAVE SEEN TOO MANY OF THE DESTRUCTIVE BREED OF LATE--
--BUT YOU HAVE TAUGHT ME OF THE SELFLESS AND CREATIVE SIDES OF HUMANITY.

THEIR HANDS TOUCH BRIEFLY, AND THE PANTHER WISHES HE COULD STAY WITHIN THE SHELTERED SUCCOR OF HER WARMTH ...BUT SHE HAS GIVEN HIM THE STRENGTH TO TURN AND TREAD CAT-LIKE ONTO THE BECKONING BRIDGE.
HE GOES TO ANOTHER BATTLE, TAKU. THE LAST FIGHT SCARRED BOTH HE AND YOU.
THE SPIRIT CAN BE BROKEN AS EASILY AS BONES, MISS LYNNE--

--AND THE AGONY OF THAT SCAR CUTS TWICE AS DEEP--
--AND OFTEN TAKES TWICE AS LONG TO MEND.
YOU'VE GOT IT TOGETHER, TAKU. THERE AREN'T ANY SPLINTS FOR THE MIND.

AND SOMETIMES WE ARE NOT EVEN AWARE ANYTHING IS BROKEN.
COULD WE GO NOW, TAKU? SUDDENLY I'M COLD ...SO VERY COLD.

THE BRIDGE HAS SPANNED CENTURIES TO ITS UNKNOWN DESTINATION. ITS MAKER AND ORIGINAL PURPOSE ARE GENERATIONS FORGOTTEN--
--EXCEPT IN LEGENDS!
THE PANTHER FEELS THE SCARLET HAZE CONSUME THEM, THE CHILL TURNING STEADILY COLDER AS THE BRIDGE PROTESTS THEIR PASSING, SWAYING WITH TREACHEROUS REPRISAL!
THE WIND TEARS AT THEM, AND THE THREE OF THEM ARE BATHED IN THE CRUEL, PINK MIST--
--UNTIL, LIKE THE SUN, THEY ARE SLICED RAW BY IT--
--AS IF THE LEGENDS WERE AWARE THAT A MERE MORTAL DARED INVADE THEIR BOUNDARIES--
--AND THAT, FOR ALL PRACTICAL PURPOSES, HE DARED TO DO IT... ALONE!
PANTHER-DEVIL!
I... I WAS JU.. JUST WONDERING IF YOU WERE WARM ENOUGH.
MAKE IT QUICK, TAYETE. IF YOU ARE TRYING TO STALL FOR TIME YOU MIGHT HAVE NO TIME LEFT AT ALL!
THEIR BREATH FORMS INTO VAPOR, REMINDING THEM THAT IT IS THE CEASELESS PUMPING OF THEIR LUNGS WHICH KEEPS THEM ALIVE.
TAYETE IS CONVINCED. T'CHALLA IS NOT HUMAN. IT IS A DECEPTION THE PANTHER IS IN NO HURRY TO DISCREDIT.
AND THEN IT IS THERE BEFORE THEM. THE LAND OF THE CHILLING MIST! IT IS AS BLEAK AS HIS MEMORIES OF THE RAID ON KILLMONGER'S COMMAND VILLAGE
THE TWO BLEAKNESSES, SPIRITUAL AND PHYSICAL, COMBINE. AND HE STANDS, DWARFED BY THE IMMENSITY OF HIS SURROUNDINGS...
...ASSAULTED BY THE MAGNITUDE OF HIS TASK. AND HE WONDERS, DARKLY, IF ANY ACTION HE TAKES WILL RETURN WAKANDA TO TRANQUILITY... OR IF ANY PATH HE TAKES WILL END IN INSIGNIFICANCE!

THE CHILL FACTOR IS RISING TOWARDS 50 DEGREES BELOW ZERO. ERIK KILLMONGER DOES NOT SEEM TO NOTICE, NOR DOES THE ANKLE DEEP SNOW SLOW HIS ARROGANT STRIDE!
THEY ARE NEARING THE ALTAR OF RESSURECTION, AND HE IS ANXIOUS FOR THE RITUALS TO BEGIN. SOMBRE WILL BE WAITING... FOR HE IS THE ORACLE OF THE RESSURECTION ALTAR!
I NO LONGER FEAR THIS PLACE. THE FIRST TIME WE CROSSED THAT BRIDGE, I COULD NOT STOP SWEATING. THE COLD NUMBED ME, BUT I COULD NOT STOP SWEATING.
YOU WERE NOT THE SAME BEING THEN.
HEEL, PREYY! STAY WITH ME!
YOU LIVED IN IGNORANCE BACK THEN, KING CADAVER. AND THE TITLE OF "KING OF ANYTHING" WAS NOT IN YOUR FUTURE IN THOSE DAYS.
BUT IT IS NOW!
NOW YOU ARE KING CADAVER... JUST AS I AM NO LONGER N'JADAKA, BUT ERIK KILLMONGER. I LIKE THE INSOLENCE OF THE NAME ERIK... BUT YOU CANNOT APPRECIATE THAT SINCE YOU HAVE NEVER LIVED IN WESTERN CIVILIZATION.
AND THIS IS THE PLACE WHERE YOUR TRANSFORMATION BEGAN. MORTAL CONCERNS ARE PAST YOU, YOUR MENTAL PROWESS HAS BEEN INCREASED TEN-FOLD... MEN WHO WERE ONCE YOUR EQUAL ARE NOW SUBJECT TO YOUR MARAUDING THEIR MINDS--
--THOUGH HOW THAT IDEALISTIC CHILD, T'CHALLA, MANAGED TO KEEP YOU FROM PLUNDERING HIS TENDER LITTLE PSYCHE IS A PUZZLEMENT.
HE IS RESOURCEFUL. DON'T YOU CONTEMPLATE T'CHALLA'S MOVEMENTS WHILE YOU ARE AWAY FROM WAKANDA?
"NEVER!"

THE ENTRANCE IS CHISELLED IN IRIDESCENT ICE, THAT SHIFTS COLORS... AN **ELEMENTAL KALEIDOSCOPE,** FRAGMENTING DESIGNS IN SHADES OF DEPTHLESS WHITES AND BURNING AMETHYST.

THE CAVERN HAS THE ATMOSPHERE OF A **MONASTERY** ...SACRED, ECHOING SILENCE OFF ITS ROCK-HEWN CEILINGS. AN **UNNATURAL HEAT** PULSES RHYTHMICALLY, CLASHING WITH THE GLACIAL AIR BEYOND ITS PORTAL.

**SOMBRE** APPEARS FROM THE FUMES, ALMOST AS IF HE IS A PART OF THEM... AND HIS PLACID WELCOME IS COUNTERED BY **SOULLESS EYES,** GLEAMING BEHIND A MASK THAT HAS BEEN **WELDED** TO FLESH!

WELCOME, ERIK. I TRUST YOU HAD A **SAFE** JOURNEY?

AH, I SEE THE **GOOD KING** IS WITH YOU.

YES. AND HE SPEAKS OF **RESOURCES,** SOMBRE. AND I WAS ABOUT TO TELL HIM, RESOURCES COME FROM THE **LAND...**

...AND THIS LAND IS NOT T'CHALLA'S ANYMORE. IT IS **MINE!**

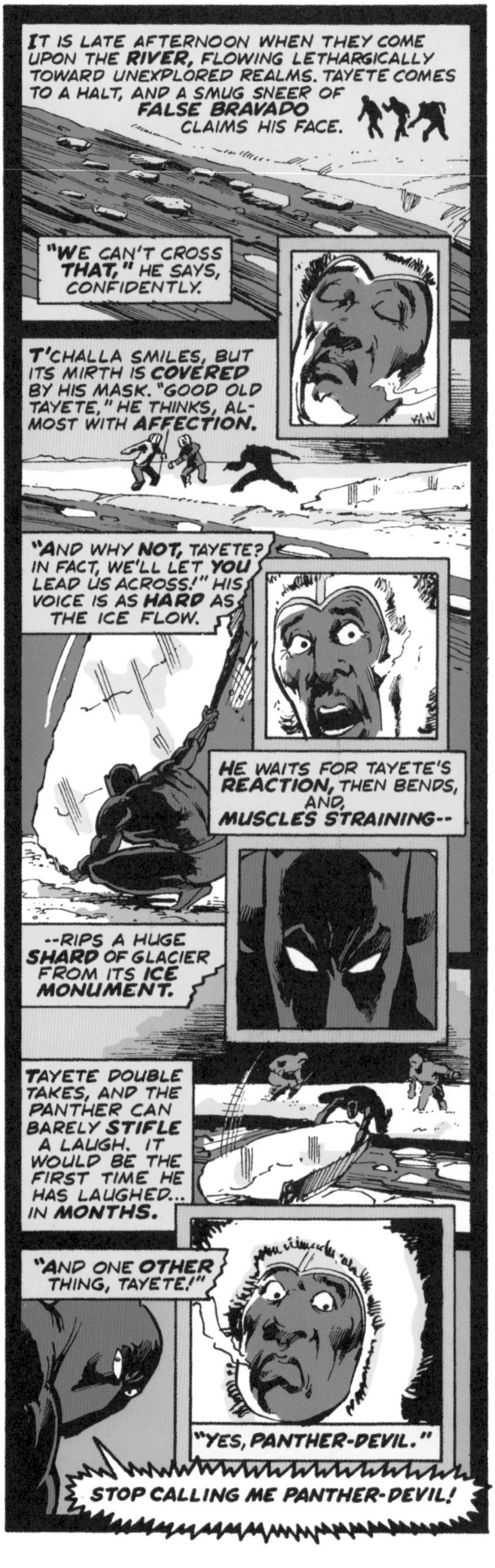

**I**T IS LATE AFTERNOON WHEN THEY COME UPON THE **RIVER,** FLOWING LETHARGICALLY TOWARD UNEXPLORED REALMS. TAYETE COMES TO A HALT, AND A SMUG SNEER OF **FALSE BRAVADO** CLAIMS HIS FACE.

"**W**E CAN'T CROSS **THAT,**" HE SAYS, CONFIDENTLY.

**T'**CHALLA SMILES, BUT ITS MIRTH IS **COVERED** BY HIS MASK. "GOOD OLD TAYETE," HE THINKS, ALMOST WITH **AFFECTION.**

"**A**ND WHY **NOT,** TAYETE? IN FACT, WE'LL LET **YOU** LEAD US ACROSS!" HIS VOICE IS AS **HARD** AS THE ICE FLOW.

**HE** WAITS FOR TAYETE'S **REACTION,** THEN BENDS, AND, **MUSCLES STRAINING--**

--RIPS A HUGE **SHARD** OF GLACIER FROM ITS **ICE MONUMENT.**

**T**AYETE DOUBLE TAKES, AND THE PANTHER CAN BARELY **STIFLE** A LAUGH. IT WOULD BE THE FIRST TIME HE HAS LAUGHED... IN **MONTHS.**

"**A**ND ONE **OTHER** THING, TAYETE!"

"YES, PANTHER-DEVIL."

**STOP CALLING ME PANTHER-DEVIL!**

NOW COME FORWARD, TAYETE. IF ANY MORE TIME IS WASTED, I'LL HELP YOU ACROSS.
HE'S NOT SERIOUS, IS HE, KAZIBE? PANTHER-DE... I MEAN, YOU AREN'T SERIOUS ABOUT...
TAYETE, PLEASE, DON'T ANGER HIM!
NOW?
RIGHT NOW!
THE FROST CURRENT SURGES PAST ICEBERGS... AND THEY ARE LIKE FROZEN DREAMS TURNED TO BITTER ILLUSIONS!
CAREFUL, TAYETE. ONE SLIP AND DEATH IS AS SWIFT AS THE RIVER'S FLOW!
BUT IT IS NOT SLIPPING TAYETE HAS TO WORRY ABOUT. THE ICE, LIKE THE PANTHER'S DREAMS, SHATTERS!
THE PANTHER HAS NOT LIED! THE TOUCH OF THAT LIQUID IS DEATH!
THE PANTHER TENSES FOR THE LEAP, AND THEN SPRINGS... TENSION UNLEASHED... EYES JUDGING THE DISTANCE TO THE OPPOSITE SHORE!
THE SHEER MOMENTUM OF HIS LEAP CARRIES BOTH OF THEM TO SAFETY.
YOUR LUCK HAS NOT YET RUN OUT, TAYETE.
EVEN IF YOU'D MANAGED TO SWIM ASHORE, THE MOST RAGING FIRE COULD NOT STOP THE ONSLAUGHT OF FROSTBITE!
NIGHT COMES. AND THE WIND-CHILL FACTOR WILL REACH MORE THAN 100 DEGREES BELOW ZERO. THEN, ANY HEAVY BREATHING WILL TURN THE TISSUE OF YOUR LUNGS TO ICE!
NOW WHERE WOULD KILLMONGER HEAD?
UP THERE... RESSURECTION ALTAR WAITS.
AND AGAIN, THE ENORMITY OF THIS LAND AND HIS TASK ENGULF HIM ...AND HE WISHES IT WERE DONE ...ONE WAY ...OR THE OTHER!

THE CEREMONY IS NEARLY OVER.
KILLMONGER HAS NO IDEA WHEN THE PIECE OF BURNT-OUT STAR, BLAZING SUPER-NOVAE IN ITS CELESTIAL WAKE, CRASHED TO EARTH. HE HAS NEVER SEEN WHAT IT LOOKS LIKE. THE CAVERN IS ITS COFFIN!
FROM THE RADIENT DEPTHS, QUASAR-LIKE RAYS BATHE THE ALTAR IN LAMBENT STRENGTH. IT IS AN ODD DESCRIPTION, CONSIDERS KILLMONGER, BUT IT MOST ACCURATELY DEFINES THE EFFECT OF THESE CORUSCANT BEAMS.
FLESH BECOMES MALLEABLE, LIKE DRIPPING WAX. HUMAN FEATURES TURN TO HOT LIQUID... THEN RESOLIDIFY--
--INTO NEW SHAPES... WITHIN... AND WITHOUT!
THE FIRST TIME YOU BROUGHT HIM HERE, HE WAS A NORMAL MAN AND SCREAMED WHEN WE STRAPPED HIM TO THE ALTAR.
HE IS NO LONGER AFRAID.
SOMBRE HAS BEEN EXPOSED TO THESE RAYS FOR SO LONG, THAT UNDER HIS ROBES HE SEEMS WRAITH-LIKE!
NATURALLY. CADAVER HAS BEEN RESURRECTED. HIS FORMER LIFE HAS CEASED TO EXIST.
FROM THE ASHES OF FLESH COME SUPERIOR PHOENIXES! WHAT DOES PHYSICAL APPEARANCE MATTER TO HIM NOW, SOMBRE ...OR TO YOU?
THE RAYS HAVE TRANSFORMED HIM FROM MERE HUMAN... AND THERE ARE FEW HUMANS THAT ARE CONTENT WITH WHAT THEY ARE.
IF THAT WERE NOT THE CASE, I WOULD HAVE NO FOLLOWERS TO OVERTHROW WAKANDA'S GREAT DREAMER, T'CHALLA.
PERHAPS YOU'D CARE TO TELL ME ABOUT IT IN PERSON, KILLMONGER!

OR IS BACKSTABBING MORE YOUR STYLE?
KAZIBE, DON'T HE KNOW? YOU JUST DON'T SAY THINGS LIKE THAT TO KILLMONGER.
KILLMONGER TURNS ABOUT, NONCHALANTLY.. AS IF THE PANTHER'S ARRIVAL WERE A WEARISOME, BUT EXPECTED NUISANCE!
HEARTBEATS MEASURE SECONDS OF SILENT CONFLICT!
AND THEN, THEY BOTH MOVE TO ATTACK!
IT HAS BEEN NEAR THREE MONTHS OF BLOODSHED SINCE THESE TWO ADVERSARIES HAVE FACED EACH OTHER--
--THREE MONTHS THAT BECOMES THE DISTANCE BETWEEN ONE OF THOSE HEARTBEATS, AS IF THIS NEW FIGHT IS AN EXTENSION OF THE FIRST!

THIS MOMENT HAS BEEN LONG AWAITED, KILLMONGER!
YOU WAITED FOR SO SHORT A MOMENT?
A MOMENT OF AMUSEMENT, NO LESS.

TO THE PANTHER'S ASTONISHMENT, KILLMONGER'S FACE DOES NOT EXPRESS DEFEAT--
--RATHER, HE IS OVERWHELMED BY HIS FOE'S SUPERIORITY! HE IS KILLMONGER'S TAYETE!!
HE IS A CHILD ONCE MORE, HAND WRESTLING WITH HIS FATHER...AND THOUGH HE CAN BARELY WAGE A CONTEST, HIS FATHER LETS HIM WIN!

THOSE DAYS ARE GONE! LIKE HIS DREAMS!
YOU SEE T'CHALLA, YOU ARE NO MORE THAN A MOMENTARY DIVERSION!
EFFORTLESSLY, KILLMONGER HURTLES HIM OVER THE EDGE OF THE PIT... AND TOWARDS INCINERATION!!

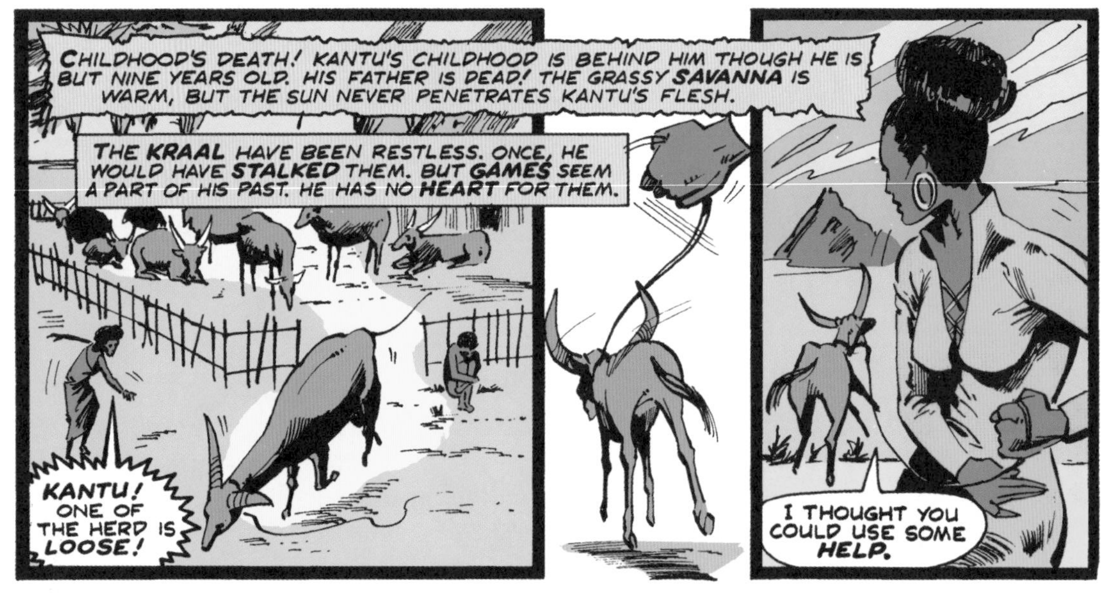
CHILDHOOD'S DEATH! KANTU'S CHILDHOOD IS BEHIND HIM THOUGH HE IS BUT NINE YEARS OLD. HIS FATHER IS DEAD! THE GRASSY SAVANNA IS WARM, BUT THE SUN NEVER PENETRATES KANTU'S FLESH.
THE KRAAL HAVE BEEN RESTLESS. ONCE, HE WOULD HAVE STALKED THEM. BUT GAMES SEEM A PART OF HIS PAST. HE HAS NO HEART FOR THEM.
KANTU! ONE OF THE HERD IS LOOSE!
I THOUGHT YOU COULD USE SOME HELP.

WHAT HELP COULD YOU GIVE ME? DO YOU COME TO TAKE ME BACK TO THAT HOS-PE-TAAL? I TRUST YOU NO MORE THAN I DO ALL THOSE INDOOR SUNS.
ONCE I TRUSTED OUR HERBALIST, MENDINAO ...BUT NOW HE STAYS WITH THESE MEN CALLED DOCK-TORS. DO YOU KNOW OF DOCK-TORS?
I'VE HAD SOME RUN-INS WITH 'EM. MENDINAO LAID SOME HEAVY RAP ON ME, THAT YOU MIGHT NEED HELP...
WHAT WITH THE FARM HERE... AND YOUR SON.

OUT-WORLDER, KEEP YOUR HANDS OFF MY SON!

MY HUSBAND HAS BEEN TAKEN FROM ME, I'LL NOT HAVE MY SON TAKEN ALSO.
CAN'T YOU LEAVE A WOMAN TO MOURN WITH DIGNITY?
I CANNOT STEAL YOUR DIGNITY... NOR THE DEPTH AND HONESTY OF YOUR SORROW... FOR IF I COULD, IT WOULD BE BUT SHALLOW GRIEF... AND IT WOULD BE HONEST IN WORDS ONLY.
I DO NOT UNDERSTAND YOU, OUT-WORLDER.
I KNOW.

BUT WE BOTH UNDERSTAND HURT AND SORROW.
PER-HAPS WE CAN HELP EASE EACH OTHER'S PAIN!

PAIN-- SCALDING HEAT PIERCES HIS FLESH--
--BUT HE FORCES THE HURT FROM HIS MIND! HE IS THE GRACEFUL CAT--
--SPLENDID IN HIS PERFORMANCE... BOUNDING FROM ONE BRANCH TO THE NEXT!
THE PANTHER CATAPULTS OFF THE CRYSTALIZED WALLS OF THE PIT--
--BEFORE HIS HANDS CAN SLIDE HIM INTO THE PULSING HELL BELOW!
IF HE FAILS, HE IS DEAD. IT IS AS SIMPLE AS THAT!
HE DOES NOT FAIL!
TAYETE AND KAZIBE GASP IN UNISON. TAYETE'S SUSPICIONS ARE CONFIRMED. THE PANTHER IS A DEMON INCARNATE!
THE TIME MAY BE FLEETINGLY SHORT, KILLMONGER--
--BUT ARE YOU STILL SURE IT IS A MOMENT OF AMUSEMENT?
KILLMONGER SMILES IN ANSWER.
SOME-THING BURNS INTO THE PANTHER'S FLESH LIKE THE TOUCH OF A BRANDING IRON CARVING ITS MARK INTO A SIDE OF BEEF!
IT IS THE ACID TOUCH OF...SOMBRE!

HE AWAKES TO SENSATIONS.
INTENSE COLD!
THE ACHE OF HUNGER!
AND THE KNOWLEDGE HE IS NOT ALONE!
HE TURNS OVER CAUTIOUSLY, LETTING HIS EYES ADJUST TO THE BLEAK CRIMSON MOON'S STATEMENT.
THEY LEFT TAYETE'S SPEAR! PROBABLY KILLMONGER'S SENSE OF HUMOR ...LET THE "GREAT DREAMER" THINK HE HAS A CHANCE AT SURVIVAL!
IT IS THEN HE SEES THE GLACIAL WOLVES THEIR EYES GLEAMING MALEVOLENT YELLOW!
SNARLING, BARING WICKEDLY CURVING TEETH, THEY PERFORM IN A COMPLEX, BRUTAL MINUET OF LIFE AND DEATH!
STARVATION SONG HARMONIZING IN THE PACK'S COLLECTIVE STOMACH! THE PACK MOVES AS ONE. THEY ARE SUPERB BEASTS, THEIR MATTED FUR GREY AND THICK AGAINST MOANING FROST WIND.
SALIVA TURNS TO ICE RIVULETS AS THE FIRST WOLF LEADS THE ATTACK!

TO FLEE WOULD LEAVE HIM AT THE PACK'S MERCY. THEY WOULD BRING HIM DOWN INTO THE SNOW, RIPPING HUGE CHUNKS OF MEAT FROM HIM--
THE COLD IS BLISTERING, BUT THE PANTHER BREAKS INTO A CHILLING SWEAT. THE SHEEN HARDENS ON HIS FLESH, ENCASING HIM IN A FRIGID, TRANSPARENT SHROUD!
HE STANDS FAST! THERE IS NO OTHER COURSE OF ACTION. HIS OPTIONS ARE FEW... NONE OF THEM PROMISE ESCAPE! THE FIRST WOLF'S UNDERSIDE IS SOFT AND YIELDS BEFORE HIS ONE WEAPON!
--UNTIL ONLY BLOOD STAINS REMAIN ON THE PRISTINE WHITE, SCREAMING THE TALE OF VIOLENCE THAT HAD CLAIMED HIS LIFE!

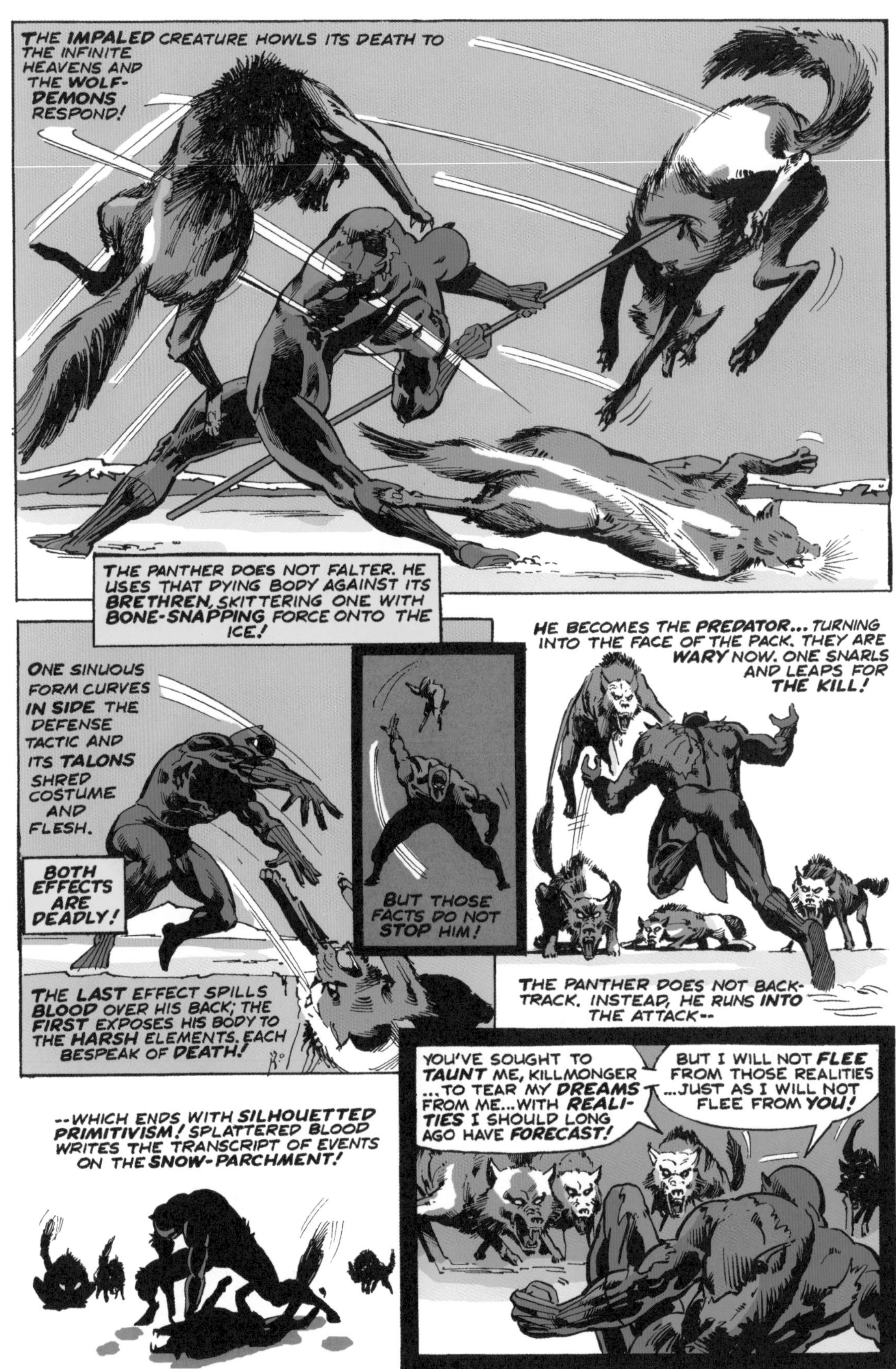
THE IMPALED CREATURE HOWLS ITS DEATH TO THE INFINITE HEAVENS AND THE WOLF-DEMONS RESPOND!
THE PANTHER DOES NOT FALTER. HE USES THAT DYING BODY AGAINST ITS BRETHREN, SKITTERING ONE WITH BONE-SNAPPING FORCE ONTO THE ICE!
ONE SINUOUS FORM CURVES IN SIDE THE DEFENSE TACTIC AND ITS TALONS SHRED COSTUME AND FLESH.
BOTH EFFECTS ARE DEADLY!
THE LAST EFFECT SPILLS BLOOD OVER HIS BACK; THE FIRST EXPOSES HIS BODY TO THE HARSH ELEMENTS. EACH BESPEAK OF DEATH!
BUT THOSE FACTS DO NOT STOP HIM!
HE BECOMES THE PREDATOR... TURNING INTO THE FACE OF THE PACK. THEY ARE WARY NOW. ONE SNARLS AND LEAPS FOR THE KILL!
THE PANTHER DOES NOT BACK-TRACK. INSTEAD, HE RUNS INTO THE ATTACK--
--WHICH ENDS WITH SILHOUETTED PRIMITIVISM! SPLATTERED BLOOD WRITES THE TRANSCRIPT OF EVENTS ON THE SNOW-PARCHMENT!
YOU'VE SOUGHT TO TAUNT ME, KILLMONGER ...TO TEAR MY DREAMS FROM ME...WITH REALI-TIES I SHOULD LONG AGO HAVE FORECAST!
BUT I WILL NOT FLEE FROM THOSE REALITIES ...JUST AS I WILL NOT FLEE FROM YOU!

YOU HAVE LEFT ME HERE AS SO MUCH CARRION!
BUT YOU HAVE UNDER-ESTIMATED ME, KILLMON-GER!
THE PACK AS A UNIFIED PRESENCE IS BROKEN. ONE LAST FORM HURTLES OVER THE BATTLE-FIELD, DRIVEN BY THE ETERNAL FORCE... HUNGER!

HE TRIES TO CONTROL HIS BREATHING. AL-READY, HE FEELS THE COLD AIR SUCKING INTO HIS LUNGS... AND IT SEARS A FROST-SCAR WITHIN HIS CHEST!
THE PANTHER IGNORES THE PAIN. HE BRACES HIMSELF... AND ABSORBS THE IMPACT.

IMMEDIATELY, HE IS TO HIS FEET. WAITING! THE REMAINING WOLVES STUDY HIM--

--AND THEIR DECISION IS AS ONE. SOMEWHERE ON THE BARREN HO-RIZON THERE IS OTHER PREY. IN-STINCT TELLS THEM, IT IS SAFER TO SEEK IT OUT THAN STAY.

ALONE.

HE SEEKS SHELTER... BUT NOT FROM HIS THOUGHTS. MONICA HAS GIVEN HIM INNER STRENGTH. W'KABI AND TAKU HAVE BEEN A GREAT AID. BUT THE TASK ITSELF MUST BE FINALLY FACED BY HIM.
HE FACES THE IMMENSITY OF HIS TASK. IT IS STRIPPED OF ITS ILLUSION, BUT NOT ITS PROMISE!

IT BEGINS--
--A LONELY VIGIL THAT LASTS THE DARK NIGHT HOURS AND INTO THE FIRST LIGHT OF DAWN'S REPRIEVE!
ALONE.

# *JUNGLE ACTION* #13,
# JANUARY 1975

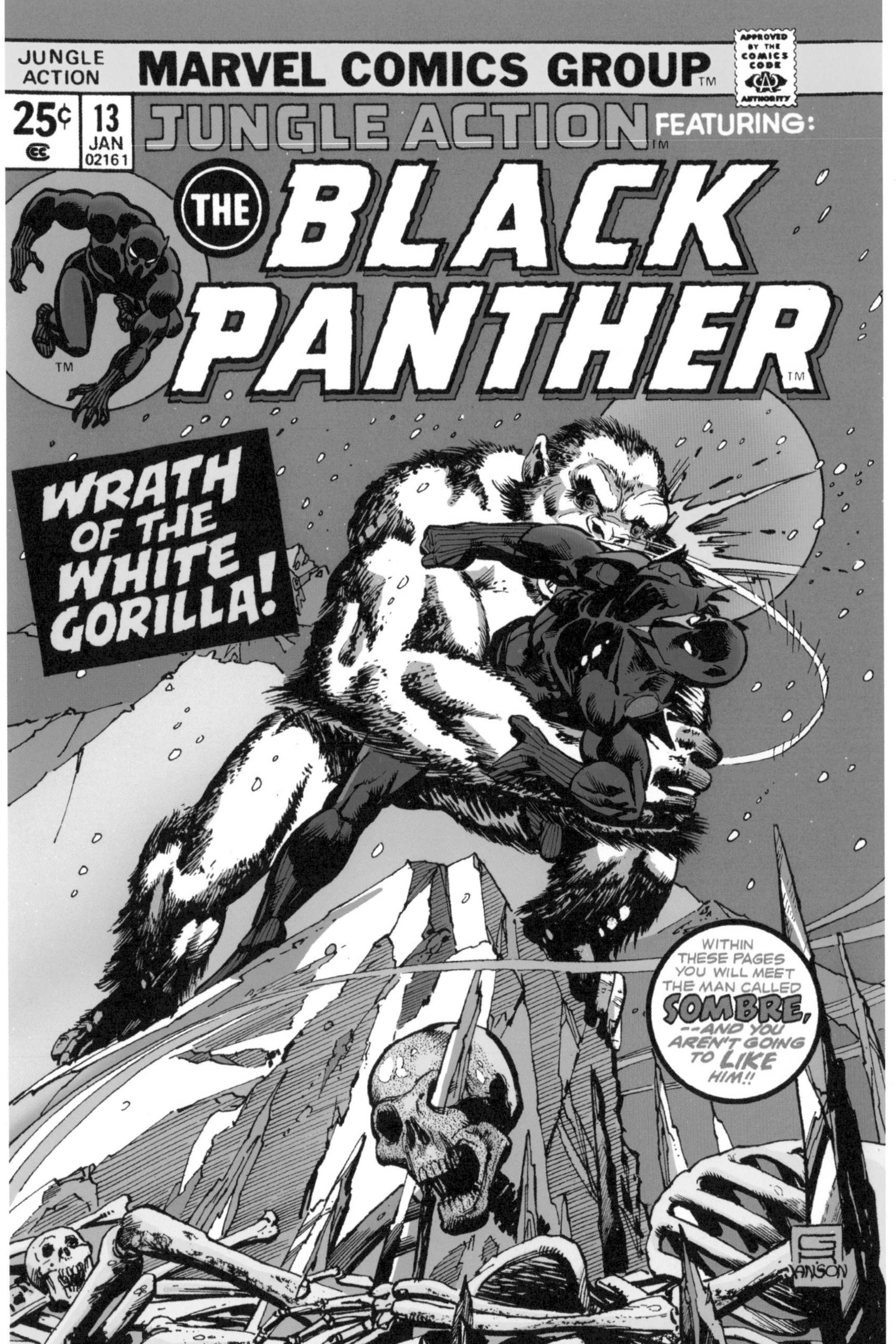
JUNGLE ACTION
MARVEL COMICS GROUP
APPROVED BY THE COMICS CODE AUTHORITY
25¢
13
JAN
02161
JUNGLE ACTION FEATURING:
THE BLACK PANTHER
WRATH OF THE WHITE GORILLA!
WITHIN THESE PAGES YOU WILL MEET THE MAN CALLED SOMBRE, --AND YOU AREN'T GOING TO LIKE HIM!!
JANSON

# Stan Lee PRESENTS: THE BLACK PANTHER!™

DON McGREGOR *Writer* · BILLY GRAHAM *Pencils* · CRAIG RUSSELL *Inker* · TOM PALMER, *Colorist* · JOE ROSEN, *Letterer* · ROY THOMAS *Editor*

THE PANTHER'S UNIFORM IS MATTED WITH DRIED BLOOD!
HE HAS PROWLED THE VAST NIGHT WITH THE SLEEK, PANTHERISH STRIDE OF THE BLACK CAT ON THE SCENT OF AN ANCIENT ENEMY... OR OF NEW PREY!
HE HAS PIERCED THE SHADOWS WITH BROODING AMBER EYES! AND NOW THE SCENT BECOMES OVERPOWERING. HE HAS FOLLOWED THE SPORE BACK TO THAT HATED PLACE...
RESURRECTION ALTAR!
WATCH OUT, JAKAK! IT'S THAT PANTHER-DEVIL! GET OUT OF MY WAY AND I'LL SEAR HIM IN HALF!
BUT HOW CAN IT BE HIM, WENZORI?
WE WERE WITH KILLMONGER WHEN WE LEFT HIM FOR DEAD... LEFT HIM FOR THE WOLVES OF THE MIST TO DEVOUR!!

I WOULDN'T IMAGINE YOU GET MANY VISITORS ...DROPPING IN UNEXPECTEDLY--
--BUT I THINK I'VE JUST LOCATED THE WELCOME MAT!
AND I'M CERTAIN YOU WOULDN'T TURN A WEARY WAYFARER AWAY.
HE HAS NOT SPOKEN FOR 24 HOURS, AND THE WORDS COME FROM BLISTERED LIPS, DEEPLY SPLIT BY THE GLACIAL COLD.
DRIED BLOOD IS ON HIS TONGUE, AND SPEAKING HAS RIPPED THE HEALING WOUND OPEN SO THAT FRESH BLOOD SPILLS INTO HIS MOUTH.
HE WONDERS IF THEY HAVE UNDERSTOOD ONE WORD OF HIS CLEVER REPARTEE.
I DON'T KNOW HOW YOU ESCAPED THOSE DEVIL-WOLVES AND THEIR RAVENOUS APPETITES--
--BUT IT IS A SHORT-LIVED VICTORY!
HE IS THE AGILE CAT, SENSING A TRAP AND ASTOUNDINGLY ESCAPING IT!
JAKAK, THE WOLVES ARE NOT THE DEVILS.
HE IS!
LOOK AT HIS EYES!
JAKAK WIELDS THE WEAPON EXPERTLY. IT IS A COMBINATION OF NUNCHAKU AND MACE... AND ITS DESIGN HAS ONLY ONE PURPOSE--
--TO RIP FLESH AND CARVE BONE TO THE MARROW! IT SADDENS THE PANTHER THAT SUCH INGENUITY SHOULD BE WASTED TO DEVISE ANOTHER METHOD OF KILLING.

ONE MORE WEAPON ADDED TO KILLMONGER'S ARSENAL ...AS IF IT IS ONLY THE WEAPONS OR THE POWERS THAT GIVE HIS FOLLOWERS IDENTITY.
HE POUNCES, HURTLING LITHE AND DARKLY TOWARD HIS ENEMY. THE MACE-NUNCHAKU'S JAGGED BOLTS FIND FLESH AND TEARS IT FROM HIS BACK, OPENING A NEW WOUND NEAR THE WELTS THE WOLVES HAD RAKED INTO HIM THE NIGHT BEFORE.
I'LL ASK BUT ONCE! WHERE IS KILLMONGER?
DOES HE HOLD REIGN INSIDE THE ALTAR?
KILLMONGER'S GONE!
HE LEFT THIS MORNING. WITH KING CADAVER. ONLY SOMBRE STAYS HERE ETERNALLY.
HE IS THE ORACLE OF RESURRECTION ALTAR...AND WE'LL BRING HIM YOUR BODY TO THROW INTO THE ABYSS.
HEY! WHAT ARE YOU--
DOING?
BLOOD AND DEATH? IS THIS ALL I AM TO HEAR FOR THE REST OF MY DAYS?
COULD YOU NOT FIND PLEASURE IN THE ACT OF LOVE--
--OR HAVE YOU BECOME SO PERVERTED THAT YOU FIND EXCITEMENT AND ENTERTAINMENT ONLY IN BRUTALITY?

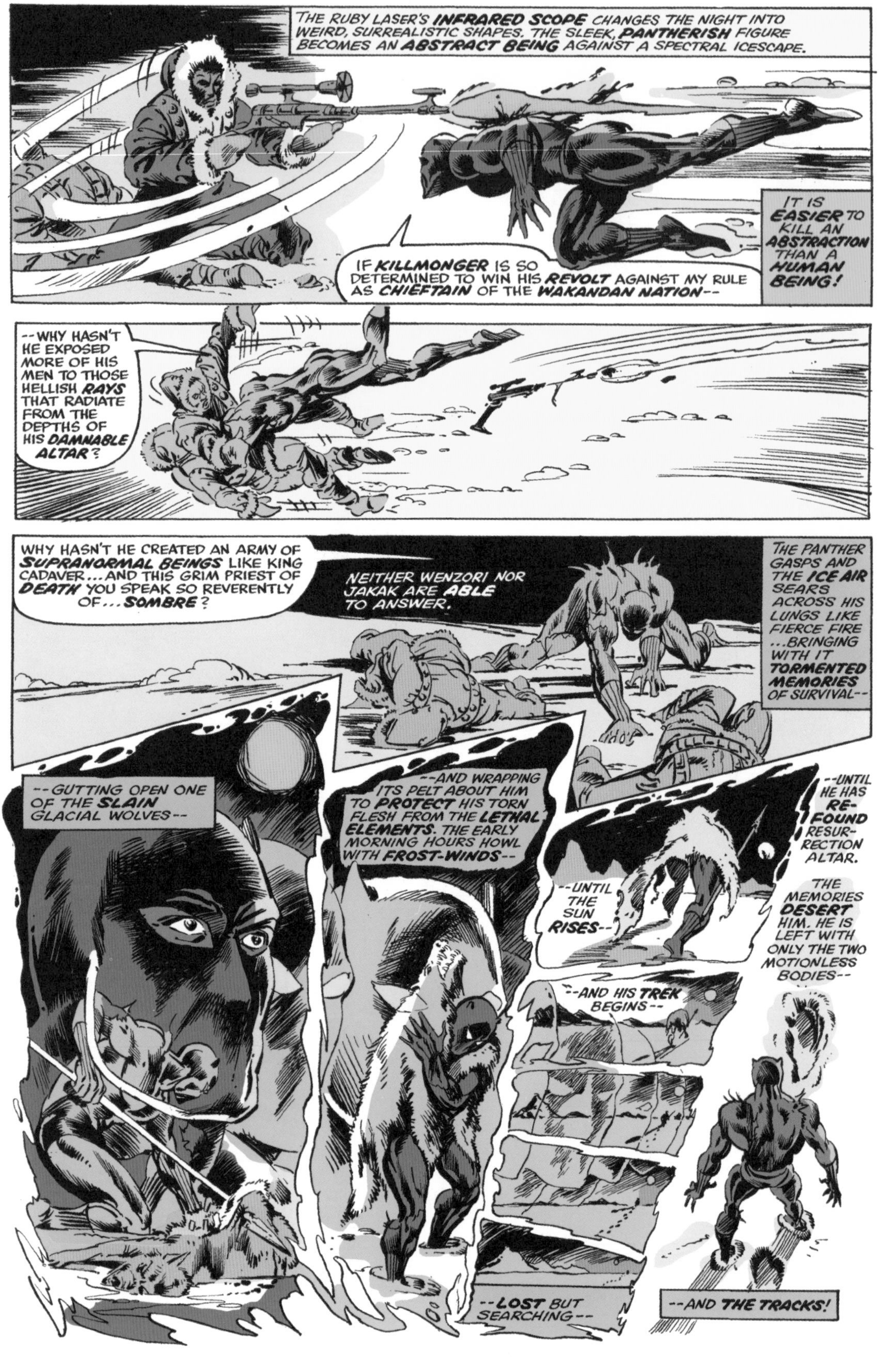

THE RUBY LASER'S **INFRARED SCOPE** CHANGES THE NIGHT INTO WEIRD, SURREALISTIC SHAPES. THE SLEEK, **PANTHERISH** FIGURE BECOMES AN **ABSTRACT BEING** AGAINST A SPECTRAL ICESCAPE.

IT IS **EASIER** TO KILL AN **ABSTRACTION** THAN A **HUMAN BEING!**

IF **KILLMONGER** IS SO DETERMINED TO WIN HIS **REVOLT** AGAINST MY RULE AS **CHIEFTAIN** OF THE **WAKANDAN NATION**--

--WHY HASN'T HE EXPOSED MORE OF HIS MEN TO THOSE HELLISH **RAYS** THAT RADIATE FROM THE DEPTHS OF HIS **DAMNABLE ALTAR**?

WHY HASN'T HE CREATED AN ARMY OF **SUPRANORMAL BEINGS** LIKE KING CADAVER... AND THIS GRIM PRIEST OF **DEATH** YOU SPEAK SO REVERENTLY OF... **SOMBRE**?

NEITHER WENZORI NOR JAKAK ARE **ABLE** TO ANSWER.

THE PANTHER GASPS AND THE **ICE AIR** SEARS ACROSS HIS LUNGS LIKE FIERCE FIRE ...BRINGING WITH IT **TORMENTED MEMORIES** OF SURVIVAL--

--GUTTING OPEN ONE OF THE **SLAIN** GLACIAL WOLVES--

--AND WRAPPING ITS PELT ABOUT HIM TO **PROTECT** HIS TORN FLESH FROM THE **LETHAL ELEMENTS**. THE EARLY MORNING HOURS HOWL WITH **FROST-WINDS**--

--UNTIL THE SUN **RISES**--

--UNTIL HE HAS **RE-FOUND** RESURRECTION ALTAR.

THE MEMORIES **DESERT** HIM. HE IS LEFT WITH ONLY THE TWO MOTIONLESS BODIES--

--AND HIS **TREK** BEGINS--

--**LOST** BUT SEARCHING--

--AND **THE TRACKS!**

IT APPEARS NEITHER OF YOU WILL BE ABLE TO ANSWER FOR SOME TIME--
--AND KILLMONGER COULD WELL HAVE OTHER GUARDS AROUND THE OUTER PERIMETER OF THE ALTAR. THE TRACKS POSE A MORE INTRIGUING QUESTION--
--AND IT IS DOUBTFUL THAT KILLMONGER WOULD TRUST UNDERLINGS WITH MUCH INFORMATION.
THE PANTHER IS ONLY PARTLY RIGHT!
THE TRACKS ARE GOUGED DEEP INTO THE SNOW AS IF SEEKING PERMANENCE AGAINST AN UNPERMANENT ENVIRONMENT.
THE PANTHER MOVES AS THE GREAT CAT, STALKING IMPULSIVELY.
THE TRACKS POSSESS HIM! WHATEVER HAS MADE THEM MUST BE OLYMPIAN IN SIZE--AND HE WONDERS IF KILLMONGER HAS EXPOSED MORE MEN TO THE PULSING RAYS WITHIN RESURRECTION ALTAR.
HE SHOULD HAVE ASKED WENZORI AND JAKAK.
TRUE, THEY COULD NOT HAVE TOLD HIM ANYTHING ABOUT THE BLAZING COMET THAT CREATED THE CAVERN. THEY ALSO DID NOT KNOW WHAT THOSE RAYS WERE, THOUGH THEY'D ONCE HEARD SOMBRE SAY IT PULSED WITH ENERGY LIKE THAT FROM DISTANT QUASARS!
BUT THEY COULD HAVE TOLD HIM THAT THOSE RAYS OFTEN PRODUCED UNPREDICTABLE RESULTS UPON HUMANITY... AND THAT MOST OF THOSE CHANGES WERE DEADLY!
THEY COULD ALSO HAVE TOLD HIM OF THE RUMORS...THAT SOMBRE TAKES THOSE VICTIMS AND CARRIES THEM TO THE LEGENDARY WHITE GORILLAS, WHERE THE CORPSES ARE LEFT AS OFFERINGS.
WENZORI AND JAKAK COULD HAVE TOLD HIM THAT AND OF THE RUMOR THAT SOMBRE COMMUNES WITH THOSE MYTHICAL GODS.
IT IS MORE THAN RUMOR. IT IS FACT! AND SOMBRE, HIDDEN BY ROBES AND A MASK THAT HAS BEEN SEARED INTO HIS FLESH BY THE RAYS, WATCHES MALEVOLENTLY... WAITING TO STRIKE!

THE SUN NEVER PENETRATES SERPENT VALLEY! IT IS BANISHED FROM THE LUSH, PRIMEVAL INTERIOR BY THE DENSE CLOUD FOREST THAT HAS BEEN THE ONLY "SKY" THIS LAND HAS EVER HAD. YET, THE MIST WHICH SWIRLS IN SERPENTINE ABANDON IS HUMID, HEATED BY SOME INNER SOURCE.
ERIK KILLMONGER MAINTAINS HIS BRISK, TIRELESS PACE. THE OTHERS SWEAT PROFUSELY, BUT KILLMONGER'S BROW REMAINS DRY AND HE SEEMS NOT TO NOTICE THE SWELTERING VAPOR.
KILLMONGER? DO YOU REALLY THINK IT WISE TO TRAVEL WHERE SERPENTS DWELL?
TAYETE AND KAZIBE, ALONG WITH THE REST OF THE REGIMENT, NOTICE IT. THEY ARE ALSO APPREHENSIVE, ANOTHER HUMAN FRAILTY TO WHICH KILLMONGER SEEMS IMMUNE!
YOU HAVEN'T SEEN ANY SERPENTS YET, HAVE YOU, TAYETE?
NO!! OF COURSE NOT! I'D HAVE GIVEN THEM WIDE BERTH IF I HAD. RIGHT, KAZIBE?
RIGHT. IT DOES NOT BODE WELL TO RAISE THE WRATH OF SERPENTS.
BUT T'CHALLA IS THE PANTHER-DEVIL, AND HE WON'T BE PLEASED WITH SUCH DOINGS.
YOUR PANTHER-DEVIL IS PROBABLY DEAD--FILLING THE STOMACHS OF SOME CONTENTED WOLVES--
--OR EVEN IF HE ISN'T, THERE IS NOT A THING HE CAN DO TO STOP MY ATTACK. BUT THIS REMINDS ME, KAZIBE--
WE WILL NOT AVOID ANY SUCH SERPENTS, KAZIBE, THOSE SERPENTS... IF THEY EXIST... ARE OUR PURPOSE FOR ENTERING THE VALLEY. SOMBRE IS THE ONLY OTHER HUMAN IN DECADES TO HAVE TROD THIS GROUND.
HE HAS TOLD ME OF MAMMOTHS THAT DEFY EVOLUTION... MAGNIFICENT CREATURES WE COULD PUT TO EXCELLENT USE WHEN WE RAID CENTRAL WAKANDA AND TAKE OVER T'CHALLA'S PALACE AND THRONE!
IT WAS YOU AND TAYETE THAT LED T'CHALLA TO RESURRECTION ALTAR. AND WHILE YOUR WEAKNESS HAS NOT IN THE LEAST HINDERED THE PROGRESS OF OUR EFFORTS... YOU HAVE DISPLEASED--ME!!

THE SPIKED BELT LASHES OUT IN COUNTERPOINT TO KILLMONGER'S CALMLY SPOKEN WORDS. KAZIBE'S FLESH RIPS UNDER THE SPIKES FROM CHEST TO STOMACH. HE IS DEFENSLESS.
KILLMONGER! YOU... YOU'LL KILL KAZIBE!
PL...PLEASE...DON'T... DON'T MAKE ME HAVE TO STOP YOU.
STOP ME? YOU, TAYETE? YOU'D STOP ERIK KILLMONGER?
YOU HAVE LESS CHANCE THAN T'CHALLA... YOUR PANTHER-DEVIL--
I TREAT MY LIEUTENANTS WITH RESPECT DUE THEIR RANKS. BUT BETRAYAL FOR ANY REASON EARNS BUT ONE REWARD.
AND WHAT OF IT, TAYETE?
WHAT'LL YOU DO ABOUT IT WHILE HE BEGS FOR MERCY HE WILL NOT RECEIVE.
NOW, TAYETE... DO YOU WANT TO CRAWL?
I...I WON'T LE...LET YOU KI... KILL KAZIBE. COU... COULDN'T WE...WE TALK ABOUT THIS?
KILLMONGER'S FACE IS IMPLACABLE. HIS EYES ARE DARK WITH EBON COLD WHICH, MYSIFYINGLY, CHANGES TO EBON FLAME! HE BEGINS TO LAUGH, RAUCOUSLY.
WELL DONE, TAYETE.
YOU SURPRISED ME. I DIDN'T THINK YOU CAPABLE OF SUCH LOYALTY!
PICK UP YOUR WHIMPERING FRIEND AND LET US PROCEED. YOU MAY YET REDEEM YOURSELVES.
BUT HURRY, TAYETE. LEST I CHANGE MY MIND. COME, I'LL LET YOU HAVE FIRST CHANCE AT BREAKING ONE OF THESE TREMENDOUS CREATURES.
YOU... RISKED YOUR LIFE FOR ME.
WHAT ELSE WOULD ONE WITH MY COURAGE DO?
I ONLY WISH I DIDN'T HAVE TO DO IT AT THE EXPENSE OF MY OWN LIFE.

THE SKY IS SWEPT WITH AN ARTIST'S PASSION... BEFORE IT HAS BEEN SOURED!
THE PANTHER IS MOVED BY A COMPULSIVE FORCE THAT IS KIN TO THE KIND THAT DRIVES AN ARTIST ONWARD, HARDLY AWARE OF WHAT HE IS PURSUING... SOMETIMES COMPLETELY UNAWARE OF WHAT HE IS STRIVING TO ACHIEVE.
IT IS A NIGHT WHEN A MAN CAN REACH AND BELIEVE HE CAN TOUCH THE STARS--
--THAT HE IS A PART OF THE COSMOLOGICAL SCHEME OF THINGS!
A NIGHT WHEN A MAN COULD BELIEVE HE IS AN INTEGRAL PART OF THE UNIVERSE.
NOT OMNIPOTENT. NOT SUPERIOR.
JUST UNIQUE AND UNTO HIMSELF.
THE PANTHER KNOWS HE IS APPROACHING THE TRAIL'S END...THAT HE HAS NEARLY REACHED ITS DESTINATION--
--AND HE IS HESITANT. HIS OWN DESTINATION SEEMED INSEPARABLY LINKED WITH THAT OF THE TRACKS.
THERE IS A RISING OF UNEARTHLY VOICES FROM BEYOND, BECKONING HIM TOWARD THE EDGE--
--AND THE VIEW THAT LIES BEFORE HIM IS STAGGERING!

THERE ARE TWO MAJOR RELIGIONS IN WAKANDA. T'CHALLA WEARS THE SACRED ATTIRE OF THE PANTHER RELIGION. IT IS TORN AND CRUSTED WITH BLOOD AND SWEAT, BUT IT IS NO LESS SACRED A GARMENT.
IT WOULD BE A TERRIBLE AGONY FOR A MAN TO MEET HIS GODS... ESPECIALLY GODS THAT HE NEVER BELIEVED IN!
THE REGAL, SAVAGE BEINGS THAT CONGREGATE BELOW HIM ARE THE FOUNDATIONS OF WAKANDA'S SECOND RELIGION.
THEY HAVE THE STATURE OF GODS... THE AWE-INSPIRING WHITE GORILLAS!
SOMBRE STANDS IN THEIR MIDST, PURPLE VELVET ROBES SWIRLING. HE IS A PERVERTED MONK WHO RADIATES EVIL NOT SERENITY... HIS ARMS RAISED IN FALSE SUPPLICATION!
YOU HAVE SENSED MY PRESENCE AS I APPROACHED. AND YOU ARE AWARE THERE WAS A SECOND PRESENCE... NOT FAR FROM MY OWN.
YOU WONDER WHERE IS MY OFFERING TO YOU! ...YES, THERE IS AN OFFERING.
BUT IT IS A LIVE OFFERING!
ABOVE YOU, GREAT ONES! THERE IS YOUR SACRIFICE!

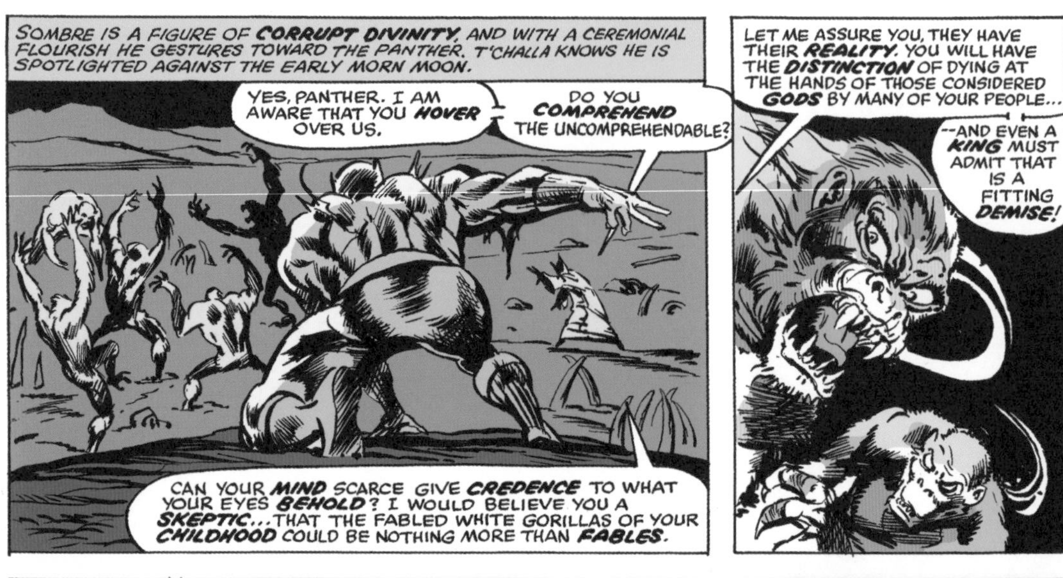
SOMBRE IS A FIGURE OF CORRUPT DIVINITY, AND WITH A CEREMONIAL FLOURISH HE GESTURES TOWARD THE PANTHER. T'CHALLA KNOWS HE IS SPOTLIGHTED AGAINST THE EARLY MORN MOON.
YES, PANTHER. I AM AWARE THAT YOU HOVER OVER US.
DO YOU COMPREHEND THE UNCOMPREHENDABLE?
CAN YOUR MIND SCARCE GIVE CREDENCE TO WHAT YOUR EYES BEHOLD? I WOULD BELIEVE YOU A SKEPTIC... THAT THE FABLED WHITE GORILLAS OF YOUR CHILDHOOD COULD BE NOTHING MORE THAN FABLES.
LET ME ASSURE YOU, THEY HAVE THEIR REALITY. YOU WILL HAVE THE DISTINCTION OF DYING AT THE HANDS OF THOSE CONSIDERED GODS BY MANY OF YOUR PEOPLE...
--AND EVEN A KING MUST ADMIT THAT IS A FITTING DEMISE!

THEY ARE OVERPOWERING, ANCIENT SPECIMENS TO SOME FORGOTTEN ERA WHEN EARLY WAKANDAN LEGENDS WERE AT THEIR BIRTH. A WANDERER, PERHAPS DARING A NEW FRONTIER OF ICE AND SNOW, GLIMPSED THE TOWERING, GOD-LIKE BEINGS AND RETURNED TO HOME, HUMBLED AND MEEK BY WHAT HE HAD SEEN. AND A RELIGION HAD BEEN FORMED!!
THE PANTHER CALCULATES THAT THE LARGEST BEING STANDS AT LEAST TWELVE FEET TALL. ITS WEIGHT IS INCALCULABLE.
YOU COMMUNE WITH THEM, SOMBRE. YOU STAND AMONG GODS... DO NOT MAKE THE MISTAKE OF THINKING YOU HOLD SUCH GLORY!

YOU HAVE A WAY WITH WORDS, PANTHER... BUT TURN. LOOK BEHIND YOU.
WHAT DEVIOUS CHARADE DO YOU PLY NOW, SOMBRE?

IT IS NO CHARADE!
HE IS STAGGERED BY ITS IMMENSITY! THIS IS NO GOD OF LOVE OR CHARITY. THIS IS A VENGEFUL GOD, RISING FULL AND MALEVOLENT--
--DEMANDING ITS TRIBUTE!

THE MEDICAL CENTER IS A STUDY IN ANACHRONISM. MONICA LYNNE GIVES KAROTA SUPPORT AS THEY NEAR THE BUILDING AND SENSES THE WOMAN'S HORROR. IT IS AS IF THIS STRUCTURE IS A DEMON SHE CANNOT FATHOM... A DEMON THAT ARROGANTLY FLAUNTS ITSELF BESIDE THE HIGH-CEILINGED, THATCHED ROOFS OF THE HOMES IN CENTRAL WAKANDA.
THE EXAMINATION ROOMS BLEND AFRICAN SCULPTURE WITH MODERN EQUIPMENT. TRIBAL HERBALISTS WORK ALONGSIDE SKILLED SURGEONS... BUT THE EFFORTS AT EASING THE CULTURAL CLASH HAVE NOT ENTIRELY SUCCEEDED.
YOU HAVE MALNUTRITION, KAROTA. YOU HAVEN'T EATEN WELL SINCE YOUR HUSBAND WAS... SLAIN BY KILLMONGER'S AIDES.
WAKANDA HOS

MAL-NUT-RICHON?
WILL MY SON, KANTU, CATCH THIS?
NO, NO, KAROTA. IT'S NOT CONTAGIOUS.

WE'LL ONLY HAVE TO BE INSIDE FOR A FEW MOMENTS. AND MENDINAO WILL GIVE YOU A FEW VITAMIN SHOTS.
VITE-A-MINS?
WHAT ARE VITE-A-MINS?
WELL... THEY'RE ...UH... VITAMINS ARE... UHM...
THEY'RE WHAT CURES MALNUTRITION.

KAROTA, YOU ACT LIKE A CHILD. MENDINAO HAS TENDED YOU... AND YOUR MOTHER BEFORE YOU.
DID NOT MY POULTICES BREAK YOUR FEVER?

WOULD I BE IN THIS PLACE IF IT HURT OUR PEOPLE?
STOP!
MENDINAO, WHAT IS THIS THING YOU DO TO ME?
DON'T BE AFRAID, KAROTA.

KAROTA! THIS IS ONLY A KIND OF POULTICE.
YOU NEVER STABBED KAROTA WITH POULTICES, MENDINAO.
YOU HAVE BECOME AS THE OUTWORLDERS! I SHOULD NEVER HAVE TRUSTED T'CHALLA'S WOMAN'S WORDS.
I'LL GO AFTER HER, MENDINAO.
BUT TRUST IS A FRAGILE CONCEPT THAT IS EASY PREY TO... DISTRUST.

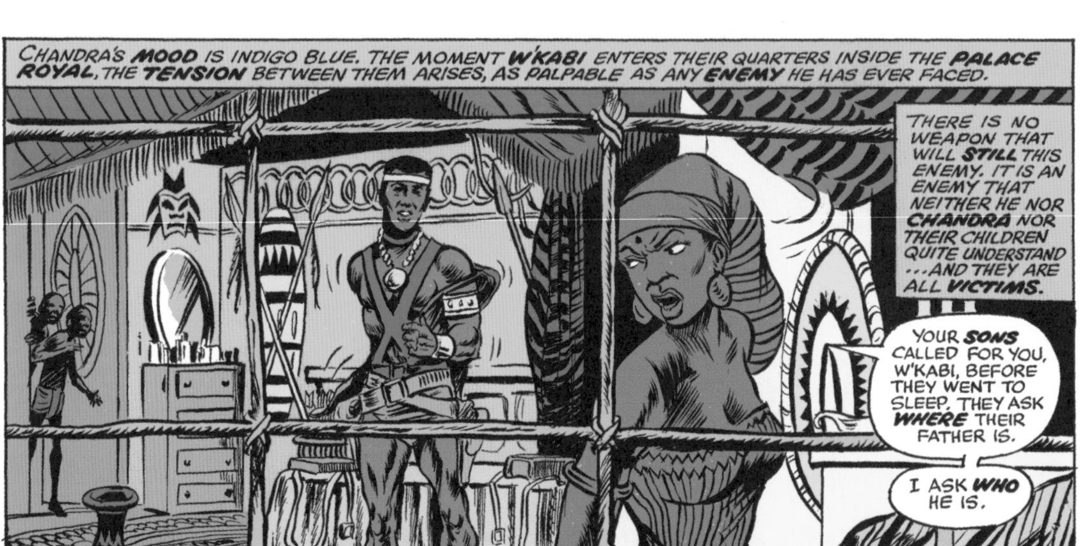
CHANDRA'S MOOD IS INDIGO BLUE. THE MOMENT W'KABI ENTERS THEIR QUARTERS INSIDE THE PALACE ROYAL, THE TENSION BETWEEN THEM ARISES, AS PALPABLE AS ANY ENEMY HE HAS EVER FACED.
THERE IS NO WEAPON THAT WILL STILL THIS ENEMY. IT IS AN ENEMY THAT NEITHER HE NOR CHANDRA NOR THEIR CHILDREN QUITE UNDERSTAND ...AND THEY ARE ALL VICTIMS.
YOUR SONS CALLED FOR YOU, W'KABI, BEFORE THEY WENT TO SLEEP. THEY ASK WHERE THEIR FATHER IS.
I ASK WHO HE IS.

I'D ASK THE SAME OF YOU, CHANDRA. ONCE YOU WELCOMED ME WITH AFFECTION... BUT THESE NIGHTS THERE IS ONLY HOSTILITY.
T'CHALLA IS GONE... NO ONE KNOWS FOR HOW LONG. AS HEAD OF COURT SECURITY I AM LEFT IN CHARGE... WITH OUR RESTRICTION CELLS CROWDED WITH KILLMONGER'S MURDERERS.

I'M SURPRISED! YOU'RE ACTUALLY TAKING OFF YOUR ARMAMENT. DON'T YOU FEEL LOST WITHOUT IT, W'KABI?
AFTER ALL, YOU'VE TURNED OUR QUARTERS INTO A MUSEUM FOR WEAPONS!

EVEN HERE THE WALLS CLOSE IN ON ME. I WON'T ALLOW THAT, CHANDRA!

THE IRATE MILITANT COMMANDS! I'VE WATCHED YOU SWAGGER PAST YOUR PRISONERS, W'KA... UHHH!
WWHHARCK!

WAIT, CHANDRA!! I SPEAK WORDS THAT DO NOT EXPRESS WHAT I FEEL...AND ACT OUT OF DESPERATION!

I AM NOT ONE OF YOUR PRISONERS, W'KABI.
AND I WILL NOT BE TREATED AS SUCH!

THE NIGHT IS UNMERCIFULLY LONG!
THE WHITE GORILLA BATTERS AT THE PANTHER, AND HE IS FRAIL AND TRIVIAL BEFORE ITS SIZE AND POWER.
IN THE DAZED MURAL OF PAIN, CAMPFIRES DANCE BEFORE HIS EYES...TURNING WOOD TO CINDERS WITH CRACKLING MELODIES. HE IS SEVEN YEARS OLD AND ONLY THE SON OF A CHIEFTAIN. HE HAS YET TO WEAR THE SACROSANCT UNIFORM OF THE BLACK PANTHER--
--YET TO UNDERGO THE SPIRITUAL AND PHYSICAL RITUALS THAT WILL BESTOW HIS SHARPENED SENSES AND AGILITY.
HE LISTENS TO THE ELDERS TALKING. FABLES AND MYTHS WEAVE LIMITLESS HORIZONS WITHIN HIS MIND--
IT WAS BEFORE THOSE CAMPFIRES THAT MENDINAO FIRST SPOKE OF THE WHITE GORILLAS...DROPPING HIS VOICE DRAMATICALLY FOR THE BENEFIT OF YOUNG EARS.
--AND THEY TAKE THE SHAPE OF VISIONS THAT WILL ONE DAY SHAPE THE MAN... THE LEADER OF THE WAKANDANS.
THERE, GREAT ONES! IN A MOMENT, YOU WILL HAVE YOUR OFFERING...SLIGHT THOUGH IT IS.
THE CAMPFIRES HAVE BEEN EXTINGUISHED!

THE DEATH-GRIP CONVEYS ONE OTHER IMPRESSION. WARMTH! THE TEMPERATURE OF AN ANIMAL, HUMAN OR OTHERWISE!
HE DOES WHAT HE MUST... BEFORE HIS RIB-CAGE CRACKS JAGGEDLY AND HIS BONES ARE ADDED TO THE SNOW-SWEPT GRAVE-YARD!
THE HUGE HANDS GRASP HIM. ITS GRIP CRUSHES THE AIR FROM HIS LUNGS, AND ITS CLAWS RIP INTO HIS CHEST AND STOMACH! HE IS AT THE MOMENT OF DEATH... CONFRONTED BY A GOD!
BLOOD SEEPS FROM ITS WOUND, BLINDING IT... ITS GOD-HOOD EBBS WITH ITS LOSS.
KILL HIM, GREAT ONE!
THE BEHEMOTH GROPES ABOUT, SEARCHING FOR THE OFFERING THAT HAS CAUSED IT SUCH INTENSE AGONY. IT ONLY SEEMS TO RESPOND TO SOMBRE'S CHANTS.
IT BECOMES CLEAR, SOMBRE. IT WAS YOU WHO MANIPULATED THIS NIGHT... YOU WHO TRIED TO ACT AS A GOD.
MY LEGENDS HAVE BEEN GIVEN THE VULNERABILITY OF FLESH, SOMBRE--
--AND HAVE LOST THEIR GRANDIOSE MYTHOLOGY!
BUT THAT IS A GRANDNESS YOU'VE NEVER HAD, AND YOU'D BETTER PRAY I DIE AT ITS HANDS... BECAUSE IF I SURVIVE... I'LL BE COMING AFTER YOU!

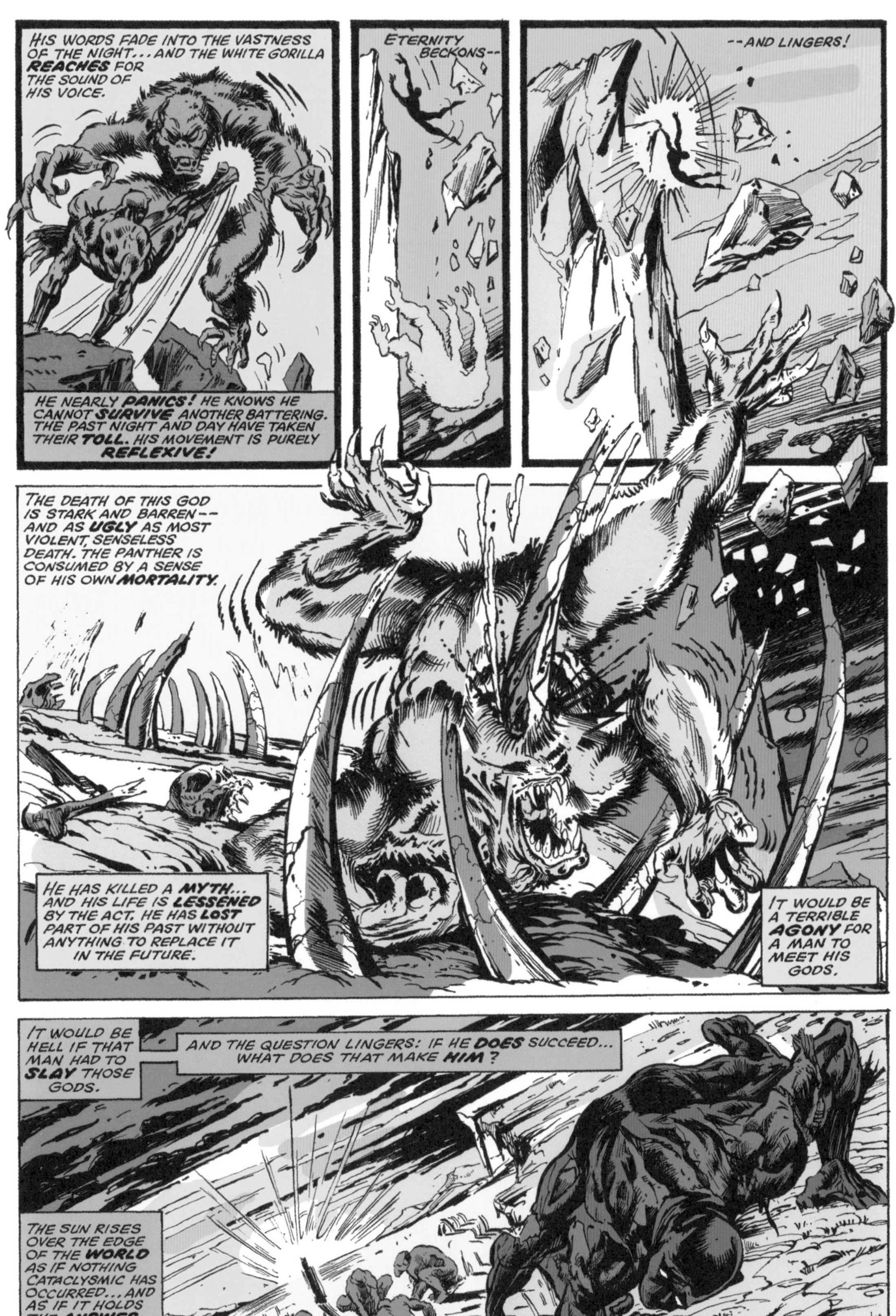
HIS WORDS FADE INTO THE VASTNESS OF THE NIGHT... AND THE WHITE GORILLA REACHES FOR THE SOUND OF HIS VOICE.
HE NEARLY PANICS! HE KNOWS HE CANNOT SURVIVE ANOTHER BATTERING. THE PAST NIGHT AND DAY HAVE TAKEN THEIR TOLL. HIS MOVEMENT IS PURELY REFLEXIVE!
ETERNITY BECKONS--
--AND LINGERS!
THE DEATH OF THIS GOD IS STARK AND BARREN-- AND AS UGLY AS MOST VIOLENT, SENSELESS DEATH. THE PANTHER IS CONSUMED BY A SENSE OF HIS OWN MORTALITY.
HE HAS KILLED A MYTH... AND HIS LIFE IS LESSENED BY THE ACT. HE HAS LOST PART OF HIS PAST WITHOUT ANYTHING TO REPLACE IT IN THE FUTURE.
IT WOULD BE A TERRIBLE AGONY FOR A MAN TO MEET HIS GODS.
IT WOULD BE HELL IF THAT MAN HAD TO SLAY THOSE GODS.
AND THE QUESTION LINGERS: IF HE DOES SUCCEED... WHAT DOES THAT MAKE HIM?
THE SUN RISES OVER THE EDGE OF THE WORLD AS IF NOTHING CATACLYSMIC HAS OCCURRED... AND AS IF IT HOLDS THE ANSWER ...BUT ISN'T SPEAKING!

VENOMM
HE'S EVEN DEADLIER THAN HIS NAME IMPLIES!

# *JUNGLE ACTION* #14,
# MARCH 1975

JUNGLE ACTION
MARVEL COMICS GROUP
APPROVED BY THE COMICS CODE AUTHORITY
25¢
14 MAR 02161
JUNGLE ACTION FEATURING:
THE BLACK PANTHER
SEE T'CHALLA BATTLE AS NEVER BEFORE AGAINST THE BEHEMOTHS FROM BEYOND TIME!
THERE ARE SERPENTS IN PARADISE
AND THEY'RE NOT JUST YOUR EVERYDAY GARTER SNAKES!

Stan Lee PRESENTS: THE BLACK PANTHER!
THE PANTHER'S YELLOWISH EYES ARE GRIM. SOMBRE STRIDES BELOW HIM, ROBES, PURPLE AND VELVET, CUTTING THROUGH THE SUFFOCATING MIST. THE STALKING IS FINALLY AT AN END.
IT HAS BEEN A LONG DESCENT FROM THE LAND OF THE CHILLING MIST TO THE HUMID SHROUD OF SERPENT VALLEY... THREE DAYS AND NIGHTS OF TRACKING, WITH ONLY UNANSWERED QUESTIONS TO FILL THE EMPTY HOURS...QUESTIONS THAT ARE OPEN WOUNDS OF INDECISION AND THAT ARE ALMOST AS PAINFUL AS THE HEALING WELTS THAT SCAR HIS FLESH.
QUESTION: WHAT PROVES A NATION'S ACHIEVEMENT? TECHNOLOGICAL ADVANCEMENT OR INDIVIDUAL CONTENTMENT? HE IS NOT AS POSITIVE OF THE ANSWER AS HE ONCE WAS, BUT IT IS THE ONE QUESTION HE COMPLETELY UNDERSTANDS.
CONTINUING PANTHER'S RAGE
THERE ARE SERPENTS LURKING IN PARADISE
BUT THE TIME FOR QUESTIONS ...HAS PASSED.
DON McGREGOR-WRITER
BILLY GRAHAM-ARTIST
PABLO MARCOS-INKER
LEN WEIN EDITOR
G JETTER-LETTERER
G.OLIVER WEIN COLORIST

THE MOIST VAPOR WEAVES A MACABRE FRAMEWORK, RISING IN SWELTERING WAVES FROM THE FETID MARSH INTERIOR--
--SINUOUSLY CARESSING THE GNARLED TREES AND ARTHRITIC BRANCHES, AN AFRICAN GOTHIC SETTING.
THE PANTHER HAS CROUCHED IN THIS POSITION BEFORE; SENSES ALERT; UNAWARE THAT HE HAS STOPPED BREATHING, LISTENING, WITHOUT REALIZING IT, FOR ANY ALIEN SOUND THAT MIGHT AFFECT THE IMMINENT CONFLICT! A PORTRAIT OF SUPPLE TENSION.
TAUT WITH THE KNOWLEDGE THAT THE VIOLENCE IS ABOUT TO BEGIN AGAIN, THE PANTHER LEAPS.
--AND THE IMPACT IS QUICK AND BRUTAL--
HE WISHES THERE WERE SOME OTHER WAY TO RESOLVE THIS CONFLICT.
THERE ISN'T!
DID YOU THINK I WOULD NOT FOLLOW YOUR SICKENING SPORE FROM RESURRECTION ALTAR, SOMBRE?
NO ANSWER? HOW ABOUT THIS, THEN, SOMBRE? YOU THOUGHT I'D BE IN NO CONDITION TO FOLLOW YOU BECAUSE OF THE WOUNDS I'D RECEIVED FROM THE WHITE GORILLA
BUT YOU WERE LUCKY TO ESCAPE YOURSELF, WEREN'T YOU? IT WAS ONLY THEIR MOURNING WHICH GAVE YOU TIME TO FLEE BEFORE THEY TURNED UPON YOU!
SOMBRE REACHES OUT, AND THE PANTHER TRIES YANKING HIS HEAD BEYOND THE TALONED GRIP.

--BUT FAILS!
FINGERS, BLISTERED AND TALONED, TIGHTEN ABOUT HIS THROAT, AND THE TOUCH OF THAT MOULDERING FLESH IS ACIDITIC--
--BURNING THE SOFT TISSUE OF THE PANTHER'S THROAT!

SWEAT DRIPS INTO THE PANTHER'S EYES, MOMENTARILY BLINDING HIM!
DON'T PANIC!
DON'T PANIC! SOME DISTANT MIND-ECHO CRIES WHILE HE LUNGES UPWARD INTO SOMBRE'S CHEST CAVITY.

THERE IS HARDLY ANY RESISTANCE, AS IF BENEATH THE ROBES, SOMBRE IS THE CONSISTENCY OF DAMP CORPSE-ASH!

A MOAN ESCAPES THE PANTHER'S LIPS, THE BLACK CAT RELUCTANTLY GIVING VOICE TO ITS PAIN--

--FOR THE TORN FLESH WHICH HAS BEEN HEALING TEARS APART--
--AGONIZINGLY!
KILLING A WHITE GORILLA SHOULD HAVE BEEN TANTAMOUNT TO KILLING A RELIGIOUS BELIEF.

BUT YOU HAVE NO TIME LEFT FOR THEOLOGICAL CRISES, PANTHER.
YOU SHOULD HAVE RETURNED TO THE SAFETY OF CENTRAL WAKANDA WHILE YOU HAD THE CHANCE--
WHERE YOUR LOVED ONES COULD HAVE CONVINCED YOU OF YOUR WORTH.

INSTEAD, YOU WILL DIE HERE, PANTHER--
--AND NONE OF YOUR FOLLOWERS WILL EVER FIND YOUR REMAINS!

SOMBRE DOES NOT HAVE TO SUCK BLOOD WITH ANY VAMPIRIC COMPULSION. HE IS NOT A VAMPIRE IN THE LITERAL TRANSLATION OF THE WORD.

HE HAS MERELY THE ABILITY TO DRINK BLOOD, HIS HUMANITY REDUCED TO CINDERS BENEATH THE VIBRANT RAYS OF HIS SHRINE... RESURECTION ALTAR.

THE TEETH PUNCTURE HIS NECK, RENDING, AND THE MORNING MIST DIMS... AFTERNOON IS BLACK... AND NIGHT WILL NEVER ARRIVE!
WHY ARE YOU TWO FIGHTING?
IF YOU ARE HARDLY MORE THAN STRANGERS--
--WHY DO YOU BATTLE AS IF YOU HAVE WAGED THIS WAR ALL YOUR LIVES?
A QUESTION? DID HE ASK IT? WAS IT A QUESTION DIMLY REMEMBERED FROM EARLY MORN HOURS?
OR HAD THE MIST BEEN GIVEN VOICE? WAS IT A WIND OF LAMENT, A DIRGE FOR SENSELESS DEATH... AND PURPOSELESS LIFE?
WHATEVER... SOMBRE IS DISTRACTED.
YOU CAME TO THIS HELLISH PLACE, SOMBRE--
YOU CAME HERE TO FIND KILLMONGER, TO TELL HIM I DID NOT DIE AT THE FANGS OF DEVIL-WOLVES... AND THAT, SADLY, I KILLED ONE OF THE WHITE GORILLAS!
SOMBRE BECOMES SWIRLS OF PURPLE VELVET... LIKE STAINED GLASS MELTING! AND THEN HE HITS THE MARSH!
THE PANTHER GLARES AMBER HATRED. SOMBRE WOULD HAVE EMOTIONLESSLY KILLED HIM, WOULDN'T HE?
LET HIM SUFFER THE SAME FATE THEN AND TO HELL WITH HIM!
EXCEPT--
SOMBRE RETURNS THE GLARE. HIS EYES REMAIN MERCILESS AND THERE IS THE SUGGESTION OF A SMILE--
--UNNERVING ACCEPTANCE OF INEVITABLE DEATH!
THE QUAGMIRE IS A MUD GRAVE, SUCKED INTO THE MOUTH AND LUNGS SILENTLY STRANGLING.
AND MEMORIES OF THAT DAMNABLE SMILE!
THE PANTHER REACHES OUT, AND HIS WOUNDS TEAR WIDER. BLOOD RIVERS BEGIN THEIR JOURNIES.
HE IS A MAN WITH A CONSCIENCE---
--WHO KNOWS THAT DEATH IS NOT MERELY POETIC SLOW MOTION AND SPURTING CATCHUP.
DEATH IS INTIMATE... AND DIMINISHES ITS PERPETRATORS.

QUIETUDE.
AS IF THE MORNING HAD NEVER BEEN BROKEN BY COMBAT, AS IF DEATH HAD NOT —TAKEN PLACE.

THE MARSHLAND STRETCHES DESOLATELY. THE MOMENT WILL LIVE ONLY IN HIS THOUGHTS.
THE QUIET REMAINS, UNBROKEN, BUT HE PAUSES. THERE IS THE FAINT SCENT OF SOMETHING UNDEFINED.
--PERHAPS IMAGINED.

AND THEN HE REMEMBERS THE VOICE.
THERE HAD BEEN A VOICE, HADN'T THERE? BACK WHEN THE AFTERNOON WAS TURNING BLACK AND HIS WOUNDS DRIPPED BLOOD ANEW.
OR WAS THAT PART OF HIS IMAGINATION ALSO.
HE SPRINGS, HALF SNARLING, THE CAUTIOUS CAT SEEKING THE UNSEEN.

DOES THIS MAN'S DEATH MEAN YOU HAVE WON, INTRUDER?
DOES THIS MEAN YOU WILL TAKE YOUR INSANITY AND LEAVE SERPENT VALLEY?
THE VOICE IS LIGHT AND MERRY. IT DOES NOT BELONG IN THIS PLACE...AND ITS TONE IS A PARADOX.
HE GLIMPSES THE FIGURE, VAGUELY, PERCHED HIGH IN THE NETWORK OF CHOKING VINE AND MIST... AND GRACEFULLY HE PROPELS HIMSELF UPWARD!
WHO ARE YOU? ONE OF KILLMONGER'S SENTRIES?
KILLMONGER? IS THAT ANOTHER MAN YOU WISH TO FIGHT?
AND WHAT END WILL THERE BE THIS TIME?

SOMETIMES I THINK THERE WILL BE NO END TO IT!
THE HIGH PITCHED VOICE IS WITHOUT ANIMOSITY. AN INQUIRY PLEASANTLY PUT INTO VOCAL TERMS, SOUNDING ALMOST--
--ALMOST... THE PANTHER REJECTS THE TERM, LEAPING UNERRINGLY AT THE FURTIVE FIGURE-
--ALMOST...HE RELENTS, HANDS ABOUT TO CLUTCH HIS TARGET, ALMOST PIXIE-ISH, REMINISCENT OF SAGE PYGMIS OR CAREFREE ELVES OR WOODLAND NYMPHS.
NYMPHS?
THAT TERM HE FIRMLY REJECTS. NYMPHS ARE TINY, PERFECTLY SCULPTURED FEMALES ...CARTOONISTS' DELIGHTS...AND THIS FIGURE IS ANYTHING BUT THAT.
--AND MISSES!!
FLUIDLY, HE BRUSHES PAST THE LAST CLINGING MOSS, GAUGING DISTANCE AND SPEED--
THE PANTHER NEARLY LAUGHS ALOUD. IT IS A GOOD THING TAYETE AND KAZIBE AREN'T HERE TO SEE THIS. MONICA WOULD LAUGH, BUT IT WOULD BE GAIETY AND HER TOUCH WOULD BE SOOTHING--
--ENOUGH TO MAKE A MAN WHOLE!
ARE YOU LOOKING FOR ME?
HOW DID YOU DO THAT?
WHERE ARE YOU?
DOES IT MATTER?
I ASK AGAIN. WHO ARE YOU?
WOULD A NAME MEAN ANYTHING TO YOU? WOULD IT GIVE YOU AN IDENTITY TO FIGHT?
I DON'T WANT TO FIGHT YOU. I'M AFTER KILL-MONGER. I WANT TO KNOW WHY HE'S ENTERED THIS TREACHEROUS TERRAIN.
DO YOU KNOW WHERE KILLMONGER IS?
CAN'T YOU PICK UP HIS SCENT?

HE HAS PASSED BY HERE--
--AND HE WASN'T ALONE! YOU'RE RIGHT, WHO-EVER YOU ARE!
MOKADI.
WHO...OR WHAT...ARE YOU?
WHAT DO YOU WANT ME TO BE?
DO YOU COME FROM HERE? DO YOU KNOW WHY THIS PLACE IS CALLED SERPENT VALLEY?
WHY DO YOU THINK IT HAS SUCH A NAME?
ARE THERE SERPENTS HERE?
WHO ARE THE SERPENTS? AND HOW MANY BREEDS OF SERPENTS ARE THERE?
YOU ANSWER QUESTIONS WITH QUESTIONS.

I HAVE NO ANSWERS. YOU ARE THE ONE WHO MOVES AND ACTS AS IF HE HAS ALL THE ANSWERS.
HE DOESN'T!

AND WHAT ARE YOU, MOKADI? THE EMBODIMENT OF A JUDGE AND JURY?
AND WHY DO YOU FOLLOW ME?
DON'T YOU KNOW WHY?

NO. BUT I KNOW KILL-MONGER AND HIS MEN ARE CLOSE AT HAND--
--AND I REMEMBER INNOCENTS SLAUGHTERED TO FURTHER HIS ATTACK IN GAINING THE THRONE OF CENTRAL WAKANDA!

OR ARE YOU EVEN AWARE THERE IS A LAND BEYOND THE MIST THAT HOVERS OVER YOUR VALLEY?
AND IF I WAS, WHAT WOULD I SEE?
A BEAUTIFUL LAND.


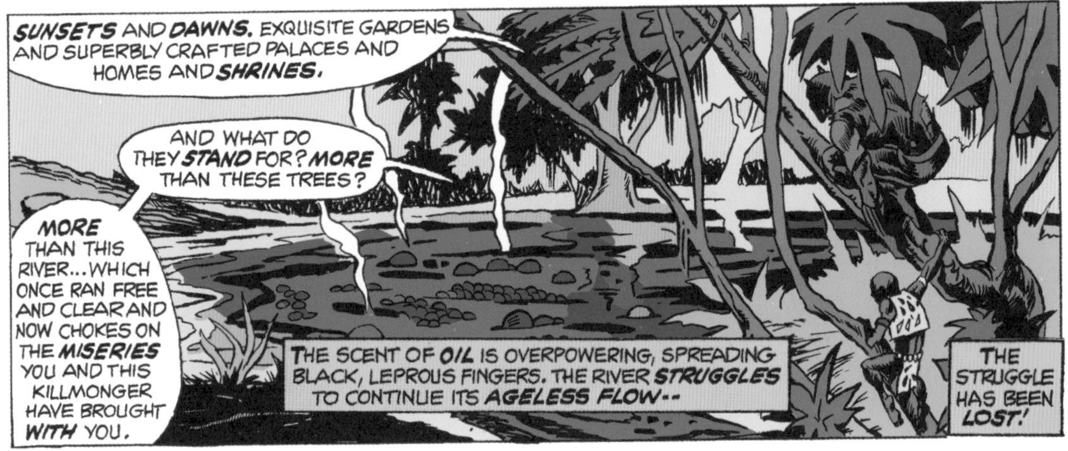

SUNSETS AND DAWNS. EXQUISITE GARDENS AND SUPERBLY CRAFTED PALACES AND HOMES AND SHRINES.
AND WHAT DO THEY STAND FOR? MORE THAN THESE TREES?
MORE THAN THIS RIVER...WHICH ONCE RAN FREE AND CLEAR AND NOW CHOKES ON THE MISERIES YOU AND THIS KILLMONGER HAVE BROUGHT WITH YOU.
THE SCENT OF OIL IS OVERPOWERING, SPREADING BLACK, LEPROUS FINGERS. THE RIVER STRUGGLES TO CONTINUE ITS AGELESS FLOW--
THE STRUGGLE HAS BEEN LOST!

THE VALLEY IS APTLY NAMED. IT IS EVOLUTION DENIED, TIME STANDING AS STAGNANT AS THE AIR AND WATER. NOON HAS ALMOST ARRIVED, BRINGING WITH IT AN OPPRESSIVE HEAT THAT DOES NOT COME FROM ANY VISIBLE SUN BUT LEAVES FLESH GLISTENING WITH SWEAT.
THE BEHEMOTHS ARE DESCENDENTS OF THE BRACHIOSAURUS. THEY WEIGH NEAR 50 TONS, AND THEY GROWL WORDLESS ANGER. THE MEN EMPTYING BARRELS OF THE THICK, FOUL LIQUID WHICH IMPRISONS THE BEASTS ARE STILL TERRIFIED OF THEM.
KILLMONGER IS IN GOOD SPIRITS. THE DAY HAS GONE WELL. TAYETE AND KAZIBE, AS THE OTHERS OF HIS REGIMENT, FEAR THAT THE CREATURE WILL REND THE NETS, PULL FREE FROM THE SLUDGE.
BUT KILLMONGER KNOWS THEIR EFFORTS ARE IN VAIN, AND HE FEELS THE TREMENDOUS POWER OF THESE MAGNIFICENT ANACHRONISMS AS IF IT IS A PART OF HIS OWN STRENGTH, A MINDLESS FORCE THAT HE CAN MAKE PERFORM AT HIS COMMAND--
--TO SHATTER A THRONE...TO REDUCE STONE TO RUBBLE...TO LEAD A CONQUEROR'S ASSAULT!
LAUGH, TAYETE! NOW YOU CAN RELAX.
AFTER WE CAPTURE A FEW MORE OF THESE SUPERB SPECIMENS, WE'LL BE ABLE TO LEAVE SERPENT VALLEY. OF COURSE, I REALIZE YOU HAVE NO FEAR OF THIS PLACE.
PERHAPS I'LL LET YOU TRAIN WITH MY ELITE MILITIA AND LEARN HOW TO RIDE THESE CREATURES WHEN WE TRAMPLE THROUGH CENTRAL WAKANDA.
YOU'D LIKE THAT, WOULDN'T YOU, TAYETE?

COME, TAYETE. YOUR BALANCE SHOULD BE BETTER THAN THAT.
KILL...KILLMONGER?
YES, KAZIBE?
SPEAK QUICKLY... AND I HOPE YOU HAVE LEARNED YOUR LESSON--
UH...KI... KILLMONGER.
UH...KILLMONGER?
--FOR LEADING T'CHALLA TO THE LAND OF THE CHILLING MIST COULD HAVE LED HIM HERE. NOT THAT IT WOULD HAVE CHANGED ANYTHING.
YES, KAZIBE? WHAT IS IT? HURRY BEFORE YOU TRY MY PATIENCE.
I DON'T MEAN TO INTERRUPT..
--BUT DON'T YOU THINK TAYETE COULD...UH ...DROWN IN THAT STUFF?
THERE'S NOT A CHANCE OF THAT, KAZIBE. TAYETE IS JUST ANXIOUS TO JOIN THE OTHERS.
THAT'S RIGHT, ISN'T IT, TAYETE?
SU...SURE.
I THINK.
FRAIL FIGURES MERGED IN... TRAGEDIES.
THE GRACEFUL WINGS FLUTTER. WEAK BIRD-TRILLING SEEMS TO ASK WHAT HAS HAPPENED TO THE GIFT OF FLIGHT.
HANDS REACHING.--
ONE HAND REACHING FIRST.
THE BIRD DOES NOT HAVE SENTIENT THOUGHT, BUT ITS EYES ARE NEARLY HUMAN. THEY BLEED WITH PANIC.
TAYETE, IF WE LOST TIME SAVING EACH HELPLESS STRAY ON OUR ROAD TO GREATNESS--
IT MAKES THE SAME QUINTESSENTIAL, TRAGIC EFFORTS AS THE BEHEMOTHS,
BUT ITS PLAINTIVE DEATH-CRIES ARE LOST IN THE VASTNESS OF EVENTS.
--WE WOULD NEVER REACH OUR DESTINATION.
AS USUAL!

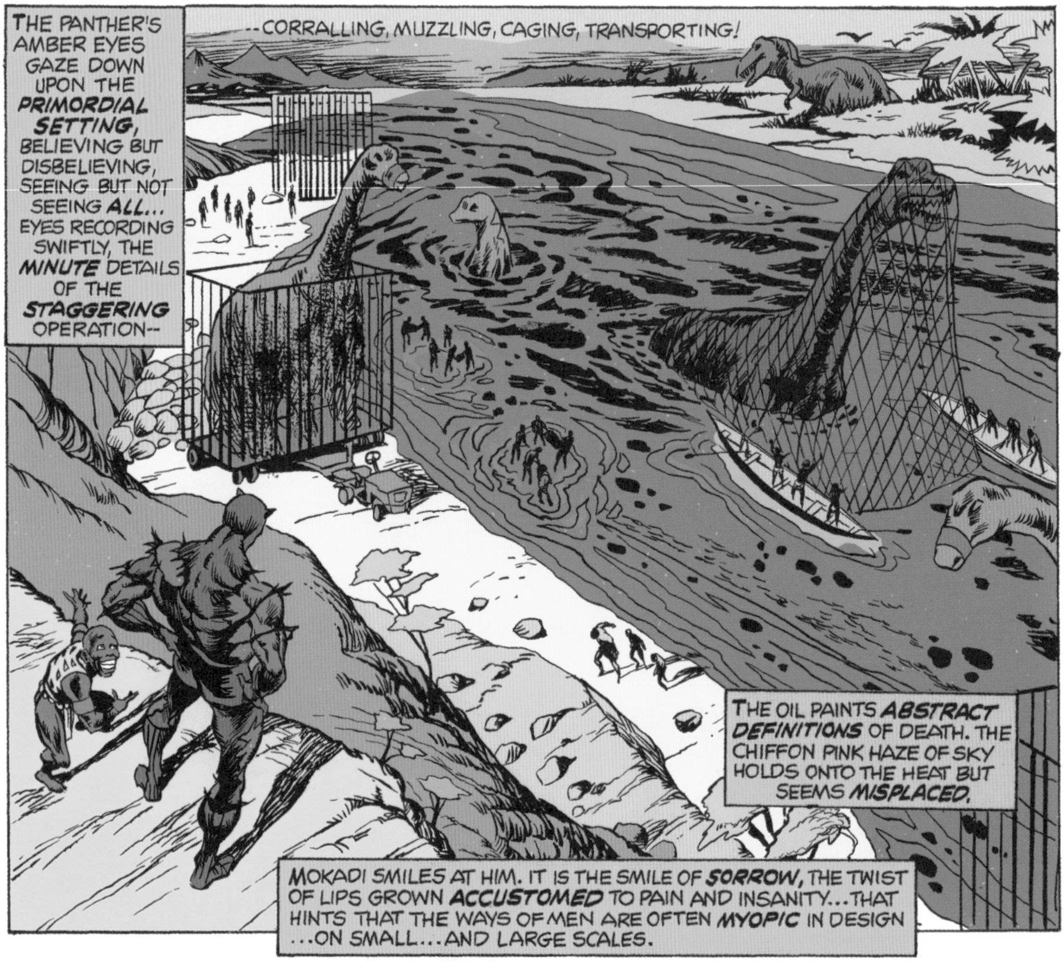

THE PANTHER'S AMBER EYES GAZE DOWN UPON THE ***PRIMORDIAL SETTING***, BELIEVING BUT DISBELIEVING, SEEING BUT NOT SEEING ***ALL***... EYES RECORDING SWIFTLY, THE ***MINUTE*** DETAILS OF THE ***STAGGERING*** OPERATION--

--CORRALLING, MUZZLING, CAGING, TRANSPORTING!

THE OIL PAINTS ***ABSTRACT DEFINITIONS*** OF DEATH. THE CHIFFON PINK HAZE OF SKY HOLDS ONTO THE HEAT BUT SEEMS ***MISPLACED.***

MOKADI SMILES AT HIM. IT IS THE SMILE OF ***SORROW***, THE TWIST OF LIPS GROWN ***ACCUSTOMED*** TO PAIN AND INSANITY... THAT HINTS THAT THE WAYS OF MEN ARE OFTEN ***MYOPIC*** IN DESIGN ...ON SMALL... AND LARGE SCALES.

DO YOU STILL HAVE ALL THE ANSWERS?
I NEVER DID, MOKADI.
THE MIND REJECTS YET ANALYSES THE SITUATION AT THE SAME TIME.
LOOK AT HIM, MOKADI. HE STRIDES ARROGANTLY... A MONUMENTAL OPPORTUNIST. ANY NEW ELEMENT AND KILLMONGER SEIZES IT. I OFTEN WONDER HOW HE JUSTI-FIES WHAT HE DOES.

SHOULD WE ONCE MORE SPEAK OF MORALITY?
I WISH WE WOULDN'T, MOKADI.
I WOULD HAVE THOUGHT IT IMPOSSIBLE TO GET THOSE STOLEN HYDRAULIC MOVERS DOWN HERE--
--BUT THEN, KILL-MONGER'S SPECIALTY IS THE IMPOSSIBLE.
HAS ANYONE EVER TOLD YOU, YOU HAVE A GREAT SENSE OF DRAMATICS, T'CHALLA?

KILLMONGER IMAGINES TAYETE'S NIGHTMARISH FRIGHT AND HE IS PLEASED. HE KNOWS THE REST OF HIS REGIMENT HOLD SIMILAR DREAD--
--LYING AWAKE IN THE DARK, LISTENING TO DISTANT PRIMAL CHALLENGES, BREATHING IN THE MIASMA OF OIL AND ROTTING VEGETATION--
--THE PAST MARAUDING THE PRESENT...AND THE MIND UNABLE TO ACCEPT THE FACT.
KILLMONGER, DID YOU SEE?
IT'S HIM. THE PANTHER-DEVIL.
TAYETE... HE TOLD YOU NOT TO CALL HIM THAT.
THIS IS NOT ANOTHER EXAMPLE OF YOUR NERVOUS FANTASIES, IS IT, TAYETE?
IF YOU DID SEE HIM IN THOSE WOODS, I SUPPOSE IT IS A STATEMENT OF HIS ENDURANCE--
--BUT IF HE'S NOT DEAD...HE SOON WILL BE.
A BUTTON IS PRESSED--
--AND A BARRED DOOR SWINGS OPEN!
THE PANTHER REELS BACKWARD. THE GUARD WHO HAS ACTIVATED THE MECHANISM FLEES.
THE CREATURE IS A TYRANNOSAURUS. ITS TAIL BATTERS AT THE CAGE WALLS, AND A SOUND COMES FROM DEEP WITHIN ITS CHEST--
MOKADI, WHOEVER YOU ARE...THIS IS NOT THE TIME FOR QUESTIONS.
--AN ANCIENT SOUND THAT INSPIRES TERROR INSIDE THE PANTHER THAT IS ALMOST KIN TO CROMAGNON TEMPERAMENT.
WHAT DO..?

CENTRAL WAKANDA SEEMS TO BE HOLDING ITS BREATH... WAITING. TRANQUILITY TEMPLE: BLOSSOMS A DREAMER CAN TOUCH, FOUNTAINS TO GENTLY KEEP THE SILENCE FROM BECOMING OPPRESSIVE. TOUCH THE SOFT PETAL, CRUSHED RED. IT DOESN'T DRIP BLOOD, DOES IT? BRUSH THE BLUE LEAVES. THEY DO NOT WEEP.
TRANQUILITY TEMPLE: A FANTASY CONSTRUCTED INTO ARCHITECTURAL AND HORTICULTURAL REALITY.
T'CHALLA IS GONE NOW. HE SHOULD HAVE BEEN BACK. BUT HE ISN'T, AND HE HAS LEFT ME IN CHARGE... TO KEEP CONTROL OF THE PRISONERS CAPTURED IN THE RAID ON KILLMONGER'S VILLAGE.
AND NOW, YOUR MOTHER AND I, LIVE IN THE SAME PLACE ...BUT ARE APART.
W'KABI LOOKS AT HIS SON KONO AND TRIES TO HOLD BACK HIS HURT. SUCH EMOTION IS NOT SUITABLE FOR ONE WHO IS HEAD OF COURT SECURITY. KONO RETURNS HIS LOOK, AND THE MISERY ENGULFS THEM BOTH...AS IF EACH WERE HOPING THE OTHER COULD SAVE THEM.
TAKU WOULD KNOW MORE OF THIS KIND OF THING THAN I. IT IS...DIFFICULT...TO LOSE HER CARING.
ONCE YOUR MOTHER AND I WERE CLOSE. I THINK THAT IS DIFFICULT FOR YOU TO IMAGINE.
WHEN WE FIRST MET, MY SON, WE WERE DIFFERENT PEOPLE. WE DID NOT HURL ACCUSATIONS AT EACH OTHER.
I FEEL HURT AND ANGER, MY SON, AND THEY MAKE ME DO THINGS THAT FORCE US FARTHER APART.
BUT WHAT WORDS DO YOU SAY...ARE THERE ANY WORDS TO SAY...TO SOMEONE YOU ONCE KNEW--
--WHO YOU CAN NO LONGER FREELY TOUCH--
--WHOSE WARMTH YOU HAVE LOST. DO YOU UNDERSTAND, MY SON?
I AM LOST!

MONICA LYNNE LOOKS PAST TAKU AND SEES THE TWO FIGURES WARMED BY BRIGHT SUNLIGHT, BUT SHE IS MORE AWARE OF THE COLD SHADOWS--
--SYMBOLIC SHADOWS REVEALED IN THEIR STANCE, BY THE BROKEN SLOPE OF SHOULDERS, THE DESPONDENT ANGLE OF LOWERED HEADS.
W'KABI SEEMS DEEPLY DISTURBED, TAKU.
PERHAPS W'KABI ONLY KNOWS ONE TYPE OF BATTLEGROUND.
IT TAKES NO MORE THAN TWO PEOPLE TO INDULGE IN WARFARE--
--AND WITH TWO, THE COMBAT IS MORE INTIMATE.

I THINK I CAN DIG WHERE YOU'RE COMING FROM, TAKU. AND LIKE MOST WARS, YOU HAVE TO LIVE THROUGH IT BEFORE YOU CAN DETERMINE THE TRUTHS AND EFFECTS OF THE BATTLE--
--AND EVEN THEN SEEKING TRUTH IS A DIFFICULT TASK, FOR ONE DOES NOT TAKE THE MAIMING RECEIVED WITHOUT A BIASED VIEW OF WHAT WENT DOWN.

I BEGIN TO SEE WHY MY CHIEFTAIN REGARDS YOU SO HIGHLY, MISS LYNNE.
YOU ARE LIKE T'CHALLA IN MANY WAYS, TAKU. YOU BOTH LISTEN WELL.
WHEN T'CHALLA FIRST BROUGHT ME TO WAKANDA FROM THE STATES, I WAS CERTAIN I HAD W'KABI PEGGED, THAT HE SPENT ALL HIS TIME HATING ME FOR BEING AN OUTWORLDER.
I THOUGHT I COULD READ W'KABI LIKE A BOOK WITHOUT HAVING TO READ AND ANALYZE PASSAGES INSIDE.

I THOUGHT HE WAS NOTHING BUT A MACHO FREAK SOLD ON MUSCLES AND MYTHS OF WAR.
BUT THERE'S MORE TO HIM, ISN'T THERE? HE'S GOING THROUGH A DEEPER THREAT WITHIN HIS HEAD. AND IF ANYONE KNOWS WHERE W'KABI'S AT, TAKU...I'LL BET IT'S YOU.
T'CHALLA CALLS YOU A COMMUNICATIONS COMMANDER. MY MAN HAS A WAY WITH WORDS AND TITLES ...BUT I THINK YOU'RE MORE AT HOME WITH HUMANS... THAN MECHANICAL TRANSMISSIONS.

I PROMISED HORATIO I WOULD VISIT HIM UPON MY RETURN, MISS LYNNE.
YOU MEAN VENOMM? IN THE THREE MONTHS HE'S BEEN HELD PRISONER, YOU'VE HAD SOME HEAVY RAP SESSIONS, HUH?
THE PHRASE "RAP" IS UNKNOWN TO ME, MISS LYNNE. I THINK I HAVE HEARD T'CHALLA USE IT, BUT HORATIO AND I HAVE NEVER HIT EACH OTHER.

I HAVE JUST COME BACK FROM KILLMONGER'S VILLAGE. HORATIO HAD KEPT MANY OF HIS SNAKES THERE AND WANTED TO KNOW WHAT HAD HAPPENED TO THEM SINCE WE RAIDED THE VILLAGE.
IT WAS A PAINFUL RETURN. I COULD NOT FORGET THE KILLING AND RECALLED THE YOUNG CHILD I CARRIED AWAY, LIMP AND BROKEN. HE BECAME MORE THAN A CHILD.
HE WAS ALL THE SPILLED BLOOD SINCE THIS REVOLUTION BEGAN.
I STOLE HIS IDENTITY FROM HIM BY DOING THAT... AND I AM SADDENED TO LOSE THE ONE FOR THE WHOLE. DO YOU UNDERSTAND?

YES, TAKU. WE FIGHT FOR THINGS WE FEAR WE'LL LOSE... AND OFTEN LOSE THEM ANYWAY.
I CANNOT IMAGINE A WORLD IN WHICH T'CHALLA IS NOT ALIVE.
NEITHER CAN I, MISS LYNNE. FOR HE IS, AT LEAST, A SEEKER OF TRUTH--
--AND THERE ARE VERY FEW OF THOSE LEFT.

THE PALACE CORRIDORS WHISPER COMPUTER MESSAGES, EACH READ-OUT SHEET A REMINDER OF T'CHALLA'S VISIONS--
THEY WOULD NOT REPLACE THE FABULOUS MESSAGE DRUMS TAKU HAD STUDIED AS A CHILD... THEY WOULD WORK BESIDE THEM.
AH, VISIONS.

I AM HERE, HORATIO. AS I PROMISED. I HAVE SEEN THE PIT WHERE YOU KEPT YOUR SNAKES...AND THEY ARE STILL THERE.

YOU'RE ONE-A THE FEW PEOPLE OUTSIDE OF ERIK THAT DON'T TREAT ME LIKE A FREAK, TAKU.
AIN'T NEVER HAD WHAT YOU'D CALL...A LOTTA "FRIENDS."

BUT REMEMBER, TAKU, I'M GONNA GET OUTTA HERE...AN' WHEN I MAKE MY BREAK... DON'T GET IN MY WAY...
I DON'T WANNA HAFTA KILL YA--
--BUT THAT WON'T STOP ME FROM DOIN' IT!

THE TYRANNOSAURUS REX HARDLY SEEMS TO NOTICE THE SINUOUS FORM IT CRUSHES IN ITS CLAW-LIKE APPENDAGE.
THE FORELIMBS RAISE, WEAKLY, RIDICULOUSLY WEAK FOR A MONSTROSITY WHICH STANDS EIGHTEEN FEET HIGH...
...ALMOST POWERLESS WHEN COMPARED AGAINST ITS WEIGHT OF EIGHT TONS--
--ALMOST USELESS IF ITS PREY WERE NOT A MAN WHOSE BACK HAS ALREADY HAD FLESH TORMENTS GASHED ACROSS IT.
HIS BLOOD FLOWS WARMLY AGAIN. IT IS A FACT HE CANNOT ESCAPE. VIOLENCE HAS ITS OWN REALITY... AND IT IS UN-GLAMORIZED AND AS PRIMEVAL AS THE SETTING WHICH THE SAVAGERY ERUPTS.
THE PANTHER'S TORN COSTUME HAS BECOME A DARK CLOTH SPONGE THAT ABSORBS THE WARMTH OF HIS BLOOD.
HE STRAINS, FORCING A KNEE BETWEEN HIMSELF AND THE TWIN TALONS. THE MOUTH IS A WET CAVERN WITH SIX INCH CURVED TEETH, AND IT SMELLS OF SWAMP MURK AND PAST CARNIVOROUS MEALS.
SALIVA, THE CONSISTENCY OF MEMBRANOUS TISSUE, FALLS UPON HIS CHEST...MIXING WITH THE RED FLUID THAT RUSHES FROM NEW WOUNDS.
THE TENDONS IN HIS LEGS ACHE WITH THE STRAIN, BUT SUDDENLY THE GRASP IS THRUST APART--
--AND HE DROPS, SLAMMING TOWARD THE EARTH.

IN MID-FLIGHT, HE EXECUTES A SUPERB SOMERSAULT--
--HITTING THE EARTH WITH AN IMPACT THAT DRIVES THE AIR OUT OF HIS LUNGS PAST SNARLING LIPS.

HIS EYES BLUR!
THE BLUR FOCUSES, AND THE BEAST IS THERE BEFORE HIM--

--AND THIS TIME IT IS AWARE OF THE TINY BLUE SPECK--

--AS IF ITS EYES HAVE ACTUALLY BECOME TRANSFIXED BY ITS MINISCULE MOVEMENTS.
HE CLAWS DESPERATELY AT THE CLIFFSIDE, TEARING HIS WOUNDS OPEN WIDER, THE BLOOD COLLECTING AT THE SMALL OF HIS BACK.

HE LOOKS PAST THE RAVENOUS MOUTH FOR SOME SIGHT OF MOKADI.
GONE.
VANISHED? AS ABRUPTLY AS HE APPEARED.
OR IS HE TRAPPED BELOW, MANGLED FLESH LEFT IN THE CREATURE'S WAKE? AND WHY DOES THE NAME MOKADI FLIRT TANTALYZINGLY AT HIS SUBCONSCIOUS, AS IF HE HAS PAST KNOWLEDGE OF ITS NAME?

RAGGED YET ELEGANT--
--TORN BUT UNIFIED--
--CLOUD AND SKY AS DISTANT WITNESSES!

HE SPRINGS INTO THE AFTERNOON AIR, AND FOR A MOMENT, ALL THE PARTICIPANTS IN THE **PRIMORDIAL CONFLICT** ARE CAPTURED IN **SPLENDID** MOVEMENT--

--THE **POETIC SYMMETRY** OF BODY AND LIMB AND MIND COMBINING TO ONE EFFECT.

HE CATCHES AT THE TREE, AND IT NEARLY **WRENCHES** HIS ARMS OUT OF THEIR SOCKETS--

--BUT HE **CLINGS** TO THE SAPLING AND IT **BENDS** UNDER HIS WEIGHT.

IT CURVES TO THE GROUND, QUIVERING WITH **UNLEASHED** POWER--

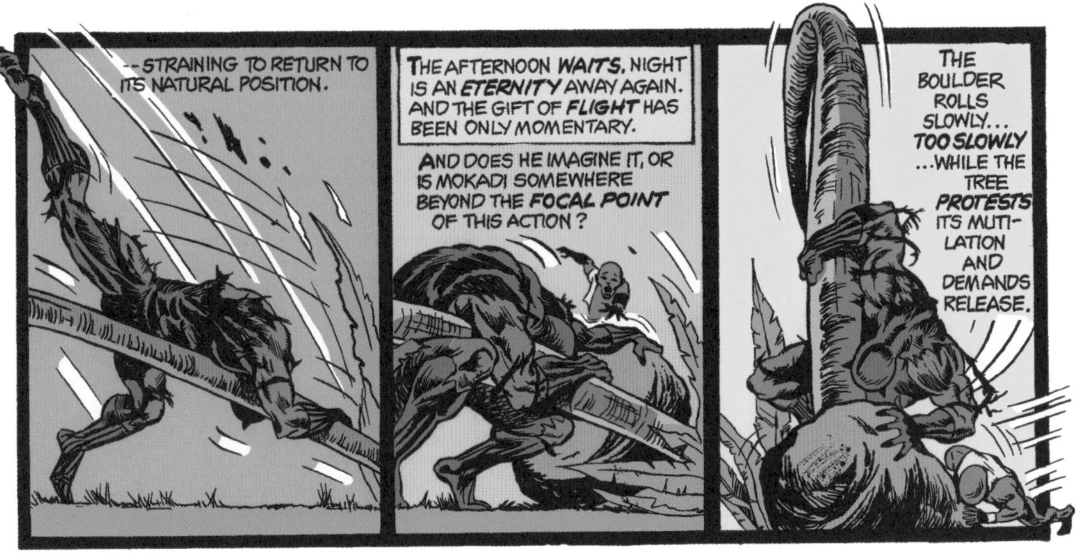

--STRAINING TO RETURN TO ITS NATURAL POSITION.
THE AFTERNOON WAITS. NIGHT IS AN ETERNITY AWAY AGAIN. AND THE GIFT OF FLIGHT HAS BEEN ONLY MOMENTARY.
AND DOES HE IMAGINE IT, OR IS MOKADI SOMEWHERE BEYOND THE FOCAL POINT OF THIS ACTION?
THE BOULDER ROLLS SLOWLY... TOO SLOWLY ...WHILE THE TREE PROTESTS ITS MUTILATION AND DEMANDS RELEASE.

GOLIATH AT THE INSTANT OF HIS DOWNFALL--
--NEVER ABLE TO COMPREHEND THE TURN OF EVENTS!
AND BLOOD CLAIMS THE AFTERNOON.
"MOKADI," HE CALLS WEAKLY, TREMBLING. HE IS VAGUELY AWARE THAT KILLMONGER HAS LEFT. "MOKADI," HE WHISPERS, THEN REALIZES THE SPRITE IS GONE.
WAS HE EVER REALLY THERE? HE HAS HEARD THE WORD MOKADI BEFORE. TO THE BOMITABA TRIBE IN THE LIKUALA REGION OF AFRICA THE TERM MEANS...
SPIRIT.
QUESTIONS.
YOU HAVE TO ASK THE QUESTIONS --BUT BEFORE YOU CAN ASK YOU MUST LEARN WHAT THE QUESTIONS ARE.
WHO WERE YOU, MOKADI? A THOUGHT MIRROR OR SAGE PYGMI?
LIMPLY, HE LEAVES THE SCENE. HE MUST SEEK HERBS TO SALVE HIS WOUNDS.
WHO ARE THE SERPENTS? AND HOW MANY BREEDS ARE THERE?
A FEW CRUCIAL ELEMENTS OF THE SCENE ARE MISSED.
FOR SOME, NIGHT DOES NOT ARRIVE.
AS USUAL.

# *JUNGLE ACTION* #15,
# MAY 1975

JUNGLE ACTION
MARVEL COMICS GROUP
APPROVED BY THE COMICS CODE AUTHORITY
25¢
15 MAY 02161
JUNGLE ACTION
THE BLACK PANTHER
PREHISTORIC DEATH LOOMS HIGH ABOVE WAKANDA--FLESH-PIERCING DOOM WAITS BELOW!
THERE IS DANGER APLENTY IN THE FOREST OF THORNS! GET THE POINT, PILGRIM?
THE BLACK PANTHER IS ABOUT TO!

Stan Lee PRESENTS: THE BLACK PANTHER!™
DON MCGREGOR WRITER
BILLY GRAHAM ARTIST
DAN GREEN INKER
KAREN MANTLO, LETTERER GLYNIS OLIVER WEIN, COLORIST
LEN WEIN EDITOR
THORNS IN THE FLESH THORNS IN THE MIND
PANTHER'S RAGE CONTINUES:
INSECURITY! IT STABS INTO THE BRAIN AND LAYS CLAIM TO ITS TERRITORY!
ITS THORNS OF SELF-DOUBT WILL RIP YOUR PSYCHE AS WELL AS YOUR FLESH--
--AND ITS MARKS MAY LAST A LIFETIME OF CRYPTIC, NEAR UNCIPHERABLE COM-PULSIONS THAT LEAD YOU TOWARD... DESTRUCTION!
THE FOREST OF THORNS IS SILENT AND THICK WITH THE SCENT OF CACTUS RIPENING IN THE TROPIC HEAT. THE BLACK PANTHER'S ACUTE SENSES BURN WITH THE ODOR OF THE BRIARS--
--AND THUS, HE IS NOT YET AWARE OF...
SALAMANDER K'RUEL!

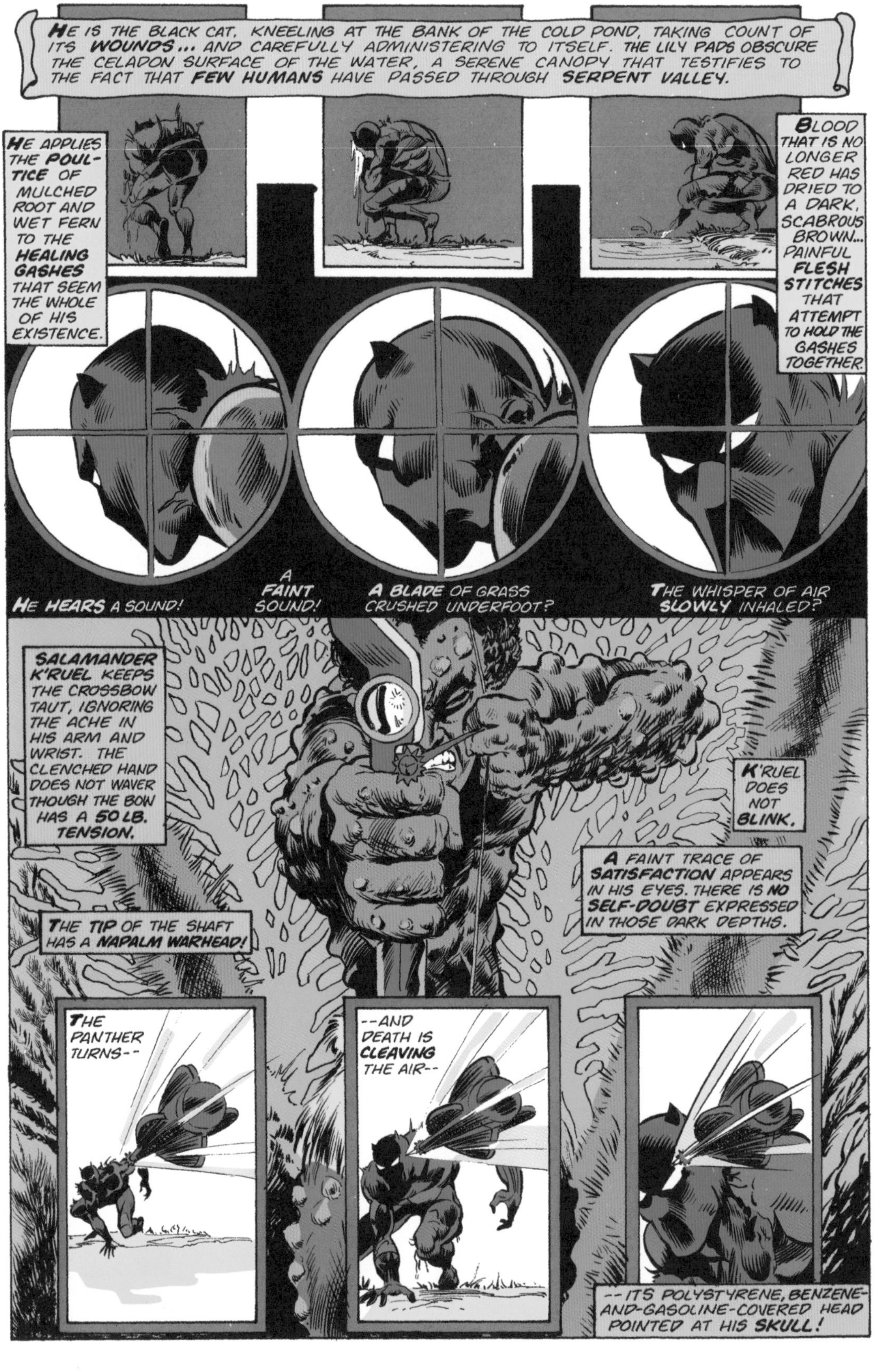

HE IS THE BLACK CAT, KNEELING AT THE BANK OF THE COLD POND, TAKING COUNT OF ITS **WOUNDS...** AND CAREFULLY ADMINISTERING TO ITSELF. THE LILY PADS OBSCURE THE CELADON SURFACE OF THE WATER, A SERENE CANOPY THAT TESTIFIES TO THE FACT THAT **FEW HUMANS** HAVE PASSED THROUGH **SERPENT VALLEY**.

HE APPLIES THE **POULTICE** OF MULCHED ROOT AND WET FERN TO THE **HEALING GASHES** THAT SEEM THE WHOLE OF HIS EXISTENCE.

BLOOD THAT IS NO LONGER RED HAS DRIED TO A DARK, SCABROUS BROWN... PAINFUL **FLESH STITCHES** THAT ATTEMPT **TO HOLD THE GASHES TOGETHER**.

**HE HEARS** A SOUND!

A **FAINT** SOUND!

**A BLADE** OF GRASS CRUSHED UNDERFOOT?

THE WHISPER OF AIR **SLOWLY** INHALED?

**SALAMANDER K'RUEL** KEEPS THE CROSSBOW TAUT, IGNORING THE ACHE IN HIS ARM AND WRIST. THE CLENCHED HAND DOES NOT WAVER THOUGH THE BOW HAS A **50 LB. TENSION.**

**K'RUEL** DOES NOT **BLINK.**

**A** FAINT TRACE OF **SATISFACTION** APPEARS IN HIS EYES. THERE IS **NO SELF-DOUBT** EXPRESSED IN THOSE DARK DEPTHS.

THE **TIP** OF THE SHAFT HAS A **NAPALM WARHEAD!**

THE PANTHER TURNS--

--AND DEATH IS **CLEAVING** THE AIR--

--ITS POLYSTYRENE, BENZENE-AND-GASOLINE-COVERED HEAD POINTED AT HIS **SKULL!**

DESPITE THE SWOLLEN WELTS THAT TEAR ACROSS HIS CHEST--
--DRIVING AWAY FROM THE MOMENTUM OF THE ARROW!
THERE ISN'T TIME LEFT TO CHECK FOR ANY INFECTION THAT MIGHT FESTER IN THE IN THE WOUNDS HE HAS RECEIVED IN THE PAST WEEK.
--SLICING JUST PAST HIS LEFT NIPPLE ABOVE THE HEARTLINE, THE PANTHER MOVES SPLENDIDLY--
EVEN THE SACRED RITES HE HAS UNDERGONE AS CHIEFTAIN OF THE WAKANDAS TO BECOME THE BLACK PANTHER WILL NOT SAVE HIM IF GANGRENE SETS IN.
THERE IS NO TIME LEFT AT ALL!
BRAASSH!!
HE IS STILL TWO DAYS JOURNEY FROM CENTRAL WAKANDA AND ANY OF ITS ADVANCED SURGERY AND MEDICAL CARE.
THE EXPLOSION SHATTERS THE PLACID GLADE. WILDERNESS SONNETS DIE IN THE BLAST. THE CELADON CANOPY HAS NO DEFENSE AGAINST INCENDIARY EXPLOSIVES.
IT SELDOM DOES!
THE THUNDER FADES... AND THE GLADE IS STILL ONCE MORE...
IT WAS THAT PANTHER-DEVIL, SALAMANDER.
IT HAD TO BE HIM.
KILLMONGER WAS RIGHT TO LEAVE US BEHIND... TO GUARD HIS TRAIL BACK TO OUR VILLAGE.
SALAMANDER K'RUEL'S VOICE IS LIKE LIGHTNING HELD IN CHECK. "YES, BUT THEN ERIK KILLMONGER SELDOM LEAVES ANYTHING TO CHANCE, M'HALAK!
"I KNEW HE WOULD OVERTHROW T'CHALLA'S REIGN. KNEW IT THAT FIRST DAY ERIK CAME TO OUR HILL VILLAGE... AND TOLD US WHAT HIS REVOLUTION WOULD MEAN TO US."
"IT WOULD SEEM THE PANTHER HAD MANY LIVES--
"BUT THIS... WAS HIS LAST LIFE!"

--BUT NOT TODAY.
SELF-DOUBT. IT CAN PARALYSE ONE INTO INACTIVITY. IT CRIPPLES THE MIND... AND THEREFORE CRIPPLES THE BODY.
SALAMANDER K'RUEL IS NOT BOTHERED BY SUCH NICETIES AS SELF-DOUBT.
YOU DO NOT DIE EASY, CHIEFTAIN OF THE WAKANDAS!
THAT'S A TITLE YOU SHOULD SAVOR. YOU WON'T HAVE IT FOR MUCH LONGER.
AFTER A COUP THE MAGNITUDE OF YOUR DEATH--
--I WONDER WHAT TITLE KILLMONGER WILL BESTOW UPON ME.
LOOKING FOR SOMETHING?
I THINK YOU'VE FOUND IT!
SELF-DOUBT. THE PANTHER HAS HAD IT AS A CONSTANT COMPANION... TO HAUNT HIS NIGHTS AND DARKEN THE SUNLIGHT. THE FIGHT SEEMS ENDLESS, AND IF THERE IS AN END, WHAT WILL IT SOLVE? ONE DAY IT MIGHT MAKE FOR INTERESTING HISTORY TEXT-BOOKS--
THE BOW HUMS VIOLENTLY AND THE PANTHER LEAPS, MAGNIFICENTLY--
SHOOOSH!
--OVER THORNS THAT JUT VICIOUSLY FROM TWISTED LIMBS--
--AND UNDER THE LETHAL SHAFT!
THUMP...
IT THUDS INTO THE PULP SURFACE OF CACTUS--

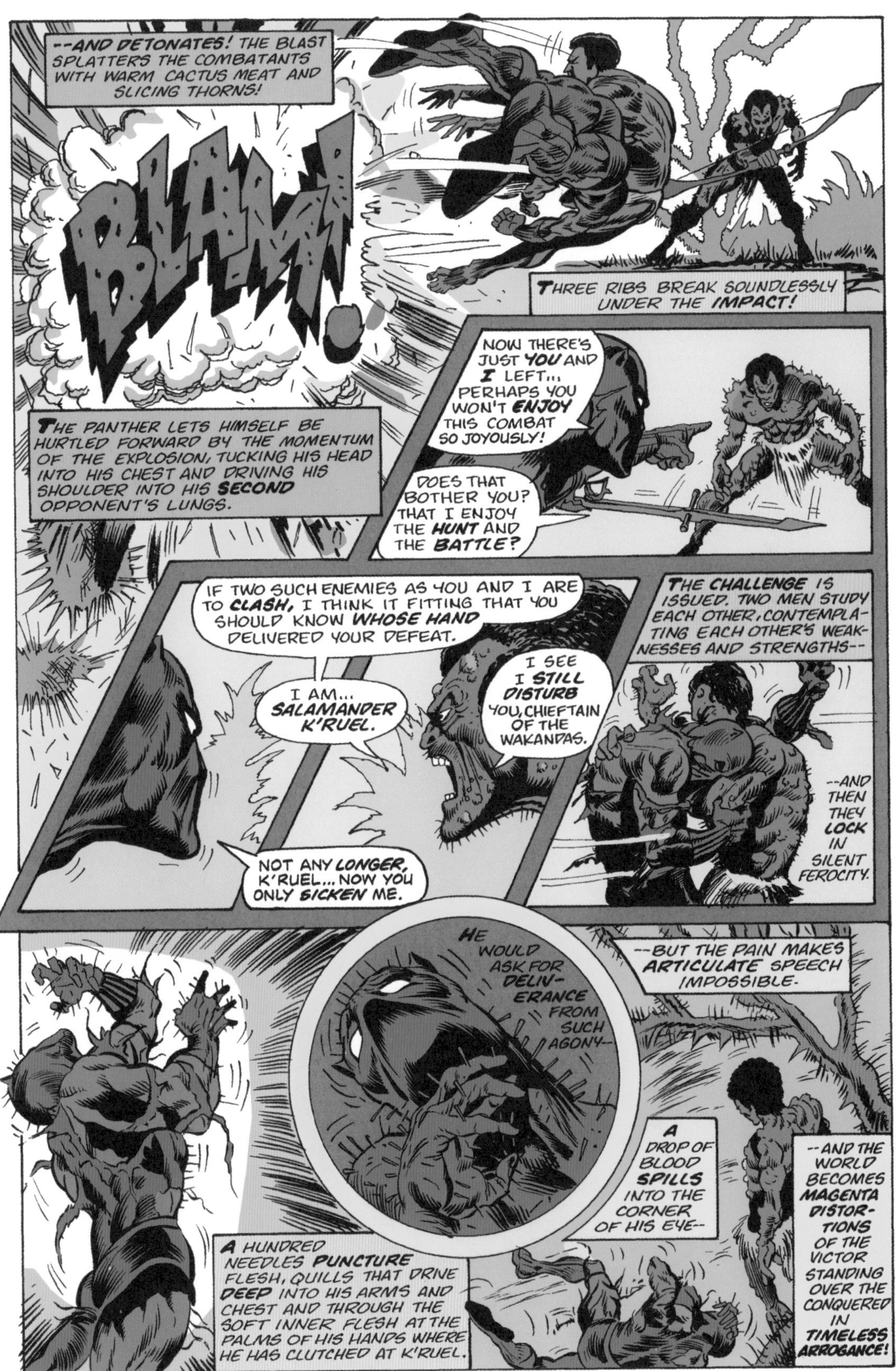
--AND DETONATES! THE BLAST SPLATTERS THE COMBATANTS WITH WARM CACTUS MEAT AND SLICING THORNS!
BLAM!
THREE RIBS BREAK SOUNDLESSLY UNDER THE IMPACT!
THE PANTHER LETS HIMSELF BE HURTLED FORWARD BY THE MOMENTUM OF THE EXPLOSION, TUCKING HIS HEAD INTO HIS CHEST AND DRIVING HIS SHOULDER INTO HIS SECOND OPPONENT'S LUNGS.
NOW THERE'S JUST YOU AND I LEFT... PERHAPS YOU WON'T ENJOY THIS COMBAT SO JOYOUSLY!
DOES THAT BOTHER YOU? THAT I ENJOY THE HUNT AND THE BATTLE?
IF TWO SUCH ENEMIES AS YOU AND I ARE TO CLASH, I THINK IT FITTING THAT YOU SHOULD KNOW WHOSE HAND DELIVERED YOUR DEFEAT.
I AM... SALAMANDER K'RUEL.
I SEE I STILL DISTURB YOU, CHIEFTAIN OF THE WAKANDAS.
NOT ANY LONGER, K'RUEL... NOW YOU ONLY SICKEN ME.
THE CHALLENGE IS ISSUED. TWO MEN STUDY EACH OTHER, CONTEMPLATING EACH OTHER'S WEAKNESSES AND STRENGTHS--
--AND THEN THEY LOCK IN SILENT FEROCITY.
A HUNDRED NEEDLES PUNCTURE FLESH, QUILLS THAT DRIVE DEEP INTO HIS ARMS AND CHEST AND THROUGH THE SOFT INNER FLESH AT THE PALMS OF HIS HANDS WHERE HE HAS CLUTCHED AT K'RUEL.
HE WOULD ASK FOR DELIVERANCE FROM SUCH AGONY--
--BUT THE PAIN MAKES ARTICULATE SPEECH IMPOSSIBLE.
A DROP OF BLOOD SPILLS INTO THE CORNER OF HIS EYE--
--AND THE WORLD BECOMES MAGENTA DISTORTIONS OF THE VICTOR STANDING OVER THE CONQUERED IN TIMELESS ARROGANCE!

UNCONSCIOUSNESS GIVES WAY TO PAIN; INTENSE, SEARING TORMENT THAT BLINDS HIS OPENING EYES. HIS SENSES ARE POSSESSED BY A COLLAGE OF WOUNDS, OLD AND NEW, BLENDING IN ONE TOTAL, EXCRUCIATING COMMENT. HE TURNS THE SCREAM THAT RISES TO HIS LIPS INTO A SNARL, BRACING HIMSELF AGAINST THE PAIN, FORCING HIS EYES TO SEE PAST THE LANCING SHAFTS OF LIGHT.
K'RUEL STANDS BEFORE HIM, BUT HE DOES NOT TRY TO MOVE. HE MUST UNDERSTAND THE TRAP FIRST.
I'VE SENT THE OTHERS HOBBLING AHEAD. I WANTED TO WAIT UNTIL YOU'D REVIVED BEFORE I LEFT TO REJOIN KILLMONGER.
YOU MIGHT THINK IT WASN'T SPORTING OF ME NOT TO WARN YOU ABOUT THE POWERS THAT I GAINED FROM RESURRECTION ALTAR. I CALL IT STRATEGY! NO HARD FEELINGS, I TRUST?
THOSE RAYS, WHATEVER THEY WERE, KILLED MANY OF THE MEN KILLMONGER HAD EXPOSED TO THEM! I DIDN'T LEARN THAT 'TILL AFTER I'D BEEN STRAPPED TO THE ALTAR.
BUT DON'T YOU HAVE ANY PARTING WORDS? NO CLEVER SHOUTS ABOUT HOW I CAN'T GET AWAY WITH THIS? HOW SAD. I'D REALLY BEEN LOOKING FORWARD TO IT.
I MUST BE LEAVING. YOU'VE DETAINED ME LONG ENOUGH AS IT IS. BUT I'LL RETURN. WITH KILLMONGER! BY THEN, THE SALAMANDERS IN THIS FOREST WILL HAVE SWARMED OVER YOUR BODY... AND THE PTERODACTYLS, LOOKING FOR A MEAL... WILL HAVE FOUND ONE!
YOU LOOK ASTONISHED. THAT CAN ONLY MEAN YOU HAVEN'T SEEN ANY OF THE FLYING REPTILES IN SERPENT VALLEY!
TAKE MY WORD FOR IT, CHIEFTAIN OF THE WAKANDAS. THEY EXIST!
GOOD-DAY, CHIEFTAIN OF THE WAKANDAS!

THE MIDMORNING HEAT CLINGS TO THE NETWORK OF BRAMBLES AND CACTUS. K'RUEL WALKS AWAY SLOWLY, FLAUNTING HIS FREEDOM. THE PANTHER DOES **NOT MOVE** UNTIL K'RUEL'S FIGURE HAS BEEN LOST AMID THE THORNED BRANCHES.

HIS EYES BEGIN TO TEAR AND TURNS THE DRIED BLOOD THERE TO RUSTY RIVULETS DRIPPING DOWN THE SIDE OF HIS FACE!
CONTROL YOUR BREATHING, HE COMMANDS VOICELESSLY. SHUT OUT THE PAIN! CONCENTRATE ON LIVING THROUGH THE NEXT BREATH UNTIL YOU HAVE FOUND A WAY TO COPE WITH THE PAIN.
THE CORDS TIGHTEN ABOUT HIS WRISTS AS HE STRAINS AGAINST THEM HE GASPS ALOUD!
THE MOVEMENT PUSHES HIS UPPER ARMS INTO THE CACTUS. GREEN SPIKES SLICE INTO HIS FLESH!
CRUELTY. IT'S A WORD YOU UNDERSTAND LIKE THE WORD PAIN... YOU GIVE IT A VAGUE DEFINITION AND FILE IT AWAY, HOPING YOU NEVER HAVE TO LEARN WHAT THE WORD REALLY MEANS.
HE WISHES THE TORTURE WEREN'T SO MINDLESS, THAT IT HAD A POINT, A REASON THAT WOULD JUSTIFY SUCH INHUMANITY.
BUT REASONS ARE SCARCE... MORE FOR FICTION THAN LIFE.
SELF-DOUBT. WHEN DID SUCH INDECISION BECOME A DECISIVE FEATURE IN HIS LIFE? WHEN HE BECAME A RULER AND HAD TO MAKE DECISIONS?
THERE IS ALWAYS SOMEONE WHO WILL HATE WHATEVER DECISION YOU MAKE... NO MATTER HOW LONG YOU TAKE IN DELIBERATION! YOU CAN NEVER SATISFY ALL OF THE PEOPLE. IS THAT AN ORIGINAL THOUGHT, T'CHALLA?
SHADOWS LENGTHEN ACROSS THE DRY LAND, ADVANCED SENTINELS ANNOUNCING THE ARRIVAL OF DUSK...
...AND DELIRIUM IS MERGED WITH SHADOWS, TURNING THE DARK SHAPES INTO MONSTROUS THINGS HE MUST COMBAT AS FIERCELY AS THE PAIN!

MEMORIES. HELTER-SKELTER, UNRELATED MOMENTS FROM HIS PAST CLOUD THE PASSAGE OF TIME. THE CACTUS LIMBS BLUR. THE LANDSCAPE IS TRANSFORMED. HIS FATHER, T'CHAKA, IS STILL ALIVE, AND T'CHALLA IS TEN YEARS OLD AND HIS FUTURE IS SHAPED IN GOLDEN AFTERNOONS THAT HAVE NOTHING TO DO WITH BEING IMPALED ON DOZENS OF PIERCING THORNS.
THE ELDERS WILL TELL YOU THAT YOU MUST MASTER THE ARTS OF MANHOOD--
--BUT IF YOU LEARN THEM AT THE EXPENSE OF THE ART OF CHILDHOOD, MY SON, YOU WILL LEARN ONLY SELF-DECEPTION.
I WILL ALWAYS LOVE THIS PLACE!
SELF-DECEPTION? IS THAT THE SAME THING AS SELF-DOUBT?
BUT YOU CAN LOSE THAT LOVE.
THE DAYS FOR CONTEMPLATING THE PASSAGE OF THE SUN THROUGH BEAUTIFUL SKIES ARE FEW. THERE IS LITTLE TIME TO LET THE MIND WONDER WHILE SAVORING THE WARMTH OF THE SUN ON YOUR FLESH.
YOU LOOSE THESE THINGS EASILY.
NEVER, MY FATHER. I WILL NEVER LOSE THEM.
YOU CAN LOSE THEM WITHOUT EVEN KNOWING IT HAS HAPPENED.
THEY WILL TEACH YOU WHAT YOU SHOULD SEEK. THEY WILL SHOW YOU THE PROPER THINGS TO WANT AND DESIRE--
--AND THUS, YOU MAY LOSE WHAT THE INNER SPIRIT NEEDS FOR REST.
THE IMAGERY FADES, THE PANTHER TRIES DESPERATELY TO BRING IT BACK, BUT THE ONLY IMAGE THAT REMAINS IS HIS FATHER PLACING THE TRIBAL HEADDRESS BACK ON HIS HEAD. THE MOMENT FOR SAVORING THE SUN WAS PAST.

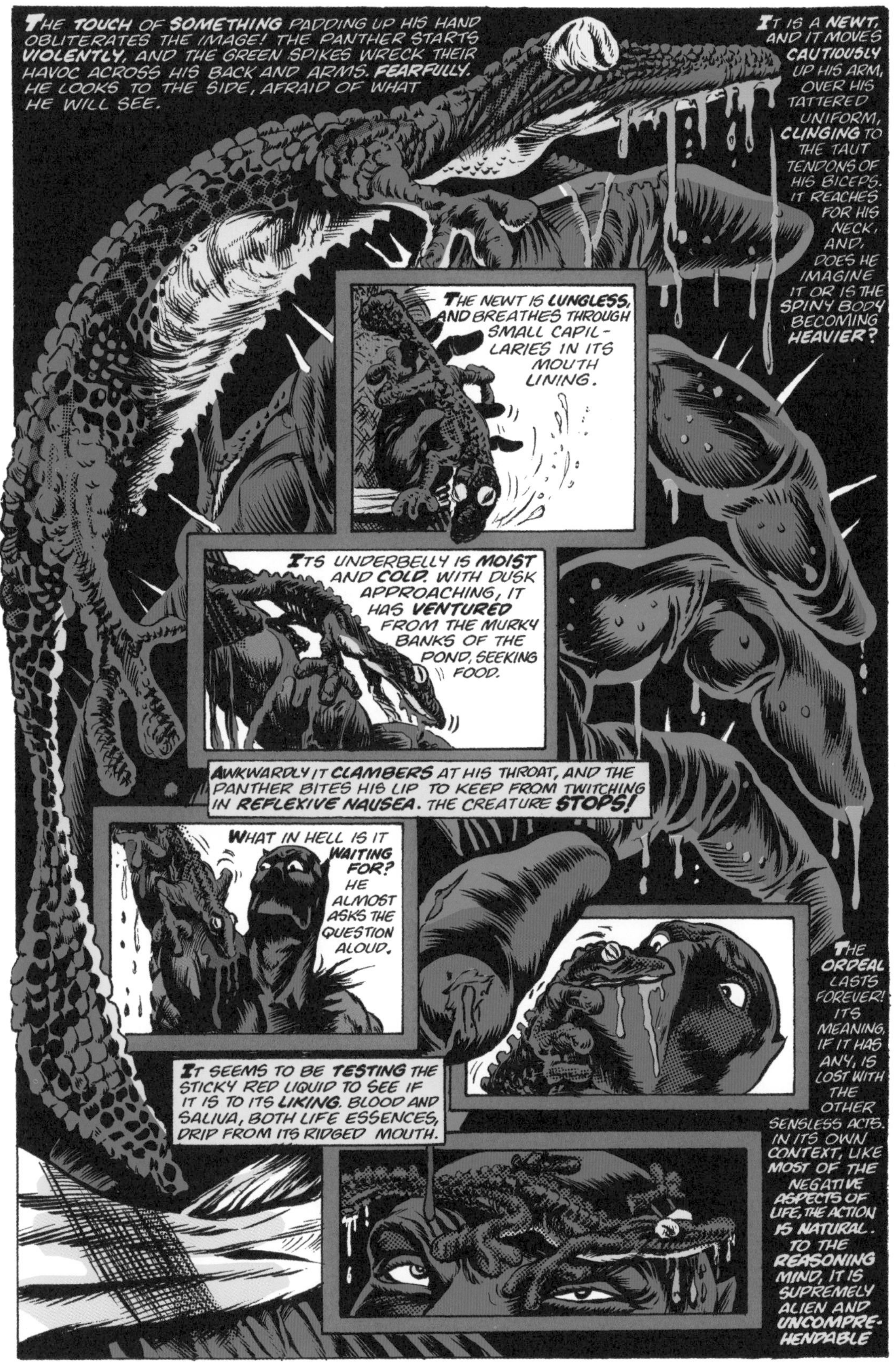
THE TOUCH OF SOMETHING PADDING UP HIS HAND OBLITERATES THE IMAGE! THE PANTHER STARTS VIOLENTLY, AND THE GREEN SPIKES WRECK THEIR HAVOC ACROSS HIS BACK AND ARMS. FEARFULLY, HE LOOKS TO THE SIDE, AFRAID OF WHAT HE WILL SEE.
IT IS A NEWT, AND IT MOVES CAUTIOUSLY UP HIS ARM, OVER HIS TATTERED UNIFORM, CLINGING TO THE TAUT TENDONS OF HIS BICEPS. IT REACHES FOR HIS NECK, AND, DOES HE IMAGINE IT OR IS THE SPINY BODY BECOMING HEAVIER?
THE NEWT IS LUNGLESS, AND BREATHES THROUGH SMALL CAPIL-LARIES IN ITS MOUTH LINING.
ITS UNDERBELLY IS MOIST AND COLD. WITH DUSK APPROACHING, IT HAS VENTURED FROM THE MURKY BANKS OF THE POND, SEEKING FOOD.
AWKWARDLY IT CLAMBERS AT HIS THROAT, AND THE PANTHER BITES HIS LIP TO KEEP FROM TWITCHING IN REFLEXIVE NAUSEA. THE CREATURE STOPS!
WHAT IN HELL IS IT WAITING FOR?
HE ALMOST ASKS THE QUESTION ALOUD.
IT SEEMS TO BE TESTING THE STICKY RED LIQUID TO SEE IF IT IS TO ITS LIKING. BLOOD AND SALIVA, BOTH LIFE ESSENCES, DRIP FROM ITS RIDGED MOUTH.
THE ORDEAL LASTS FOREVER! ITS MEANING, IF IT HAS ANY, IS LOST WITH THE OTHER SENSLESS ACTS. IN ITS OWN CONTEXT, LIKE MOST OF THE NEGATIVE ASPECTS OF LIFE, THE ACTION IS NATURAL. TO THE REASONING MIND, IT IS SUPREMELY ALIEN AND UNCOMPRE-HENDABLE

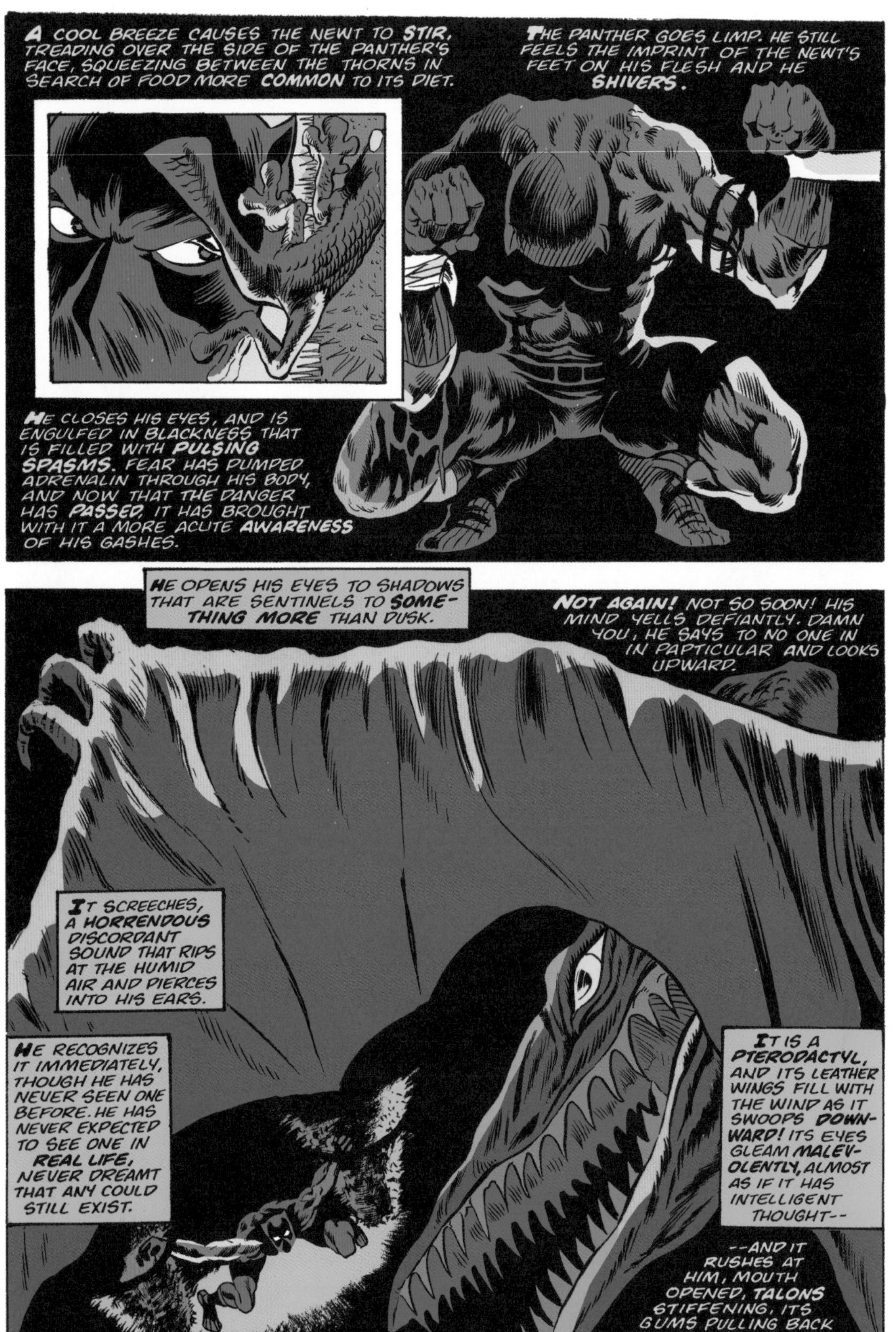
A COOL BREEZE CAUSES THE NEWT TO STIR, TREADING OVER THE SIDE OF THE PANTHER'S FACE, SQUEEZING BETWEEN THE THORNS IN SEARCH OF FOOD MORE COMMON TO ITS DIET.
THE PANTHER GOES LIMP. HE STILL FEELS THE IMPRINT OF THE NEWT'S FEET ON HIS FLESH AND HE SHIVERS.
HE CLOSES HIS EYES, AND IS ENGULFED IN BLACKNESS THAT IS FILLED WITH PULSING SPASMS. FEAR HAS PUMPED ADRENALIN THROUGH HIS BODY, AND NOW THAT THE DANGER HAS PASSED, IT HAS BROUGHT WITH IT A MORE ACUTE AWARENESS OF HIS GASHES.
HE OPENS HIS EYES TO SHADOWS THAT ARE SENTINELS TO SOMETHING MORE THAN DUSK.
NOT AGAIN! NOT SO SOON! HIS MIND YELLS DEFIANTLY. DAMN YOU, HE SAYS TO NO ONE IN IN PAPTICULAR AND LOOKS UPWARD.
IT SCREECHES, A HORRENDOUS DISCORDANT SOUND THAT RIPS AT THE HUMID AIR AND PIERCES INTO HIS EARS.
HE RECOGNIZES IT IMMEDIATELY, THOUGH HE HAS NEVER SEEN ONE BEFORE. HE HAS NEVER EXPECTED TO SEE ONE IN REAL LIFE, NEVER DREAMT THAT ANY COULD STILL EXIST.
IT IS A PTERODACTYL, AND ITS LEATHER WINGS FILL WITH THE WIND AS IT SWOOPS DOWNWARD! ITS EYES GLEAM MALEVOLENTLY, ALMOST AS IF IT HAS INTELLIGENT THOUGHT--
--AND IT RUSHES AT HIM, MOUTH OPENED, TALONS STIFFENING, ITS GUMS PULLING BACK FROM ITS BLACKISH, DISCOLORED TEETH.

HE IGNORES THE THORNS! SELF-DOUBT IS BANISHED BEHIND SURVIVAL INSTINCTS.
ITS FIRST SWOOP RAKES ACROSS THE CACTUS, SPILLING OUT GREEN-YELLOW LIQUID INTERIORS! THE CORDS SEVER AND THE PANTHER REACHES TO UNTIE THE OTHERS.
BUT HIS FINGERS ARE NUMB AND REFUSE TO RESPOND!
THE SECOND DESCENT IS BRUTAL. THE WINGED REPTILLIAN REACHES FOR THE SQUIRMING MORSEL, ITS TREMENDOUS VEINED WINGS BATTERING THE LIVING STAKE THAT THE PANTHER HAS BEEN LASHED AGAINST.
THE CACTUS SPLITS JAGGEDLY, THRUSTING SEVERAL OF ITS THORNS IN THIN GROOVES UP THE PANTHER'S BACK, AS IF UNWILLING TO GIVE UP ITS TENANT.
THE PTERODACTYL IS JUST AS ADAMANT! THE PANTHER TWISTS AND LUNGES, BUT THE EFFORT IS FUTILE, AND HE IS BORNE ALOFT, HELPLESS, BONE HARD TALONS CRUSHING HIS ARMS!
THE MAMMOTH CREATURE SHRIEKS ITS VICTORY, AND THE BRILLIANT DUSK SKY-LINE SWEEPS AWAY BENEATH THEM.
THERE IS A NOTE OF FINALITY IN THE DYING COLORS!

TWO DAYS JOURNEY AWAY IN A WORLD FURTHER DISTANT AND WHERE PTERODACTYLS ARE CONSIDERED HISTORY AND ENTERTAINMENT, THE SAME NOTE OF FINALITY IS STRUCK. THE SUN SETS IN MOLTEN DEATH OVER THE FARMLAND OUTSIDE CENTRAL WAKANDA. MONICA LYNNE STROLLS THROUGH THE TWILIGHT WITH TAKU.
KAROTA'S SMALL FARM SPREADS OUT BEFORE THEM.
KAROTA'S BEEN SO DOWN SINCE I TOOK HER TO YOUR MODERN HOSPITAL.

A SIMPLE INNOCULATION IS THE SAME THING TO HER AS HAVING A NIGHTMARE COME DOWN 'ROUND YOUR HEAD. MAN, DID IT SPOOK HER, TAKU.
I USE THE WORD LITERALLY. OR DOESN'T THAT WORD HAVE THE SAME CONNOTATIONS IN WAKANDA THAT IT DOES IN THE STATES?
YOU MEAN THE RACIAL SLUR?
I'M NOT TALKIN' 'BOUT THE C.I.A.

IT COMES TO ME THIS MIGHT BE ONE OF THE FEW PLACES IN THE WORLD THE C.I.A. ISN'T LISTENING. BUT BACK TO KAROTA.
SHE THINKS WE PUT THE SCREWS TO HER. T'CHALLA HAS SPOKEN OF CULTURE SHOCK. THE GOOD OLD U.S. OF A. SUFFERS FROM TRANSIENCE... BUT IN WAKANDA IT'S DOWN-RIGHT INTENSIFIED!

T'CHALLA SAW ONLY THE BENEFICIAL THINGS TECHNOLOGY COULD BRING HIS LAND... PERHAPS HE CHOSE TO IGNORE ANYTHING THAT THREATENED HIS DREAM--
--OR ELSE CONVINCED HIM-SELF HE COULD OVER-COME ANY SETBACK THAT MIGHT ARISE.
EVERYONE IS SEEKING PARADISE. THERE MUST BE A TRUTH ABOUT PARADISE THAT SCHOLARS HAVE OVERLOOKED.
"TRUTH IS ELUSIVE QUICKSILVER ... OPEN THE FINGERS... IT IS GONE!" TAKU REPLIES.

HELLO, KANTU. WHAT HAS HAPPENED TO THE BRAVE WARRIOR? DON'T I EVEN GET A GREETING?
LOOK AT HIM, TAKU. HE DOES NOT IMAGINE OR DREAM ANYMORE.
KILLMONGER'S MEN KILLED HIS FATHER ... IT'S ALMOST AS IF THEY'VE KILLED HIM.
VERY ELOQUENT THE WAY YOU PUT IT BEFORE, TAKU. QUICKSILVER TRUTH.
ONCE I THOUGHT I'D TOUCHED SOME BASIC TRUTHS.
HEY, LISTEN, TAKU, HAVE YOU EVER SEEN THESE GUYS IN THE CIRCUS THAT TWIRL PLATES ON TOP OF A LINE OF POLES.
TRICK IS, SEE, HE'S HE'S GOT TO KEEP 'EM ALL SPINNIN'... SPINNIN' ANY OF THE PLATES THAT START TO FALL.
PERSPECTIVE IS LIKE THAT. YOU KNOW WHERE I'M COMING FROM?
I MEAN, YOU START TO GAIN SOME INSIGHT ON A SUBJECT... FROM LOVE TO BIOLOGY ... WHATEVER ... AND YOU STUDY THAT SUBJECT, 'TILL YOU THINK YOU'RE ON TOP OF IT!
AND. SUDDENLY SOME OTHER AREA COMES AT... HITS YOU LIKE A CEMENT WALL. AND YOU REALIZE YOU KNOW NEXT TO NOTHING ABOUT THIS NEW SUBJECT SO YOU RUSH OVER THERE AND TRY TO DECIPHER ITS MYSTERIES.
I DID NOT THINK YOU WOULD DARE TO COME BACK HERE, OUT-WORLDER.
AND ON IT GOES, TILL YOU REALIZE YOU'VE NEGLECTED ALL THE OTHER TOPICS.
I DO NOT NEED YOUR HELP TO MAKE DINNER.
ALL THE PLATES START TO WOBBLE--
--AND IF THEY SMASH UPON THE FLOOR--
--YOU'LL BE LIKE KAROTA AND KANTU... LEFT ALONE IN THE DARK.
YOU ARE ONE OF T'CHALLA'S TRIBUNAL. DO YOU HEAR HOW HIS WOMAN BABBLES ON?
BE GENTLE, KAROTA. T'CHALLA HAS BEEN GONE OVER A WEEK.
I THINK SHE NEEDS YOU.

THE PALACE ROYAL REFLECTS THE SUNSET ORCHESTRATION: THE TONE OF FINALITY TURNING DARKER: SUBDUED TO A GRIM, MONOCHROMATIC HUE.
W'KABI AND CHANDRA'S QUARTERS INSIDE THE PALACE ARE LIKE A PRISON. THEY ARE EACH TRAPPED, EACH SEEKING AN EXIT... THOUGH NIETHER HAS ANY IDEA WHERE THEIR EXITS WILL LEAD!


W'KABI AND CHANDRA TRY TO EXPRESS FEELINGS THAT THEY HAVE YET TO LEARN HOW TO ARTICULATE, BUT THEY SPEAK NONETHELESS, AS IF COMPELLED TO MEET AS CONTEMPORARY GLADIATORS AGAINST AN OPPONENT THAT HAS BECOME THEMSELVES!

YOU WON'T UNDERSTAND, W'KABI.

ANYTHING I SAY WILL ONLY HURT YOU... AND I HAVE NO WISH TO DO THAT. YOU WILL NOT BELIEVE ME, OF COURSE, BUT THAT IS TRUE.

W'KABI FEELS THE ANGER RISING IN HIM AS IF IT IS AN INDEPENDENT CREATURE HE CANNOT CONTROL.

YOU SAY I DO NOT UNDERSTAND. YOU ARE RIGHT, CHANDRA, I DO NOT UNDERSTAND!

"YOU RIP OUR LIVES. YOU SEE ME AS HEAD OF COURT SECURITY AND NOTHING MORE.

"YOU HAVE TURNED OUR LIVES TOGETHER INTO A... A JOB... NOTHING MORE... NO ONE COULD HAVE TOLD ME THAT ONE DAY THAT WAS WHAT OUR LOVE WOULD BECOME!"

AT TIMES, THEY WEAKEN!

AT TIMES, THEY ARE FIERCE!

UNFORTUNATELY, THEY ARE SELDOM WEAK OR FIERCE AT THE SAME MOMENT.

AND A TOUCH MAY BE TRANSFORMED FROM SOLIDIFYING TWO INTO ONE. NOW, IT IS A WEAKNESS THAT MIGHT BE USED!

THE UPPER MOUNTAIN REGIONS OF WAKANDA SEE THE LAST NOTE OF FINALITY LINGER BEFORE THE NIGHT DESCENDS. ERIK KILLMONGER MOVES OUT OF THE SHADOWS SURROUNDING HIS VILLAGE.
HIS DARK EYES ARE WITHOUT EXPRESSION AS HE SURVEYS THE DESTRUCTION!
KING CADAVER DOES NOT TAKE THE EVENT SO CALMLY!

ERIK! THEY FOUND OUR VILLAGE AND THEY'VE LEVELED IT TO THE GROUND!

IT WAS T'CHALLA'S MEN THAT DID THIS. WHAT DO YOU THINK HAPPENED TO LORD KARNAJ AND THE DEAR BARON?

KILLMONGER LOOKS AT CADAVER, INTO THE VEINED, MESMERIZING EYES OF CADAVER'S BLISTERED FACE; AND THE HARD FACE BREAKS INTO A TIGHT SMILE THAT SHOWS GENUINE AMUSEMENT.
A SUPERIOR ENEMY GRANTING HIS FOE AN UNFORSEEN VICTORY.
SO T'CHALLA THOUGHT HE'D TRIUMPHED OVER US BEFORE HE WENT TO SERPENT VALLEY. HE DIED WITH TRIUMPH ON HIS LIPS.

BUT I NEVER GAVE T'CHALLA MUCH CONTEMPLATION IN LIFE ... IT WOULD BE FOOL-HARDY TO DO SO NOW THAT HE IS DEAD!
AND WE WILL GAIN OUR VENGEANCE FOR CENTRAL WAKANDA'S ATTACK... WHEN WE CHARGE THROUGH THEIR PRECIOUS PALACE ROYAL WITH THOSE MAGNIFICENT BEHEMOTHS WE HAVE TAKEN FROM SERPENT VALLEY.
OUR TRIUMPH, KING CADAVER, IS ONLY WEEKS AWAY.
AND THE ONLY SURVIVORS WILL PAY HOMAGE TO US!

SERPENT VALLEY TWISTS BELOW THE PANTHER IN A JAGGED CONFUSION OF GREEN LIMBS--
--AND SHARP, UPTHRUST THORNS!
THE TIPS OF THE TALONS PLUNGE INTO THE PANTHER'S CHEST. HIS CAPTOR SCREECHES ITS ANNOYANCE WHEN HE PROTESTS VIOLENTLY.
AND ITS WEAK HINDLIMBS LOSE ITS GRASP ON HIM!!
FALLING--
--HURTLING DOWNWARD--
--THE RUSH OF AIR STEALING SOUND FROM HIS LIPS--
--REACHING INSANELY FOR THE DIMINISHING FORM OF THE REPTILE. HE'D WANTED TO GET AWAY--
--BUT NOT THIS FAR AWAY.
THE THORNED LIMBS LIFT TOWARD HIM, AS IF ANXIOUS TO RECEIVE AN OFFERING!
AND HE SEES THE THORNS DRIPPING BLOOD!
RENDING!
UNYIELDING!
EYES AND CHEEKS AND LIPS AND NECK, ALL EXPOSED TO THE CARVING EDGES.
ALL THE GRACEFUL ACROBATICS IN THE WORLD CANNOT SAVE HIM FROM--
DEATH!!

A SCREAMING POUNDS IN HIS TEMPLES. IS IT HIS SCREAM OR--

NO! IT IS THE PTERODACTYL, WINGS WIDE-SPREAD, GLIDING OBSCENELY TOWARD ITS DINNER!
STEADY, BIG FELLOW!
THE WORDS ARE GASPED OUT FROM DISTORTED LIPS. HIS HANDS GROPE, SLIDING--
SLIDING!!
SLIDING OVER THE LEATHERY TEXTURE OF WINGS.
ITS DULL, UNWITTING EYE GLARES BACK AT HIM WITH PRIMEVAL ANGER, BRUTISH AND LETHAL IN ITS INTENT!
HIS FINGERS SLIDE OVER THE NECK, ACHINGLY SEEKING A GRIP!
HIS REPRIEVE FADES WITH EACH LOST INCH.
AND THEN HE HAS IT, ONE HAND CLOSING OVER A BULGING BONE THAT SWELLS BENEATH THE HIDE. AND THAT ONE HAND-HOLD BECOMES AN ARMLOCK--
--AND THE ARMLOCK ALLOWS HIM TO HOIST HIMSELF ASTRIDE THE WINGED REPTILE.
THE PTERODACTYL TRIES TO DISLODGE HIM, BUT HE GAINS HIS BALANCE, STANDING UNDEFEATED. SELF-DOUBT IS DISCARDED!
TORN AND HAGGARD, WEARY AND SPENT, BUT RELEASED AND UNCONQUERED!

K'RUEL WALKS LIESURELY, CONFIDENTLY. HE HAS LEFT HIS TWO WOUNDED AIDES BEHIND, WAVING TO THEM WITH JAUNTY GOOD SPIRITS AND CLIMBS STEADILY OUT OF SERPENT VALLEY WITHOUT REALLY SEEING HIS SURROUNDINGS.
HE DOES NOT SEE THE IMMENSE SHADOW THAT SWALLOWS HIM!

BUT HE DOES HEAR THE DULL, RYTHMIC HAMMERING AT THE AIR, A SOUND LIKE TATTERED CURTAINS MONOTONOUSLY PLAYING ETERNAL CHANTS FOR DAYS WHEN THEY WERE WHOLE.
K'RUEL LOOKS UP!

AND FOR AN INSTANT, HE IS ASTONISHED! HE IS A MAN WHO HAS FELT HIS FLESH DISINTEGRATE BURSTING INTO LIQUID BUBBLES, AND THEREFORE--
--HE DOES NOT ASTONISH EASILY.

SHADOWS ON THE SKYLINE, NIGHTMARES ON THE WING! IT IS IMPOSSIBLE, OF COURSE, BUT IF IT ISN'T, HE ALREADY HAS AN ARROW FITTED INTO THE CROSSBOW TO MAKE SURE IT'S IMPOSSIBLE.
NICE AND EASY DOES IT, BIG FELLOW!
K'RUEL HEARS THE VOICE. HE DOES NOT UTTER A SNEERING, "CHIEFTAIN OF THE WAKANDAS!"

BUT THE WORDS "PANTHER-DEVIL" ARE CLOSE ON HIS LIPS.
YOU'D BETTER MAKE THAT FIRST SHOT COUNT K'RUEL--
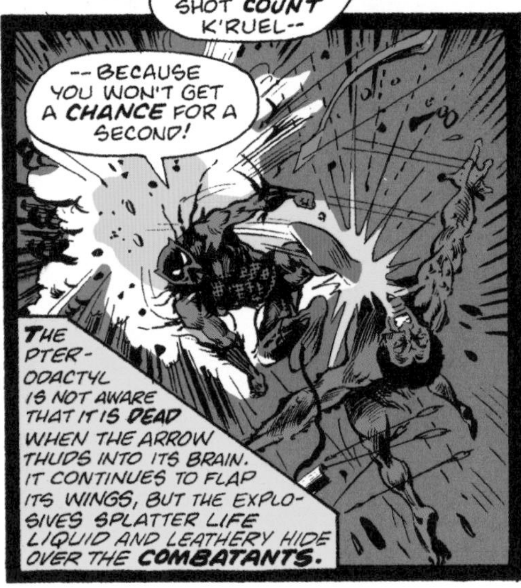
--BECAUSE YOU WON'T GET A CHANCE FOR A SECOND!
THE PTERODACTYL IS NOT AWARE THAT IT IS DEAD WHEN THE ARROW THUDS INTO ITS BRAIN. IT CONTINUES TO FLAP ITS WINGS, BUT THE EXPLOSIVES SPLATTER LIFE LIQUID AND LEATHERY HIDE OVER THE COMBATANTS.

I HOPE YOU WON'T THINK THIS UNSPORTING OF ME, K'RUEL, BUT THE LAST TIME WE TOUCHED, IT WAS A PIERCING EXPERIENCE!
NO HARD FEELINGS, I TRUST?
K'RUEL DOES NOT ANSWER.
HE CAN'T!

THE TREK BEGINS. DURING THE NEXT TWO DAYS, THE JOURNEY SEEMS ENDLESS. DELIRIUM SETS IN. THE SHROUDLIKE MISTS OF SERPENT VALLEY ARE FINALLY LEFT BEHIND, THE MIST COVERING THE VALLEY'S INTERIOR LIKE SUBCONSCIOUS SCAR TISSUE HIDING VICIOUS VISIONS.
DAYS AND NIGHTS BLEND.
RETURNING HOME.
HADN'T HE DONE THAT ONCE BEFORE?
HAS LIFE BECOME A CONTINUAL JOURNEY BACK HOME?

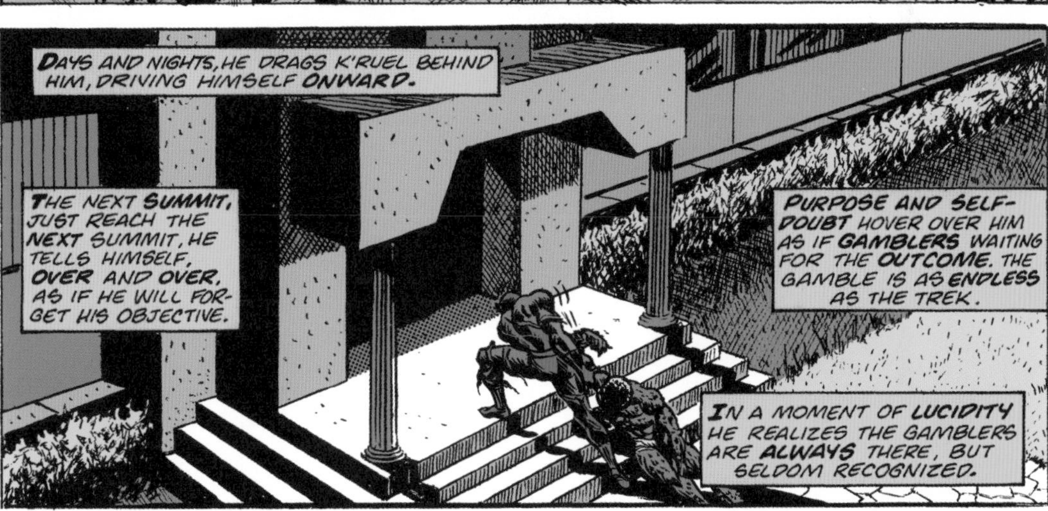
DAYS AND NIGHTS, HE DRAGS K'RUEL BEHIND HIM, DRIVING HIMSELF ONWARD.
THE NEXT SUMMIT, JUST REACH THE NEXT SUMMIT, HE TELLS HIMSELF, OVER AND OVER, AS IF HE WILL FORGET HIS OBJECTIVE.
PURPOSE AND SELF-DOUBT HOVER OVER HIM AS IF GAMBLERS WAITING FOR THE OUTCOME. THE GAMBLE IS AS ENDLESS AS THE TREK.
IN A MOMENT OF LUCIDITY HE REALIZES THE GAMBLERS ARE ALWAYS THERE, BUT SELDOM RECOGNIZED.

HOME! NO ONE SOUNDS ANY TRUMPETS OF TRIUMPH!
HE COLLAPSES BEFORE THE PALACE ROYAL AND BARELY FEELS MONICA'S TOUCH, GENTLY STROKING AT HIS TEMPLES.
TAKU, IT'S T'CHALLA. HE'S HURT! BADLY!
GO GET MENDINAO.
THE BLACK PANTHER DOES NOT MOVE. HE WANTS TO TELL HER OF SALVATION AND RESOLUTIONS--
--BUT NOW THAT HE'S FOUND THEM, THERE ISN'T ANY HURRY.
NONE AT ALL.
NEXT VENOMM RETURNS ALONG WITH OUR LETTERS PAGE, JUNGLE REACTIONS. WE'LL BE LOOKING FOR YOUR RESPONSE. TILL THEN, HANG IN THERE, PEOPLE!

# *JUNGLE ACTION* #16,
JULY 1975

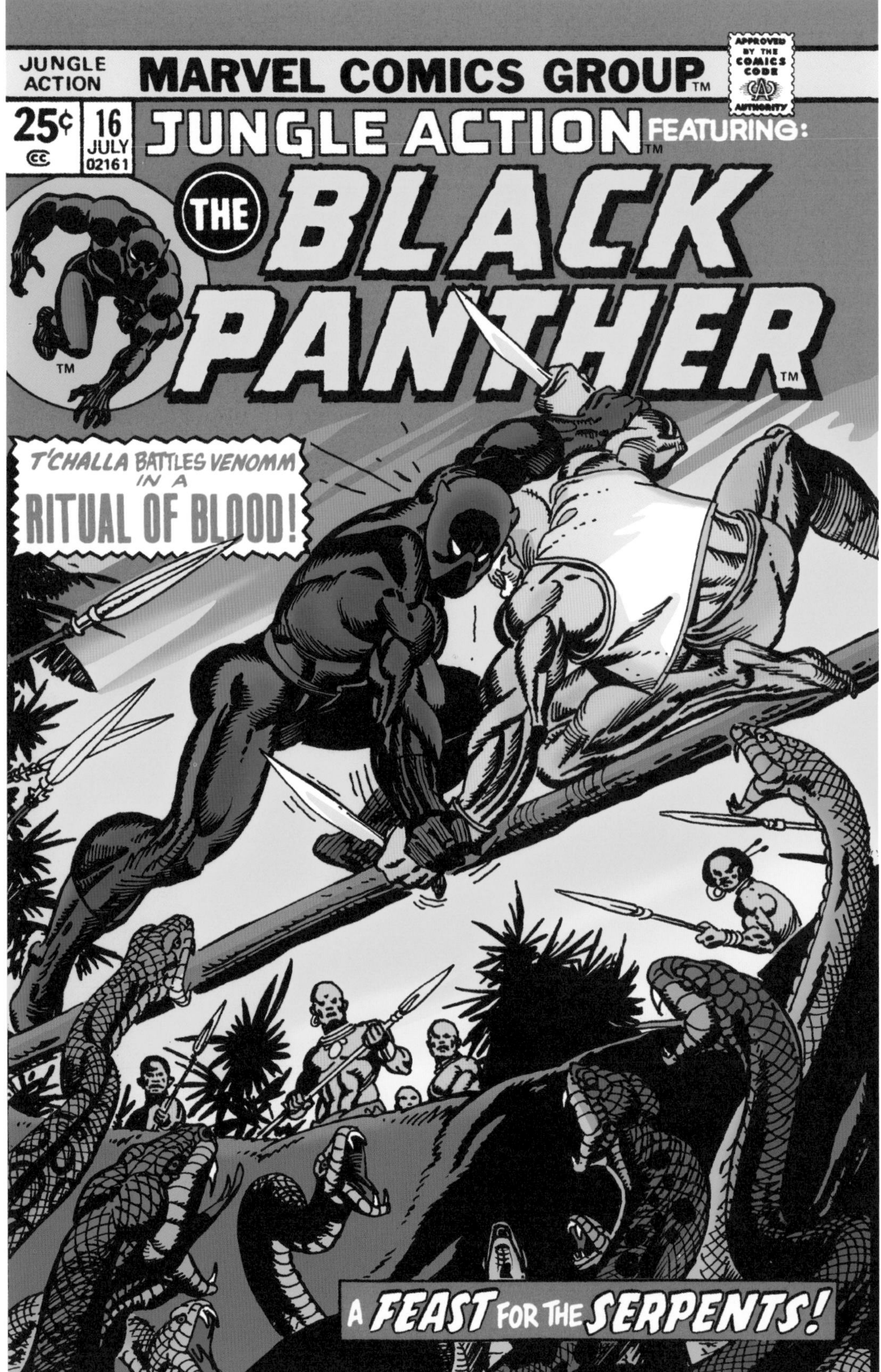
JUNGLE ACTION
MARVEL COMICS GROUP
25¢
16
JULY
02161
JUNGLE ACTION FEATURING:
THE BLACK PANTHER
T'CHALLA BATTLES VENOMM IN A RITUAL OF BLOOD!
A FEAST FOR THE SERPENTS!

Stan Lee PRESENTS:
BLACK PANTHER!™
CONTINUING PANTHER'S RAGE: PART ELEVEN.
SOME LOVERS NEED REVOLUTIONS!
SOME LOVERS FORGE THEIR COMMITMENTS TO EACH OTHER WITH THE SAME COMPULSIVE FERVOR THEY USE IN PURSUING THEIR CAUSES. THE CHANTS AND SLOGANS ARE THEIR LOVE SONG.
THE BLACK PANTHER AND MONICA LYNNE FEEL THE WARM WATER CLOSE OVER THEIR HEADS AS THE MAGNIFICENT TURTLES SLASH DOWNWARD OBLIVIOUS TO THEIR RIDERS' PRESENCE. THE CURRENT SWIRLS WITH TAUNTING TURQUOISE TREASURES RIPPLED BY SCARLET STREAKS. THE SETTING IS IDYLLIC POSTCARD PURITY COMBINED WITH THE FULFILLMENT OF ROMANTIC FANTASIES.
AND ALL OUR PAST DECADES HAVE SEEN REVOLUTIONS!
SOME LOVERS DON'T GIVE A DAMN ABOUT REVOLUTIONS!
BUT REVOLUTIONS HAVE A WAY OF NOT BEING IGNORED!
WAR AND CAUSES AND SOCIETY DICTATES ARE INTRUDERS THAT THREATEN THEIR IDYLLIC MOMENTS. THE POSTCARD IS MARRED.
DON McGREGOR WRITER
BILLY GRAHAM ARTIST
GLYNIS WEIN COLORIST
JANICE CHIANG LETTERER
LEN WEIN EDITOR

SOME LOVERS WHISPER, "I CAN'T MAKE IT ALONE," AND TAKE THE RISK. THEY REACH OUT. THEY TOUCH AND TAKE ANOTHER RISK. THEY GIVE THE TOUCH MEANING.
LOVE WITH AFFECTION. EXPENSES MAXIMUM.
THE SEA TURTLES EXECUTE A SUPERB ARABESQUE. THE PANTHER AND MONICA MOVE IN UNISON ...GLIDING...AND THE WATER CLOSES AND OPENS AT THEIR PASSAGE. THEY POSE AND PERFORM, EACH MOVEMENT MADE FOR THE OTHER.
THE TWO TETHERED REPTILES CAME FROM DISTANT SEASCAPES, BORN ON A HOSTILE SHORELINE WITH THE SURF OFFERING SURVIVAL ... IF ONLY THE NEWBORN COULD REACH ITS SHELTER!
DEATH WAS THEIR MOST IMMEDIATE ACCOMODATION IN THE FIRST MOMENTS OF LIFE... AND THE ACCOMODATORS WERE MAN AND VULTURES AND POISONS. THEY HAVE STARTED IN PANIC AND LEARNED TRANQUILITY IN THE OCEAN'S DEPTHS.
THE PANTHER AND MONICA ARE RELEASED FROM THE OCEAN'S DEPTHS ...AND THE AFRICAN SUN IS DECEPTIVELY TRANQUIL.
THE PANIC SEEMS TO BE BEHIND THEM.
THEY'RE WRONG!

OH MAN, IS IT GOOD TO HAVE YOU BACK, T'CHALLA. THE SUNSETS AND DAWNS LOST THEIR MEANING WHILE YOU WERE AWAY. YOUR ABSENCE MAKES A REAL CHANGE IN CENTRAL WAKANDA.
IT WASN'T UNTIL THOSE LONG HOURS I SPENT IN SERPENT VALLEY, TRYING TO RETURN HOME--
--THAT I FINALLY REALIZED WHAT THE REAL CHANGE IN WAKANDA WAS.
OH, I WAS ALWAYS AWARE THAT THE COMPUTERS AND MACHINERY HAS AFFECTED OUR LIFESTYLE... BUT NEVER BEYOND THE MORE OBVIOUS CHANGES.
IN MY FATHER'S DAY... DOESN'T THAT MAKE ME SOUND ANCIENT?... WAKANDAN LIFE WAS CONCERNED WITH ONE THING: DAILY SURVIVAL.
TO HARVEST ENOUGH FOOD TO EAT.
TO BUILD A HOME.
ALL THE ADVANCEMENTS I BROUGHT TO OUR LAND CHANGED OUR PRIORITIES. 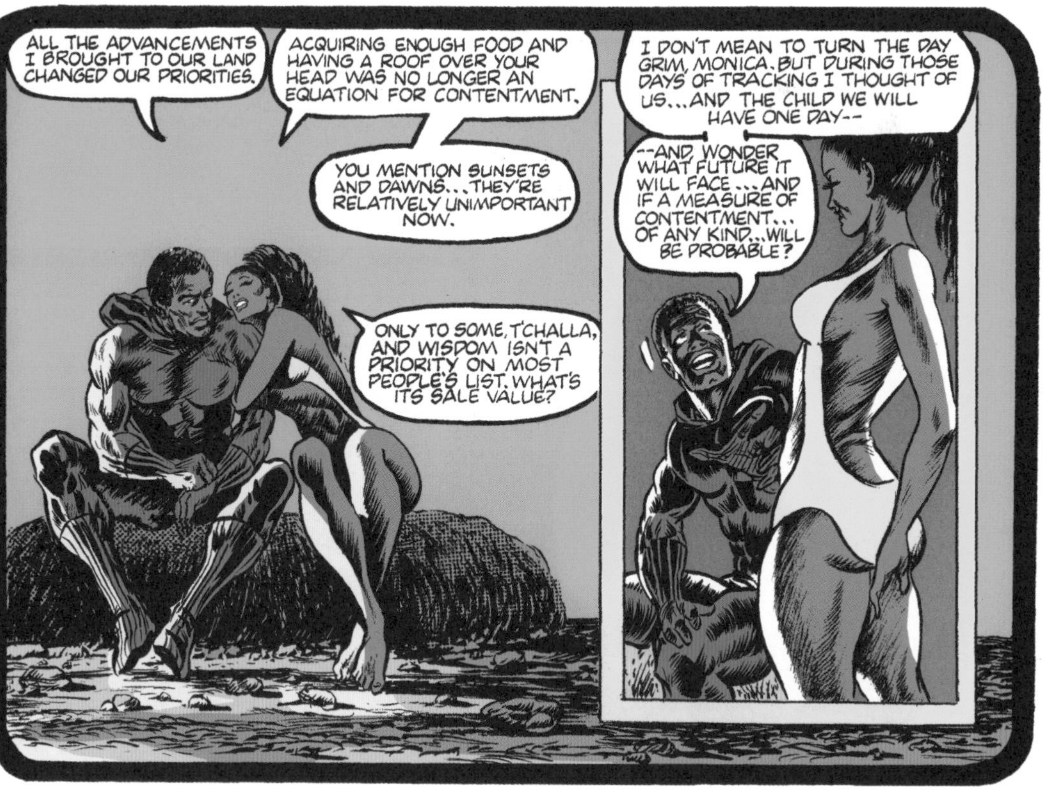
ACQUIRING ENOUGH FOOD AND HAVING A ROOF OVER YOUR HEAD WAS NO LONGER AN EQUATION FOR CONTENTMENT.
YOU MENTION SUNSETS AND DAWNS... THEY'RE RELATIVELY UNIMPORTANT NOW.
ONLY TO SOME, T'CHALLA, AND WISDOM ISN'T A PRIORITY ON MOST PEOPLE'S LIST. WHAT'S ITS SALE VALUE?
I DON'T MEAN TO TURN THE DAY GRIM, MONICA. BUT DURING THOSE DAYS OF TRACKING I THOUGHT OF US... AND THE CHILD WE WILL HAVE ONE DAY--
--AND WONDER WHAT FUTURE IT WILL FACE... AND IF A MEASURE OF CONTENTMENT... OF ANY KIND... WILL BE PROBABLE?

WAKANDA BECOMES A PALPABLE BACKDROP, A **CANVAS** MARKING THE ROUTE OF A COPPER SUN, A CHART FOR A MIDNOON ZEPHYR FLIRTING WITH THE TREES. THEY HOLD ON TO EACH OTHER'S HAND AS IF TO CONFIRM THE OTHER'S REALITY. "AH, YOU AND TAKU," MONICA SIGHS, AND HER SIGH **REFLECTS** THE CONTENTMENT THE DAY HAS DELIVERED. IF ONLY THERE COULD BE **MORE** DAYS LIKE THIS ONE! "SOMETIMES YOU AND HE ARE SO MUCH **ALIKE**." T'CHALLA LOOKS AT HER WITH AFFECTION. SHE FILLS THE DAY. THE CANVAS **LOSES** ITS SUN AND WIND. "WE'RE NOT SO MUCH ALIKE. TAKU IS A... **POET**, THOUGH AS FAR AS I KNOW, HE HAS **NEVER** SPOKEN IN **RHYMES**. BUT A POET NONETHELESS. PERHAPS THAT'S WHY YOU FEEL A CERTAIN KINSHIP."

"I THINK YOU HAVE A TOUCH OF THE POET YOURSELF, T'CHALLA." SHE STUDIES HIS HAND, LOST IN HIS LIFE LINE.
"I PRIDED MYSELF ON THAT ONCE," HE REPLIES AND HIS VOICE IS FILLED WITH MEMORIES. "I SHIPPED IN CONCERT PIANISTS, SURROUNDED MYSELF WITH CULTURAL ELEGANCE FROM ALL THE WORLD'S COUNTRIES AND CUSTOMS; AND THEN, I LEARNED, BRIEFLY, WHAT REAL POETRY WAS. I'M AFRAID MUCH OF KILLMONGER'S REVOLUTION HAS CAUSED ME TO LOSE A GREAT DEAL OF MY EMPATHY. BUT TAKU, HE STILL LISTENS, SENSES, EVALUATES.
"INSIDE, HE IS SIMULTANEOUSLY OUTRAGED BY THE SAVAGERY OF MEN. YET, MOST OFTEN, I THINK HE IS MERELY BEMUSED BY THEIR PURPOSES AND INTRIGUES."
"HE'S NEVER STATED THAT, I'LL BET," MONICA COMMENTS.
"TO SPEAK, WOULD BE ONLY TO REPEAT IDEAS HE HAS ALREADY LEARNED AND WORDS, SPOKEN TOO OFTEN; BECOME RITUAL... TRUTHS TURNED TO A CLICHE' ARSENAL... AND THE WORDS LOSE THEIR MEANING."

YOU'RE BEAUTIFUL WHEN YOU'RE WET.
ARE YOU GOING TO SAY SOMETHING CORNY?
YES. AND THE CRITICS WILL HOWL, BUT LOVERS DON'T NEED CRITICS--
--AND CRITICS DON'T NEED LOVERS.
VERY PROFOUND, MY JUNGLE LORD.
SHOULD WE PLAY TARZAN? AMERICANS LOVE TARZAN, DON'T THEY?
I PREFER OTHER TYPES OF PLAY.
AND I JUST WANTED TO SAY... I THINK YOU'RE BEAUTIFUL, TOO.

VENOMM LOOKS AROUND HIS CELL, AND DESPITE TAKU'S PRESENCE THE BITTERNESS CLAIMS HIM... MUCH LIKE IT DOES DURING THE LOST HOURS OF THE NIGHT... WATCHING THE SHADOWS ENACT FLITTERING MESSAGES OF FREEDOM.
A YEAR? HAS IT ONLY BEEN A YEAR SINCE HE WAS PLACED INTO THIS PRISON? A PRISON IS A PRISON EVEN IF IT IS INSIDE A JUNGLE KING'S ROYAL PALACE.

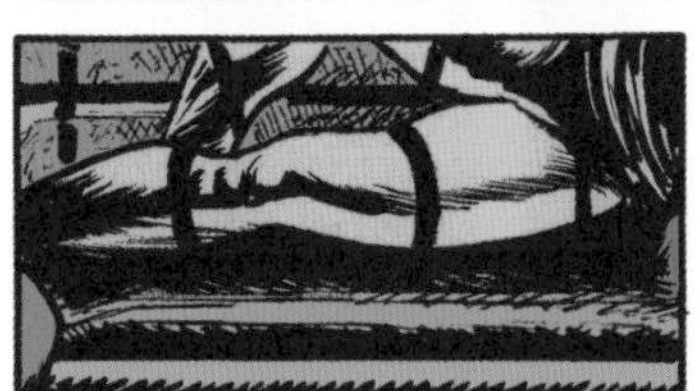

THE SERVICE HAS BEEN EXCELLENT, BUT I'LL BE WANTING NEW ACCOMODATIONS, THANK YOU, VENOMM THINKS--

--AND FOR A MOMENT FEELS THAT HIS THOUGHTS ARE OPEN TO TAKU.
YOU ARE SILENT, HORATIO. ANOTHER ATTACK OF ANGER PERHAPS?
I HOPED THE MANY TIMES WE HAVE SPENT IN COMMUNICATION WOULD HAVE EASED YOUR ANGER... THAT PERHAPS YOU MIGHT GO BACK TO WRITING POETRY.

I AIN'T WRITTEN A POEM SINCE I WAS NINE YEARS OLD, TAKU. 'SIDES, THE STUFF WAS JUNK LEASTWAYS, THAT'S WHAT THEY SAID.

WORDS EXPRESS, HOWEVER INADEQUATELY, OUR FEARS AND DESIRES.
OUR FEARS AND DESIRES SHOULD NOT BE SCORNED NO MATTER HOW INADEQUATELY THEY ARE EXPRESSED.

YOU REALLY BELIEVE THAT MUMBO-JUMBO, TAKU?
HEY, YOU'RE SOMETHING ELSE MAN.

BUT I'M GONNA TELL YA, WORDS DON'T MEAN NUTHIN'... THEY'RE ONLY WORDS.
LOOK, THE WORLD'S HAD EDJICATED GUYS LEARNING THE WORLD FOR YEARS, RIGHT? SHOOTIN' OFF THEIR BIG MOUTHS, FOR WHAT? NUTHIN'! THEY'RE ONLY TALKIN' AND WRITIN' TO THEMSELVES! THEY AIN'T SAYIN' A DAMN THING OUT ON THE STREETS.
I MEAN, YOU REALLY THINK YOUR WORDS ARE GONNA MAKE ME FORGET I'VE SPENT A YEAR OF MY LIFE IN A RITZY CAGE?
FLOWERY SPEECHES TO PLEASE EACH OTHER IS ALL IT COMES DOWN TO.
ANYHOW, LEOPARDS DON'T CHANGE THEIR SPOTS, TAKU. AN' I'M ONE LEOPARD THAT DON'T LIKE CAGES. 'SIDES, I FEEL LIKE A KEPT WOMAN.
YOU TREATED ME RIGHT TAKU, I'LL GIVE YOU THAT. BUT YOU CAN'T TAKE AWAY THESE BARS.
YOU HAVE OTHER BARS THAN THESE KEEPING YOU PRISONER, HORATIO, AND THOSE YOU WILL HAVE TO BREAK YOURSELF.
THERE'S ONE THING ABOUT MY SNAKES, TAKU. THEY DON'T TALK BACK AS MUCH AS YOU.

THE BARS SLIDE UPWARD WITH A SLIGHT ELECTRONIC WHISPER... A DISTURBING SOUND THAT STILL SLICES THROUGH W'KABI'S EARS. IT DOESN'T MATTER THAT SUCH ICY SIGHS HAVE EXISTED IN WAKANDA FOR NEAR A DECADE.
I HAVE SOME MORE QUESTIONS FOR YOU, VENOMM.
GO AHEAD AN' ASK. NUTHIN'S GONNA STOP YOU ANYWAYS.
TRUE. BUT YOU FAIL TO ANSWER.
YOU NOTICED THAT, DIDJA?
YOU USE SARCASM AS A WEAPON... PERHAPS YOUR SARCASM CAN TELL ME HOW KILLMONGER GOT A WHITE INTO WAKANDA.
VENOMM IS AMUSED. "YEAH. WHEN YOU TALK ABOUT MINORITIES, GUESS I TAKE THE CAKE, DON'T I? BEEN THAT WAY SINCE THAT ACID ATE AWAY MOSTA MY FACE. ANYHOW, SO YA WANTA KNOW HOW A WHITE BWANA GOT HERE. GOES BACK TO WHEN YOUR MAIN MAN, THE PANTHER, WAS STATESIDE WITH THE AVENGERS.
"ERIK HAS ALREADY TAKEN ON THE NAME KILLMONGER. BUT HE GAVE HIS REAL NAME, N'JADAKA, WHEN HE CRASHED THE AVENGERS' PAD AND GAVE THE PANTHER HIS SOB STORY.
THE PANTHER FELL FOR IT, JUST LIKE ERIK SAID HE WOULD. HE TOLD THE PANTHER HOW HE'D BEEN KIDNAPPED FROM WAKANDA DURING THE RAID THAT KLAW MADE ON YOUR HAND.
"THEN HE LAID IT ON THICK 'BOUT HOW HE WANTED TO RETURN HOME.
"SURE ENUFF, COUPLE DAYS LATER, THERE'S THIS FANCY RIG LANDIN' ON TOP OF THE TENEMENT ERIK HAD IN HARLEM. ERIK HADDA LIVE IN HARLEM. CERTAINLY WASN'T GOING TO BE ALLOWED TO LIVE IN FOREST HILLS.
AND WHILE THEY PACKED--
"I SLIPPED INTO THE BACK COMPARTMENT. ERIK HAD EVERYTHING FIGGERED, BELIEVE ME!

"ALL THE TIME THE PANTHER WAS HELPIN' ERIK MOVE THINGS, ERIK PLAYED IT STRAIGHT. NEVER LET ON ONCE HOW MUCH HE HATED THE PANTHER'S GUTS.
"YOU HAVE NEVER TOLD US WHY YOUR LEADER HATES OUR CHIEFTAIN WITH SUCH FURY," W'KABI PROBES INTENSELY.
"IT REALLY STARTED WHEN T'CHALLA'S OLD MAN WHO FIRST STARTED USING THIS STUFF YOU HAVE ON THE GROUND --WHAT'S IT CALLED?"
"VIBRANIUM," TAKU OFFERS PLACIDLY.
"YEAH, THAT STUFF. ERIK ALWAYS BLAMED THAT WHOLE SCENE WHERE HE WAS KIDNAPPED BY KLAW'S MEN ON ... I FORGET THE NAME OF T'CHALLA'S OLD MAN."
W'KABI TENSES AT SUCH DISRESPECT. "T'CHAKA," HE ANSWERS.
"YEAH, HIM," VENOMM CONTINUES. "KLAW'S MEN KILLED ERIK'S MOTHER AND FATHER RIGHT IN FRONT'A HIM. SINCE THAT TIME ERIK WAS KINDA LIKE THE KID IN THEM OLD WESTERNS WHO DON'T THINK OF NUTHIN' BUT WASTIN' THE BAD GUYS.
"I MUSTA SEEN THAT PITCHER A MILLYUN TIMES," VENOMM SAYS FONDLY.
"ANYHOW, WITH ALL THE JUNK ERIK BROUGHT ON BOARD THE PLANE, THE PANTHER NEVER EVEN SUSPECTED I WAS WHAT'CHA CALL A STOWAWAY.
"THAT'S LIKE WHEN YOU HIDE ON A SHIP AN' NOBODY KNOWS YOU'RE THERE."
VENOMM HAS HARDLY FINISHED SPEAKING THE SENTENCE WHEN HE LEAPS!
A KNIFE BLADE CARVES THE AIR AS HIS ARM LOCKS AROUND TAKU'S THROAT--
--AND W'KABI'S DRAWN WEAPON IS AIMED AT A HUMAN SHIELD.

W'KABI'S FINGER TIGHTENS ON THE SMOOTH, CURVED INSIDE OF THE TRIGGER--
--AND THE METAL IS SLICK WITH HIS SWEAT!
SURE, GO AHEAD, W'KABI. WHYN'T YOU PULL THE TRIGGER AND SEE WHAT HAPPENS?
WHAT MAKES YOU THINK I WON'T, VENOMM?
COME OFF IT, MAN. YOU AIN'T GONNA BLOW TAKU AWAY JUST TO NAIL MY HIDE.
YOU ARE COUNTING ON ME NOT TO BE AS RUTHLESS AS YOU ARE, VENOMM.
BUT YOU HAVE MADE A MISTAKE IF YOU THINK I AM ANYTHING LIKE TAKU.
IF YOU MAKE ONE WRONG MOVE... JUST ONE!
BUT I'M NOT GOING TO MAKE ANY WRONG MOVE W'KABI--
--AN' YOUR TIME HAS RUN OUT. THROW DOWN THE GUN!
HORATIO, YOU FLEE DEEPER INTO YOUR MAZE OF SELF-IMPRISONMENT.
TAKU, I GOTTA HAND IT TO YOU. YOU SURE GOT SOME COOL.
BUT I SCARE YOU, DON'T I, W'KABI? AND I SHOULD!
I'LL USE THIS BLADE. YOU WANT TO SEE WHAT HIS WINDPIPE LOOKS LIKE? YOU JUST KEEP HOLDIN' ONTO THAT GUN!
THE HAMMER MOVES BACKWARD EVER SO SLOWLY. IT IS NEAR ITS LIMIT. ANOTHER OUNCE OF PRESSURE ON THE TRIGGER AND IT WILL SEND ITS MISSILE SCREAMING INTO THE ROOM.
VENOMM TRIES TO READ W'KABI'S EYES!...
HE WON'T PULL THE TRIGGER! HE WON'T DARE!
BUT THEN HE SEES THE DANGEROUS FIRE IN W'KABI'S EYES... AND HE IS NOT SO SURE!

THE HAND, THE FINGER, THE EYES, ALL REMAIN STEADY RIGHT UNTIL THE MOMENT W'KABI MAKES HIS DECISION.
SMART MOVE, W'KABI. YOU HAD ME GOING THERE FOR A MOMENT.
NOW KICK THE GUN OVER... REAL GENTLE!
SO FAR YOU DONE GOOD, BOY.
NOW LET'S SEE YOU TAKE THE OTHER GUN OUT...UH UH... WITH TWO FINGERS ...YEAH, THAT'S NICE.
HOW FAR DO YOU THINK YOU'LL GET?
IF THERE'S A DUMB QUESTION THAT CAN BE ASKED YOU'LL FIND IT, WON'T YOU?
HORATIO?
NUTHIN' YOU CAN SAY WILL CHANGE THINGS, TAKU. I AIN'T SOME LOST CAUSE FOR YOU TA WORK ON.
YOU WERE NEVER A CAUSE TO ME, HORATIO WALTERS. I THOUGHT YOU UNDERSTOOD THAT.
THIS AIN'T A T.V. SHOW IN THE STATES, TAKU... IT'S MY LIFE! IF THINGS COULDA WORKED OUT DIFFERENT THAN THIS, I'D GONE THAT ROUTE.
BUT I GOTTA USE THE CARDS I'M DEALT.
VENOMM IS RIGHT! THIS IS NOT TELEVISION PREACHING DANGEROUS PRIME-TIME VISIONS OF VIOLENCE, WHERE METAL SELDOM TEARS FLESH AND BLOOD IS OBVIOUSLY A FICTITIOUS ELEMENT BORNE OF FERTILE IMAGINATIONS.
IT IS SEVERAL SECONDS OF VIOLENCE SHREDDING THE PAST AND ALTERING THE FUTURE. IN REAL LIFE IT HAPPENS THAT WAY!
IT'S POSSIBLE VENOMM IS NOT EVEN AWARE OF THAT!
THE SHADOWS OF APPROACHING NIGHT REACH ACROSS THE ROOM, SHADOW GAMES BEGINNING THEIR NIGHTLY PERFORMANCE. BUT... THIS TIME, VENOMM IS NOT IN THE AUDIENCE.
BECAUSE THEY ARE NOT PAPIER-MACHE BUT MADE OUT OF FLESH AND BLOOD, THE TWO MEN LIE VERY STILL!
VERY!

AND A HALF HOUR LATER ONE FIGURE STILL LIES MOTIONLESS.
A TRACE OF BLOOD DRIES ON THE CEMENT, AND IT SPEAKS TO THE PANTHER AND MONICA IN A LANGUAGE THAT HAS TORN LOVERS FROM EACH OTHER'S SIDES SINCE MANKIND FIRST ESTABLISHED WAR AS A "NECESSARY" PART OF LIFE.
MONICA, RUN OVER TO THE HOSPITAL. GET MENDINAO.
QUICKLY!
ARE YOU ALRIGHT, TAKU?
THERE ARE MORE IMPORTANT QUESTIONS YOU SHOULD ASK, MY CHIEFTAIN.
SUCH AS HOW HORATIO CAME TO ESCAPE. HE TURNED ON ME SO ABRUPTLY... AND THOUGH I SENSED HIS DISCONTENT, I WAS STILL TAKEN UNAWARE. I SHOULD HAVE WARNED W'KABI.
W'KABI IS AN ALERT WARRIOR. YOU DID NOT NEED TO WARN HIM. ONE CANNOT PREPARE FOR EVERY EVENTUALITY.
T'CHALLA HOVERS OVER W'KABI'S BODY WHILE HE LISTENS TO TAKU, AND HE HEARS THE WORDS BUT DOES NOT TRULY COMPREHEND THEM. NIGHT MUSIC GIVES WAY TO FOOTFALLS AND THE APPEARANCE OF MENDINAO.
VENOMM MAY BE THE TRAGIC FIGURE YOU DECLARE HIM TO BE, TAKU--
--BUT NO AMOUNT OF TRAGEDY EXCUSES WHAT HE HAS DONE HERE.
HE WILL NOT RESPOND TO THE HERBAL CURE THAT I HAVE LEARNED FROM MY FATHER.
YOUR FOREIGN TRAINED MEDICS WILL HAVE TO GET HIM TO A HOSPITAL.
IT IS HARD TO ACCEPT. ONE STRIKE AND HE IS FELLED.
A MAN CAN SURVIVE A HUNDRED WOUNDS, MY CHIEFTAIN--
--BUT ONLY ONE IS NEEDED TO SLAY HIM.
AH, T'CHALLA, WHY DOES THE LIGHT OF TOMORROW ALWAYS LOOK DIM?
I DON'T HAVE AN ANSWER, MONICA, ...BUT I DO KNOW WHERE VENOMM WILL HEAD--
--AND I'LL BE WAITING FOR HIM!
THE SONAR CRAFT LIFTS INTO THE COPPER SKY, AS IF A PROJECTILE CATAPULTED TOWARD THE GLARING SUN. A HARSH WITNESS TO HARSH EVENTS!

VENOMM SURVEYS THE VILLAGE OF N'JADAKA. THE HUNGRY CRY OF A SCAVENGER SPEARS THE SILENCE, AND HE PEERS INTO THE GREY WASTELAND AND REMEMBERS THE ROUTINE SOUNDS OF DAILY EXISTENCE.
GONE!
FREE, VENOMM THINKS. AND TAKU HAS TOLD ME THAT MY SNAKES ARE STILL IN THE PIT!
INEXPLICABLY, HE DOES NOT FEEL ANY JOY!

ONLY EMPTINESS LEFT.
THE SMOULDERING CHARRED WOOD HAS CEASED BURNING MORE THAN TWO MONTHS PAST, BUT THE CINDER OF COMBAT STILL REMAINS, CAUGHT IN THE ASHES AND SMOKE THAT RISES AS IF IN SUPPLICATION TO THE PASSIONLESS JUDGEMENT OF THE SUN.
HE HEARS THEM FIRST BEFORE HE ACTUALLY VIEWS THEM.

HE IS THE SNAKE CHARMER ABSOLUTE WHO KNOWS HIS SUBJECT WELL.
MINDLESS SAVE FOR HIS MIND!
DIRECTIONLESS SAVE FOR ANY DIRECTION HE COMMANDS!
HE DOES NOT SPEAK TO THEM. THEY WOULD NOT HEAR HIM IF HE DID. BUT FROM THEIR MOVEMENT AS THEY SLIDE SINUOUSLY OVER ONE ANOTHER, HE KNOWS THEY HAVE SENSED HIS PRESENCE FROM THE VIBRATIONS TRANSMITTED THROUGH THE GROUND.
SEVERED TONGUES FLICKER MEASURING HIS IMAGE. ONE COULD ALMOST SWEAR THEY ANTICIPATE HIS FIRST COMMAND!

THE SHORELINE IS A BROODING LANDSCAPE, SPLIT WINE RACING UP THE CARPET OF SAND.
THE AIR IS ALIVE... BUZZING WITH THE FURIOUS HUM OF COUNTLESS MOSQUITOS. THE PANTHER HAS BEEN IN PLACES WHERE THE MOSQUITOS ARE SO THICK THAT TO BREATH IS TO SUCK THEM INTO YOUR NOSTRILS.
HE IS THE BLACK CAT, PAUSING FROM ITS STALKING STRIDE...AMBER EYES PERCEIVING A FIGURE UNRELATED TO HIS PURSUIT.
IT IS KANTU, AND AS HE LOOKS INTO THE SAD DEPTHS OF THOSE YOUNG EYES HE SEES REFLECTIONS OF HIMSELF, MOURNING FOR HIS FATHER, UNABLE TO ACCEPT HIS FATHER'S DEATH.
HE CAME TO THE RIVER THEN AND ASKED IT QUESTIONS... BUT DID NOT LISTEN FOR ANY ANSWERS.
KANTU? WHAT ARE YOU DOING HERE, SON?
MY CHIEFTAIN...
THERE'S NO NEED TO BE SO FORMAL.
BESIDES, I INTRUDED ON YOUR THOUGHTS. I ONCE TOLD A FRIEND THAT "A MAN GOES TO BROOD WHERE IT'S MOST ISOLATED. UNLESS HE HAS SOMEONE TO LISTEN TO HIS SILENCES."
THIS MAN... THE ONE WHO IS CALLED KI--KILLMONGER... IT IS HIS FAULT MY FATHER IS DEAD. I COULD KILL HIM!
I WOULD TELL YOU I UNDERSTAND YOUR GRIEF, BUT YOU COULD NOT BELIEVE THAT, COULD YOU, KANTU?
ONE THING YOU CAN BELIEVE ...YOUR MOTHER FEELS THE SAME LOSS.
I HAVE NEVER SEEN THIS MAN, MY CHIEFTAIN, BUT I HATE HIM.
THE PANTHER BOWS HIS HEAD, AND THE TWO OF THEM STARE INTO THE HARSH EYE OF THE SUN.
ONE ASKS IF THERE IS ANY HOPE LEFT AT ALL.
THE OTHER DOES NOT KNOW THE WORDS TO ASK SUCH A QUESTION, BUT WONDERS THE SAME THING.

THE BLACK CAT DOES NOT ASK ANY QUESTIONS. IT NEEDS VERY FEW ANSWERS OR TRUTHS.
THE PANTHER PROWLS THE NIGHTSCAPE, AND HE IS THAT BLACK CAT, TREADING HIS DOMAIN. HE CEASES TO THINK OF KANTU AND W'KABI THE MOMENT HE CATCHES THE FIRST HINT OF CARBON TAINTING THE AIR.
HE BECOMES CAUTIOUS.
TESTING.
IDENTIFYING SHADOWS.
YES, VENOMM HAS BEEN HERE AND IS PROBABLY STILL NEARBY.
A BREATHING STILL-LIFE PORTRAIT--
--POISED--
--READY TO POUNCE!
THE SUN RETIRES TO ITS CHAMBERS--
--AND FAILS TO WITNESS THE DAY'S FINAL ACT.
AND THEN THE PATIENT CAT HAS SEPARATED HIS PREY FROM ALL THE OTHER SHAPES... AND MAKES HIS PRESENCE KNOWN!
VENOMM!
FIGGERED I BETTER COME OUT INTO THE OPEN OR YOU'D WAIT 'TILL HELL FROZE OVER.
TOOK YOU LONG ENUFF TO GET HERE.
CLEVER RIDDLES WON'T STAY MY HAND, VENOMM. I'VE LITTLE USE FOR MORE VIOLENCE ... BUT I AM NOT LETTING YOU WALK AWAY FROM HERE AFTER WHAT YOU HAVE DONE TO W'KABI.

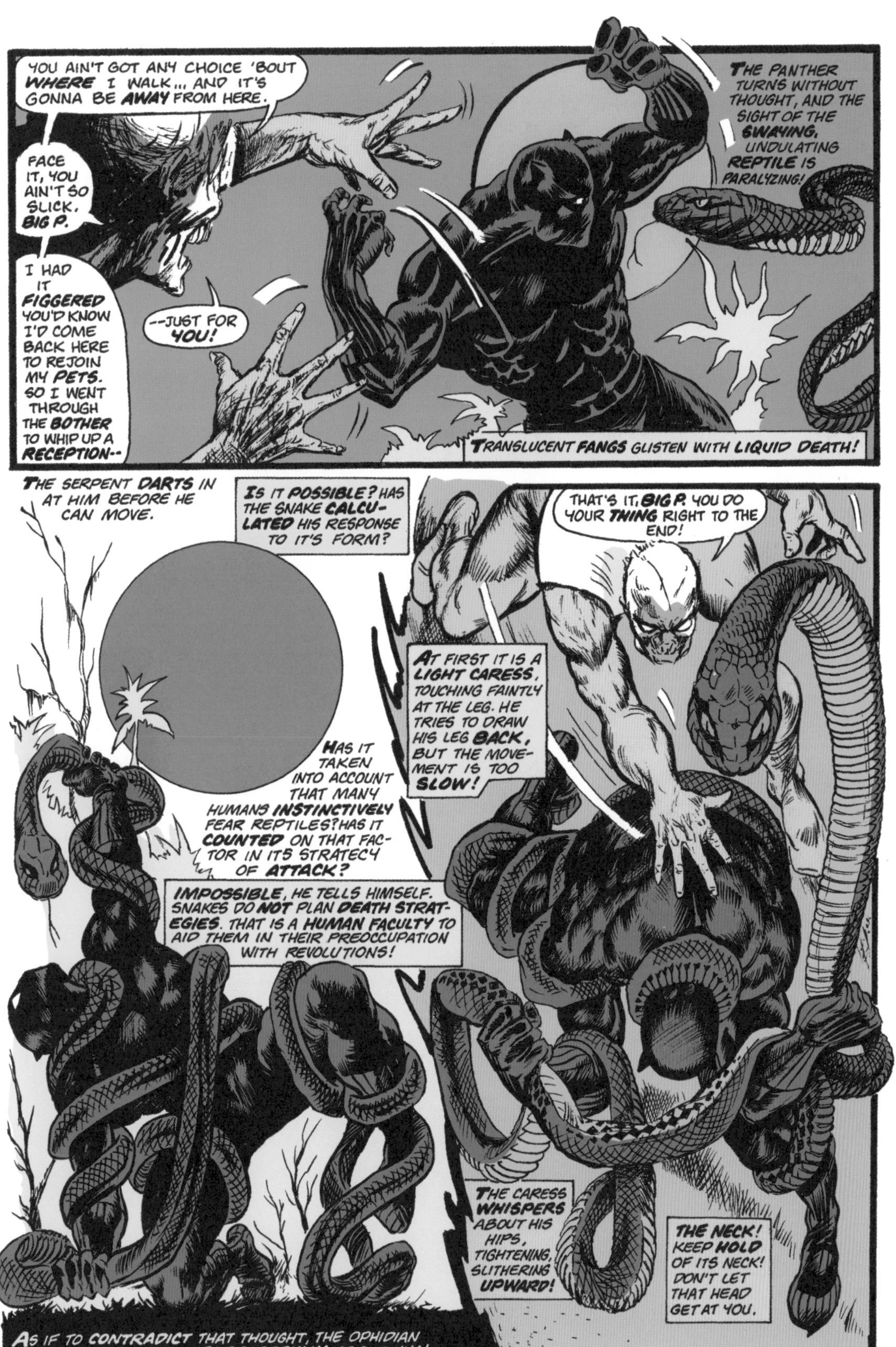
YOU AIN'T GOT ANY CHOICE 'BOUT WHERE I WALK... AND IT'S GONNA BE AWAY FROM HERE.
FACE IT, YOU AIN'T SO SLICK, BIG P.
I HAD IT FIGGERED YOU'D KNOW I'D COME BACK HERE TO REJOIN MY PETS. SO I WENT THROUGH THE BOTHER TO WHIP UP A RECEPTION--
--JUST FOR YOU!
THE PANTHER TURNS WITHOUT THOUGHT, AND THE SIGHT OF THE SWAYING, UNDULATING REPTILE IS PARALYZING!
TRANSLUCENT FANGS GLISTEN WITH LIQUID DEATH!
THE SERPENT DARTS IN AT HIM BEFORE HE CAN MOVE.
IS IT POSSIBLE? HAS THE SNAKE CALCULATED HIS RESPONSE TO IT'S FORM?
THAT'S IT, BIG P. YOU DO YOUR THING RIGHT TO THE END!
AT FIRST IT IS A LIGHT CARESS, TOUCHING FAINTLY AT THE LEG. HE TRIES TO DRAW HIS LEG BACK, BUT THE MOVEMENT IS TOO SLOW!
HAS IT TAKEN INTO ACCOUNT THAT MANY HUMANS INSTINCTIVELY FEAR REPTILES? HAS IT COUNTED ON THAT FACTOR IN ITS STRATEGY OF ATTACK?
IMPOSSIBLE, HE TELLS HIMSELF. SNAKES DO NOT PLAN DEATH STRATEGIES. THAT IS A HUMAN FACULTY TO AID THEM IN THEIR PREOCCUPATION WITH REVOLUTIONS!
THE CARESS WHISPERS ABOUT HIS HIPS, TIGHTENING, SLITHERING UPWARD!
THE NECK! KEEP HOLD OF ITS NECK! DON'T LET THAT HEAD GET AT YOU.
AS IF TO CONTRADICT THAT THOUGHT, THE OPHIDIAN SHAPE WRAPS ITSELF PURPOSEFULLY ABOUT HIM!

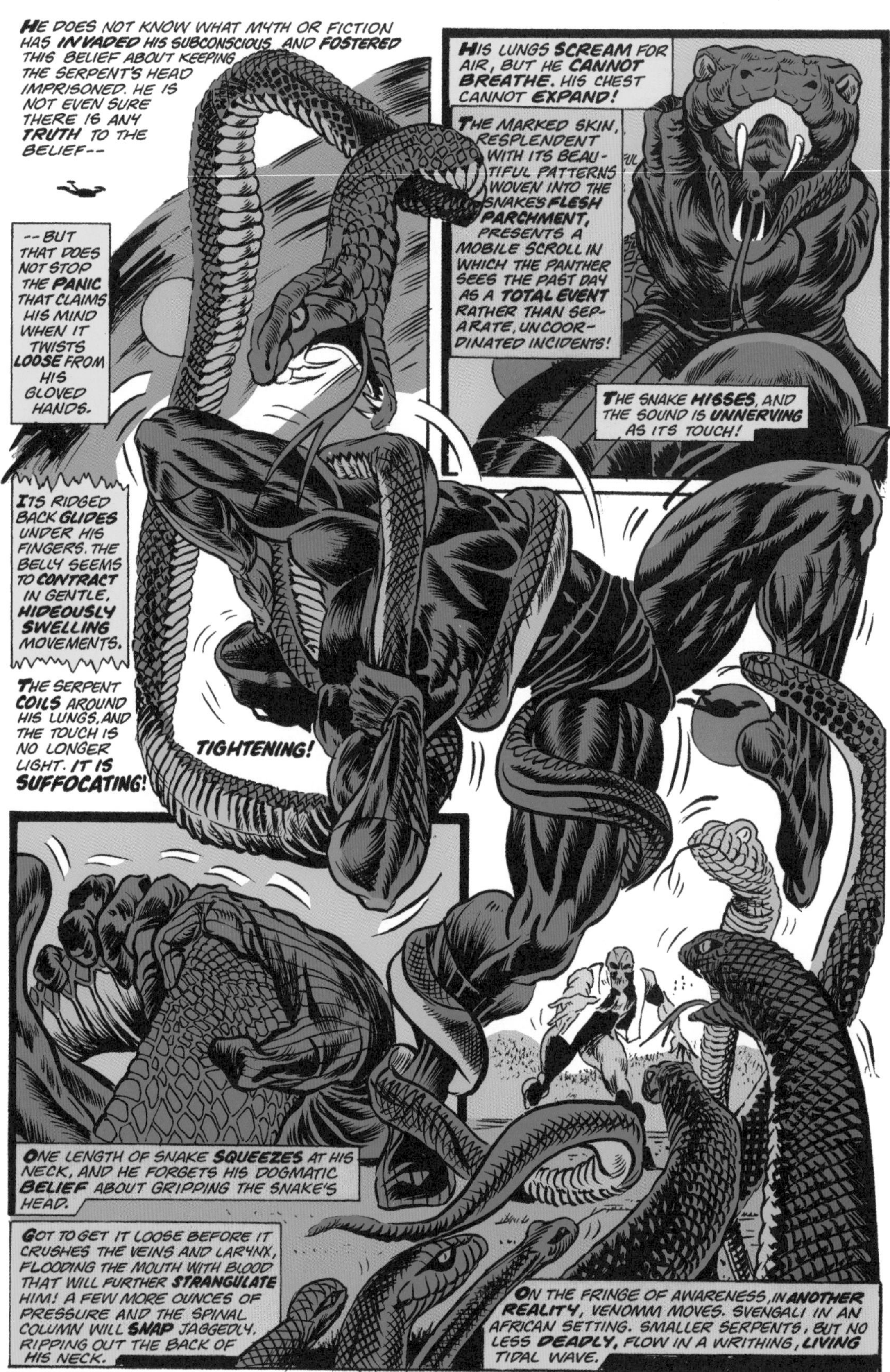
HE DOES NOT KNOW WHAT MYTH OR FICTION HAS INVADED HIS SUBCONSCIOUS AND FOSTERED THIS BELIEF ABOUT KEEPING THE SERPENT'S HEAD IMPRISONED. HE IS NOT EVEN SURE THERE IS ANY TRUTH TO THE BELIEF--
--BUT THAT DOES NOT STOP THE PANIC THAT CLAIMS HIS MIND WHEN IT TWISTS LOOSE FROM HIS GLOVED HANDS.
HIS LUNGS SCREAM FOR AIR, BUT HE CANNOT BREATHE. HIS CHEST CANNOT EXPAND!
THE MARKED SKIN, RESPLENDENT WITH ITS BEAUTIFUL PATTERNS WOVEN INTO THE SNAKE'S FLESH PARCHMENT, PRESENTS A MOBILE SCROLL IN WHICH THE PANTHER SEES THE PAST DAY AS A TOTAL EVENT RATHER THAN SEPARATE, UNCOORDINATED INCIDENTS!
THE SNAKE HISSES, AND THE SOUND IS UNNERVING AS ITS TOUCH!
ITS RIDGED BACK GLIDES UNDER HIS FINGERS. THE BELLY SEEMS TO CONTRACT IN GENTLE, HIDEOUSLY SWELLING MOVEMENTS.
THE SERPENT COILS AROUND HIS LUNGS, AND THE TOUCH IS NO LONGER LIGHT. IT IS SUFFOCATING!
TIGHTENING!
ONE LENGTH OF SNAKE SQUEEZES AT HIS NECK, AND HE FORGETS HIS DOGMATIC BELIEF ABOUT GRIPPING THE SNAKE'S HEAD.
GOT TO GET IT LOOSE BEFORE IT CRUSHES THE VEINS AND LARYNX, FLOODING THE MOUTH WITH BLOOD THAT WILL FURTHER STRANGULATE HIM! A FEW MORE OUNCES OF PRESSURE AND THE SPINAL COLUMN WILL SNAP JAGGEDLY, RIPPING OUT THE BACK OF HIS NECK.
ON THE FRINGE OF AWARENESS, IN ANOTHER REALITY, VENOMM MOVES. SVENGALI IN AN AFRICAN SETTING. SMALLER SERPENTS, BUT NO LESS DEADLY, FLOW IN A WRITHING, LIVING TIDAL WAVE.

A SHAPE APPEARS AGAINST THE MOON, A DARK BLEMISH, AN INSTRUMENT FOR REVOLUTIONS AND RETRIBUTION. IT IS THE SONAR SKIMMER THE PANTHER LEFT BEHIND!
COME ON, BIG P. LET'S HEAR ONE A YOUR SERMONETTES!
CASE YOU'RE GETTIN' LONESOME, I'VE SENT FOR SOME MORE COMPANY TO LIVEN UP THE PARTY.
BUT IT CANNOT REACH HIM IN TIME. ALREADY, THE BLOOD AND OXYGEN DRAIN FROM HIS BRAIN. STARVATION BRINGS ON HALLUCINATIONS!
AN' I SEE YOU DIDN'T COME WITHOUT SOME EXTRA GUESTS YOURSELF. FUNNY, NOT THE WAY I THOUGHT YOU'D PLAY IT!
THE PANTHER FORCES HIMSELF FROM HIS KNEES.
HE RISES TO HIS FEET, STRAINING, LEGS TREMBLING. THE EFFORT IS MIRACULOUS.
HE STAGGERS BUT REMAINS ERECT, DIGGING HIS FINGERS INTO THE MEAT OF THE SNAKE AND SWINGING WITH ALL THE STRENGTH HE CAN MUSTER!
ONCE: HIS FINGERS BATTER UNNOTICED INTO THE ROCK ALONG WITH THE SERPENT'S HEAD. THE FLESH OVER HIS KNUCKLES SPLITS TO THE BONE!
TWICE; THE TONGUE STIFFENS IN DEATH. THE CONTRACTIONS TIGHTENING THE SNAKE ABOUT HIM SUDDENLY CEASE.
TRIUMPH MAKES HIM BELIEVE THE ORDEAL IS OVER.
IT ISN'T!
HE FALLS TRYING TO RELEARN HOW TO BREATHE, THOUGH EACH BREATH RIPS LIKE RAZORS ACROSS HIS LUNGS.
TAKU?
MY CHIEFTAIN.
YOU AND KANTU. ALL... ALWAYS SO FORMAL. EVEN WH... WHEN YOU'RE TRYING TO SAVE MY LIFE.
A HAND GRIPS HIS ARM, AND HE RETURNS THE GRIP.
AND THEY FACE THE ONSLAUGHT OF SERPENTS AS ONE UNIFIED AGAINST THE SEETHING TURBULENT MASS.
IF THEY DIE, IT WILL BE AS ONE!

TAKU, GET OUTTA THERE!
NO, HORATIO. YOU MUST KILL ME TOO IF YOU ARE GOING TO KILL T'CHALLA.
OH, MAN, YOU'RE TOO MUCH, TAKU. YOU HANG IN THERE WITH 'JOE JUNGLE LORD' AN' YOU'LL GET YOUR EARS PIERCED!
HE'S GONNA DIE ANYWAY, TAKU. IN THE NAME OF THE REVOLUTION. ERIK'LL SEE TA THAT.

ALL OUR PAST DECADES HAVE SEEN REVOLUTIONS, HORATIO.
AND WHAT IS SOLVED?

MEN LIKE YOU AND I DIE... THE REVOLUTION ITSELF DIES...
REVOLUTIONS GIVE ONE THE ILLUSION THEY ARE DOING SOMETHING WITH THEIR LIVES.

OKAY, OKAY. I'LL STOP THE SNAKES.
BUT YOU AIN'T ALWAYS RIGHT, TAKU. SEE, REVOLUTIONS CHANGE THINGS, THAT'S WHAT THEY DO.
AND THAT AIN'T NO ILLUSION, TAKU. DIDN'T YOU NEVER THINK OF THAT?
AND SOME-TIMES THOSE CHANGES ARE BETTER'N WHAT'S GONE DOWN BEFORE.

YOU CAN ALSO HIDE FROM YOURSELF IN A REVOLUTION'S MAZES--
AND IF YOU BETRAY YOURSELF IN THE COURSE OF EVENTS, THE MAZE'S EXIT WILL LEAVE YOU EMPTY STILL.
AND THE MOON SEEMS RE-SIGNED TO THE ACTIONS... OF REVOLUTIONS... AND MEN.
THE SNAKES FOLLOW VENOMM'S LANGUID RETREAT, BUT HE IS STILL A SOLITARY FIG-URE, STILL SUR-ROUNDED BY DARKNESS--
--AND STILL WITHOUT ANY DESTINATION!
-FIN-

# *JUNGLE ACTION* #17,
# SEPTEMBER 1975

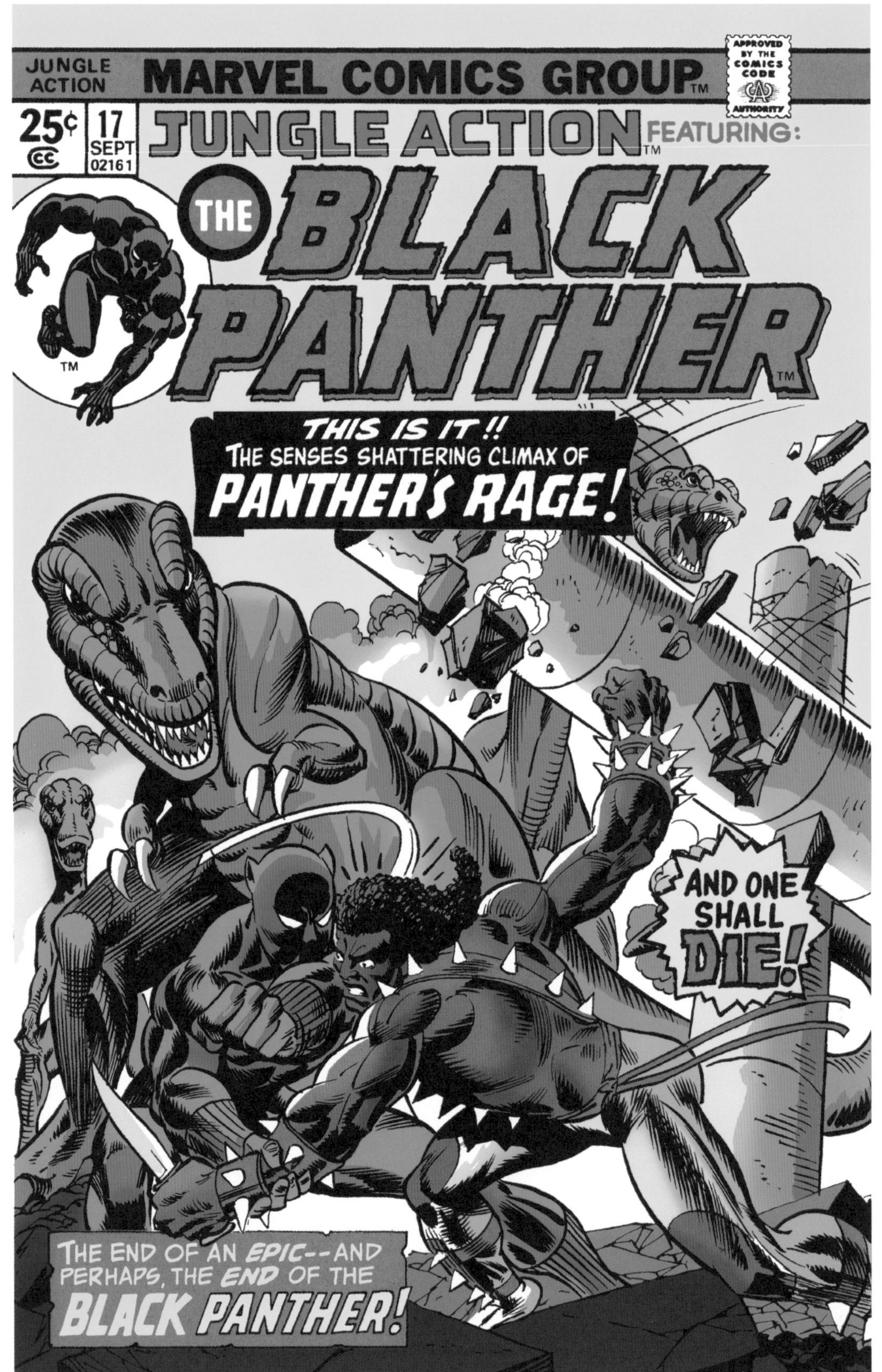
JUNGLE ACTION
MARVEL COMICS GROUP
APPROVED BY THE COMICS CODE AUTHORITY
25¢
CC
17
SEPT
02161
JUNGLE ACTION FEATURING:
THE BLACK PANTHER
THIS IS IT!!
THE SENSES SHATTERING CLIMAX OF
PANTHER'S RAGE!
AND ONE SHALL DIE!
THE END OF AN EPIC--AND PERHAPS, THE END OF THE
BLACK PANTHER!

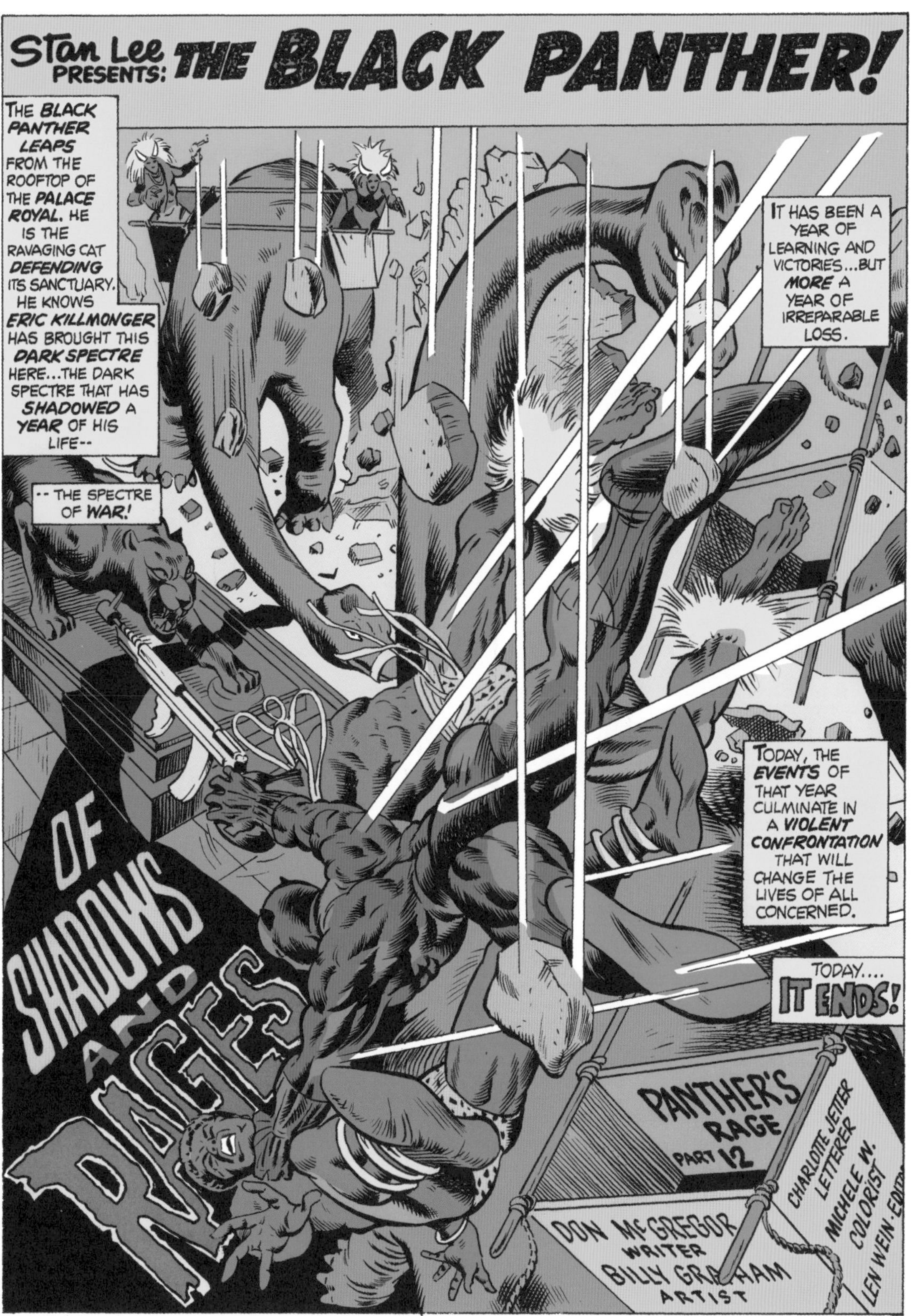
Stan Lee PRESENTS: THE BLACK PANTHER!
THE BLACK PANTHER LEAPS FROM THE ROOFTOP OF THE PALACE ROYAL. HE IS THE RAVAGING CAT DEFENDING ITS SANCTUARY. HE KNOWS ERIC KILLMONGER HAS BROUGHT THIS DARK SPECTRE HERE...THE DARK SPECTRE THAT HAS SHADOWED A YEAR OF HIS LIFE--
--THE SPECTRE OF WAR!
IT HAS BEEN A YEAR OF LEARNING AND VICTORIES...BUT MORE A YEAR OF IRREPARABLE LOSS.
TODAY, THE EVENTS OF THAT YEAR CULMINATE IN A VIOLENT CONFRONTATION THAT WILL CHANGE THE LIVES OF ALL CONCERNED.
TODAY.... IT ENDS!
OF SHADOWS AND RAGES
PANTHER'S RAGE PART 12
DON McGREGOR WRITER
BILLY GRAHAM ARTIST
CHARLOTTE JETTER LETTERER
MICHELE W. COLORIST
LEN WEIN-EDITOR

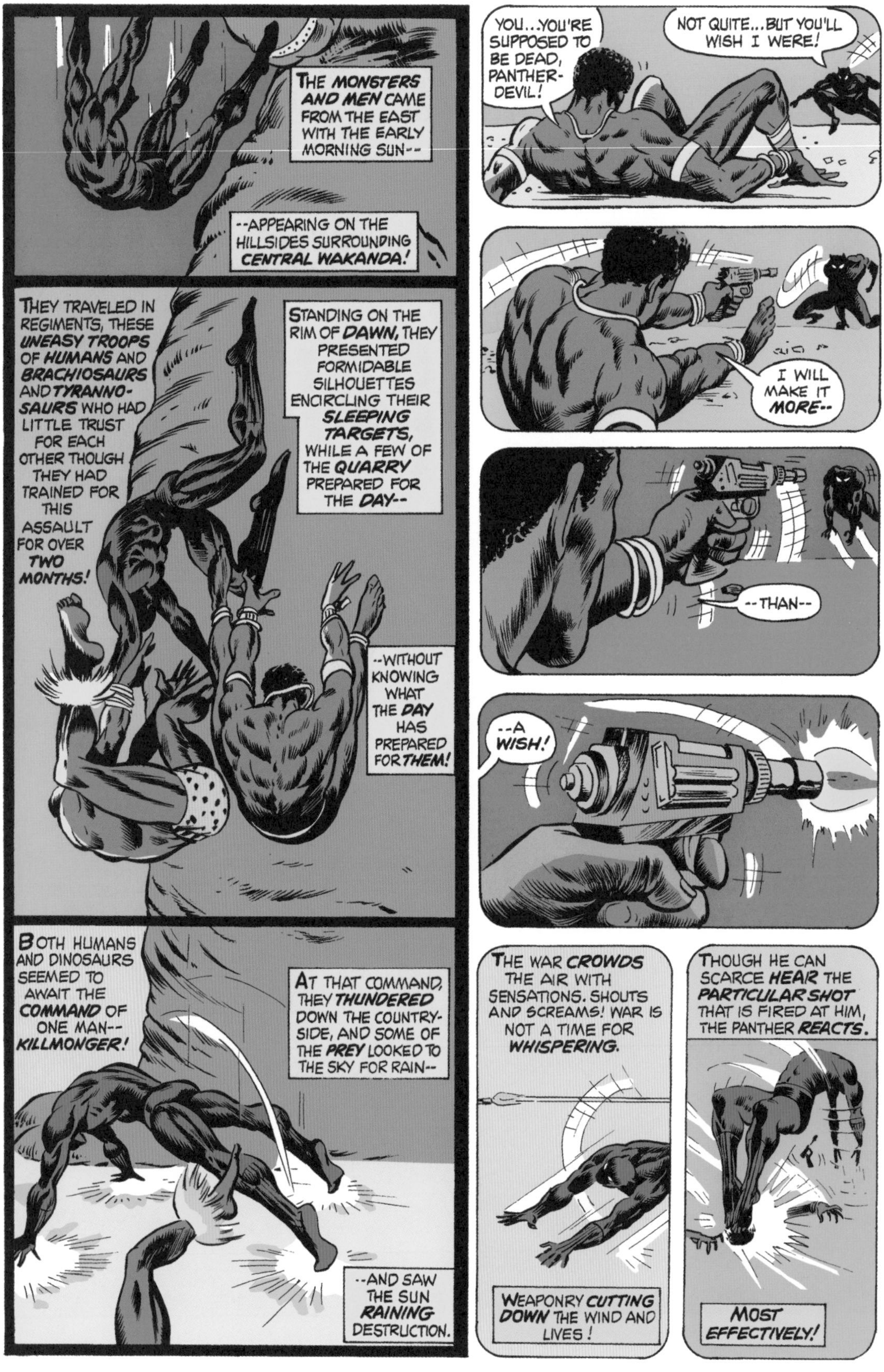

THE MONSTERS AND MEN CAME FROM THE EAST WITH THE EARLY MORNING SUN--

--APPEARING ON THE HILLSIDES SURROUNDING CENTRAL WAKANDA!

THEY TRAVELED IN REGIMENTS, THESE UNEASY TROOPS OF HUMANS AND BRACHIOSAURS AND TYRANNO-SAURS WHO HAD LITTLE TRUST FOR EACH OTHER THOUGH THEY HAD TRAINED FOR THIS ASSAULT FOR OVER TWO MONTHS!

STANDING ON THE RIM OF DAWN, THEY PRESENTED FORMIDABLE SILHOUETTES ENCIRCLING THEIR SLEEPING TARGETS, WHILE A FEW OF THE QUARRY PREPARED FOR THE DAY--

--WITHOUT KNOWING WHAT THE DAY HAS PREPARED FOR THEM!

BOTH HUMANS AND DINOSAURS SEEMED TO AWAIT THE COMMAND OF ONE MAN--KILLMONGER!

AT THAT COMMAND, THEY THUNDERED DOWN THE COUNTRY-SIDE, AND SOME OF THE PREY LOOKED TO THE SKY FOR RAIN--

--AND SAW THE SUN RAINING DESTRUCTION.

YOU...YOU'RE SUPPOSED TO BE DEAD, PANTHER-DEVIL!
NOT QUITE...BUT YOU'LL WISH I WERE!

I WILL MAKE IT MORE--

--THAN--

--A WISH!

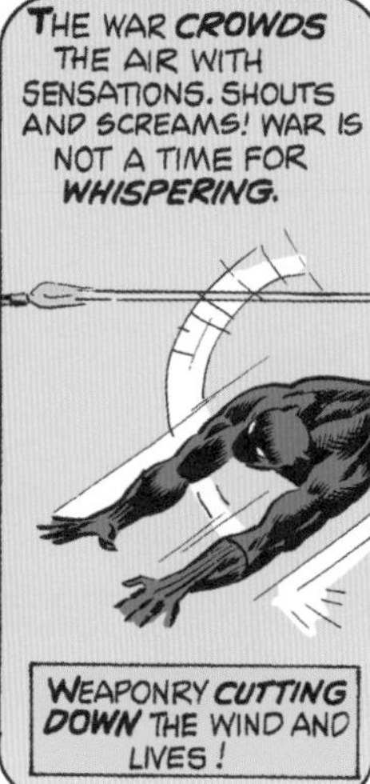

THE WAR CROWDS THE AIR WITH SENSATIONS. SHOUTS AND SCREAMS! WAR IS NOT A TIME FOR WHISPERING.
WEAPONRY CUTTING DOWN THE WIND AND LIVES!

THOUGH HE CAN SCARCE HEAR THE PARTICULAR SHOT THAT IS FIRED AT HIM, THE PANTHER REACTS.

MOST EFFECTIVELY!

THE PANTHER TURNS WITH ANIMAL CAUTION, SURVEYING THE CLASH BETWEEN HIS SECURITY FORCES AND KILLMONGER'S WARRIORS.
HIS AMBER EYES REGISTER A SILENT SNARL: "DON'T... PLEASE DON'T DESTROY IT ALL!" AND THEY ALSO SEE MONICA LYNNE, AND THE THREAT BECOMES MORE THAN THE DESTRUCTION OF A DREAM TO WHICH HE WAS ONCE PRISONER!

LASERS SCORCH THE AIR AND SCAR THE GROUND! THE LIGHT HAS BEEN HARNESSED JUST AS THE DINO-SAURS HAVE BEEN BY THE ELECTRICAL BITS THAT CLAMP INTO THEIR MOUTHS AND KEEP THEM FROM STAMPEDING--
--AND NOW THE LIGHT OFFERS THE DARKNESS OF DEATH!
THE PANTHER LEAPS--

--SUPERBLY--
--USING THE SIDE OF THE BEHEMOTH AS A CATAPULT--

--AND VAULTING OVER ITS HUGE, BROAD BACK--
--HE DROPS NIMBLY ON THE OTHER SIDE IN LESS THAN FIFTEEN SECONDS!

YOU DO THAT WELL, T'CHALLA, BUT BELIEVE ME, I WASN'T GOING TO FAINT OR FREEZE--
I WAS WELL ON MY WAY TO GETTING MYSELF OUT OF THERE... BUT FAST!
ARE YOU ALL RIGHT?
AM I ALL RIGHT? YOU'RE THE ONE THAT DOVE OFF A ROOFTOP, GOT YOURSELF SHOT AT AND JUST SCALED THAT REJECT FROM KING KONG... AND YOU ASK ME IF I'M ALL RIGHT?

IT'S FRIGHTENING, ISN'T IT?
VERY! WHEN IT STARTED, I THOUGHT THOSE RAGGED PROPHETS WHO PREDICT THE END OF THE WORLD WERE HAVING THEIR DAY!

"THEY'RE NOT...BUT KILLMONGER IS HAVING HIS!", T'CHALLA STATES...AND HIS EYES EXPRESS MORE THAN HIS WORDS!

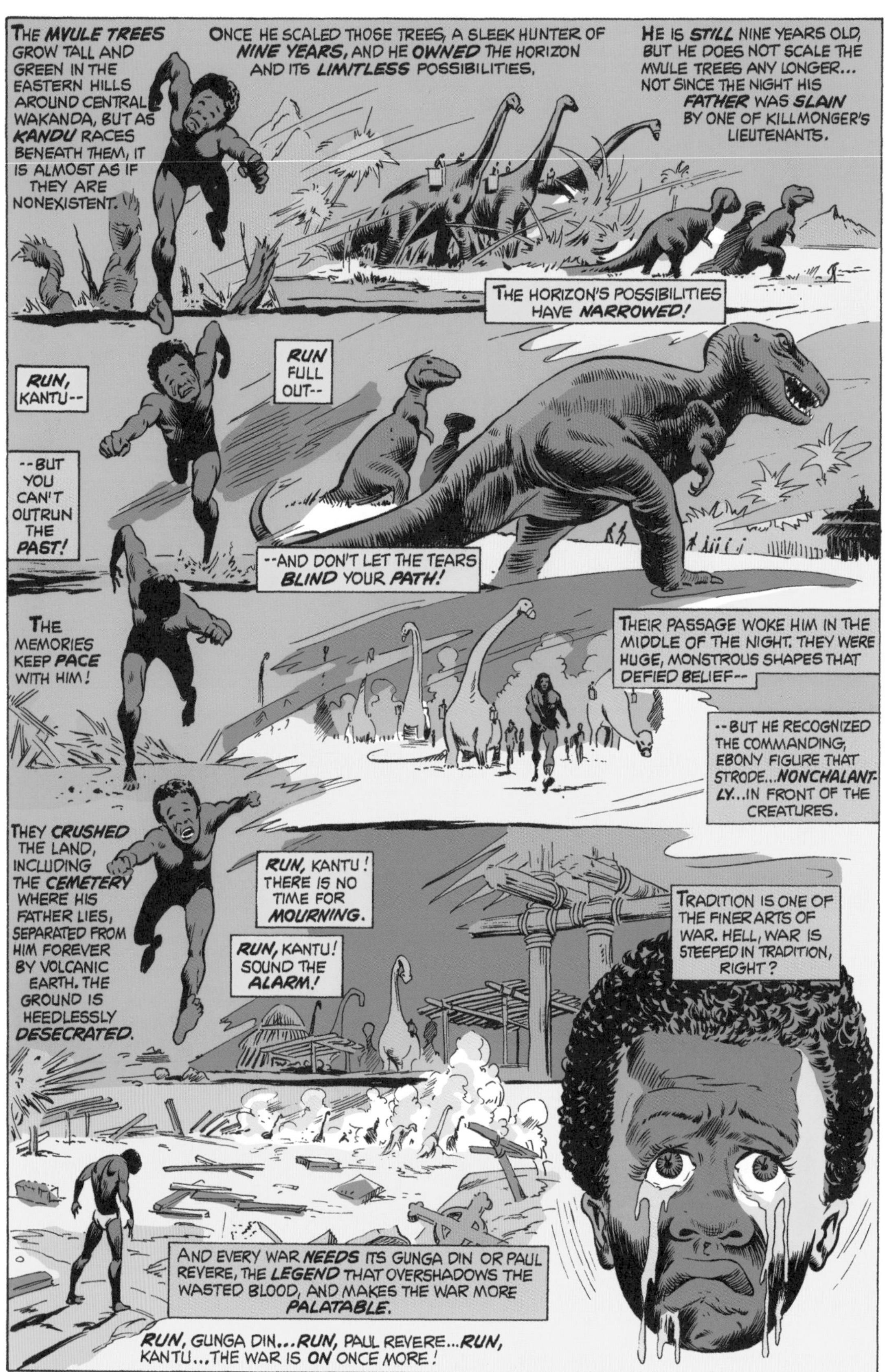
THE MVULE TREES GROW TALL AND GREEN IN THE EASTERN HILLS AROUND CENTRAL WAKANDA, BUT AS KANDU RACES BENEATH THEM, IT IS ALMOST AS IF THEY ARE NONEXISTENT.
ONCE HE SCALED THOSE TREES, A SLEEK HUNTER OF NINE YEARS, AND HE OWNED THE HORIZON AND ITS LIMITLESS POSSIBILITIES.
HE IS STILL NINE YEARS OLD, BUT HE DOES NOT SCALE THE MVULE TREES ANY LONGER... NOT SINCE THE NIGHT HIS FATHER WAS SLAIN BY ONE OF KILLMONGER'S LIEUTENANTS.
THE HORIZON'S POSSIBILITIES HAVE NARROWED!
RUN, KANTU--
RUN FULL OUT--
--BUT YOU CAN'T OUTRUN THE PAST!
--AND DON'T LET THE TEARS BLIND YOUR PATH!
THE MEMORIES KEEP PACE WITH HIM!
THEIR PASSAGE WOKE HIM IN THE MIDDLE OF THE NIGHT. THEY WERE HUGE, MONSTROUS SHAPES THAT DEFIED BELIEF--
--BUT HE RECOGNIZED THE COMMANDING, EBONY FIGURE THAT STRODE...NONCHALANT-LY...IN FRONT OF THE CREATURES.
THEY CRUSHED THE LAND, INCLUDING THE CEMETERY WHERE HIS FATHER LIES, SEPARATED FROM HIM FOREVER BY VOLCANIC EARTH. THE GROUND IS HEEDLESSLY DESECRATED.
RUN, KANTU! THERE IS NO TIME FOR MOURNING.
RUN, KANTU! SOUND THE ALARM!
TRADITION IS ONE OF THE FINER ARTS OF WAR. HELL, WAR IS STEEPED IN TRADITION, RIGHT?
AND EVERY WAR NEEDS ITS GUNGA DIN OR PAUL REVERE, THE LEGEND THAT OVERSHADOWS THE WASTED BLOOD, AND MAKES THE WAR MORE PALATABLE.
RUN, GUNGA DIN...RUN, PAUL REVERE...RUN, KANTU...THE WAR IS ON ONCE MORE!

MORNING IS WELL UNDER WAY... AND SO IS THE ASSAULT. GUNGA DIN IS LATE!
THE ELEGANT MARBLE COLUMNS OF THE PALACE, IMBUED WITH THEIR OWN LUSTROUS SWIRLS OF INNER FLAMING COLOR, SHATTER BENEATH THE ONSLAUGHT--
--THEIR BEAUTY AND ELEGANCE TRAMPLED TO MEANINGLESS DEBRIS!
THE FIRST COUNTERATTACK FORCE OF SONAR GLIDERS OPEN FIRE, DECAPITATING ONE OF THE TYRANNOSAURS-
--AND THE LUDICROUSLY GROTESQUE REMAINS HURTLE DOWNWARD!
I'VE GOT TO REACH KILLMONGER.
T'CHALLA...I... I DON'T WANT YOU KILLED!
I DIDN'T WANT ANY OF THIS, MONICA--BUT I HAVEN'T BEEN LEFT MUCH CHOICE, HAVE I?
THE MOUTH OPENS IN PROTEST, A GROWL ERUPTING FROM A THROAT THAT IS TORN RAGGEDLY AND DOES NOT YET REALIZE IT IS NO LONGER SUPPOSED TO WORK!
RADIO SONAR GLIDER SECTOR TWO, TAKU...AND TELL THEM TO OVERTAKE THAT REGIMENT. AND TELL THEM NOT TO FAIL!
I'M COMING FOR YOU, KILL-MONGER ...AND NOTHING'S GOING TO STOP ME!
THE HEAD ALONE IS TREMENDOUSLY HEAVY...HEAVY ENOUGH TO CRUSH HUMAN FLESH AND BONE!
WHICH IT ALMOST DOES!
MY CHIEFTAIN, WE HAVE JUST RECEIVED WORD FROM THE HOSPITAL COMPOUND!
SOME OF THE CREATURES ARE BEING DIRECTED STRAIGHT AT IT!

THEY STAND ON THE PERIMETERS OF VIOLENCE...AND THE WAR SEPARATES THEM. THAT LINE IS DISTINCT, BUT THE OTHER ELEMENTS THAT DIVIDE THEM ARE LESS DEFINED. IDEOLOGIES IN CONFLICT...NOW LOST!
PLACE A THOUSAND WARRIORS IN MY PATH, KILLMONGER--
--AND HOWEVER MANY MONSTERS YOU CAN MUSTER...AND IT'S STILL NOT ENOUGH TO STOP ME!
IT'S HIM! THE PANTHER-DEVIL IS COMING THIS WAY, KAZIBE!
MEEE?! IT'S YOU HE'S AFTER, TAYETE!
NO, KAZIBE! IT'S OBVIOUSLY YOU HE SEEKS! LOOK AT THE WAY HE'S GLARING RIGHT AT YOU.
ME?
BUT DON'T WORRY...
I'LL PROTECT YOU!
I WON'T MOVE FROM THIS SPOT--
--AND HE CAN'T MAKE ME.
GET OUT OF MY WAY, TAYETE!
YES, PANTHER-DEVIL. RIGHT AWAY, PANTHER-DEVIL.
AND STOP CALLING ME PANTHER-DEVIL!

LIVES/ CRIMSON/ SPLATTERED/ SPILLING/ FILLING A NEVER ENDING OCEAN/ DEPTHS OF PAIN AND LOSS/ ALGAE OF GRIEF AND DEATH/ CORAL WAVING TATTERED RIBBONS OF FLESH. IDEOLOGY CONSUMED BY THE BRUTAL ACTS PERPETRATED IN ITS NAME.
YOU MOVED, TAYETE!
I KNOW I MOVED. DON'T YOU THINK I KNOW THAT? BUT GUESS WHAT?
WHAT?
I HOPE HE GETS KILLMONGER!
TAYETE, WHAT ARE YOU SAYING? KILLMONGER WILL CUT OUT BOTH OUR TONGUES FOR WHAT YOURS HAS SAID!
"GOOD MORNING, T'CHALLA. I HADN'T EXPECTED TO SEE YOU HERE. I'D THOUGHT WE'D SPOKEN OUR FINAL WORDS BACK IN SERPENT VALLEY. YOU DO DISPLAY SOME TALENT AT SURVIVAL!
"AND YOU ARE STILL AS PERSISTENT IN YOUR FOOLISHNESS. YOU WANT A FIELD OF HONOR TO BATTLE ON, T'CHALLA. BLOODSHED WITH DIGNITY!
"IF YOU WEREN'T SUCH A DREAMER, YOU'D REALIZE THERE IS NO DIGNITY IN ANY OF THIS.
BUT I'M GLAD YOU'RE NOT DEAD. THIS IS HOW IT SHOULD BE. THE LAST BATTLE WOULD BE ANTI-CLIMACTIC IF YOU WEREN'T HERE.
COME T'CHALLA. FIGHT YOUR WAY TO ME. IF YOU CAN'T...YOU'RE NOT WORTH THE TIME I'VE SPENT TALKING TO YOU.
I'LL BE WAITING FOR YOU WHERE WE FIRST MET--
"--AT WARRIOR FALLS.
"IT WILL GIVE OUR BATTLE A SENSE OF SYMMETRY!"

W'KABI IS CERTAIN HE WILL NEVER GET USED TO THE ODOR THAT FILLS HIS HOSPITAL ROOM-- MORTALITY SMOTHERED BY DISINFECTANT. THE FEW TRIBAL DECORATIONS ON THE WALL ARE FAMILIAR... BUT THEY ARE ONLY TOKEN REMINDERS OF WAKANDAN TRADITION.
AND W'KABI IS NOT QUITE SURE HE TRUSTS THE STRANGE THINGS THAT PUNCTURE HIS ARM AND FEED HIM. A MAN EATS THROUGH HIS MOUTH... NOT HIS ARM!
PLASMA
WHOLE BLOOD
I'M SORRY THIS HAD TO HAPPEN, W'KABI. LIFE HAS BEEN DIFFICULT ENOUGH FOR BOTH OF US WITH-OUT EITHER OF US BEING HURT ANYMORE.
HIS SONS DO NOT SEEM TO UNDERSTAND IT EITHER, NOR WHY THEIR FATHER IS IN THIS PLACE. W'KABI WISHES CHANDRA WOULD REACH OUT AND TOUCH HIM TENDERLY...AND CURSES HIMSELF FOR HAVING SUCH A NEED.
T'CHALLA WAS HERE LAST NIGHT. HE TRIED TO SPEAK TO ME OF LOVE, CHANDRA.
BUT WHAT DOES HE KNOW OF IT? RIVER-SIDE WHISPERS? HE KNOWS NOTHING ABOUT THE NIGHTS I LIE BESIDE YOU, LISTENING TO YOU SLEEP AND KNOWING I'D STILL BE LOCKED OUT IF YOU WERE AWAKE.
IT HAS BEEN LONG SINCE I HAD SOMEONE ...DESIRE ME.
DON'T MAKE IT EVEN MORE DIFFICULT, W'KABI. I TOLD YOU... I WAS LOST IN YOUR SHADOW.
BUT I NEVER TRIED TO DO THAT TO YOU.
I DID NOT SAY YOU DID. I MERELY SAID, THAT IS WHAT HAPPENED.
CHANDRA LOOKS OUT THE WINDOW, AS IF ESCAPE FROM THE OPPRESSIVE ROOM AND HER LIFE LIES RIGHT OUTSIDE THE GLASS.
NOT TODAY, IT DOESN'T!

THE PALACE ARCHITECTURE HOLDS FIRM FOR ONE LAST MOMENT, BEFORE THE BRACHIOSAUR'S WEIGHT FORCES IT INWARD. THE INTRICATELY HAND-CRAFTED FRIEZE-WORK RIPS APART.
ONCE THOSE ROCK-CARVED MURALS TOLD A STORY...A SUBLIME PARABLE IN PICTURES COMPLETE WITH MORAL. A STORY TO CHARM THE HEART AND MIND.
MOST OF THOSE WHO SPENT TIME IN THE PALACE HAD ALREADY FORGOTTEN THE STORY'S EXISTENCE...IT WAS MERELY ETCHINGS ON THE WALLS BY WHICH THEY PASSED.
THEY SELDOM CONSIDERED ITS MORAL...NOW THEY'LL NEVER HAVE THE TIME.
THE HUGE PANTHER STATUE WHICH HELD REIN OVER THE THRONE ROOM CRUMPLES TO BLUE-BLACK DUST.

THE BRACHIOSAURS TRY TO REAR AWAY FROM THE BUILDING. THE FLOORING GIVES UNDER THEIR TREAD.

AND ONE LEG BATTERS THROUGH THE PRISON CELLS.

THE PRISONERS MAKE THE MOST OF IT.

BETTER GET A STEP ON IT, KARNAJ, BEFORE THE REST OF THIS PLACE COMES DOWN ON US AND KEEPS US HERE PERMANENTLY.

I KEEP TELLING YOU, IT'S LORD KARNAJ.

OH YEAH. I KEEP FORGETTING, KARNAJ.

KILLMONGER'S FINALLY DONE WHAT HE'D SAID HE'D DO.... BRING THIS PLACE DOWN AROUND T'CHALLA'S EARS!

LET ME GET MY HANDS ON ONE OF MY SONIC DISRUPTORS, MALICE... AND I'LL MAKE SURE YOU REMEMBER.

HEY...WAIT... HELP ME OUTTA HERE.

SORRY, FRIEND ...YOU'RE ON YOUR OWN!

AND AS THEY FLEE THE RUINS, ONE MAN WATCHES ...VENOMM!

ONE OTHER OBSERVES THEIR FLIGHT--
THE WAR FILLS THE AIR AND LAND, A KALEIDOSCOPE OF COMBAT. DUST AND SMOKE SHROUD MUCH OF WHAT OCCURS.
BUT ONE FIGURE CAN'T BE MISSED.
HE SEEMS TO BE EVERYWHERE... LASHING OUT... RELEASING THE RAGE THAT HE HAS KEPT RESTRAINED FOR NEAR A YEAR.
THE BLACK PANTHER LEAPS DIRECTLY INTO THE CENTER OF THE HOLOCAUST--
--AND HE DOESN'T STOP THERE!
LET ME GET MY HANDS ON A WEAPON. JUST ONE!

NLY THIS ONE
ES SOMETHING
OUT
YOU'VE HAD YOUR CHANCE, KARNAJ!
AND THAT GOES FOR YOU, TOO, MACABRE!

THE HOSPITAL FLOOR BUCKLES BENEATH THEIR FEET.
THE WARMTH OF CHANDRA'S HAND IS REMINISCENT OF YESTERDAY, CLOSE AND PRIVATE--
--A TOUCH THEY LOST IN A THOUSAND CARELESS, FORGOTTEN HOURS!
W'KABI KNOWS WHAT HAS SLAIN THE BEAST. NOT BEAUTY, BUT SONAR GLIDERS ARMED WITH DEADLY LASERS. HE'D OVERSEEN THEIR INSTALLATION HIMSELF, EVEN THOUGH HE DISTRUSTED THE OUTWORLDER WEAPONS!

HIS CHILDREN'S NAMES ARE ON HIS LIPS WHEN THE WORDS ARE CHANGED INTO A SCREAM THAT NEVER PAUSES FOR BREATH--
--AND USHERS IN A WORLD OF NIGHTMARE BLACK!

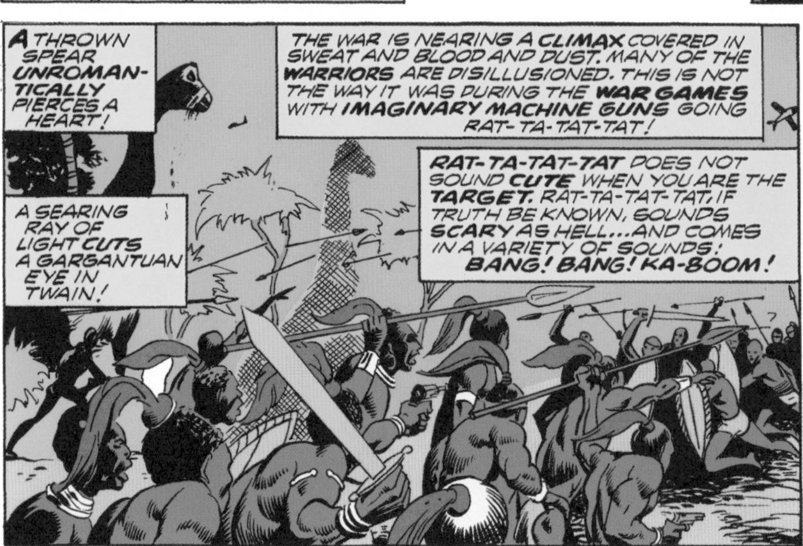
A THROWN SPEAR UNROMANTICALLY PIERCES A HEART!
THE WAR IS NEARING A CLIMAX COVERED IN SWEAT AND BLOOD AND DUST. MANY OF THE WARRIORS ARE DISILLUSIONED. THIS IS NOT THE WAY IT WAS DURING THE WAR GAMES WITH IMAGINARY MACHINE GUNS GOING RAT-TA-TAT-TAT!
A SEARING RAY OF LIGHT CUTS A GARGANTUAN EYE IN TWAIN!
RAT-TA-TAT-TAT DOES NOT SOUND CUTE WHEN YOU ARE THE TARGET. RAT-TA-TAT-TAT, IF TRUTH BE KNOWN, SOUNDS SCARY AS HELL... AND COMES IN A VARIETY OF SOUNDS: BANG! BANG! KA-BOOM!

AND SOMETIMES EVEN SILENTLY! BUT THE END RESULT IS USUALLY THE SAME.
DESTRUCTION!

WE HAVE NOT MET BEFORE, TAKU! ALLOW ME TO INTRODUCE MYSELF! I AM KING CADAVER!
AND THE KING CAN INVADE YOUR MIND! FEEL IT?
OF COURSE YOU DO!

KILLMONGER'S REPORT ON YOU SAYS YOU PRIDE YOURSELF ON YOUR ELOQUENCE! I THINK IT ONLY FAIR THAT YOU REALIZE THAT YOUR AWARENESS OF MY MIND RIPPING THROUGH YOUR OWN... WILL BE YOUR LAST LITERATE THOUGHT!
FOR ONE SO RATIONAL AS YOURSELF, WHAT BETTER FATE THAN LIVING THE REST OF YOUR LIFE WITHOUT CONTROL OF YOUR THOUGHTS OR BODY--
--IF... YOU CAN CALL THAT LIVING!

TAKU MOANS, CLUTCHING AT HIS HEAD AS IF HE CAN TEAR THE AGONIZING INTRUDER FROM HIS MIND. HE CAN'T.
HIS FINGERS RIP AT HIS TEMPLES, BUT THE PAINFUL INVADER IS INSIDE, WHERE THE MIND STAYS IN SECLUSION, RIPPING OPEN PERSONAL MEMORIES WITH ZEALOUS DELIGHT. PRIVACY HIDEOUSLY VIOLATED!
THE FORCE IS YANKED FROM HIS MIND... ALMOST AS VIOLENTLY AS IT HAD THRUST ITSELF INWARD.
CADAVER, YOU ALWAYS DID GIVE ME THE CREEPS!
NEVER KNEW WHEN YOU WERE GONNA TRY WORMIN' YOUR WAY INTO MY MIND! THAT'S A KINDA SICK POWER YOU GOT YOURSELF THERE, KINGIE!
LIKE THE WAY I HANDLE THAT WHIP?
NOT TOO MUCH, HUH?
HECK WITH YA IF YOU CAN'T TAKE A JOKE!
CADAVER SEEKS OUT THE MAN WHO HAS ATTACKED HIM, AND HIS EYES PULSE FEAR-SOMELY--
--AND THEN PULSE WITH GENUINE FEAR. A BRACHIO-SAUR TAKES A ROUTINE STEP--
--AND CADAVER CALLS FOR IT TO HALT!
IT DOESN'T!
YOU OKAY, TAKU? YOU LOOK KINDA PALE!
IN A MANNER'A SPEAKIN', THAT IS!
NOW AIN'T THAT A KICK... FIRST TIME I EVER SEEN YOU AT A LOSS FOR WORDS!
YOU WERE RIGHT, HORATIO ...WHAT HE DID WAS SICK! I CANNOT BANISH THE MEMORY!
YEAH... WELL... LOOKS LIKE THE WAR IS KINDA GOIN' AGAINST ERIK ON THIS END!
VENOMM, FOR WHAT YOU DID, I'M GOING TO TAKE YOU APART!
MALICE, THIS IS GOING TO HURT YOU--
--A LOT MORE THAN IT WILL ME!

HE BEGAN HIS ROLE AS THE BLACK PANTHER WITH A GREAT LOVE THAT HE THOUGHT COULD NEVER BE DIMINISHED. AND IN THOSE DAYS HE LEAPT UP THE ROCKY MOUNTAINSIDE WITH GRACEFUL ABANDON. WARRIOR FALLS 'FROTHING FURY HAS LASTED MORE THAN A YEAR, AN INCREDIBLE TORRENT OF ANGRY THUNDER SLASHING DOWNWARD WITH HEART STOPPING FORCE.
HE SPRINGS TOWARD HIS ENEMY, FROM ON PRECARIOUS HOLD TO THE NEXT, AS IF TRYIN TO GO BEYOND HIS OWN LIMITATIONS--
KILLMONGER
THIS IS WHERE IT ENDS, KILLMONGER--
--ONE WAY ...OR THE OTHER!
THAT FIRST YEAR WHEN HE UNDERWENT THE SACRED PANTHER RITUALS WAS EXCITING, AND HE WAS ALWAYS PUSHING HIMSELF TO SEE JUST HOW FAR HE WOULD DARE... AND LEARN WHAT HE COULD ACHIEVE.
HE DIDN'T ALWAYS SUCCEED, BUT HE WAS ALONE THEN, AND EACH ATTEMP WAS NOT MET WITH CRITICISM WITHIN HIS OWN HOUSE (THE COURT TRIBUNAL JUDGEMENT FIGURES CASTING VAGUE RECRIMINATIONS, THOUGH NONE OF TH SEEMED TO AGREE ON WHAT WAS WRON BEYOND THE OBVIOUS THREAT THAT KILLMONGER PRESENTED.

--UNTIL HE ARRIVES AT A SPOT ABOVE KILLMONGER!

THIS IS THE PANTHER OF OLD... SURE AND CONFIDENT OF HIS PURPOSE. HE LUNGES THROUGH THE AIR, ANTICIPATING THE CLASH, STEELING HIMSELF FOR THE FIRST IMPACT.

IT TOOK YOU LONG ENOUGH, T'CHALLA!

I WON'T MAKE YOU WAIT THAT LONG FOR THIS DRAMATIC ENDING YOU SPEAK OF!

YOUR TALENT FOR SURVIVAL HAS REGRET-TABLY RUN OUT!

LOOD BATTLE FOCUSED DOWN TO HESE TWO... ONE SLEEK AND ANTHERISH... THE OTHER SUPERBLY ARROGANT.

ah, FINALLY... A REACTION!
I WAS BEGINNING TO THINK YOU WERE NOT SUBJECT TO PAIN THE WAY THE REST OF US ARE!
IT ALMOST MAKES YOU HUMAN!
BUT YOU BETTER GET USED TO FEELING PAIN RATHER THAN JUST CAUSING IT, KILLMONGER--
BECAUSE I'M BRINGING IT ALL BACK TO YOU!
FOR ALL YOUR VICTIMS ...AND FOR THE SURVIVORS YOU LEFT TO MOURN!
I'M NOT CHASING SHADOWS ANYMORE, KILLMONGER, THE WAY YOU HAD ME PURSUING THEM--
--AND I'M NOT TWITCHING AT MY EVERY FAULT... REAL OR IMAGINED!
THAT GASH ISN'T YOUR IMAGINATION, T'CHALLA!
YOU GIVE CREDIT TO YOUR NAMESAKE, BUT YOU STILL CAN'T EVADE THESE SPIKES, T'CHALLA!
HOW MANY TIMES CAN YOU WITHSTAND THEIR BITE... BEFORE YOU FALL? SIX TIMES? A DOZEN?
AND WHEN YOU FALL THIS TIME, YOU WON'T BE GETTING UP AGAIN, T'CHALLA! NO RAGGED, BLOODIED, VICTORIOUS FIGURE STAGGERING AWAY TRIUMPHANTLY!
JUST A CORPSE... IN A TORN UNIFORM WHOSE MEANING WILL SOON BE FORGOTTEN!

SINCE YOU BEGAN THIS WAR, KILLMONGER, YOU'VE BEEN POSITIVE THAN WHEN IT ENDED, YOU WOULD BE THE WINNER!
AND THE SHADOWS I CHASED ALSO STALKED ME IN TURN! I WAS AFRAID TO OVERTAKE THE SHADOWS... OR LET THEM OVERTAKE ME! FOR THEY CONCEALED ALL THE GUILTS I LEFT UNVOICED!
I TRIED TO PRETEND I WASN'T AFRAID OF THEM! BUT THANKS TO YOU, KILLMONGER, I CAN LOOK UPON THOSE SHADOWS--
--AND WHILE I HAVE YET TO CONQUER THEM--
--I AM NO LONGER THEIR SLAVE!
AND I AM NO LONGER AFRAID OF THEM--
--OR YOU!
THEN YOU ARE MORE FOOLISH THAN I THOUGHT... FOR THIS BELT WILL TEAR OUT YOUR THROAT AND LEAVE YOUR PRETTY WORDS SCATTERED IN THE DUST!
NO, T'CHALLA! YOU CANNOT CHEAT ME OF YOUR DEATH AGAIN! I'VE WANTED MY HANDS TO FEEL THE LIFE LEAVE YOUR BODY!
FREEFALL!
THE PANTHER HURTLES OVER THE EDGE INTO THE ABYSS, THE ROCKY CLIFFSIDE FALLING SHARPLY AWAY TO A PANORAMA OF AIR AND RAINBOW SPRAY THAT MARKS A LIQUID COFFIN.
THE PANORAMA RUSHES PAST HIM AS HIS FALL GAINS SPEED! THE AIR IS FORCED OUT OF HIS LUNGS... WHISTLING PAST SNARLING LIPS AND NOSTRILS!
HE IGNORES THE TERROR AND THE VIEW, AND TWISTS INTO A NEAR IMPOSSIBLE TURN THAT CURVES HIM BACK TOWARD THE CLIFF.
HIS FINGERS RIP OPEN AGAINST THE ROCK, BUT THE HANDHOLD IS ENOUGH TO PROPEL HIM UPWARD... A DARKLY CLAD NEMESIS FROM WHICH KILLMONGER CAN NEVER BE RID!
DON'T HURRY AWAY, KILLMONGER! WE'RE NOT FINISHED YET!
HE AVOIDS THOSE SPIKES, WHILE HIS GLOVED FISTS BATTER KILLMONGER'S FACE AND CHEST. BLOOD BURST BRILLIANTLY INTO THE DAYLIGHT.
YOU'VE WANTED THE SAME THING I HAVE ALL ALONG, HAVEN'T YOU, T'CHALLA?
GO AHEAD! YOU'VE BESTED ME! EXACT YOUR VENGEANCE!
AND MAKE ME A MARTYR TO MY FOLLOWERS...AND TO SOME OF YOUR PEOPLE! IT COULD WELL BE THE LAST TIME YOU CALL THEM SUCH!

KILLMONGER'S WORDS END WITH A LAUGH... A WORDLESS INSULT THAT CONFUSES THE PANTHER.
THE LAUGHTER IS UNNERVING... BUT IT IS THE BRUTAL MOVEMENT OF KILLMONGER'S HUGE, BARBED HANDS THAT FOLLOWS THE LAUGHTER AND LENDS IT A DIFFERENT MEANING.
LAUGHTER IN THE FACE OF DEFEAT? HAS KILLMONGER LOST WHATEVER LITTLE SANITY HE HAD LEFT?
HE STRUGGLES TO BREAK FREE...AND THAT PLEASES KILLMONGER AS IT ALLOWS HIM TO EXHIBIT HIS SUPERIOR STRENGTH.
HIS BLOOD IS BRIGHT AGAINST THE DARK OF HIS UNIFORM. ANOTHER UNIFORM TORN AND BLOODIED. HOW MANY DOES THAT MAKE THIS YEAR, HIS MIND ASKS.
KILLMONGER SPEAKS, AND HIS WORDS ARE VERBAL LAUGHTER.
DID YOU REALLY BELIEVE YOU'D BESTED ME, T'CHALLA? I WAS ONLY HAVING SOME SPORT WITH YOU... BEFORE I ENDED IT!
I'M NOT LEAVING THE FALLS TO CHANCE YOUR DEATH THIS TIME... THIS TIME I'LL BREAK YOUR BACKBONE... AND THEN I'LL STAND OVER YOU AND WATCH YOU SLOWLY DIE!
THIS IS THE REAL END, T'CHALLA--
--AND YOU'RE RIGHT--
-- I ALWAYS KNEW IT WOULD END THIS WAY!

KANTU CHARGES TOWARD THE FRAY, SCREAMING HIS RAGE IN A HIGH PITCHED VOICE THAT BREAKS. IT IS A TINY VOICE LOST IN VAST EVENTS, AND KILLMONGER IS ONE WHO HAS IGNORED THE ROARS OF DINOSAURS AND TURNED HIS BACK ON THEM. THIS IS ONE VOICE HE SHOULDN'T IGNORE!
THE PANTHER AND KILLMONGER'S EYES LOCK FOR ONE LAST TIME. THE EYES HOLD NO PANIC, RATHER A TRACE OF ANNOYANCE... AN UNSPOKEN "WHAT THE HELL IS HAPPENING?"
IT IS OVER WITH A SILENT DESCENT. KILLMONGER HITS THE CRASHING WHITE RAPIDS AND DISAPPEARS UNDER THE SURFACE.
NEITHER THE PANTHER NOR KANTU SPEAK. THEY LOOK AT EACH OTHER AS IF THEY ARE SOMEHOW INEXPLICABLY ENTWINED. YOUTH AND ADULT FACING THE SAME ADVERSARY IN TIMELESS, VIOLENT ARENAS.
THEY WALK INTO THE FAMILIAR SUN AND FEEL ITS WARMTH FOR THE FIRST TIME THAT DAY. THE WAR HAS ENDED... AND THE ONLY SURVIVORS... ARE VICTIMS THEMSELVES!
-fin-

# *JUNGLE ACTION* #18,
# NOVEMBER 1975

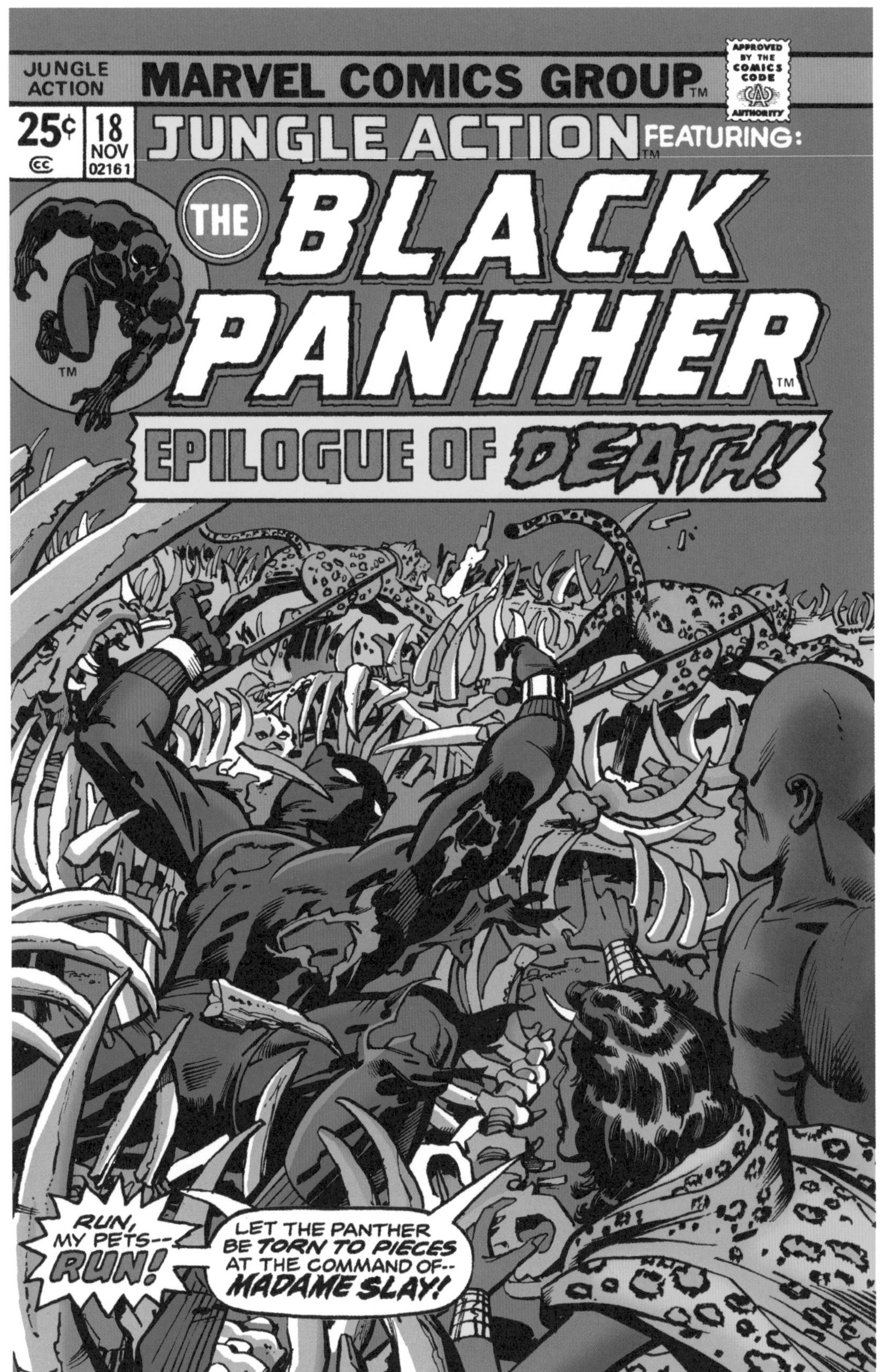
JUNGLE ACTION
MARVEL COMICS GROUP TM
APPROVED BY THE COMICS CODE AUTHORITY
25¢
18 NOV 02161
JUNGLE ACTION TM FEATURING:
THE BLACK PANTHER TM
EPILOGUE OF DEATH!
RUN, MY PETS-- RUN!
LET THE PANTHER BE TORN TO PIECES AT THE COMMAND OF-- MADAME SLAY!

Stan Lee PRESENTS:
BLACK PANTHER!
EPILOGUE!
AFTERMATH!
A STUDY IN ASHES AND RUIN.
DON McGREGOR WRITER
BOB McLEOD INKER
BILLY GRAHAM ARTIST
LETTERER DAVE HUNT
COLORIST GLYNIS OLIVER WEIN
MARV WOLFMAN EDITOR
A LIVING PANTHER SURVEYS THE WRECKAGE FROM ATOP A STONE PANTHER WHICH ONCE GUARDED THE THRONE ROOM OF HIS PALACE ROYAL. NOW ONLY THE DECAPITATED AND RAVAGED HEAD REMAINS TO OVERLOOK THE THRONE ROOM THAT FELL WHEN ITS GUARDIAN DID!

PIANO KEYS SOUND NOTES THAT TOUCH THE AIR--
--AND THE PAIN EASES FROM THE PANTHER'S AMBER EYES.
HE GLIDES INTO THE AIR LIKE A GREAT BLACK CAT SOOTHED BY GENTLE MUSIC--

--AND AS HE LANDS AMID HIS LOST DREAMS, THE MUSIC CHANGES TEMPO, LURING HIM TOWARD ITS PLAYER.
THE KEYS TRIP LIGHTLY ONE AFTER THE OTHER, THE MELODY MORE OPTIMISTIC ABOUT LIFE THAN HIS REFLECTIONS.
PUT THE DREAM BACK TOGETHER AS IF A SHATTERED CITY AND ELOQUENT TEMPLES WERE BUT PUZZLE PIECES TORN ASUNDER BY A BERSERK CHILD.

ALL THE PERSONAL TINY TREASURES ARE IRREPARABLY CRUSHED. THE ACQUIREMENTS OF A LIFETIME ARE TAKEN AWAY. THE LITTLE ITEMS AND MEMENTOES YOU SWEAR YOU CAN'T DO WITHOUT.
MONICA LYNN'S FINGERS SPEAK TENDERLY ACROSS THE KEYBOARD. SOME THINGS HAVE NOT BEEN LOST.
YOU'VE DISCOVERED THE NEW PIANO.
IT'S NICE TO HEAR YOU PLAY AGAIN.

IT DOESN'T SEEM LIKE TWO MONTHS HAVE PASSED SINCE KILLMONGER SMASHED THE LAST ONE... ALONG WITH EVERYTHING ELSE.
TOOK THAT LONG TO GET A NEW ONE SHIPPED IN. I MISSED YOUR MUSIC. I STILL HAVE A FONDNESS FOR THE PIANO--

--EVEN THOUGH IT'S NOT A NATURAL INSTRUMENT IN WAKANDA.
I KINDA GUESSED. W'KABI MUST'VE LOVED THAT... EVEN YOUR TASTE IN MUSIC IS CORRUPTED BY THE OUTWORLDERS.
OF COURSE, I KNOW YOU HOLD DEAR MUCH WAKANDAN MUSIC... BUT THIS MELODY... LET'S JUST SAY... MUSIC'S THE WAY I SPEAK BEST.
NO FOXY LADY TALK. THINK OF IT AS A WOMAN TELLING A MAN SHE LOVES TO LOOK AT HIM...
...EVEN WHEN HE HAS A COWL OVER HIS FACE.

BACK IN FUN CITY, I USED A HIP ATTITUDE AS A DEFENSE. YOU SPEAK A LITTLE STREET LINGO AND A LOTTA STRAIGHTS SEE YOU AS A THREAT. A NEW IMAGE IN AMERICA... US BLACK "WIMMEN" ARE SUPPOSED TO BE "WITH IT."
HOW COME NOBODY TRIES TO SEE INSIDE UNLESS YOU'RE HURTIN'? IS IT ONLY HURT THAT MAKES A PERSON REAL?
NO. BUT HURT MAKES A FEW PEOPLE STOP AND TRY TO SEE INSIDE.
I LIKE THAT. IT'D MAKE A GOOD LYRIC FOR A SONG.

I'M SORRY TO INTERRUPT YOUR QUIET TALK, MY CHIEFTAIN. I KNOW YOU HAVE LITTLE TIME FOR SUCH MOMENTS.
I GUESS IT CAN'T BE HELPED, TAKU. HAVE YOU GOT THE CRAFT READY TO TAKE OFF THAT'S GOING TO TAKE VENOMM BACK TO HIS HOMELAND?

HORATIO!
TAKU TAKES CARE'A EVERYTHING, JOE JUNGLE-LORD.
YEAH...TAKU I KNOW. YOU AIN'T SUPPOSED TO TALK OUTTA LINE TO THE KING.
YOU THINK KILLMONGER WRECKING THIS PLACE GAVE YOU TROUBLE, YOU'RE LUCKY YOU GOT THEM... WHAT'CHA CALL 'EM ...DINOSAURS BACK WHERE THEY COME FROM.
THEM THINGS STARTED REPRODUCIN' ...THAT MEANS LIKE WHEN YOU HAVE KIDS... WELL, THAT'S WHEN YOU'D HAVE TROUBLE, BIG P.
REAL TROUBLE!

MORE TROUBLE THAN BROKEN ELEVATOR SHAFTS, VENOMM?
OH, YEAH. A LOT MORE. DON'T YOU THINK SO, TAKU?
HEY!! WHATTA YA DOIN'?
TAKE THE STAIRS, TAKU, WHILE VENOMM CONTINUES HIS THESIS.
I'LL MEET YOU AT THE VERTICAL LAUNCHING SECTOR.

THE PANTHER DISAPPEARS SWIFTLY, BLENDING INTO THE DARK DEPTHS THAT HOUSE THE ONE SECTION OF CENTRAL WAKANDA THAT REMAINED UNTOUCHED BY THE WAR: THE UNDERGROUND COMPUTERIZED COMPLEX!
THESUS? WHAT'S A THESUS?

YOU SURE THIS THING IS WORKING RIGHT, TAKU?
I AIN'T GOT MUCH DESIRE TO GO DOWN THE WAY GEORGE OF THE JUNGLE DID.
THE PANTHER STRIDES PAST SLEEK, STERILE SILVER WALLS THAT CAST BACK HIS IMAGE IN FLAT METALLIC MOVEMENT THAT HAS LOST ITS FLESH AND BLOOD DEPTH.
THE VAST CHAMBERS ARE ALIVE WITH THE SOUND OF ACTIVITY. PAINTED METAL STEMS REACH FOR THE DISTANT CEILING--
--UNNATURAL ROOTS UNDER THE SOIL--
--BLOOMING TECHNOLOGY ABOVE THE LAND.

IS THE CRAFT SET FOR FLIGHT, TAYETE AND KAZIBE?
OH, YES. I'VE JUST BEEN SHOWING KAZIBE HOW THIS THING WORKS. HE'S STILL A BIT AFRAID OF THESE WONDER MACHINES.

I AM GLAD I CAN FREE YOU FROM THESE CHAINS, HORATIO.
WE LIVE IN BONDAGE... TO OUR PAST AND TO THE DEMANDS OF OTHERS. AT TIMES, IT SEEMS EASIER TO BE FREE OF LINKAGES OF CHAIN.

THAT'S REAL CUTE, TAKU. DIDN'T UNNERSTAND A WORD OF IT. BUT IT'S CUTE.
UUUHHH ...COULD YOU HOLD UP A MINUTE... I THINK I'M--
--STUCK.

I AM STUCK!
PANTHER-DEVIL, TELL THEM TO STOP THIS INFERNAL BEAST!
RRIIIPPP!
TAYETE... I DON'T HAVE THE HEART TO TELL YOU TO QUIT CALLING ME PANTHER DEVIL.

THE AMBER PAGODA IS SURROUNDED BY SOFT SOUNDS. WHISPERING LEAVES SPEAKING THE VOICE OF THE WIND... RIVER CURRENTS FLIRTING WITH THE SUN.
W'KABI AND CHANDRA'S CHILDREN STAND AT THE RIVER'S EDGE, BUT LOOK TOWARD THE DOORWAY WHERE THEIR PARENTS STAND AS SEPARATE SILHOUETTES THEY HOPE WILL JOIN.

THEY DO NOT UNDERSTAND THE GESTURES AND POSTURES OF DEPRESSION AND SORROW--
--BUT THEY DO KNOW SOMETHING IS... WRONG!
THEY SAY THIS ISN'T THE COWARDLY WAY OUT... ENDING IT ALL FACE TO FACE--
--BUT I THINK IT'D HAVE BEEN EASIER ON BOTH OF US IF WE'D KEPT IT LESS PERSONAL.

THAT'S WHAT WE BECAME, CHANDRA--
--LESS PERSONAL.
THERE IS A WORD I SHOULD HAVE LEARNED BEFORE... AFFECTION... I NEVER KNEW WHAT IT MEANT TO ME UNTIL MY NEED FOR IT WAS SO GREAT...

...AND I COULD NO LONGER GIVE IT. YES, I KNOW. I ONCE THOUGHT AFFECTION IMPORTANT... IT SEEMS LESS SO NOW.
WE CHANGE POSITIONS.
COME, CHILDREN.
WHERE ARE YOU GOING?

AWAY. NOT FAR ENOUGH TO ESCAPE THE GUILT THAT HOUNDS ME. I CAN'T GO THAT FAR.
ARGUMENTS FLARE IN W'KABI'S MIND: LIVING WITH GUILT DOES NOT ATONE FOR THE ACTS THAT BOTHER YOU... IT MERELY RUINS YOUR LIFE.
I LIVE WITH GUILT. EVERY ACTION. YOU'LL HAVE TO FORGIVE ME... BUT I'M TIRED OF IT.
HE STARTS TO RAISE HIS LEFT ARM TOWARD HER RETREATING FIGURE AND STOPS, REALIZING THAT IT IS A MECHANICAL ARM THAT HE LIFTS, A DEAD LIMB THAT CANNOT FEEL THE PAIN THE REST OF HIM FEELS.
AND THE RIVER SPEAKS SOFTLY OF LONELY NIGHTS!

IT IS THE MORNING AFTER THE LONELY NIGHT. A SLAUGHTER WILL HAPPEN THIS MORNING... BRUTAL... AND RUTHLESS... AND CALCULATED SLAUGHTER! AT THE MOMENT, THE TWO MEN WHO STALK THE SNARLING LEOPARD THINK THEY WILL COMMIT THE KILL.
THEY WILL SPEAR THE ANIMAL HIDE AT THE THROAT, CAREFUL NOT TO RUIN THE PELT...
...AND THEN THEY WILL TAKE TURNS BASHING IN ITS SKULL UNTIL IT CEASES TO FIGHT!
THEY ARE ALONE WITH THE MORNING AND THEIR BRUTALITY, AND SECURE IN THAT KNOWLEDGE UNTIL A FOREIGN SOUND RIPS AWAY THEIR SECURITY!
AND THEY LOOK UPON THE FACES OF THEIR EXECUTIONERS!
THERE WILL BE A SLAUGHTER THIS MORNING--
--BUT THEY... WILL BE THE VICTIMS!

THE SECOND NIGHT PASSES; A BLACK ETERNITY OF RESTLESS SLEEP AND WAKING TO EMPTY STRETCHES OF BED IN A VAST ROOM FILLED WITH THE SOUND OF HIS LONE BREATHING. W'KABI NEARLY CALLS CHANDRA'S NAME AND REALIZES THAT IT IS THE PANTHER'S VOICE HE HEARS.
WOODLAND SOMBRE IS TREACHEROUSLY PASTEL. THE SHADOWS ARE HIDDEN!
WE'RE ALMOST AT THE SPOT, W'KABI, WHERE THE SHEPHERD SAYS HE SAW HIS MYSTERIOUS CORPSES.
I SEE I DID NOT NEED TO ADVISE YOU THAT A CAUTIOUS APPROACH WOULD BE BEST, MY FRIEND.
THE MAN MUST EXAGGERATE HIS FINDINGS, MY CHIEFTAIN. SINCE KILLMONGER'S DEATH, WAKANDA HAS HAD LITTLE OF THE CRUELLY PLANNED SLAYINGS AT WHICH HE WAS A MASTER!
LET US HOPE... IT IS NOT SOMEONE COPYING... HIS STYLE!
YOU HAVE BEEN SILENT FOR LONG STRETCHES ON OUR JOURNEY. IS IT THIS THAT TROUBLES YOU?
CHANDRA HAS LEFT ME ...TO SEEK HER ...I THINK THE WORD SHE USES IS... IDENTITY. I DID NOT WISH TO BORE YOU WITH IT, MY CHIEFTAIN.
IT WOULD NOT BORE ME, MY FRIEND. I SENSED YOUR AGONY.
I GO OVER IT AND OVER IT... I WANT THERE TO BE SOME GOOD GUYS AND BAD GUYS... BUT THERE ARE NONE.
THE CHANGES IN MY LIFE... I AM ASHAMED TO ADMIT ...SCARE ME! I WAS WEAK AND LEANED ON CHANDRA. NOW I DEPEND ON AN ARM THAT IS NOT PART OF MY FLESH--
--AN ALIEN UNFEELING THING THAT RESPONDS TO MY THOUGHTS IN A MANNER I DO NOT UNDERSTAND. IT FILLS ME WITH HORROR!
IT WAS A DIFFICULT DECISION, BUT YOU HAD LOST YOUR REAL ARM. IT COULD NOT BE MENDED.
AND COUPLES SHARE DEPENDENCY. WHEN CHANDRA'S WORLD BECAME LESS DEPENDENT ON YOU... YOURS WAS STILL DEPENDENT ON HERS. IT IS A PAINFUL CHANGE WHEN THE TWO PEOPLE HAVE HAD A CLOSE HISTORY.
THEY WALK OUT INTO THE CLEARING AND STOP! THEIR DISCUSSION OF LIFE IMPALED BY THE REALITY OF DEATH!
A PASTEL DEATH SCENE WITH UNKEMPT SCAVENGERS HUNGRILY EYEING THE REMAINS.
THE HYENAS JUMP HALF-HEARTEDLY FOR PIECES OF AN AFTERNOON MEAL!

W'KABI'S REAL HAND SEPARATES THE OTHER FROM ITS WRIST. THE HORROR IS FELT ONLY IN W'KABI'S MIND.
OUR SHEPHERD DID NOT EXAGGERATE, W'KABI. SCATTER THE HYENAS WHILE I RELEASE THE BODIES.
THE TOUCH OF A BUTTON AND THE METALLIC ARM PULSATES UP INTO HIS CHEST WHERE THE ENERGY VIBRATES: A FLESH TUNING FORK! THE MIND REBELS AGAINST THE CONCEPT!

THAT SHOULD KEEP THEM AWAY. HYENAS ARE NOT AS SURE ABOUT A PREY THAT DOES NOT REMAIN STILL.
THEY'VE BEEN DEAD MORE THAN A DAY. THE SUN HAS NOT BEEN KIND TO THEM.
I HAD HOPED SUCH VIOLENCE WOULD ONLY BE DISTURBING MEMORIES.
INSTEAD, ITS SPECTER STALKS US ANEW.
THERE ARE MANY TRACKS HERE, MY CHIEFTAIN.
TWO SETS OF HUMAN PRINTS SURROUNDED BY THE TRACKS OF MANY CATS.
LEOPARDS, IT WOULD APPEAR.
AN IMPOSSIBLY HUGE HAND REACHES OUT FOR HIM, THRUST FROM THE PASTEL FOLIAGE--
--AND IMPOSSIBLY HUGE FINGERS DIG INTO THE SOFT NECK FLESH.
THE GRIP TIGHTENS AS THE IMPOSSIBLY HUGE FINGERS SEEK THE NARROW SKULL LINE BENEATH THE EAR LOBES.
THE PASTELS GO DARK!

PUT HIM DOWN--
--AND PUT HIM DOWN... NOW!
THE GIANT DOES NOT REPLY, BUT HE RELEASES W'KABI IN AN ALMOST GENTLE FASHION.
THERE IS NOTHING GENTLE ABOUT HIM WHEN HE TURNS BACK TO FACE THE PANTHER.
NOTHING GENTLE AT ALL! THERE IS NOTHING GENTLE, EITHER, ABOUT THE PANTHER'S ATTACK!
SILENTLY, THE GIANT FALLS. HE DOES NOT CRY IN OUTRAGE. HE DOES NOT HURL VINDICTIVE THREATS. HIS FACE ACCEPTS THE ACT ALMOST PASSIVELY.
THERE ARE QUESTIONS THAT YOU SHALL ANSWER, SILENT ONE.
WE CAN END THIS SENSELESS CONFLICT NOW AND SAVE EACH OTHER FROM SUFFERING A GREAT DEAL OF PAIN...
THE PANTHER SEES THE GIANT RISING, CATCHES THE SWEEPING ARC OF THE HANDS WHICH ARE CLASPED ABOUT THE BOULDER!
...OR WE CAN-- UUHHHH!
SUCKER-ED! AND HE FELL FOR IT!
THE PASTEL SETTING BECOMES QUIET. ONLY THE DISTANT SNARLS OF UNEASY LEOPARDS CARRY ON THE HUMID AIR.
THE GIANT DOES NOT SPEAK ONE WORD OF TRIUMPH!

THE PANTHER AWAKENS TO LIMBO, AND IT FLASHES DISJOINTEDLY IN HIS EYES AND MIND WITH NAUSEATING EFFECT!
IT IS NOT A PLEASANT EXPERIENCE!
THERE IS A SICK FEELING DEEP IN HIS STOMACH, AND THE SWELLING AT HIS TEMPLE IS LIKE THE MEMBRANE SURFACE OF A DRUM POUNDING OUT ITS WOUND-MESSAGE!
HE TRIES TO MOVE HIS ARMS, BUT SOMETHING RESTRAINS THEM! HE IS HELPLESS!
HE LOOKS INTO THE WOMAN'S FACE, AND THERE IS A PASSIONATE HATRED DIRECTED AT HIM.
"WHO ARE YOU?" THE PANTHER ASKS WITH LIPS THAT TRY RELEARNING HOW TO FORM WORDS. "WERE YOU THE ONE WHO KILLED THOSE MEN?"
I AM MADAM SLAY... AND I KILLED THOSE...
...KILLERS!
AND YOU NEED NOT ASK... I'M GOING TO KILL YOU, ALSO!
BUT Y KNEW S ONE VER CLOSE... ME. YO HAVEN FORGOT ERIK, H YOU
"KILLMONG THE PANT GASPS, AN FEELS SO WHAT EMBARRA AT SUCH STARK, M DRAMAT RESPONS

I CALLED HIM ERIK. HE WAS FOND OF THAT NAME. AND HE WAS AS FOND OF ME AS I WAS OF HIM!
BUT THAT'S ALL OVER NOW, ISN'T IT? IT'S PAST... BECAUSE YOU CAUSED HIS DEATH!
DON'T BOTHER DENYING IT.
I HAVEN'T BEEN LONELY. MUTE HERE IS MORE SUITABLE COMPANY THAN MOST.
ERIK TOLD ME MUTE HAD SOMETHING CALLED APHONIA... BUT THAT'S OF NO REAL CONSEQUENCE EITHER... IT'S ENOUGH TO SAY... MUTE'S NAME FITS HIM--
--ADEQUATELY!
YOU MIGHT WONDER WHY I WEAR THESE PELTS. I DO NOT WANT THAT MISUNDERSTOOD.
THOSE BEAUTIFUL ANIMALS WERE SLAIN BY MEMBERS OF YOUR RIGHTEOUS PEOPLE. I WEAR THESE HIDES AS TRIBUTE ...TO ERIK... AND TO THE SUPERB CATS WHO WERE BUTCHERED IN THEIR PRIME!
THE CLOSENESS OF THESE PELTS REMINDS ME OF THEIR GRACE AND WARMTH WHEN THEY WERE ALIVE--
--BUT MORE--
--IT KEEPS THE MEMORY OF ERIK CLOSE TO ME!

RISE PREYY! ERIK KEPT HIM AT HIS SIDE MOST OFTEN. IF PREYY COULD SPEAK I THINK HE WOULD APPRECIATE THE FACT THAT HE SHALL CAUSE--
--YOUR DEATH!!
I NEVER ACTIVELY SOUGHT LOVE, T'CHALLA...I MIGHT HAVE BEEN QUITE CONTENT WITHOUT IT--

--IF IT HAD NEVER HAPPENED. BUT IT DID!
YOU TOOK LOVE FROM ME, PERHAPS NOT BY YOUR OWN HAND... BUT IT WAS YOUR DOING!
YOU TOOK LOVE FROM ME AND I DO NOT FORGIVE YOU FOR THAT.

I CAN NEVER FORGIVE YOU FOR THAT!
TAKE HIM, PREYY!! YOU AND YOUR BROTHER TAKE HIM PAST THE ROCKY VISTAS!
ENJOY THE VIEW, T'CHALLA. THIS IS YOUR LAST JOURNEY!

THE FIRST LUNGE NEARLY TEARS HIS ARMS OUT OF THEIR SOCKETS!
HE TRIES TO GAIN HIS BALANCE, SEEKING TO GET HIS FEET BENEATH HIM--

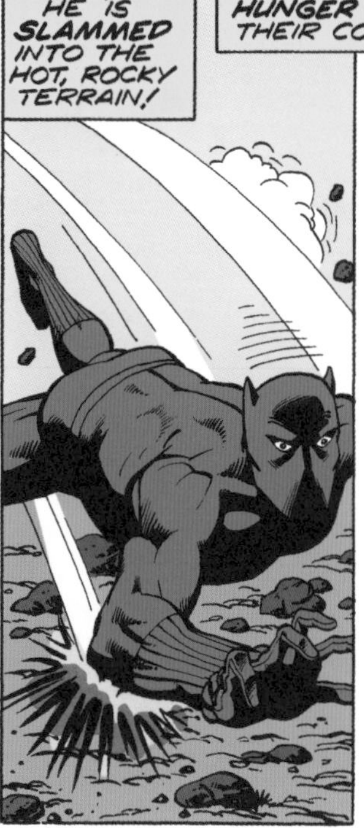
--BUT THE TETHERS DRAW TAUT ROUND THE LEOPARDS' NECKS, AND HE IS SLAMMED INTO THE HOT, ROCKY TERRAIN!

THE LEOPARDS GAIN SPEED, AND THROUGH THE BLUR OF DUST AND SWEAT THE PANTHER GLIMPSES HYENAS WATCHING THE EVENT. HE CANNOT SEE THE EAGER HUNGER ADDING COLOR TO THEIR COLORLESS EYES--
--BUT HE KNOWS IT IS THERE!

THE HYENAS ARE THE LEAST OF HIS WORRIES! THEY WILL TRAIL BEHIND--
--CAUTIOUS GOURMETS KEEPING THEIR DISTANCE--
THE PACK WILL FIGHT AMONGST THEMSELVES FOR THE DINNER THAT IS LEFT IN HIS WAKE.
--UNTIL THE SERRATED ROCK EDGES AND SHARP SKULL AND RIB BONE REMAINS HAVE CARVED A GARISHLY RED BANQUET FROM HIS FLESH!
IT WON'T BOTHER THEM AT ALL THAT THE BRIGHT RED MEAT IS QUICKLY DULLED BY LAYERS OF DUST!
CHAOTIC, WORDLESS MEMORIES OF DINOSAUR MOUTHS DEVOUR HIM WHILE HUGE, WHITE, GOD-LIKE BEINGS REND THEIR OWN MYTHOLOGY WITH TALONED CLAWS!
THEY ARE MEMORIES THAT HAVE CHANGED THE SHAPE AND COURSE OF HIS LIFE!
THE LEOPARDS SEEM TO GAIN SPEED.
RIPPING--
--SPRAWLING--
--HURTLING FORWARD--
--HIS MOVEMENTS NOT HIS OWN BUT DICTATED BY SHEER MOMENTUM!
WORDS ARE USELESS, EVEN IF HE COULD SPEAK, WHICH HE CAN'T, BECAUSE THE SUN-BAKED STONE TRAMPOLINE DOES NOT YIELD EACH TIME HE BATTERS INTO ITS SURFACE!
THE PANTHER IS POSITIVE HE HITS EVERY ROCK IN THEIR PATH!
THE TWO LEOPARDS SEEM TO SEPARATE AS IF ON CUE!
THEY HAVE RUN THIS COURSE BEFORE!
A ROCK RAZOR CURVES LETHALLY FROM THE RED EARTH, AND THE CATS RUN ON EITHER SIDE OF IT--
--LEAVING HIM DIRECTLY IN THE CENTER; HIS SOFT HUMAN FLESH RIPE FOR THIS NATURAL GUILLOTINE THAT WILL SLICE HIM IN TWAIN!

HE KNOWS THIS AS A GRAVEYARD, WITH SKELETAL REMAINS THE ONLY EVIDENCE OF FORGOTTEN VICTIMS! A CEMETERY UNATTENDED BY MOURNERS... BUT A PLACE OF DYING NONETHELESS.
THERE ARE ONLY SECONDS BEFORE THE IMPACT--
--WHEN THE SWORD-LIKE POINT OF THE ROCK WILL END ANY GRACE OR THOUGHT HE HAS LEFT!
BRUISED KNUCKLES WRAP THE DEATH-LINES ABOUT EACH WRIST--

--BURNING THE FLESH RAW!
THE POINT OF IMPACT IS CLOSER, RUSHING UP THE LANDSCAPE TO FILL HIS VISION. THERE IS NOTHING ELSE IN EXISTENCE!
HE TRIES TO BREATHE, SUCKING IN THE DUST THAT HAS A HORNET'S ANGRY STING!

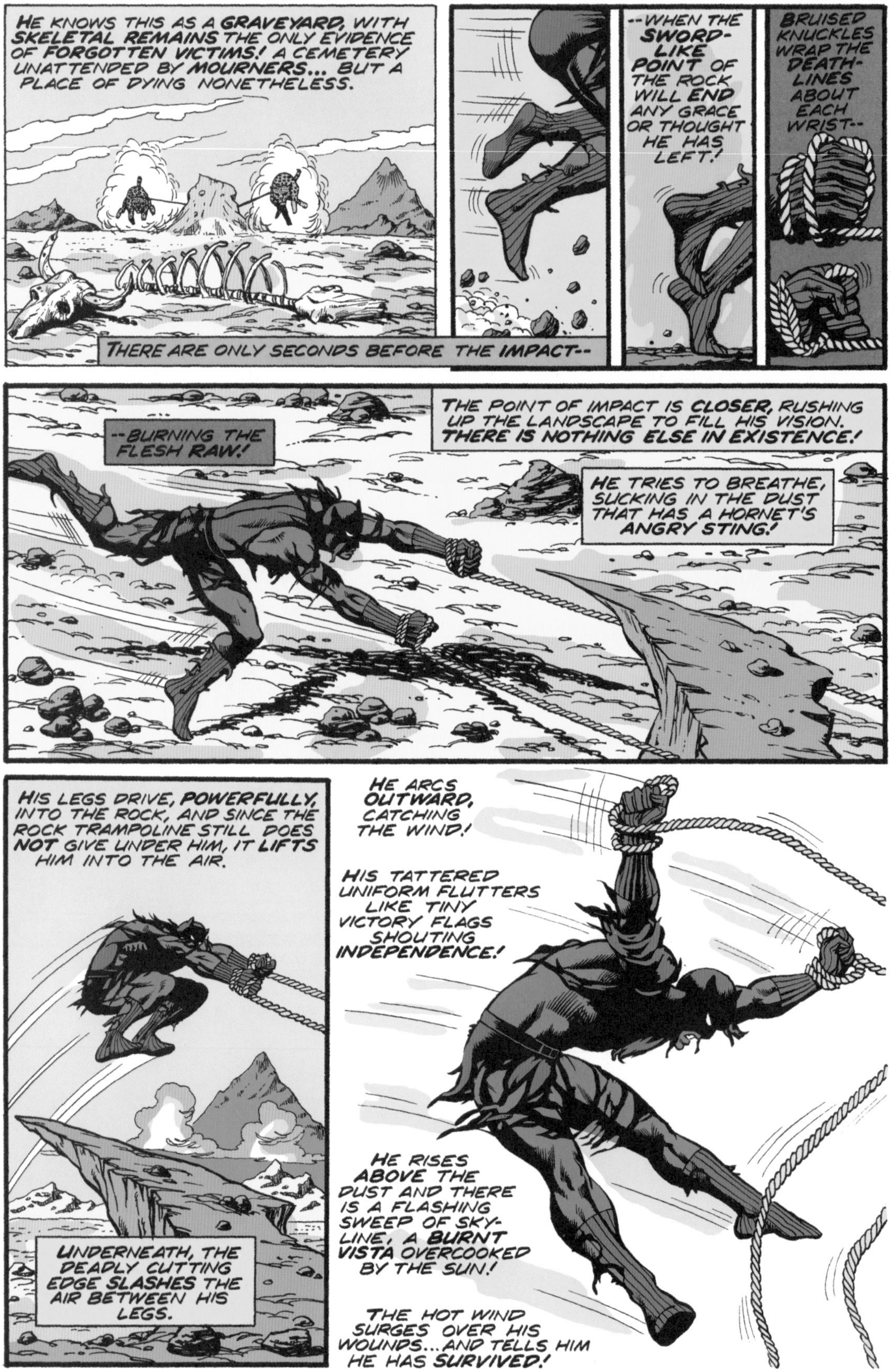

HIS LEGS DRIVE, POWERFULLY, INTO THE ROCK, AND SINCE THE ROCK TRAMPOLINE STILL DOES NOT GIVE UNDER HIM, IT LIFTS HIM INTO THE AIR.
UNDERNEATH, THE DEADLY CUTTING EDGE SLASHES THE AIR BETWEEN HIS LEGS.
HE ARCS OUTWARD, CATCHING THE WIND!
HIS TATTERED UNIFORM FLUTTERS LIKE TINY VICTORY FLAGS SHOUTING INDEPENDENCE!
HE RISES ABOVE THE DUST AND THERE IS A FLASHING SWEEP OF SKY-LINE, A BURNT VISTA OVERCOOKED BY THE SUN!
THE HOT WIND SURGES OVER HIS WOUNDS... AND TELLS HIM HE HAS SURVIVED!

THE NEXT SECONDS ARE RISKY! ONE MIS-CALCULATION... JUST ONE!... AND HE WILL CRASH BACK INTO THE DUST AND ROCK. THE HYENAS ARE AN UNSEEN AUDIENCE; THEIR LAUGHTER MOCKS HIS AUDACIOUS ATTEMPT!
HE LANDS ON THE LEOPARDS' BACKS, AND THIS SURFACE DOES GIVE BENEATH HIS BOOTS. MUSCLES RIPPLE FLUIDLY THREATENING TO DASH HIM UNDER THEIR TREAD!
HE SWAYS UNCERTAINLY. EARTH AND SKY TUG AT HIM. HE WILL NEVER BE ABLE TO SECURE HIS FOOTING!
IN ONE SECOND, THE SITUATION CHANGES. HIS FOOTING IS A CERTAINTY!
HE IS ASTRIDE THE SNARLING BEASTS, CROUCHING DEFIANTLY--
--AND THEY HEAD, INSTINCTIVELY, BACK TOWARD THE LAIR FROM WHICH HIS FUNERAL PROCESSION BEGAN!
GREY AND BLACK ARE ALIEN HUES IN THIS CEMETERY. SCULPTURED LAWNS AND DECORATIVE MARKERS ARE MISSING, BUT IT IS STILL A LAND FERTILIZED BY ROTTING CORPSES!
ONE CORPSE HAS JUST RETURNED... DEFIANTLY!
MADAM SLAY IS LESS THAN PLEASED!
MUTE!! BE CAREFUL, MUTE! HE'S COME BACK!

STRAIGHT, LADY! THE PANTHER... IS BACK!
HIS VOICE IS SHAKY WITH PAIN AND ANGER AND A PROFOUND TRACE OF SORROW!
THIS IS A DIFFERENT RAGE FROM THAT HE FELT TOWARD KILLMONGER. EVEN AS HE ATTACKS, HE KNOWS THAT IN MANY WAYS THESE PEOPLE ARE VICTIMS... WHO HAVE CHOSEN TO MAKE OTHERS... THEIR VICTIMS!

IT HAS BEEN MONTHS SINCE THE LAST BATTLE... SINCE MY HANDS ACHED SO BADLY IT TOOK WEEKS TO BE ABLE TO CLOSE THEM WITHOUT PAIN!

TWO MONTHS WITHOUT SOME-ONE TRYING TO HUMILIATE ME... OR MY HAVING TO HUMILIATE ANOTHER HUMAN BEING.
IT TAKES LONGER THAN TWO MONTHS TO FORGET BOTH!

ERIK SAID YOU ALWAYS WERE THE IDEALIST!
I STILL AM!

AND I DIDN'T LET KILL-MONGER TAKE THAT FROM ME--
--BY RIDICULE--

--OR VIOLENCE!
HE SOUGHT TO CORRUPT THAT IDEALISM... I TEMPERED WITH PRAGMATISM!
UUHHH!
I'LL TEAR YOU OPEN, T'CHALLA.
AND I'M REALLY SUR-PRISED YOU STUCK IT OUT! IDEALISTS ...WHEN FACED WITH REALITY... NORMALLY BURY THEIR HEADS LIKE OSTRICHES!

BEFORE THE DAY IS OVER YOU'LL BE BURIED, T'CHALLA--
--AND THE REST OF YOUR BODY WILL JOIN YOUR HEAD IN THE SAND!

MADAM SLAY HEARS THE BLAST AND TURNS, UNCOMPREHENDINGLY. SHE LOOKS INTO W'KABI'S FACE AND SEES THE SAME LOOK OF INCOMPREHENSION.
ILOGUE

ONCE, W'KABI WOULD HAVE AIMED TO KILL--
--BUT THOSE DAYS HAVE PASSED. MADAM SLAY TOPPLES INTO HER THRONE WITH A SICKENING SOUND THAT REMINDS HIM OF THE NIGHT VENOMM SLASHED OPEN HIS HEAD WITH A GUN BARREL.
IT IS A SOUND THAT LIVES WITH YOU FOREVER ONCE YOU HAVE HEARD IT.

HE DOES NOT UNDERSTAND HOW THIS MONSTROUS LIMB WORKS, BUT HE DOES UNDERSTAND ITS POWER!
W'KABI LOOKS AT THE SMOULDERING LENGTH OF ARM AS IF IT IS SOMETHING DANGEROUS THAT WILL TURN ON HIM.
EPILOGUE

HE DOES NOT SEE THE PANTHER'S AMBER EYES NARROW AS THEY COMPREHEND THAT THERE IS MORE TRAGEDY HERE THAN ANYTHING ELSE, AND THAT ALL OF THEM ARE HURT AND BLEEDING AND SEPARATED FROM EACH OTHER BY THAT PAIN.
EPILOG
PICK HER UP, MUTE! IT IS TIME TO LEAVE THIS PLACE.
IT IS OVER, MY CHIEFTAIN. FINALLY OVER.
W'KABI... SOMETIMES I THINK--
--IT WILL NEVER BE OVER!

# *JUNGLE ACTION* #19, JANUARY 1976

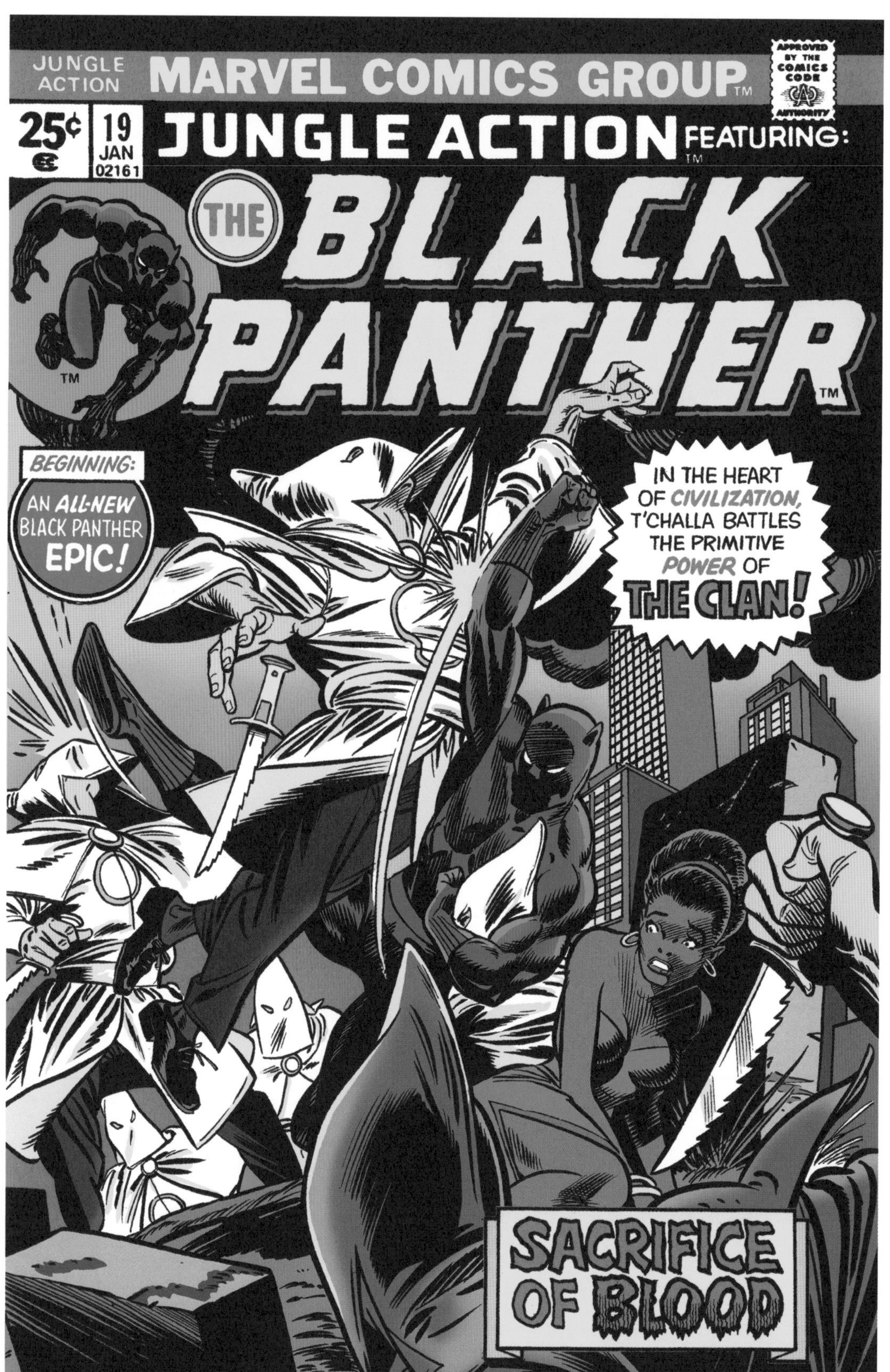
JUNGLE ACTION
MARVEL COMICS GROUP
APPROVED BY THE COMICS CODE AUTHORITY
25¢
19
JAN
02161
JUNGLE ACTION FEATURING:
THE BLACK PANTHER
BEGINNING:
AN ALL-NEW BLACK PANTHER EPIC!
IN THE HEART OF CIVILIZATION, T'CHALLA BATTLES THE PRIMITIVE POWER OF THE CLAN!
SACRIFICE OF BLOOD

Stan Lee PRESENTS: THE BLACK PANTHER!™
DON McGREGOR WRITER
BILLY GRAHAM ARTIST
BOB McLEOD INKER
D. WOHL, LETTERER P. GOLDBERG, COLORIST
MARV WOLFMAN EDITOR
THE PANTHER VS. the KLAN!
BLOOD and SACRIFICES!
THE CEMETERY IS ALIVE WITH SHADOWS.
ONE OF THE SHADOWS IS LITHE AND SILENT AS IT PASSES THROUGH THE SPIDERY NET-WORK OF BRANCHES. THE SHADOW HAS A SINGULAR IDENTITY... THE BLACK PANTHER.
THERE ARE OTHER SHADOWS. AND THESE MAKE SINISTER SOUNDS.
THE CEMETERY SEEMS TO WAIT FOR THE SHADOWS TO TAKE ON A SEMBLANCE OF LIFE-FLESH!
THEY DO!

IT IS MUGGY, UNCOMMONLY HUMID FOR A GEORGIA NIGHT SO LATE INTO THE MONTH OF SEPTEMBER. IT IS THE KIND OF NIGHT THAT SEEMS HOTTER THAN THE DAY. THE SUN HAS FLED TO A COOLER CLIMATE.
MONICA LYNNE DOES NOT SEE THE LIGHT FROM THE TORCHES. HER EYES ARE CLOSED, LOOKING INTO THE DARKNESS OF MEMORIES, TO SEE IF THEY CAN SHED SOME SORT OF TRUTH ON THE PRESENT.
THE PANTHER TESTS THE TREE LIMB, AS MIGHT SOME GREAT JUNGLE CAT. IT IS BEST TO BE CAUTIOUS, ESPECIALLY IN UNFAMILIAR TERRAIN. KNOW YOUR ENTRANCES AND EXITS!
THESE TREE LIMBS DO NOT HAVE THE RESILIENCY OF THOSE IN WAKANDA... THE BARK IS THICKER AND CARVED WITH NATURAL RIDGES.
ONE MISCALCULATION COULD BE FATAL!
NOW, BROTHERS. NOW IS THE HOUR WE STRIKE.
THE REV HAS VOICED THE WORD. THERE IS A TIME FOR MILITANCY FOR THE GREATER GLORY OF TOMORROW AND THE HEREAFTER.
WE KNOW THAT, JEDIDIAH, WE BATTLE THE ONE TRUE WAR, AND WE STRIKE FOR THE ONE, TRUE WAY!
THE PANTHER'S AMBER EYES NARROW. IN THE DISTANCE, ANOTHER SOUND PENETRATES. THIS CEMETERY CERTAINLY IS A BUSY PLACE AT NIGHT.
THIS IS MORE THAN PASSING STRANGE. THEIR APPROACH WAS AMATUERISH. HE HAD HEARD THEIR PROGRESS MORE THAN FIVE MINUTES BACK, AND HAD LEFT MONICA'S SIDE QUIETLY, TAKING TO THE TREES TO DISCOVER THE SOURCE OF THE SOUNDS.
AND HE STILL CAN'T FIGURE OUT WHAT THEY HOPE TO ACCOMPLISH.

MONICA FEELS VAGUELY UNREAL. SHE WAITS FOR SOME EMOTION TO CLAIM HER, BUT IT REFUSES TO HEAR ITS CUE. SHE CAN ONLY RECALL ONE MEMORY OF HER SISTER. THE MEMORY REPEATS ITSELF, OVER AND OVER.
A JULY DAY IN 1953 (OR WAS IT '54?) WHEN SHE WAS EIGHT YEARS OLD (OR WAS IT NINE?) AND ANGELA... HER SISTER ANGELA... WAS TEN (OR PERHAPS ELEVEN) AND THEY LIVED THROUGH THOSE FEW GRUBBY, DIRTY SUMMERS THAT WERE THE MOST SATISFYING SUMMERS SHE'D EVER HAD. BACK IN THE DAYS WHEN WE THOUGHT WE WERE IMMORTAL, MONICA THINKS, AND NOW YOU'VE DIED... AND MADE THAT A LIE, ANGELA.
BUT BACK THEN, WE DIDN'T KNOW NUTHIN' 'BOUT ANYTHING, IT SEEMS. OPPRESSION. DISCRIMINATION. WE WERE MORE INTERESTED IN THOSE FABULOUS ROADWAYS WE PUSHED OUR BANGED-UP TOY CARS THROUGH.
IT'S OBVIOUS, DEAR SISTER, THAT WE DID NOT HAVE THE SAME CHILDHOOD AS JAMES BALDWIN OR ELDRIDGE CLEAVER. OUR BITTERNESS DID NOT COME TILL MUCH LATER... AND IT NEVER WAS A PART OF OUR MAKE-UP! IN FACT, ABOUT THE ONLY THING I HATED IN THE WORLD THAT SUMMER WAS... YOU.
HERE YA GO, RUNT. MA SAID TA SHARE THIS WITH YA.
BUT I DON'T WANT A ROOT-BEER POPSICLE. YOU KNOW I DON'T LIKE NO ROOT-BEER.
TOUGH! 'CAUSE I DO!
OOPS. SORRY. THE TOP HALF'S YOURS.
NO IT ISN'T! NO IT ISN'T!

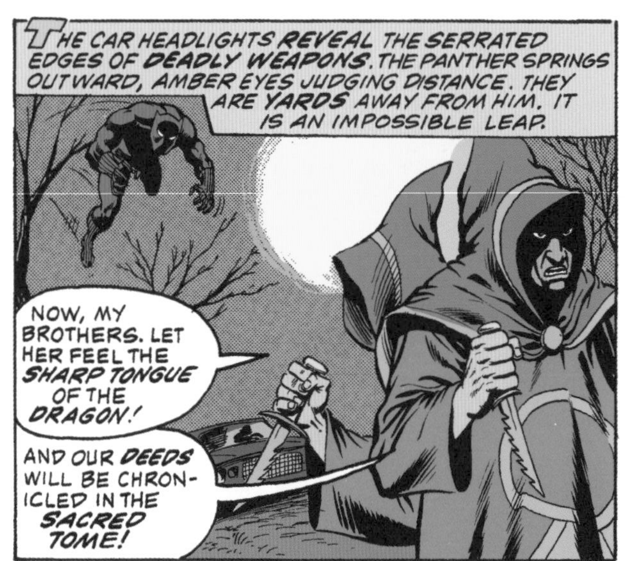

THE CAR HEADLIGHTS REVEAL THE SERRATED EDGES OF DEADLY WEAPONS. THE PANTHER SPRINGS OUTWARD, AMBER EYES JUDGING DISTANCE. THEY ARE YARDS AWAY FROM HIM. IT IS AN IMPOSSIBLE LEAP.
NOW, MY BROTHERS. LET HER FEEL THE SHARP TONGUE OF THE DRAGON!
AND OUR DEEDS WILL BE CHRONICLED IN THE SACRED TOME!

HE DROPS DOWNWARD, ANGLING TO INCREASE HIS LEAP... AND HE IS RIGHT ON TARGET!
I WAS WILLING TO GIVE ALL OF YOU THE BENEFIT OF THE DOUBT--
--BUT IT SEEMS MY FIRST IMPRESSION OF YOU WAS CORRECT.

MONICA DROPS, MUCH TO HER ATTACKER'S SURPRISE AND CHAGRIN. SHE REACHES UP TO GRIP HIS ROBES, AND HER LONG LEGS DRIVE INTO HIS STOMACH.

THE STUNT IS AMAZINGLY EFFECTIVE!

HEY, WAITAMINNIT! YOU CAN'T DO THIS!

I JUST DID!

THE PANTHER TURNS INTO THE GLARE OF HEADLIGHTS, SHUTTING HIS EYES SO THAT HE WILL NOT LOSE HIS NIGHT VISION.

SCREECH

A FOOT JAMS ONTO THE BRAKES, AND THE GRASS RIPS UP, SPEWING DIRT AND NIGHT CRAWLERS, WHILE THE SOUND OF SPLINTERING GLASS SIGNALS THE ABRUPT END TO A HUMAN FLIGHT!

ONE OF THE ROBED FIGURES REACTS, STARTLED BY THE BRIGHT LIGHTS, STARING DIRECTLY INTO THEM AS HE SEEKS TO ESCAPE.

NOW WHERE--

--DO YOU THINK--

--YOU'RE GOING?
MISS, DID YOU JUST SEE WHAT HE DID?
HE... UHM... HE JUST JUMPED RIGHT OVER THE CAR!

CONTACT!
YOU WON'T FEEL VERY WELL WHEN YOU WAKE UP--
--BUT REMEMBER THAT YOU'LL BE LUCKY THAT YOU ARE WAKING UP AT ALL. THE "TONGUE" OF THE DRAGON WOULD NOT BE SO KIND!
SPLURP!

THE MAN BEHIND THE WHEEL TURNS AND LOOKS AT THE FIGURE WHICH HANGS LIKE AN ORNAMENT THROUGH THE SHATTERED PATTERNS OF HIS WINDSHIELD.
SHATTERED. LIKE HIS LIFE HAS BEEN SHATTERED. HE THINKS. NONSENSE PATTERNS. SO MUCH FOR THE DELUSION OF A STRUCTURED LIFE.
AND THEN HE LEAPS FROM THE CAR.

THAT "BALLET DANCER" IN THE BLUE TIGHTS CAN'T HANDLE EVERYTHING BY HIMSELF!
--SO YOU CAN TAKE THIS LITTLE GESTURE AS AN INDICATION THAT I'M TAKING A HAND IN THE FRAY!

YOU OKAY?
I THINK I BROKE MY HAND.
ONE OF THE HOODED FIGURES RISES FROM THE SLUMPED BODIES OF HIS BRETHREN--
--AND HE COULD BELONG TO THE THE ORDER OF SOME BENEVO-LENT MONESTERY BUT FOR THE BLADE HE HOLDS IN HIS HANDS.
WE WILL NOT BE THWARTED... YEA, WE SHALL YET O'ERCOME!
HE LAUNCHES HIMSELF AT MONICA WITH FANATIC'S FERVOR!
FULFILL THE MISSION!
DEATH IS THE FULFILLMENT OF THAT MISSION.
BUT HE IS INTERCEPTED BEFORE THAT JAGGED BLADE CAN FIND HER FLESH.
AND IT IS DEATH THE PANTHER INTERCEPTS.
AS IF HE AND DEATH ARE INSEPARABLY LINKED.
T'CHALLA. WHAT'S HAPPENING?
HAS THE WHOLE WORLD GONE CRAZY? I THOUGHT THE VIOLENCE IN WAKANDA WOULD NEVER END. BUT IT'S EVEN HERE.
I COME BACK HOME ...AND IT'S EVEN HERE!

MY MIND KNOWS ANGELA IS DEAD... THAT SHE'S BURIED UNDER THAT STONE. AND YET IT REFUSES TO ACCEPT SHE'S REALLY THERE.
DOES A RUSHED EXPLANATION FROM MY PARENTS MAKE IT REAL? HOW LONG WILL IT TAKE TO ACCEPT THAT IT IS REAL... AND THAT THERE'S NOTHING I CAN DO THAT CAN CHANGE ANY OF THIS?
TIME!
NO EXACT AMOUNT OF TIME. JUST TIME.

I'M SORRY. I DON'T MEAN TO INTRUDE.
IT'S ALL RIGHT. THANK YOU FOR HELPING OUT.
WOULD YOU MIND NOT... SHAKING MY HAND... SO ENTHUSIAS-TICALLY?

YOU SHOULD NOT HIT A MAN IN THE SIDE OF THE HEAD WITH YOUR FIST.
THE MAN'S HEAD IS HARDER. REMEMBER THAT!

BLAST! IT ALWAYS LOOKED SO GOOD WHEN I WAS A KID, WATCHING JOCK MAHONEY PLAY THE RANGE RIDER ON T.V. HE'D LET HIS FIST COME UP FROM THE GROUND--
--AND THE BAD GUYS WOULD ALWAYS WAIT FOR IT TO HIT THEIR JAWS.

HE MUST'VE BROKEN EVERY BONE IN HIS HAND ALL THE WAY UP TO HIS ELBOW!
THIS MAN WILL NEED MEDI-CAL ATTENTION, BUT HIS WOUNDS ARE NOT SERIOUS.

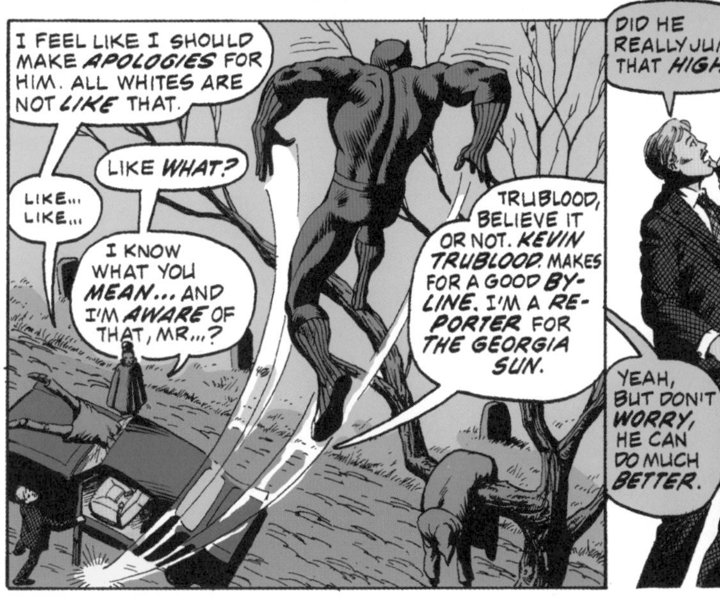
I FEEL LIKE I SHOULD MAKE APOLOGIES FOR HIM. ALL WHITES ARE NOT LIKE THAT.
LIKE WHAT?
LIKE... LIKE...
I KNOW WHAT YOU MEAN... AND I'M AWARE OF THAT, MR...?
TRUBLOOD, BELIEVE IT OR NOT. KEVIN TRUBLOOD. MAKES FOR A GOOD BY-LINE. I'M A RE-PORTER FOR THE GEORGIA SUN.

DID HE REALLY JUMP THAT HIGH?
YEAH, BUT DON'T WORRY, HE CAN DO MUCH BETTER.

THE REAL QUESTION IS, DID YOU COME OUT HERE, KNOWING I WAS AT MY SISTER'S GRAVESIDE... FOR SOME CHEAP STORY? THAT'S PRETTY CALLOUS, FRIEND.

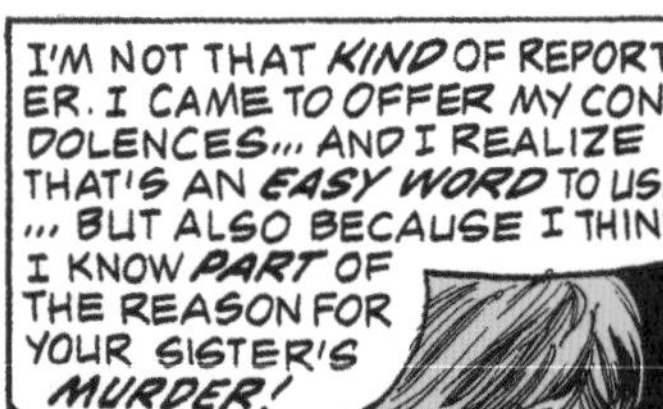

I'M NOT THAT KIND OF REPORTER. I CAME TO OFFER MY CONDOLENCES... AND I REALIZE THAT'S AN EASY WORD TO USE ... BUT ALSO BECAUSE I THINK I KNOW PART OF THE REASON FOR YOUR SISTER'S MURDER!

"NOW WHAT DOES THAT MEAN?"

"I'M NOT TRYING FOR A MELODRAMA".
I REHEARSED OUR MEETING A DOZEN TIMES ON THE WAY HERE.

I'VE BLOWN ALL MY LINES, MISS LYNNE.

NO, MS. LYNNE. ISN'T THAT THE CORRECT ADDRESS THESE DAYS?
IF YOU'D LIKE.
DON'T BE SO UPTIGHT. REMEMBER, MR. TRUBLOOD, YOU CAN'T REHEARSE LINES FOR LIFE... THAT'S ONLY FOR MOVIES.

UNFORTUNATELY... OR MAYBE FORTUNATELY... I GUESS IT DEPENDS ON HOW YOU LOOK AT IT!
I MET YOUR SISTER BEFORE HER DEATH.

I THINK SHE'D LOCKED INTO A LITTLE NEST OF CORRUPTION... NOTHING VERIFIED ... BUT SHE'D CONVINCED ME THAT HER SUSPICIONS COULD BE VALID.

SHE WORKED AT EZRA WILKINSON'S REALTY PLACE. REAL ESTATE AND POLITICS ARE VERY OFTEN... THIS CLOSE...
SHE THOUGHT THERE WERE KLAN MEMBERS NOT ONLY IN OUR TOWN'S REAL ESTATE--

--BUT ALSO OUR POLITICAL STRUCTURE.
THE KLAN!

I HAVEN'T HAD MUCH CHANCE TO TALK WITH MOM AND DAD. T'CHALLA AND I ARRIVED ONLY A FEW HOURS AGO. I HAD TO COME OUT HERE... SEE ANGELA
HE'S THAT JUNGLE KING OR SOMETHING, RIGHT?
YOU CALL HIM PANTHER-DEVIL IF YOU'D LIKE.
I'LL PASS!
I HATE TO TELL YOU THIS MR. TRUBLOOD, BUT THIS MAN'S BLACK... AND I KNOW ENOUGH ABOUT THE KLAN TO KNOW THEY HAVEN'T OPENED THEIR MEMBERSHIP DRIVE THAT WIDE.

THE MOON SEEMS UNNATURALLY HUGE; A PRISONER IN A HUMID CAGE THAT CAN NEVER ESCAPE.
THE BUILDINGS APPEAR EMPTY-- AS IF THEY HAVE NOT HAD RESIDENTS IN AGES. FADED POSTERS ADD TO THE IMPRESSION. YET WITH THE MORNING, THE DOORS SPEAK OF THE INCREDIBLE DRY SPELL.
HOTEL
IT SEEMS THE HEAT WILL BE WITH THEM FOREVER. THEY ARE AS MUCH PRISONERS OF IT AS THE MOON.

I DON'T KNOW WHAT SHERIFF TATE'S GOING TO HAVE TO SAY WHEN WE DROP THESE GUYS OFF AT HIS FRONT DOOR!
I'M NOT EVEN SURE IF HE'LL BE IN AT THIS HOUR... OR HOW HE'S GOING TO REACT TO YOU. TATE DOESN'T REACT WELL TO WHAT HE TERMS WEIRDNESS!
AND THIS IS GOING TO GIVE HIM PLENTY OF IT. HE ALREADY FEELS THE WORLD'S CHANGING FASTER'N HE CAN DEAL WITH IT!

OUR CAPTIVES HAVE REMAINED SILENT. THEY ARE INDEED LOYAL TO THEIR LEADER!
WELL, ONE THING'S FOR SURE. YOU WERE RIGHT. THEY'RE NOT WITH THE KLAN. THE KLAN'S A LOT MORE SUBTLE ABOUT ITS ACTIVITIES THESE DAYS-- RALLIES AND SUCH ARE THEIR BIG SHINDIG.
HIT THE MIDDLE AND LOWER CLASS WHITES WHERE THEY LIVE... AND BELIEVE ME, THEY'VE GOT THEIR RECRUITING SHTICK DOWN PAT.
THEY USE EVERYTHING. THE RECESSION... LIBERALISM. I TELL YA, THEY EVEN HAVE A GREAT SENSE OF DRAMA... WHAT WITH THEIR BURNING CROSSES...
...BUT THEY TRY TO KEEP ANY VIOLENCE QUIET AND NOT TRACEABLE BACK TO THEM. THEY AREN'T OVERJOYED BY BAD PRESS.

THIS IS OUR *STOP.*

POLICE

BY THE WAY, WHAT *DO* THEY CALL YOU? JUST THE PANTHER?

EITHER THE PANTHER OR... *T'CHALLA* WILL SUFFICE.

TA-CHALLA?

*WITHOUT* THE "T", KEVIN. WITHOUT THE "*T*".

PERHAPS YOU'LL BE MORE *TALKATIVE* HERE--

--SO LET'S NOT *WASTE* ANY FURTHER TIME.

OKAY, *WHAT'S* GOING ON OUT HERE? AND YOU BETTER MAKE YOUR ANSWER *QUICK!*

HENRY, YOU WANTA *PUT UP* THE ARTILLERY. HOW MANY TIMES I GOTTA TELL YOU...? YOU'RE NOT QUICK DRAW McGRAW.

NOT UNTIL WE KNOW WHAT'S *UP,* RAFE. I'M NOT GOING TO END UP WITH THE BACK OF MY HEAD *BLOWN OFF* AND FRYING ON THE SIDEWALK!

I AM NO FONDER THAN YOU OF THE PROSPECT OF *DEATH,* OFFICER.

--AND WHILE I HAVE FACED MORE *SOPHISTICATED WEAPONRY,* I KNOW THIS FIREARM CAN ACHIEVE THE *SAME* PURPOSE.

THEREFORE I HOPE *YOU* CAN UNDERSTAND MY ACTION. WE'RE BOTH MOTIVATED BY THE SAME CONCERN... *SELF PRESERVATION!*

AND SO ARE THE MEMBERS OF THE *DRAGON'S CIRCLE.* THEY SEE A CHANCE FOR *ESCAPE* DURING THE CHAOS AND TURN TO *FLEE* INTO THE NIGHT.

NONE OF THEM MAKE IT!!

THE PANTHER MOVES LIKE AN UNHARNESSED SHADOW.
HE LIFTS THEM HIGH, HOLDING THEM LIKE SOME HUMAN METAPHOR THAT CAPTURES MOMENTARILY THE SYMBOLIC STRUCTURE OF THE SCALES OF JUSTICE.
IT LASTS FOR JUST A MOMENT, PERHAPS IT NEVER REALLY EXISTED AT ALL EXCEPT IN KEVIN TRUBLOOD'S MIND.
PERHAPS THAT IS THE ONLY PLACE IT NEED EXIST.

SHERIFF RODERICK TATE IS TIRED AND NOT IN GOOD HUMOR.
HE WASN'T ASLEEP WHEN THE PHONE RANG, THOUGH HE'D BEEN GIVING SUCH AN ENDEAVOR HIS BEST. THE BED SHEETS WERE DAMP AND LIMP, CONSPIRING AGAINST ANY REST.
WELL, WHATTA YOU BOYS GOT TO SAY FOR YERSELVES?
AIN'T NO CRIME IN DRESSIN' UP. LOOK AT HIM! DRESSED LIKE HE WAS SOME KINDA AGENT FOR SATAN!

I SEEN HIM. PUT ALLA YOU T'GETHER... I SWEAR, YUH'D HAVE YERSELVES A REG'LAR COSTUME BALL!
Y'SEE, THESE HERE ARE LOCAL BOYS... WHICH DON'T GIVE 'EM NO SPECIAL LEA-WAY, LIKE THEY MIGHT THINK.
BOTH HE AND THE WOMAN HAVE LIED! HE ATTACKED US!
NOW, YOU MADE YERSELF A GOOD POINT THERE, MR. LAWYER-TYPE JEDIDIAH THORD ... CEPTIN' I NEVER KNEW YOU HAD NO DEGREE... NO SIR!
BUT SEEIN' AS YOU GOT YERSELF SO WELL EDUCATED, YOU MIGHT RECOLLECT THAT THERE'S A LAW AGAINST THE DESECRATION OF BURIAL GROUNDS.
NOW, MISS LYNNE, I CAN HEAR YOUR WORDS WITHOUT YOUR SPEAKIN' EM!

NOW YOU DON'T WANNA SPEND SOME TIME BEHIND BARS COOLIN' YOUR HEELS, YOU BETTER GET YOUR ACT T'GETHER--
--AN' TELL ME WHAT KINDA FOOL CLUB YOU BELONG TO AND JUST WHAT IT WAS YOU HOPED TO ACCOMPLISH IN THE CEMETERY.

THEY ALL LOOK AWAY, SEEKING STRENGTH IN THEIR NUMBERS. DESPITE THEIR DIFFERENT NATIONALITIES, THEY ALL HAVE A SIMILARITY. THEY'VE ALL BEEN THROUGH THE SAME INDOCTRINATION COURSE!
THEY ARE WILLING TO MAKE THEIR SACRIFICES... EVEN IF IT COSTS THEM THEIR FREEDOM...

THE HEAT LINGERS THROUGH THE NEXT DAY, A HOSTILE GUEST RELUCTANT TO LEAVE AND REJOICING IN ITS VICTIMS' TORMENT.
THE LYNNE HOUSEHOLD IS FILLED WITH THE AROMA OF COUNTRY FRIED CHICKEN, SPARE RIBS, HAMHOCKS CHIT'LINS, COLLARD GREENS AND HOMEMADE CORNBREAD.
JESSICA LYNNE HAS SPENT A LIFETIME AT THIS STOVE, IGNORING THE HEAT OUTSIDE AS WELL AS THE SUFFOCATING AIR FROM THE OVEN, AS IF SHE IS IMMUNE TO THE WEATHER.
THAT'S IMPOSSIBLE, T'CHALLA THINKS. SIMPLY IMPOSSIBLE.
WE MADE A LIFE OUT HERE. YOU DO THE BEST YOU CAN AND MAKE SOME KINDA LIFE OUTTA WHAT YOU'RE GIVEN.
PRO'BLY AIN'T MUCH TO YOU.

YOU'RE WRONG, MRS. LYNNE, AND I HAVED DINED AT BANQUETS THAT DID NOT MATCH YOUR SUPERB COOKING.
MOM STILL MAKES HER LEMONADE FRESH, LIKE WHEN WE WERE KIDS.
I MUST ADMIT, THIS IS AN INCREDIBLY DIFFERENT TYPE OF LIFE THAN I HAVE EXPERIENCED, EVEN DURING MY PREVIOUS STAY IN YOUR COUNTRY.

I THINK WE BUILT OUR LIVES... OR AT LEAST SURVIVED... BECAUSE OF THAT LEMONADE!
GUESS IT'S A WAY OF LIFE YOU DON'T SEE MUCH OF ANYMORE. IT'S PASSING AWAY!

ONE MAN. ONE WOMAN. SOMETIMES HATING EACH OTHER. SOMETIMES WILLING TO FORGIVE.
WHEN MAKIN' A FAMILY SURVIVE THRU HARD TIMES ATE UP YOUR LIFE.
IT WAS ENOUGH TO JUST GET ON THROUGH!

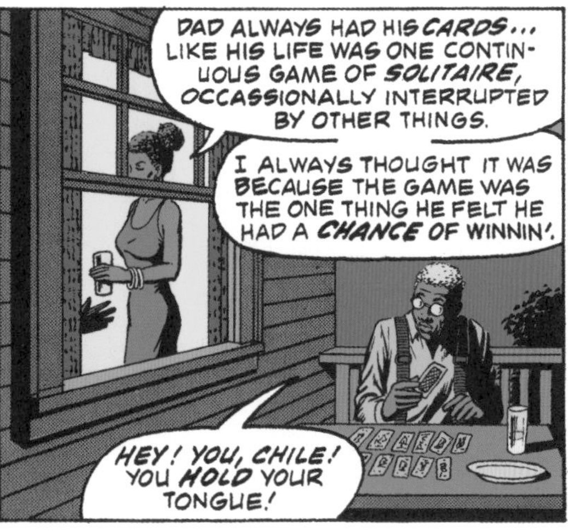
DAD ALWAYS HAD HIS CARDS... LIKE HIS LIFE WAS ONE CONTINUOUS GAME OF SOLITAIRE, OCCASSIONALLY INTERRUPTED BY OTHER THINGS.
I ALWAYS THOUGHT IT WAS BECAUSE THE GAME WAS THE ONE THING HE FELT HE HAD A CHANCE OF WINNIN'.
HEY! YOU, CHILE! YOU HOLD YOUR TONGUE!

MRS. LYNNE, YOUR COURTESY TOWARD MY PRESENCE HAS BEEN MOST... GRACIOUS... I THANK BOTH YOU AND YOUR HUSBAND FOR YOUR KINDNESS.
I HATE TO DARKEN SUCH AN ELEGANT MEAL... AND I HOPE YOU WILL NOT TAKE OFFENSE... BUT YOU SEEM TO HAVE AVOIDED TALKING ABOUT YOUR DAUGHTER'S DEATH!

THE SUBJECT IS AVOIDED DELICATELY... BUT I AM NOT SURE IT IS A SUBJECT YOU CAN HAVE THE COMFORT OF AVOIDING.
I DON'T RIGHTLY KNOW WHAT YOU MEAN!
I MEAN, WHATEVER CAUSED ANGELA'S MURDER... AND YOU HAVEN'T TALKED MUCH ABOUT IT!

IT MAY NOT BE THE LAST ACT OF VIOLENCE. THE ATTACK ON MONICA SEEMS TO PROVE THAT.
IT IS EVIDENT THAT THE PRISONERS DO NOT BELONG TO THE KLAN ITSELF... BUT TO SOMETHING CALLED THE DRAGON'S CIRCLE!

AND YET, THEY HAD KLAN ITEMS ON THEIR PERSONS. PATCHES THAT ARE ASSOCIATED WITH THE KLAN, AND A COPY OF THE KLAN NEWSPAPER.
IF THEY AREN'T A PART OF THE KLAN, WHY DID THEY HAVE ALL THOSE ITEMS ON THEM?
LOOK, I DON'T KNOW HOW IT IS WHERE YOU COME FROM... BUT THERE'S BEEN A LOT OF PAIN IN THIS FAMILY DURING THE LAST FEW WEEKS--

THE HOUSE GOES QUIET. IT SEEMS SUDDENLY DEFENSELESS, AND THE PANTHER HAS THE FEELING THAT HE IS AN INVADER IN THIS DOMAIN!
--AN THE KINDA QUESTIONS YOU'RE ASKIN' COULD BRING A LOT MORE PAIN. NOW I WOULDN'T MIND IF I THOUGHT THEM QUESTIONS WERE GONNA PROVE SOMETHING MORE THAN--
--CAUSING US MORE PAIN!
AND YET, BEYOND, IN THE SHADOWS THAT SURROUND THE HOUSE, FIGURES MOVE TOWARD THE LIGHT... READY TO RIP THE NIGHT APART.

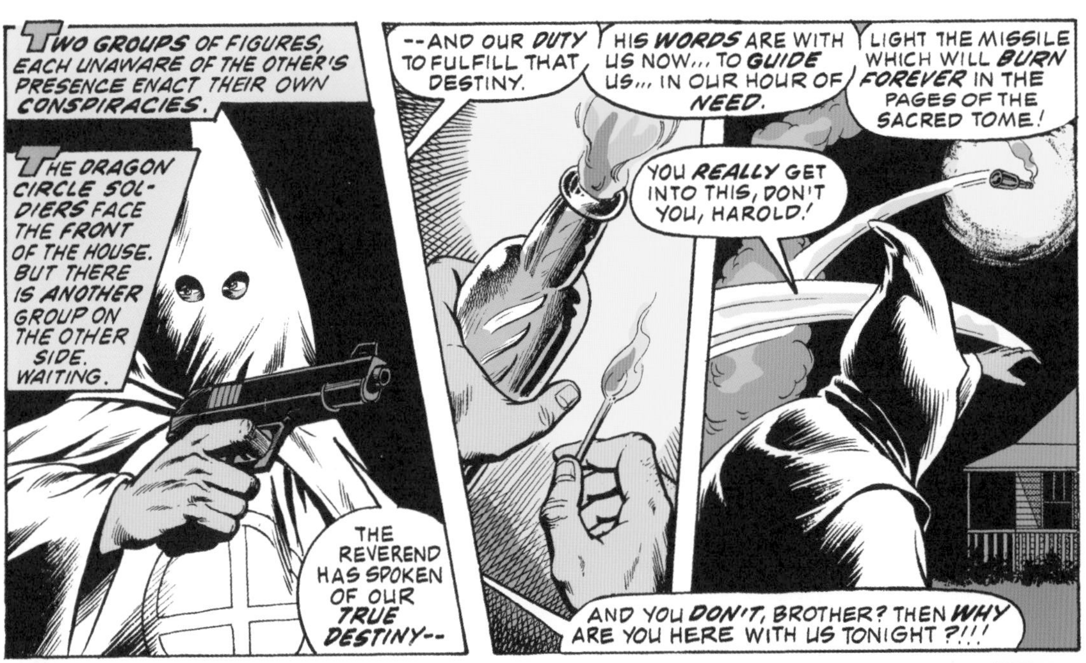

TWO GROUPS OF FIGURES, EACH UNAWARE OF THE OTHER'S PRESENCE ENACT THEIR OWN CONSPIRACIES.
THE DRAGON CIRCLE SOLDIERS FACE THE FRONT OF THE HOUSE. BUT THERE IS ANOTHER GROUP ON THE OTHER SIDE. WAITING.
THE REVEREND HAS SPOKEN OF OUR TRUE DESTINY--
--AND OUR DUTY TO FULFILL THAT DESTINY.
HIS WORDS ARE WITH US NOW... TO GUIDE US... IN OUR HOUR OF NEED.
LIGHT THE MISSILE WHICH WILL BURN FOREVER IN THE PAGES OF THE SACRED TOME!
YOU REALLY GET INTO THIS, DON'T YOU, HAROLD!
AND YOU DON'T, BROTHER? THEN WHY ARE YOU HERE WITH US TONIGHT?!!!

ON THE OPPOSITE SIDE OF THE HOUSE, THE OTHER GROUP REACTS AS THE MISSILE FLARES WITH SMOKE AND FIRE.

THEY ARE FAMILIAR WITH SUCH WEAPONS. THEY HAVE USED SUCH PRIMITIVE EXPLOSIVES IN THEIR OWN PAST.

EXCEPT, THEY WONDER AS ONE... IF THEY DIDN'T THROW THE MOLOTOV COCKTAIL... WHO DID?

NOW WHAT'S THIS? 4th OF JULY'S A LONG TIME GONE!

THE BOTTLE ARCS THROUGH THE NIGHT SKY, DROPPING TOWARD THE FRONT OF THE HOUSE.

IT IS A BOMB, T'CHALLA KNOWS IMMEDIATELY, AND THE THOUGHT IS FOLLOWED WITH A SECOND: THAT IT WILL SHATTER THE WINDOWS AND SPLINTER THE WOOD FRAMEWORK ALONG WITH THE HUMAN LIVES IT WILL TURN TO PAIN AND AGONY.

THE PANTHER SMASHES THROUGH THE WINDOW. SHARDS OF GLASS RAKE ACROSS HIS CHEST AND LEGS--

--BUT IT DOES NOT SLOW HIS LEAP. WITH ONE FLUID MOVEMENT HE SNATCHES THE BOTTLE OUT OF ITS TRAJECTORY--

--AND HURLS IT BACK WHERE IT CAME FROM!

THE NIGHT **EXPLODES**!

THE DARKNESS **BURNS** INTENSELY AT THE MOMENT OF IMPACT... AND IT BEGINS A CHAIN REACTION OF MOVEMENT.

THE PANTHER CROUCHES--

--TRYING TO **ISOLATE** THE SEPARATE SOUNDS AND SIGHTS THAT EXPLODE WITH THE SAME KIND OF **FURY** AS THE BOMB.

WHAT THE **DEVIL** IS THAT COMING AT US?

I DON'T SEE ANYTHING. **WHERE?**

OBJECTS MOVE AGAINST THE MOON AND TREES. CAR ENGINES TURN OVER, A DESPERATE SOUND SEEKING TO GAIN FLIGHT.

THE HORSES **ERUPT** INTO MOTION. THEIR **PANIC** HANGS IN THE AIR, LIKE THE ACRID SMELL OF GASOLINE AND BURNT GRASS.

THE PANTHER LEAPS!

--CHOOSING HIS INITIAL TARGET, AND HE TAKES THE HOODED RIDER OUT OF THE SADDLE.
THERE!
THE TWO OF THEM CRASH TO THE EARTH, BUT ONLY THE PANTHER LANDS ON HIS FEET!

THE DRAGON SOLDIERS ARE EQUALLY DISMAYED BY THIS REACTION TO THEIR ATTACK.
WHO ARE THESE PEOPLE?
WHO DID YOU THINK THEY ARE, HAROLD? IT'S THE KLAN!
THEN, THEY HAVE UNWITTINGLY PLAYED INTO THE FAVOR OF OUR ORDAINED DESTINY.
NOW, WHILE THEY DISTRACT THE LYNNE'S DEFENDER... WE SHALL COMPLETE OUR SANCTIONED MISSION.
GET DOWN, MOM!
DAD, WILL YOU GET RID OF THOSE CARDS? PLEASE!!
NOT ON YOUR LIFE, GIRL. ALL'S I NEED IS A RED JACK AN' I'M GONNA WIN THIS HERE GAME!
THE PANTHER COMMANDEERS ONE OF THE FOUR-WHEEL-DRIVE JEEPS AND DIRECTS IT TOWARD ITS OWNERS--
--BUT HE REACHES THEM LONG BEFORE THE VEHICLE CAN.
THAT TURKEY'S OUT OF HIS HEAD!
I'M GETTING OUT OF HERE!
I'M AFRAID YOU'RE MISTAKEN ABOUT THAT.
YOU'RE NOT GOING ANYWHERE AT THE MOMENT. NOWHERE AT ALL!

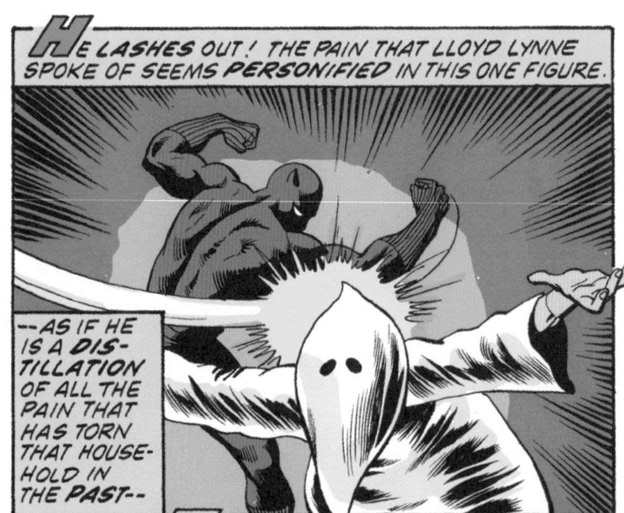

HE LASHES OUT! THE PAIN THAT LLOYD LYNNE SPOKE OF SEEMS PERSONIFIED IN THIS ONE FIGURE.
--AS IF HE IS A DISTILLATION OF ALL THE PAIN THAT HAS TORN THAT HOUSEHOLD IN THE PAST--

--AND CONTINUES TO THREATEN IT IN THE PRESENT.
THE STILL, HOT SEPTEMBER NIGHT IS ALIVE WITH BATTLEFIELD EXCLAMATIONS. BLOOD AND SACRIFICES EACH SACRIFICE EXACTING A BRUTAL PAYMENT.

THE PANTHER TURNS TO WITNESS AN EXODUS IN PROGRESS. A FANTASY NIGHTMARE OF GOBLINS AND NASTIES FLEEING FROM REAL SCARECROWS.
THEY ARE ALMOST LAUGHABLE IN THEIR SINGLE-MINDED ATTEMPT TO FIND SECLUSION IN THE DARKNESS.

THESE TWO WOULD APPEAR TO BE MEMBERS OF THE KLAN, MR. LYNNE--
--AND NOT JUST TWISTED MIMICRY OF SUCH PEOPLE.
I DON'T THINK EITHER OF THESE ORGANIZATIONS ARE GOING TO GIVE YOU THE OPTION OF LEAVING THIS ALONE.
WELL... YOU AIN'T AS BAD AS I THOUGHT WHEN I FIRST SEEN YOU... STILL KINDA WEIRD, BUT NOT BAD...
I GUESS!
HEY THERE! SEE THAT, MONICA? MY RED JACK!! KNEW IT WAS DUE TO COME UP.
TELL YOU SUMTHIN' ELSE. I DON'T MIND FIGHTIN' BACK WHEN I'M BIT, MISTER--
--AN' WHAT YOU DID, YOU DID RIGHT WELL. BUT YOU JUST CAUSED US A WHOLE LOTTA TROUBLE IN A WAY...
IT AIN'T GONNA END HERE... YOU CAN BET ON THAT!

NEXT THEY TOLD ME A MYTH I WANTED TO BELIEVE!

# *JUNGLE ACTION* #20, MARCH 1976

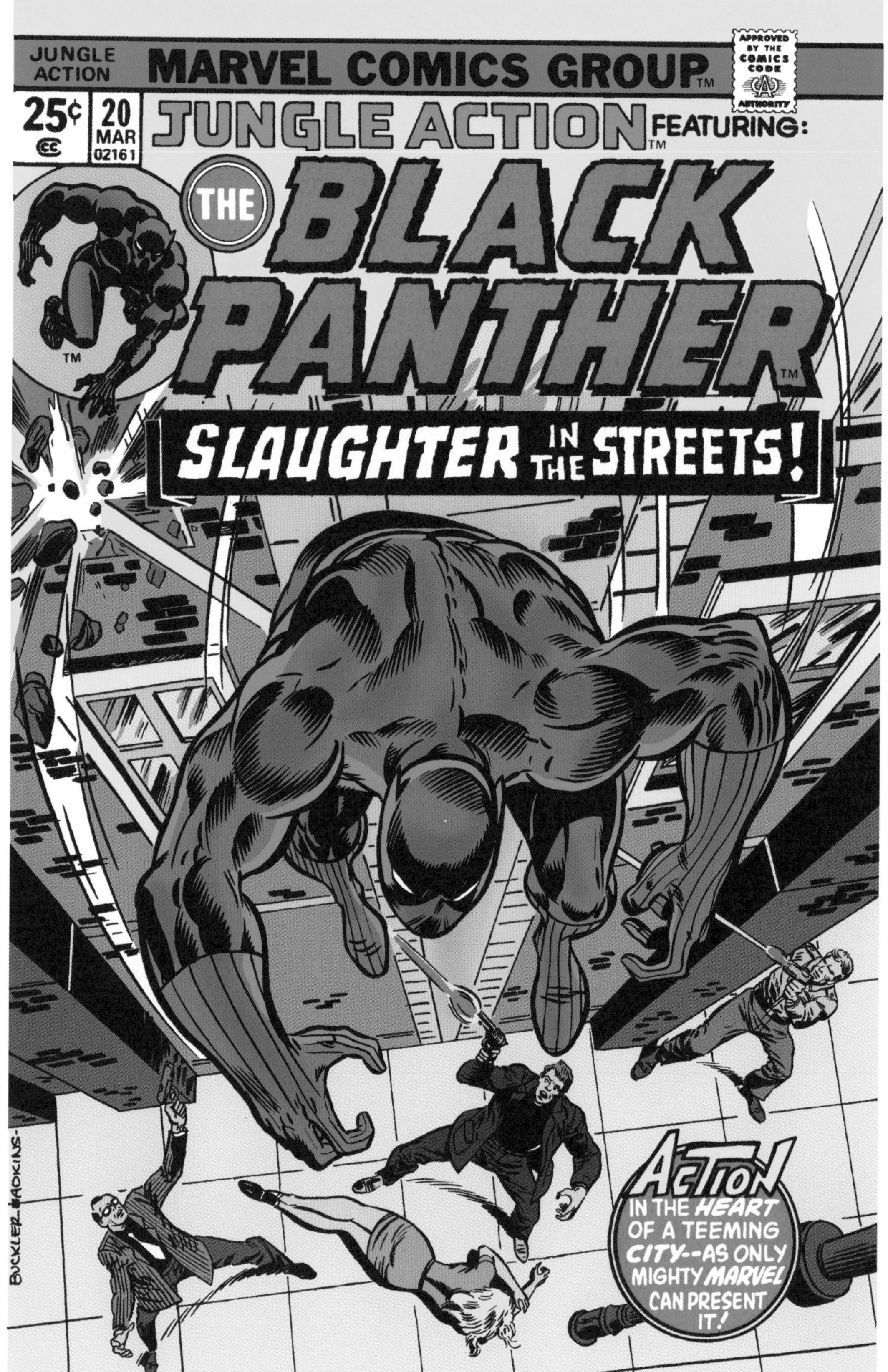
JUNGLE ACTION
MARVEL COMICS GROUP
APPROVED BY THE COMICS CODE AUTHORITY
25¢
20 MAR
02161
JUNGLE ACTION FEATURING:
THE BLACK PANTHER
SLAUGHTER IN THE STREETS!
BUCKLER & ADKINS
ACTION IN THE HEART OF A TEEMING CITY--AS ONLY MIGHTY MARVEL CAN PRESENT IT!

With the sleekness of a jungle beast, the Prince of Wakanda stalks both the concrete of the city and the undergrowth of the veldt, for when danger lurks he dons the garb of the savage cat from which he gains his name!

STAN LEE PRESENTS: THE BLACK PANTHER!™

# THE PANTHER VS. THE KLAN PART TWO

DANGEROUS!

INFLATION IN THE MIDST OF A RECESSION.

STARVATION-SPECTERS STALK THE SUPER-MARKET. HAMBURGER IS 20¢ A POUND MORE THAN IT WAS LAST WEEK? BUY IT ANYWAY. YOU HAVE TO EAT, DON'T YOU?

PAY THE RENT, THE ELECTRICITY AND THEN HOPE THERE'S ENOUGH LEFT TO PAY THE PHONE COMPANY!

## THEY TOLD ME A MYTH I WANTED TO BELIEVE

AISLE 3

CEREALS

LOTIONS

EXIT

AISLE 4

CANN

DON'T SQUEEZE THE CHARMIN, T'CHALLA.

IS IT AGAINST THE LAW, MONICA?

IN SOME PLACES.

ESPECIALLY IN PRIME-TIME LAND.

SCRIPT BY: Don McGregor

PENCILS BY: Billy Graham

INKING BY: Bob McLeod

COLORS BY: Janice Cohen

LETTERS BY: Denise Wohl

EDITING BY: Marv Wolfman

DANGEROUS!

FOR THE BLACK PANTHER AND MONICA LYNNE, THE SPECIAL OF THE DAY IS BARGAIN BASEMENT DEATH, SERVED WITH JAGGED-EDGED KNIVES THAT ARE GUARANTEED TO BE EFFECTIVE.

AND ALL SALES ARE... FINAL!

YOU'RE ATTRACTING ATTENTION.
IT WAS HARD NOT TO NOTICE.
I THINK YOU SHOULD HAVE PUT ON SOME CIVILIAN CLOTHES TO COME TO TOWN.
THEY DO NOT MASK THEIR CURIOSITY UNTIL I TURN TO LOOK AT THEM--
--AND THEN THEY AVERT THEIR GAZE. BUSILY EYEING EVERYTHING BUT ME WITH AN EMBARRASSED SHAME NOT QUITE HIDDEN IN THEIR EYES!
3
CEREALS
LOTIONS
YOU'RE A CELEBRITY... OR A SIDE-SHOW FREAK. I THINK THE JURY IS STILL OUT AS TO WHICH.
OR A THREAT, COULD BE A THIRD ALTERNATIVE. I WOULDN'T IMAGINE MANY OF THEM ARE AWARE THAT A BLACK PANTHER REALLY EXISTS.
WAKANDA IS FAR FROM THE REALM OF THEIR CONCERNS.
AS USUAL YOU ARE PRETTY MUCH ON TOP OF IT. I'M NOT SURE I WOULD HAVE BELIEVED IN A SUPER-SCIENTIFIC DISNEYLAND IN THE AFRICAN JUNGLE WHEN I LIVED HERE AS A CHILD.
ACTUALLY, I SPENT MORE THAN MY CHILDHOOD IN THIS SMALL GEORGIA TOWN... AND MUCH OF WHAT HAPPENED HERE--
--INFLUENCED THE WAY I REACTED ABOUT EVERYTHING SINCE I LEFT TO SEEK FAME AND FORTUNE.
REBECCA WINTHROP HAS NEVER LEFT THIS SMALL TOWN. NEITHER HAVE HER NINE CATS. THAT IS THE ONLY THING THE CATS AND REBECCA HAVE IN COMMON--
--BESIDES A DEPENDENCY ON EACH OTHER.

NOW'S YOUR CHANCE, HERBERT... WHILE THAT AGENT FOR SATAN IS BUSY. THE REVEREND HAS SPOKEN... YOU'VE HEARD HIS WORDS.
YEAH, BUT, ROLAND... DO I HAFTA SAY ALL THEM TERRIBLE THINGS TO HER?
FOOD FOR YOUR PETS
YOU WILL SAY THEM... FOR IT IS THE WAY TO END ALL SUCH SLURS.
APPREHEN-SIVELY, A HAND REACHES OUT...
...HOLDING THE KNIFE, SHAKING EVER SO SLIGHTLY--
--BUT THEN, THE LONG IN-DOCTRINATION SESSIONS REPEATING THEIR LESSONS IN HIS MIND, HERBERT STRIKES VIOLENTLY.
AND THE MOVE-MENTS DO NOT SUGGEST ANY HESI-TATION.
I GOT A MESSAGE FOR YOU AND YOUR FAMILY, MONICA LYNNE.
ALL'A YOU BETTER KEEP YOUR MOUTHS CLOSED TO THE NEWS-PAPERS, YOU GOT THAT? AND THE LAW.
PLEA... PLEASE, TAKE THE KNIFE... AWAY.
PLEASE.
YOU DON'T KEEP QUIET... WE ARE GOIN' TO DRAW A LINE RIGHT ACROSS YOUR THROAT...
BE A SHAME TO SEE SUCH PRETTY LIPS SPITTIN' BLOOD... BUT YOU START TALK-IN' ABOUT THE KLAN... AN' THEM INCIDENTS THE OTHER NIGHT AT THE CEMETERY WHERE YOUR SISTER LIES ROTTING IN HER GRAVE--
--AND ALL OF YOU WILL END UP LYING BESIDE HER. GOT THAT?

HE IS THE BLACK CAT, ALERT TO A THREAT IN A DOMAIN WHERE HE SHOULD NOT SUSPECT A THREAT.

REBECCA WINTHROP WATCHES HIM WHIRL WITH FELINE GRACE. SHE CANNOT SEE THE AMBER EYES THAT SEEK THE SOURCE OF DANGER--

SOUP

Bargains

--BUT SHE CAN SEE THE PANTHER'S REACTION!

REMEMBER... THERE AIN'T NO PLACE YOU CAN HIDE FROM THE KLAN.

SOUP

IT IS IMMEDIATE, SUDDEN--

--AND DEVASTATING!

IN FACT, WE'RE HOLDING US A MEETIN' AT THE OLD DEVOURING SWAMP SITE TONIGHT...

...JUST TO DECIDE WHAT TO DO ABOUT THE LYNNE FAMI...UUGGH!

IT'S NOT A MEETING YOU ARE LIKELY TO ATTEND, THEN.
IS IT?

WHAT'S GOING ON HERE?
WHERE'D HE COME FROM?
I HOPE THIS ISN'T A PURCHASE. I HAVEN'T EVEN FIGURED OUT WHAT'S A TAX-DEDUCTIBLE ITEM OR FOOD STAMP ITEM YET.

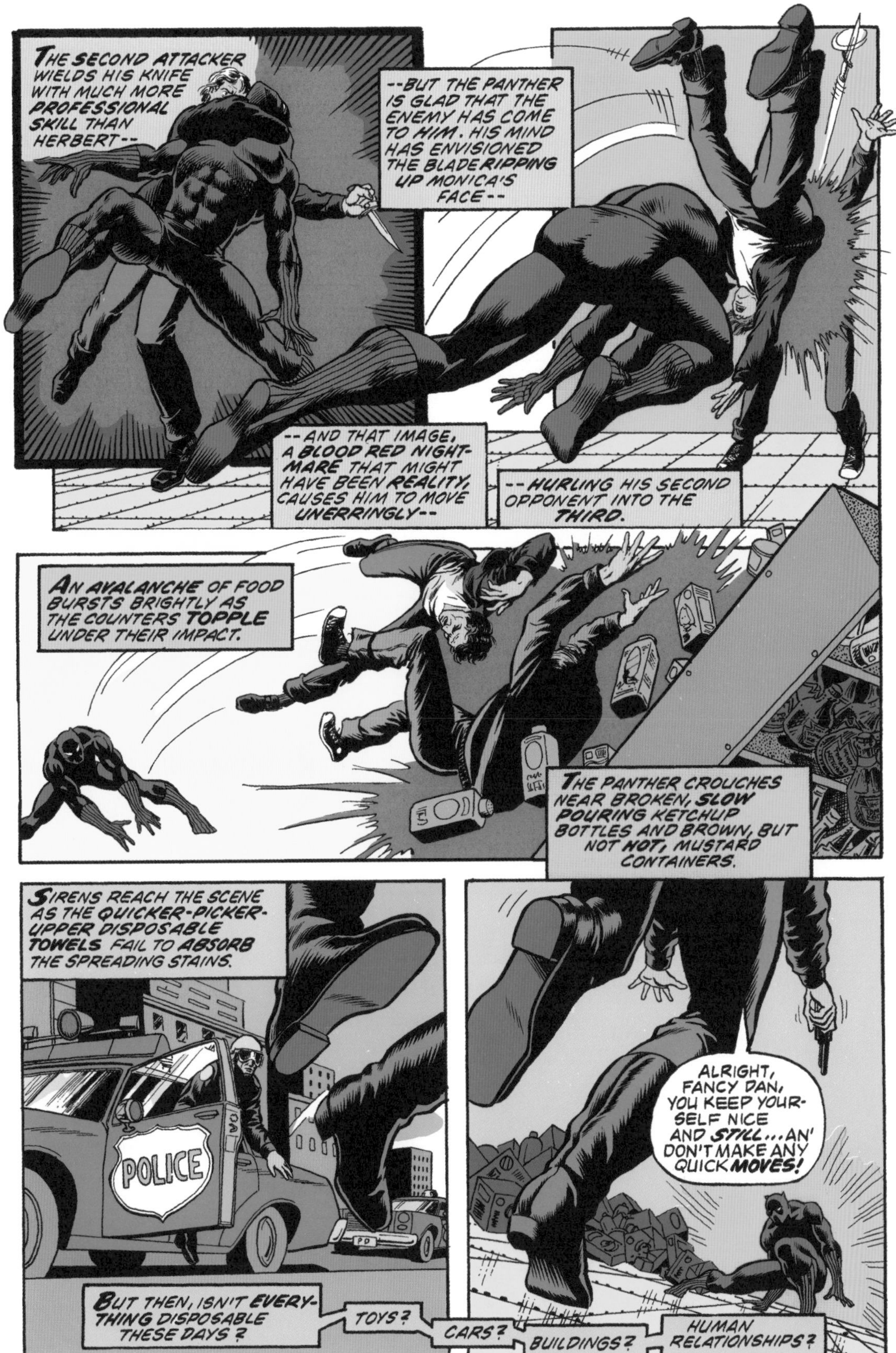
THE SECOND ATTACKER WIELDS HIS KNIFE WITH MUCH MORE PROFESSIONAL SKILL THAN HERBERT--
--BUT THE PANTHER IS GLAD THAT THE ENEMY HAS COME TO HIM. HIS MIND HAS ENVISIONED THE BLADE RIPPING UP MONICA'S FACE--
--AND THAT IMAGE, A BLOOD RED NIGHT-MARE THAT MIGHT HAVE BEEN REALITY, CAUSES HIM TO MOVE UNERRINGLY--
--HURLING HIS SECOND OPPONENT INTO THE THIRD.
AN AVALANCHE OF FOOD BURSTS BRIGHTLY AS THE COUNTERS TOPPLE UNDER THEIR IMPACT.
THE PANTHER CROUCHES NEAR BROKEN, SLOW POURING KETCHUP BOTTLES AND BROWN, BUT NOT HOT, MUSTARD CONTAINERS.
SIRENS REACH THE SCENE AS THE QUICKER-PICKER-UPPER DISPOSABLE TOWELS FAIL TO ABSORB THE SPREADING STAINS.
POLICE
ALRIGHT, FANCY DAN, YOU KEEP YOUR-SELF NICE AND STILL... AN' DON'T MAKE ANY QUICK MOVES!
BUT THEN, ISN'T EVERY-THING DISPOSABLE THESE DAYS?
TOYS?
CARS?
BUILDINGS?
HUMAN RELATIONSHIPS?

THE PANTHER STARES DOWN THE LENGTH OF NEON-LIGHTED ROOM AND SEES ONE OF HIS ATTACKERS STARTING FOR THE ELECTRONIC DOORWAYS.
HE IS NOT SURE WHICH GROUP THE MAN REPRESENTS: THE KLAN, OR THE DRAGON CIRCLE SOLDIERS.
HEY!
I JUST TOLD YOU NOT TO MOVE. NOT A MUSCLE!
YOU'VE GOT YOURSELF SOME QUESTIONS TO ANSWER.

YOUR QUESTIONS WOULD BE BETTER ASKED TO THE MEN WHO STARTED THIS CONFLICT.
I AM GOING AFTER THEM--NOW!

YOU AIN'T GOING NOWHERE--
--'AN YOU AIN'T GONNA HURT NOBODY ELSE. YOU AIN'T BEEN LISTENIN' TOO GOOD, MISTER, THAT'S YOUR PROBLEM!
BEANS
BEANS

THE PANTHERS EYES BURN FROM THE NEON LIGHTS, AND IT SLOWS HIM ENOUGH SO THAT HE CANNOT COMPLETELY AVOID THE THRUSTING PISTOL.
THE MUGGY SEPTEMBER DAY ERUPTS WITH SOUND, DROWNING OUT THE QUIET BACKGROUND MUSIC FROM THE STORE SPEAKERS.
THEY SEE HIM AS A THREAT, ATTACKING THEIR OWN, AND THEY GATHER AROUND HIM WITH VINDICTIVE FURY.
AFTER ALL, IT COULD HAVE BEEN THEM THAT HE ATTACKED.

I KNEW YOU WAS UP TO NO GOOD WHEN YOU COME LEAPIN' AT ME. SCARE A BODY HALF-TO-DEATH!
REBECCA WINTHROP SLASHES AT HIM WITH THE CAN OF CATFOOD. THE PANTHER DOES NOT LAUGH. IT TEARS HIS COSTUME AT THE SCALP, RIPS OPEN THE FLESH ABOVE THE EYEBROW.

THE SCAR WILL BE SLIGHT, HARDLY NOTICEABLE, BUT HE WILL CARRY IT FOR THE REST OF HIS LIFE.
THIS IS THE FIRST TIME THIS POLICEMAN HAS EVER HAD TO STRIKE ANOTHER HUMAN BEING, REMARKABLE CONSIDERING THE PROFESSION HE HAS CHOSEN. HE IS SICKENED BY THE SOUND OF IMPACT.
WHRAK!
WHAT DO YOU PEOPLE THINK YOU ARE DOING?
STAGING YOUR OWN IMPROVISATION OF "THE OX-BOW INCIDENT"?
HE WAS TRYING TO PROTECT ME! THOSE MEN NEARLY GUTTED ME OPEN WITH KNIVES!
SHERIFF RODERICK TATE PULLS TO A SCREECHING STOP IN THE FRONT OF THE SUPER-MARKET!
POLICE
POLICE
PD
SCRREECH!
HIS SHIRT CLINGS UNCOMFORTABLY TO HIS BACK, AND HE WONDERS HOW THE DEVIL THEY MAKE RECKLESS DRIVING LOOK SO EASY IN THOSE TELEVISION SHOWS.
INSIDE, HIS FIRST SIGHT IS OF THE PANTHER AND MONICA LYNNE... AND HE WINCES.
SHERIFF RODERICK TATE WOULD LIKE TO START HIS OWN RAMPAGE. TONIGHT, HE THINKS, WILL PROBABLY BE A GOOD NIGHT TO GO OUT AND GET RIP-ROARING DRUNK.
IF ONLY TO FORGET WHAT THE REST OF THIS DAY HAS BEEN LIKE.

YOU GOT ANYTHING UNDER THEM HELMETS?
I MEAN OTHER THAN THEM MELONS YOU SUBSTITUTE FOR BRAINS?
WHO??... SHERIFF TATE!?
I KNOW WHO I AM... BUT I GOT MY DOUBT ABOUT YOU GUYS.
YOU BEEN KEEPIN' THIS TOWN ALIVE, MISS MONICA. IT'S NOT USUALLY JUMPIN' QUITE THIS MUCH.

IT'S BEEN MORE DEADLY THAN LIVELY FOR ME, TATE. THIS IS THE SECOND ATTEMPT ON MY LIFE SINCE I HAVE COME HOME.

IT'S THE... UH... MANNER OF DRESS YOUR... FRIEND... HAS KINDA SETS PEOPLE ABACK.
Y'KNOW, IF YOU DRESSED UP ALL IN PINK 'STEADA BLUE, THEY COULD PAIR YOU WITH PETER SELLERS. BE A NATURAL!

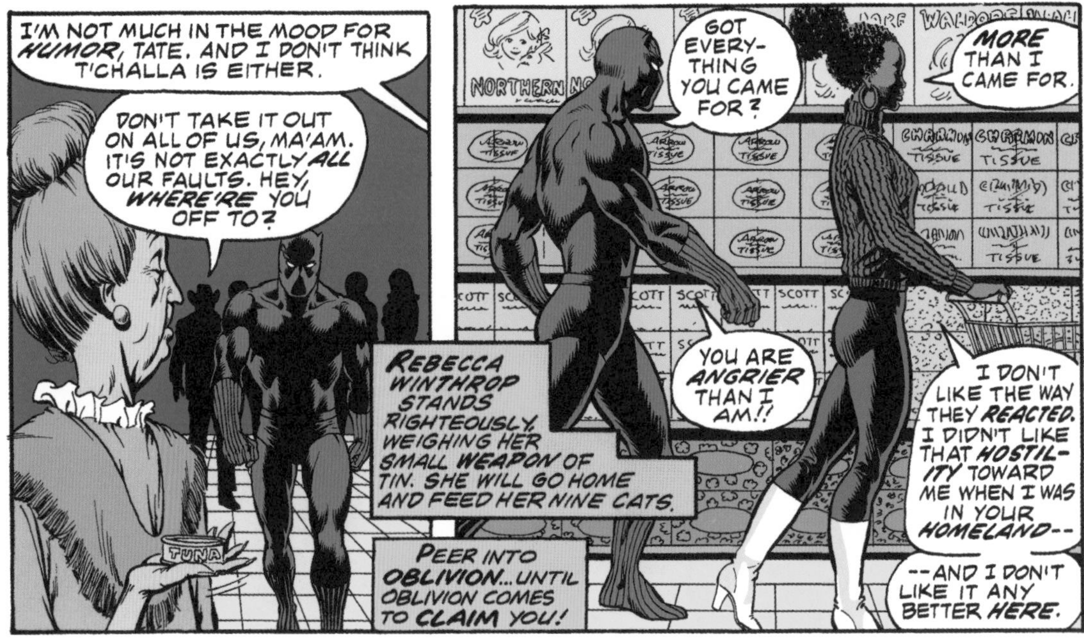
I'M NOT MUCH IN THE MOOD FOR HUMOR, TATE. AND I DON'T THINK T'CHALLA IS EITHER.
DON'T TAKE IT OUT ON ALL OF US, MA'AM. IT'S NOT EXACTLY ALL OUR FAULTS. HEY, WHERE'RE YOU OFF TO?
REBECCA WINTHROP STANDS RIGHTEOUSLY, WEIGHING HER SMALL WEAPON OF TIN. SHE WILL GO HOME AND FEED HER NINE CATS.
PEER INTO OBLIVION... UNTIL OBLIVION COMES TO CLAIM YOU!
TUNA
GOT EVERYTHING YOU CAME FOR?
MORE THAN I CAME FOR.
YOU ARE ANGRIER THAN I AM!!
I DON'T LIKE THE WAY THEY REACTED. I DIDN'T LIKE THAT HOSTILITY TOWARD ME WHEN I WAS IN YOUR HOMELAND--
--AND I DON'T LIKE IT ANY BETTER HERE.
NORTHERN
TISSUE
SCOTT

THE STORE EMPLOYEES ARE NO HAPPIER. THE SPILT FOOD COMBINES... CONGEALS... A RECIPE RUN AMOK... THE FLOOR COVERED WITH HUMPTY DUMPTY REMAINS THAT HAVE NO SOLID PARTS.
THE REPORTERS AND PHOTOGRAPHERS LOVE IT. ESPECIALLY THE SOMBER ATTIRE OF THE PANTHER.
WELL, WELL. IF IT ISN'T KEVIN TRUBLOOD OF THE GEORGIA SUN. FIGHTING REPORTER IN SHINING ARMOR.
THE ARMOR'S KIND OF TARNISHED, ROD. DON'T MUCH KNOW WHAT I BELIEVE IN THESE DAYS.
HELLO, KEVIN!
ONE THING'S FOR SURE, YOU'LL MAKE EXCITING FRONT PAGE COPY.
I WOULD BE MORE INTERESTED IN FINDING OUT WHAT HAPPENED TO THOSE DRAGON CIRCLE SOLDIERS YOU HELPED MONICA AND I BRING TO SHERIFF TATE'S HEADQUARTERS A FEW NIGHTS BACK.
MORE BAD NEWS, I'M AFRAID. JEDIDIAH THORPE AND THE OTHER MEMBERS HAVE BEEN RELEASED ON BAIL.
YOUR CURRENCY DOES SEEM TO PROCURE ALMOST ANYTHING, SHERIFF TATE.
IT WAS ALL DONE ACCORDING TO THE LAW. YOU GOT MY WORD ON THAT. NOT A THING I COULD DO. SOMEBODY WITH A LOT OF MONEY IS BEHIND THIS DRAGON CIRCLE.
THESE PUNKS DIDN'T SNEER AT US WHEN THEY LEFT THE WAY MOSTA THEM WOULD. THEY'RE DEDICATED TO SOMETHING ALL RIGHT.
I WOULD NOT SAY THEY HAD ANYTHING TO DO WITH THE KLAN, THOUGH.
I DON'T THINK THE MEN WHO ATTACKED MONICA TODAY HAD ANY AFFILIATION WITH THE KLAN EITHER!
IT IS A THOUGHT WORTH CONSIDERING, SHERIFF TATE. IT PRESENTS MANY INTRIGUING SPECULATIONS.
MANY.

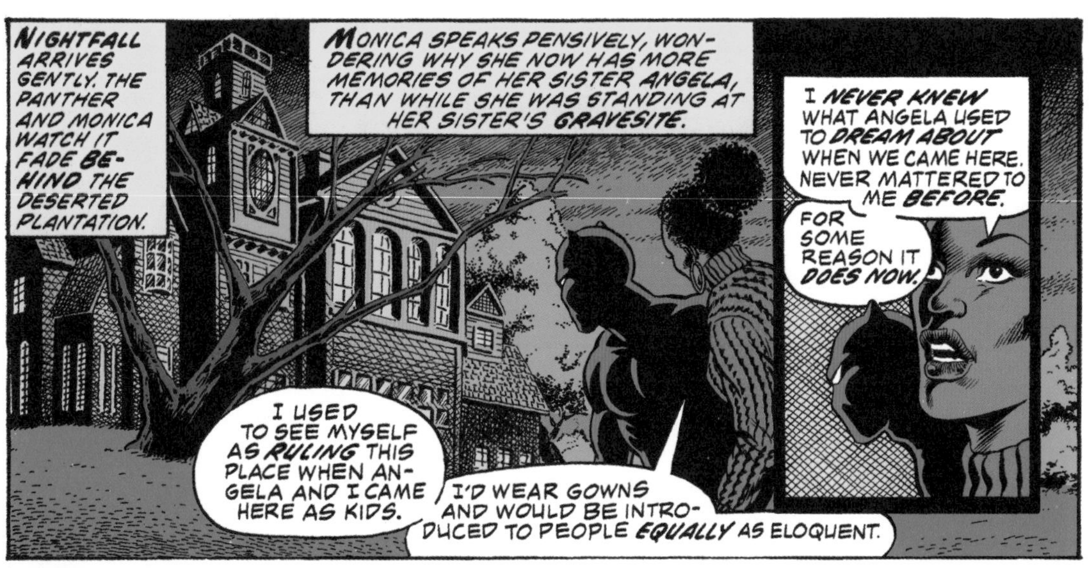

NIGHTFALL ARRIVES GENTLY. THE PANTHER AND MONICA WATCH IT FADE BEHIND THE DESERTED PLANTATION.
MONICA SPEAKS PENSIVELY, WONDERING WHY SHE NOW HAS MORE MEMORIES OF HER SISTER ANGELA, THAN WHILE SHE WAS STANDING AT HER SISTER'S GRAVESITE.
I NEVER KNEW WHAT ANGELA USED TO DREAM ABOUT WHEN WE CAME HERE. NEVER MATTERED TO ME BEFORE.
FOR SOME REASON IT DOES NOW.
I USED TO SEE MYSELF AS RULING THIS PLACE WHEN ANGELA AND I CAME HERE AS KIDS.
I'D WEAR GOWNS AND WOULD BE INTRODUCED TO PEOPLE EQUALLY AS ELOQUENT.

YOUR MOTHER AND FATHER SAY SHE WAS SUPPOSED TO HAVE... KILLED HERSELF.
SUPPOSED TO HAVE SHOT HERSELF IN THE HEAD, T'CHALLA. DON'T TRY TO SOFTEN IT!
AT TWO O'CLOCK IN THE MORNING SHE WAS SUPPOSED TO HAVE ENTERED THE REAL ESTATE OFFICES OF HER EMPLOYER, AMBROSE ELLIS--
--AND PULLED THE TRIGGER THAT BLEW HER BRAINS OUT!
REMEMBERING US HERE AS KIDS, I'D LIKE TO SAY IT WAS IMPOSSIBLE. KEVIN THINKS IT MIGHT HAVE BEEN MURDER, SINCE SHE HAD CONTACTED HIM ABOUT A POSSIBLE LAND MANIPULATION DEAL--
--THAT MIGHT HAVE INVOLVED THE KLAN!

IN 1968, SHE ONCE WROTE A LETTER FROM COLLEGE, SAYING SHE HATED GUNS.
A STUDENT SHE KNEW WAS KILLED IN A PROTEST RIOT. I REMEMBER WHAT SHE WROTE... "EVERYBODY WAS EITHER SCARED OR HATEFUL... AND WE ARE ALL DYING BECAUSE OF IT."
HOLD ME, T'CHALLA, I NEED YOU!

WE WILL FIND OUT WHAT REALLY HAPPENED. IT WILL NOT EASE THE HURT AND LOSS MUCH... KNOWLEDGE SELDOM DOES... BUT AT LEAST WE WILL KNOW THE TRUTH OF IT!
TRUTH? RIGHT NOW I NEED YOU MORE THAN THE TRUTH!

BUT DON'T PROMISE IT WILL LAST FOREVER--
--I WON'T BE ABLE TO TAKE IT IF IT DOESN'T!

FOREVER ENDS.
ALONE, WITHOUT HER WARMTH HE CROUCHES--

--DIVES--

--EXECUTING SUPERB MOONLIT ACROBATICS--

--USING TREE LIMBS AS SPRINGBOARDS--

--AND THEN THE GREAT BLACK CAT PAUSES... CALCULATING.

HE IS THE BLACK CAT ON THE PROWL--
--NOW AT THE GOAL OF HIS PURSUIT.


HE DESCENDS.

THEY ARE DRESSED IN FLOWING WHITE, BUT THERE IS NOTHING PURE OR HOLY IN THEIR DEMEANOR.

A CROSS BURNS IN THE DISTANCE. ANOTHER ONE WAITS FOR THE TORCHES TO SET IT ABLAZE.

I SUSPECT YOU HAVE BEEN AWAITING MY PRESENCE.

I HOPE YOU ARE NOT DISAPPOINTED.

LOOK OUT! HE'S HERE!

HE'S FASTER THAN OUR BROTHERS TOLD US.

THAT WON'T SAVE HIS HIDE FROM OUR SHOT-GUNS... YOU'D BETTER BELIEVE THAT.

THE STEADY SOUND OF A GRANDFATHER CLOCK DOMINATES THE LYNNE HOUSEHOLD. FOREVER MIGHT END. KEVIN TRUBLOOD'S ILLUSIONS MIGHT END.
BUT THE SOUND OF THE CLOCK CONTINUES... INEXORABLY.
T'CHALLA WENT TO DEVOURING SWAMP, KEVIN.

TO CHECK IF THERE REALLY IS A KLAN MEETING THERE TONIGHT, HUH?
YEAH, THAT'S MY MAN. GOES OFF LIKE HE'S TAKING NOTHING MORE THAN A CASUAL STROLL.


THE PANTHER'S AVENGING FORM REFLECTS THE FLARING TORCHLIGHT.

AND THE COLORS SHIFT, RED AND ORANGE, AND YELLOW, OVER THE BLUE LENGTH OF HIS STRAINING BODY.

THROUGH THE SLITS IN THE WHITE HOODS, EYES EXPRESS HATRED AND FEAR. IT IS THE ONLY SIGN OF HUMANITY ABOUT THE FIGURES.

WHY DO YOU WANT TO WRITE THIS PIECE ABOUT THE KLAN!?
I'M CERTAIN IT WASN'T FASCINATION WITH MY SISTER ANGELA, THAT MADE YOU FOLLOW THRU ON THE STORY.

SHE WAS PART OF IT. WHEN ANGELA FIRST CAME TO MY DESK WITH HER STORY--
--TELLING ME THE KLAN MIGHT BE RESPONSIBLE FOR SOME LARGE LAND MANIPULATION DEALS IN THE AREA--

--AND THAT IT MIGHT LEAD RIGHT UP ON TO OUR POLITICAL ARENA... I WAS STUNNED!
BUT I THOUGHT TO MYSELF: 'WHAT A FANTASTIC STORY. MAYBE I'LL GET A PULITZER FOR THIS!'
I HAVE THOSE KIND OF FANTASIES ... IT'S A WEAKNESS OF MINE.

THEY ARE ALL AT HIM AT ONCE. ONE OF THE FIGURES USES THE SHOTGUN AS IF IT WERE A BASEBALL BAT--
--AND SLAMS IT INTO THE PANTHER'S MIDSECTION. THE BURNING TORCHES AND CROSS DIM BEFORE HIS EYES.
AND FOR THE FIRST TIME, THE PANTHER CONSIDERS THAT QUITE POSSIBLY HE MADE A MISTAKE BY ENTERING THIS FRAY SO EMOTIONALLY.

I HAD THOSE KIND OF FANTASIES WHEN I STARTED SINGING. THAT I'D END UP ON STAGE, SIDE BY SIDE WITH ELLA FITZGERALD.
BUT WHAT YOUR SISTER WAS TELLING ME ABOUT SOUNDED AS IF IT COULD BE REAL.

THERE WASN'T ANY FANTASY INVOLVED IN WHAT I'D LEARNED ONCE I STARTED TO INVESTIGATE.
--LIKE FINDING THE FOOT OF AN ELEPHANT, AS IN THE OLD FABLE, AND, THINKING IT WAS THE WHOLE ANIMAL!
...AND I DIDN'T REALIZE BUT I'D ONLY DISCOVERED ONE TINY PART OF THE ORGANISM--

ON TOP OF THAT, OTHER PEOPLE AROUND ME... FRIENDS... RELATIVES... PEOPLE I WORKED WITH--

--THEY ALL ASKED THE SAME QUESTION: WHY DO YOU WANT TO WRITE THIS PIECE?

AND I WAS STUNNED AGAIN. MY CAPACITY FOR BEING STUNNED IS ENDLESS, I GUESS. MAYBE IT IS.

I DIDN'T THINK IT WAS A QUESTION THAT HAD TO BE ASKED. I THOUGHT IT WAS OBVIOUS WHY I WAS GOING TO WRITE THIS STORY.

ONE AGAINST THE MULTITUDES.

THE FLAMES TWIST AND TOSS OVER THE TWISTING AND TOSSING FIGURES. STROBE-LIGHT BATTLE!

THE FLAMES' GLOW LENDS A BARBAROUS ATMOSPHERE TO THE BRUTALITY. THE FLESH POUNDS AT OTHER FLESH.

WOOD BATTERS FLESH TO UGLY WELTS.

METAL BARS CLUB FLESH TO NUMBNESS.

FLESH WOUNDS THAT SPILL BLOOD.

SOMETHING WRONG WAS HAPPENING, AND I DISCOVERED IT... AND THE IDEALISM THAT HADN'T WITHERED AWAY IN ME ROSE UP AND SAID, "BLAST IT, WE'RE GOING TO DO SOMETHING ABOUT THIS CORRUPTION."
I STILL BELIEVE IN THIS COUNTRY.

I KNOW THAT'S UNFASHIONABLE THESE DAYS... AND SOMETIMES... KNOWING MUCH OF OUR HISTORY... I WONDER WHY I STILL BELIEVE.
BUT I KNOW WHY!
I BELIEVE IN THE FAIRY TALES... THE MYTHS I WAS TAUGHT IN SCHOOL... THE VALUES THIS COUNTRY WAS SUPPOSED TO STAND FOR.

I STILL WANT TO BELIEVE IN THOSE MYTHS.
IN FACT... I STILL DO!

AND IF THIS COUNTRY ISN'T PERFECT, SO WHAT! NOTHING IS!
AND WE'LL KEEP FIGHTING UNTIL AMERICA LIVES UP TO THE THINGS IT PROCLAIMED IT WAS!

TORCHLIGHT HAS OVERSEEN THIS SCENE BEFORE... IN OTHER PLACES... IN LESS SOPHISTICATED TIMES.

THE FLICKERING LIGHT REVEALS NOTHING MORE THAN THE PAIN AND LUDICROUS ACTIONS THAT BRUISED AND SWEATING MEN INFLICT UPON EACH OTHER.

A DOUBLE BARRELLED SHOTGUN PUSHES INTO THE PANTHER'S ADAM'S APPLE, AND A VOICE SPEAKS. "TIE HIM TO THE CROSS, BROTHERS--

"TIE HIM AND LET THE FLAMES CONSUME HIS FLESH! IT IS TIME THE KLAN TOOK A MORE ACTIVE ROLE AGAINST SUCH TRASH!

AND MAYBE SOMEDAY WE'LL COME CLOSE... OR AT LEAST CLOSER... TO WHAT THOSE BELIEFS WERE SUPPOSED TO BE.
YOU'RE GETTING CARRIED AWAY.
YOU'RE RIGHT! I AM GETTING CARRIED AWAY!

BECAUSE MY CHARACTER WAS QUESTIONED WHEN I SAID I WAS GOING TO DO THAT STORY--
--THAT I WAS GOING TO EXPOSE IT!
AND OTHERS TOLD ME THEY LL FIREBOMB YOU. YOU DON'T MESS WITH THE KLAN.
I HAD TO THINK ABOUT THAT. DID I HAVE THE RIGHT TO INVOLVE MY FAMILY IN THIS? HAD I APPOINTED MYSELF ON A CRUSADE... WAS I SOME BLIND LIBERAL FANATIC?

NO, I DECIDED! I'D BEEN THREATENED! I REALIZED I WAS AFRAID TO WRITE THAT STORY.
MY FRIENDS, MY RELATIVES, MY CO-WORKERS. THEY MADE ME AFRAID TO WRITE THAT STORY. AND THEY WERE AFRAID.

AND I THOUGHT, "GOOD LORD, WHAT IS AMERICA COMING TO?" WASN'T EVEN FREEDOM OF SPEECH, WHICH I TOOK TO INCLUDE THE WRITTEN WORD, INVIOLABLE?

"AND THEY ASKED ME WHAT I HOPED TO CHANGE?
"WRITE YOUR PIECE. THE KLAN'LL STILL BE HERE.
"AND THEY SAID, 'ALL THIS WILL BRING YOU IS GRIEF. THINK ON IT.

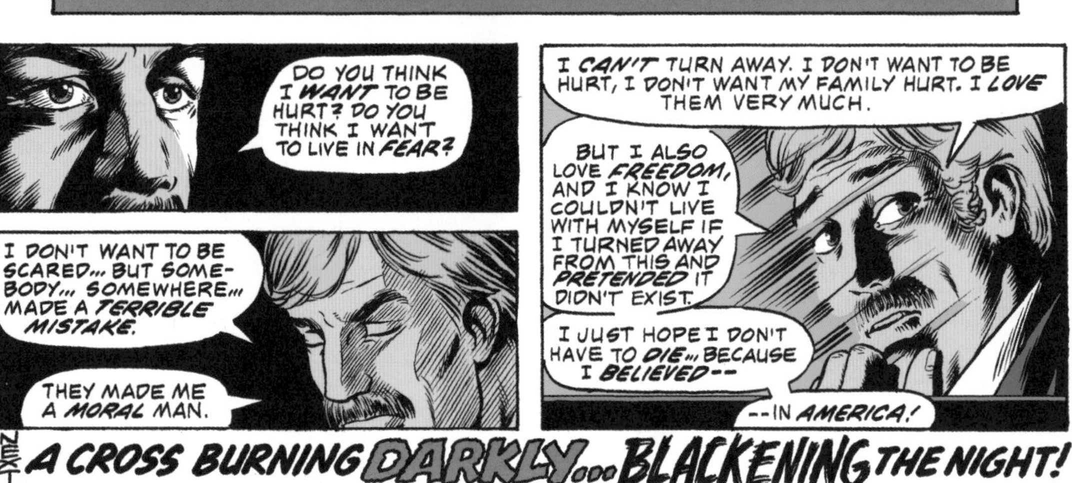

DO YOU THINK I WANT TO BE HURT? DO YOU THINK I WANT TO LIVE IN FEAR?
I DON'T WANT TO BE SCARED... BUT SOMEBODY... SOMEWHERE... MADE A TERRIBLE MISTAKE.
THEY MADE ME A MORAL MAN.
I CAN'T TURN AWAY. I DON'T WANT TO BE HURT, I DON'T WANT MY FAMILY HURT. I LOVE THEM VERY MUCH.
BUT I ALSO LOVE FREEDOM, AND I KNOW I COULDN'T LIVE WITH MYSELF IF I TURNED AWAY FROM THIS AND PRETENDED IT DIDN'T EXIST.
I JUST HOPE I DON'T HAVE TO DIE... BECAUSE I BELIEVED--
--IN AMERICA!

A CROSS BURNING DARKLY... BLACKENING THE NIGHT!

# *JUNGLE ACTION* #21,
# MAY 1976

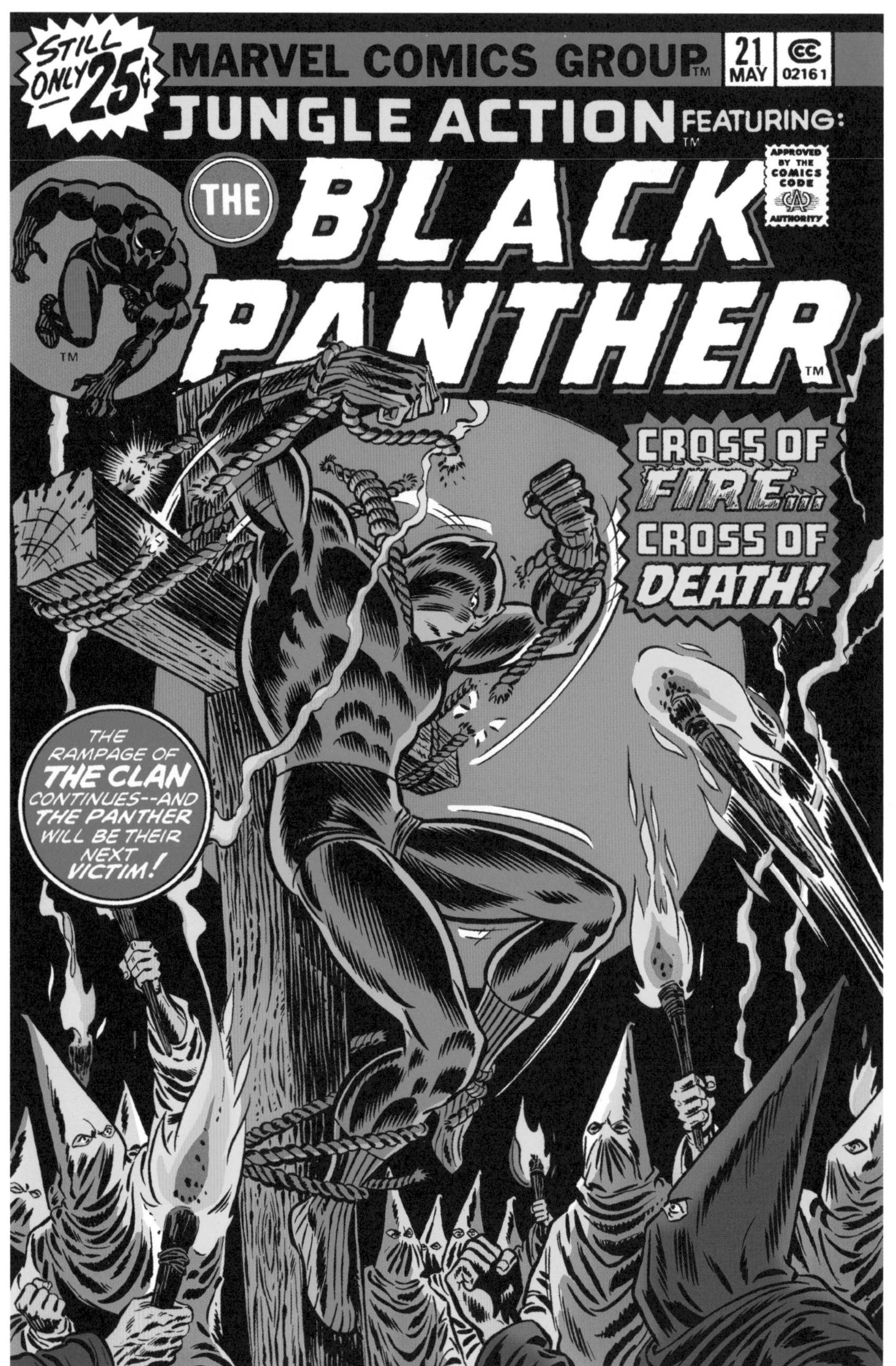
STILL ONLY 25¢
MARVEL COMICS GROUP
21 MAY
CC 02161
JUNGLE ACTION FEATURING:
APPROVED BY THE COMICS CODE AUTHORITY
THE BLACK PANTHER
CROSS OF FIRE... CROSS OF DEATH!
THE RAMPAGE OF THE CLAN CONTINUES--AND THE PANTHER WILL BE THEIR NEXT VICTIM!

With the sleekness of a jungle beast, the Prince of Wakanda stalks both the concrete of the city and the undergrowth of the veldt, for when danger lurks he dons the garb of the savage cat from which he gains his name!
Stan Lee PRESENTS: THE BLACK PANTHER! TM
A CROSS BURNING DARKLY BLACKENING the NIGHT!
THE PANTHER VS. THE KLAN!
DON McGREGOR AUTHOR
BILLY GRAHAM ARTIST
BOB McLEOD INKER
HARRY BLUMFIELD letterer
PHIL RACHELSON colorist
MARV WOLFMAN EDITOR
HE IS NOT A SYMBOLIC CHRIST!
FORGET ABOUT TURNING HIS FLESH AND BLOOD INTO SOME ESOTERIC ALLUSION TO THE PERSECUTION OF CONTEMPORARY MAN.
THIS IS THE BLACK PANTHER... KING OF THE WAKANDAS... ALSO KNOWN AS T'CHALLA.
AND HE IS MADE OF FLESH AND BLOOD. AND THE FLAMES WHICH CONSUME THE CROSS AND HIS BODY PROVE HIS HUMANITY.
AND THE DEATH-WATCHERS, DRESSED IN WHITE ROBES, REVEL AT HIS TORMENT... AND DESIRE HIS DEATH!

T'CHALLA'S BEEN GONE QUITE AWHILE. I HOPE HE CAN NAVIGATE HIMSELF AROUND DEVOURING SWAMP WITHOUT ENDING UP LOST OR IN A SINKHOLE. 'COURSE, IF THE KLAN REALLY IS HAVING A MEETING OUT THERE TONIGHT, HE COULD BE IN WORSE TROUBLE THAN THAT, HUH, MONICA?
HE WON'T GET LOST... AND HE WAS BORN TO THE TREES... THAT WON'T THROW HIM--
--BUT I'M NOT CUT OUT TO PLAY THE WOMAN'S WAITING ROLE. YOU SEE, MR. TRUBLOOD, IN ALL THE OLD MOVIES MY SISTER ANGELA AND I SAW AS A KID, THE WOMAN ALWAYS WAITED... FOR THE HERO TO RETURN.
YEAH, ANGELA-- RIGHT AFTER YOUR SISTER COMES TO MY NEWSPAPER, SHE ENDS UP DEAD-- A SUICIDE TO ALL APPEARANCES!
YET, THE WEEK BEFORE, SHE WAS ON THE VERGE OF GAINING EVIDENCE THAT THE KLAN WAS MANIPULATING A LARGE LAND TRACT WITH THE REAL ESTATE AGENCY WHERE SHE WORKED.
AND WHAT ABOUT THIS SECOND GROUP THAT'S BEEN RUNNING AROUND... THE DRAGON CIRCLE SOLDIERS? NOT EVEN T'CHALLA'S BEEN ABLE TO FIGURE HOW THEY FIT INTO THIS.
T'CHALLA.
IT SEEMS LIKE WE'VE BEEN WAITING FOR HIS RETURN FOR ETERNITIES.
HE IS THE GREAT BLACK CAT--
--AND THE GREAT BLACK CAT FEARS FLAME.
HE FEARS IT INSTINCTIVELY.
HE DOES NOT NEED TO THRUST HIS PAW INTO THE FLAME TO KNOW IT WILL CAUSE PAIN.

WAITING. SOMETIMES I THINK WE SPEND HALF OUR LIVES WAITING-- FOR MIRACLES!
BEFORE I BECAME KEVIN TRUBLOOD, BOY REPORTER, AND WAS JUST KEVIN TRUBLOOD, LUNATIC WITH A PASSION TO WRITE--
--MY WIFE AND I WOULD SAY: "WAIT'LL YOU MAKE IT AS A HOT-SHOT REPORTER, THAT'S WHEN WE'LL HAVE IT MADE."
MADE! HA! I MADE IT, ALL RIGHT--TO A LIFETIME OF DEADLINES AND WEARYING HOURS!
IN THE PROCESS, I LOST A LOT OF MY PASSION.
I REFOUND SOME OF IT, WHEN I DECIDED I'D FOLLOW YOUR SISTER'S STORY ALL THE WAY.
DAD.
YOU TWO THROUGH MAKIN' YOUR SPEECHES? THOUGHT YOU WERE PRACTICIN' FOR THE ORAL ROBERTS SHOW.
I'M GOING TO HAVE KEVIN DRIVE ME OUT TO DEVOURING SWAMP. SEE IF WE CAN'T FIND T'CHALLA.
WELL, I'M SURE NUTHIN' I'D SAY WOULD STOP YOU, CHILD... YOU'RE GONNA DO WHAT YOU WANT.
'SIDES, IT'LL GIVE YOUR MOTHER AND I SOME QUIET 'ROUND HERE. MAN'LL BE ABLE TO PLAY SOLITAIRE IN PEACE.
HE IS THE BLACK CAT--
--AND GIVEN ANY CHOICE THE BLACK CAT WILL FLEE THE HOLOCAUST.
BUT THERE ISN'T ANY CHOICE. CHOICE HAS BEEN TAKEN AWAY.
LIPS, HIDDEN BY HOODS, SPEAK. "LOOK AT THAT, WILLYA? HIS FLESH IS GONNA BE TURNED TO BLISTERS...
...AN HE HASN'T SCREAMED ONCE!"
"HE WILL," ASSURES OTHER CLOAKED LIPS.
HE IS ALSO A MAN, AND INTELLECTUALLY AND EMOTIONALLY AND PHYSICALLY... THE FIRE IS DESTROYING HIM!

HE IS AT THE CENTER OF THE INFERNO AND PAIN IS AT THE CENTER OF HIS BEING.
HE MUST CONQUER THE PAIN. HE MUST BANISH IT FROM HIS MIND IF HE IS TO SURVIVE.
BUT HE CAN'T BANISH IT, HIS MIND SCREAMS WITH FLESH-SCREAMS!!
YOU MUST!
CAN'T! DON'T YOU UNDERSTAND, A MAN CAN ONLY TAKE SO MUCH!
THINK, T'CHALLA. YOU HAVE CONQUERED PAIN BEFORE ... AND YOU HAVE SURVIVED.
BUT NOT AGONY LIKE THIS.
LIKE THIS... AND WORSE! THE HEMP ROPE TETHERED ABOUT YOUR ANKLES HAS TURNED TO ASH.
YOU WILL MAKE IT! THAT'S IT! YOU'LL ONLY HAVE THE CHANCE TO DO THIS ONCE, SO MAKE SURE YOU DO IT RIGHT THE FIRST TIME.
THE SOLES OF HIS BOOTS AFIRE, HE EXECUTES THE MOVEMENT AS IF WITHOUT A SINGLE THOUGHT... SLAMS THEM INTO THE TOP OF THE CROSS... AND IT SPLINTERS IN A FIERY SHOWER WHERE THE WOOD BURNS AT ITS MIDSECTION.
HE'S MOVING! HE SHOULD BE ROASTED BY NOW... BUT HE'S MOVING!
THE OTHERS WERE RIGHT. HE'S GOT TO BE A DEMON INCARNATE!
LIFT YOURSELF, T'CHALLA, ELSE THE MORNING LIGHT WILL FIND YOU A BLACKENED CORPSE.
WON'T MAKE IT!

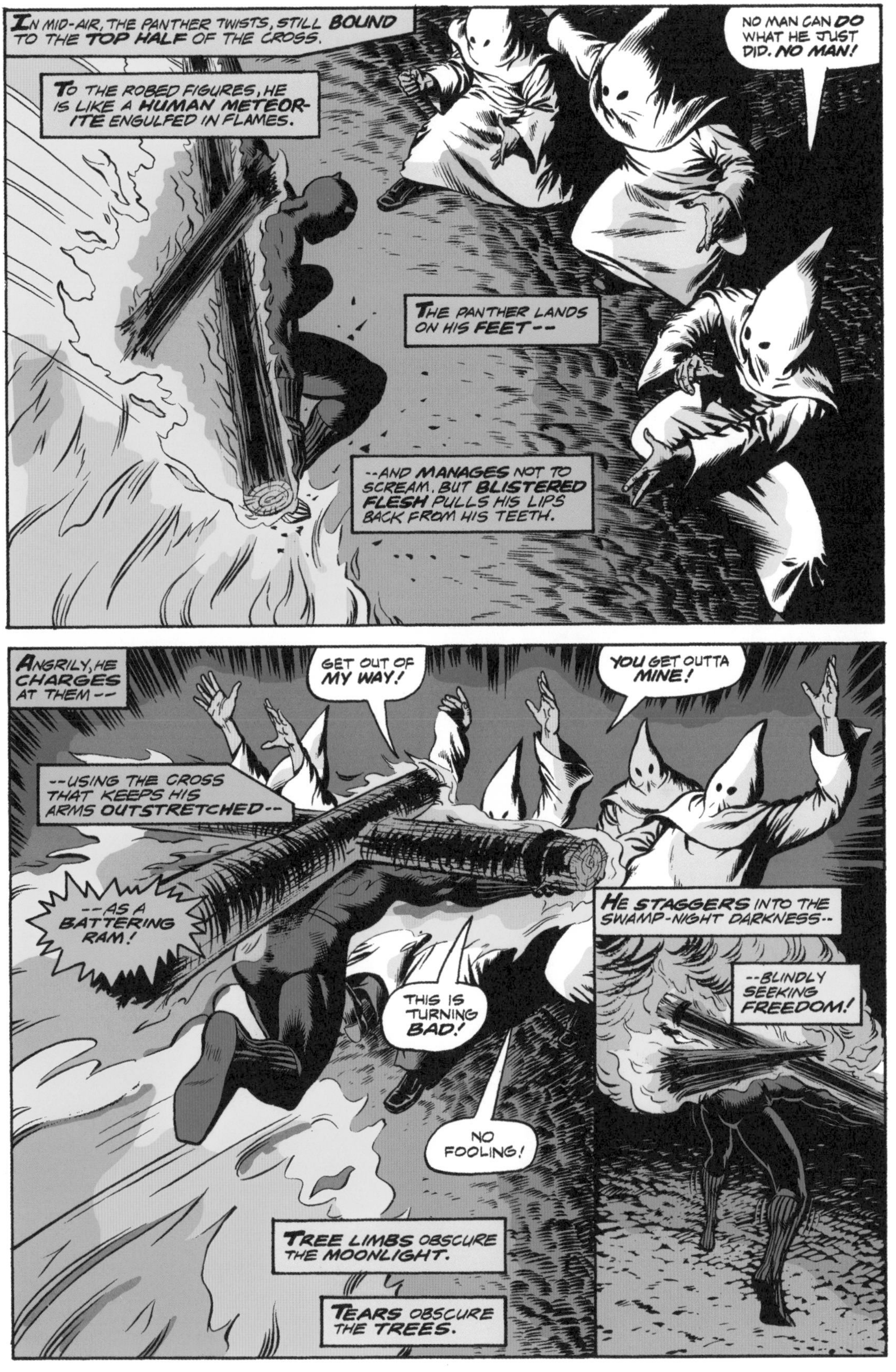

IN MID-AIR, THE PANTHER TWISTS, STILL BOUND TO THE TOP HALF OF THE CROSS.

TO THE ROBED FIGURES, HE IS LIKE A HUMAN METEORITE ENGULFED IN FLAMES.

NO MAN CAN DO WHAT HE JUST DID. NO MAN!

THE PANTHER LANDS ON HIS FEET--

--AND MANAGES NOT TO SCREAM. BUT BLISTERED FLESH PULLS HIS LIPS BACK FROM HIS TEETH.

ANGRILY, HE CHARGES AT THEM--

GET OUT OF MY WAY!

YOU GET OUTTA MINE!

--USING THE CROSS THAT KEEPS HIS ARMS OUTSTRETCHED--

--AS A BATTERING RAM!

THIS IS TURNING BAD!

NO FOOLING!

TREE LIMBS OBSCURE THE MOONLIGHT.

TEARS OBSCURE THE TREES.

HE STAGGERS INTO THE SWAMP-NIGHT DARKNESS--

--BLINDLY SEEKING FREEDOM!

HE STAGGERS! THE PAIN IS EMBODIED IN HIS FLESH--
--AND HE CANNOT ESCAPE HIS OWN BODY.
THE NIGHTMARE DESCENDS AND CLINGS TO HIM LIKE THE MOSS WRAPPED AROUND THE CYPRESS.

NIGHT SILENCE.
NIGHT SOUND.
HE IS UNAWARE THAT THE SHOUTS HAVE DIMINISHED, SWALLOWED BY THE SWAMP.
BLINDLY, HE FORAGES ABOUT.
THE PAIN REMAINS LASHED TO HIM, AND HE MOANS!

THE EARTH TURNS TO SPONGE, AND WATER RISES TO ITS SURFACE BENEATH HIS GLOVED HANDS.

HE CRAWLS THOSE LAST INCHES--

--CRAWLS FOR AN AGONIZING ETERNITY WHERE ILLUSION AND REALITY MERGE.

INTELLECT SLAUGHTERED!

HE IS ONLY THE PAIN, CONSUMING, ENGULFING, TOTAL PAIN.

HIS FINGERS SINK INTO MUD, AND SLICKLY-GREEN MARSH WATER CLINGS TO HIS WOUNDS AND DRIPS BACK INTO THE SOURCE FROM WHENCE IT CAME--

--AND HE REMAINS THERE, UNWILLING TO RISE, FOR HE IS NOT LAZARUS EITHER. HE IS ONLY FLESH AND BLOOD... AND THEY HAVE DESTROYED THAT!

No!
HE CANNOT LET THEM DESTROY HIM! HE CANNOT ALLOW THEM THAT VICTORY!
"I WILL SURVIVE," AND HE TRIES TO SPEAK THE WORDS AS A CHALLENGE--
IT'S GETTING KIND OF COOL.
YEAH, SORRY ABOUT THE BROKEN WINDSHIELD.
THAT'S A STRANGE THING TO APOLOGIZE FOR, KEVIN.
--BUT HIS LIPS WILL NOT FORM THE WORDS AND HIS TONGUE REMAINS STIFF AGAINST THE TOP OF HIS MOUTH.
WHY SURVIVE? WHY NOT SUCCUMB TO THE LANGUAGE OF THE PAIN?
COME ON, HE SPEAKS ANGRILY, CHIDING HIMSELF... YOU HAVE TRAVELLED THIS IDENTITY LABYRINTH BEFORE.
IT WAS T'CHALLA WHO THREW ONE OF THOSE DRAGON CIRCLE CLOWNS THROUGH IT.
YOU WOULDN'T BELIEVE THE TROUBLE I'M HAVING GETTING A WINDSHIELD TO REPLACE IT. ODD SIZE, SAYS THE GUY AT THE REPAIR SHOP, BUT IT SHOULD ONLY TAKE A COUPLE MORE WEEKS TO GET IT IN.
IS IT A JOURNEY YOU MUST RETURN TO ENDLESSLY...
...SEEKING RESOLUTIONS TO PROBLEMS YOUR PAST CONVINCED YOU WERE RESOLVED?
THE DEBATE PUSHES THE PAIN BACK, AND HE EXHALES AND BREATHES WITH THE PAIN, AND FINALLY THE WILDERNESS IS BEHIND HIM.
AUTOMOBILE LIGHTS PROMISE AID--
I'LL GIVE HIM CREDIT... HE ALWAYS SAYS IT WITH A SMILE...EVEN WHEN HE TOLD ME THAT THREE WEEKS AGO.
KEVIN?
--AND PASS ON, FAILING TO DELIVER.
THE TEXTURE OF THE TARN STAYS WITH HIM, TURNING COLDER, YET IT IS COMFORTING.
HE HAS NOT BEEN RAISED TO AVOID THE DIRT AND DOES NOT DRAW AWAY FROM IT DISDAINFULLY. HE IS WAKANDAN; THE EARTH IS A PART OF HIM.
AND NOW IT IS THE ONLY COMFORTING ELEMENT LEFT IN HIS UNIVERSE.
I KNOW. WE HAVEN'T FOUND HIM YET. DID YOU REALLY THINK WE WOULD?
I...KEPT... HOPING.

THEY SHOULD BE THE ONES WHO FIND HIM, THINKS MONICA. THAT'S THE WAY IT'S SUPPOSED TO WORK OUT.
BUT LIFE IS SELDOM IMBUED WITH SUCH SIMPLICITY. IT ALL GETS SO COMPLEX SOMEWHERE ALONG THE WAY--
--AS IF LOST WITH ONE'S YOUTHFUL INNOCENCE!
PHONE
THE TONE OF HER MOTHER'S VOICE TELLS HER AUTOMATICALLY WHAT HAS HAPPENED... NOT THE DETAILS-- THE ESSENCE OF IT... BUT SHE LISTENS ANYWAY.
CALM DOWN, MOM. PLEASE. I CAN'T UNDERSTAND A WORD YOU'RE SAYING.

WHAT'S THAT ?! THEY FOUND HIM WHERE ?... YES, MOM, I KNOW WHERE THAT IS ... MOM, THE HOSPITAL... WHAT HOSPITAL DID THEY TAKE HIM TO ?
YES, MOM, I KNOW YOU SAW HIM... I CAN IMAGINE HOW BAD IT LOOKED. I'VE SEEN HIM HURT BEFORE--

PHONE
--AND PROBABLY WILL AGAIN...

I GUESS I DON'T LOOK VERY REGAL, DO I? A LITTLE TORN AROUND THE EDGES.
YOUR EDGES ARE FINE.
SUPERHEROES ARE SUPPOSED TO BE IMPERVIOUS TO PAIN, AREN'T THEY?
I'VE HEARD THAT.
THEN WHY DOES THIS ...HURT SO MUCH?
HOW COULD THEY DO THIS TO YOU? THEY'RE SUPPOSED TO BE HUMAN BEINGS. HOW COULD THEY DO A THING LIKE THIS?

AH, PEOPLE PERPETRATE PSYCHOLOGICAL PUNISHMENTS ON EACH OTHER EVERY DAY... OFTEN VERY CALCULATED... BUT IT SEEMS LESS CRUEL EVEN IF IT ISN'T... WE'RE BLISSFULLY UNAWARE OF THE MAIMING OF MINDS... BUT THIS... OH, LORD, THIS!
YOUR HAND IS STRENGTH ...IT SEEMS YOUR HAND IS ALWAYS GIVING ME STRENGTH.

YOU GIVE ME THE SAME. IT'S EASY TO KEEP LOVE ALIVE WHEN THINGS ARE GOING WELL ...IT'S WHEN YOU'RE DOWN AND OUT THAT IT GETS MORE DIFFICULT.
YOU TALKED TO ME OF LOVE ONCE... IT SEEMS SO LONG AGO. WE ATE ROAST KRAAL VENISON, AND I ADORED YOU. BUT RIGHT NOW, WHAT I FEEL FOR YOU, IS LESS FLAMBOYANT... SUBTLER...
I WANT YOU HEALED. AND I'LL REALLY WANT YOU WHEN YOU'RE WELL... AND I'LL BE HERE UNTIL YOU ARE.

SHERIFF RODERICK TATE STUDIES THE PEOPLE GATHERED IN THE HOSPITAL. HE NEARLY SMILES AT LLOYD LYNNE WHEN HE SPOTS THE PLAYING CARDS HELD IN THE MAN'S HANDS. HE IS NOT SURE HE WOULD RECOGNIZE THE MAN WITHOUT THOSE CARDS
YOU'RE COMING ALONG RIGHT WELL. DOCS ARE STILL TRYIN' TO FIGURE HOW YOU CAN BE MENDIN' WITHIN A COUPLE OF WEEKS' TIME. YOU GOT 'EM PUZZLED, BOY.
THERE IS A CEREMONY I UNDERGO TWICE A YEAR, SHERIFF TATE... IT IS VERY RIGOROUS... VERY PRIVATE. I HOPE YOU CAN RESPECT THAT.

SAME AS I HOPE YOU CAN RESPECT THE FACT I DON'T WANT TO LOSE ANOTHER DAUGHTER.
AIN'T BEEN CLEARED UP WHETHER OR NOT ANGELA KILLED HERSELF AS THEY SAY...
...OR WAS MURDERED AS MR. TRUBLOOD SUSPICIONS.

WE ALL HAVE TOO MUCH LOSS IN OUR LIVES, MR. LYNNE.
BUT ONE CANNOT RUN FROM THE LOSS... OR YOU END UP LOSING EVEN MORE.

THOSE'RE EASY WORDS TO SAY.
YOU ARE VERY PERCEPTIVE, MR. LYNNE--AND UNFORTUNATELY CORRECT. IT CAN BE DIFFICULT TO DISTINGUISH BETWEEN HONEST GRIEF AND MARTYRISM. NEITHER IS EASY TO SURVIVE.
WHAT'D YOU SAY?
I MERELY AGREED WITH YOU.

T'CHALLA, WHAT YOU'VE SAID IS FINE... AND MAYBE EVEN IMPORTANT... BUT WHILE YOU'VE BEEN IN HERE, EVENTS HAVE BEEN HAPPENING. THE KLAN IS HOLDING A LEGITIMATE RALLY TOMORROW NIGHT.
THEN PERHAPS WE'LL ATTEND.
I WAS HOPING YOU'D SAY THAT.

NOW WAITAMINNIT, YOU TWO! I DON'T WANT YOU GOIN' IN THERE BUSTIN' THINGS UP. THEY GOT THEMSELVES A PERMIT, YOU GOT THAT?
NOW I'M NOT SAYIN' THERE'S A LAW THAT CAN STOP YOU FROM GOING DOWN THERE... BUT YOU ARE SURELY GONNA STIR UP A HORNET'S NEST--
--AND I'D'A THOUGHT YOU GOT STUNG ENOUGH ALREADY!
WELL, EITHER WAY, I'VE HAD ENOUGH OF THAT! YOU BREAK THE LAW, YOU KNOW WHAT I'LL DO WITH YOUR CARCASSES! IT'S MY UNDERSTANDIN' YOU PEOPLE WANT'A KNOW MORE ABOUT ANGELA'S DEATH, SO LET'S TALK ABOUT THAT. NOTHIN' ELSE.

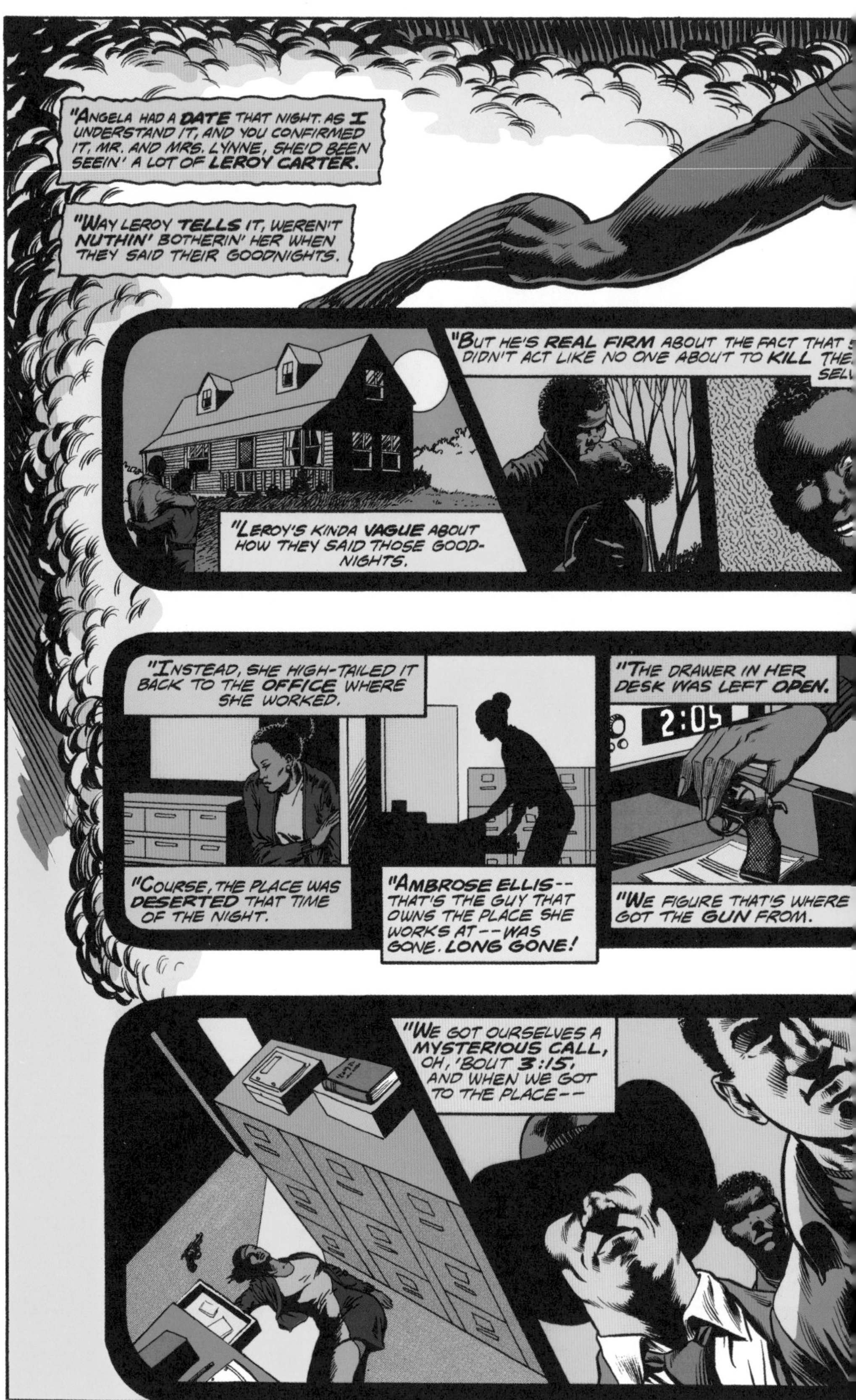
"ANGELA HAD A DATE THAT NIGHT. AS I UNDERSTAND IT, AND YOU CONFIRMED IT, MR. AND MRS. LYNNE, SHE'D BEEN SEEIN' A LOT OF LEROY CARTER.
"WAY LEROY TELLS IT, WEREN'T NUTHIN' BOTHERIN' HER WHEN THEY SAID THEIR GOODNIGHTS.
"LEROY'S KINDA VAGUE ABOUT HOW THEY SAID THOSE GOOD-NIGHTS.
"BUT HE'S REAL FIRM ABOUT THE FACT THAT
DIDN'T ACT LIKE NO ONE ABOUT TO KILL
"INSTEAD, SHE HIGH-TAILED IT BACK TO THE OFFICE WHERE SHE WORKED.
"COURSE, THE PLACE WAS DESERTED THAT TIME OF THE NIGHT.
"AMBROSE ELLIS-- THAT'S THE GUY THAT OWNS THE PLACE SHE WORKS AT--WAS GONE. LONG GONE!
"THE DRAWER IN HER DESK WAS LEFT OPEN.
2:05
"WE FIGURE THAT'S WHERE
GOT THE GUN FROM.
"WE GOT OURSELVES A MYSTERIOUS CALL, OH, 'BOUT 3:15, AND WHEN WE GOT TO THE PLACE--

"ANYHOW, LEROY SAID HE LEFT HER SIDE AT TWO IN THE MORNIN'--
"--AND IT WOULD APPEAR SHE HAD HIM FOOLED, 'CAUSE SHE NEVER DID GO INSIDE THE HOUSE. THAT'S NOT LIKE A LADY WITHOUT ANY BOTHERS.
IT WAS A SMALL GUN, BUT CLOSE... WELL, I'M NOT NA PAIN YOU FOLKS WITH THE DETAILS.
"BULLET PASSED RIGHT THROUGH HER TEMPLE.
"MAYBE THERE'S SOME COMFORT KNOWING SHE HADDA DIE QUICK.
'S HAD ONE'A THEM CY-SMANTZY CLOCKS T FLIP THE TIME.
"--IT WAS ALREADY OVER.
"CLOCK WAS STOPPED AT 2:06. LOTTA GRIEF CAME TO YOU FOLKS AN' LEROY... NOT TO MENTION OTHER FRIENDS...
2:06
"...THOUGH NONE OF THEM KNEW TILL 'MORNIN' LIGHT HOW EMPTY'A DAY IT TRULY WAS GONNA BE.
TATE FINISHES, AND THE ROOM IS SILENT LIKE THAT OF A WAKE.

IT IS NIGHTFALL, AND THE MAIN EVENT OF THIS GATHERING SHOULD COMMENCE. IT IS, AFTER ALL, A RECRUITING RALLY.

THE IMPERIAL WIZARD, HARRISON K. STRYKER, SURVEYS THE ASSEMBLAGE. THE ATTENDANCE IS SATISFACTORY... EVEN IF MOST OF THE PEOPLE HAVE EXPECTED A COUNTY FAIR EXHIBITION. THEY SEEM TO MISS THE COTTON CANDY AND THE GUT-BUSTER RIDES.

THE BORED AND DISCONTENTED STIR AMIDST THEIR FELLOWS... LIKELY CANDIDATES FOR THE INITIATION RITES.

STRYKER SMILES. THERE ARE A LOT OF YOUNG PEOPLE ATTENDING THE MEETING. A GOOD SIGN. A VERY GOOD SIGN.

NOW THAT THE CHAPLAIN HAS FINISHED OUR PRAYER, IT IS MY PLEASURE TO ADDRESS YOU GOOD PEOPLE...

...TO LET YOU KNOW THAT YOUR PLIGHT IN AMERICA TODAY IS NOT AS HOPELESS AS YOU FEAR--

--AND TO GIVE YOU MEANS TO FIGHT YOUR FEARS!!

YOU WILL NOTE THAT WE DON'T COVER OUR FACES THIS NIGHT. WE ARE PROUD... DO YOU HEAR?...PROUD OF WHAT WE ARE.

AND TONIGHT, WE GIVE YOU THE OPPORTUNITY TO JOIN OUR RANKS... AND THE CHANCE TO CONQUER THOSE FEARS.

I WANT TO DEMONSTRATE A POINT... ONE THAT AFFECTS EACH WHITE IN THIS AUDIENCE.
PLEASE WELCOME MRS. CRANDALL AND HER SON, JIMMY.
NOW I ASK YOU, WHO WILL FIGHT FOR THIS WHITE CHILD... IF WHITE PEOPLE DON'T FIGHT FOR HIS RIGHTS?!
WHO WILL PUT BREAD AND MEAT ON YOUR TABLES TO FEED YOUR CHILDREN... IF BLACKS CONTINUE TO STEAL THE JOBS THAT RIGHTFULLY BELONG TO YOU AND YOUR SONS?!
FOR THE EMPLOYERS FEAR ALSO. THEY FEAR REPERCUSSIONS IF THEY DO NOT GIVE THOSE JOBS TO THE BLACKS.
AND ALL OF YOU KNOW... I SPEAK THE TRUTH!
WILL YOU LISTEN TO THAT? AND THOSE PEOPLE ARE PROBABLY EATING IT UP.
PEOPLE USE DECEIT AND TREACHERY... EVEN ON PEOPLE THEY MIGHT ONCE HAVE LOVED. THEY STOP SEEING THEM AS PEOPLE.
YEAH... AND THEY SEE THEMSELVES AS THE GOOD GUYS. THEY WEAR THE WHITE HATS. TRY FIGHTING SOMEBODY CONVINCED OF THAT.
YOU'LL NEVER GET THROUGH TO THEM.
BUT ONE MUST TRY, RIGHT, KEVIN? ELSE... WHY ARE WE HERE?

WHEN OUR MEMBERSHIP HAS THRIVED WE WILL ESTABLISH A LEGAL MOVEMENT THAT WILL RESOUND WITH OUR VOICES. AND ONCE AGAIN, WE WILL HAVE TRUE REPRESENTATION IN OUR GOVERNMENT.
OUR COUNTRY AND OUR ARTS ARE CONTROLLED BY ANTI-CHRIST JEWS WHO BRAND THE KLAN WITH IMAGES OF SLAUGHTERING THE SUPPOSEDLY OPPRESSED BLACK MAN.
THAT'S QUITE AN ACCUSATION. YOU GIVING ANYBODY THE FREEDOM TO COUNTER THAT?

ARE YOU OPEN FOR A QUESTION AND ANSWER SESSION?
EVEN IF YOU'RE NOT... LET ME ASK JUST ONE --WHY DID YOU BURN THIS MAN ON A CROSS TWO WEEKS BACK?
A CROSS IS SUPPOSED TO BE A DECENT SYMBOL, LEAST THAT'S WHAT I WAS TAUGHT.
WHAT KIND OF TERROR TACTICS ARE THESE, MISTER? ARE YOU ATTEMPTING TO TURN THIS PEACEFUL RALLY INTO A RIOT WITH YOUR ABSURDLY SLANDEROUS ATTACKS?
WE HAVE NOT BURNED ANY MAN.

NO!? WHY NOT LET THESE GOOD PEOPLE JUDGE FOR THEMSELVES?
WOULD YOU LIKE TO SEE HIS BLISTERED FLESH?
THAT SHOULD BE TESTIMONY ENOUGH!

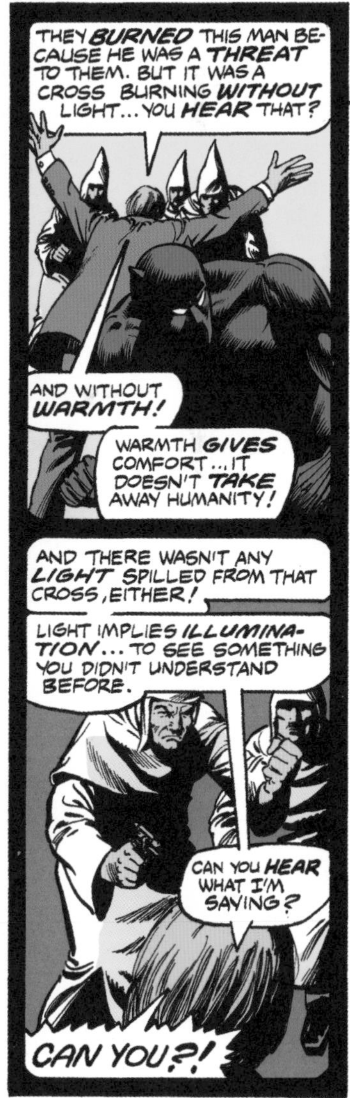
THEY BURNED THIS MAN BECAUSE HE WAS A THREAT TO THEM. BUT IT WAS A CROSS BURNING WITHOUT LIGHT... YOU HEAR THAT?
AND WITHOUT WARMTH!
WARMTH GIVES COMFORT... IT DOESN'T TAKE AWAY HUMANITY!
AND THERE WASN'T ANY LIGHT SPILLED FROM THAT CROSS, EITHER!
LIGHT IMPLIES ILLUMINATION... TO SEE SOMETHING YOU DIDN'T UNDERSTAND BEFORE.
CAN YOU HEAR WHAT I'M SAYING?
CAN YOU?!

I'M SORRY TO RUIN YOUR "GOOD TIME." AND I KNOW THIS ISN'T ANYTHING YOU WANT TO HEAR.
I'LL GIVE IT TO YOU STRAIGHT... THOSE BURNING CROSSES ...THEY'RE ...THEY'RE A CORRUPTION... YEAH, THAT'S THE WORD I WANT...
...A CORRUPTION OF THE WORD "LIGHT"!
AND THE NIGHT'S DARK ENOUGH ALREADY WITHOUT BLACKENING IT FURTHER, PEOPLE.

YOU'RE SICK, BOY! SOMEBODY'S GONNA HAFTA DO SOMETHIN' 'BOUT ALL YOUR RANTIN' 'N' RAVIN!
WE CAN'T HAVE YOU GOIN' 'BOUT SCARIN' THE FOLKS!

AND I CANNOT HAVE YOU MAIMING A MAN--
--MERELY BECAUSE HE HAS SPOKEN WITH PASSION!

YOU COME HERE LOOKING FOR TROUBLE... AND YOU'VE SURELY FOUND...
...IIITT.
WE CAME HERE LOOKING FOR THE TRUTH--
--AND NOT A DISTORTION FABRICATED FROM HALF-TRUTHS.

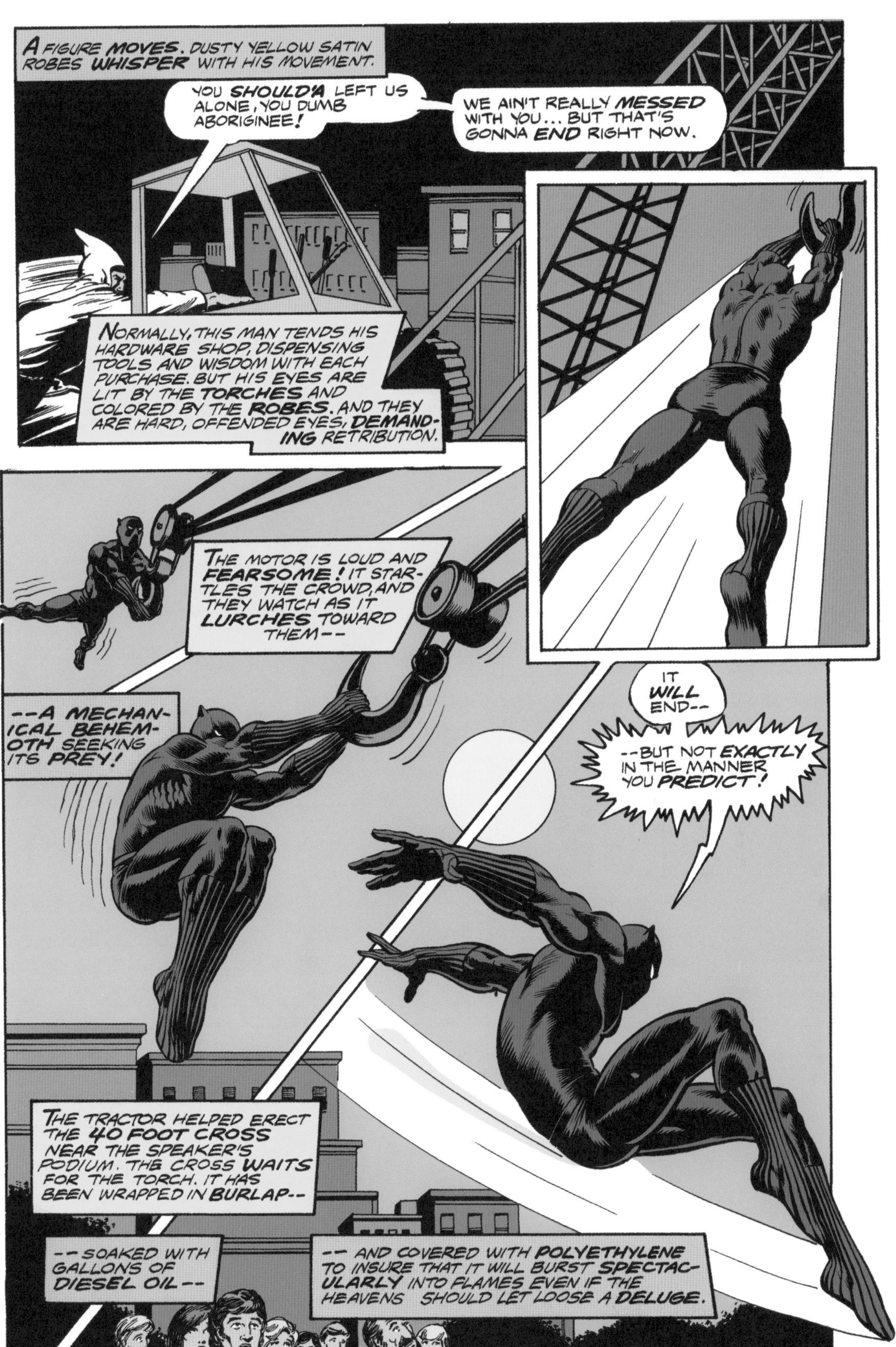
A FIGURE MOVES. DUSTY YELLOW SATIN ROBES WHISPER WITH HIS MOVEMENT.
YOU SHOULD'A LEFT US ALONE, YOU DUMB ABORIGINEE!
WE AIN'T REALLY MESSED WITH YOU... BUT THAT'S GONNA END RIGHT NOW.
NORMALLY, THIS MAN TENDS HIS HARDWARE SHOP, DISPENSING TOOLS AND WISDOM WITH EACH PURCHASE. BUT HIS EYES ARE LIT BY THE TORCHES AND COLORED BY THE ROBES. AND THEY ARE HARD, OFFENDED EYES, DEMANDING RETRIBUTION.
THE MOTOR IS LOUD AND FEARSOME! IT STARTLES THE CROWD, AND THEY WATCH AS IT LURCHES TOWARD THEM--
--A MECHANICAL BEHEMOTH SEEKING ITS PREY!
IT WILL END--
--BUT NOT EXACTLY IN THE MANNER YOU PREDICT!
THE TRACTOR HELPED ERECT THE 40 FOOT CROSS NEAR THE SPEAKER'S PODIUM. THE CROSS WAITS FOR THE TORCH. IT HAS BEEN WRAPPED IN BURLAP--
--SOAKED WITH GALLONS OF DIESEL OIL--
--AND COVERED WITH POLYETHYLENE TO INSURE THAT IT WILL BURST SPECTACULARLY INTO FLAMES EVEN IF THE HEAVENS SHOULD LET LOOSE A DELUGE.

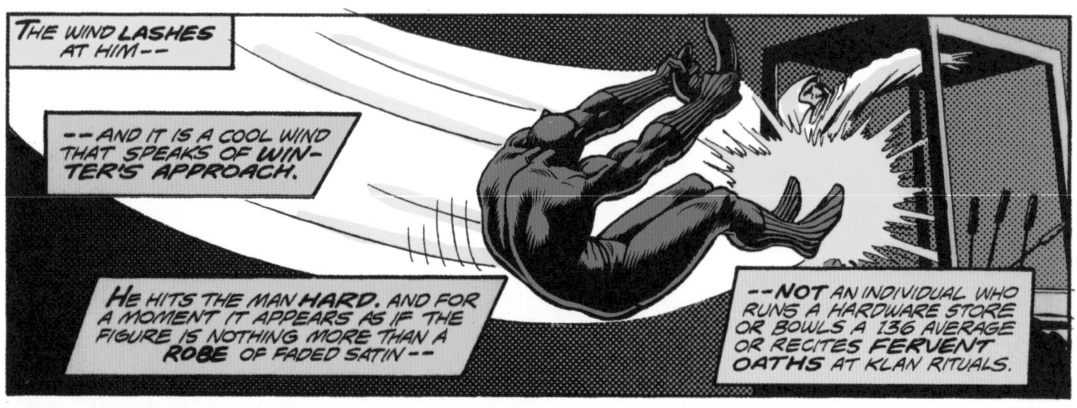
THE WIND LASHES AT HIM--
--AND IT IS A COOL WIND THAT SPEAKS OF WINTER'S APPROACH.
HE HITS THE MAN HARD. AND FOR A MOMENT IT APPEARS AS IF THE FIGURE IS NOTHING MORE THAN A ROBE OF FADED SATIN--
--NOT AN INDIVIDUAL WHO RUNS A HARDWARE STORE OR BOWLS A 136 AVERAGE OR RECITES FERVENT OATHS AT KLAN RITUALS.

JUST A ROBE, CLOAKING INDIVIDUALITY.
THE PANTHER'S FLESH BURNS AGONIZINGLY. THE SWING HAS STRETCHED THE TENDER, HEALING WOUNDS.

HE BLINKS AGAINST THE ONSLAUGHT OF PAIN--
--AND CLIMBS TO THE TOP OF THE CAB, SEEKING KEVIN AND THE LYNNE FAMILY AMID THE CROWD.
THE WOUNDS BEGIN TO THROB--BLOOD MESSAGES RUSHING SIGNALS TO THE BRAIN.

TOO SOON! THE MESSAGE CROWDS OUT HIS OTHER SENSES. TOO SOON. THE BODY SCREAMS WITH THE PUNISHMENT IT HAS TAKEN.
A HAND RAISES FROM THE CROWD. THE GESTURE GOES UNNOTICED.
THE NARROW "V" OF THE SIGHT IS FILLED WITH THE BACK OF THE PANTHER'S HEAD!
BENEATH HIS COWL IS HAIR AND FLESH AND BONE AND BLOOD. ONE BULLET WILL TEAR THROUGH ALL OF THAT.

AN ASSASSIN'S TICKET TO GLORY: THE SLOW RETRACTION OF A GUN HAMMER--
--THE CALCULATED SQUEEZING OF THE TRIGGER--
--AND THOUGHTS BLASTED INTO DEATH'S INFINITY!

YOU AIN'T GONNA KILL HIM, DAMN YOU!
HE AIN'T DONE NUTHIN' THAT DESERVES KILLIN'... AN' IF YOU PEOPLE REALLY DID KILL MY LITTLE GIRL... I'LL MAKE SURE THAT'S THE LAST THING YOU TAKE FROM ME.
THIS HERE'S LLOYD LYNNE SPEAKING. YOU GOT MY NAME RIGHT? LLOYD LYNNE! YOU REMEMBER IT... AND YOU REMEMBER MY LITTLE GIRL'S NAME, TOO.
MR. LYNNE!
GET OUT OF HIS LINE OF FIRE!

THE GUN SWINGS TOWARD LLOYD'S HEAD AS THE LAST OF THE DECK OF CARDS FLUTTERS TOWARD THE EARTH. A JACK OF HEARTS ON A QUEEN OF SPADES. KINGS FILLING EMPTY SPACES. INEVITABLE LOSS CONQUERED BY A SINGLE UPTURNED CARD.
GONE. THE CARDS ARE SCATTERED.

THEY ARE TRAMPLED BENEATH THE CROWD. THE HOUSE IS BANK-RUPT!
BUT ONE LAST CARD HAS YET TO BE PLAYED!

GUESS I OUGHTTA THANK YOU, HUH? YOU SAVED MY CARCASS, THAT'S FOR SURE.
NOT BEFORE YOU RISKED YOUR OWN LIFE TO SAVE MINE.
I FIGGER YOU DON'T THINK MUCH'A ME.
I THINK A GREAT DEAL OF YOU, MR. LYNNE.

DO YOU NOW? WELL... MEBBE I MEANT... I SOMETIMES DON'T THINK MUCH'A ME. BUT THAT'S NO NEVER MIND, I GUESS.
SEE, I GOT TO THINKIN' ...WATCHIN' YOU... AND LISTENING TO THIS REPORTER FELLA ALL THE TIME GIVIN' HIS SERMONS... THAT MAYBE I SHOULD'A FOUGHT MORE--
--AND MAYBE THERE'S SOMETHIN' TO WIN IF YOU DO. LEAST-WAYS, DON'T SEEM LIKE YOU'LL LOSE YOURSELF.
MR. LYNNE, YOU ARE BEGIN-NING TO MAKE KEVIN AND I APPEAR INELOQUENT.
NOW WHAT'S THAT S'POSED TO MEAN?
IT MEANS, WE'RE GLAD YOU'RE WITH US, MR. LYNNE.
THE ENTERTAINMENT IS OVER. THE TIRED AND DISCONTENT FADE INTO THE SEPTEMBER NIGHT--
--WAITING FOR OCTOBER'S RESURRECTION!

NEXT THE SOUL STRANGLER! AND THE BLACK PANTHER FIGHTING IN 1876! HOW DO WE MANAGE THAT? CHECK US OUT NEXT ISSUE!

APPENDIX ONE

# "PANTHER'S CHRONICLES" BY DON MCGREGOR

This essay by Don McGregor first appeared as the *Introduction to Marvel Masterworks: The Black Panther*, Volume One.

# PANTHER'S CHRONICLES
## BY DON MCGREGOR

The amazing thing is that these comics you hold in your hands exist at all.

Good, bad, or indifferent, in the 1970s, when these were originally written and drawn, there was only a short time frame between 1973 and 1976 where there was a tiny gap at Marvel Comics where this kind of book, and a few others, could become a reality.

In the early '70s, the Marvel Comics Universe was expanding rapidly. New titles were continually being added to the line. It is almost a rule in this industry that there are always too few people to truly oversee the production of all the books a company puts out. By 1973, new people were being added to the staff, as not only new monthly and bi-monthly comics were being added, but Marvel was exploding into the black-and-white comics magazine market, as well.

By 1977, it is my sincere belief that you would never be holding this book in your hands. These stories would have been weeded out and never allowed to grow.

It was a different time, the early '70s, and what many people take for granted now in storytelling media—and especially what can or can't be in comics—then was *verboten*. Writing about race, or sexual preferences other than heterosexual were virtually nil. In the world of comics these and other topics were considered a taboo.

Many of the rules in comics are unwritten, but get inside the conclave, and they are there, some insidiously, some absurd, some shrewd. But the rules are there, and it didn't take long for me to begin to realize they shaped what I could do as a storyteller.

In 1972 I had been hired to work on staff as a proofreader. I came from Rhode Island, and I'd been telling and writing stories and loving comics as long back as I have active memory.

I have read that I was saved from life as a security guard when I was offered the job at Marvel Comics. I did work as a security guard. I also worked for my grandfather's company, who printed, among other things, the patches the astronauts wore on their flights to the moon.

I had worked in a bank, for a while, where I observed the offices and class structure of power and money. I worked at the Providence *Journal*, and reviewed books of authors like Evan Hunter, whom I loved dearly, and who influenced me greatly as a writer.

I worked at a movie theater where I got to view all the parts of unrated films before they were shown to Rhode Island's appointed "civics committee" that would decide what could be seen and not seen in the State. You didn't have to accede to their dictates; they couldn't force you; but when license renewal time came around you might find it hard to get it renewed. Should have prepared me for the travel to New York and the world of comics, but somehow I guess I believed all the Bullpen Bulletin pages, and that this place of writers and artists would be different.

I worked for the National Guard in the Military Police in a time when riots exploded in this country. I could have retired at 45, full medical benefits, and a government retirement program. Except you can get court-martialed for telling a lieutenant, "I'm tired of being subservient to mental incompetence," saluting, and doing an about face out of his office.

I write about these jobs, and the fact that when the offer came to work at Marvel Comics I was living in a three bedroom house, with a fireplace, with a garage, with a bay window view of a pond with lily pads, within three walking blocks of a private stretch of Atlantic Ocean beach.

I had my daughter, Lauren, who was about three years old at the time.

I walked away from it all for a $125.00 a week job at Marvel Comics.

I did that. No one "saved" me from a life as a security guard. I'm just setting the record straight here. I could have simply stayed within that safe place, writing for Warren Magazines, trekking around New York City to magazines like *Mike Shayne*, *Mystery Magazine*, and others, trying to sell my short stories.

I'd already proven I was a writer. I didn't need validation.

I came to Marvel Comics because I loved Marvel Comics. As the line burgeoned, one of my jobs was to read all the reprint titles. One of the titles was *Jungle Action*, a collection of jungle genre comics from the 1950s, mostly detailing white men and women saving Africans or being threatened by them.

I voiced a lament that I thought it was a shame that in 1973 Marvel was printing these stories, and couldn't we have a black African hero. I was not thinking of the Black Panther, and it was really a lament, because I was in no position to change anything.

Sometime later, during an editorial meeting, it was announced that several of the reprint titles would feature new material. Now, it was one of those unwritten rules that if you worked in editorial you would be given things to write, to supplement that $125.00 a week. It was at such a meeting that I learned I would be given Killraven (in *Amazing Adventures*) and *Jungle Action*, with the Black Panther in Wakanda, to write.

Thus began a profound three years, both professionally and personally, one of intense gratification as a storyteller, but also continual anxiety. It was an intense time; it was an exciting time. It was a time of fulfillment; it was a time of frustration. It was a time when the storyteller in me was challenged, again and again, and I learned, then, that a writer doesn't just have to make a decision of what kind of writer he/she will be, they will have to make that decision time after time, until their last story is written.

Jim Salicrup kindly lent me all the comics that featured the Black Panther, because mine were still back in Rhode Island, I guess. In those days, you could read every book with a character before starting to write a series. It would become part of what I would try to do. Learn what I liked, and learn what I didn't, and see what I could bring to a character, without violating its own mythos.

I immediately felt that the stories had to be about Wakandans, that already the Black Panther character had been compromised. Why would an African chieftain decide to be a school teacher in Harlem? And leave his people adrift, without leadership?

I also realized that Wakanda was a concept, but that detailing how the country worked had never been explored. On top of that, it would make me shake my head at how many white villains managed to locate this super secret society.

That meant, if the stories were situated in Wakanda, all the major characters would have to be Wakandan. And that meant all of the characters save one would be black. That was a decision that would cause me conflict during the unfolding of "Panther's Rage." An all-black cast in a comic book, from a major company, at that time? Wasn't happening.

Believe me, no one in the editorial hallowed halls was applauding this approach. In fact, I can't recall a single, encouraging word from editorial during the entire run of the series.

I realize now that it is part of who I am as a writer, but once undertaking a series, I was already concerned about what I would write about after "Panther's Rage." Before I'd written a single page, I had decided these should be done as big visual stories, and that when this storyline ended I would set the second in South Africa, with the Panther searching for his mother, and deal with the oppression of Apartheid.

I didn't know it at the time, but I had been given these two titles to write, because they were expected to die.

DC had trouble selling Tarzan by Joe Kubert, and jungle strips weren't considered big sellers in comics. I think there were high expectations for Killraven, but when there were three different writers and three different artists for the first three issues before I took over, it was seen as a death-knell for the series.

No one, including me, expected the reaction from the readers, from the fans, for these books, and they were invaluable voices for me in the maelstrom about them. I often wished some of the letter writers were in editorial (in time they would be), where I often felt isolated, and knew it was unwise to reveal anything you wanted to do as a storyteller. If you were told, "No," and you did it anyway, then you had committed an open act of defiance.

I learned, some time after these books were published, that what I hadn't been told was I'd been given the chance to write, and the books had failed, but that I could still stay on staff. When I learned this, in some darkened hours of late night, I found I could still be moved to tears at how manipulative so much of it was. I was learning about one-eyed jacks.

The reason people did not mind me on staff wasn't because I was particularly good at it, but I had no agenda to become editor-in-chief, or if I did, I was going about it in the most incomprehensible manner ever.

On the other hand, from the get-go, with the comics, I was lucky, because I met some terrific artists, who became friends, and more than that, allies, and beyond that, took all that anguish and determination I had as a writer and brought the stories visually to life. Only because Rich Buckler wanted to do the Panther and had believed in what I wanted to do, did he draw the first three chapters of "Panther's Rage." If Rich hadn't insisted they let him draw it, the title wasn't important enough, it wouldn't have an artist of his stature on it.

The only people I ever spoke to about these stories were the artists. They were the only ones who were in on what I hoped to do. Speak to other writers, they'd either want to tell you how to do it; or it would get to people who would say "No."

I knew right out of the gate that "Panther's Rage" would be like a chapter serial. You can see that approach in the first issue. T'Challa is actually thrown off a cliff. One of the edicts I am glad came down was that they didn't want only cliffhangers, which allowed each chapter to become a component of the whole.

I never told anyone but Rich that the entire series would be titled "Panther's Rage." If I had, I truly suspect it would not have been allowed. What I did was, I had the title logo photostatted, and when the finished art came in for the next chapter, I would shoot the logo down and paste it on the first page. Since *Jungle Action* was a low-priority book, it was seldom read until after it saw publication, and that's how the "Panther's Rage" came to be.

Originally, I know I recall this accurately, I had "Rage" planned for ten chapters. I'm not sure why, since I loved the old Republic serials, and traditionally they were comprised of twelve to thirteen chapters, which is what "Panther's Rage" did end up being. The series lengthened during the trek started in *Jungle Action* #12. I realized that I could not encompass all the locales and thematic elements that I wanted to explore in the series during the writing of those issues.

Rich Buckler helped me find a place to live in the Bronx, near where he lived. At night, I would go to Rich's place, and I would stand in Panther poses, while he drew. We designed pages together.

In *Jungle Action* #8, I wrote my first scene with Taku and Venomm, the first characters I ever wrote who were gay. I could not bring these characters out of the closet at the time. It is not enough for a writer to want to do something in this medium. You have to find a way that it can become a paper reality, held in hands, seen by eyes, read and experienced. I was already under the gun with the interracial aspect of Killraven, and the all-black cast in *Jungle Action*. If it had come out at that time that Taku and Venomm were homosexual, I have no doubt that when I was called into the inner sanctums that time, it could quite possibly be the last time I was called.

It wouldn't be until 1978, and *Detectives Inc.*, that I would find someone who would represent all kinds of people in comics. That was Eclipse's Dean Mullaney, and because of him, I was able to include gays in comics, outright, for the first time.

I had no political agenda in this, merely a human one. It always puzzled me that if the bottom color in comics was supposed to be green, why was there such abhorrence of diversity?

*Jungle Action* #8 was Rich's last Panther for a long while. The title page "Malice By Crimson Moonlight" was directly inspired by Steranko's *S.H.I.E.L.D.* double-page title spread for "Dark Moon Rise, Hell Hound Kill." We didn't do it as good.

In that issue I also did something crazy, but that I had to do if I wanted a book that wouldn't make me wince. I determined that I couldn't live with a five-page reprint in the back of the book. It would always be there, taunting me, stabbing me. I had to find a way that would make it so that the reprint stories wouldn't have to be used, but it couldn't cost the company money. With the help of friends like Alex Simmons, Jim Salicrup and Rich, I came up with ways to do back-up features—maps, pinups, story recaps. I know Alex worked on the finished drawings for T'Challa's Wakandan Palace, and was glad we could incorporate a toilet in the place. You take your victories where you can get them.

Doing these features would cause some hostility with some of the other writers. I could never have foreseen this. I was confronted, after working hours, by several irate writers. The consensus was that I was making them look bad. I was giving the company work for free. I understood their position. I also understood that I had to live with these books. I was giving everything I had to create them. I just wanted a book I didn't have to cringe every time I looked at it.

I did the backups for the readers. And me. And those outdated stories didn't have to be a part of *Jungle Action*.

I have no idea how Gil Kane came to draw *Jungle Action* #9. If some writers were angling to get off series when they felt sales figures were going down so some other writer would be on the title and get the blame, it makes my eyebrows rise that Gil was given "But Now The Spears Are Broken," on a book that was really still low priority, on which the fan mail was just beginning to increase and become more and more personal and analytical.

I do know that Danny Crespi, bless him, did the title page logo. He told me to tuck the art in the stack of production work he had and he would get to it. Danny was head of production then, and I think he and John Verpoorten took me under their wing, perhaps suspecting this place was going to swallow me up. I thank both of them for their kindness to me, when there were times I felt so isolated, in a place where I wanted to belong.

Issue #9's sequence where Zatama is murdered almost killed me as a writer.

Since I worked during the day on staff, I wrote the books at night. I don't know how many nights I worked on that scene. I hated everything that I wrote. It all sounded so trite. Each version seemed like I'd read it before. It was one of those times that made me hold my head so it wouldn't splatter and make me wonder what made me think I could be a writer.

Eventually, I settled for a caption from one draft, one from another, until it was something I could live with. I knew I had to get past the page. I feel, in looking back on it, that I wanted too much to come from Zatama's death, and I had not earned it as a writer.

But this is another thing the storyteller learns, that everyone reacts differently, and a couple of decades later, Jon Cooke, of *Comic Book Artist* magazine, would talk to me about how this page affected him. And I told him how it almost broke me as a writer.

So go figure.

My artistic luck held with *Jungle Action* #10. My old friend Billy Graham became the artist. Now I had an ally on both titles I was writing: Craig Russell on Killraven; Billy Graham on the Panther. Billy often gave me a place to stay when I was first trying to sell my stories in New York City. When the Billy Graham drawn *Sabre* run is finally collected I'll write about our many adventures during that time. Billy was one of the few truly Renaissance people I have ever met. He was effervescent, although that was often his word for me. I remember the momentous, dramatic first time we met; and I recall the last words we ever spoke together.

With Billy on "Panther's Rage" I could try any visual layout I wanted. Billy had no problem with it, and encouraged me to do so. Klaus Janson continued to ink the book; Glynis Oliver was coloring the book, and I lucked out there, too, because if Glynis hadn't wanted to do the book, her talent would have been considered wasted on "Panther's Rage." Glynis didn't stay on the book because of me, although we always got along famously, but because the Wakandan locale was so different from much of what she had to color, which was primarily New York City.

I had definite ideas about the color in "Panther's Rage." The moon was not supposed to ever be a pale yellow. There was always a Frank Frazetta moon in the sky, as I would tell Billy and Glynis. And the ambiance of Wakanda should always show. It was distinct, magical reality. There were certain kinds of blues that I felt were perfect for the Panther, and others that would dull his figure in night, so lighting on him was always of key import to me. And Billy and Glynis got it.

In *Jungle Action* #11, I had a sequence where I wanted the panels to fade out into the past, and later to fade in back to the present. When you're dealing with a complex visual like that, you have to confer with everybody at their separate phase of the book, so they know what it is you are trying to pull off, and what they need to do to make it work.

I took a lot of extra time working on that sequence, but this brings up a catch-22. How much time does the creative person devote to the work? A writer gets paid the same amount of money for spending ten minutes on a page or spending two days.

I was never as lucky with lettering as I was with art and coloring. But I understand that this was a low priority book. If I were a letterer and I had a book that paid a certain amount of money for two words or 22 words, or six balloons vs. 13 balloons, I can understand why a letterer would say, "Keep me away from, Don!"

This brings me to another aspect that I had to think about right from the beginning. These were bi-monthly books. If I wrote Taku or W'Kabi out for a single issue, for instance, that meant that the readers did not see that character for four months. If I omitted one of them for two issues there would be half a year that the audience didn't see those characters. A half a year is a long time to ask the reader to have any kind of emotional commitment to the character.

That was always a factor. I had thirteen pages in the beginning. How do you get the characters in there, have a scene that is theirs? How do you reintroduce that character in the new chapter so it isn't something the devoted followers have read before, yet make it so new readers know who they are with.

I had to face that question each issue.

The upside to creating your own supporting cast was that you could more or less do things with them without having to ask permission. If you wanted the Panther and Monica to marry, you'd have to get a committee to agree that such a thing could happen. If W'Kabi lost an arm, that was considered your character, and you didn't have to consult to do it. Another unwritten rule to be learned at that time.

The fan mail was increasing. It was very exciting and again, intense. People were evaluating the books, relating to them. A storyteller can't ask for more than that.

I sometimes felt I was climbing a steep mountain. The more acclaim the books would get, the more rewarding the efforts. Yet, there was a part of me that feared that with the next book, that would be it, I would have stepped off the edge of the mountain, to plummet into the abyss.

The reactions from some other writers in the business were bizarre. "How come I don't get letters like this?" How the hell would I know? I don't write the letters. Others said, "Too many type-written letters, means your books are going to die!"

The books that were believed to be dead, and somehow were still surviving.

The letter writers gave me hope when I was back in the lonely hours writing the books.

Of course, you may think you know what people are going to get from a story, but during the course of creating these books, one of the other things I learned is, you can never tell what someone will get from a story.

In "The God Killer" I was sure it examined the nature of religious belief, and that we all have a potential to be the God Killer of what we learned in our youth, or that we sustain that belief and become committed to it. We received one letter threatening to bomb the Marvel Comics offices because this anonymous reader believed I was advocating that all black people kill all whites!

Whoa!

I played with something besides the Panther in issue #13. For the first year of the series we always saw W'Kabi as T'Challa's counselor of War, and in that context of W'Kabi's playing devil's advocate to T'Challa. In comics, often readers perceive what a character's purpose is in the series. We had never seen W'Kabi outside of his work; in this issue I introduced his wife, Chandra, and the domestic turbulence in their home, and its affect on their kids.

Readers responded. Interviewers would ask many questions about it. People began to see W'Kabi in a new way, and would have to re-examine who he was. Kind of like real life.

I would return to this theme later in *Detectives Inc: A Terror of Dying Dreams*, and it would help inspire Malcolm Deeley to publish a book titled *Poets Against Abuse*, to help raise money for victims of domestic violence.

Gil Kane penciled all the series' dinosaur covers. I was told that was because Gil liked to draw dinosaurs. Everybody has their own thing.

In the original coloring for *Jungle Action* #15, when I saw Billy's art, I thought the panels where T'Challa was tied to the cactus were strips of his outfit over his shoulders. Glynis colored it as blood, and I thought, that makes it more real. But someone complained in the Bullpen that we were doing "comics for sailors," whatever that meant, and people were suddenly offended.

Now, along the way, issue after issue, editorial wanted to know where the white people were. Always, "Where are the white people?" And my response was, "This is a hidden, technologically advanced African nation. Where are the white people supposed to come from?!"

They wanted the Avengers in there. They wanted white people helping the black people out. I'm sure part of their reasoning was, if you guest-star the established white characters, you have bigger sales. I have no idea if that is true. Maybe. Maybe not. But here's the thing, we were doing something unheard of in comics, and the books hadn't died, as predicted, they were still limping along, or however they were selling. And maybe, just maybe, we were giving something to some people somewhere. I felt there could be something of importance about this.

It was my decision. I did not want the black hero to have to rely on white heroes to save the day for him. I stood firm on it, then. I stand firm on it now.

I did not foresee the reaction, though, when Kantu comes to T'Challa's aid, and kills his father's murderer. To me, T'Challa had won the important fights we all face as individuals, and there was triumph for both him and Kantu. But damn, was there agitation at this unrevealed final moment!

As I wrote earlier, this was a tumultuous time for me, professionally and personally. I often felt as if I were in that old circus act, the one where the performer spins plates on top of tall sticks. I felt I'd spin one plate, the writing; spin another, my marriage; the editorial job, another; but whatever plates weren't being spun were wobbling.

I quit the editorial job toward the end of "Panther's Rage." Now, here's the upside of being on staff. You can always be around, and it's hard for people to screw around with your books without you trying to save them somehow. If you're not there, anything can happen.

But my life was coming apart, and I knew I couldn't keep this pace going, so I thought I could save my marriage and quit. It didn't help.

I also knew I could not write about South Africa and Apartheid at that time. It would require too much research, and I was already overextended, physically and emotionally. I decided to write The Panther vs. The Klan instead. It was America's bi-centennial, and I would joke that it was my birthday gift.

And there was an uproar about the Klan.

My response was, "Hey, you wanted white people, I gave you white people. There's no satisfying you folks."

Billy called and asked me if I really wanted to do this. "They aren't going to come get me up in Harlem, Don."

I said to Billy, 'Oh, come on, Billy. They can take a joke, can't they?"

"No," Billy replied, "they can't, Don."

I could not oversee that series the way I had "Panther's Rage." My marriage ended. I was going to court to make sure I got to see my daughter, Lauren. The day I moved out of the house, I came back to my apartment only to hear the phone ringing. It was my ex-wife telling me I had to head up to Rhode Island, that my dad had had a heart attack and they didn't know if he was going to make it through the next day.

I write about this, because as the books are being produced, all of your life is being affected. I had always seen "The Panther vs. The Klan" story as being about separatist groups. Not just the Klan. But what I saw happening in America, the groups who felt their way was the only way, the only right way, and that the violence they used against other people was justified. I always intended to bring other characters like Wind Eagle and the Soul Strangler into the mix.

I think the separatist theme is only intensified, and more valid these days.

To my recollection, in the color comics, the only time I came into conflict with the Comics Code Authority was on issue #21's Panther burning on the cross cover. They claimed that the cover was sacrilegious and showcased torture and bondage. All true. And all valid for a writer to examine.

Originally, T'Challa was tied back on the cross, and as penciled by Rich Buckler, it captured the pain and horror of the moment. It was moving. It was startling. The cover that was published has super-hero drama, but destroys everything I tried to build up within the first pages of "A Cross Burning Darkly, Blackening The Night."

I loved the opening line, and still do: "This is not a symbolic Christ figure."

There was only so much of this type of thing being done in comics in those days. I wanted the hurt and loss of human life caught. Some folks think being a writer is glamorous. Certainly not the days you spend trying to experience burning, or being tear gassed, or…well, you get the idea. It's long and it's painful. I think a lot of people cared about T'Challa, and the cruelty and inhumane treatment to someone they cared about would have a visceral impact that would stay long after they'd put the comic down.

Now, some will claim that my writing about the Klan killed the series. That sales then dropped. That may be the case.

But I would like to offer one different approach that could have been tried, and may have worked or may not have worked. If the people hadn't been so afraid of the subject matter, so hostile to my doing it, if those in charge had gone to the outside media and made them aware of what comics were now handling in terms of subject matter, maybe it would have helped sales.

When I was writing "Panther's Quest" in 1989, Jim Salicrup suggested we go down to the promotion people. Jim had no stake in this. It wasn't a book he was editing. He just knew that Nelson Mandela was in New York, and maybe promotion could get a column in the news about Marvel doing a series on South Africa and Apartheid. The woman was needlessly scornful to Jim. There were only certain ways to promote comics. She wanted me to go to a signing that was happening that day, on a book I had nothing to with, and take time away from the creators who were there promoting their book, a book I knew nothing about. That's what she knew how to do; and she didn't want to have to explore a new way of promotion.

I'm just saying, maybe if the Klan storyline had been embraced rather than feared, maybe the ending wouldn't have been the same.

Or maybe it would.

When I was taken off the Panther, I was told it was because I was too close to the black experience.

I looked at my white hands.

Later, someone said that the editor was just treating me like a jilted girlfriend, and that "Mr. Sincerity," me, wanted to believe it. I don't know how this person knows the conversation took place, because there was just the two of us present when it occurred.

However, I knew the books were gone. And it was in a time when I was fighting to see my daughter, going to court, facing things I never knew I'd have to face. A lot of that is a grey time for me. Living in Rhode Island, in that house? I scarcely recalled what daily life was like then. The time period during the divorce and the comics' cancellation are fog enshrouded. I suspect my friends recall them more vividly than I do.

And T'Challa was gone. At the time, I thought forever.

I was wrong. The Panther would come back into my life. In the '80s. But that's another story. There's always another story. Hopefully one you'll see in a volume like this.

Be kind to each other. Be kind to yourselves. And hang in there!

Don McGregor

**2010**

# DEDICATION:

This is for my Grandson,

NIKOLAS MOURITZEN

Whose Mommy was only around three to five years old when these books were written.

I rocked him in one arm for nights when he was two weeks old, which he will never remember, until my arm ached from the elbow down.

And he'll probably never recall the affectionate nicknames, Nick-At-Night and Red Alert Nick.

But he might recall learning to swim up in that special lake my daughter and all our family love.
And in some later year, he might enjoy having this book dedicated to him.

And for
My Granddaughter,

MIA ISABELLA McGREGOR

Who is only one but already loves to grab books and look at pictures with her large, beautiful eyes that capture the heart and bring smiles to faces and that hopefully, sometimes, when she is older, this book will bring a smile to her face, and maybe she'll have some small remembrance of pointing at me and saying, "Baby! Baby!" and me asking her, "Who's the baby? You? Or me?"

## APPENDIX TWO

# *JUNGLE ACTION #7*

# PLOT SYNOPSIS

This appendix features reproductions of pages from Don McGregor's first typescripts of the *Jungle Action* #7 plot synopsis.

DEATH REGIMENTS BENEATH WAKANDA

by Don McGregor
2121 Grand Concourse
APT 6H
Bronx, N.Y.

PAGE ONE: Three small panels run down the left hand side of the page, inside of which are either stats from specific panels from last issue's PANTHER'S RAGE, or small silhouette shots representing incidents from last issue. Copy narrates what has gone before. Atop those three panels, a circular shape, the Panther astride it, in which reads PANTHER'S RAGE CONCLUDES.

The huge burst panel shows Killmonger throwing the Panther over the falls.

PAGES TWO and THREE: Both pages combine in one effect, showing the brutal descent of the Panther from top to bottom of the falls. Panic rushes in at him along with the sweeping surge of water, but the Panther fights both the panic and his downward sweep. He kicks himself off jutting rocks, strategically holds his breath past the breaking point, takes the few collisions that he cannot avoid in places that will not break bones.

Killmonger leaves the scene when the Panther is out of sight and calls Kazibe and Tayete to follow him back to the settlement. Now that the Panther is out of the way, their plans can surge forward. Confusion will rein in Wakanda over their chieftain's death, and during that confusion Killmonger will strengthen his stronghold over Wakanda.

PAGE FOUR: Idyllic sight at the edge of the RIVER OF GRACE AND WISDOM. The river flows lightly here. WE open into scene with small panels which widen into major establishing panel. MONICA LYNNE stands upon the stone steps leading down into the inviting water. With her, is one of T'Challa's court hand-maidens, TANZIKA. Tanzika is a lovely young lady herself, dressed in flowing white robes. But the attitude between the two is reserved and only superficially congenial. Tanzika, as with most other Wakandas, are putout by the Panther's reappearance, bringing along this outsider, a commoner at that, to their realm.

Tanzika tells Monica she may bathe here. If she needs help later, Tanzika tells her she will be under the nearby pagoda. Monica slips off her robe and goes into the river. While she washes, she is unaware that a dark figure, OUR HERO, floats toward her, lying face down in the water. At the last moment, she sights him, pulls him from the water and onto the shore. WE do not know if he is alive or dead here.

DEATH REGIMENTS BENEATH WAKANDA - SYNOPSIS Pg. 2.

PAGE FIVE: WE open on a pair of eyes, and reflected in those pupils are serpents heads. In the next panel, WE see a pair of hands moving almost hypnotically and there is a huge, terrifying reptile swaying before the hand.

KILLMONGER, TAYETE and KAZIBE walk onto the scene and WE see full figure for the first time, the impressive sight of HORATION VENOMM. Tayete and Kazibe react startledly to the sight of this man who already has one serpent wrapped about him.

WE are in a village area, and Venomm is inside a fenced off area where there are cages of reptiles. Small bowls contain potions inside these cages. AS WE watch the remaining serpent crawls toward the kneeling Venomm and wraps itself about the muscular, white figure. Kazibe shakes his head. "I haven't ever gotten used to that guy," he admits, to which Killmonger grins.

PAGE SIX: Venomm walks over to Killmonger. Killmonger tells him the Panther is dead. "We no longer move forward haltingly, Horatio! Our major obstacle--turned out to be no obstacle at all. I promised you a place where you could carry on your reptillian practices, but also a place where you would be accepted. That place is here. The time is now!"

Killmonger tells Venomm to return to the minds. "If the Wakandians think the death of their leader is startling, wait till they see what else we've been up to. And while overseeing the minin operations, you might also make sure that the death regiments prepare for the coming battles."

Venomm agrees, leaves and Kazibe mutters about trusting this white man with the ugly face. Killmonger lays waste to Kazibe. "There was a time when I heard such talk daily, Kazibe...except the talk was about <u>my</u> flesh...You should beware, lest Horation ever hear your sentiments. He does not wear those serpents for...decoration!"

PAGE SEVEN: Back in Central Wakanda, just outside of <u>TRANQUILITY TEMPLE</u>. Huge flames leap up from ornately carved fireplaces. It is the scene of a feast, <u>wild exotic dishes</u> served to T'Challa, Monica, W'KABI, TAKU, and others. Sitting in the crowd is <u>ZATAMA</u>, ayouthful, rebellious figure who isn't much in accord with what the Panther is saying.

The Panther is dressed in ceremonial costume, complete with feathers and elaborate design. He has survived the falls, but bandages are wrapped about his chest. And now, as they feast, the Panther tells them about Killmonger and WE flip into flashback, those panels contained inside the flames that <u>roast</u> the <u>delicacies</u> cooking in huge, open <u>tortoise shells</u>. "I knew him as N'JADAKA--not Killmonger. And I met first, back in the lands across these waters--but his origins are here! He told me that during Klaw's first attack upon Wakanda, the raid that killed my father, T'Chaka (SEE F.F. #53), Klaw's men attacked the smaller village sites, looting and killing many of the populace, kidnapping some of the young men as slaves to be used in mining the valuable Vibranium ore. N'Jadaka was among those captured.

PAGE EIGHT: The story continues, flashbacks scenes visually depicting the history lesson: "When I used Klaw's own weapon upon him, his men retreated, using those young men as hostages. N'Jadaka was among those, but soon after reaching American shores, he made good his escape."

"He was embittered even back then. Not having any idea how he could get back to Wakanda, or ever where it was located, he soon landed in an orphanage. His athletic ability, honed to an edge here, was exploited in his new home, and he managed a scholarship to a university. As black unrest and social upheaval dominated the AMERICAN scene and he joined a violent radical group. I learned much of this after he contacted me. When the Black Panther came to America to fight alongside the Avengers, he immediately knew whom I was and desired to return to his homeland. When he chose the name Erik Killmonger, I cannot guess, nor do I know how he has become so powerful in so few years. But he must be made to pay for the suffering he has caused!"

Now WE are back into the present and ZATAMA accuses. "Your only answer to all of this is violence, T'Challa!" Before T'Challa can argue, Taku interrupts. "My Chieftain, a lone white man has been sighted near BLACK WARRIOR FALLS!" T'Challa reacts.

PAGE NINE: "And I have a strong idea whom he might be," he mutters and is off, once again, Monica calling to him. Sunset is falling as WE cut scenes.

WE open on Kazibe and Tayete, walking beside the falls. Something looms above them, hidden in the overhead jungle foliage. Tayete strides arrogantly. "I'll tell you one thing, Kazibe, that Panther ought to thank his Gods that it was Killmonger that finished him off...I would not have been so merciful." A hand comes down, grips Tayete by the throat and lifts him right off the ground until he is face to face with the Panther. "Perhaps, then, I'll not be merciful either." Kazibe, still on the ground, moans. "I don't believe it! I refuse to believe it!" "I've waited for some of Killmonger's crew to pass here. These falls seem to hold much fascination for your leader and his employs." "You'd best let us go," Tayete says weakly. "The death regiments are only right behind us." "Death regiments?" The Panther muses. "Then perhaps they'll be more use than both of you." He flings Tayete down into Kazibe, knocking them both unconcious. Then he drags them into the foliage and secrets himself.

PAGE TEN: The death regiments, in full regalia, pass, unaware that the Panther lurks nearby. And he follows them as they disappear under the falls. Build for suspense. What is on the other side? The Panther enters.

DEATH REGIMENTS BENEATH WAKANDA SYNOPSIS PAGE FOUR

PAGE ELEVEN: A few small panels open the page as WE lead downward in a dark narrow passageway that opens into the huge panel of--A MINING OPERATION, UNDER THE SACRED MOUND OF VIBRANIUM. Killmonger's men are hollowing out from within. An incredible sight of bluish luminosity and errie design. One small panel is insert at the bottom of the page as a double pronged whip end wraps about the Panther's face and neck.

PAGE TWELVE: Pulled off balance, the Panther still lands on his feet as Venomm reveals himself. One of the snakes hisses, throws it's deadly poison at the Panther, who deftly avoids it and pulls Venomm, off balance. The Panther kicks between these deadly serpents. One lunges for his face and the Panther yanks himself aside and off a great cliff edge. Darkness and sure death beckon beneath him. And grinning, Venomm strides over and steps on one of the Panther's hands.

PAGE THIRTEEN: Now, the Panther does the incredible. The one hand that still holds earth, he suddenly lets go. The only thing holding him aloft is the fact that Venomm's boot is holding him there. If Venomm lifts that foot, the Panther plunges to his death.

But before, Venomm can do so, the Panther uses that free hand to reach powerfully upward, grabbing Venomm by his leg. He yanks Venomm over his head and the snakes fly downward. The Panther, still holding onto Venomm, whose life, at this moment, is entirely in the Panther's hands, climbs onto the ledge.

PAGE FOURTEEN: The Panther yanks Venomm up and lays into him savagely. Finally, when Venomm lies at his feet, the Panther stands over him, victorious. Grimly, he pulls Venomm up to him. "You and your leader, Killmomger, have spread terrorism over this land that is as corrosive as your name. In your mere passing, you have destroyed many lives. Some destroy in subtle ways, but you have left a wake of destruction--and I shall follow that trail, I shall take on any of Killmonger's aides...until we both stand face to face once more...~~andxtherexisxonlyxhimxandxI~~ and that time....shall be the final battle...for one of us!"

NEXT: AN EVIL MOST SUPERNATURAL
and
MALICE--she's too vicious for any fairy tale!

I have met many who destroy in a subtle manner—

Respect!
Speak not to me of respect.
To attain such one must first respect the human condition--
--and you and your leader have wantonly

# Suggestions for Further Reading

## BLACK PANTHER COLLECTIONS

Jack Kirby, Ed Hannigan, Peter B. Gillis, Denys Cowan, et al., *Black Panther Epic Collection: Revenge of the Black Panther*

This collection features Kirby's return to the Black Panther in 1977 with the character's first ongoing solo series. It also includes the conclusion of "The Panther vs. the Klan" story arc in *Marvel Premiere* (1979–1980) and a 1988 miniseries about T'Challa's encounters in South Africa.

Christopher Priest, Mark Texeira, et al., *Black Panther by Christopher Priest: The Complete Collection*

This multivolume set, which covers the Black Panther's longest continuous run, from 1998 to 2003, is widely embraced by critics for its sharply satirical reinvention of Marvel's super hero. These issues also introduce Everett K. Ross, Zuri, and the Dora Milaje.

Reginald Hudlin, Peter Milligan, John Romita Jr., et al., *Black Panther by Reginald Hudlin: The Complete Collection*

The comics in this collection from 2005 to 2008 recall the Black Panther's origins and enlarge T'Challa's family through his sister, Shuri, and a brief marriage to the X-Men's Storm.

David Liss, Francesco Francavilla, et al., *Black Panther: The Man Without Fear—The Complete Collection*

When T'Challa gives up his crown after the "Doomwar" event, he takes over for Daredevil and must defend Hell's Kitchen without the benefit of his powers in this run from 2010 to 2012.

Ta-Nehisi Coates, Brian Stelfreeze, and Chris Sprouse, *Black Panther, Vol. 1: A Nation Under Our Feet*

T'Challa returns to the throne in Wakanda in the hardcover collection of this first story arc by Coates, Stelfreeze, and Sprouse from 2016 to 2017. He confronts a new set of challenges from insurgent factions within his country, including the People and the Midnight Angels.

Roxane Gay, Ta-Nehisi Coates, Alitha Martinez, et al., *Black Panther: World of Wakanda*

This 2017 series centers the stories of Ayo and Aneka of the Midnight Angels, who are as devoted to each other as they are to Wakanda.

Ta-Nehisi Coates, Evan Narcisse, Paul Renaud, et al., *Rise of the Black Panther*

This 2018 series revisits T'Challa's youth and traces the early years of his path to the mantle of Black Panther.

Nnedi Okorafor, Aaron Covington, André Lima Araújo, et al., *Black Panther: Long Live the King*

The six-issue series from 2018 features stand-alone stories about the Black Panther.

Nnedi Okorafor, Vita Ayala, Leonardo Romero, et al., *Shuri: The Search for Black Panther*

The volume collects the issues from 2018 to 2019 in the first ongoing solo series about T'Challa's sister, Shuri. Wakanda's techno-scientific genius teams up with an ensemble of Marvel heroes including Iron Man, Spider-Man, and Ms. Marvel.

Kyle Baker, Vita Ayala, Juan Samu, and Arianna Florean, *Marvel Action: Black Panther*

Black Panther and Shuri work together to solve mysteries and defeat villains in these stories for younger audiences, which debuted in 2019.

## RESOURCES FOR STUDENTS AND SCHOLARS

Eli Boonin-Vail, "'The Body of the Nation': Ta-Nehisi Coates' *Black Panther* and the Black Literary Tradition," *Inks: The Journal of the Comics Studies Society* 4, no. 2 (2020): 135–55.

Todd Steven Burroughs, *Marvel's Black Panther: A Comic Book Biography, from Stan Lee to Ta-Nehisi Coates*. New York: Diasporic Africa Press, 2018.

andré carrington, "Desiring Blackness: A Queer Orientation to Marvel's Black Panther, 1998–2016," *American Literature* 90, no. 2 (2018): 221–50.

Julian C. Chambliss, "An Archetype or a Token?: The Challenge of the Black Panther," in *Marvel Comics into Film: Essays on Adaptations Since the 1940s*, eds. Matthew J. McEniry, Robert Moses Peaslee, and Robert G. Weiner. Jefferson, NC: McFarland & Company, 2016: 189–97.

Dennis Culver, *Marvel's Black Panther: The Illustrated History of a King: The Complete Comics Chronology*. San Rafael, CA: Insight Editions, 2018.

Joseph J. Darowski, ed. *The Ages of the Black Panther: Essays on the King of Wakanda in Comic Books*. Jefferson, NC: McFarland & Company, 2020.

Ramzi Fawaz, *The New Mutants: Superheroes and the Radical Imagination of American Comics*. New York: New York University Press, 2016.

Sheena C. Howard, ed. *Why Wakanda Matters: What Black Panther Reveals About Psychology, Identity, and Communication*. Dallas, TX: BenBella Books, 2021.

Sean Howe, *Marvel Comics: The Untold Story*. New York: Harper, 2012.

Travis Langley and Alex Simmons, eds. *Black Panther Psychology: Hidden Kingdoms*. New York: Sterling Publishing, 2019.

Rob Lendrum, "The Super Black Macho, One Baaad Mutha: Black Superhero Masculinity in 1970s Mainstream Comic Books," *Extrapolation* 46, no. 3 (2005): 360–72.

Martin Lund, "'Introducing the Sensational Black Panther!': *Fantastic Four* #52–53, the Cold War, and Marvel's Imagined Africa," *The Comics Grid: Journal of Comics Scholarship* 6, no. 1 (2016), http://doi.org/10.16995/cg.80.

Adilifu Nama, *Super Black: American Pop Culture and Black Superheroes*. Austin: University of Texas Press, 2011.

Anna Peppard, "'A Cross Burning Darkly, Blackening the Night': Reading Racialized Spectacles of Conflict and Bondage in Marvel's Early Black Panther Comics," *Studies in Comics* 9, no. 1 (2018): 59–85.

William Schulte and Nathaniel Frederick, "Black Panther and Black Agency: Constructing Cultural Nationalism in Comic Books Featuring Black Panther, 1973–1979," *Journal of Graphic Novels and Comics* 11, no. 3 (2020): 296–314.

Tucker Stone and David Brothers, "Fear of a Black Panther," *The Comics Journal*, February 16, 2018. http://www.tcj.com/fear-of-a-black-panther.

David Taft Terry, "Imagining a Strange New World: Racial Integration and Social Justice Advocacy in Marvel Comics, 1966–1980," in *Soul Thieves: The Appropriation and Misrepresentation of African American Popular Culture*, eds. Tamara Lizette Brown and Baruti N. Kopano. New York: Palgrave Macmillan, 2014.

Rebecca Wanzo, "And All Our Past Decades Have Seen Revolutions: The Long Decolonization of Black Panther," *The Black Scholar*, February 19, 2018, https://www.theblackscholar.org/past-decades-seen-revolutions-long-decolonization-black-panther-rebecca-wanzo.

Bradford W. Wright, *Comic Book Nation: The Transformation of Youth Culture in America*. Baltimore: Johns Hopkins University Press, 2003.

# Notes

## SERIES INTRODUCTION

1. Variations on this phrase greet the reader at the head of several Superman stories in the late 1930s. See Jerry Siegel, ed., *The Superman Chronicles*, vol. 1 (DC Comics, 2006).
2. Mike Benton, *Superhero Comics of the Golden Age: The Illustrated History* (Taylor, 1992), 65.
3. See Jean-Paul Gabilliet, *Of Comics and Men: A Cultural History of American Comics*, trans. Bart Beaty and Nick Nguyen (University Press of Mississippi, 2010), pages 3–8 for the economic history of the early American comic book industry.
4. Ian Gordon, *Comic Strips and Consumer Culture, 1890–1945* (Smithsonian Institution Press, 1998), 135–51.
5. Gabilliet, 34.
6. See Benton, 57–62. It should be noted that the Green Arrow and Aquaman also clung to life as backup features, and that Superman still enjoyed respectable sales—boosted by the success of *The Adventures of Superman* television show. Plastic Man was canceled, however, when Quality Comics folded in 1956.
7. *Mad*—one of the most original and influential comic books of the 1950s—featured an acclaimed Superman parody by Harvey Kurtzman and Wallace Wood entitled "Superduperman" in #4 (1953); it was followed by "Bat Boy and Rubin" in *Mad* #8 (1953) and "Woman Wonder" in *Mad* #10 (1954).
8. For a detailed account of these failed revivals, see Bill Schelly, *American Comic Book Chronicles: The 1950s* (TwoMorrows, 2013), 95–102. For a cultural history of the moral panic over comics, see David Hajdu, *The Ten-Cent Plague: The Great Comic-Book Scare and How It Changed America* (Farrar, Straus and Giroux, 2008).
9. The company also introduced the Martian Manhunter as a backup strip in the pages of *Detective Comics* in 1955. Although notable as DC's first new superpowered character in years, the Manhunter made no discernible difference to sales, and his impact upon fandom—and the larger super hero genre—does not compare with that of the Flash's revival.
10. In the 1940s, Goodman's comic book company was generally known as Timely. Betweeen 1951 and 1957, it was called Atlas. It had no single name between 1958 and 1961.
11. Goodman was one of the publishers who attempted to revive the genre in 1954, but he swiftly abandoned super heroes again when sales proved weak.

12. See *Penguin Classics Marvel Collection: The Fantastic Four* for a detailed discussion of Lee and Kirby's groundbreaking work on this series.
13. This achievement is even more impressive if we consider that Lee, Lieber, and Kirby also launched a Western title—*The Rawhide Kid*, in August of 1960, which they continued to work on—as well as a solo Human Torch strip for the pages of *Strange Tales*. In addition, Lee was also continuously working on Marvel's girl-oriented books, such as *Millie the Model* (with artist Stan Goldberg) and *Patsy and Hedy* (with artist Al Hartley). Although inevitably overshadowed today by Marvel's super heroes, the company continued to produce numerous titles in other genres under Lee's general editorship during these early years.
14. This phrase served as the headline for one of the first pieces of significant media coverage of the company—an article by Nat Freedland that appeared in the *New York Herald Tribune Sunday Magazine*, January 9, 1966.
15. Stan Lee, speaking at the 1975 San Diego Comic-Con, as cited in John Morrow, ed., *Kirby and Lee: Stuf' Said!: The Complex Genesis of the Marvel Universe, in Its Creators' Own Words* (TwoMorrows, 2018), 119–120. As Jean-Paul Gabilliet notes, Lee always spoke as if he "invented this method of work, but [Will] Eisner had already been practicing it in his studio at the end of the 1930s." See Gabilliet, 127.
16. For a brilliant discussion of authorship, ownership, and the comic book industry, see Shawna Kidman, *Comic Books Incorporated: How the Business of Comics Became the Business of Hollywood* (University of California Press, 2019), 91–135.

## VOLUME INTRODUCTION

*I would like to thank Ben Saunders and Brannon Costello for their generous assistance on early drafts of this essay.*

1. Adilifu Nama, *Super Black: American Pop Culture and Black Superheroes* (Austin: University of Texas Press, 2011), 39–53; Crystal Am Nelson, "And They Started Sayin' 'Black Power!,'" *Feminist Media Histories* 4, no. 3 (2018): 30–48; Charles W. Henebry, "A Tale of Two Panthers: T'Challa and the Black Panther Party for Self-Defense," in *The Ages of the Black Panther: Essays on the King of Wakanda in Comic Books*, ed. Joseph J. Darowski (Jefferson, NC: McFarland & Company, 2020), 36–63. See also "Lowndes County Freedom Organization Founded," *SNCC Digital Gateway*, https://snccdigital.org/events/lowndes-county-freedom-organization-founded.
2. Dennis Culver, *Marvel's Black Panther: The Illustrated History of a King* (San Rafael, CA: Insight Editions, 2018), 13; Gina M. DiNicolo, *The Black Panthers: A Story of Race, War, and Courage: The 761st Tank Battalion in World War II* (Yardley, PA: Westholme Publishing, 2014), 41–43.
3. Stokely Carmichael, "Black Power and Its Challenges" (lecture, Students for a Democratic Society, UC Berkeley, October 29, 1966).
4. For example, see Evan Narcisse, "The Politics of Marvel's Black Panther," *Kotaku*, May 5, 2016, www.kotaku.com/the-politics-of-the-black-panther-1766701304; Sean Howe, *Marvel Comics: The Untold Story* (New York: Harper, 2012); and Martin Lund, "'Introducing the Sensational Black Panther!': *Fantastic Four* #52–53, the Cold War, and Marvel's Imagined Africa," *The Comics Grid: Journal of Comics Scholarship* 6, no. 1 (2016), http://doi.org/10.16995/cg.80.
5. Nama, *Super Black*, 43–44. See also Tim Posada, "Afrofuturism, Power, and Marvel Comics's *Black Panther*," *The Journal of Popular Culture* 52, no. 3 (2019): 629.

6. Ben Saunders, "Introduction" to *Penguin Classics Marvel Edition: The Fantastic Four* (New York: Penguin Classics, forthcoming).
7. Lund, "'Introducing the Sensational Black Panther!,'" 13.
8. Bradford W. Wright, *Comic Book Nation: The Transformation of Youth Culture in America* (Baltimore: Johns Hopkins University Press, 2003), 36. See also Mike Benton, *The Comic Book in America: An Illustrated History* (Dallas: Taylor Publishing Company, 1989).
9. Howe, *Marvel Comics: The Untold Story*, 86. For more on the "ironic self-awareness" that Lee and Kirby often brought to the mixing of genres in *Fantastic Four*, see Saunders, "Introduction" to *Penguin Classics Marvel Edition: The Fantastic Four* (New York: Penguin Classics, forthcoming).
10. Ramzi Fawaz, *The New Mutants: Superheroes and the Radical Imagination of American Comics* (New York: New York University Press, 2016), 118.
11. Fawaz, *The New Mutants*, 119.
12. Culver, *Marvel's Black Panther*, 40.
13. David Taft Terry, "Imagining a Strange New World: Racial Integration and Social Justice Advocacy in Marvel Comics, 1966–1980," in *Soul Thieves: The Appropriation and Misrepresentation of African American Popular Culture*, eds. Tamara Lizette Brown and Baruti N. Kopano (New York: Palgrave Macmillan, 2014), 160.
14. Quoted in Culver, *Marvel's Black Panther*, 40.
15. Rebecca Wanzo, "And All Our Past Decades Have Seen Revolutions: The Long Decolonization of Black Panther," *The Black Scholar*, February 19, 2018, https://www.theblackscholar.org/past-decades-seen-revolutions-long-decolonization-black-panther-rebecca-wanzo.
16. Don McGregor, "Panther's Chronicles," 361.
17. Todd Steven Burroughs, "The Spy King—How Christopher Priest's Panther Forever Shook Up the Avengers," in *Marvel's Black Panther: A Comic Book Biography, from Stan Lee to Ta-Nehisi Coates* (New York: Diasporic Africa Press, 2018), 108.
18. James Heath Lantz, "Irreverent Panels: The Comics Career of Billy Graham," *Back Issue!* #114 (August 2019), 20.
19. Don McGregor, "Panther's Chronicles," 360.
20. Terry, "Imagining a Strange New World," in *Soul Thieves*, 155.
21. Julian C. Chambliss, "A Different Nation: Continuing a Legacy of Decolonization in Black Panther," in *The Ages of the Black Panther: Essays on the King of Wakanda in Comic Books*, ed. Joseph J. Darowski (Jefferson, NC: McFarland & Company, 2020), 208.
22. José Alaniz, "Wakanda Speaks: Animals and Animacy in 'Panther's Rage,'" in *The Ages of the Black Panther: Essays on the King of Wakanda in Comic Books*, ed. Joseph J. Darowski (Jefferson, NC: McFarland & Company, 2020), 83.
23. Rob Lendrum, "The Super Black Macho, One Baaad Mutha: Black Superhero Masculinity in 1970s Mainstream Comic Books," *Extrapolation* 46, no. 3 (2005): 366.
24. Anna Peppard, "'A Cross Burning Darkly, Blackening the Night': Reading Racialized Spectacles of Conflict and Bondage in Marvel's Early Black Panther Comics," *Studies in Comics* 9, no. 1 (2018): 76.
25. "The Panther vs. the Klan" story would continue in *Black Panther* #14–15 (1979) and conclude in *Marvel Premiere* #51–53 (1979–1980).

## ALSO AVAILABLE FROM THE PENGUIN CLASSICS MARVEL COLLECTION

All titles in the Penguin Classics Marvel Collection are available as collector-worthy hardcover editions as well as signature Penguin Classics black spine paperback editions.

**THE AMAZING SPIDER-MAN**

Stan Lee and Steve Ditko

Foreword by Jason Reynolds
Introduction by Ben Saunders

**CAPTAIN AMERICA**

Jack Kirby, Joe Simon, Stan Lee, Jim Steranko, and John Romita Sr.

Foreword by Gene Luen Yang
Introduction by Ben Saunders

**BLACK PANTHER**

Don McGregor, Rich Buckler, Billy Graham, Stan Lee, and Jack Kirby

Foreword by Nnedi Okorafor
Introduction by Qiana J. Whitted

**Series Editor: Ben Saunders**

More titles in the Penguin Classics Marvel Collection to come; visit prh.com/penguinclassics for more information.